THE BERKELEY STUDENT REVOLT

SEYMOUR MARTIN LIPSET is professor of sociology and a member of the Center for International Affairs at Harvard University. He has been professor of sociology and director of the Institute of International Studies at the University of California, Berkeley, and Henry Ford Visiting Research Professor of Political Science and Sociology at Yale. He has also been visiting professor at the University of Warsaw and the Free University of Berlin. He is author of, among other books, *Political Man* (A330), *The First New Nation* (A597) and *Agrarian Socialism* (A606), and co-author of *Union Democracy* (A296).

SHELDON S. WOLIN teaches Political Theory at the University of California, Berkeley, where he is a Professor of Political Science. He was educated at Oberlin, Harvard, and Oxford, and has taught at Oberlin and Northwestern. He is author of *Politics and Vision, Continuity and Innovation in Western Political Thought,* and of several articles dealing with political theory.

The Berkeley Student Revolt

FACTS AND INTERPRETATIONS

EDITED BY

SEYMOUR MARTIN LIPSET

AND

SHELDON S. WOLIN

Anchor Books
Doubleday & Company, Inc.
Garden City, New York

The Anchor Books edition is the first publication of
The Berkeley Student Revolt: Facts and Interpretations

Anchor Books edition: 1965

Library of Congress Catalog Card Number 65–20058

The publisher wishes to thank the magazines and publishers who have given permission to reprint the following articles:

Max Heirich and Sam Kaplan, "Yesterday's Discord," *California Monthly*, February 1965. Copyright © 1965 by the California Alumni Association.

Clark Kerr, Selections from *The Uses of the University*, 1963, published by Harvard University Press. Copyright 1963 by the President and Fellows and Harvard College, reprinted by permission of the publishers.

Harold Taylor, "The Academic Industry: A Discussion of Clark Kerr's *The Uses of the University*," reprinted from *Commentary*, December 1964. Copyright © 1964 by the American Jewish Committee.

Bradford Cleaveland, "A Letter to Undergraduates," *Slate Supplement Report*, Vol. 1, No. 4, Berkeley, California, September 1964.

Richard Fallenbaum, "University Abdicates Social Responsibility," *The Cal Reporter*, Berkeley, California, May 13, 1963.

The Editors of *California Monthly*, "Chronology of Events: Three Months of Crisis," *California Monthly*, February 1965. Copyright © 1965 by the California Alumni Association.

Mervin D. Field, "The UC Student Protests: California Poll," *California Poll*, February 2, 1965. Copyright 1965 by Field Research Corporation.

"The Position of the Free Speech Movement on Speech and Political Activity," *California Monthly*, February 1965. Copyright © 1965 by the California Alumni Association.

Mario Savio, "An End to History," *Humanity, an arena of critique and commitment*, No. 2, December 1964.

Jack Weinberg, "The Free Speech Movement and Civil Rights," *Campus Corelator*, January 1965. Copyright 1965 by Campus Corelator.

"State Campus Safety Imperiled," an editorial; "Clark Kerr Blames Peking But 'Muscovites' Active," "Big UC Revolt—The House That Kerr Built," *Tocsin*, October 10, 1964, Oakland, California. Copyright by Tocsin, Inc., 1964.

Clark Kerr, "A Message to Alumni," "Statement by President Clark Kerr, November 12, 1964," "Statement by President Clark Kerr, December 3, 1964," *California Monthly*, February 1965. Copyright © 1965 by the California Alumni Association.

Henry F. May, "Statement," *California Monthly*, February 1965. Copyright © 1965 by the California Alumni Association.

Herbert McClosky, "Statement on Academic Senate Resolution of December 8, 1964," Berkeley *Daily Gazette*, December 15, 1964.

Henry Stapp, "Reflections on the Crisis at Berkeley," *Daily Californian*, December 18, 1964.

Daniel I. Arnon, "An Answer to a Letter by a Pro-FSM Student," Berkeley *Daily Gazette*, February 10, 1965.

Nathan Glazer, "What Happened at Berkeley," reprinted from *Commentary*, February 1965. Copyright © 1965 by the American Jewish Committee.

Edward Strong, "Statement Read at the Meeting of the Academic Senate, Berkeley Division," *University Bulletin,* Vol. 13, No. 19, December 14, 1964.

Martin Meyerson, "Statement by Acting Chancellor Martin Meyerson," *University Bulletin,* Vol. 13, No. 21, January 11, 1965.

CONTENTS

INTRODUCTION

The daily life of a university is usually not newsworthy. Occasionally the outside world takes notice when some university scientist reports a new discovery, when a statesman uses the occasion of an honorary degree to deliver an important political pronouncement, or when a group of students organizes an absurd escapade to relieve the tedium of academic routines. During the fall of 1964 the Berkeley campus of the University of California became the center of a widening circle of attention, but for none of the reasons mentioned above. To be sure, the events were political, but they did not take the usual form of campus politics. Students were involved, but their behavior was very different from the stereotypes of Joe College or Campus Queen.

As the result of a series of events unprecedented in American university history, the Berkeley campus community lived in a state of unrelieved tension and continuous agitation from September until January. The immediate cause was an announcement by campus officials that a twenty-six-foot strip of land at the entrance to the campus, previously thought by most students and faculty to belong to the City of Berkeley, was the property of the university and subject, therefore, to existing university regulations dealing with political activity. This particular strip happened to be the place where students traditionally conducted political activity involving solicitation of funds and members for off-campus political-action groups, without interference. A student protest movement was rapidly organized, the Free Speech Movement (FSM), and it advanced demands for the drastic reform of university rules and regulations affecting student political activity on campus. A running battle, which lasted almost the entire semester, developed between the administration and the FSM. Before the dispute had run its course, the faculty was drawn in, and the effects of the controversy were registered throughout the entire state. The governor became involved; members of the state legislature began to take sides; thousands of letters and telegrams were sent by alumni, prominent citizens, and interested individuals and groups. Meanwhile the campus was the scene of many unacademic events. There were endless protest meetings, rallies, and silent vigils, with crowds sometimes reaching as many as 7000; there were repeated violations of university rules and civil laws; on two occasions hundreds of police were massed on campus, and the threat of violence seemed immediate and inevitable; three sit-ins occurred, the last culminating in the occupation of the central administration building by 800 students and their forcible removal by an almost equal number of police; and a sympathy strike, launched by teaching assistants, severely interrupted classroom routines. One of the world's largest and most famous centers of learning was brought to the edge of collapse.

The events of the semester have an importance that far transcends its immediate local consequences. The University of California has often been viewed as a prototype of the future form of public education in this country and even abroad. It is a vast system and hence enjoys many of the advantages of large-scale organization; its student population is huge but highly selected; its tuition costs are almost nominal, when measured against comparable private institutions, but its operating budget is, by any standard, staggering; and despite the traditional academic snobbery against state universities, it has attracted a distinguished faculty. Yet the institution became the target of organized student discontent and of strong faculty criticism. The students insisted that the atmosphere and condition of the university were conducive neither to free expression nor to good education. Whatever the merits of the student case, the fact that a fundamental institution of our society was subjected to such criticism and assault is reason enough for believing that these events and the reactions to them deserve wide attention.

Similarly, the events tell us something about the new generation of students, or, at least, about its more articulate and aggressive spokesmen. It is not our purpose here to praise or blame the students involved, only to point to some of the obvious characteristics that they displayed. High on the list of the obvious is the markedly political interests of this new student generation. Another is their preoccupation with protest, their sensitivity to social abuses—both of which may appear highly developed or overly developed, depending upon one's preferences. One could easily enumerate many more characteristics, but the basic point is that these Berkeley students are representative of many in their generation, not just those on a single campus.

Finally, some old and enduring issues were argued again during these months: the nature of political freedom and its place on a university campus; the proper relation between means and ends; and the spirit of the laws and governance appropriate to an academic community.

The purpose of this collection of essays is to convey to a wider audience a sense of what took place and what the participants thought and felt. The articles, statements, and documents reflect the powerful feelings aroused by the events; even the editors of this volume were in disagreement. Nevertheless, we have tried to assemble a collection that would represent as wide a range of significant views as possible. An attempt has also been made to assist the reader by providing a detailed chronological account of the events.

Undoubtedly more essays will appear in the near future and many of them may possess greater detachment, but we believe that much is to be gained by assembling a record of what men thought and felt at the time. Men do not always see more clearly when they see from a distance. We have also been compelled to exercise our judgment in choosing what seemed most relevant from the mass of pamphlets, manifestoes, broadsides, and proposals that appeared at the time. In addition, a few of the essays were commissioned for this volume and have not appeared elsewhere. We feel that there is justification for this practice, since in each case the contributors played an important part in some of the events. In several cases, too, we have allowed contributors to introduce slight revisions in works that were produced under very trying conditions; no one, to our knowledge, has revised his position or his interpretation.

The editors are deeply conscious of two omissions. First, no one has carefully analyzed the intricacies of faculty politics during the period in question. Second, certain crucial items could not be included, because the necessary permissions were unobtainable from the journal which held the copyright. The articles by Lewis Feuer, Paul Jacobs, Steve Weissman, and Clark Kerr that appeared in *The New Leader* were important losses.

We must also ask the reader to be tolerant of the frequent repetition which appears throughout. Many authors have set out their own summaries of the events as a preliminary to analysis. A ruthless editor would have deleted most of this material, but we have not, because the summaries have almost always been integrally connected with the authors' argument. We decided, therefore, to reprint each article as it was written. In any case, there is some advantage to allowing this repetition, since it gives the readers an opportunity to see how expert analysts and close participants can "see" the same set of events quite differently.

We are very grateful to the contributors to this volume and to their original publishers for giving us permission to reprint their articles. We also owe a debt of gratitude to the magazines of original printing for publication rights. Sondra Betsch and Nathan Glazer helped us considerably in locating materials and in designing the contents of the book.

Since the main actors who made this book possible were the students of the University of California, we are directing all royalties from this book to the Special Opportunity Scholarship Program designed "to help young people from economic, racial, occupational, or other backgrounds that normally would tend to discourage hopes for a college education."

Seymour Martin Lipset

Sheldon S. Wolin

Berkeley, California
February 15, 1965

I

Students and Politics

The Berkeley outbreak is but one of a vast number of student protest movements. Two articles, one analyzing the factors that predispose university students everywhere to activist politics, and the other presenting the history of past student protests at Berkeley, begin the background of the story.

UNIVERSITY STUDENT POLITICS

BY SEYMOUR MARTIN LIPSET,
PROFESSOR OF SOCIOLOGY, BERKELEY

Interest in the character, intensity, and extent of university student involvement in politics has increased sharply in recent years. In the United States, much of the civil-rights revolution has been manned by students, in both the North and the South. The recent disturbances at the Berkeley campus of the University of California, which appear to resemble events observed in recent years only on the campuses of underdeveloped nations, were in large measure an outgrowth of controversies that stemmed from the demands of students involved in civil-rights activities to use the university as a base for their off-campus demonstrations and sit-ins. During 1964, student demonstrations played a major role in unseating governments in Bolivia, South Vietnam, and the Sudan. The Syngman Rhee regime in Korea was finally overthrown in 1960 as a result of student demonstrations, and similar actions have been directed against the military regime during the past year. Mass demonstrations in Japan, manned almost entirely by students and directed against the passage of the Japanese-American Security treaty, prevented President Eisenhower from visiting that country in 1960. The list of countries in Asia, Africa, and Latin America in which student political activity has formed a major threat to the stability of the polity could be extended almost indefinitely.

In the Communist countries, also, students have played a major role in efforts to change the status quo. This was especially true in Poland and Hungary in 1956. In Poland, the chief organ of criticism was a student journal, *Po Prustu* (*Plain Talk*), which served as the main rallying point for the liberal elements as long as it was permitted to exist. In Hungary, too, university students were a major force among the groups taking part in the uprising. In the Soviet Union, students have played an important role in demands for reform, insisting on more freedom and more intellectual integrity. A former student of Moscow University reports that while "it is difficult to give exact figures . . . my estimate of the proportion of Soviet students whose political discontent was revealed during the thaw of 1956 would be from one-fourth to one-third of the total. With the exception of the professional activists, the remaining played the familiar role of 'the masses': their attitude toward the political avant-garde was sometimes sympathetic, sometimes uncomprehending, but rarely hostile." In Communist China, the year 1957 witnessed the "Hundred Flowers" campaign in which open criticism was encouraged by the Party. The results startled the regime, since for five weeks it was exposed to a barrage of sharp attacks by older intellectuals and students. As René Goldman, a French journalist present in China at the time reported: "What really shook the party was a feeling that it faced the loss of its control over the youth. Young people brought up under Communist rule had become the loudest in denouncing the party which had vested its hopes in them." Yugoslavia also faced student protest in the late fifties.

The efforts by the rulers of Communist countries to repress student political activities may be explained in part by their awareness of the importance of student movements in undermining the pre-Communist regimes of these countries. In nineteenth-century Russia, university students were almost the only group to engage in demonstrations demanding freedom and economic reform, from the middle of the century onward. Student disorders occurred almost annually at the University of Moscow from the late eighties to the Revolution of 1905. Historians report that the Russian workers learned the value of street demonstrations from students. In China students helped greatly in bringing about the downfall of the Manchu Dynasty at the turn of the century. Student politics reached a second climax in May 1919, when the huge student demonstration that began in Peking inaugurated the second Chinese revolution. In the 1930s student movements, demonstrations, and strikes played a major role in undermining Chiang Kaishek, and following World War II, student riots contributed greatly to the final downfall of the Nationalist regime.

It is interesting to note that shortly before he died, C. Wright Mills, in seeking to specify the conditions favoring social revolution, challenged the Marxist beliefs in the political potential of the working class as an agency of "historic change," and suggested that the record of revolutionary movements indicated students and intellectuals are more likely than the proletariat to be the "immediate radical agency of change."

The special political behavior of students, their greater propensity to participate in radical or other protest movements, is an outgrowth of elements specific to the situation and environment of university life, disposing students toward deviant behavior. University students are generally at an age defined as biologically adult; many non-students of the same age have already entered upon adult activities, marrying, earning money, and spending it as they wish. Students are often at the age where they may vote and marry, and many do both. Yet few university students earn all their livelihood; many remain financially dependent on their parents, and the society at large still treats them in many ways as adolescents without responsibilities, permitting and even approving their "sowing of wild oats." They may even violate the law in various ways without being punished. (At Santa Barbara, not too long ago, a student was killed during a fraternity initiation; at Berkeley this past fall, a police car was surrounded and held captive by student demonstrators who used its roof as a speakers' podium for thirty-six hours. In neither case was anyone punished.) In many countries, particularly in Latin America, police are restricted by law from entering university precincts; campuses are privileged sanctuaries to which students may flee after carrying out attacks against institutions of the surrounding society.

If students are defined as socially irresponsible, they are also encouraged to be idealistic. Value-transmitting agencies such as the family, church, and school, tend to present morality in absolute, right or wrong terms. The famed German sociologist Max Weber observed that youth has a tendency to follow "a pure ethic of absolute ends," while mature men tend to espouse an "ethic of responsibility." The advocate of the first fears that any compromise on matters of principle will endanger the "salvation of the soul"; the proponent of the second fears that an unwillingness to confront the complex "realities of life" may result in the "goals . . . [being] damaged and discredited for generations, because responsibility for *consequences* is lacking." University students, though well educated, have generally not established a sense of close involvement with adult institutions; experience has not hardened them to imperfection. Their libidos are unanchored; their capacity for identification with categories of universal scope, with mankind, the oppressed, the poor and miserable, is greater than it was earlier or than it will be later in life. Their contact with the articulated moral and political standards of their society is abstract; they encounter them as principles promulgated by older persons, as imposed by authority, rather than as maxims incorporated into and blurred by their own experience. Increasingly in the modern world, which includes the highly educated sector of the emerging nations, equality, efficiency, justice, and economic well-being are represented as the values of the good society. Poverty, racial discrimination, caste systems, social inequality, administrative and political corruption, and cultural backwardness are all violations of such principles. In all countries, of course, reality is usually at variance with principles, and young persons feel this strongly. Educated young people everywhere thus tend to support idealistic movements which take the ideologies and values of the adult world more seriously than does the adult world itself. Youthful idealism, even when it leads to sharp rejection of adult practices and the use of extremist methods is often expected and respected by older people.

An opinion survey based on a random sample of University of Warsaw students reports that those students who were most committed to socialism and its egalitarian ideals were much more likely to have actively participated in the demonstrations against the regime in 1956, than were those who had less faith in, or were opposed to, socialism as a goal. In Berkeley during this past fall, the study of the University of California student body by Robert Somers printed here indicates that the factor most highly associated with support for the student demonstrations and sit-ins, the demands of which were the elimination of all campus controls on any form of political activity, is commitment to political liberalism.

Another factor that affects the likelihood of young people to deviate from accepted adult norms rests on the need of new generations to differentiate themselves from older ones, in effect, from their parents. Such needs are most prevalent in societies that stress individualism, the need for separate identity, characteristic of most Western countries. However, even in the more traditional societies of the underdeveloped world, the university system itself represents an incursion of modern individualistic values stressing creativity and innovation.

The relations of youth with the parental generation is also complicated by the fact that the institutions within which they have been socialized before entering the university, the family, church, and school are more likely to be concerned with transmitting the values of older generations, with shielding youth from the effects of changes that erode older beliefs, than with preparing youth to cope with change. But since youth become aware of major changes in values, even if teachers, parents, and preachers do not discuss or frown on such changes, the relative "conservatism" of adult educators will serve to undermine their authority and to lead young people to think they know more and better than their elders. This attitude may predispose them to support innovating concepts and organizations as soon as they reach the freedom from familial restraint provided by the university.

The particular attraction of extremist movements to young

people, the willingness among those most disposed to question ancient verities in the name of freedom to accept uncritically new doctrinaire solutions, may be related to the very uncertainty about what is right and wrong inherent in the situation of many university students. At a university, youth learn that there are attractive values and ways of life that differ sharply from those urged on them by their parents. This contact with a variety of possibilities not taught within the family is confusing, and rather than remain in a state of doubt, many youth seek a new certainty in beliefs opposed to those taught at home. Radical movements give young people an idealistic rationale for breaking with their families, especially when parents are perceived as supporters of the reactionary system.

A major source of tensions which fosters the availability of young people for organized "deviance" is their situation as socially "marginal" individuals, as people whose status and future are not yet established. The student has left the security of the family, and does not yet have the security and emotional involvement he will attain on entering his own occupational career and marriage. The longer and more intensive this insecurity concerning career and marriage, the less likely is the recognition that it flows from anxiety about an inherently ambiguous personal situation, and the greater the tendency to blame it on society and the adult world. Many will seek a socially acceptable explanation for their fear of possible personal failure, and this is often readily available in the ideologies of radical social movements.

The extent to which students will seek and accept such ideological outlets is related to their degree of uncertainty about the future. Those studying for courses that do not readily lead to a secure career should be more available for rebelliousness than those in fields of study that resemble apprenticeships to a definite position, e.g., engineering, preparation for schoolteaching, and the like. The most insecure of all are those who hope to be creative intellectuals, and consequently those in the liberal arts (more the humanistic than the scientific disciplines), especially graduate students, should be expected to play a leading role in student protest, a hypothesis that research on the subject bears out.

Studies of support for extremist movements in many countries indicate that social dislocation, changing from one significant environment to another, predisposes individuals to accept new values, ideologies, and affiliations in the religious and political spheres. University-student communities probably contain a larger proportion of socially displaced individuals than any other type. Many students, sometimes almost all, on most campuses, have left home, have changed communities, have given up old friends, and must adapt to a totally new environment. One would expect, therefore, to find a disproportionate number of extremists among them. And, in line with these assumptions, research on student behavior indicates that student political activists and supporters of more radical politics are more likely to be found among those students who are living away from home than among those who live with their families and commute to school.

In addition to the various sources of motivation for student radicalism, there are factors inherent in the ecological structure of universities that facilitate collective action. Like a vast factory, a large campus brings together great numbers of people in similar life situations, in close proximity to each other, who can acquire a sense of solidarity and wield real power. At Berkeley, there are close to 30,000 students, at Mexico City over 65,000, at Buenos Aires over 70,000, at Calcutta more than 100,000, at Rome about 50,000, at the University of Paris over 75,000, and at Moscow over 30,000. It is relatively easy to reach students; leaflets handed out at the campus gates will usually do the job. These conditions facilitate quick communication, foster solidarity, and help to arouse melodramatic action.

The need of a younger generation to establish its independence corresponds to the tactic of radical activist movements to seek recruits among those who are not well integrated in the institutional system. The fact that students constitute the group that is most available for radical social movements because of its social situation, discontents, and accessibility, is not lost on movements seeking support. Communist parties, particularly, have concentrated considerable resources on university campuses in the United States and other countries for precisely these reasons. In many of the underdeveloped countries, most parties seriously concern themselves with student politics, though the more extreme ones are almost always much stronger on the campuses than in the nation as a whole. Thus the concentrated efforts to reach students with political messages should be added to the list of factors predisposing and exposing students to political activism.

On a comparative level, it is clear that the extent of political concern among students in different countries is in part a function of the degree of tension in the larger polity. In societies that have a stable democratic order with legitimate government and opposition, as in the United States and much of western Europe, students may be disproportionately to the left of non-students of similar social strata, but on the whole they exhibit much less interest in politics and give less support to extremist groups than do students in those nations that have unstable polities. It has been argued that the greater significance of radical student politics in Latin America reflects characteristics of the national political structures. In conditions of political tension, where the existing adult elites and counter-elites are badly organized and ineffectual, student political organizations are likely to be important. Thus countries in which governments may be easily toppled by the political action of the military are often the same nations as those in which student political activity is of major importance. South Korea, Bolivia, the Sudan, and South Vietnam are the most recent cases in point.

National university systems vary in academic standards and in the extent to which they require students to toe the mark. The greater the pressures placed on students to work hard in order to retain their position in the university, the less they will participate in politics of any kind. In much of Latin America, India and Japan, students are not faced with the need of taking rigorous, severely competitive, regular examinations. Among faculties and departments within the universities, similar variations also hold. Fields like the natural sciences, which require more concentrated study and work than the humanities or social sciences, will inhibit the inclination of students toward active politics.

The greater the number of years the student spends at the university, the greater the likelihood of significant student activity. Where the university system permits students to "hang around" for years, to finish at their own discretion, one finds the phenomenon of the professional student, from whose ranks political leaders and activists are likely to be recruited. Observers of student politics in much of Latin America and southern Asia have pointed to the presence there of such "professional students," many of whom are not enrolled, as being "often the catalysts who agitate lambs into lions." Currently in large centers of graduate training in the United States, one also finds "students" who remain in the university community for many years, nominally preparing for doctoral examinations or supposedly writing theses. Many commentaries on the upheaval at Berkeley have pointed to the significant role played by the large number of semipermanent "graduate students" in creating the Bohemian and politicized atmosphere there.

The quality of the relationships between students and their teachers, which depends in part on the traditions of the various university systems and on the student-faculty ratio, affects the extent to which students feel committed to, or alienated from, the academic culture. Where there is a drastic separation between students and teachers, where faculty must depend on extra-university employment because of low salaries, or where there is a very great number of students per faculty member, students are more likely to engage in radical political activities to express their discontent.

Participation in politics may be viewed as an alternative to other forms of student extracurricular activities. Universities in many parts of the underdeveloped world, in Latin America, the Near East, and parts of Asia, have almost no organized extracurricular activity other than political. In the United States, organized sports were expressly introduced into colleges and universities to divert the adolescent energy that in many college communities had gone into brawls and "town and gown" riots. Determined but unsuccessful efforts to provide alternative activities in order to reduce the energies available for political activity, have been attempted in universities in the Arab world and in Japan.

It should be noted in conclusion that even though radical and extremist attitudes and actions occur frequently among highly politicized students, most students in most countries are not so politicized, and insofar as they have political beliefs, these are conservative, moderate, or liberal. Surveys of student attitudes in many universities of Latin America and Asia indicate that the large majority in most of them do not support radical politics. The discrepancy between the image of students in these nations as predominantly leftist and the data reported in the opinion surveys is a consequence of the fact that the less radical the politics of students, the less likely they are to be interested in or take part in any form of politics. Hence one finds the majority of the politically interested and active students located toward the far left of the political spectrum, creating the public impression that most students agree with this position, when in fact this is not the case.

Basic to any understanding of the critical political stance which characterizes the politics of the university community, whether faculty or student, as compared to the predominant politics of other privileged high-status sections of the population, is the fact that those engaged in intellectually creative activities, whether inside or outside of the academy, are involved in an enterprise requiring them to criticize, revise, and supplant tradition. They value new discoveries and innovation, not the reproduction, copying, and transmission of old discoveries and ideas. Originality, departure from what is established and officially accepted, is a central value in the outlook of the modern intellectual. Universities by their stress on scientific discipline and detachment from the idols of the marketplace, have nurtured a critical attitude. Especially in the social sciences has there been a tension between the affirmation of the dominant systems of practice and belief and a critical attitude toward these systems. And it is the anti-tradition and anti-Establishment attitudes of modern intellectual life that provide a point of departure for and help legitimate student politics which are generally to the left of national politics on many campuses of the world.

In general, however, it may be said that where the society, the university, and the student are committed to the fullest development of research and teaching in an atmosphere of complete academic freedom, and where adequate resources are available in the form of faculty, libraries, laboratories, and financial support, students are less likely to engage in extreme forms of political activity and are more likely to allow themselves to be assimilated into the corporate life of the university as an institution devoted to the interpretation of what is inherited, the discovery of new truths, and the training of students to do both of these and to prepare themselves for careers based on these activities. Universities to be successful must form a community that embraces students as well as faculty and research workers. Universities must develop a culture of their own, whose concerns are in many ways sharply distinct from those of groups political or others outside the campus. This culture must transcend the bodies of specific knowledge which are taught and cultivated, and foster a scholarly ethos of attitudes and sensibilities, of standards and canons of judgment which must be assimilated and cannot be explicitly taught. These tasks of the university cannot be performed without the assimilation of the student body into the university community, which is a graded community, inevitably hierarchical by virtue of differences in age and competence. This task is not an easy one, but on its effective performance depends the success of the university in fulfilling its essential tasks.

A high incidence of intense student political activity is in some sense an indication of the failure of a university as an academic community, particularly since in most cases such activity involves a rejection of the intellectual leadership of the faculty, a denigration of scholarship to a more lowly status than that of politics within the university itself. And where a campus becomes highly politicized as many have in some parts of the underdeveloped world, academic freedom, the principal condition for a meaningful university life, is threatened, if not destroyed. Where professors must worry about the political reactions of students and colleagues, there is no freedom to teach, study, or do research. Few student movements may be in a position to overturn governments, but they may sharply weaken or even destroy the independence of the university. Thus the problem of student politics is more than academic for both the academy and for society.

YESTERDAY'S DISCORD*

BY MAX HEIRICH AND SAM KAPLAN[1]

GRADUATE STUDENTS, DEPARTMENT OF SOCIOLOGY, BERKELEY

Mass student outbursts are nothing new on the Berkeley campus. A review of the last thirty-five years of them shows they have differed greatly in form, purpose, and number of participants. And these differences can be related both to national and international events and to the composition of the student body. But one thing is clear: almost every year, except under unusual circumstances, at least a part of the student body engages in crowd outbursts that make things temporarily uncomfortable for administration, faculty, other students, Berkeley townspeople, and sometimes, the public at large.

The last thirty-five years can be conveniently divided into four periods of characteristic student political styles. For ease, each period can be conventionally named according to the decade in which it flowered; of course, no period coincides precisely with a decade. The most recent period, for instance, seems to have begun in about 1957; when it will end, no one can be sure.

Until the end of the twenties or so, at least according to the recollections of campus old-timers, mass student activity was "traditional" and strictly non-political. Football games and other social events were the focus of collective energies; and particularly exciting victories on the gridiron were often followed by good-natured, exuberant marches into downtown Berkeley. At times, the students became heady enough with victory and their own massed energy to rock trollies off their tracks.

A proper accounting of the last thirty-five years begins, however, with the thirties. The tenor of campus life changed—it was, of course, the depression. But student activity was not much concerned with the economic issues of the depression. Instead, students engaged in a continuing protest about the breakdown of disarmament and the approach of war. This lasted throughout the decade, until late into 1941, when America finally entered the Second World War. Annual strikes—a grandiose name for what actually happened—for peace were the major feature of the period.

From 1941 through the late forties, the campus became quiet, as campuses were everywhere. Neither football nor politics provided sufficient focus—so it would seem—for collective

* From *California Monthly*, February 1965.

[1] The authors would like to acknowledge the research assistance of Dan Kirchnet.

outbursts; and if the late forties might have been expected to see a release of student energies in demonstrations of some kind, the heavy preponderance of veterans in the student body right after the war and then the coming of the Korean War seems to have put a damper on them.

For a time, the fifties were the period of the "Silent Generation." But the student body was silent only in the sense that the students of the twenties were silent: that is, they were not political. For they did engage in massive, energetic crowd behavior—it was the time when panty raids were invented and enjoyed a national vogue. U.C. had a particularly vigorous panty raid in 1956.

But in the late fifties, student political protest arose again. The "Silent Generation" enjoyed only a short stay. The protests of the fifties, however, were strikingly different from those of the thirties, though there were some similarities. For one thing, while these protests emerged over many issues, they were mostly connected with civil rights and civil liberties. Sometimes they were transformed from simple demonstrations to mass picketing and various kinds of sit-ins. This period, clearly enough, is still with us. It gives no sign of subsiding; if anything, it does not yet appear to have reached its crest. And already its collective activities seem to involve a great many more students than those of earlier decades. The present period, in fact, even seems to have enlisted the energies of more students than ever took part in football victory marches or panty raids.

What accounts for these fluctuations in collective student outbursts? Why do some periods seem to produce mainly short-run displays of footloose animal spirits, lacking much political content, while others, like the present, produce sustained, organized political activity? And why and how do the periods of mainly political action—chiefly the thirties and the present—differ in their concerns and tactics?

When we look back on the thirties, we are apt to think of the primary domestic fact of the time, the Great Depression. But the students at Berkeley did not engage themselves with the economic issues of the welfare state that was coming into existence under the New Deal of Franklin Roosevelt. Rather, the thirties were marked most prominently by continuing student agitation aimed at focusing public opinion against the international rush toward war.

Although the organized protest on campus was not about welfare issues, we can see in the tactics the students adopted a reflection of one of the economic matters taking place in American society. The favorite tactic of the protestant students was the "strike"—and it seems likely that this method had been borrowed from the widespread industrial conflict that marked the American economy through most of the thirties.

The campus strike, however, was a pale copy of the industrial strike. There were campus strikes against war, or against "War and Fascism," every year from 1935 through 1941, but they never involved much more than a one-hour rally at Sather Gate, with students being urged to stay away from classes during the meeting. In short, the strike was purely symbolic: by taking part, one declared oneself in sympathy with the aims of the protest group, but without trying to paralyze the University's educational and administrative activities.

The 1935 strike, as the first of the series, has special interest, not the least because of the problems of students' civil liberties that accompanied it.

This 1935 strike was part of a worldwide student protest against "War and Fascism" scheduled for April 12. Its worldwide leaders were hoping that 200,000 students throughout the world would participate; one of the strike leaders in California hoped that 10,000 students in the state would join. On the Berkeley campus, the announcement of the intended strike had a number of varied effects. One was that the Associated Students, which refused to approve campus participation in the strike, met in executive, or secret, session to establish a special forum for discussion of the issues involved as an alternative to the strike or other more spontaneous activity. The campus groups with pacifist platforms—YMCA, YWCA, and the Wesley Foundation—also refused to endorse the strike, arguing that it would be a poor method to combat either war or fascism.

Meanwhile, a group known as the Anti-War Week Committee announced it would distribute handbills in late March in support of the strike. This dragged into the arena the bull of civil liberties—and by the horns. Berkeley had a municipal ordinance requiring a five-dollar permit for any group distributing pamphlets. The Anti-War Week Committee denounced the ordinance as being aimed solely at commercial activities and went ahead with handing out their pamphlets *sans* permit.

Nine students were promptly arrested at Sather Gate on March 20. By the time the arraignment was held, however, the number of students involved had doubled, nine additional students having distributed handbills without a permit in protest at the first batch of arrests. The arraignment was bedlam. The eighteen students pled not guilty on constitutional grounds, but not before trying to cross-examine the prosecutor and the judge with question after question. "I am not here to answer your questions at this time," the judge said. "The purpose of this trial is to ascertain whether or not you are guilty of violating the ordinance as is charged." The judge also had to warn the spectators, most of whom were faculty, civil officials, and student sympathizers, that he would have to clear the court if they did not stop laughing so much.

At Sather Gate, the same day, 15 graduate students and teaching fellows protested the arraignment by handing out literature themselves. They were not arrested. And in early April the Berkeley City Council announced that the handbill statute would be altered to permit the unmolested distribution of anti-war material. On April 10, two days before the scheduled strike, the charges against the eighteen pamphleteering students were dismissed, and the police guaranteed the strike leader protection against vigilantes.

Just how effective the one-hour strike on the 12th was, the student newspaper, the *Daily Californian* does not say, although it does report that 3,500 attended a rally at Sather Gate after the administration refused to grant permission for a meeting on campus. (At this time, the student body numbered 12,000.) In those days, the area beyond Sather Gate was city property—it was not until the late fifties, after the construction of Sproul Hall, that off-campus rallies were forced out as far as Telegraph and Bancroft.

Thus, the first "strike against War and Fascism" was a kind of microcosm of the usual course of mass student politics. First, a small minority of students attempt to engage in protest action. Then the administration, or other students, or public officials try to restrict the protest in some way. The issue then becomes the defense of free speech and the number of people involved begins to swell as civil libertarians come to the support of the protesting students. And this, in turn, generates more interest in the protest and more sympathy for the students.

A similar pattern can be found in a strike that was called at Berkeley the year before not in protest against war but in defense of free speech. In October, 1934, five students at UCLA were suspended for alleged Communistic activities, largely because they had held an illegal meeting to discuss the state election campaign issues. One of the suspended students was the president of the UCLA student body. At the same time, the editor of the student paper at the University of Santa Clara was removed for condemning ROTC. A general protest promptly developed on several campuses throughout the state about the rights of students to express themselves freely. At UCLA, about 2,000 students met to oppose the suspensions, while at Berkeley a sympathy strike was called over both the suspensions of the UCLA students and the removal of the University of Santa Clara editor. As was usual during the decade, the strike was called for one hour only, during the time of a rally at Sather Gate. The strike was called for the 10–11 a.m. hour on Monday, November 5. The ASUC Executive Committee and President Sproul called on students to ignore the strike, with the president adding that the usual penalties would be invoked for those missing class.

For their part, the demonstrators declared that they did not wish to interfere with any students who wanted to attend classes, but they insisted "on the right of all students to walk out of their ten o'clock classes if they so desire." The strike committee urged a four-point program: 1) unconditional reinstatement of the five suspended UCLA students, 2) prevention of the formation of student vigilante groups at UCLA and San Jose State College, 3) unconditional reinstatement of student editors at Santa Clara University, which had suspended them for peace editorials, and 4) the end of statewide suppression of academic freedom.

The meeting at Sather Gate turned into a shambles. About a thousand students were on hand, and most of them heckled and booed the protest speakers into submission. The leaders of the demonstration then tried to quell the heckling by presenting a woman speaker. She cried, "We have a constitution that guarantees free speech and assemblage!" But before she could get much further, a shower of eggs and tomatoes burst about her, and she burst into tears, sobbing, "You might have the courtesy to listen." At that point, various ASUC leaders went through the crowd, urging restraint and encouraging students to return to classes, but the throng refused to disperse until 11:30 a.m. By then, a girl had clawed and scratched a student about to throw a tomato; and at the last moment one student who was getting ready to hurl a lemon cream pie changed his mind and distributed pieces of it among the crowd as a "form of refreshment."

For the next two weeks, the pattern of growing support on the free speech issue emerged. The Berkeley provost, Dr. Munroe Deutsch, declared his appreciation to the strike group for taking their meeting off-campus after having been denied permission to meet on campus, and added that "I most deeply regret the fact that students of the University did not permit those who wished to express themselves to state their views freely." Dr. Deutsch also went on to declare that the response of the students to the rally showed "absolutely" that they "have little sympathy with any effort of this kind to disrupt the work of the University."

An investigation of the violence at the strike rally followed, the investigation producing the intelligence that some 22 students, mostly senior fraternity men, served as "undercover agents," to quote the *Daily Cal,* to gather information on campus radicalism for the American Legion. The chairman of the Legion's Americanism Committee stated that reports of Communism at the university were "vastly exaggerated."

Even earlier in the decade there had been occasional violence over political activities. A group of students attempting to pass out anti-war leaflets at the Army-Navy game played in Memorial Stadium on Armistice Day, 1932, was set upon by a joint expeditionary force of soldiers and sailors. According to the *Daily Cal,* the students were "rudely dispersed."

In 1933, two students selling the newspaper of a campus group known as the Social Problems Club, which some people accused of being a Communist organization, were attacked outside Sather Gate by home-made tear-gas bombs, one of the students being hospitalized with burns. The same club had taken a hand in the mixed reception planned for some 800 Japanese naval cadets who visited the campus in April, 1933. The cadets were with the fleet of Japanese battleships that had anchored in San Francisco Bay. The club meant to oppose imperialism of all sorts, but cautiously added that they held no special claim against the Japanese people. At Sather Gate, speakers protested militarism—this was at the time of Japan's invasion of Manchuria—and banners were displayed. But the cadets, as it turned out, were taken on a walking tour of the campus, starting at the stadium, and by the time they reached Sather Gate, the demonstration had ended, not the least because police broke it up on the grounds that so many people had gathered they were impeding traffic.

Here we see a student response to particular international events—the Manchurian invasion—triggered off by a connected local matter—the arrival of the Japanese fleet. But this protest has the recurrent feature of the decade: the anti-war theme. So it is not surprising that students took the only local opportunity they had to protest against war: they worked for a voluntary, rather than compulsory, ROTC.

In 1934 the same Social Problems Club conducted an unofficial straw poll on a compulsory military training program on campus, against the wishes of President Sproul, with about 1,200 students voting 2 to 1 against compulsory ROTC. The ASUC executive committee joined in and sent President Sproul a resolution urging a voluntary program. Nonetheless, ROTC remained compulsory. Later in the decade there were further student efforts in favor of voluntary ROTC, but such protests disappeared—as did other kinds of protests—with America's participation in the Second World War.

As for anti-war rallies and strikes, they continued to the end of the period. One striking change occurred in 1936. Where before the ASUC had opposed the anti-war rallies, now it supported and sponsored them. In 1936, Norman Thomas was invited to speak. Though he was originally asked to address an official university meeting in the Greek Theater, he ended up speaking at Sather Gate when the administration turned down an ASUC request that the program also include talks by three students, one from ASUC, another from a campus religious group, and a third from student left-wing groups. Five thousand attended the off-campus meeting. Two weeks later Rule 11, requiring presidential approval for off-campus speakers and use of campus facilities by non-approved groups, appeared.

The next year (1937), the peace rally was on campus, in Harmon Gymnasium. University exercises were suspended for an hour as four students spoke. The meeting of about 4,500 unanimously approved resolutions against compulsory ROTC and for the establishment of a permanent student peace committee. Here we see another pattern: a protest at first reviled, later becoming officially legitimate.

Nonetheless, some students felt that the administration still exercised offensive power in the choice of speakers. In 1938, the executive committee of the U.C. branch of the American Student Union complained that the administration was trying to harass plans for peace meetings. The American Student Union branch eventually threatened a peace strike and rally separate from the one officially sponsored by the ASUC. The unofficial meeting at Sather Gate, featuring playwright Lillian Hellman and the former Socialist mayor of Berkeley, J. Stitt Wilson, as speakers, drew about 1,200 people. About 2,000 attended the official meeting. Earlier in the year, when Peace Strike planners suggested sending medical aid to Spain, Sproul announced Rule 17. It replaced Rule 11 and also forbade fund-raising for off-campus causes.

By 1941, enrollment at Berkeley had grown to about 14,000. The war in Europe was well underway and various student groups wanted to make it clear, in their slogan, that "the Yanks are *not* coming." In April, according to the San Francisco *Chronicle,* 20 square blocks around campus were plastered with posters saying: "War — What For? — Strike for Peace." About 2,000 students appeared at another Gate rally, once again on the usual peace strike date of April 22. The students passed resolutions calling on the Federal government not to increase armament expenditures; at the same time, they urged the defense of civil liberties against the Dies Committee, the Yorty Committee, and the Ku Klux Klan. Two days later, there was another peace strike at Sather Gate, this one sponsored by the California Youth Legislature. Resolutions were passed against convoys. And the former president of the ASUC peace committee explained that he had resigned because the administration had refused to permit the committee to present certain speakers who were, from the administration's perspective, anyway, "not respectable enough." In addition, he said, all attempts to have a meeting which would express the committee's opinions along with others had failed. This meeting of 3,000 was the last political protest of any size on campus for a number of years.

For purposes of discussing the political behavior of students on the Berkeley campus, the years from 1941 through the mid-fifties are not very revealing. As at most other American schools during these years, the student body was quiescent.

The reasons are not far to seek. During the Second World War itself, the campus population was largely composed of men in military service undergoing various specialized kinds of training. The discipline of their days at U.C. made student politics unlikely, even if they had the inclination to take part. But it seems probable that they did not have the inclination either. After all, their focus was inescapably on the war, whose threatened dangers created great internal cohesion and loyalty in the nation at large.

With the end of the war, campus life returned to normal only in the sense that the students were all civilians. In every other sense, it was a new period in American higher education. The student body was predominantly composed of returning veterans, and for them there was time to be made up, against careers deferred. Under the aegis of the GI Bill, hundreds of thousands of veterans entered college; for many, it was their first chance at higher education; for most, the emphasis was on getting done. Those years, with their makeshift classroom buildings, were intense ones on campuses, but the veterans could not have been less interested in the usual round of campus social life and politics.

By the time the great wave of veterans had passed over campus and left, the Korean War developed, presenting to undergraduates the specter of the draft and, perhaps, a focus on the world that left little concern for campus events.

We can speak, therefore, of the period from about 1941 through 1952 as a time when the students focused outwardly so much—on the war, on jobs, on the Korean War—that the campus as an arena of political life seemed to hold little interest.

Somewhat overlapping this period and continuing on into the late fifties was a quite different era. The students of the time were known as the "Silent Generation," largely because of their apparent apathy to large issues. Contrasted with the student generation which last had gone to school without the pressures of war, these students did seem lacking in public interest. Yet to speak of them as "silent" is to mislead a little, for it suggests that they withdrew into purely personal concerns. There seems little doubt that most students did withdraw from public life, perhaps because they wanted to escape the oppressiveness of politics during the McCarthy era.

The early fifties were quiet at Berkeley, certainly much quieter in politics than the thirties or the period to follow, the period we are now in. Yet the early fifties were not without their political excitement: they were the years at Berkeley of the long struggle over the special loyalty oath for faculty.

But the history of the time gives little space to student participation in the struggle.

As for non-political excitement—well, there were football games and panty raids. In those years football victories were welcomed with huge bonfires on Piedmont Avenue, kept burning by fraternity men who hurled furniture from their houses. Residents remember the street fires reaching the height of telephone poles. And there was the great panty raid of 1956, nearly a riot, with thousands of students surging around the dorms and the sororities. So much damage was caused that police had to be called out and a judge eventually awarded the sororities involved $4,500 in damages to repay the cost of lost underwear. Taking such boisterous behavior into account, perhaps we had better speak of the period as a time of "fun and withdrawal."

There is no precise way to date the end of this brief period at Berkeley. But it was clearly at an end in 1957 with the formation of TASC—Toward an Active Student Community. The name itself suggests the re-emergence of student interest in political action. TASC's major engagement was in a struggle over civil liberties, rather than over any substantive issues. So far, this has been the major focus of the present period, except for student involvement in civil rights work. One of TASC's earliest confrontations with the problem of civil liberties occurred when at a Socialist street meeting in October, 1957, an unidentified man was observed taking pictures of participants. TASC promptly condemned "photography of, or taking names of observers of Sather Gate street meetings by public or private agencies for the purpose of discriminating against those individuals as violation of rights of freedom of speech and freedom of assembly."

Meanwhile, the campaign for the abolition of compulsory ROTC also re-emerged. In the fall of 1956, in an ASUC election, the male undergraduates had voted in favor of a resolution to make ROTC voluntary; a year later the ASUC president presented the Regents with the results of the referendum. The Regents sent the proposal to a committee for study. At the same time, during the fall of 1957, TASC regrouped as SLATE, the name being adopted because the organization decided to run a slate of candidates in the fall ASUC elections. SLATE's campaign was another sign of the quickening political interest on campus. In the election, all was tumult. The SLATE candidates were disqualified and later requalified by different branches of ASUC. The *Daily Californian* reported that students from fraternities and sororities were detected stuffing ballot boxes against SLATE candidates. At any rate, SLATE lost narrowly, and decided in February, 1958, to become a permanent party.

For the spring election, SLATE prepared the first of its

campaign programs. The group singled out three main issues: it called for the end to discrimination in fraternities and sororities, for the establishment of a Fair Bear price policy in rents for student living quarters and wages for student workers and for the protection of academic freedom. Another wild campaign followed, with one actual election voided because SLATE candidates had been left off the ballot. Finally, SLATE captured two ASUC seats and lost two in the run-offs.

All this took place against a backdrop of administration efforts to redefine the vexatious problem of what constituted legitimate issues for student politics. In October, 1957, following a year's campaign by student organizations, a new liberalized interpretation of Rule 17 was presented. The new interpretation permitted nonrecognized off-campus groups composed entirely of U.C. students to use campus facilities for programs of special interest to the student body. In turn, the sponsoring groups would have to request the use of facilities and receive approval from the dean of students, while submitting promotional material for approval a week before the meeting. Groups would also be obliged to pay for any required special services, such as police protection. Off-campus speakers would have to file an application with the dean a week prior to the speeches, receive certification by a faculty or a senior staff adviser, and, where appropriate, obtain a recommendation from the chairman of an academic department. Finally, such off-campus groups would not be allowed to solicit party memberships or religious conversions.

In 1958, the administration at Berkeley underwent a major change in personnel. President Sproul retired and was replaced by Clark Kerr, who had been Berkeley's chancellor. Glenn Seaborg became chancellor; Edward Strong became vice chancellor; and Alex Sherriffs became Vice Chancellor of Student Affairs, a post newly created by Kerr and Seaborg "to facilitate relations and communications among students, faculty, and administration."

That fall, the *Daily Cal* expressed its disapproval of Rule 17 and the relocation of the free speech area to Telegraph and Bancroft. It "appears strange to us," went the newspaper's editorial of September 18, 1958, "and a little bit disillusioning that any university should have to take such an effort to relocate speakers off campus."

In December, the ASUC Executive Committee asked the administration to restore the Sather Gate tradition of free speech. Since the area just to the south of the Gate was now University property, this would have permitted unrecognized off-campus groups and speakers to speak without permission on campus. No official action was taken by the chancellor's office. The same month, Dean of Students Hurford Stone ordered an end to ASUC election rallies because SLATE had held an unauthorized meeting at Sather Gate. The dean declared that the rally had blocked traffic. Within three days, however, the dean withdrew the ban, explaining that he had received an apology from SLATE and that, in any event, the ban would handicap all students, not just those in SLATE.

During the same fall, the accelerating spread of student involvement in political issues spilled over into new areas. The Interfraternity Council, for example, declared itself against discrimination in fraternities. In part, this was a response to various off-campus activities. A brief had been filed with the State Attorney General's office in behalf of 15 minority organizations in California asking that the university be found in violation of the U.S. Constitution because of fraternity and sorority discrimination. The matter found its way into that autumn's race for the governorship. The Democratic candidate (and eventual winner), Attorney-General Brown, promised an end to Greek discrimination, while Republican Senator Knowland said that social organizations should be allowed free choice of their members.

In another area, the Academic Senate passed a motion directing professors not to reveal information to any outside party about a student's political beliefs and history when the professor had obtained that information in classroom discussion. The resolution specifically mentioned three "outside parties"; civil service, military intelligence, and the F.B.I.

In the spring semester of 1959, the U.C. chapter of the American Association of University Professors urged the administration to pull the University out of the National Defense Education Act program because it required a special loyalty oath from students.

The administration, meanwhile, continued to seek a formula that would make it clear that students engaged in off-campus political activities did not speak for the University. Vice Chancellor Sherriffs reminded the student body in early March that a 1946 regulation of the Regents forbade a student to engage in "any off-campus activities in which he shall do anything intended, or which does, convey the impression that he represents the University or the student body" unless he held written authorization to do so. Violation was grounds for dismissal.

Five days later the issue became pressing. SLATE sought permission to hold a campus rally in behalf of a local "fair housing" proposition (which eventually failed of passage). Permission was denied, Dean Stone observing that SLATE's identification with the university would give the impression that the university endorsed the proposition. The old pattern emerged again. Three days after Dean Stone announced the ban, a protest rally held by an ad hoc committee met at Sather Gate both to support the housing proposition and to demonstrate against the dean's refusal to permit the original rally.

Then, on April 8, the state Attorney-General's office issued an informal opinion that SLATE could not be prohibited from engaging in off-campus activity. The opinion added, however, that the university "may prohibit the use of its facilities at its own discretion."

During the summer, the Regents ruled that U.C. sororities and fraternities must remove any charter requirements for membership based on race, religion, or national origin by September 1, 1964.

The next school year saw the further rising of the tide of student political involvement. SLATE candidate David Armor reopened the controversy over voluntary ROTC; and on October 20, a university freshman, Frederick L. Moore, the son of an Air Force officer, began a hunger fast on the steps of Sproul Hall to protest compulsory ROTC. On the second day, after long-distance phone conversations with his parents, he ended his fast and withdrew from the university, but not, he said, in protest. The same day SLATE held a rally at Sather Gate to criticize the Regents for not taking action on ROTC, it having been about three years since the undergraduate males had voted in favor of making it voluntary and two years since their position had been presented formally to the Regents.

Then, on October 23, President Kerr issued his famous rules on political activity by students. These have become known since as the Kerr Directives. They are: 1) the preamble of the student government constitution on each campus shall be changed to make it clear that the student governments are directly responsible to the appropriate chancellor's office, 2) student governments are forbidden to speak on off-campus issues, 3) amendments to student government constitutions are subject to the prior approval of campus officials, 4) to be recognized, student organizations must have an active adviser who is a faculty member or a senior staff member; such groups must declare their purposes to be compatible with the educational objectives of the university; they must not be affiliated with any partisan political or religious group; and they must not have as one of their purposes the advocacy of positions on off-campus issues.

In addition, Rule 17 was modified. It had declared a university "responsibility" to have qualified outside speakers on important public matters. This was changed to state that the university recognizes the intellectual value of campus discussion of public issues.

Protests against the Kerr Directives were widespread. The *Daily Californian* and student papers at the Riverside and Santa Barbara campuses complained that the directives infringed on the tradition of student government; the student government at UCLA condemned the directives by resolution; and students at Riverside picketed the chancellor's office.

In April, the Regents were presented with a faculty committee report on ROTC as well as speeches from the student body presidents at Berkeley, UCLA, Davis, and Santa Barbara. The Regents announced they could take no action until the faculty report was received by the Defense Department.

There were other issues. SLATE held a rally to protest capital punishment and the scheduled execution of Caryl Chessman; 50 students went to Sacramento to picket the State Capitol and present to the legislature a petition signed by 384 faculty members urging the abolition of the death penalty. A smaller group of students marched from campus to San Quentin when Chessman was executed.

In another demonstration, Berkeley students began picketing two downtown variety stores, Kress and Woolworth's, to protest the arrest of 180 students who had tried to sit-in at various store restaurants in Nashville to break down segregation.

However feverish the pace of so much political activity, it was all mere preliminary to the massive protest largely directed by U.C. students against the House Un-American Activities Committee when it met in May in San Francisco. Part of the demonstration was inspired by the news that a Berkeley schoolteacher under investigation by HUAC would not be rehired. At the climax of the demonstrations, policemen turned hoses on the students and washed them down the steps of City Hall. Of the 63 persons arrested, only one faced trial and he was acquitted. Two U.C. students from England, however, were denied extension of their visas when it turned out that they had participated in the City Hall demonstrations.

If we look back over these protests, we see that except for ROTC, they all revolve around the issues of civil rights, mainly for Negroes, and civil liberties—the protection of free speech, of action according to conscience, of the rights of students to manage their own affairs. Generally speaking, the protests that attracted the most sympathy were those which caught up both strands: civil rights as the object of the original protest, and then the civil liberties of the students taking part.

Despite the incessant struggle between the students and the administration over the definition of the limits of student political involvement, the controversy had so far exclusively been carried out in debate, each side appealing to the public and to one another according to certain rules of the game. Through the present period, at least until the Free Speech Movement of 1964, both sides showed great patience, a willingness to adhere to the rules, and a conviction that ultimately victory would go to the side with the better reasons.

The next academic year, 1960–61, was marked by further controversies over free speech. There were also some substantive quarrels. In mid-October, the *Daily Cal* editorial board voted to endorse a group of SLATE candidates in an ASUC election. The Executive Committee of ASUC immediately ordered revision of the paper's bylaws to give Ex Com "final authority with respect to the supervision and direction of its (the *Daily Cal's*) affairs, policies and conduct." All but one of the staff resigned and established a new paper, *The Independent Californian*.

The Independent was able to print within a week a copy of an "All-University Editorial" from the student papers at the UCLA, Santa Barbara, and Riverside campuses, condemning the Executive Committee for changing the *Daily Cal* bylaws. An attempt to remove the *Daily Cal* from student politics by placing a consultative board in charge of its operations failed to win the necessary two-thirds vote in an ASUC referendum, so the Executive Committee retained control.

Once again, ROTC became a focus of student politics. SLATE picketed Harmon Gymnasium during ROTC classes. The Regents voted in December to postpone any action on whether to make ROTC voluntary. Then, in February, a picket, sophomore James Creighton, learned he had failed ROTC because he had picketed in his uniform after a warning that such action in uniform was improper and subject to discipline. Despite pleas from the ASUC's student forum and the National Student Association, the Academic Senate eventually rejected a motion to raise Creighton's grade in his ROTC course from the F he had received to the B which was his previous average.

And again, that year, the administration tried to draw a workable line between permitted and forbidden political activity by students. In February, 1961, President Kerr modified regulations to allow the exhibition or distribution of non-commercial literature on campus, providing that the purveyors of it complied with the rules of the chief campus officer—at Berkeley, the chancellor. Kerr's modification followed a lawsuit brought by UCLA student Joel Peck against the Regents to win the right to circulate literature on campus. At the time, UCLA banned the distribution of all types of literature.

In April, the administration attempted to clarify two regulations relating to rights of free speech. The chancellor (now Strong after Seaborg was appointed to serve on the Atomic Energy Commission) ruled that persons and organizations unconnected with the university would not be allowed to post, exhibit, or distribute literature on campus. And the administration clarified Rule 6, which forbids university faculty, staff, and students from communicating with members of state or Federal legislatures on policies or legislation affecting the university. Vice Chancellor Sherriffs modified Rule 6 to say that individuals would be permitted to take stands, but that they would not be allowed to use the university's name while doing so.

About two weeks later, another Rule 6 clarification was forthcoming. Chancellor Strong declared that individuals or groups of individuals were free to communicate with the state or Federal government on policies or legislation applying to the university, provided that the communication was accompanied by a statement that the views were private, that the communication was not made on a university letterhead, and provided that the chancellor's office had reviewed and approved the communication.

In May, the administration became embroiled in a controversy over the scheduled appearance of Malcolm X, spokesman for the "Black Muslims." The chancellor forbade Malcolm's appearance on the ground that his speech would violate university and state regulations aimed at enforcing the separation of church and state. The student NAACP protested that Malcolm suffered differential treatment in being refused permission to speak. The campus NAACP chapter observed that the Rev. Billy Graham, Bishop James Pike, Rabbi Alvin Fine, and the Rev. Roy Nichols had all appeared on campus since May, 1958. The Executive Committee of ASUC censured the administration; and 161 professors signed a petition to the administration protesting the refusal of permission.

In view of so much controversy, it was perhaps not surprising that during the spring semester of 1961 some members of the state legislature began to complain about free speech at the university. Assemblyman Louis Francis introduced a bill—which never reached the floor—to prohibit teachers from "espousing their own alien political philosophies" in the classroom. Francis declared: "We are sick and tired of supporting ultra-liberal left-wing professors on your campus."

A week later, however, the assembly moved by a vote of 77–0 to print a letter in its journal demanding that Assemblyman Francis retract his charges of Communist activity on university campuses. At almost the same time, State Senator Hugh Burns announced imminent publication of his committee's report on Communist activity on the Berkeley campus. "Most kitchens have their cockroaches," Burns said, "and most universities have their Communists."

It was also at this time that a storm broke out over the campus appearance of Frank Wilkinson, who had refused to testify at a HUAC hearing and been sentenced to a year in prison for contempt of Congress. Three hundred citizens from the Bay Area picketed the State Capitol in protest, while Senator Burns and Assemblyman Don Mulford, whose district includes the university, warned that SLATE, which sponsored Wilkinson's speech, would soon be "exposed for what it is"—and lose its campus privileges. President Kerr replied that

SLATE had approval to present Wilkinson (whose speech drew 3,500). Chancellor Strong added that supporters of HUAC had already presented speakers on campus in defense of their opinions.

Early in the summer, just after the end of finals, SLATE lost university recognition for identifying itself as a "campus political party" in a letter sent to the student paper at Ohio State University.

On August 1, 1961, President Kerr issued new statewide rules which, again, were designed to try to effect some *modus vivendi* for campus political groups, their right to speak, and the administration. Kerr's new rules prohibited political and social action groups from establishing headquarters on campus and from using the university's name to describe themselves. Groups were allowed to use university facilities upon application for special meetings or other events, subject to the availability of space and the nature of the speaker's topic.

Six weeks into the next academic year (1961–62), an exchange of letters in the *Daily Cal* between two members of SLATE and President Kerr served to continue the debate on the legitimate political rights of students. Ken Cloke, a SLATE representative to the Executive Committee of the ASUC, claimed that the Kerr Directives were a definite cause of student apathy on campus because of the limits they placed on political activity. Cloke added that the chancellor had permitted student government to exist, but only within ever-narrowing boundaries. The rule that prohibited a stand by student government on off-campus issues, said Cloke, was one of those regulations that undermined student political interest and involvement.

Cloke and another SLATE representative, Roger Hollander, expanded this claim in a *Daily Cal* column two weeks later. Cloke and Hollander argued: 1) A true open forum is hindered by the requirement that one week's notice must be given for a rally or meeting, since it makes the spontaneous public discussion of issues impossible on campus, especially under emergency situations. 2) "Relegating social and political actions to off-campus status is detrimental to the educational process . . ." The university must prepare students for participation in society, and that includes teaching them to put ideas into action, as well as to consider ideas objectively. 3) The California constitution cannot be invoked in defense of the prohibition of social and political action on campus. The constitution (Article IX, Section 9) is meant to protect the University from outside forces which might try to influence its policies for political or sectarian reasons. It is not meant to restrict the actions of on-campus groups, such as SLATE. 4) Something must be behind the decisions, without precedent, to eliminate previously existing student rights. What forces are behind these decisions?

President Kerr replied two days later in an open letter to the *Daily Cal*. Essentially, Kerr answered the question in Point Four of the Cloke-Hollander column: what forces are behind the decision to eliminate previously-held student rights? It is not true, Kerr said, that previously-held student rights have been eliminated. The claim that they have is an example of the "Big Myth" technique at work. And if Cloke and Hollander really believe that the Kerr Directives are less liberal than older rules, let them request a restoration of the old Rule 17, the Sproul statement of 1940, and the associated rulings. If the ASUC's Executive Committee asks for this restoration, Kerr declared, those older regulations will be immediately brought into force on the Berkeley campus in place of the Kerr Directives. (ASUC promptly voted 11–4, the four SLATE representatives opposed, to support the Kerr Directives.)

The next day, Cloke and Hollander answered in another open letter, declaring themselves shocked and surprised by Kerr's response. They said that their original article had referred only to the requirement of a one-week notification for campus meetings, and the ruling that the executive committee could not use a disclaimer of official affiliation with U.C., and hence could make no comment on off-campus issues. Not all student rights had been withdrawn, but only these two. "We ask: can it be denied that certain rights which existed previously for students, do, in fact, not exist at present?"

They also reject Kerr's offer to restore the old regulations in place of the Kerr Directives. The question, they said, is not whether the new rules are more or less liberal than President Sproul's or even whether they are in need of reform. The question, declared Cloke and Hollander, is whether the administration has a right to set down arbitrary regulations governing the political behavior of individuals and student groups. "In a democratic society, the source of authority for such regulations is rightfully derived from the society's constituents, which in the case of a student community are the students and not the university administration." There the exchange of letters ended.

In mid-March, 1962, the administration moved to provide an alternative to the requirement of prior notice for public meetings by designating a campus "Hyde Park," an area which could be available for public discussion at any time and on any topic. The site selected, the lower plaza behind the Student Union, however, raised objections from some students, who observed that few people crossed the plaza. They added that while establishment of a free speech area was a step in the right direction, students should be allowed to speak anywhere on campus.

In the meantime, the one-week notification had been reduced to 72 hours. The Student Civil Liberties Union, however, asked for a further reduction, to 24 hours. SCLU asked for three other changes as well: that the administration need only be notified of intended meetings, without need for getting approval; that any group composed of only university-connected people—students, faculty, and staff—would be allowed to use campus facilities for meetings, whether or not the group was officially recognized; and that the administration would take as its responsibility the appointment of a faculty adviser to groups which could not find a suitable person, the adviser to possess no veto power over the group's activities.

Other efforts in the direction of establishing satisfactory rules governing student political activity were made. The ASUC executive committee, for instance, requested that President Kerr grant it permission to decide what was and was not an off-campus issue. Kerr, trying to work out another troublesome problem, faculty rights in the political arena, proposed that the Academic Senate adopt a rule forbidding faculty from identifying themselves as professors at U.C. whenever they took part in non-educational activities.

Thus the '61–'62 year was marked by almost incessant debate among students, faculty, and administration as each sought to preserve his rights and protect his position. But there was more than debate. Throughout the year, students had held a number of unauthorized rallies and vigils, often in connection with nuclear testing. Usually the rallies were ignored, but on one occasion, in March, 1962, a rally protesting resumption of atmospheric testing by the United States was dispersed by campus police at the request—so said the *Daily Cal*—of the dean of students' office.

One rally, by its timing, also suggests the development of student chagrin over the limits placed on the power of ASUC to take stands on off-campus issues. Indeed, the rally, a protest against the tactics of the House Un-American Activities Committee, suggests resentment over the ASUC's willingness to abide by the Kerr Directives. The rally, in which about 450 students participated, came the day after the president of ASUC ruled that a proposed motion condemning HUAC was in violation of the Directives, Dean Katherine Towle having observed that the resolution constituted "social or political action."

Finally, '61–'62 saw an end to the long debate over compulsory ROTC. In May, President Kerr presented a proposal to the Regents without disclosing its contents; and at their meeting of June 29, the Regents voted to make ROTC voluntary.

At the start of the next academic year, President Kerr announced that off-campus political groups would be allowed to use university facilities provided their meetings were not used to "plan or implement any social or political action."

At almost the same time, Chancellor Strong ruled that two propositions on the state ballot that fall could be considered on-campus issues, so that ASUC was free to take stands on them. One, Proposition 1A, was a school bond issue providing 92.5 million dollars for the university. The other was Proposition 24, which, among other things, would have required the dismissal of any university employee who refused to answer the questions of a legislative committee or subcommittee or who pleaded the Fifth Amendment. The ASUC Senate responded the next day by endorsing 1A and denouncing 24.

During the gubernatorial race, meanwhile, Republican candidate Richard Nixon pledged to forbid persons who had violated the Subversive Control Act of 1951 or who had taken the Fifth Amendment from speaking on state-supported campuses. President Kerr declared in answer that the Regents, not the governor, will decide who can speak at the university, and added: "The university is an open forum. We have confidence in the judgment, wisdom, and cultural faculties of our students."

But further, Kerr observed, a Regents policy of 1951, reaffirmed in 1961, closes the campus to speakers from the American Communist Party; and speeches incompatible with the educational purposes of the university are forbidden under the Kerr Directives, which also declare that speakers may not use the university to involve the university in controversial issues of the day. Kerr reasserted this view a few days later. The non-conformist, as contrasted with the conspirator, serves humanity, the president said, "and the university is one of his havens." Outside forces will not be allowed to restrict freedom of speech and inquiry at the university. "When freedom of thought and expression has died on a university campus, it has died everywhere."

That fall, a year-old suit by the American Civil Liberties Union in behalf of four students at the Riverside campus to bring an end to the university's ban on Communist speakers was appealed to the Riverside Superior Court. The suit argued that the ban was an infringement on the students' right of free speech; the university replied that it was a private corporation chartered under state law, so that the ban was merely a policy decision of Regents, not a denial of Constitutional rights.

Before the matter was settled in the courts, however, the university moved to strike down the ban. During the spring semester of 1963, Herbert Aptheker, editor of the theoretical journal of the American Communist Party, was denied permission to speak on campus, as required by Rule 5. Earlier, the campus chapter of the American Association of University Professors had called on the Regents to abolish the ban. Soon after Aptheker was denied, an advertisement, signed by 300 faculty members and graduate students, appeared in the *Daily Cal* to denounce the ban on Communist speakers as "a repudiation of the democratic principles of freedom of speech and the right of dissent." Then, in April, undergraduates voted 2,947 to 847 in an ASUC referendum to ask the Regents to remove the ban. The next day, Chancellor Strong agreed that the ban was inconsistent with the university's open forum policy, but added that he could not give permission for Communists to speak since the ban continued in force. At their June meeting, the Regents voted 15–2 to revoke the ban. The Regents also established three qualifications to be invoked at the discretion of the chancellor. These qualifications were that meetings were to be chaired by a tenured faculty member, that speakers be subject to questions from the audience, and that speakers be balanced in debate by a speaker holding an opposing opinion.

A month later, Albert J. (Mickey) Lima, the first American Communist to speak on campus since the 1951 ruling of the Regents, drew a crowd of about one thousand students. The *Daily Cal* characterized the student reaction as "blah"—boredom.

During the year, some old issues were brought to resolution, at least temporarily. The ASUC Senate created an independent control board for the *Daily Californian,* thus getting it out of the jurisdiction of the Senate for the first time since the early fall of 1960. And the Federal government repealed the part of the loyalty oath required in the National Defense Education Act which had provoked the AAUP chapter to request that the university withdraw from the program in 1959.

And also during the year, as during the previous year, the university came under attack from "outside forces" complaining about campus policies. An Alameda County detective claimed in a speech to the Berkeley Realty Board that "the Bay Area is the Communist center of the United States, and most of the Communist activity in the area is centered at the university." He blamed the university's adherence to "the doctrine of academic freedom"; the doctrine, he said, permits students to participate in "all outward activities" without being stopped. A University spokesman noted only that the University does not employ Communists and that President Kerr would not "dignify the charge with a full statement."

In June, a state senate subcommittee issued the Burns Report, which claimed that "apostles of class struggle" use the academic freedom of the university to camouflage themselves and take part in Communist-front organizations. The report, formally known as the 12th Biennial Report of the Senate Fact-Finding Subcommittee on Un-American Activities, added that pro-Castro committees and former leaders of SLATE "are now running gigantic fronts for Communist movements . . . we wonder why any radicals—right, left or any other sort —are tolerated."

What the Burns Report probably had in mind, at least in part, were several demonstrations on campus during the '62-'63 academic year. At the time of the Cuban missile crisis in October, 1,500 students attended a noon-to-midnight rally sponsored off-campus by the Young Socialist Alliance. The *Daily Cal* reported that most of the students in attendance did not want war, but could see no alternative. The next day, SLATE held a rally at Wheeler Oak in Dwinelle Plaza to protest the American blockade of Cuba. A straw poll of the crowd found students favoring the blockade by a ratio of seven to one. SLATE also sponsored a 40-man picket line in November to demonstrate against the McCarran Act and the Federal Subversive Activities Control Board.

For the most part, however, the continuing debate over student political rights was confined, as in past years, to a dialogue. Even action turned out to be collective debate. The ASUC, while continuing to abide by the Kerr Directives, sought, for example, to learn whether schools similar to U.C. had comparable regulations. It found in a survey of 20 schools with student bodies of more than 8,000 that only one, the University of Arizona, had similarly restrictive rules. Student governments of three other schools, Pennsylvania State, Western Michigan University, and Illinois, made a practice of not engaging in off-campus affairs. The student governments of the remaining 16 schools made use of their right to take stands on off-campus issues.

If the major demonstrations for two years had been about nuclear testing, the Cuban crisis, and some remnants of the loyalty controversies of the early 'fifties, the academic year of 1963-64 was one long run of civil rights protests which drew ever-broader support. The first rally of the year, held by 300 students at Telegraph and Bancroft, met to protest the Federal ban on travel to Cuba, but five days later about 700 students gathered to hear James Farmer, national director of CORE, urge them to give more than their sympathies to the civil rights movement.

A week after, a storm broke over a racial incident involving university participation in an annual football festival sponsored by Berkeley's Junior Chamber of Commerce. Lynn Sims, a Negro student who was vice president of the junior class at U.C., had been chosen to escort one of the girls competing in the queen contest that was a part of the festival. The

JayCees, however, requested Sims not to escort her. The university launched an investigation, the JayCees apologized, but the university withdrew from the festival. With that the JayCees abandoned the festival themselves, and it was scheduled elsewhere for the '64 football season.

Berkeley CORE, meanwhile, began urging local merchants to advertise that they were "equal opportunity employers" as part of a program to increase Negro and other minority employment in previously all-white firms. CORE also asked the merchants to hire a "fair proportion" of minority employees within three months.

From another angle, emphasis was brought to bear on the civil rights campaign. Local newspapers began interviewing students at Stanford and Berkeley who had just returned from summer work for civil rights in Mississippi.

Then, in November, came the first picketing of a firm to get it to hire additional minority members. This was the picketing of a drive-in restaurant, Mel's, in San Francisco. Police arrested 111. On November 8, Mel's in Berkeley was picketed, 180 taking part under the leadership of a high school group. Campus CORE refused to endorse the picket, arguing that it was politically motivated since one of Mel's co-owners was a candidate in San Francisco's mayoralty race. (He lost.) Campus CORE was also unhappy because no provision was made to monitor the picket line in order to prevent violence. After three days more of picketing, Berkeley CORE claimed victory.

On November 21, Berkeley CORE announced it planned to picket Sather Gate and downtown firms during Christmas. The Sather Gate stores, however, reached an agreement with CORE in early December and CORE said it would picket only downtown. A week later the Sather Gate merchants declared they were cancelling their agreement with CORE and would negotiate only on a city-wide basis through the Berkeley Chamber of Commerce. The Christmas picketing, however, did not produce an agreement.

In February, there was another picket, this time by campus CORE, of a Lucky Supermarket on Telegraph. Bay Area CORE chapters were using a new tactic, the "shop-in." CORE members filled a basket with groceries, unloaded it at a check-stand, and left the store. After ten days of picketing and "shopping-in," CORE and Lucky's signed a hiring agreement, affecting all Lucky stores in the Bay Area. As many as one hundred students had picketed the Telegraph Avenue store at one time. On the day that the Lucky agreement was announced, a picket line was established outside the Sheraton-Palace Hotel in San Francisco. One court order had limited the number of pickets to nine, another forbade singing and chanting. When 100 pickets started to march, police moved in and arrested 81 demonstrators, 19 dropping out to avoid arrest. The next day the two restraining orders were ruled invalid by Superior Court on the grounds that demonstrators had not been properly served notice. Meanwhile, another 42 students had been arrested, bringing the total to 123. Of the total, 60 were U.C. students. These numbers may be a bit misleading, since some students may have been involved in both demonstrations.

On Friday night, March 6, a thousand demonstrators, mainly students, appeared at the Sheraton-Palace to test the court orders, which by now had been properly served. By Sunday night, the number picketing had swollen to 2,000. After 767 demonstrators were arrested for blocking the hotel lobby during what turned out to be the last day of the protest, the Hotel Owners Association signed an agreement promising to hire more members of minority groups. Of the 767 arrested, 100 were from U.C.

On March 16, picketing began at a Cadillac agency in San Francisco; this time 100 were arrested, nearly 20 of them from U.C. Eventually, more than 1,000 took part in Auto Row demonstrations. Trials against those arrested dragged on through the semester and into the summer, with those found guilty getting jail sentences, sometimes suspended sentences, and fines.

One response to these massive demonstrations came from two state legislators. Assemblyman Don Mulford termed the sit-ins "anarchy" and called for legislative action. The president pro-tem of the state senate, Hugh Burns, advocated expulsion of students arrested for illegal acts. "The state universities," Burns said, "should instruct their students that under our form of government they have legal redress for real or fancied wrongs."

President Kerr used a Charter Day address at the Davis campus to reply to these views. Such proposals, Kerr declared, are both impractical and improper. Kerr also addressed a warning to those who plan civil disobedience: "Those who deliberately violate a specific law . . . bear the heavy moral responsibility of determining that there is no other effective recourse within the body of the law and that the cause of justice which they seek to serve outweighs the exceedingly grave consequences of an act which weakens the total fabric of the law."

It seems likely, in retrospect, that the employment of civil disobedience in behalf of civil rights protests was adopted from the tactics of the southern civil rights movement. After all, many U.C. students had been south. In addition, many events had contributed to a growing sense of outrage among some students about what they regarded as the slow progress of the civil rights struggle. The bombing of a church in Birmingham that killed four Negro children occurred at the start of the school year; and many campus events served to focus attention on the issue.

In October, for instance, Malcolm X was allowed to speak on campus (overturning an earlier ruling that such addresses had to be prohibited on grounds of maintaining the separation of church and state). Malcolm's speech attracted a crowd from seven to eight thousand.

In March, various campus living groups held a "Freedom Fast" at Sunday night meals, the money saved being sent to southern Negroes who had lost jobs because they tried to vote. And later that month, a U.C. Negro student, claiming that campus police had treated him in a discriminatory fashion by requiring him to show a registration card, charged brutality and later filed a $106,000 damage suit against the University. From 50 to 60 students picketed Sproul demanding that the administration apologize to the student.

This was also the year in which President Kennedy was assassinated. The President had been a great hero to many students; his Charter Day address in 1962 had drawn an enormous and tumultuous welcome; and the Peace Corps has had greater recruiting success on the Berkeley campus than at any other school in the nation. Some observers have suggested that the murder of the President galvanized many students into more vigorous and militant action.

In contrast with earlier years, it is striking how the '63–'64 campus debate shifted away from the issue of student rights to a concern with civil rights in general, especially those of Negroes. The single major proposal of the year for some revision in the uneasy balance of administrative powers and student rights came from SLATE, which suggested that policy-making power in the university be transferred from the Regents and the administration to the faculty and students. The university treated the proposal lightly. "Well, it's Big Game Week," said a spokesman, "and SLATE seems to have been affected by it." He added that the state constitution provides for a Board of Regents whose members hold 16-year terms precisely to protect them from pressure.

Here then, is the chronology of student activity on campus. It is, in brief, a record of anti-war protest in the thirties, quiet during the forties, fun and withdrawal in the early fifties, and then a resurgence of political concern, gradually accelerating, in the late fifties and early sixties.

Some connections between events in the great society and events on campus are clear. In the thirties, the demonstrations against war were clearly a response to the deterioration of international peace; the tactics, the strike in an attenuated form, borrowed from the labor militance of the era. But the present period of political engagement is quite different. There is, first, a much greater concern with the internal issue of who shall regulate student conduct on political matters, and how. At the same time, the political concerns are part of the time: war and civil rights, mainly. And the major tactics appear to be borrowed straight from the civil rights movement.

And what about the quiet period between? The war, it seems clear, changed the composition of the student body so thoroughly that protest was almost out of the question.

But with the late fifties, we can see a return to politics. What inspired it? Perhaps the lifting of the McCarthyite strains of the early fifties; perhaps the growing national focus on what was to become the civil rights movement. The Supreme Court decision of 1954, followed by the slow changes of the succeeding years, and then the dramatic breakthrough of the Montgomery bus boycott may have had the effect of teaching a whole generation of students that alteration of what they considered unjust laws could best be achieved through collective action, including civil disobedience.

The period from 1954 through the end of the fifties offers, too, a kind of model of what has been happening at Berkeley. The legal break that came with the decision against public school segregation was followed by a period of hope that legal recourse could be employed to integrate the schools. But after three or four years, leaders of the civil rights movement found the legal process heartlessly slow so they turned to collective militancy.

Similarly, the years from '56 through '63 at Berkeley appear, on the basis of this chronology, to have been a time of continuing—one might almost say incessant—debate on the internal issue of student political rights and privileges. With all the changes of rules, the clarifications, the charges and counter-charges, it seems no one was ever satisfied that really workable and equitable procedures had been developed.

And the very militancy of the Bay Area civil rights movement in '63–'64 which seemed to divert student attention from the issue of student political rights had the consequence of further provoking outside forces into disapproval of the freedom the students did have, thus building up greater pressure against the administration. At the same time, the students, caught up in the movement, felt a greater need for freedom just because they were embarking on a course fraught with unusual and unpredictable risks. And the great concern over civil rights had another effect: it brought into student politics a great many more students than had participated in the past. This, too, increased both internal and external pressures on the University administration—at the same time that it prepared many students to defend what they considered a just cause through disciplined collective action.

Against this backdrop, the student revolt of the fall of 1964 seems less like a sudden and surprising explosion from within the body politic of the university, but rather the natural out-growth of eight years of expanding student political involve-ment, and of an increasing conflict over the proper limits of student rights to express their views, listen to the views of others, and finally take action for the causes they favor.

II

Problems in the Multiversity—
The Future Foreseen and Advocated

Although there was no one in Berkeley at the beginning of September 1964 who foresaw what was coming, at least two men, Clark Kerr and Bradford Cleaveland, did have an inkling. In his Godkin Lectures at Harvard in April 1963, Kerr stated, "the undergraduate students are restless. Recent changes in the American university have done them little good. . . . There is an incipient revolt of undergraduate students against the faculty. . . . (they) are coming to look upon themselves more as a 'class'; some may even feel like a 'lumpen proletariat.' Lack of faculty concern for teaching, endless rules and requirements, and impersonality are the inciting causes." And in an open "Letter to Undergraduates" distributed in early September by SLATE, a student political party which is a coalition of many of the militant groups and students who were later to form the core of the FSM, Bradford Cleaveland, a former graduate student in political science, wrote that unless the Regents granted all the demands he suggested were necessary for educational reform Berkeley students should "start a program of agitation, petitioning, rallies, etc., in which the final resort will be CIVIL DISOBEDIENCE. In the long run there is the possibility that you will find it necessary to perform civil disobedience at a couple of major University ceremonies." And Cleaveland told the Berkeley students that "if you get this far you will also have witnessed nation-wide publicity which will have exposed Berkeley for the undergraduate sham that it is."

The publications that include these analyses and recommendations are presented in this section. With them are other articles by Cleaveland and another spokesman for SLATE, Richard Fallenbaum. The selection from Clark Kerr's Godkin Lectures are followed by a critique of his views by Harold Taylor. The section concludes with the Charter Day address presented by President Kerr on May 5th, 1964. This address was presented as an answer to pressure on the University from the right, from those who demanded that the University expel students who are convicted for participation in civil rights sit-ins. In this talk Kerr reiterated his position that the university

*would not punish students for off-campus activities. The other
side of this position, that the university would not allow students to use campus facilities for off-campus action is what
was to become the issue of the Fall semester.*

SELECTIONS FROM *THE USES OF THE UNIVERSITY**
BY CLARK KERR
PRESIDENT, UNIVERSITY OF CALIFORNIA

The title, "The Uses of the University," implies a generally
optimistic tone, for it is not the *misuses* of the university that
will mainly concern us. At the same time, however, it is well
to note that in the discussion that follows, analysis should not
be confused with approval or description with defense.

Multiversity President, Giant or Mediator-Initiator

It is sometimes said that the American multiversity president is a two-faced character. This is not so. If he were, he
could not survive. He is a many-faced character, in the sense
that he must face in many directions at once while contriving
to turn his back on no important group. In this he is different
in degree from his counterparts of rectors and vice chancellors, since they face in fewer directions because their institutions have fewer doors and windows to the outside world. The
difference, however, is not one of kind. And intensities of relationships vary greatly; the rector of a Latin American university, from this point of view, may well have the most trying
task of all, though he is less intertwined in a range of relationships than the North American university president.

The university president in the United States is expected to
be a friend of the students, a colleague of the faculty, a good
fellow with the alumni, a sound administrator with the trustees, a good speaker with the public, an astute bargainer with
the foundations and the federal agencies, a politician with the
state legislature, a friend of industry, labor, and agriculture, a
persuasive diplomat with donors, a champion of education
generally, a supporter of the professions (particularly law and
medicine), a spokesman to the press, a scholar in his own
right, a public servant at the state and national levels, a dev-
otee of opera and football equally, a decent human being, a
good husband and father, an active member of a church.
Above all he must enjoy traveling in airplanes, eating his meals
in public, and attending public ceremonies. No one can be all
of these things. Some succeed at being none.

He should be firm, yet gentle; sensitive to others, insensitive

* (Cambridge: Harvard University Press, 1963), pp. 29–41, 86–105,
118–23.

to himself; look to the past and the future, yet be firmly planted in the present; both visionary and sound; affable, yet reflective; know the value of a dollar and realize that ideas cannot be bought; inspiring in his visions yet cautious in what he does; a man of principle yet able to make a deal; a man with broad perspective who will follow the details conscientiously; a good American but ready to criticize the status quo fearlessly; a seeker of truth where the truth may not hurt too much; a source of public policy pronouncements when they do not reflect on his own institution. He should sound like a mouse at home and look like a lion abroad. He is one of the marginal men in a democratic society—of whom there are many others—on the margin of many groups, many ideas, many endeavors, many characteristics. He is a marginal man but at the very center of the total process.

Who is he really?

To Flexner, he was a hero-figure, "a daring pioneer" who filled an "impossible post" yet some of his accomplishments were "little short of miraculous"; thus the "forceful president" —the Gilman, the Eliot, the Harper. The necessary revolutions came from on high. There should be Giants in the Groves. To Thorstein Veblen he was a "Captain of Erudition,"[1] and Veblen did not think well of captains. To Upton Sinclair, the university president was "the most universal faker and most variegated prevaricator that has yet appeared in the civilized world."[2]

To the faculty, he is usually not a hero-figure. Hutchins observed that the faculty really "prefer anarchy to any form of government"[3]—particularly the presidential form.

The issue is whether the president should be "leader" or "officeholder," as Hutchins phrased it; "educator" or "caretaker," as Harold W. Dodds[4] stated it; "creator" or "inheritor," as Frederick Rudolph[5] saw it; "initiator" as viewed by James L. Morrill[6] or consensus-seeker as viewed by John D. Millett;[7] the wielder of power or the persuader, as visualized

---

[1] Thorstein Veblen, *The Higher Learning in America* (Stanford, Calif.: Academic Reprints, 1954), p. 85.

[2] Upton Sinclair, *The Goose-Step: A Study of American Education* (Pasadena: John Regan & Co., 1923), pp. 382–384.

[3] Robert Maynard Hutchins, *Freedom, Education and The Fund: Essays and Addresses, 1946–1956* (New York: Meridian Books, 1956), pp. 167–196.

[4] Harold W. Dodds, *The Academic President—Educator or Caretaker?* (New York: McGraw-Hill, 1962).

[5] Frederick Rudolph, *The American College and University: A History* (New York: Alfred A. Knopf, 1962), p. 492.

[6] James Lewis Morrill, *The Ongoing State University* (Minneapolis: University of Minnesota Press, 1960), p. 48.

[7] John D. Millett, *The Academic Community: An Essay on Organization* (New York: McGraw-Hill, 1962), p. 259.

by Henry M. Wriston;[8] "pump" or "bottleneck" as categorized by Eric Ashby.[9]

The case for leadership has been strongly put by Hutchins. A university needs a purpose, "a vision of the end." If it is to have a "vision," the president must identify it; and, without vision, there is "aimlessness" and the "vast chaos of the American university." "The administrator must accept a special responsibility for the discussion, clarification, definition and proclamation of this end." He must be a "troublemaker, for every change in education is a change in the habits of some members of the faculty." For all this he needs the great "moral virtues" of "courage," "fortitude," "justice," and "prudence." In looking for administrators who really thought and wrote about the "end" of their institution, Hutchins particularly identified Marcus Aurelius as the great prototype.[10] Lowell, too, believed a president should have a "plan" and that although the faculty was "entitled to propose changes," the plan should not basically be subject to interference. He also had the rather quaint idea that the president should "never feel hurried" or "work . . . under pressure."[11]

There were such leaders in higher education. Hutchins was one. Lowell was another; and so was Eliot. When Eliot was asked by a faculty member of the medical school how it could be after eighty years of managing its own affairs the faculty had to accommodate to so many changes, he could answer, "There is a new president."[12] Even in Oxford, of all places, as it belatedly adapted to the new world of scholarship, Benjamin Jowett as Master of Balliol could set as his rule: "Never retract, never explain. Get it done and let them howl."[13] Lord Bryce could comment in his *American Commonwealth* on the great authority of the president in the American university, on his "almost monarchical position."[14]

But the day of the monarchs has passed—the day when Benjamin Ide Wheeler could ride his white horse across the Berkeley campus or Nicholas Murray Butler rule from Morningside Heights. Flexner rather sadly recorded that "the day of the excessively autocratic president is . . . over. He has done a great service . . ." Paul Lazarsfeld could observe the "aca-

[8] Henry M. Wriston, *Academic Procession: Reflections of a College President* (New York: Columbia University Press, 1959), p. 172.

[9] Eric Ashby, "The Administrator: Bottleneck or Pump?" *Daedalus*, Spring 1962, pp. 264–278.

[10] Hutchins, pp. 169, 177.

[11] A. Lawrence Lowell, *What a University President Has Learned* (New York: Macmillan, 1938), pp. 12, 19.

[12] Rudolph, p. 291.

[13] James Morris, "Is Oxford Out of This World?" *Horizon*, January 1963, p. 86.

[14] James Bryce, *The American Commonwealth*, new edition (New York: Macmillan, 1914), II, 718–719.

demic power vacuum" that resulted—leadership no longer taken by the president nor assumed by the faculty, with the result of little "institutional development."[15] Hutchins was the last of the giants in the sense that he was the last of the university presidents who really tried to change his institution and higher education in any fundamental way. Instead of the not always so agreeable autocracy, there is now the usually benevolent bureaucracy, as in so much of the rest of the world. Instead of the Captain of Erudition or even David Riesman's "staff sergeant," there is the Captain of the Bureaucracy who is sometimes a galley slave on his own ship; and "no great revolutionary figure is likely to appear."[16]

The role of giant was never a happy one. Hutchins concluded that the administrator has many ways to lose, and no way to win, and came to acknowledge that patience, which he once called a "delusion and a snare," was also a virtue. "It is one thing to get things done. It is another to make them last." The experience of Tappan at Michigan was typical of many, as Angell later saw it: "Tappan was the largest figure of a man that ever appeared on the Michigan campus. And he was stung to death by gnats."[17]

The giant was seldom popular with the faculty and was often bitterly opposed, as in the "revolution" against Wheeler at California. And faculty government gained strength as faculties gained distinction. The experiences of Tappan, Wheeler, Hutchins, even Thomas Jefferson, are part of the lore of the university presidency. So are those of Wayland, who resigned from Brown in frustration after vainly trying something new, Woodrow Wilson with all his battles over innovations at Princeton, and many others.

Moreover, the university has changed; it has become bigger and more complex, more tensed with checks and balances. As Rudolph saw it, there came to be "a delicate balance of interests, a polite tug of war, a blending of emphases." The presidency was "an office fraught with so many perils, shot through with so many ambiguities, an office that was many things to many men."[18] There are more elements to conciliate, fewer in a position to be led. The university has become the multiversity and the nature of the presidency has followed this change.

Also, the times have changed. The giants were innovators during a wave of innovation, to use the terms of Joseph Schumpeter drawn from another context. The American uni-

[15] Paul F. Lazarsfeld, "The Sociology of Empirical Social Research," *American Sociological Review*, December 1962, pp. 751–767.

[16] David Riesman, *Constraint and Variety in American Education* (Garden City, N.Y.: Doubleday, 1958), pp. 30–32.

[17] Ernest Earnest, *Academic Procession* (Indianapolis: Bobbs-Merrill, 1953), p. 74.

[18] Rudolph, p. 423.

versity required vast renovation to meet the needs of the changing and growing nation. As Eliot said in his inaugural address, "The university must accommodate itself promptly to significant changes in the character of the people for whom it exists." The title of Wilson's inaugural address was, "Princeton for the Nation's Service." They and others helped take what had been denominational colleges and turned them into modern national universities. They were not inventors—the Germans did the inventing—but they came along at a stage in history when massive innovation was the order of the day. The giants today, when found at all, are more likely to be in a few of the old Latin American universities undergoing modernization or the new British universities in the midst of an intense discussion of educational policy.

The giants had performed "a great service," but gentler hands were needed. University administration reverted to the more standard British model of "government by consent and after consultation."[19] There is a "kind of lawlessness"[20] in any large university with many separate sources of initiative and power; and the task is to keep this lawlessness within reasonable bounds. The president must seek "consensus" in a situation when there is a "struggle for power" among groups that share it.[21] "The president must use power economically, and persuasion to the fullest extent."[22] As Allan Nevins sees it, "The sharpest strain on growth lies not in finding the teachers, but expert administrators," and the new type of president required by the large universities "will be a coordinator rather than a creative leader . . . an expert executive, a tactful moderator. . . ."[23]

Academic government has taken the form of the Guild, as in the colleges of Oxford and Cambridge until recent times; of the Manor, as in Columbia under Butler; and of the United Nations, as in the modern multiversity. There are several "nations" of students, of faculty, of alumni, of trustees, of public groups. Each has its territory, its jurisdiction, its form of government. Each can declare war on the others; some have the power of veto. Each can settle its own problems by a majority vote, but altogether they form no single constituency. It is a pluralistic society with multiple cultures. Coexistence is more likely than unity. Peace is one priority item, progress another.

The president in the multiversity is leader, educator, creator, initiator, wielder of power, pomp; he is *also* officeholder,

[19] Eric Ashby, "Self-Government in Modern British Universities," *Science and Freedom,* December 1956, p. 10.
[20] Theodore Caplow and Reece J. McGee, *The Academic Marketplace* (New York: Basic Books, 1958), p. 206.
[21] Millett, p. 224.
[22] Wriston, p. 172.
[23] Nevins, pp. 118–119.

caretaker, inheritor, consensus-seeker, persuader, bottleneck. But he is mostly a mediator.

The first task of the mediator is peace—how he may "the Two-and-Seventy jarring Sects confute." Peace within the student body, the faculty, the trustees; and peace between and among them. Peace between the "Two Cultures" and the "Three Cultures" and their subcultures; among all the ideas competing for support. Peace between the internal environment of the academic community and the external society that surrounds and sometimes almost engulfs it. But peace has its attributes. There is the "workable compromise" of the day that resolves the current problem. Beyond this lies the effective solution that enhances the long-run distinction and character of the institution. In seeking it, there are some things that should not be compromised, like freedom and quality—then the mediator needs to become the gladiator. The dividing lines between these two roles may not be as clear as crystal, but they are at least as fragile.

The second task is progress; institutional and personal survival are not enough. A multiversity is inherently a conservative institution but with radical functions. There are so many groups with a legitimate interest in the status quo, so many veto groups; yet the university must serve a knowledge explosion and a population explosion simultaneously. The president becomes the central mediator among the values of the past, the prospects for the future, and the realities of the present. He is the mediator among groups and institutions moving at different rates of speed and sometimes in different directions; a carrier of change—as infectious and sometimes as feared as a "Typhoid Mary." He is not an innovator for the sake of innovation, but he must be sensitive to the fruitful innovation. He has no new and bold "vision of the end." He is driven more by necessity than by voices in the air. "Innovation" may be the historical "measurement of success," the great characterizing feature of the "giants of the past";[24] but innovations sometimes succeed best when they have no obvious author. Lowell once observed that a president "cannot both do things and get credit for them"—that he should not "cackle like a hen that laid an egg."

The ends are already given—the preservation of the eternal truths, the creation of new knowledge, the improvement of service wherever truth and knowledge of high order may serve the needs of man. The ends are there; the means must be ever improved in a competitive dynamic environment. There is no single "end" to be discovered; there are several ends and many groups to be served.

The quality of the mediation is subject to judgment on two

[24] Dodds, p. 43.

grounds, the keeping of the peace and the furthering of progress—the resolution of inter-personal and inter-group warfare, and the reconciliation of the tug of the anchor to the past with the pull of the Holy Grail of the future. Unfortunately peace and progress are more frequently enemies than friends; and since, in the long run, progress is more important than peace to a university, the effective mediator must, at times, sacrifice peace to progress. The ultimate test is whether the mediation permits progress to be made fast enough and in the right directions, whether the needed innovations take precedence over the conservatism of the institution. Mediators, though less dramatic than giants, are not a homogenized group; they only look that way.

They also appear to some people to be doing very little of consequence. Yet their role is absolutely essential if carried out constructively. They serve something of the function of the clerk of the meeting for the Quakers—the person who keeps the business moving, draws forth ideas, seeks the "sense of the meeting." David Riesman has suggested the term "evocator." The techniques must be those of the mediator; but to the techniques may also be added the goals of the innovator. The essence of the role, when adequately performed, is perhaps best conveyed by the term "mediator-initiator."

Power is not necessary to the task, though there must be a consciousness of power. The president must police its use by the constituent groups, so that none will have too much or too little or use it too unwisely. To make the multiversity work really effectively, the moderates need to be in control of each power center and there needs to be an attitude of tolerance between and among the power centers, with few territorial ambitions. When the extremists get in control of the students, the faculty, or the trustees with class warfare concepts, then the "delicate balance of interests" becomes an actual war.

The usual axiom is that power should be commensurate with responsibility, but, for the president, the *opportunity to persuade* should be commensurate with the responsibility. He must have ready access to each center of power, a fair chance in each forum of opinion, a chance to paint reality in place of illusion and to argue the cause of reason as he sees it.

Not all presidents seek to be constructive mediators amid their complexities. One famous president of a New York university succeeded in being at home only five months in five years. Some find it more pleasant to attend meetings, visit projects abroad, even give lectures at other universities; and at home they attend ceremonial functions, go to the local clubs, and allow the winds of controversy to swirl past them. Others look for "visions." But most presidents are in the control tower helping the real pilots make their landings without crashes, even in the fog.

Hutchins wrote of the four moral virtues for a university president. I should like to suggest a slightly different three—judgment, courage, and fortitude—but the greatest of these is fortitude since others have so little charity. The mediator, whether in government or industry or labor relations or domestic quarrels, is always subject to some abuse. He wins few clear-cut victories; he must aim more at avoiding the worst than seizing the best. He must find satisfaction in being *equally* distasteful to each of his constituencies; he must reconcile himself to the harsh reality that successes are shrouded in silence while failures are spotlighted in notoriety. The president of the multiversity must be content to hold its constituent elements loosely together and to move the whole enterprise another foot ahead in what often seems an unequal race with history.

The multiversity is a confusing place for the student. He has problems of establishing his identity and sense of security within it. But it offers him a vast range of choices, enough literally to stagger the mind. In this range of choices he encounters the opportunities and the dilemmas of freedom. The casualty rate is high. The walking wounded are many. *Lernfreiheit*—the freedom of the student to pick and choose, to stay or to move on—is triumphant.

Life has changed also for the faculty member. The multiversity is in the mainstream of events. To the teacher and the researcher have been added the consultant and the administrator. Teaching is less central than it once was for most faculty members; research has become more important. This has given rise to what has been called the "non-teacher"—"the higher a man's standing, the less he has to do with students" —and to a threefold class structure of what used to be "the faculty": those who only do research, those who only teach (and they are largely in an auxiliary role), and those who still do some of both. In one university I know, the proportions at the Ph.D. level or its equivalent are roughly one researcher to two teachers to four who do both.

Consulting work and other sources of additional income have given rise to what is called the "affluent professor," a category that does include some but by no means all of the faculty. Additionally, many faculty members, with their research assistants and teaching assistants, their departments and institutes, have become administrators. A professor's life has become, it is said, "a rat race of business and activity, managing contracts and projects, guiding teams and assistants, bossing crews of technicians, making numerous trips, sitting on committees for government agencies, and engaging in other distractions necessary to keep the whole frenetic business from collapse."

The intellectual world has been fractionalized as interests have become much more diverse; and there are fewer common topics of conversation at the faculty clubs. Faculty government has become more cumbersome, more the avocation of active minorities; and there are real questions whether it can work effectively on a large scale, whether it can agree on more than preservation of the status quo. Faculty members are less members of the particular university and more colleagues within their national academic discipline groups.

But there are many compensations. "The American professoriate" is no longer, as Flexner once called it, "a proletariat." Salaries and status have risen considerably. The faculty member is more a fully participating member of society, rather than a creature on the periphery; some are at the very center of national and world events. Research opportunities have been enormously increased. The faculty member within the big mechanism and with all his opportunities has a new sense of independence from the domination of the administration or his colleagues; much administration has been effectively decentralized to the level of the individual professor. In particular, he has a choice of roles and mixtures of roles to suit his taste as never before. He need not leave the Groves for the Acropolis unless he wishes; but he can, if he wishes. He may even become, as some have, essentially a professional man with his home office and basic retainer on the campus of the multiversity but with his clients scattered from coast to coast. He can also even remain the professor of old, as many do. There are several patterns of life from which to choose. So the professor too has greater freedom. *Lehrfreiheit,* in the old German sense of the freedom of the professor to do as he pleases, also is triumphant.

What is the justification of the modern American multiversity? History is one answer. Consistency with the surrounding society is another. Beyond that, it has few peers in the preservation and dissemination and examination of the eternal truths; no living peers in the search for new knowledge; and no peers in all history among institutions of higher learning in serving so many of the segments of an advancing civilization. Inconsistent internally as an institution, it is consistently productive. Torn by change, it has the stability of freedom. Though it has not a single soul to call its own, its members pay their devotions to truth.

The multiversity in America is perhaps best seen at work, adapting and growing, as it responded to the massive impact of federal programs beginning with World War II. A vast transformation has taken place without a revolution, for a time almost without notice being taken. The multiversity has demonstrated how adaptive it can be to new opportunities for creativity; how responsive to money; how eagerly it can play a new and useful role; how fast it can change while pretending that nothing has happened at all; how fast it can neglect some of its ancient virtues. What are the current realities of the federal grant university?

The Second Transformation

The American university is currently undergoing its second great transformation. The first occurred during roughly the last quarter of the nineteenth century, when the land grant movement and German intellectualism were together bringing extraordinary change. The current transformation will cover roughly the quarter century after World War II. The university is being called upon to educate previously unimagined numbers of students; to respond to the expanding claims of national service; to merge its activities with industry as never before; to adapt to and rechannel new intellectual currents. By the end of this period, there will be a truly American university, an institution unique in world history, an institution not looking to other models but serving, itself, as a model for universities in other parts of the globe. This is not said in boast. It is simply that the imperatives that have molded the American university are at work around the world.

Each nation, as it has become influential, has tended to develop the leading intellectual institutions of its world—Greece, the Italian cities, France, Spain, England, Germany, and now the United States. The great universities have developed in the great periods of the great political entities of history. Today, more than ever, education is inextricably involved in the quality of a nation. It has been estimated that over the last thirty years nearly half of our national growth can be explained by the greater education of our people and by better technology, which is also largely a product of the educational system.[25]

So many of the hopes and fears of the American people are now related to our educational system and particularly to our universities—the hope for longer life, for getting into outer space, for a higher standard of living; our fears of Russian or Chinese supremacy, of the bomb and annihilation, of individual loss of purpose in the changing world. For all these reasons and others, the university has become a prime instrument of national purpose. This is new. This is the essence of the transformation now engulfing our universities.

The knowledge industry. Basic to this transformation is the growth of the "knowledge industry," which is coming to permeate government and business and to draw into it more and more people raised to higher and higher levels of skill.

[25] Edward F. Denison, *Sources of Economic Growth in the United States* (New York: Committee for Economic Development, 1962).

The production, distribution, and consumption of "knowledge" in all its forms is said to account for 29 percent of gross national product, according to Fritz Machlup's calculations; and "knowledge production" is growing at about twice the rate of the rest of the economy.[26] Knowledge has certainly never in history been so central to the conduct of an entire society. What the railroads did for the second half of the last century and the automobile for the first half of this century may be done for the second half of this century by the knowledge industry: that is, to serve as the focal point for national growth. And the university is at the center of the knowledge process.

The university historically has been growing in concentric circles. It started with philosophy in Greece, and a library—the first great one—at Alexandria. It spread to the ancient professions, and then to science. It permeated agriculture and now industry. Originally it served the elites of society, then the middle class as well, and now it includes the children of all, regardless of social and economic background.

Spatially the modern university often reflects its history, with the library and the humanities and social sciences at the center of the campus, extending out to the professional schools and scientific laboratories, and surrounded by industry, interspersed with residence halls, apartments, and boarding houses. An almost ideal location for a modern university is to be sandwiched between a middle-class district on its way to becoming a slum and an ultramodern industrial park—so that the students may live in the one and the faculty consult in the other. M.I.T. finds itself happily ensconced between the decaying sections of Cambridge and Technology Square.

Universities have become "bait" to be dangled in front of industry, with drawing power greater than low taxes or cheap labor. Route 128 around Boston and the great developing industrial complexes in the San Francisco Bay Area and Southern California reflect the universities in these areas. The Gilpatric report for the Department of Defense explained that 41 percent of defense contracts for research in the fiscal year 1961 were concentrated in California, 12 percent in New York, and 6 percent in Massachusetts, for a total of nearly 60 percent, in part because these were also "centers of learning."[27] Sterling Forest outside New York City seeks to attract industry by location next to a new university campus.[28] In

---

[26] Fritz Machlup, *The Production and Distribution of Knowledge in the United States* (Princeton, N.J.: Princeton University Press, 1962), pp. 374, 399.

[27] Roswell L. Gilpatric, *The Changing Patterns of Defense Procurement*, issued by the Office of the Secretary of Defense, June 19, 1962, p. 7.

[28] John Fischer, "The Editor's Easy Chair," *Harper's Magazine*, September 1961, pp. 10–16.

California, new industrial laboratories were located next to two new university campuses before the first building was built on either of these campuses.

Sometimes industry will reach into a university laboratory to extract the newest ideas almost before they are born. Instead of waiting outside the gates, agents are working the corridors. They also work the placement offices. And the university, in turn, reaches into industry, as through the Stanford Research Institute.

The new connection of the university with the rise and fall of industrial areas has brought about an inter-university and interregional competition unmatched in history except by the universities and their *Länder* in nineteenth-century Germany. Texas and Pittsburgh seek to imitate what California and Boston have known; so also do Iowa, Seattle, and nearly all the rest. A vast campaign is on to see that the university center of each industrial complex shall not be "second best."

It is often through new academic specialties and through athletics that the universities seeking to rise in the academic hierarchy can most quickly and easily attract national attention—and also by hiring great and visible academic stars. The mark of a university "on the make" is a mad scramble for football stars and professorial luminaries. The former do little studying and the latter little teaching, and so they form a neat combination of muscle and intellect.

The university and segments of industry are becoming more alike. As the university becomes tied into the world of work, the professor—at least in the natural and some of the social sciences—takes on the characteristics of an entrepreneur. Industry, with its scientists and technicians, learns an uncomfortable bit about academic freedom and the handling of intellectual personnel. The two worlds are merging physically and psychologically.

The rise of Ideopolis. University centers have a tendency to coalesce. Allan Nevins has put it this way: "Observers of higher education can now foresee the inexorable emergence of an entirely new landscape. It will no longer show us a nation dotted by high academic peaks with lesser hills between; it will be a landscape dominated by mountain ranges."[29] The highest peaks of the future will rise from the highest plateaus.

One such plateau runs from Boston to Washington. At the universities and laboratories situated along this range are found 46 percent of the American Nobel Prize winners in the sciences and 40 percent of the members of the National Academy of Sciences. A second range with its peaks runs along the California coast. C. P. Snow has written: "And now

[29] Allan Nevins, *The State Universities and Democracy* (Urbana: University of Illinois Press, 1962), p. 114.

the scientific achievement of the United States is moving at a rate we all ought to marvel at. Think of the astonishing constellation of talent, particularly in the physical sciences, all down the California coast, from Berkeley and Stanford to Pasadena and Los Angeles. There is nothing like that concentration of talent anywhere in the world. It sometimes surprises Europeans to realize how much of the pure science of the entire West is being carried out in the United States. Curiously enough, it often surprises Americans too. At a guess, the figure is something like 80 percent, and might easily be higher."[30]

The California mountain range has 36 percent of the Nobel laureates in science and 20 percent of the members of the National Academy of Sciences. The Big Ten and Chicago constitute a third range of academic peaks, with 10 percent of the Nobel laureates and 14 percent of the members of the National Academy of Sciences. These three groupings of universities—the East Coast, California, and the Big Ten and Chicago—currently produce over three quarters of the doctorates conferred in the United States. Another range may be in the process of development in the Texas-Louisiana area.

This concentration of talent partly follows history—the location of the older private and public universities. Partly it follows industrial strengths and population centers. But it also has its own logic. No one university can cover all specialties, or cover them well enough so that there is a sufficient cluster of close intellectual colleagues. The scholar dislikes intellectual isolation and good scholars tend to swarm together. These swarms are extraordinarily productive environments. No library can be complete; nor any graduate curriculum. Some laboratories, to be well used, must be used by more than one university. Thus the Big Ten and Chicago, through their Committee on Institutional Cooperation, are merging their library resources, creating a "common market" for graduate students, diversifying their research laboratories on a common-use basis, and parceling out foreign language specializations. Something similar is happening in the University of California system, and between Berkeley and Stanford. Harvard and M.I.T., Princeton and Pennsylvania, among others, run joint research enterprises.

These clustering universities, in turn, have clustering around them scientifically oriented industrial and governmental enterprises. To match the drawing power of the great metropolis, there now arrives the new Ideopolis. The isolated mountain can no longer dominate the landscape; the constellation is greater than the single star and adds to the brightness of the sky.

[30] C. P. Snow, 110th anniversary banquet speech, Washington University, St. Louis, Mo., Feb. 23, 1963.

There are other possible patterns for development. France and Russia have not made their universities so central to the life of society. They have segregated their research institutes to a substantial degree and established separate institutions for much of their technical training. Also, both have set up their universities on a regional basis with one university having a monopoly in the region. Both France and Russia, however, are now making their universities more central mechanisms, and Paris and Moscow, in particular, are the dominating institutions. Nevertheless, their basic pattern is quite different from the American, and, I think, not as productive.

With these national, industrial, and academic pulls upon them, universities need to be quickly responsive to opportunities, readily adaptable to change. Yet they are basically conservative institutions. Jacques Barzun in his *House of Intellect* presents this "House" from an inward looking and idealistic point of view, as one opposed to the "corruption" of science, to modern art, to foundations with their interdisciplinary projects, and so forth, regretting that the "House" is no longer "a company apart."[31] However, the "City of Intellect" of the modern university also must look outward and to reality; it cannot be "a company apart." This conflict between internal and external dynamics has always been a difficult one for universities but never so intense as at present when the imperatives of change press so unmercifully against the necessities of internal harmony.

Conservative Institutions—Dynamic Environment

There are two great clichés about the university. One pictures it as a radical institution, when in fact it is most conservative in its institutional conduct. The other pictures it as autonomous, a cloister, when the historical fact is that it has always responded, but seldom so quickly as today, to the desires and demands of external groups—sometimes for love, sometimes for gain, increasingly willingly, and, in some cases, too eagerly. The external view is that the university is radical; the internal reality is that it is conservative. The internal illusion is that it is a law unto itself; the external reality is that it is governed by history.

The university's gate of Janus leads inward as well as outward, and inside the gate the social landscape changes remarkably. When one looks inward toward the "ivory tower," he sees a different "looking-glass land." Here, to get somewhere, you must run twice as slowly. This is as it must be. The university, as an institution, needs to create an environment that gives to its faculty members:

[31] Jacques Barzun, *The House of Intellect* (New York: Harper, 1959).

a sense of stability—they should not fear constant change that distracts them from their work;

a sense of security—they should not need to worry about the attacks against them from outside the gate;

a sense of continuity—they should not be concerned that their work and the structure of their lives will be greatly disrupted;

a sense of equity—they should not be suspicious that others are being treated better than they are.

Inventiveness should be left to the individual faculty member within the protection and solidity of the surrounding institutional structure. Galileo within the conservative institution of Padua in his day, Erasmus at Oxford and Freiburg, Newton at Cambridge helped start the enormous metamorphosis from which the modern world emerged. But their institutions, as institutions, were stolidly changeless.

The faculty guild. "Nothing should ever be done for the first time" was the wry conclusion of F. M. Cornford from his vantage point as a classicist at Cambridge University at the turn of the century when Cambridge was stirring with responses to the modern world. He added that "Nothing is ever done until every one is convinced that it ought to be done, and has been convinced for so long that it is now time to do something else."[32] John Stuart Mill had looked upon the British universities of his day as largely unrelated to the progress of national life. Harold Laski, a century after Mill, felt that Oxford and Cambridge operated under a form of "syndicalism," which he considered the antithesis of the social usefulness he sought, and that they were only partly saved by being shaken up by royal commissions every thirty or forty years. Flexner referred to universities generally as "institutions usually regarded as conservative, frequently even as strongholds of reaction," and added that "institutions as such tend for quite obvious reasons to lag behind the life which they express and further."[33]

With reference to the American scene, Frederick Rudolph in his recent authoritative study of American colleges and universities concluded that "Resistance to fundamental reform was ingrained in the American collegiate and university tradition, as over three hundred years of history demonstrated. . . . Except on rare occasions, the historic policy of the American college and university [was]: drift, reluctant accommodation, belated recognition that while no one was looking,

[32] F. M. Cornford, *Microcosmographia Academica Being a Guide for the Young Academic Politician* (Cambridge, Eng.: Dunster House, 1923), p. 32.

[33] Harold Laski, "The American College President," *Harper's Monthly Magazine*, February 1932, p. 319; Abraham Flexner, *Universities: American English German* (New York: Oxford University Press, 1930), p. 5.

change had in fact taken place."[34] Nevitt Sanford, after a study of more contemporary focus, observed that there have been few innovations at all and even fewer "initiated by college or university faculties"; when a movement for reform has come, "it is the collective faculty who usually seem to be dragging their feet."[35]

There is a kind of "guild mentality" in the academic profession, as in many others. The guild was isolationist toward society, devoted to producer as against consumer sovereignty, and committed more to guild rules than to quick adaptation to popular demand. The guild was egalitarian, full of senatorial courtesy, selective of its own members. It was also a "sort of club" as Snow has characterized the colleges of Cambridge and Oxford,[36] and an "oligarchy of senior professors" as Ashby has noted about these same institutions.[37] In Germany, the faculty was more a class structure than a guild—a class structure intimately tied into the class structure of the surrounding society, hierarchical rather than fraternal.

The self-contained guild idea is still an attractive ideal. One recent call to faculty members is to "close our gates," become "masters within our walls," assume a "posture of offence" against the surrounding society.[38] Yet, except in a few situations, the faculty guild has never been a fully self-governing guild in reality, and almost never a company of "free agents,"[39] much as it might like to believe itself one. However, the guild idea, the "Republic of Scholars," is often and understandably the faculty member's vision of "pie-in-the-sky."

Some of history has swirled past the "guild"; some has disrupted it; some has transformed it; some has swept it entirely away. Much of the Renaissance occurred completely outside the university. The university was generally allied against the Reformation, although bitter fights were fought within many universities, and in some the reformers emerged triumphant. The industrial, democratic, and scientific revolutions have gradually moved in on the universities and changed them almost beyond recognition. Some revolutions, like the

[34] Frederick Rudolph, *The American College and University: A History* (New York: Alfred A. Knopf, 1962), p. 491.

[35] Nevitt Sanford, "Higher Education as a Social Problem," in Sanford, ed., *The American College: A Psychological and Social Interpretation of the Higher Learning* (New York: John Wiley & Sons, 1962), p. 19.

[36] C. P. Snow, *The Masters* (New York: Macmillan, 1951), Appendix, p. 382.

[37] Eric Ashby, "Self-Government in Modern British Universities," *Science and Freedom*, December 1956, p. 10.

[38] Frank Pinner, "The Crisis of the State Universities: Analysis and Remedies," in Sanford, ed., p. 91.

[39] Logan Wilson, *Academic Man* (London: Oxford University Press, 1942), p. 71.

French and Russian, placed the "guild" fully under state control, although it has regained some of its ancient rights in France. In all of these intellectual and social revolutions, the university, as an institution, was initially more a "stronghold of reaction" than a revolutionary force, although the ideas of its individual members have often been a stimulus to change.

Eric Ashby has said that policy should "seep gradually upward" within the guild.[40] Sometimes it has. In Oxford and Cambridge, research of extraordinary quality developed when the guild was still in control and still devoted to the classics. But, generally, change, when it has come, has been initiated or at least assisted from outside the gates, as the case of England today so decisively demonstrates. The educational revolution now going on there comes from the outside and above, and finds its greatest proponents in the Labor Party.

The individual faculty member, and particularly the political liberal on the faculty, is often torn between the "guild" and the "socialist" views of the university. The guild view stands for self-determination, and for resistance against the administration and the trustees; the socialist view, for service to society which the administration and the trustees often represent. The guild view is elitist toward the external environment, conservative toward internal change, conformist in relation to the opinion of colleagues. The socialist view is democratic toward society, radical toward change, and nonconformist. And the political liberal is drawn toward both views. Here is a paradox. Few institutions are so conservative as the universities about their own affairs while their members are so liberal about the affairs of others; and sometimes the most liberal faculty member in one context is the most conservative in another. The natural radical, within the context of the guild, is radically conservative. The faculty member who gets arrested as a "freedom rider" in the South is a flaming supporter of unanimous prior faculty consent to any change whatsoever on his campus in the North. The door to the faculty club leads both out and in.

Change is a traumatic experience for an academic community, as for others. The Yale faculty in 1828 rejected in theory, while proving in practice, that colleges "by being immovably moored to the same station . . . serve only to measure the rapid current of improvement which is passing by them."[41] In a very real sense, the faculty is the university—its most productive element, its source of distinction. And faculty members are properly partners in the enterprise with areas

---

[40] Ashby, p. 5.
[41] *Reports of the Course of Instruction in Yale College by a Committee of the Corporation and the Academical Faculty* (New Haven, Conn.: Hezekiah Howe, 1828), in *American Journal of Science and Arts*, Vol. 15 (January 1829), p. 298.

reserved for their exclusive control. Yet when change comes it is rarely at the instigation of this group of partners as a collective body. The group is more likely to accept or reject or comment, than to devise and propose. The group serves a purpose as a balance wheel—resisting some things that should be resisted, insisting on more thorough discussion of some things that should be more thoroughly discussed, delaying some developments where delay gives time to adjust more gracefully to the inevitable. All this yields a greater sense of order and stability.

Institutional changes are coming, however, in areas under faculty control or influence. Some of the needed revisions will be troublesome. In many places, curricula and calendars will need to be restudied; undergraduate teaching renovated; faculty concepts of equality of treatment revised; mechanization of some elements of instruction installed; some fields of study (like biology) revolutionized. These changes will come in the face of much faculty hesitation and even some resistance. At least two changes, however, will have faculty support. One will be directed toward overcoming the fractionalization of the intellectual world, and the other will call for procedures devised to make administration more personal, including faculty administration.

The faculty world seems to sense a loss of unity—intellectual and communal unity. In large measure this can be attributed to "the overwhelming predominance of things that are new over things that are old" and to what Robert Oppenheimer calls "a thinning of common knowledge."[42] Knowledge is now in so many bits and pieces and administration so distant that faculty members are increasingly figures in a "lonely crowd," intellectually and institutionally. It is a sad commentary on the "community of masters" when its elements come together in interchange only when they coalesce feverishly over a grievance about some episode related to a change of the calendar or a parking fee.

Quite fortunately, however, there is a kind of senatorial courtesy within the collective faculty about changes desired by a single member, or a few. Changes initiated from the outside, as in the development of the federal grant university, which also have their internal supporters, are especially easy to accomplish. The individual faculty member seeking something new has, in turn, often found his greatest encouragement and leverage coming from the outside; the individual scholar is the inventor, the outside agency the force for innovation. The inventing faculty member almost instinctively knows that internal change will come more easily if he obtains the exter-

[42] J. Robert Oppenheimer, "Science and the Human Community," in Charles Frankel, ed., *Issues in University Education* (New York: Harper, 1959), pp. 56, 58.

nal support of a foundation or a federal agency. These outside-to-inside and inside-to-outside alliances have been great sources of progress.

Much change also takes place largely outside collective faculty purview, outside the "veto groups" of the academic community—in the new department or institute, the new project, the new campus. The institute, in particular, has been as much the vehicle of innovation in recent years as the department has been the vault of tradition. Change comes more through spawning the new than reforming the old.

When change does come, it may be by the slow process of persuasion, or by subversion as through the inside-outside alliance, or by evasion as in the new enterprise, or by external decision. The academic community, regardless of the particular process involved, is more changed than changing; change is more unplanned than planned.

"Remembrance of things past." If the collective faculties represent the present, the collective alumni represent the past —as much the best of the past as the faculty the best of the present. The alumni are oriented toward their own undergraduate days. There seems to be a rising sense of alumni concern as the rate of change rises. Generally it is over the preservation of an emphasis on teaching as against research; of the beauty of the old campus as against the asphalt and concrete and glass of the recent "improvements"; of the quality of remembered undergraduate life in its totality; of the old admission requirements which let the old grads get in; of athletic teams that never lost a game; of the spirit of the "halls of ivy" as against the technological materialism of the federal grant university; of the integrity of the old alma mater against the blandishments from Washington. The older and the smaller and the more private and the more distinguished the university, the greater the intensity of these concerns.

If the alumni are concerned, the undergraduate students are restless. Recent changes in the American university have done them little good—lower teaching loads for the faculty, larger classes, the use of substitute teachers for the regular faculty, the choice of faculty members based on research accomplishments rather than instructional capacity, the fragmentation of knowledge into endless subdivisions. There is an incipient revolt of undergraduate students against the faculty; the revolt that used to be against the faculty *in loco parentis* is now against the faculty *in absentia.* The students find themselves under a blanket of impersonal rules for admissions, for scholarships, for examinations, for degrees. It is interesting to watch how a faculty intent on few rules for itself can fashion such a plethora of them for the students. The students also want to be treated as distinct individuals.

If the faculty looks on itself as a guild, the undergraduate students are coming to look upon themselves more as a "class"; some may even feel like a "lumpen proletariat." Lack of faculty concern for teaching, endless rules and requirements, and impersonality are the inciting causes. A few of the "nonconformists" have another kind of revolt in mind. They seek, instead, to turn the university, on the Latin American or Japanese models, into a fortress from which they can sally forth with impunity to make their attacks on society.

If federal grants for research brought a major revolution, then the resultant student sense of neglect may bring a minor counterrevolt, although the target of the revolt is a most elusive one.

The big state universities are most vulnerable to charges of neglect of students. The private universities, tied more to tradition, to student tuition, to alumni support, to smaller size, have generally far better preserved their devotion to undergraduate life.

In inter-university competition, the distribution of the ablest students, as shown by the statistics on scholarship winners, is a telling point. A university's share of the ablest students is an important element in its ranking: how attractive is its educational program to the students most entitled to make a choice?

Student pressures for better undergraduate instruction may be supplemented by the complaints of parents, who think their children are being sacrificed on the altar of research. Also, the public at large, whose attention has been riveted on the elementary and secondary schools as the "population bulge" has affected them, may now turn its attention increasingly to the university level when the "bulge" reaches there. Generally the public is more interested in quality of instruction than in quantity of research. The spotlight which the universities have helped turn on the teaching of others at lower levels may now be turned on their own.

Changes Still to Come

There has been some success, but there are some problems still to be fully faced; and they are problems of consequence.

One is the improvement of undergraduate instruction in the university. It will require the solution of many sub-problems: how to give adequate recognition to the teaching skill as well as to the research performance of the faculty; how to create a curriculum that serves the needs of the student as well as the research interests of the teacher; how to prepare the generalist as well as the specialist in an age of specialization looking for better generalizations; how to treat the individual student as a unique human being in the mass student body; how to make the university seem smaller even as it grows larger; how to establish a range of contact between faculty and students broader than the one-way route across the lectern or through the television screen; how to raise educational policy again to the forefront of faculty concerns. Increasingly, also, the better institutions will need to keep in mind that many of their undergraduate students will be going on to graduate school, and therefore that they need individual attention as pre-graduate students.

Another major task is to create a more unified intellectual world. We need to make contact between the two, the three, the many cultures; to open channels of intelligent conversation across the disciplines and divisions; to close the gap between C. P. Snow's "Luddites" and scientists;[43] to answer fragmentation with general theories and sensitivities. Even philosophy, which once was the hub of the intellectual universe, is now itself fragmented into such diverse specialties as mathematics and semantics. However, the physical sciences are drawing together as new discoveries create more basic general theories; the biological sciences may be pulled together in the process now going on; the social sciences might be unified around the study of organizations and the relations of individuals to and within them. Chemistry and social psychology may come to be central focalizing fields. As knowledge is drawn together, if in fact it is, a faculty may again become a community of masters; but "a sense of the unity . . . of all knowledge"[44] is still a very long way off.

A third problem is to relate administration more directly to individual faculty and students in the massive institution. We need to decentralize below the campus level to the operating agencies; to make the collective faculty a more vital, dynamic, progressive force as it now is only at the departmental level; to bridge the growing chasm between the department that does the teaching and the institute that does the research, with the faculty member torn between; to make the old departments and divisions more compatible with the new divisions of knowledge; to make it possible for an institution to see itself in totality rather than just piecemeal and in the sweep of history rather than just at a moment of time; to bring an understanding of both internal and external realities to all those intimately related to the process, so that there may be greater understanding; to see to it that administration serves and stimulates rather than rules the institution, that it be expendable when necessary and flexible all the time; to assure that the university can do better what it does best: to solve the whole range of governmental problems within the university.

Additionally, there is the urgent issue of how to preserve a margin for excellence in a populist society, when more and

---

[43] C. P. Snow, *The Two Cultures and the Scientific Revolution* (New York: Cambridge University Press, 1959).

[44] Karl Jaspers, *The Idea of the University*, trans. H. A. T. Reiche and H. F. Vanderschmidt (Boston: Beacon Press, 1959), p. 46.

more of the money is being spent on behalf of all of the people. The great university is of necessity elitist—the elite of merit —but it operates in an environment dedicated to an egalitarian philosophy. How may the contribution of the elite be made clear to the egalitarians, and how may an aristocracy of intellect justify itself to a democracy of all men? It was equality of opportunity, not equality *per se,* that animated the founding fathers and the progress of the American system; but the forces of populist equality have never been silent, the battle between Jeffersonianism and Jacksonianism never finally settled.

If there are to be new departures, they are most likely to come on the campuses of those old, private universities which have prided themselves on control of their own destiny, and on the totally new campuses of the state universities in America and the new public universities in Britain. The university for the twenty-first century is more likely to emerge from these environments than from any others. Out of the pride of the old and the vacuum of the new may come the means to make undergraduate life more exciting, intellectual discourse more meaningful, administration more human. And perhaps there will arise a more dynamic demonstration of how excellence makes democracy more vital and its survival more assured. Then the universities may rise to "the heights of the times" and overcome "their inspirational poverty."[45]

George Beadle, president of the University of Chicago, once implied that the very large American university (but not his own) might be like the dinosaur which "became extinct because he grew larger and larger and then sacrificed the evolutionary flexibility he needed to meet changing conditions";[46] its body became too large for its brain. David Riesman has spoken of the leading American universities as "directionless . . . as far as major innovations are concerned";[47] they have run out of foreign models to imitate; they have lost their "ferment." The fact is that they are not directionless; they have been moving in clear directions and with considerable speed; there has been no "stalemate." But these directions have not been set as much by the university's visions of its destiny as by the external environment, including the federal government, the foundations, the surrounding and sometimes engulfing industry.

The university has been embraced and led down the garden path by its environmental suitors; it has been so attractive and so accommodating; who could resist it and why would it, in turn, want to resist?

45 Sir Walter Moberly, *The Crisis in the University* (London: SCM Press, 1949), p. 20.
46 George W. Beadle, "The University of X," *Context,* Fall 1961.
47 Riesman, p. 64.

But the really new problems of today and tomorrow may lend themselves less to solutions by external authority; they may be inherently problems for internal resolution. The university may now again need to find out whether it has a brain as well as a body.

THE ACADEMIC INDUSTRY
A DISCUSSION OF CLARK KERR'S *The Uses of the University**
BY HAROLD TAYLOR,
FORMER PRESIDENT OF SARAH LAWRENCE COLLEGE

The argument of Mr. Kerr's book is that the American university is the center of the knowledge industry in this country. There is a heavy demand for certain kinds of knowledge and knowledgeable people to move the society toward the goals it has set for itself, and the university exists to meet these demands. "The process cannot be stopped. The results cannot be foreseen. It remains to adapt." The universities able to adapt quickly and effectively will be the great universities of the future.

Mr. Kerr makes a parallel argument about the administration of the university. The president of the university presides over a loosely held set of bureaucracies; he mediates the forces at work among them, feeling their strength, deciding which ones are to be encouraged, which ones blocked, and which ones are so powerful that they would, if opposed, sweep the president away with them. There are varieties of interest groups, all of them legitimate—the students, the faculty, the alumni, the community, the voters, the government, industry, agriculture, "society." The president has to see that each one of the interests gets its fair hearing, its fair share of legitimate attention and remains in balance with the others.

The president is therefore not an educational leader, nor should he try to be. The faculty would not allow it, and his managerial duties prevent it. Mr. Kerr is suspicious of "vision," as he puts it. That day is over. The president is now a "mediator-initiator," although what the mediator can initiate in the system Mr. Kerr describes, God only knows. In the biggest places, a half-billion-dollar budget, tens of thousands of students, a hundred-million-dollar building program, a political apparatus, government contracts, and hundreds of administrative details, get in the way of any hope of doing anything about education. The president has to have the *opportunity to persuade* (Mr. Kerr's italics), but he must remember that the mediator "wins few clear-cut victories; he must aim more at avoiding the worst than seizing the best. He

* From *Commentary*, December 1964.

must find satisfaction in being *equally* distasteful to each of his constituencies; he must reconcile himself to the harsh reality that successes are shrouded in silence while failures are spotlighted in notoriety."

But why not seize the best? Why be distasteful to all constituencies? Why submit to the genteel cynicism of the academics? We are told by Mr. Kerr of the enormous growth in power of the organized intellect within the knowledge industry. We are told nothing about the way in which the power can be directed, by the president of the university, among others, toward ideal ends. "The ends are there," says Mr. Kerr, "the means must be ever improved in a competitive dynamic environment."

The ends are not there. They change all the time, and the means determine the ends. If a president buys scholars and his coaches buy football players, this defines the ends he is seeking—prestige and money. If the president is simply an executive with all the equipment of the "mediator-initiator," and his twin purpose is "the keeping of the peace and the furthering of progress," how does he choose which means for what ends? How does he decide what kind of peace is to be kept, what kind of progress is to be made, and what direction it should take? Or, for that matter, who decides what education is and what direction it should take? Not the faculty, since, as Mr. Kerr points out, they are not interested in education or educational policy. Not the students, they are never consulted. Not the vice-presidents and deans who, under the present system, are middle-management mediators in their own right, administering sections of the knowledge industry. Who then? The alumni? The Board of Regents? The state legislature? The government? A committee of outside experts?

A university, no matter how big, must be a university, not a "multiversity," and if it exists as a collection of activities held together only by a common name—if, as Mr. Kerr says, "it has been embraced and led down the garden path by its environmental suitors," isn't it time that it shocked itself by its own situation and discovered at last "whether it has a brain as well as a body"? How can we, in view of Mr. Kerr's account of the seduction of the university by money and prestige, his statements about the scandalous neglect of undergraduates, the entrepreneurship among faculty members in the field of government contracts, the manipulative attitudes which have replaced the idea of comradeship among scholars and students—how can we accept, condone, or advocate a philosophy of mediation when the responsibility of the university is to give intellectual and cultural leadership?

The university is becoming organized so that competitive success by its members (high grades and prestige for students, high salaries and prestige for faculty members) is the criterion of value and reward. The society is so organized that competitive success in the economic and social system is the mark of American virtue. Then from what corner of the entire culture, if not from the universities, will come those ideas and criticisms which take the society out of its narrow orbit of self-acceptance?

The President of the United States is a mediator, in Mr. Kerr's terms. If that is all he is, he becomes a president like General Eisenhower, and decisions are made by the equilibrium of forces, not by the exercise of thought and imagination.

The big universities have changed in precisely the ways Mr. Kerr has described. They have become corporations for producing, transmitting, and marketing knowledge, and in the process have lost their intellectual and moral identity. At the time that they should have been creative centers for the development of strategies for peace, disarmament, and world unity, they were busy with defense department contracts. When the educational problem of the Negro was getting worse by the day, they were busy making admission requirements more and more favorable to the white middle-class student from privileged environments. When the social habits and material ambition of the citizens were following the lead of the advertising agencies, the universities were producing graduates whose intellectual equipment was suited to reading advertising copy. When the public schools were groping for ways of improving the intellectual content of their curriculum, the universities were sneering at teachers colleges and schools of education as the province of the intellectually unfit and the spiritually slothful. At a time when political and social movements have been promoting authoritarian causes on a basis of anti-intellectualism, the universities have frowned on political action by liberal student activists.

In the face of all this, Mr. Kerr seeks a proper balance among competing interests, both in the relative importance attaching to the divisions of knowledge—the social sciences, the humanities, the creative arts, the natural sciences—and in the relative importance of teaching, research, professional education, general education, community service.

What is wrong with Mr. Kerr's argument is that the pluralism of American society, while one of its primary characteristics, is not a pluralism devoid of all values, spreading in all directions like the content of a marsh. A poem is greater than a stock dividend, students are more important than projects, although all are necessary parts of the university structure. The university may be "a mechanism held together by administrative rules and powered by money," but the power of the money must be used to achieve certain large aims which it is up to the educators in the universities to decide. I do not see how the university president and his colleagues can run away from this. Nor do I see why the classical view of the European university should be held up as a model for universities everywhere else. I am weary of seeing Flexner, Newman, von Humboldt, and the rest cited as those who have given us the definition of the university, with deviations considered to be defections from intellectual virtue. The American land-grant university is a new institution, and need deliver no apology for deviating from German, British, or early American models. These were the agencies of a class society and existed to create an elite of the educated to govern in matters of taste, religion, economics, and politics. The land-grant university in America possesses its own particular genius. It was developed to serve the needs of a new kind of society in which the intellectual life was not to be divorced from the practical. Mr. Kerr's idea of a university designed to serve the needs of society is one which accepts the reality of a pluralism of social need and purpose. But it is still too narrow to define the university's mission.

The major component missing in Mr. Kerr's conception is the use of the university to inform, enlighten, and enrich the lives of the students. It is clear from those passages of the book in which Mr. Kerr deals with students that in the scale of university interests they are close to the bottom. Mr. Kerr describes their plight, but has no plan of rescue. In his suggestions for the use of federal funds for education appear ideas for federal research centers, the continued support of research projects, a National Foundation for Higher Education, graduate fellowships, a national Council of Advisors on Education, but the most he can produce for students is to suggest that "federal agencies should permit, even encourage, post-doctoral fellows and research professors to teach one-quarter or even one-third time at no cost to the institution," and that teaching assistantships should be taken as seriously as research assistantships and fellowships.

But this palliative will hardly do. For the university, no matter how large and no matter how diverse its activities, exists within the society as the major force to keep the society intellectually honest and politically healthy. The students, and especially the undergraduates, are the instruments of cultural and social change, their minds are the means through which a society seeks its own future.

The production of knowledge and of knowledgeable people possessing marketable skills could presumably be done elsewhere than in the universities. Some business corporations and government agencies already do it, and American style and efficiency in organization make this comparatively easy, given the funds and a few first-rate executives. The hard task is to develop an educational community in which the central values of intellect and sensibility are shared by all its members without regard to the particular form of knowledge or skill possessed by the individuals in it.

What saves a university from becoming a training institute or a research institute is the student body, and the mark of a true university is whether or not it takes its students seriously. They constitute the intellectual resources without which knowledge remains inert and social progress becomes impossible. To neglect them is to indicate that one is prepared to accept a role for the university as the servant of society, and as a place where faculty members, research scholars, and educational administrators band together to further interests peculiar to themselves and their clients.

UNIVERSITY ABDICATES SOCIAL RESPONSIBILITY*
BY RICHARD FALLENBAUM

One of the first tasks of anybody interested in the nature of education at the university is to ask the question: what does the university think of itself, how does it see its role in society, what does it conceive to be its contribution to solving the problems of existence in the twentieth century? With an answer to this kind of question one would have a better understanding of why the university treats its students as it does and what it hopes to accomplish by it. Yet one of the most striking findings of any study of the public aspect of the university-speeches, reports, pamphlets, etc.—is the complete lack of any formulation of responsible social objectives particularly in the area of education. This is not to say that the university has no goals. On the contrary, the university seems dedicated to the task of building itself into a vast academic empire. To this end it seeks to nurture and tap every demand in the burgeoning academic market. The university responds to the rising clamor for admissions by providing more places for students. The government embarks on an arms race or a space race and the university dutifully provides hydrogen bombs and satellites. Many university undertakings are valuable but many others are ridiculous and even dangerous. The only quality that is common to them all is that they increase the university's size and prestige.

How is it possible for the university to operate in such a social and moral vacuum? The answer is implicit in every major document concerning the university, but it has never been as explicitly set forth as in President Kerr's speeches at Harvard three weeks ago (at the time of this article). Clark Kerr's answer to the charge of academic aimlessness is essentially that

* From *The Cal Reporter* (SLATE newspaper), Berkeley, May 13, 1963, pp. 1, 3.

it is a shame, of course, but there is nothing that can be done about it. At one time, the argument runs, universities *did* have an idea of what needed to be done in society, and the men who ran them attempted with varying success to turn their institutions to these tasks. Since then conditions have changed and many of the academic visions have lost their relevance. But according to Kerr, something more fundamental has also happened. Not only has a new era made some ideas irrelevant to the conduct of the modern university, it has made *all* ideas irrelevant. Somehow, somewhere in the quite recent past the university became a prisoner and slave of the irresistable forces of history. As a result of that fateful event the modern educational leader must, Kerr argues, abandon his petty illusions (I almost said "petty bourgeois illusions") and fall in step with history. His function, to use Kerr's imagery, is of a mechanic servicing a vast educational machine. His duty is to adjust the complex mechanism so that the many forces fed into it do not produce a breakdown. Kerr's argument is in many ways brilliant and not without a certain pathos. But the fact of the matter is that Kerr has nailed his flag to one of the most widely discredited intellectual conceptions. History is not a separate *thing* with its own logic and imperatives. It is the sum of men's choices about their own lives, the consequences of which define the choices we have. Kerr would rather not face up to these choices, so he says they do not exist and defends himself by assuming a stance of militant impotence. Being an informed man Kerr recognizes the existence of some pressing concerns such as survival and the loss of individual purpose. But he simply gives them a polite nod and returns to his tinkering.

The same sort of historical determinism seems to permeate every segment of the university. Close to home, for example, the committee that set up the breadth requirements for undergraduates introduced its report with a somewhat more disguised and conservative version. "(We) have assumed that the College of Letters and Science, which has existed in its present form for the last forty years has had during these years a definite purpose, and has achieved results in which we may take reasonable satisfaction." Any recognition of changes in the intellectual and social environment that has occurred these forty years is not evident in the report.

The effect of this social aimlessness on the individual students, particularly the undergraduate, is that the education he receives at Cal has very little relevance to his prospects in life and to the alternatives open to him. If survival and alienation are critical problems to everybody including the student, why is not education aimed at uncovering the issues and explaining the alternatives? But this is not done, and the student's four-year-stay here is painfully dull and frustrating. What makes that time tolerable is the social and intellectual contacts with other students and the promise of respectability and economic gain.

To its credit the university seems to have realized that something is wrong and is taking the initiative, President Kerr's determinism the contrary notwithstanding, to break the pattern. Its diagnosis is that undergraduates do not receive adequate faculty attention. Its prescription for undergraduates is the British system of higher education. This is being put into effect on the Santa Cruz campus with its cluster of small more-or-less self-contained colleges. This and all other admirable educational experiments are, however, in danger of failing. The hostility towards ideas and vision implicit in Kerr's theory leads to the adoption of cute slogans, gimmicks and piecemeal solutions. Unless men like Kerr face up to the fundamental social issues to which they so blithely give lip service the future for the university is more chaos, for the students more frustration and pain, and for mankind the continuing drift towards oblivion.

A LETTER TO UNDERGRADUATES*

BY BRADFORD CLEAVELAND,

FORMER GRADUATE STUDENT

DEPARTMENT OF POLITICAL SCIENCE, BERKELEY

Dear Undergraduates,

On May 13, 1963, SLATE published the *Cal Reporter,* a newspaper which charged this university with a total failure to educate undergraduates. The paper said that the university pushed the myth that you, as undergraduates, are "training for leadership," when in reality you are training for obedience; that you leave the university with a basic suspicion of intellectuals, and fear of the kinds of thought necessary for you to meet the 20th century world-in-revolution. The theme of a quote from Bertrand Russell ran through the paper:

> We are faced with the paradoxical fact that education has become one of the chief obstacles of intelligence and freedom of thought.

This is not a *minor* charge. The charges were clearly focused upon your situation as an undergraduate, and not the graduate schools. The response to the newspaper was astonishing. The *Daily Cal* made the coy comment that SLATE had again emerged like a "grouchy bear," but that it offered no "constructive solutions." This casual and inappropriate response represented the views of a great many of you and your

* *Slate Supplement Report,* Vol. I, No. 4, Berkeley, September 1964.

professors and administrators. But those charges were not minor, they were *seriously radical*, and for the *Daily Cal* to suggest that we all sit around picking our noses while asking for "constructive solutions" is astonishing!! If the rising waters of a flood threaten to immerse you in death and suffocation, it would be more than ridiculous to reflect on "constructive solutions." Or:

There Is No Blueprint for an Educational Revolution!!!

It was like this: on the one hand there was substantial agreement that the university stamps out consciousness like a super-Madison-Avenue-machine; on the other, people saying, "So what?" or "Bring me a detailed and exhaustive plan." *But there is no plan for kicking twenty thousand people* IN THEIR ASSES! No plan will stop excessive greed, timidity, and selling out. At best the university is a pathway to the club of "tough-minded-liberal-realists" in America, who sit in comfortable armchairs talking radical while clutching hysterically at respectability in a world explosive with revolution. At worst the university destroys your desires to see reality and to suffer reality with optimism, at the time when you most need to learn that painful art. In between those two poles is mostly garbage: Bus. Ad. Ph.D. candidates "on the make"; departmental enclaves of "clever and brilliant" students who will become hack critics; and thousands of trainees for high-class trades which will become obsolete in ten years.

Dear undergraduate, let me make this crystal-clear for you. There is a contrast which exists on this campus between the common (and sometimes beautiful) illusions which we have all had, and what actually happens! . . . a gap which seems to be reaching catastrophic proportions. I will offer two sets of utterly obvious facts to show you that a violent contrast does exist; and that the university is a grotesque perversion of the conditions necessary for your freedom to learn reality and to suffer it with optimism. The first set of facts is your Charter Day Ceremony, the second is the essentials of your undergraduate routine—a grotesque perversion of your freedom to learn.

Your Undergraduate Routine

The *Cal Reporter's* charges were that the routine life of the university is *destructive* of anything we know of educational tradition: especially at the level where we might reasonably expect to see painstaking efforts to give mass education its highest expression—at your level as undergraduate. In the place of such efforts, your routine is comprised of a systematic psychological and spiritual brutality inflicted by a faculty of "well-meaning and nice" men who have decided that your situation is hopeless when it comes to actually participating in serious learning. As an undergraduate you receive a four-year-long series of sharp staccatos: eight semesters, forty courses, one hundred twenty or more units, fifteen hundred to two thousand impersonal lectures, and over three hundred over-sized "discussion" meetings. Approaching what is normally associated with learning—reading, writing, and exams—your situation becomes absurd. Over a period of four years you receive close to fifty bibliographies, ranging in length from one to eight pages, you are examined on more than one hundred occasions, and you are expected to write forty to seventy-five papers. As you well know, reading means "getting into" hundreds of books, many of which are secondary sources, in a superficial manner. You must cheat to keep up. If you don't cheat you are forced to perform without time to think in depth, and consequently you must hand in papers and exams which are almost as shameful as the ones you've cheated on. You repeat to yourselves over and over as an undergraduate that "It doesn't make any difference . . . it's the grade that counts," a threadbare and worn phrase (if you are lucky enough to make it to the third or fourth year) used as commonly as your word "regurgitation" in place of "exam." You know the measure of truth in those bits of slang: it *is* nauseous . . . you almost *do* "puke up your work" to professors. I personally have known students who have gotten physically sick by merely reflecting upon their routine. In the sciences and technical fields your courses are bluntly and destructively rigorous. . . . you become impatient with "that social sciences and humanities crap." How did you get to be such puppets? You *perform*. But when do you think? Dutifully and obediently you follow, as a herd of grade-worshiping sheep. If you are strong at all, you do this with some sense of shame, or if you are weak, you do it with a studied cynicism . . . as jaded youth with parched imaginations that go no further than oak-paneled rooms at the end of the line . . . BUT WHETHER YOU ARE STRONG OR WEAK YOU PERFORM LIKE TRAINED SEALS, AND LIKE SHEEP YOU FOLLOW . . . WITH THE THOROUGHBRED PHI BETA KAPPA SHEEP LEADING YOU!! up the golden stairway to the omnipotent A, to the Happy Consciousness, to success and a very parochial mind. This is the core of your dutiful daily lives, and your homage to respectability. Reluctantly or otherwise, you permit it to be applied by administrators who use computers on you as much because they are afraid of personal contact with you as for the reason that they wish to keep the assembly line moving efficiently. You permit professors to extract your performance by the coercion of grades. Why do you permit this apostasy of learning . . . a process which prevents you from extending your thought beyond a shallow dilettantism?

IF THE FACTS OF YOUR UNDERGRADUATE EXISTENCE WERE
SOLELY DETERMINED BY THE "COURSE/GRADE/UNIT SYS-
TEM," YOUR "INCIPIENT REVOLT," TO WHICH PRESIDENT
KERR HIMSELF IRRESPONSIBLY ALLUDED IN THE GODKIN
LECTURES, WOULD PROBABLY HAVE ALREADY OCCURRED.[1]

The reason why, dear undergraduates, you permit your
minds to be abused, is because you are given a magnificent
bread and circus. What a pain reliever! . . . these "extra-
curricular" activities. Coming to you from your ASUC student "government," other special bureaucracies such as the
Committee on Arts and Lectures, and added to by more intellectual offerings from departmental and special-grants lecture series, is a semesterly tidal wave of exciting and highly intense stimuli which dazzles you away from the fact that you
are obstructed from learning, or even questioning whether you
should be learning while you are here. This bread and circus
assures you that the world is really *not* in the midst of anything so serious as *revolution,* much less within your own
sacred borders!! From the powerfully entertaining to the scho-
lastically intellectual you get films, debates, art exhibits, athletics, drama, "spirit" groups, recreation, seductions of hundreds of social groups; this pyrotechnical explosion of *Kultur*
is something terribly "other directed"; happily away from your
puppetlike performance in the course/grade/unit procedural
core. Your attention is diverted away from your treadmill to
the candied goodness of the bread and circus. Hopefully, when
you get your bachelor's degree, you will step up to higher
plateaus, where many kinds of "success" await you. You are
blinded to the fact that you are really getting something of
terrible importance while you are here:

TRAINING IN THE CAPACITY FOR UNQUESTIONING OBEDI-
ENCE TO A COMPLEX FLOOD OF TRIVIAL BUREAUCRATIC
RULES. IN THE NAME OF HUMAN LEARNING YOU ACQUIRE
THE CAPACITY TO BE DOCILE IN THE FACE OF RULES.
WHILE YOU ARE TRAINING, THE RULES WHICH TELL YOU
HOW TO GO ABOUT YOUR TRAINING ARE DISPLACING YOUR
FREEDOM TO THINK . . . SKILL AND OBEDIENCE ARE WHAT
YOU ACQUIRE.

Aren't you the least bit aware that such a capacity is not
only necessary for life in America's giant public and private

[1] "There is an incipient revolt of undergraduate students against the
faculty; the revolt that used to be against the faculty in loco parentis is
now against the faculty in absentia," from page 103 of *The Uses of the
University,* Harvard, 1963 (Godkin Lectures given in 1963 at Harvard).
Kerr's comments throughout the book on higher education are made
from the vantage point of a sort of disinterested observer, as though the
president was not talking about his own "multiversity," or as though he
was really nothing more than a bureaucrat-employee of the Regents. Or,
as Kerr himself puts it, ". . . he is mostly a mediator," on p. 36.

corporations, but that it is also a first-class ticket to a traditional form of statehood under the designation of tyranny?
No matter how well trimmed you keep your grassy lawns in
suburbia after you get your bachelor's degree, your moral
and spiritual servitude will not be reduced. If you have attended a Charter Day ceremony and can recall the feelings
you had, you might feel the temptation to say that it is this
indictment which is grotesque, and *not* the university . . . but
you are the university . . . it is *your* life I have described in
its essentials.

Has it ever occurred to you, dear undergraduate, that human learning is a painful and exhilarating process which comes
from asking the kinds of questions which YOU would like to
ask: "WHY AM I IN THE UNIVERSITY? WHAT IS KNOWLEDGE?
WHAT IS EXTREMISM, AFTER ALL, AND HOW DOES POLITICAL
EXTREMISM AFFECT ME? In your present situation, if you *insisted* on . . . now listen . . . if you *insisted* on the freedom
to spend large amounts of time in a singleminded devotion to
pursuing such questions, you would soon begin to feel rather
out of it . . . you would be a kook. Any question of a fundamental, or a general character; or any question which hits you
personally in a deep way, can only be considered naïve and
stupid. Can you conceive of taking any such question and
studying, talking, and reading about it for an entire semester
—free of any other requirement—or for an entire year, or even
more time? Without interference, but only earnest guidance
from "teachers"? Or is it that you must always attend to that
"other" paper, the "midterm next week," or the "reading in
another course"? Or is it that you do this half the time and say
to hell with it the rest of the time: go to an art film, or to
Strawberry Canyon, or to an exciting lecture for a one-night
stand on the topic of Western Civilization?

Dear undergraduate, you *know* what really happens to you.
You almost don't have to be told. It is as though the BENEFAC-
TORS OF THE FRUITS OF LEARNING said to you, "Here, take
this beautiful piece of fruit . . ." and you do, and you try to
take a bite, when "STOP!!" you are being offered another piece
of fruit, another, and then another. At the same time, before
you really begin to taste and speculate about the taste of any
one piece of fruit, your FRUIT BENEFACTORS, and FRUIT BENE-
FACTORS' ASSISTANTS, are demanding that you describe in detail the intricate beauty of each piece; they become impatient
if you do not describe the fruit "properly," and they penalize
you for thoughtful slowness by calling it stupidity, and by lowering your respectability rating. Most of you learn to hate the
fruits of learning. But there are a few of you—the "clever and
brilliant"—(preferably transfers from the Ivy League), who
learn in a terrific quickness, to take quick little bites from
the large and beautiful fruits and then furiously hurl them as

far away as possible. You clever ones learn to devour the small fruits of skill and training; those fruits are your "security insurance" in life, or perhaps you think they will lead you later to an XKE and sexy-intelligent-wife-in-silk-dress. You perform your tricks well: smiling up at your benefactors and saying "delicious . . . excellent!"

Charter Day

It is the Charter Day ceremony in which your illusions achieve their most refined expression. In this ceremony there are loud pronouncements of university intentions. The university is portrayed as a great champion and advocate of the noble aim of education for all. The ceremony leaves the impression that the University of California not only provides training; that it not only provides for economic ascent, but that it goes much further by providing something more fundamental and ennobling under the designation of education. The university claims to "produce" enlightened citizens with a heightened awareness of the moral, philosophical, and spiritual values of civilized life. All of the accoutrements of glory are present in this state-wide celebration: solemn music, processions, colorful robes, and impressive ritual. Attended by thousands of students, a well-polished public with many celebrities, and with major national and international press coverage, the ceremony is elevating and beautiful. The speeches are confident gestures of power and rather traditional majesty. The over-all purpose of the ceremony is a peculiar mixture of exaltation of statesmen, educators, and education. The podium is always shared by President Kerr with figures such as Stevenson, U Thant, and Kennedy. The university is placed proudly in the widest context—the world—unbashfully professing itself as a benefactor of free thought, intelligence, and the search for wisdom. The university is seen as playing a major role in the creation of world centers of learning, as well as continuing the rich tradition of education in the Western world. If you have attended this ceremony, you might easily have been overcome with the feeling that only detractors and scoffers of the worst sort would dare criticize such a "Citadel of Learning."

But SLATE *did* criticize; the indictment implied that the Charter Day ceremony is an unmerciful sham; an example of unparalleled demagoguery. And many of you who have been elevated by Charter Day *agreed* with the *Cal Reporter's* charges . . . as did the *Daily Cal,* by implication, when it blandly fretted that no constructive solutions had been offered. Why the confusion; and why did the *Daily Cal* have such a posture? In order to answer this I will turn to the other of the "two sets of utterly obvious facts" I said I would use to prove that a violent contrast exists on this campus.

Dear Undergraduates!!

I am no longer interested in cajoling you, arguing with you, or describing, to you something you already know. What I am about to say to you at this point concerns you more directly. I will entreat you to furiously throw your comforting feelings of duty and responsibility for this institution to the winds and act on your situation. This institution, affectionately called "Cal" by many of you, or, as the *Daily Cal* might put it, "the Big U," does not deserve a response of loyalty and allegiance from you. There is only one proper response to Berkeley from undergraduates: that you *organize and split this campus wide open!*

FROM THIS POINT ON, DO NOT MISUNDERSTAND ME. MY INTENTION IS TO CONVINCE YOU THAT YOU DO NOTHING LESS THAN BEGIN AN OPEN, FIERCE, AND THOROUGHGOING REBELLION ON THIS CAMPUS.

I would like to briefly explain to you now why such a course of action is necessary, and how, if such a revolt were conducted with unrelenting toughness and courage, it could spread to other campuses across the country and cause a fundamental change in your own futures.

I have used the phrase "world-in-revolution" several times to this point. I would like to say to you now that most of you are incompetent to deal with that phrase. It is a phrase which betrays a distinct view of reality . . . a view of reality out of which might grow an effective "opposition" in the present American scene where the only opposition seems to be crystallizing along reactionary lines. "World-in-revolution" is a phrase . . . a view of reality which contains a large measure of truth, one which is certainly debatable. BUT IT IS NOT DEBATED BY YOU. The catastrophic gap between the incubator world of your multiversity and the world of reality is represented by your ignorance of what "world-in-revolution" means. The university teaches you to bury your heads in the sand, trembling in ignorance of the American black revolution for civil rights, the impending revolution in automation, and likewise in ignorance of political revolutions, which, like thunderclapping salvos, explode the world over. The multiversity is the slickest appeal ever made for you to fortify your organization-man mentalities, for you to lead privatized lives in which it is a virtue for you to go greedily "on the make." In urging you to rebellion, I have action in mind, not further understanding. What more is there to understand when you can so easily discover that a Peace Corpsman who left Cal is now living in Nigeria in a separate small house with the conveniences of suburban America, plus two houseboys, and that a young girl civil-rights worker from the Bay Area who goes to Mississippi lives in abject poverty with a family of eleven black American citizens, in a shack with no running water, with lice, with rats, and in constant fear for her life?

In this multiversity, you will not learn so much as a cursory meaning of what a world-in-revolution means to you. You will not learn the utterly profound fact of what a revolution is:

THAT A REVOLUTION COMES ABOUT WHEN ENORMOUS NUMBERS OF FELLOW HUMAN BEINGS ARE OPPRESSED TO POINTS FAR BEYOND WHAT WE BLANDLY LABEL AN "IN-TOLERABLE SET OF CONDITIONS."

Nor will you learn that to be a counter-revolutionary is to go about the business of slaughtering enormous numbers of human beings whose inflamed spirits and starved stomachs force them to cry out for the freedoms which you spit upon in your apathy.

AND YOU WILL LEARN MOST OF ALL NOT TO ENTERTAIN SO MUCH AS THE POSSIBILITY THAT AMERICAN FOREIGN POLICY IN KOREA AND SOUTH VIET NAM ARE PRECISELY COUNTER-REVOLUTIONARY . . . THAT THE AMERICAN NA-TION IS INVOLVED IN DESTROYING POPULAR NATIONAL REVOLUTIONS, AND APPEARS TO BE GETTING ITSELF LOCKED MORE AND MORE IN THAT SUICIDAL AND INHUMANE POL-ICY.

You will learn not to entertain such thoughts, even though such statements have been made on the floor of the U. S. Senate (by Wayne Morse, U. S. Senator from Oregon), where nobody seems to have taken these fantastic charges seriously. And you will learn not to react when you hear other Americans say, "After all, God's on our side, we're savin' those illiterate savages from the Commies, even if we gotta mutilate 'em to do it, Goddamit!!"

You will not learn that, at home, here in the good ole U.S.A., in the civil-rights revolution which is now going on, the phrase "white backlash" is the simplest way to say "the bigotry of the majority"; that "white backlash" is a counter-revolutionary phrase, used by "scholars," so-called liberals, advocated by conservatives, or used by anyone else who adopts the hideous posture of "studying," or analyzing the "problem" of the black man in America. Nor will you learn that the real meaning of "white backlash" is: "Don't bug me nigger . . . you're buggin' me with that civil disobedience . . . now stop that, or we'll show you who has the tear gas, cattle prods, and shotguns!!"

Is it really necessary for thirty thousand black and white Americans to march up Telegraph Avenue to Bancroft Way, many of them fellow students, chanting for the rights of black Americans, before you see the contrast between your world of Oskie Dolls, fraternity boys on drunken weekend blasts where alcohol is transformed from joy into arrogance, and cute *Daily Cal* stories on Ludwig? How long will it take you to see the meaning of a casual remark I heard recently: "The fraternity system is to education as the South is to the United States?"

Is this too simplistic a view of your lot as undergraduates? You might say in protest that only a few students are in the ASUC "government" of political castrates who think they are training for leadership; that the *Daily Cal* is merely a handful of sellouts "going on the make" in that jaded commercial enterprise called the press, which is owned in large part by the Regents of this university. You might say that many students scorn the old "Saturday virtues" of beer cans and bermudas, along with the peculiar fraternity brand of the little-marlbora-man complex. "It's all on the way out," you might say, "we're growin' up . . . our answers are 'blowin on the wind.'" Really? Will you say that? Then I say to you, what about the dormitory undergraduates? Last year the Regents arrogantly denied some dorm students permission to set up a small campus radio station. No pretenses . . . the Regents simply said that dorm "boys" were incapable of responsibility in the matter and incompetent to use the airways. Kerr's whimpering protest to the Regents took the disgusting form of publicly saying that the boys were merely "engineering types," who only wished to express their tinkering mentality. Two SLATE students came to the side of the engineers in a *Daily Cal* letter. Do you recall how those virile young American engineering students responded to the whole affair? THEY AGREED WITH THE REGENTS AND KERR!!

Proceed. You might say that there are many students who do not live in organized living groups; that the independents are more mature. I will concede this point, but only if you agree that you are judging by mere appearances. For it is true that in the realm of what may only be called social "style," the independent who has broken ties with organized living has taken a slight step forward. After all, some of them even look *European!* The Jean-Paul Belmondo coolness, the stylized life of the terribly cosmopolitan Terrace, and all the rest. Of course, the majority of independents have little or no politics, and where it really counts—that puppetlike performance for grades, that scramble after grades and respectability—they do the same as the rest of you.

Regarding the radicals, those who are now going to jail in the civil-rights revolution: they are beginning to learn what the world-in-revolution means. I would make only one irreverent comment to them. They shouldn't bitch because the whole campus doesn't go to jail with them: because they are the real leaders on the campus, and yet while *on the campus* they too become sheep. They take the flunkings of professors who penalize them for attending a San Francisco court rather than a Berkeley class; the same professors who donate money to the civil-rights fight as long as it stays three thousand miles away in the South.

The only large group of students I personally respect, other than the Freedom Fighters, are the dropouts. Ignominious lot! What a fate . . . that one would be forced to give up that little registration card with respectability written all over it! This "Hidden Community" of unseemly hangers-on in Berkeley now numbers in the thousands. Those most bugged by this "element" are the ASUC types. They screech, "You can't even tell them from students sometimes (although some are very dirty) . . . and they're using *our* student union!" If they have flunked out (or dropped out) of the university how can they deserve respect? Well . . . if I thought it was a virtue to perform like sheep I wouldn't be urging revolt. The fact is that these students are the real ones. Many have had the guts to cut their social umbilical cords, become genuinely *free,* and to begin coughing up their own mistakes. They don't take the fatal step which the Cowell Psychiatric Clinic calls "regressive:" which means to go back to Mama, or, God forbid, to a junior college. They face life in its own terms, and many do something rather shocking around Berkeley: they learn to read a book. And I might add that many of them are also Freedom Fighters. (Incidentally, do you know the latest figures? According to Cowell, close to fifty per cent of those of you who are graced with the mantle of "freshman at Cal," are eliminated by the end of the third year.)

Are you aware that the most salient characteristic of the "multiversity" is massive production of specialized excellence? SPECIALIZED EXCELLENCE. It will be some time before machines will displace the super-trades; thus massive training centers are necessary. But why do we insist upon calling them educational centers rather than training centers?

> THE MULTIVERSITY IS NOT AN EDUCATIONAL CENTER, BUT A HIGHLY EFFICIENT INDUSTRY: IT PRODUCES BOMBS, OTHER WAR MACHINES, A FEW TOKEN "PEACEFUL" MACHINES, AND ENORMOUS NUMBERS OF SAFE, HIGHLY SKILLED, AND RESPECTABLE AUTOMATONS TO MEET THE IMMEDIATE NEEDS OF BUSINESS AND GOVERNMENT.

We all know that this is necessary to some extent for the maintenance of "American know-how"; otherwise the system would collapse and anarchy would reign, etc. But the forbidden fruit is to ask the devastating question WHY? WHY ONLY *know-how?* Or is it that we wish to produce the largest population of highly skilled idiots ever known to man? We may safely say that graduate schools should perform the function of training for specialized excellence . . . but even then not exclusively. And if you will recall, we are discussing the matter of undergraduate freedom to learn. What has occurred when undergraduate education is eradicated; whether it be for the excuse of "too many students," or "exploding knowledge," or in the name of political expedience during the "Cold War"?

WHEN THIS OCCURS IN PUBLIC UNIVERSITIES, THE RESULT IS ABANDONMENT OF THE AMERICAN DEMOCRATIC EXPERIMENT IN WHICH THE RADICAL PROPOSITION OF EDUCATION FOR ALL IS THE CENTRAL AXIOM.

Dear undergraduate, your "learning" has come to an impasse. Below the level of formal responsibility (the Regents, president, and chancellors), the Academic Senate (the faculty) itself is guilty of a massive and disastrous default. It is said that the Regents have given to the faculty the power and responsibility to deal with your learning. To put it mildly, the Academic Senate has turned that power and responsibility into a sham, an unused fiction. If this be true, then who is responsible for seeing to it that the faculty do something? We can cancel out President Kerr: he has already admitted publicly that he is incompetent to attend to the matter of undergraduate learning. That takes us back up the bureaucratic ladder again . . . do you know what the phrase "The Regents of the University of California" means? Following is the meaning of that phrase:

Edward CARTER: Chairman of the Board of Regents, Director, Broadway-Hale Retail Stores, Northrup Aircraft, Pacific Tel & Tel, and First Western Bank; Dorothy CHANDLER: Director, L.A. *Times,* and wife of Norman CHANDLER of the Southern California News Publishing empire; William COBLENTZ: corporation lawyer, San Francisco; Frederick DUTTON: U. S. Assistant Secretary of State; Mrs. William Randolph HEARST: ("housewife"), of the Hearst national newspaper empire; Mrs. Edward HELLER: ("housewife"), widow and heir to Edward HELLER, Director, Permanente Cement, Wells Fargo Bank, Schwabacher & Fry partner, and Pacific Intermountain Express; William E. FORBES: Southern California Music Company; Lawrence KENNEDY: attorney, Redding, California, (just prior to Mr. Kennedy's appointment as a Regent, it was strongly urged that it might be appropriate to appoint an *educator* to the Board of Regents); Donald H. MC LAUGHLIN: ("mining geologist"), Director, Homestake Mining Company, one of the largest gold mining operations in the world, recent interests in uranium mining, Director, Western Airlines, American Trust, and a Peruvian copper-mining operation; Samuel MOSHER: Director, Signal Gas & Oil, and Long Beach Oil Development Company, which was accused publicly a few months ago, by Lieutenant Governor Glenn Anderson, of trying to wrest public control of a recently discovered state owned oil field off Long Beach with a projected worth of over 3 billion . . . enough to shake up the world market and give California Petroleum men a virtual monopoly; Edwin PAULEY: Director, Pauley Oil, Western Airlines; William Matson ROTH: U. S. Special Deputy for Trade Relations, Director, National Life Insurance, Matson Shipping, Honolulu Oil, Pacific Intermountain Express; Norton SIMON: Director, Hunt Foods, McCalls, Wesson Oil & Snowdrift, and also "land developer"; Phillip BOYD: former mayor of Palm Springs, Director, Deep Canyon Properties, Security National Bank; John CANADAY: Vice President, Lockheed Aircraft, Director, Corporate Public Relations, Lockheed Aircraft; and Regent number sixteen on our list is the one and only representative of organized labor (the most reactionary element in labor at that): Cornelius HAGGERTY: President, Construction and Building Trades Council, AFL-CIO.

In these men you find substantial ownership and control of the vital raw materials and service industries in the West: communications, the press, television, air and surface transportation, fuel, and finance; virtually enough power to make or break five governors and ten university presidents. The board members are appointed for terms of sixteen years by the governor. There are also ex-officio members, ONE OF WHOM IS AN EDUCATOR: Clark Kerr. I would like to ask you to think for a moment about the "public" character of these men. In the first place, who even knows them? . . . except a few of us who are aware that they are "famous" or "very wealthy men." What do they do? AND WHY? FOR WHOSE INTEREST?

Dear undergraduate, there is perhaps no other set of questions, in the political realm, of greater importance for you. Let us return for a moment to the matter of who is responsible for your freedom to learn. As I said a moment ago, the Regents have delegated power and responsibility to the Academic Senates of the eight campuses. Let us just call the Academic Senate the "faculty," which is the automatic membership of the Senate. At any rate, there is something terribly wrong here. If we assume that the faculty is incompetent to effect the necessary changes, then it would seem of the greatest urgency that the Regents themselves do something to correct the situation. If the Regents do not act, then we must conclude that they are (1) satisfied; or (2) incompetent; or (3) both. Two things are certain: (1) as corporate men of power, the Regents are getting precisely what they most desire—enormous numbers of highly skilled graduates to fill the corporate structure and to keep it running smoothly; (2) IT IS DEBATABLE, from their own point of view, whether the Regents would find it practical to "educate" these skilled people as well as to *train* them. Why? To put the answer very crudely: the Regents, who run private corporations, just as the politicians who run public corporations, desire highly skilled, but politically and economically *dumb* "personnel." The politicians have, of course, even made laws to that effect . . . in the form of such legislation as the Hatch Act, which forbids partisan politics in government bureaucracies. Consequently, if the faculty refuses to face the problem of educating undergraduates, but instead is encouraged, and agrees, to make only piecemeal reform which only slightly lessens pressures in some areas while making them more severe in other areas, the Regents might be said to be very happy with such a course of action . . . in fact that is what they are doing. The course/grade/unit system will probably be "adjusted," and the bread and circus will become more intense and dazzling: note the priority in the university building program . . . first you build the student-union complex, then an auditorium which will be the "largest this side of the Mississippi," and "sometime in the future" will come an undergraduate library. But why do private and public corporate men act this way?

> FROM TIME IMMEMORIAL, MEN OF POWER HAVE CONSIDERED IT WISE TO KEEP THEIR CONSTITUENTS AT A LEVEL OF IGNORANCE WHEREBY THE PROCESS OF RULING THEM IS MOST EASILY ACCOMPLISHED.

Or are we to entertain the possibility that the Regents have upset the applecart of history? Have they become revolutionaries? It is true that they recently removed the ban on Communist speakers on campus. Of course, they resisted for fifteen years . . . since the McCarthy era. And during the McCarthy era they were able to force the Academic Senate into adopting a loyalty oath. If you can forgive the faculty of a university for *that,* you can forgive them for *anything.* Many professors did not forgive the Senate, however, and resigned. The spine of this faculty, close to forty professors, left in disgust, left scars behind which will never heal. Moreover, what the hell difference does it make whether you hear a Communist every year or so. Most of you would laugh at him . . . like laughing at a movement which involves the entire world! If any one of you wisely decided to study a Communist speaker's proposals, to think about them, to read about them seriously, you not only would find it *impossible from the standpoint of time,* but you would also be considered a heretic by your fellow "students." It is probably accurate to say that the removal of the speaker ban on Communists was a great contribution on the symbolic level . . . like a Charter Day ceremony. Politically, it was very wise.

Speaking of politics, what relation exists between the university and the U. S. Government? Aside from providing trained personnel for public corporations (agencies, bureaus, etc.) as in private ones, is there as direct a relation between the university and government as between the university and the Regents? Yes, it seems that the university, or shall we call a spade a spade—the Regents—it seems that the Regents are snuggled up pretty tightly to the seats of power in Washington (though it is difficult to tell who-hugs-whom the hardest in Washington):

> Item—from the *Cal Reporter*, May 13, 1963, "According to the Financial Report of 1961–62, the U. S. Government spent about 227 millions on Special Projects. These included 150 millions for Lawrence Radiation Laboratory (U.C.), 76 millions for Los Alamos Radiation Lab (U.C.). The income for the entire University (eight campuses) excluding these special projects was 250 millions."

Let us summarize for a moment. Your learning opportunities are limited to "getting ahead," or acquiring a skill to do so. You are obstructed from the realities of the twentieth-century world-in-revolution. You are left with the conclusion that the Regents are conducting a major love affair with the U. S. Government, both of whom are not particularly anxious to see you "get smart" for fear that you might become radical student politicos. In conducting this love affair with the government, the Regents have left the matter of "educating" the infant-undergraduate to the adolescent faculty, knowing that they cannot do the job properly. The major implication in all of this is that if you wish to remain infants then you can . . . but if you wish to deny your infantile character then you must realize that you can't talk to your adolescent baby-sitters, the faculty, about your corrupt daddies, the Regents. The reason is simple: the baby-sitters are afraid of their daddies. No . . . if you really want to do something then you must stand up straight, like the young men and women you really are, and begin to SPEAK what you feel, to speak loudly, strongly, and to say your highest ideals, your deepest dreams, to pull out all of the stops, to let go and to tell the world . . . SPEAK TO THE WORLD AND TELL THEM THAT YOU WANT TO LIVE!!!

Have I sufficiently taken care of your objections? If not, chances are that what remains is *fear,* and that is *your* problem. If I have taken care of your objections, then you might be asking, HOW DO YOU START A REBELLION ON THE CAMPUS? That's a tough one—and you might have to get tough in order to be heard. You also know that you will need legitimate demands behind your slogans of FREEDOM NOW! THE FREEDOM TO KNOW AND TO LEARN!!

Demands?

1. *Immediate commitment of the university to the total elimination of the course/grade/unit system of undergraduate learning in the social sciences and humanities.*

2. *Immediate disbanding of all university dorm and living group rules which prescribe hours and which provide for a system of student-imposed discipline, thereby dividing students against themselves.*

3. *Immediate negotiations on the establishment of a permanent student voice which is effective (that is, independent) in running university affairs.*

4. *Immediate efforts to begin recruitment of an undergraduate teaching faculty to handle undergraduate learning in social sciences and humanities.*

5. *Immediate negotiations regarding two methods of undergraduate learning which provide for the basic freedom required in learning:*
   a. *A terminal examination system which will be voluntary and an option with "b."*
   b. *Immediate creation of undergraduate programs of a wide variety in which the student will be given careful, but minimal guidance, without courses, grades, and units.*

6. *Immediate establishment of a university committee to deal with these demands on the Berkeley campus.*

Go to the top. Make your demands to the Regents. If they refuse to give you an audience: start a program of agitation, petitioning, rallies, etc., in which the final resort will be CIVIL DISOBEDIENCE. In the long run there is the possibility that you will find it necessary to perform civil disobedience at a couple of major university public ceremonies. Depending on the resistance, you might consider adding the following two demands:

7. *Resignation of Clark Kerr. Resignation of top administrators who might employ slick diverting tactics.*

8. *Reconstitution of the Board of Regents, either through firing or expansion, perhaps both.*

If you find such additional demands necessary you are likely to find it necessary to take your demands to Sacramento, where you will get to know such people such as Hale Champion, State Director of Finance, who seems to have a slight distaste for knowledge and sees education in terms of the dollar sign. Or you might get to know Don Moskovitz, an assistant press secretary to Brown and educational advisor. You will find few allies there, with the exception of Thomas Braden. Max Rafferty, of course, is out of the question . . . would have you all in knickers made of old American flags if he could.

If it is necessary to go this far beyond formal "channels," and if you have the guts to get there, you will begin to learn how tough it is to effect radical change. If the *Daily Cal* decides to support you at various times along the way (very unlikely), they will be duly chastised by the so-called "Publications Board," and then the students' editors might have the guts to walk out (doubly unlikely). If such a walkout occurs again, as it did a couple of years ago, it might be wise to consider an effective picket to try to keep out the same types of fraternity scabs who took over last time in an action which was traitorous to the undergraduates.

And if you get this far you will also have witnessed nationwide publicity which will have exposed Berkeley for the undergraduate sham that it is. Not to say that the public in general will feel that way, what with the press "redbaiting" you, but that students all over the country will read between the lines. By this time you may also be able to call for a mass student strike . . . something which seems unthinkable at present. If a miracle occurs, or two, you might even get to say that you were the seeds of an educational revolution unlike anything which has ever occurred. Remember one thing:

> "The task of genius, and man is nothing if not genius,
> is to keep the miracle alive, to live always in the miracle,
> to make the miracle more and more miraculous, to swear
> allegiance to nothing, but live only miraculously, think
> miraculously, to die miraculously."
>
> *Henry Miller*

EDUCATION, REVOLUTIONS, AND CITADELS*
BY BRADFORD CLEAVELAND

It is the *revolutionary character* of the present American educational situation which is least mentioned. The following discussion attempts to define elements in American education that distinguish it as revolutionary and insists that there is a desperate need for recognizing it as such. Urgency in this matter proceeds from the fact that education, as never before in history, is becoming a political issue. Shifts in the alliance between education and authority have produced a variety of deep and politically explosive disputes in history, but never has education emerged in the political arena so ill-defined, confused, and with dimensions so immense as today in American

* Written and distributed in mimeographed form, September 1964.

life. While this occurs, the intellectual dialogue concerning education suffers from evasiveness; actions toward improvement are timid ploys for minute change. The primary source of responsibility for the chaos in American education is not the citizen but the intellectual. In the present world of revolution, there is an evasion by intellectuals of the one worthwhile revolution, the only "necessary revolution" . . . the revolution in education. Ironically, present American citizen support for education, albeit innocent and vulgarized, can be characterized as springing from a revolutionary proposition. Our attempt will focus on this matter first. Secondly, we will turn to a major cause of intellectual evasion of regarding education as revolution. Finally, we will examine one of the results of advancing education in a form contrary to education itself, by assessing that recent reality in American life so penetratingly labeled the "multiversity" by President Clark Kerr of the University of California.

Education As Revolution

There are two elements in American education that distinguish it as revolutionary. Both are contained in the proposition *state education for all*. The first of these two elements represents a revolution already accomplished. It is best expressed in the words of Alexander Meiklejohn:

> From church to state! In three centuries we . . . have transferred from one of these institutions to the other the task of shaping the minds and characters of our youth. Do we realize what we have done? This is revolution. It is the most fundamental aspect of the social transformation which has brought us from the medieval to the modern world. As compared with it the changes in the gaining and holding of property, the making and enforcing of laws, even the expression in literature and art, are secondary and superficial. In the transition from the medieval to the modern form of human living I doubt if any other change is as significant as the substitution of political teaching for religious. We have changed our procedure for determining what kind of beings human beings shall be.[1]

The second element is a recent revolutionary ideal. The noble character of that goal and the desire for its implementation has seen Americans place a deep public trust in educators and politicians. This ideal is best stated in the words of Robert Hutchins, in his book *Some Observations on American Education:*

[1] Meiklejohn's words are taken from his book *Education between Two Worlds*, Harper, 1942, page 4.

I have selected as the central theme of the book the question of whether it is possible to have true education in a country that insists on something called education for everybody. I believe it is. I believe the doctrine of education for all is America's greatest contribution to the theory and practice of democracy.[2]

The first element in American education which distinguishes it as revolutionary is, then, education by the state; the second, education for all. Unfortunately, it is not a truism to say that the proposition of state education for all contains two revolutionary goals, one accomplished and one recently undertaken. The truth of that proposition is neither obvious nor well-known. The accomplishment of transferring education from church to state is a revolution for the simple reason that the state, in spite of generations of counterclaims, became heir to moral education. In a way more profound and complex than readily acknowledged, the state is now the repository of morality. The notion of education for all is likewise revolutionary, having come into its present form as an ideal in American life after centuries of struggle in the West for man's liberation through freedom from ignorance. Even if we accept the qualification of education for all as meaning educational "opportunity" for all, the commitment is nonetheless to a revolutionary ideal. It is revolutionary because widespread education which is meaningful would include knowledge not only of principles of justice and the moral ambiguities inherent in political life, but knowledge of the uses and abuses of power, and this in turn would be inimical to the traditional uses of power. No state or political authority in the past has undertaken the task of educating its constituency in this sense. Past regimes have especially avoided any serious commitment to educating those who suffer most from the various dislocations which occur in a political order. But in the United States we have committed ourselves, in public policy, to educational opportunity for all; especially to those who are in greatest need!

As mentioned earlier, after centuries of struggle in Western tradition, it is possible to say that the American people have demonstrated their desire and willingness to use their wealth for supporting the proposition of education for all . . . which is to say education for themselves. If there is a consensus in modern American life, it must be said to rest in large part

---

[2] Hutchins' book *Some Observations on American Education,* was published by Cambridge University Press, 1956. His words are taken from the introduction to the book, page xiii. It is time for both Meiklejohn and Hutchins to receive credit for their heroic gestures in American life. Their lives have included long and impassioned efforts to persuade professional scholars and intelligent citizens to attend to the complexities of a qualitative assessment of higher education.

upon the matter of education: the citizens accept education as "necessary for survival." But the proposition of state education for all, as we shall see, has not proceeded in substance. It would seem that the revolutionary proposition of state education for all would arouse no small amount of enthusiasm in public men and educators. Such an enthusiasm would include the conviction that educational revolution calls for discussion which leads to action of a radical variety as opposed to mere reflection and occasional minor manipulations of the present system. In place of decisive action we seem to be continually submerging ourselves more deeply in "understanding"; we *know* that education is of radical importance for reworking our moral, political, and economic concepts, and in an all too casual manner we thoughtlessly proclaim that education is fundamental to the immediate revolutions in civil rights, unemployment, and automation.

Everyone knows a great deal, we all know which way we ought to go, but nobody is willing to move. If at last someone were to overcome the reflection within him and happened to act, then immediately thousands of reflections would form an outward obstacle. Only a proposal to reconsider a plan is greeted with enthusiasm; action is met with indolence. Some of the superior and self-satisfied find the enthusiasm of the man who tried to act ridiculous, others are envious because he made the beginning when, after all, they *knew* just as well as he did what should be done—but did not do it. Still others use the fact that someone has acted in order to produce numerous critical observations and give vent to a store of arguments, demonstrating how much more sensibly the thing could have been done; others, again, busy themselves guessing the outcome and, if possible, influencing events a little so as to favor their own hypothesis."[3]

Kierkegaard's words, though written in 1846, are devastatingly appropriate to large numbers of American intellectuals in mid-century American life. Rather than taking up the proposition of state education for all and using it as a means for concerning themselves with the world in revolution, they are permissive and indolent. For it is true that while intellectuals have abdicated discussion leading toward action by passively reflecting on the matter, politicians and high-level educators are using the proposition of state education for all as a political myth in the most noxious sense, while educational institutions themselves are undergoing a major transformation which is destructive of education itself.

[3] Soren Kierkegaard, *The Present Age*, Oxford, 1949, p. 60.

Education As Cold War

The notion we use to designate our contingencies on the level of generality is "Cold War." The ideological, economic, and technological revolutions which are occurring are placed in that general political context. Before we proceed to a description of what the Cold War is "doing to education," by turning to that citadel of training called the "multiversity," it will be necessary to meet a major objection to regarding education as revolution.

It is an objection which is said to emanate from the nature of the Cold War itself. That is, education in the humane sense is not possible during "war." But this is an objection which comes from a mistaken view of the Cold War. It is a view which places an excessive emphasis on the warlike aspects of the Cold War and consequently calls for an implacable expediency. The extensive national sacrifices, it might be said, demanded by the Cold War in the realm of education means sacrifice of serious and extended liberal learning in favor of extensive training for specialized excellence. Just as in all-out war, this will serve two vital functions. First, it will provide for national survival through weaponry, and long-range superiority in technology. Secondly, it will reduce the potentially schismatic and devisive effects which are always claimed as emanating from liberal learning. Consistent with this expedient of displacing learning with training is the use of political myth after the fashion of wartime propaganda. "Education for all" is such a myth, and its accoutrements are all of the rich symbols of Western civilized educational tradition. Vital parts of this tradition are notions of man's historic struggle for liberation through knowledge, freedom from ignorance, and the search for wisdom. In addition to the use of these inspiring notions from history, the state must adopt the pretense of benefactor of the fruits of learning for all; the doors of learning must appear as having been heroically thrown open to all citizens. This viewpoint is found in its deadliest form in reactionary American "political philosophers" who call for the extinction of liberal learning along with "liberalism." Conservative writers support them somewhat vaguely, and liberals stand resigned, in reflection, to the temporary postponement of learning.[4]

Lacking space, we will state only the essential points in retort. Generally, by placing the emphasis on the "war" aspect

[4] Willmoore Kendall, Leo Strauss, and Eric Voegelin are leading reactionaries; conservative writers such as Russell Kirk and William Buckley appear regularly in the *National Review*. The liberals are entrenched en masse "inside" educational *institutions* and maintain a passive control from within while writing slick and evasive articles for numerous journals outside the academy.

of the Cold War, vital distinctions between demands placed upon intellectuals and educational institutions during all-out wars of massive violence are mistaken for the challenges facing us during a Cold War. The use of the concept of *détente* is an example in this confusion. Détente, in the context of the Cold War alone, is hardly capable of definition and is in continual dispute. The *real* détente came into being in the transformation of massive wars of violence into Cold War. It is blindness to ignore the fact that massive violence has been pervasively exchanged for ideological warfare. Moreover, economic and technological strife has also taken some of the burden away from mass murder and helped to make the predominating mode of violence not all-out war, but revolutions and counter-revolutions. The expected duration of the Cold War, as a factor in itself, should make us pause from the temptation of suspending liberal learning, for such suspension might, for all practical purposes, mean destruction of liberal learning.

On the level of ideological conflict, it would seem insane to engage in that conflict while destroying the source of our raw material: freedom of thought and intelligence. It is only through the massive application of liberal learning that the "freedom," for which we claim a monopoly, can exist. This is made clear by considering the mode of violence in the Cold War. Repeatedly, the United States is being forced into the role of counter-revolutionary power clothed in excessive moral pretensions. This is indeed new clothing: for it is true that we do not employ simple terror—the only means of extinguishing revolution—as traditionally used. We are using terror in the name of human freedom! Traditional counter-revolution, as ugly and villainous as it has been, has never seen the use of terror in such a grotesque manner. Confused citizens follow this grisly process through the press. It is a sad irony to hear intellectuals decrying an immoral press—"disinterested" intellectuals; some withdrawing into privatism, others gingerly snuggling up to the seats of power and venturing out after a little *Realpolitik* as "hardheaded realists."

During the Cold War the protagonists of education and intellectual honesty face a challenge which is immense: the challenge of discussion and action to bring authenticity into the revolutionary proposition of state education for all. It is a necessary revolution made essential by the nature of the Cold War itself. The Cold War is a "war" which is itself in dispute; it is a highly controversial and unique political situation because controversy as such has become a condition for survival. War *cannot* be declared, as it were. Nuclear stalemate itself has caused a diffusion of war into modes other than massive violence. The world political scene is so inundated by strife derived from moral, economic, and technological dimensions, of the politics of modernity, that if the United States continues to pursue a foreign policy in which power alone is axiomatic, the result will be disastrous. If the United States continues to conduct counter-revolutions through terror in the name of freedom, we will establish only our own irrevocable barbarism. The controversial character of the Cold War, as distinct from wars of massive violence, is made poignant even on the floor of the U. S. Senate, where it is possible to solicit a public audience in opposition to the present policy of careening down a path of counter-revolution strewn with the mutilated populations of countries such as Korea and Vietnam. But the tragedy of the twentieth-century intellectual will not be his absence from the floor of the U. S. Senate, nor even his abstinence from genuine criticism in matters of public policy. The Cold War is a diffused conflict of long duration, and the main tragedy of the educator and intellectual will be their silence of "long duration" in the proximity of American youth in the colleges and universities where they not only wish to know about the problems of the Cold War, and terrific domestic problems, but wish as well to learn the art of thinking about them.

The Cold War détente from all-out war emerged abruptly and crystallized in American consciousness with the jolt of Sputnik. At that point, American education had nearly finished giving birth to the revolutionary proposition of education for all. Simultaneously, "Education for All" became one with "Survival," and closing missile gaps became the aim of education.

Nonetheless, characteristic of the distinction between World War and Cold War, the transformation from one to the other brought great relief to the American people. On the educational scene, the end of World War II saw the departure of hundreds of thousands of enlisted and officer military personnel from campuses. But temporary war buildings, dorms, and barracks began refilling rapidly with civilian youth who brought with them more than the simple pressure of numbers. The creation of massive technological training centers on the level of higher education, through the use of "education for all for survival of the human race" as a propaganda slogan, brought tremendous wealth to the academy. At the level of the college, or undergraduate learning, it spelled disaster.

Clark Kerr's Citadel of Training

The "multiversity" has arrived. More than a year has passed since it appeared in full regalia in the public spotlight. Since the Harvard Godkin Lectures of May 1963, by President Clark Kerr of the University of California, in which he defined the multiversity, there has been an almost deadening silence. Aside from a few flippant allusions to Berkeley as the "L.A. of the intellect," or "Brave New World arrived," there has been no serious discussion. It is as though we must all postpone debate, and liberal learning as well, until the end of the Cold War, or until the arrival of some "new philosophy" from Providence, which will solve the contradictions of an American "democracy" which is opposing democratic revolutions within her own borders, and catastrophically losing counter-revolutions because of a pathological view of our "mission" in the world. The multiversity is the most recent arrival on the American scene to assert that attempts toward basic unities in social and political life are illegitimate. It is an institutional attempt to deny moral dimensions in politics, economics, and social life. Most important it has severed learning at its source: it has eradicated any semblance of education in the one area where we most expect it to reside—undergraduate learning.

The state of California appears to have undertaken, more nobly than any other state, the aim of education for all. At the present time, close to fifty per cent of the college-age youth in California enter some institution of higher education. The impressiveness of this figure is obliterated by the attrition rate: over fifty per cent. However, the California Master Plan for Higher Education (engineered into existence by Kerr) dominates the entire educational apparatus of the state. Due largely to Kerr and the Berkeley model of the multiversity, California has the most highly planned and rational system of education in the nation. Kerr, the former chancellor of the Berkeley campus of the eight-campus university system, is now a national power image in higher education. As a public system of higher education, the University of California surpasses all others in the illusive sphere of "prestige." It seems to surpass all others as a center of raw political power, second only to Harvard and competing only with Yale as a brain center for waging the Cold War; the Washington-Berkeley circuit, as the Ivy League-Washington circuit, is heavily trafficked. While Kerr's multiversity commands such attention, it has no substantial educational policy, and Kerr's position, as expressed in the Godkin Lectures, is a posture inimical to openly confronting the issues we have raised or the complexities of educational philosophy. To whom is Kerr responsible?

In answering this question all of the worst characteristics of what might be called the "bureaucratization of life" emerge. Is Kerr responsible to the state legislature, the governor, the people? All of these, but only by way of diffuse influence. He is actually the appointee of the traditional body of trustees, or Regents, as they are called in California. This body of men, almost wholly unknown to the public, are appointed by the governor for terms of sixteen years. They hold the power of the multiversity and determine the broadest dimensions of its educational policy, or lack thereof. But on the other hand they have theoretically delegated the matter of educational policy two steps down in the bureaucracy, past the president and chancellors of the eight campuses, to the level of the faculty's so-called "Academic Senates." At this point the determination of educational policy remains an unused fiction.

Of the sixteen Regents who run the multiversity (eight more are ex-officio members), fifteen are men of enormous corporate wealth and power. They own major proportions of western United States interests in petroleum, mining, banking, the press, and transportation. There is one representative from organized labor. The one Regent "educator" is an ex-officio member of the board, Kerr himself.

Kerr, the most publicly "visible" of those who run the multiversity, considers himself a liberal. He has publicly joined with politicians and educators in the advocacy of the noble aim of educating the people. His public speeches, with those of other educators and politicians, have left a common understanding with the people of the state that the University of California not only provides opportunity for economic ascent, but that it provides something more fundamental and ennobling under the designation of education. An example is the annual Charter Day ceremony. All of the accoutrements of glory are present in this state-wide celebration: solemn music, processions, colorful robes, and impressive ritual. Attended by thousands of students, a well-polished public of celebrities, with major coverage by the press, the ceremony is elevating and beautiful. The speeches are confident gestures of power and rather traditional majesty. The over-all purpose of the ceremony is a mixture of exaltation of statesmen and education. The podium is always shared by Kerr with figures such as Stevenson, U Thant, Kennedy, and Dean Rusk. The University of California is placed in the widest context—the world—proudly portrayed as a vanguard of freedom of thought and intelligence, and is seen as playing a major role in continuation of the rich tradition of Western civilized education. Participants in such a ceremony are overwhelmed with the feeling that only scoffers and detractors of the worst sort would dare criticize such a university. But the routine life of the University of California is inimical to anything we know of Western educational tradition, whether it be English, German, or American.

The salient characteristic of the multiversity is massive production of specialized excellence. The multiversity is actually not an educational center but a highly efficient industry engaged in producing skilled individuals to meet the immediate needs of business or government. It is a foregone conclusion that graduate schools should perform this function to a large extent but by no means exclusively. Moreover, it is only possible to totally eradicate education by destroying its traditional bulwark: undergraduate learning.

Undergraduate learning at the multiversity, under Kerr's regime, has come to an impasse. It is best characterized by quoting a statement by Bertrand Russell: "We are faced with the paradox that education has become one of the chief obstacles of intelligence and freedom of thought."[5]

Below the level of formal power and responsibility (the Regents, president, and chancellors), the faculty itself is guilty of a massive and disastrous default. More concerned with their own increasingly affluent specialized careers, they have permitted an administrative process to displace, and become an obstruction to, extended thought and learning for the undergraduate. Professors have made a gift of the undergraduate learning situation to the bureaucrat.

The bureaucrats have destroyed education. To give this charge substance it is unnecessary to appeal either to the "empirical data of the social scientist," or to the "finished product" of the undergraduate college and the effects of this "product" on the culture and politics of American life. It is sufficient to describe the procedural core of the undergraduate experience and the peculiar context into which it fits in the multiversity.

The process is a four-year-long series of sharp staccatos: eight semesters, forty courses, one hundred twenty or more "units," ten to fifteen impersonal lectures *per week*, and one to three oversized discussion meetings per week led by poorly paid and unlearned graduate students. Approaching what might be of more substance: reading, writing, and examinations, the situation becomes absurd. Over a period of four years a student receives close to forty bibliographies, ranging in length from one to eight pages, is examined on more than one hundred occasions, and is expected to write from forty to seventy-five papers. Reading means "getting into" hundreds of books, most of which are dull secondary sources, in a superficial manner. Examination is commonly known as "regurgitation." Writing is plagiarized in many cases; otherwise it is poor and generally superficial. In the sciences, courses are excessively rigorous in competition with the "soft" humanities. This process is the very core of the undergraduate experience. It is applied by administrators in large part by the use of computers. It is extracted by professors through the coercion of grades.

If the facts of undergraduate existence were solely determined by such a procedural core, the "incipient revolt," to

---

[5] The author is at a loss in not being able to find the source of this statement by Russell, having carried it as a part of his intellectual baggage for a number of years; certain, however, that it comes from one of Russell's terse monologues on education.

which Kerr himself irresponsibly alludes in the Godkin Lectures, would probably have already occurred.[6] But the greatest advantage of the multiversity concept is its inclusiveness. For the undergraduate this means the panoply of pain relieving ingredients within the context of the multiversity, but "outside the classroom." In this respect the campus presents the student with a magnificent *panem et circenses*. Emanating from the student "government," special adjunctive bureaucracies such as Berkeley's Committee on Arts and Lectures, and added to by more intellectual offerings from departmental and special grants lecture series, comes a plethora of exciting and highly intense stimuli ranging from the highly entertaining to the highly intellectual. Films, debates, art exhibits, athletics, drama (light and tragic), spirit groups, recreation, seductions of hundreds of social groups; this pyrotechnical explosion of *Kultur* represents something terribly "other-directed"; happily away from the nauseousness of the procedural core.

Need we say that it is insane to expect learning to occur in this two-sided situation of forced procedural performance inundated by dazzling stimulation? Extended thought cannot occur; it is either obstructed or dissolved in the grand spectacle. There is a cynical objection that pretends to dispel this view. It is said that the undergraduate "who really desires an education" can acquire one. This is patently false. It is the highly intelligent and sensitive student who suffers most. He is painfully aware that *there is no time to think,* few places to think, and fewer students interested or capable of extended dialogue. The view that the best education occurs when the student is challenged does not apply to the multiversity. The student is not challenged by the profundities of Western thought, its weaknesses and polarities, its relation to action, and the exciting prospect of a lifetime search for wisdom. On rare occasions the student only gains a paltry and meager view of that enormous challenge; the access to such challenge is itself obstructed by the procedural core as applied in an absolutistic sense by administrators and professors, and the confusion and frustration of meeting that obstruction is deflected into the dazzling bread and circus. Opportunity for manipulation of the program by the "bright student" is nonexistent. The number of students in honors courses is negligible, enrollment in them does not relieve students of require-

---

[6] "There is an incipient revolt of undergraduate students against the faculty; the revolt that used to be against the faculty in loco parentis is now against the faculty in absentia," from page 103 of *The Uses of the University* (Godkin Lectures in book form), Harvard, 1963. Kerr's comments on higher education throughout the book are made from the vantage point of a sort of Eichmann-like third party, or almost disinterested observer, as though the president was really nothing more than a bureaucrat-employee of the Regents. Or, as Kerr himself prefers to put it ". . . he is mostly a mediator." p. 36.

ments, and since they are negligible in number and ineffective as a means of getting around requirements, they are insignificant as hopeful exceptions in the general situation. Furthermore, this objection that education is possible "in spite of the system" attests to an attitude of far greater importance in the multiversity. There is a cancerous cynicism which regards honesty, simple inquiry, openness, and the ingenuous response as stupidity. In this atmosphere the notion of education for all is discarded as pedestrian and passe. The fact is that the multiversity *has* devised a curriculum and a context in which the ingenuity of even the superior student is defeated, and the multiversity *has* used the noble banner of education for all while cynically overthrowing education in the name of training for the contingencies of the Cold War. The sole response thus far to this kind of criticism of higher education and the multiversity has been that professors have modified their courses by becoming either more dazzling in the classroom and adding to the stimuli of the undergraduate, or by "tightening up" courses and becoming more rigorous, thereby worsening the situation.

It is unfortunate that most students depart from the multiversity without sufficient awareness of the distinction between education and training. In the multiversity, they are unlike the superior student who at least becomes aware (usually too late) of the deficiencies of the situation. The great majority are diverted from seriously confronting their situation by the bread and circus, and by the prospect of a clean, "high-paying" job after graduation. And somehow, as a part of this non-political role toward which they are headed, most of them think of themselves rather casually as "future leaders."

Conclusion

The catastrophic effect of the multiversity phenomenon on human learning is informed not by its peculiarity in American education, but by the fact that the Berkeley and Harvard-MIT scenes are two giants moving forward slowly in definition of the form and substance of American education. These two giants seem to be fixed in their paths, and it is little wonder that the "revolutionary character" of the present American educational situation is least mentioned. But there are shoddy seams in the present educational establishment that will soon threaten to burst from assaults from without. A giant wave of moral indignation does not appear far off. It threatens to make McCarthyism pale in significance; is already stirring in conservative journals. Is it conceivable that the assaults will be met with a great moral courage, dedicated through education to arousing an apathetic American people who ignore the terrible problems of racism, poverty, and automation-unemployment, in the name of privatism; a moral courage directed at destruction of the studied cynicism of American students in their regard for American foreign policy? Or will those assaults be met with the willingness of liberals to abandon their heritage totally through passive reflection, "tragic" pessimism, and their own special brand of privatism which is *not* ignorant of massive social injustice?

Privatism and political primitivism in American life in general can be seen as deeply related to the evasion of implications which followed the transfer of education from church to state. This is no small matter and is doubled in importance by the public adoption of the goal of education for all. Only by the willingness of those in centers of education to open debate on this issue, an issue which cannot stop short of a fundamental confrontation of the polarities in American political philosophy; only by such a confrontation and forthright debate can the two forms of privatism be overcome in a humane fashion. The timidity of intellectuals in and around the academy on this matter betrays itself in the aggressive response of those same intellectuals to their academic departments, to foundations, and to the federal government, by the establishment of morally and politically "neutral" careers of great affluence in research enclaves or institutes.

Education as revolution is an imperative which must express itself first at the level of undergraduate learning. It is not for want of plans or logistical arrangements that this matter will be postponed further, but for lack of courage and the will to sacrifice indolent reflection based on excessive greed. For the "sacrifices" of the Cold War have not been sacrifices in the usual sense within the academy. They have meant great material gains; the sacrifice has been that of conscience. Consequently, change can only come from redeemed conscience. The will to retain and increase the authenticity of the American experiment in civilized living through freedom with order, must be created by instructors and professors within themselves, and by themselves to begin with. Refusal to do this means the alternative of waiting for the flames of reaction to lick at their feet. The only other possibility is that of the students arriving first, having been aroused from without, and shaming the academy into drastic changes.

THE UNIVERSITY: CIVIL RIGHTS AND CIVIC RESPONSIBILITIES*
BY CLARK KERR, PRESIDENT, UNIVERSITY OF CALIFORNIA

The United States of America is engaged today in what future historians will undoubtedly call a period of profound social change; in a struggle to bring to complete reality the great American ideal of freedom and equality for all American citizens, in a renewed attack against the forces of fear and ignorance that have kept the promise unfulfilled for some American citizens for more than one hundred years. The realization of this ideal will be one of the great victories for the human spirit, and it now seems certain that destiny has given to our generation the grave opportunity to witness and to contribute to this historic victory.

The University of California, as an integral part of the society it serves, is devoted to the fulfillment of this American dream. The university is also devoted to much else that is central to the proper conduct of a nation conceived in the spirit of justice and freedom and dedicated to the propriety of means as well as to the desirability of ends. I should like to speak briefly today of the university's contributions both to the achievement of this dream of equality and to the support of methods worthy of the dream itself.

The University of California has stood for nearly a century as a great portal to equality of opportunity in this state—a portal open to all able young people. Many thousands of students to whom other doors were closed have walked through that portal to make their contributions to the nation—including the first American Negro to win the Nobel Prize and the first great Negro athlete to break the color bar in professional sports.

Throughout its history, the university has supported policies and programs which contribute to equality of opportunity.

We admit students from all segments of society and from all areas of the world, our sole concern being for their past achievements and their future promise.

We select faculty and employees on the basis of demonstrated capacity to perform, and we work with the State Fair Employment Practices Commission to assure that these policies are not subverted in practice at any level. Our staff presently includes a somewhat higher proportion of minority group members than the proportion of these minorities in the total population.

* Address presented at the Charter Day Ceremonies, Davis Campus, May 5, 1964.

We refuse to make our Housing Office facilities available to landlords who discriminate.

We deny our athletic facilities to colleges or universities whose teams are segregated.

We have served notice that no student organization, however closely or historically connected with the university, can use the name or the facilities of the university after September 1, 1964, unless it has eliminated discriminatory requirements in the selection of its members.

We have sponsored research by many faculty members in many fields on the effects of segregation and the problems of integration.

We have sponsored conferences on nearly all aspects of integration in nearly all parts of the state.

We have undertaken a program to identify academically promising high school students from disadvantaged backgrounds and to help them qualify for a university education.

The University of California has conducted its own affairs in the conviction that "all men are created equal" and has sought by example and by idea to share that conviction with the society we serve.

It is a fact of history, however regrettable, that social change is often accompanied by tensions and frictions which occasionally erupt into civil disturbances. Some of the controversies of this current period of social change have given rise to questions about the university's position, both institutionally and in relation to the actions of a few citizens who happen also to be university students, faculty members, or employees. This is perhaps an opportune time for me to state again the position of the university.

First and foremost, the university is fully and inalterably committed to the principles of democratic government upon which this nation was founded, among which is the rule of law. Only under a rule of law can all citizens be assured full rights and liberties, or redress when those rights or liberties are denied. Respect for the law of the land is imperative to the survival of democratic government. Those who deliberately violate a specific law, to test it or to call public attention to what they believe to be an injustice, must be prepared to accept the lawful consequences of their actions, which consequences may follow them for much of their lives; and they bear the very heavy moral responsibility of determining that there is no other effective recourse within the body of law and that the cause of justice which they seek to serve outweighs the exceedingly grave consequences of an act which weakens the total fabric of the law. Those individuals who enter into such an act may be paying merely lip service to democratic ideals while in actuality serving the cause of anarchy or some other cause.

The University of California assumes responsibility for the preservation of law and order upon its campuses. The university deplores disrespect for the law on the part of any citizens, whatever their organizational ties.

It has recently been suggested that the university should also assume responsibility for the off-campus actions of individual students by expelling those who are arrested or convicted for illegal kinds of participation in civil rights demonstrations. I should like to state briefly why I believe this proposal to be both impractical and improper.

The university now has a total enrollment of more than 60,000 students on seven different campuses; soon the figure will exceed 100,000 on nine campuses. The university must and will maintain academic and campus discipline among this huge number of students. But we cannot possibly maintain surveillance over the off-campus actions of more than 60,000 students, even if we wanted to do so, in their home towns, in their home states, their home countries, or whatever parts of the state or the world they may visit in their roles as individual citizens.

But there are more important considerations. A rule which arbitrarily provides for expulsion after a given number of arrests or convictions could work grave inequities. Let me indicate a few of the questions which would immediately arise. What about arrests culminating in acquittals? What about cases in which some participants in mass demonstrations are acquitted and others convicted by different juries? What about convictions in which the judge suspends the sentence because of mitigating circumstances? What about convictions in southern states where local laws are much more restrictive? What about convictions which are appealed to higher courts? And, of course, what about arrests for a broad spectrum of other types of offenses, ranging from felonies to traffic violations to over-indulgence in Big Game fervor?

The American judicial system provides that persons shall not be tried twice, and sentenced twice, for the same offense. A single court conducts the case and imposes a single sentence. The court does not rule that a violator shall be barred from further use of tax-supported institutions—schools, postal service, highway system, public parks—nor are these public entities expected to take official note of and impose additional penalties upon violators. I see no reason today to depart from these traditional American principles of law and jurisprudence by having the university impose a second trial or a second penalty. A citizen who is not also a student would have no such second trial or second penalty. It would be manifestly unfair to treat the citizen who is also a student differently from the citizen who is not also a student.

There are still other principles at stake. The American society is a pluralistic society, with many centers of power and many sets of rules and relationships and many spheres of action and concern. The emergence of a pluralistic rather than a monolithic form of society in the United States was no happenstance; rather, it was the inevitable concomitant of our belief in democratic government and the importance of the individual. Many different centers of power will prevent any one center, particularly the state, from becoming all-powerful. Many different organizations, each with limited relationships to its members, will prevent any one organization from dominating the life of the individual.

Just as there are many separate organizations in a democratic society, so also the individual has many separate relationships to these organizations. He may be at one and the same time the member of a family, a student in a university, a participant in a church, an employee of a business, and a citizen of the state; and in each of these relationships he will have certain rights and responsibilities. The relationship to the family is inherently different from that to the university or to the state. The relationship to the university is as a student, subject to the rules of the university and proper performance within the university; to the state as a citizen subject to the laws of the state. The university can no more act as though it were the state, than the state can act as though it were the university. We have a system based upon separation of powers, not only within the public, but also within the private spheres of action, and between public and private spheres. The university relates to its students as students. It is not also the family, or the church, or the state. This is the most basic consideration of all.

I say again as I have said before that the activities of students acting as private citizens off-campus on non-university matters are outside the sphere of the university. (1) The student is an individual and his individuality should be respected by the university. The university should seek to govern him and discipline him only in areas of direct university concern. (2) The student is also an independent citizen. As student, the university assumes certain responsibilities for his proper conduct. As citizen, the state assumes certain responsibilities. (3) The punishment, for students and citizens, should fit the crime. One punishment, not two, should fit one crime. A citizen because he is a student should not be penalized more than his fellow citizen who is not a student. There should be equal treatment under the law.

There is another side to this coin. Just as the university cannot and should not follow the student into his family life or his church life or his activities as a citizen off the campus, so also the students, individually or collectively, should not and cannot take the name of the university with them as they move into religious or political or other non-university activities; nor should they nor can they use university facilities in connection with such affairs. The university has resisted and will continue to resist such efforts by students, just as it has resisted and will continue to resist the suggestions of others that the university take on some of the functions of the state. The university is an independent educational institution. It is not a partisan political or sectarian religious institution; nor is it an enforcement arm of the state. It will not accede to pressures for either form of exploitation of its name, its facilities, its authority. The university will not allow students or others connected with it to use it to further their non-university political or social or religious causes nor will it allow those outside the university to use it for non-university purposes. The university will remain what it always has been—a university devoted to instruction, research, and public service wherever knowledge can serve society.

In conclusion, may I say that the University of California does share, in its instructional functions, along with other educational institutions, with churches, with families, a deep responsibility to help equip our students with the training, the knowledge, and the understanding to care wisely and effectively about the future of our free society. In meeting this responsibility, the university supports the powers of persuasion as against the use of force, the application of decent means to decent ends, the constructive act as against the destructive blow, respect for the rights of others, opposition to passion and hate, the reasoned argument as against the simplistic slogan, enlightenment in place of blind prejudice and ignorance. Only thus, by supporting means worthy of the ideals of our American society, can the University of California best help to bring to reality in the urgent present the ageless vision "that all men are created equal"; can it also best serve a society based on "the consent of the governed."

III

The History of a Student Revolt

The story of the Berkeley upheaval has been told in a myriad of articles in magazines and newspapers. The academic articles, theses, and books are still to come. Before entering into a discussion of how and why these events occurred we would like to describe what occurred. This section contains two selections. The first is an excellent detailed Chronology prepared by the editors of the California Monthly, *the alumni magazine of Berkeley. The second presents the reactions of the people of California as revealed to the California Poll.*

CHRONOLOGY OF EVENTS: THREE MONTHS OF CRISIS
BY THE EDITORS OF *California Monthly*

The following chronology traces events of the "free speech" controversy at Berkeley from September 10, 1964, through January 4, 1965.

September 10

A letter authored by "a former student" and distributed with the *Slate Supplement Report* called for an "open, fierce and thoroughgoing rebellion" on the Berkeley campus. Although the letter did not relate specifically to the "free speech issue," it sounded the rallying cry for subsequent events:

"The University does not deserve a response of loyalty and allegiance from you. There is only one proper response to Berkeley from undergraduates: that you ORGANIZE AND SPLIT THIS CAMPUS WIDE OPEN! . . .

"Go to the top. Make your demands to the Regents. If they refuse to give you an audience: start a program of agitation, petitioning, rallies, etc., in which the final resort will be CIVIL DISOBEDIENCE. In the long run, there is the possibility that you will find it necessary to perform civil disobedience at a couple of major University public ceremonies . . ."

September 15

The Ad Hoc Committee to End Discrimination—led by former Berkeley student and Slate founder Michael Myerson and by Tracy Sims, leader of the Palace Hotel demonstrations—announced plans to picket the *Oakland Tribune* for the third Friday in a row, and held a noon rally at the Bancroft and Telegraph entrance to the Berkeley campus.

September 16

1. Presidents or chairmen and advisers of all student organizations received a letter from Dean of Students Katherine A. Towle, dated Sept. 14, announcing that, effective Sept. 21, tables would no longer be permitted in the 26-foot strip of University property at the Bancroft and Telegraph entrance, and that advocative literature and activities on off-campus political issues also would be prohibited:

> "Provisions of the policy of the Regents concerning 'Use of University Facilities' will be strictly enforced in all areas designated as property of the Regents . . . including the 26-foot strip of brick walkway at the campus entrance on Bancroft Way and Telegraph Avenue . . ."

> (*Small copper plaques, imprinted: "Property of The Regents, University of California. Permission to enter or pass over is revocable at any time," outline University campuses' boundaries. A series of these plaques is located parallel to Bancroft Way, about 26 feet outside the large concrete posts at the Bancroft-Telegraph entrance to the campus. The new policy did not apply to an approximately eight-foot-wide strip of City of Berkeley sidewalk located between the plaques and the Bancroft Way curb.*)

> "Specifically," Dean Towle's letter said, "Section III of the (Regents') policy . . . prohibits the use of University facilities 'for the purpose of soliciting party membership or supporting or opposing particular candidates or propositions in local, state or national elections,' except that Chief Campus Officers 'shall establish rules under which candidates for public office (or their designated representatives) may be afforded like opportunity to speak upon the campuses at meetings where the audience is limited to the campus community.' Similarly, Chief Campus Officers 'shall establish rules under which persons supporting or opposing propositions in state or local elections may be afforded like opportunity to speak upon the campuses at meetings where the audience is limited to the campus community.'

> "Section III also prohibits the use of University facilities 'for the purpose of religious worship, exercise or

conversion.' Section IV of the policy states further that
University facilities 'may not be used for the purpose of
raising money to aid projects not directly connected with
some authorized activity of the University . . .'

"Now that the so-called 'speaker ban' is gone," Dean
Towle's letter continued, "and the open forum is a reality, student organizations have ample opportunity to present to campus audiences on a 'special event' basis an
unlimited number of speakers on a variety of subjects,
provided the few basic rules concerning notification and
sponsorship are observed . . . The 'Hyde Park' area in the
Student Union Plaza is also available for impromptu, un-
scheduled speeches by students and staff.

"It should be noted also that this area on Bancroft Way
. . . has now been added to the list of designated areas
for the distribution of handbills, circulars or pamphlets
by University students and staff in accordance with
Berkeley campus policy. Posters, easels and card tables
will not be permitted in this area because of interference
with the flow of (pedestrian) traffic. University facilities
may not, of course, be used to support or advocate off-
campus political or social action.

"We ask for the cooperation of every student and student organization in observing the full implementation of
these policies. If you have any questions, please do not
hesitate to come to the Office of the Dean of Students,
201 Sproul Hall."

Explaining the new ruling, Dean Towle said, "The growing use and misuse of the area has made it imperative that the
University enforce throughout the campus the policy long ago
set down by the Regents." Only leniency on the part of the
administration slowed enforcement of these rules in the past,
she said, but more strict enforcement had been under discussion for some time, she added.

Berkeley Chancellor Edward W. Strong, in a report to the
Berkeley Division of the Academic Senate dated October 26,
said:

"The situation was brought to a head by the multiplied
activity incidental to the primary election, the Republican
convention, and the forthcoming fall elections. Representatives of the Chancellor's Office, the Dean of Students
Office, the Campus Police, the Public Affairs Office, and
the ASUC had the problem on the agenda of meetings on
July 22, July 29, and September 4. They agreed that the
situation would worsen during the political campaign,
and steps should be taken at the beginning of the semester
to assure use of the area in accordance with University
rules . . ."

2. Arthur Goldberg, former chairman of Slate, announced lawyers representing Slate and other interested groups would meet tomorrow (Sept. 17) to decide possible legal action. Goldberg called the new policy "another in a long series of acts to curtail either right or left wing political action on campus . . .

"As the students become more and more aware of America's social problems, and come to take an active part in their solution, the University moves proportionally the other way to prevent all exposure of political action being taken.

"The most important thing is to make this campus a market place for ideas. But, the University is trying to prevent the exposure of any new creative political solutions to the problems that every American realizes are facing this society in the mid-Sixties."

September 17

Representatives of 18 student organizations met with Dean Towle to point out what they considered to be the unfairness and purposelessness of the new enforcement policy. The student groups asked for:

1) Advocacy of any political viewpoint or action or to be able to distribute literature to that effect in the Bancroft-Telegraph area.

2) Permission to distribute literature from tables, from which they can attract, by means of posters, interested people. They said they do not want to force literature on pedestrians, but rather hand out literature to those who approach them.

Student spokesmen offered to conduct a traffic flow survey, and to police for violations of university rules regarding placement of posters on university property. Most of the groups also indicated they would be willing to forego collection of money in the area.

Dean Towle answered that Regents' policy is clearly set down for all on-campus areas, including Bancroft-Telegraph, and that the university administration is under obligation to enforce that policy.

Dean Towle also charged, during the meeting, that, although the university had repeatedly asked for cooperation from groups using the Bancroft-Telegraph area, it received little in the matter of poster and table placement. "Some of the students have been both impudent and impertinent," she added.

Dean Towle implied it might be possible for the University to substitute the Hyde Park area in the Student Union Plaza for the Bancroft-Telegraph area. This offer was rejected. The students agreed to submit a list of written suggestions to the Dean of Students for the possible use of the Bancroft-Telegraph area and the Hyde Park area, although Dean Towle said further use of the Bancroft-Telegraph area was "almost out of the question."

The students insisted on their right, and "duty to society" to remain at their south entrance posts.

September 18

The 18 student organizations affected by the Bancroft-Telegraph controversy petitioned the Dean of Students for the use of the Bancroft-Telegraph area, under the following conditions:

"1. Tables for student organizations at Bancroft and Telegraph will be manned at all times.

"2. The organizations shall provide their own tables and chairs; no University property shall be borrowed.

"3. There shall be no more than one table in front of each pillar and one at each side of the entrance way. No tables shall be placed in front of the entrance posts.

"4. No posters shall be attached to posts or pillars. Posters shall be attached to tables only.

"5. We (students) shall make every effort to see that provisions 1–4 are carried out and shall publish such rules and distribute them to the various student organizations.

"6. The tables at Bancroft and Telegraph may be used to distribute literature advocating action on current issues with the understanding that the student organizations do not represent the University of California—thus these organizations will not use the name of the University and will dissociate themselves from the University as an institution.

"7. Donations may be accepted at the tables."

September 20

At an evening meeting, most of the groups affected by the new university policy agreed to picket, conduct vigils, rallies and touch off civil disobedience, if the university stands firm on the Bancroft-Telegraph politics ban after a meeting with Dean Towle, scheduled for 10:30 a.m. the next morning.

September 21

1. Dean Towle met with representatives of student groups affected by the new university rules for the Bancroft-Telegraph area. She accepted most of the proposals submitted by the students on Sept. 18: she would allow groups to set up a regulated number of tables with posters attached in the area,

and she would allow distribution of informative—as opposed to advocative—literature from them. Dean Towle also announced the establishment "on an experimental basis" of a second "Hyde Park" free-speech area at the entrance to Sproul Hall:

"Individuals are free to speak at will in these areas," she said, "provided they are registered students or staff of the University of California and observe the policies pertaining to use of University facilities. Since the University reserves such areas of the campus for student and staff use, those who speak should be prepared to identify themselves as students or staff of the University. It is suggested that speakers use as their podium the raised part of the wall on either side of the main stairway or the lower steps flanking the main stairway. Because of possible disturbance to persons working in Sproul Hall offices, voice amplifiers will not be permitted. There must be no interference with traffic or the conduct of University business."

Dean Towle refused permission to advocate specific action and to recruit individuals for specific causes. Also prohibited was solicitation of funds and donations "to aid projects not directly connected with some authorized activity of the University . . .

"It is not permissible, in materials distributed on University property, to urge a specific vote, call for direct social or political action, or to seek to recruit individuals for such action," Dean Towle said.

The students refused to accept Dean Towle's concessions. Picketing, demonstrations and vigils would be conducted, they said, until satisfaction was obtained from the university:

Jackie Goldberg, spokesman for the protesting groups, insisted "the University has not gone far enough in allowing us to promote the kind of society we're interested in.

"We're allowed to say why we think something is good or bad, but we're not allowed to distribute information as to what to do about it. Inaction is the rule, rather than the exception, in our society and on this campus. And, education is and should be more than academics.

"We don't want to be armchair intellectuals. For a hundred years, people have talked and talked and done nothing. We want to help the students decide where they fit into the political spectrum and what they can do about their beliefs. We want to help build a better society."

Dean Towle replied: "We have tried to be as fair as possible —but university policy is clearly stated in this area." The non-advocative restriction is not directed specifically at students, Dean Towle explained. Even non-students invited to speak on campus are informed that on-campus advocacy of direct political or social action is prohibited.

Dr. Saxton Pope, special assistant to Vice Chancellor Alex Sherriffs, who was present at the meeting, said the university was trying to discourage "advocacy of action without thought."

2. Approximately 75 students held an all-night vigil on Sproul Hall steps.

September 22

The ASUC Senate (by a vote of 11–5) requested the Regents "to allow free political and social action to be effected by students at the Bancroft entrance to the University of California, up to the posts accepted as the traditional entrance." The senate motion also requested the privilege of soliciting funds for off-campus activity. These privileges were also requested for eight other campus locations where only non-advocative literature is now permitted. The ASUC Senate also began circulation of a petition to gather student grassroots support, and discussed the possibility of the ASUC purchasing the disputed land and establishing it as a free speech area. The senate also proposed establishment of a board of control to prevent congestion in the area and to protect students from "overt confrontation" by leaflet distributors. Commenting on the senate's motion, Men's Residence Hall Representative Mike Adams said, "Advocacy of action makes our society a viable one, and is central to the entire educational process." Alumni Representative Wayne Hooper urged the senate not to "use the petition as a crutch. Don't wait for the students to pat you on the backside before you take a stand of your own."

September 23

Chancellor Strong issued the following statement:

"I call attention to the following facts concerning student use of University-owned property at the Telegraph-Bancroft entry to the campus. The Open Forum policy of the University is being fully maintained. Any student or staff member is free to address a campus audience in the 'Hyde Park' areas in the heart of the campus. Printed materials on issues and candidates can be distributed by bona fide student groups in nine places on campus, including the Telegraph-Bancroft location. A full spectrum of political and social views can be heard on campus, and candidates themselves can be invited to speak on campus.

"The University, rightly, as an educational institution, maintains an open forum for the free discussion of ideas and issues. Its facilities are not to be used for the mounting of social and political action directed at the surrounding community. The University has held firmly to the principles set forth by President Kerr in his Charter Day Address on the Davis Campus May 5, 1964:

"'The activities of students acting as private citizens off-campus on non-University matters are outside the sphere of the University . . . Just as the University cannot and should not follow the student into his family life or his church life or his activities as a citizen off the campus, so also the students, individually or collectively, should not and cannot take the name of the University with them as they move into religious or political or other non-University facilities in connection with such affairs . . . The University will not allow students or others connected with it to use it to further their non-University political or social or religious causes, nor will it allow those outside the University to use it for non-University purposes'."

September 25

University President Clark Kerr condemned the student demonstrations, and disagreed with the protestors that you must have action in order to learn:

"The Dean of Students has met many requests of the students. The line the University draws will be an acceptable one . . .

"I don't think you have to have action to have intellectual opportunity. Their actions—collecting money and picketing—aren't high intellectual activity . . . These actions are not necessary for the intellectual development of the students. If that were so, why teach history? We can't live in ancient Greece . . .

"The University is an educational institution that has been given to the Regents as a trust to administer for educational reasons, and not to be used for direct political action. It wouldn't be proper. It is not right to use the University as a basis from which people organize and undertake direct action in the surrounding community."

September 27

Spokesmen for the combined liberal and conservative student political groups announced plans to picket tomorrow's (Sept. 28) university meeting: the groups would simultaneously set up tables at Sather Gate and hold a rally in front of Wheeler Hall, without giving the required prior notice to the university administration. While the university meeting is in progress the students would march to the university meeting. Politically conservative protestors would participate only in the march, since the other activities violated university regulations.

September 28

Chancellor Edward W. Strong announced a substantial concession—that campaign literature advocating "yes" and "no" votes on propositions and candidates, campaign buttons and bumper strips could now be distributed at Bancroft-Telegraph and at eight other campus locations—as pickets formed in front of Wheeler Hall and marched to the university meeting. Chancellor Strong's liberalization of regulations—a result, he said, of a "reinterpretation of Regents' policy"—was a direct contradiction to Dean Towle's statements earlier in the dispute. Dean Towle had stated Regents' policy prohibited distribution of literature advocating either a "yes" or a "no" vote.

Arthur Goldberg, one of the protest leaders, said: "And you're asking me if picketing is effective?"

Another protest spokesman said:

> "The Bancroft-Telegraph issue has alerted us to the free speech issue all over campus. We won't stop now until we've made the entire campus a bastion of free speech."

Commenting on the student pickets disruption of the University Meeting, ASUC President Charles Powell said:

> "Placards like 'Sproul Hall Will Fall' and constant heckling and disruption among an audience . . . are . . . unnecessary at this stage of the issue, and a reflection of student sentiment of which I can no longer be proud."

September 29

1. Several tables were set up on campus at both Bancroft-Telegraph and in front of Sather Gate. Only one or two of the tables had the required permits from the University. (According to the dean of students office, permits were issued only to "qualified organizations" that promised not to solicit money or members, or initiate or advocate any off-campus activity other than voting.) Most of the organizations represented by tables would not make this promise and, in fact, were conducting such activities.

Dean of Men Arleigh Williams and university police officers informed each of the tables that some of the activities being conducted were illegal; a few times they asked for identification from students manning the tables. Dean Williams said: "Every effort will be made to remove those tables." But, he did not indicate if such an effort would involve action on the part of University police.

Arthur Goldberg, a protest leader, was asked to make an appointment with Dean Williams.

2. Representatives of protest groups met at 10:30 p.m. to plan future action.

September 30

1. At noon, University Friends of the Student Non-Violent Coordinating Committee (SNCC) and Campus Congress of Racial Equality (CORE) set up tables at Sather Gate. Neither had permits from the Dean of Students Office. According to Mario Savio, SNCC spokesman, the student groups were denied permits because it was suspected that they would attempt to collect funds for off-campus political or social action. According to Brian Turner, who set up the SNCC table, funds *were* being collected, in direct violation of University regulations.

University administration representatives approached each table, and took the names of those manning the tables. Five students—Mark Bravo, Brian Turner, Donald Hatch, Elizabeth Gardiner Stapleton, and David Goins—were requested to appear before Dean of Men Arleigh Williams at 3:00 p.m. for disciplinary action. That action triggered what was to become the first of the Sproul Hall sit-ins.

2. At 3:00 p.m.—under the direction of Mario Savio, Arthur Goldberg and Sandor Fuchs—more than 500 students and protestors appeared outside Dean Williams' office. Savio, Goldberg and others stood on a narrow balcony outside the second floor lobby of Sproul Hall, shouting to passing students and those gathered on Sproul Hall steps, urging them to join the growing mass seated and standing outside the Dean of Students Office.

Savio, the apparent spokesman for the protestors, presented a petition signed by more than 500 students:

"We the undersigned have jointly manned tables at Sather Gate, realizing that we were in violation of University edicts to the contrary. We realize we may be subject to expulsion."

Savio then issued two demands:

1) That everyone in the group who signed be treated exactly the same as the students who were summoned into Dean Williams' office, and

2) That all charges should be dropped until the University clarifies its policy, and it is clear whether or not there has been any violation.

Savio stated the group was absolutely firm on the first point, but might give a little on the second.

Dean Williams answered Savio's demands:

"I can not make any guarantee to concede to any request. We are dealing only with observed violations, not
unobserved violations. And, we will continue to do this."

Dean Williams thereupon cancelled a scheduled 4:00 p.m.
meeting with the leaders of all the groups protesting the
university's policy.

At 4:00 p.m., Dean Williams asked the original five students, plus the three demonstration leaders, to enter his office
to discuss disciplinary action. None of the eight people summoned entered the dean's office.

Savio then announced that, since it appeared none of their
demands had been met, that they would remain in Sproul
Hall throughout the night:

"We want equal action," Savio declared. "And, that's
no action, because they can't take action against all these
people who are here. They're scared. We're staying."

Money was collected—Slate announced a sizeable contribution—for food. By 5:00 p.m., women students were preparing
sandwiches in a second floor alcove.

3. At about midnight Chancellor Edward W. Strong issued
the following statement:

"Students and student organizations today enjoy the
fullest privileges in the history of the University, including discussing and advocacy on a broad spectrum of political and social issues. Some students demand on-campus solicitation of funds and planning and recruitment of
off-campus social and political action. The University cannot allow its facilities to be so used without endangering
its future as an independent educational institution. The
issue now has been carried far beyond the bounds of discussion by a small minority of students. These students
should recognize the fullness of the privileges extended
to them by the University, and ask themselves whether
they wish to take further actions damaging to the University.

"The University cannot and will not allow students to
engage in deliberate violation of law and order on campus. The Slate Supplement Report this fall urged 'open,
fierce and thoroughgoing rebellion on the campus . . . in
which the final resort will be Civil Disobedience.' Individual students must ask themselves whether they wish to
be a part of such action.

"When violations occur, the University must then take
disciplinary steps. Such action is being taken. Eight students were informed individually by a representative of
the Office of the Dean of Students that they were in vio-

lation of University regulations and were asked to desist. Each of the eight students refused to do so. I regret that these eight students by their willful misconduct in deliberately violating rules of the University have made it necessary for me to suspend them indefinitely from the University. I stand ready as always to meet with the officers of any student organization to discuss the policies of the University."

4. "I really don't know what to say," Mario Savio told the group of students sitting-in in Sproul Hall, when he heard Chancellor Strong's statement. "If you won't take this as the official statement of the group, I think they're (the administration) all a bunch of bastards."

Savio, one of the eight students suspended, acted as spokesman for the protestors. He said the issue will be met with continued protest. The three points of future protest action will be:

1) A fight for the dropping of disciplinary action against the suspended students;
2) A continuation of the fight for the demands on the free speech areas, including a proposed meeting with Chancellor Strong, and
3) The stipulation that no disciplinary action be taken against any students participating in further demonstrations.

Savio went on to say that the problem was that parts of Clark Kerr's Multiversity Machine, the students, "had broken down and were gumming up the works." So, naturally, the university had decided to expel the parts which weren't running smoothly. His analogy was cheered by the demonstrators.

As the evening progressed the demonstrators continued their sit-in, lie-in, and representatives of the various political organizations supporting the "Free Speech Movement" (FSM) —the name born that evening—met to plan future moves.

October 1

1. The first Sproul Hall sit-in broke up at approximately 2:40 a.m., when demonstrators voted to leave the premises. Before leaving, they announced a rally to be held at noon on Sproul Hall steps.
2. Several mimeographed fliers appeared on campus, calling for student and faculty support for the suspended students and announcing a "Free Speech Rally" at noon on Sproul Hall steps.
3. At approximately 10:00 a.m. two tables were set up outside Sather Gate, and one at the foot of Sproul Hall steps.
4. At approximately 11:45 a.m. Deans George S. Murphy

and Peter Van Houten, with University Police Lieutenant Merrill F. Chandler approached and spoke to a man who was soliciting funds at the Campus CORE table at the foot of Sproul Hall steps. The man, later identified as Jack Weinberg, a former student, refused to identify himself or to leave the table. Lieutenant Chandler arrested the man for trespassing. Weinberg went limp. Instead of carrying Weinberg into police headquarters in Sproul Hall, University police moved a police car into the area where students were gathering for the noon rally, intending to remove Weinberg by auto.

The crowd chanted "Release him! Release him!" About 100 students promptly lay down in front of the police car, another 80 or so sat behind it. Mario Savio removed his shoes and climbed on top of it, urging the gathering crowd to join in.

By noon, about 300 demonstrators surrounded the immobile police car; by 12:30 p.m., several thousand students were crowded around the car—which became the focal point and rostrum for the next 32 hours of student demonstrations.

Weinberg remained inside the captured police car throughout the two-day demonstration. He was fed sandwiches and milk through an open window.

Savio demanded Weinberg's release and the lifting of University prohibitions against soliciting funds and memberships on campus:

> "We were going to hold a rally. We didn't know how to get the people. But, we've got them now, thanks to the University . . .
>
> "Strong must say no to the suspensions. He must agree to meet with the political organizations. And, there must be no disciplinary action against anyone before the meeting!
>
> "And, I'm publicly serving notice that we're going to continue direct action until they (the Administration) accede. I suggest that we go into that building (Sproul Hall) and sit on the desks and chairs and make it impossible for them to continue their work."

Charles Powell, ASUC president, took Savio's place atop the stranded car:

> "I can see now that your cause is just," Powell said. He asked that, instead of a mob scene in Sproul Hall, only he and Savio enter the building to meet with Dean Williams.

The crowd demanded that Savio and Powell negotiate Weinberg's release, and termination of the eight student suspensions, and suspension of administration action against any protestors until the matter had been arbitrated.

Dean Arleigh Williams told Savio and Powell that the matter was out of his jurisdiction. He referred them to Chancellor Strong, with whom they discussed the problem.

Chancellor Strong refused Savio's demands. He said the university would not give in to pressure, the suspensions would stand, and that a meeting was possible only if the demonstrations ceased.

Savio and Powell returned from their meeting with Chancellor Strong at about 1:45 p.m.

Powell offered to have the ASUC Senate attempt to deal with the entire situation concerning the university's edict. The crowd refused Powell's offer, and he left.

At approximately 2:30 p.m., Savio suggested the demonstrators force their way into Sproul Hall, in order to hinder operations of the administration there:

> "I recommend that 500 of you stay here around this auto and others join me in taking our request back to the deans."

Savio then led about 150 students into Sproul Hall, where they sat outside the dean of students office.

About 4:00 p.m., the demonstrators inside now numbered about 400, voted to pack solidly in front of the door to the deans' office, and not allow anyone out. Deans Peter Van Houten and Arleigh Williams were trapped within the office by this maneuver.

The situation remained static until about 5:30 p.m. when Savio, again atop the automobile, announced "a committee of independent faculty members" would try to make contact with high administration officials. If contact was made, the group decided, the students in Sproul Hall would be notified and would leave the building. The students also voted to have the faculty committee notify them as soon as contact was made with the administration. Within a short time, contact was made with Vice Chancellor Alex Sherriffs, but a breakdown in communications prevented the students being notified.

At 6:15 p.m., 45 minutes before the scheduled closing, campus and Berkeley police officers began closing the front doors of Sproul Hall. Angered, about 100 of the approximately 2000 students outside Sproul Hall charged the doors, packing them to prevent their closing. Two police officers were pulled to the floor; one lost his hat and shoes (which were returned to him as he escaped into the building) and was bitten on the leg. About 20 police officers took up stations at the foot of the main stairway leading from the Sproul Hall lobby to the second floor, where the deans' offices are. The students took up positions on the lobby floor.

After a long discussion, the demonstrators outside decided to form a united front, and ordered those inside the building to come outside to join them on the mall. All but five of those inside Sproul Hall at the time obeyed the summons. The remaining five were left unmolested. The demonstrations then continued around the police car on the mall between Sproul Hall and the Student Union.

5. Demonstration leaders met in a closed meeting at 10:00 p.m. They decided:

1) The demonstrators would attempt to remain on the steps and in the mall through Family Day on Saturday, Oct. 3.

2) Tables would be set up at Sather Gate, separate from the Sproul Hall demonstrations, in the hope that more people would be suspended.

3) A rally would be held at noon tomorrow (Oct. 2), centering around the car carrying Weinberg.

4) After the rally, groups of demonstrators again would move into the second floor of Sproul Hall and block off the Dean of Students Office.

6. At 11:15 p.m. small groups of anti-demonstration demonstrators began converging on the mall from all directions, swelling the crowd to about 2500. At this point, the demonstration degenerated into a shouting, singing, swearing and egg throwing contest. The demonstrators sang "We Shall Overcome!" The anti-demonstration forces shouted "Mickey Mouse!"

7. California Governor Edmund G. Brown issued the following statement:

"I support fully the stand of U.C. President Clark Kerr and Berkeley Chancellor Edward W. Strong.

"This is not a matter of freedom of speech on the campuses. I and President Kerr and the Regents have long fought to maintain freedom of speech and an Open Forum policy on all the campuses of the University.

"This is purely and simply an attempt on the part of the students to use the campuses of the University unlawfully by soliciting funds and recruiting students for off-campus activities.

"This will not be tolerated. We must have—and will continue to have—law and order on our campuses."

8. Berkeley Chancellor Edward W. Strong issued the following statement:

"Because two facts respecting University policies on students and student organizations are still being misunderstood or misrepresented by some persons, I want again to emphasize these two facts:

"1) The University's policy prohibiting planning and recruiting on campus for off-campus political and social action, and prohibiting also the solicitation or receipt of funds for such purposes is now and has always been the unchanged policy of the University.

"2) The University has not restricted or curtailed freedom of speech of students on campus by any change of its own Open Forum policy.

"No instance of a newly imposed restriction or curtailment of freedom of speech on campus can be truthfully alleged for the simple reason that none exists.

"Freedom of speech by students on campus is not the issue. The issue is one presented by deliberate violations of University rules and regulations by some students in an attempt to bring about a change of the University policy prohibiting use of University facilities by political, social and action groups."

9. Charles Powell, ASUC president, issued the following statement:

"The facts are these:

"The prohibition on the solicitation of funds and membership on campus for partisan issues is not a ruling of the Chancellor or of President Clark Kerr.

"It is, in fact, a State law.

"Therefore, the only rational and proper action at this point is to seek changes in the law. Those opportunities are not here on the campus—but in the houses of the State Legislature.

"In a conference with President Kerr, I have been told that mob violence and mass demonstrations directed at the Administration will, in no way, do anything to alleviate the problem.

"In fact, we are indeed losing support among the Regents for concessions which have already been made.

"I am certain, and President Kerr has confirmed this fear, that if demonstrations such as today's continue, we will lose the Open Forum policy.

"This is a tradition for which all students and President Kerr have fought long and hard, and one which we need not lose.

"I appeal to my fellow students.

"I ask that you not oppose the Administration—the Administration can do nothing to meet the demands being made.

"But this I do ask, write your State legislators, then give your full-hearted support to the ASUC Senate which will ask the property at Bancroft and Telegraph be deeded to the City of Berkeley for municipal administration.

"Above all, I ask you to discontinue demonstrations which are endangering lives, property, and the Open

Forum policy which the entire University community enjoys."

10. Mona Hutchins, vice president of the University Society of Individualists, a conservative group, issued the following statement:

"The conservative campus groups fully agree with the purpose of the sit-ins in Sproul Hall. Individual members of our organizations have expressed their sympathy by joining in the picketing on the steps of the Hall, and will continue to do so.

"However, our belief in lawful redress of grievances prevents us from joining the sit-ins. But, let no one mistake our intent. The United Front still stands."

October 2

1. The *Daily Californian*, the campus student newspaper, printed the following editorial, bordered in black and signed by the Senior Editorial Board:

"Last night the students became a near mob, with a police car for their symbol.

"The demonstrators surrounded a police car in front of Sproul Hall as a banner for their disobedience against University authority. It became a symbol of their power. And yet when an opposition force appeared late last night from the fraternities and residence halls, the demonstrators appealed to the police to maintain 'law and order.'

"No one can rationally justify the simultaneous defiance of authority on one hand, the expectation of protection on the other.

"We feel that, under these circumstances, the demonstrations have dissolved into a morass of distorted goals, inconsistent means, and blindness to their fallibility.

"The demonstrators say that the campus administration is no longer open for discussion. How can the demonstrators themselves be open for rational discussion when the basic issues of solicitation of funds, recruitment of members and 'mounting social and political action' have been wholly overshadowed by defiance?

"The antagonists of late last night exhibited something just as dangerous. They overflowed with an explosive singsong belligerence. They went to Sproul Hall with anger and without reason—and almost touched off a riot.

"The entire Open Forum policy has been threatened by the action of both of these student groups. The concept of the Open Forum will continue to be in jeopardy at the hands of persons completely outside the University if the same irrational and rash challenges to the Administration's final decision continue.

"The Administration has drawn the line at what it believes is the last concession on the University level. We completely believe they are telling the truth.

"Those who espouse over-simplified concepts of the issues and solutions, will tell you otherwise.

"The University has drawn the last line it can.

"We therefore suggest that the emotional commitment of the past two weeks needs a drastic reappraisal. We urge the students to think by themselves—not by the group."

2. At 1:30 a.m., as conflicts between demonstrators and anti-demonstration demonstrators threatened to erupt into a full-blown riot, Father James Fisher of Newman Hall mounted the police car. The crowd fell silent as he pleaded for peace—and got it.

Demonstrations around the stranded police car, still containing Jack Weinberg, continued throughout the day. Sproul Hall was locked, except for one police-guarded door at the south end through which those with legitimate business inside could pass. A pup tent was pitched on one of the lawns. The entire mall area was littered with sleeping bags, blankets, books, and the debris of the all-night vigil.

Speakers continued to harangue the crowd from the top of the sagging police car, gathering momentum as noon approached. At noon, lunch-time onlookers enlarged the crowd to close to 4000 persons.

3. At 10:30 a.m., after President Kerr and Chancellor Strong agreed that the situation had to be brought under control, a high-level meeting of administrators, deans and representatives of at least four law enforcement agencies was held to formulate plans for handling the demonstrations. At 11:55 a.m., representatives of the governor's office and the president's office joined the session. (It was agreed that Chancellor Strong would read a statement at 6:00 p.m., declaring the assembled group an unlawful assemblage and asking the crowd to disperse. To enforce Chancellor Strong's declaration, plans also were drawn up for a mass movement of police officers onto the campus for the purpose of arresting those demonstrators who refused to comply with Chancellor Strong's request to disperse.)

4. At about 4:15 p.m., demonstration spokesmen asked to meet with President Kerr. President Kerr and Chancellor Strong agreed to meet with the protest leaders at 5:00 p.m.

5. At 4:45 p.m. police officers from Oakland, Alameda County, Berkeley and the California Highway Patrol began marching onto the campus, taking up positions at the north

and south ends of Sproul Hall and on Barrows Lane, behind
the administration building. Some 500 officers, including over
100 motorcycle police, were on hand by 5:30 p.m., some
armed with long riot sticks.

As the police arrived, onlookers and protest sympathizers
swelled the crowd between Sproul Hall and the Student Union
to more than 7000. Spectators lined the Student Union balcony and the roof of the Dining Commons.

As the possibility of police action against the demonstrators
increased, protestors were instructed on "how to be arrested"
(remove sharp objects from pockets, remove valuable rings
and watches, loosen clothing, pack closely together, do not
link arms, go limp) and were counseled on their legal rights
(give only your name and address, ask to see your lawyer, do
not make any statements). All persons with small children,
those under 18 years of age, non-citizens, and those on parole
or probation were advised to leave.

And, as six campus police officers penetrated the periphery
of the crowd—in an effort to reinforce the stranded police car
—the demonstrators packed themselves solidly around the car.

6. At about 5:30 p.m., the demonstrators were informed
that the meeting between protest leaders and university officials was in progress at University House, and that President
Kerr had promised no police action until after that meeting.
Participating in the negotiations were President Kerr, Chancellor Strong, members of an informal faculty group, student
leaders, representatives of the Inter-Faith Council, and nine
demonstration spokesmen. A six-point agreement was reached
and was signed by President Kerr and the demonstration
spokesmen. The meeting was disbanded at 7:15 p.m.

7. At approximately 7:20 p.m., the crowd was informed
that an agreement had been reached, and that the protest
spokesmen were en route from University House to present
it to the demonstrators.

8. At 7:30 p.m., with President Kerr and Chancellor Strong
watching from the steps of Sproul Hall (the crowd was un-
aware of their presence), Mario Savio mounted the flattened
roof of the police car to read the agreement:

"1) The student demonstrators shall desist from all
forms of their illegal protest against University regulations.

"2) A committee representing students (including
leaders of the demonstration), faculty, and administration will immediately be set up to conduct discussions and
hearing into all aspects of political behavior on campus
and its control, and to make recommendations to the
administration.

"3) The arrested man will be booked, released on his

own recognizance, and the University (complainant) will not press charges.

"4) The duration of the suspension of the suspended students will be submitted within one week to the Student Conduct Committee of the Academic Senate.

"5) Activity may be continued by student organizations in accordance with existing University regulations.

"6) The President of the University has already declared his willingness to support deeding certain University property at the end of Telegraph Avenue to the City of Berkeley or to the ASUC."

(The agreement was signed by Clark Kerr, Jo Freeman, Paul C. Cahill, Sandor Fuchs, Robert Wolfson, David Jessup, Jackie Goldberg, Eric Levine, Mario Savio and Thomas Miller.)

At 7:40 p.m., Mario Savio said:

"Let us agree by acclamation to accept this document. I ask you to rise quietly and with dignity, and go home."

9. At 7:50 p.m., President Clark Kerr held a news conference in Sproul Hall. Chancellor Strong was present, but did not take part. Outside the window, the students were dispersing. The police officers had been dismissed. President Kerr said: "Law and order have been restored without the use of force." University rules remain unchanged, he said. The arrested non-student trespasser (Jack Weinberg) has been booked by police. Although the university agreed not to press charges, President Kerr said he could not speak for the district attorney. The eight suspended students remain suspended. Their cases will be reviewed, under the regular procedures, by a faculty committee. The faculty committee's suggestions may, or may not, be accepted by Chancellor Strong. Final disposition is still in the hands of the administration, President Kerr stressed.

Chancellor Strong, the President continued, will issue appointments to the special ad hoc committee to be established under point two of the agreement. Four students, four faculty members and four administration representatives will be named to the committee. Two of the students will be named from among those who negotiated the agreement with President Kerr.

October 3

Edward W. Carter, chairman of the University Board of Regents, issued the following statement:

"Law and order have been re-established on the Berkeley campus of the University of California. That this was accomplished without violence is a tribute to President

Clark Kerr and his administrative staff. All applicable University rules remain unchanged; the non-student arrested has been booked by the police; the eight suspended students are still on suspension, and the regular procedures for review of student conduct and grievances are functioning.

"A faculty committee will review individual cases in an orderly manner, and in due course will make recommendations for their disposition by the properly constituted administrative authorities.

"It is regrettable that a relatively small number of students, together with certain off-campus agitators should have precipitated so unfortunate an incident."

October 4

1. California Governor Edmund G. Brown pledged to maintain law and order on university campuses and asked President Kerr to prepare, "as soon as possible," a full and complete report on the student demonstration:

"I would like a detailed account of its causes, what actions were taken and why, what issues were involved, and what recommendations you have for preventing similar situations in the future."

2. President Clark Kerr, answering Governor Brown's request, said the administration "has already begun an investigation and analysis" of the demonstrations. Kerr's statement said, in part:

"Law and order were restored to the Berkeley campus without the use of force—a result the Governor desired as much as I.

". . . All applicable University rules remain unchanged; the non-student arrested as a trespasser has been booked by the police. The eight suspended students are still under suspension and the regular procedures for review of student conduct and grievances are functioning."

President Kerr described the situation as "highly complicated . . .

"Students with left-wing and right-wing political orientation are more active than ever before. Off-campus elements excite this orientation. As a consequence, the historical position of the University against being made a base for political direct action is placed under unusual attack.

"At the same time, the world and national situations have most unfortunately placed more emphasis in the minds of a few students on direct action, even outside the limits of the law, than on compliance with law and order and democratic process.

"Nevertheless, the University is fully responsible for the maintenance of law and order and the guarantee that it remain an educational institution."

3. Various reactions were inspired by the student protest demonstrations:

1) Ernest Besig, executive director of the Northern California chapter of the American Civil Liberties Union (ACLU), disputed the University's interpretation of the State Constitutional clause relating to political and sectarian activity on the campus (Article IX, Section 9, *see Appendix*). His statement was issued October 1: "The ACLU does not share the opinion of the University Administration that the constitutional ban on political and sectarian activity is aimed at students."

Bessig said the ACLU Board of Directors would consider intervening on behalf of the eight suspended students.

2) The Executive Committee of the Association of California State College Professors expressed support for the student protestors: "Participation in social action, whether it is political or non-political ought not only to be permitted, but actively encouraged, so long as it does not interfere with the regular instructional program . . ."

3) The Inter-Faith Staff Workers and Student Leaders, a local religious group, supported the aims of the protestors: "We affirm the right of members of the campus community to solicit funds, distribute literature and recruit members for involvement in common action."

4) Cal Students for Goldwater supported the Regents' right to regulate as they deem necessary and complained of the non-enforcement of rules applying to campus political activities, according to Morris E. Hurley, vice president.

4. Chancellor Strong's office issued a statement outlining plans to implement the agreement reached between protestors and President Kerr last Friday night:

1) Tomorrow (Oct. 5), Chancellor Strong will send the names of the eight suspended students to the Faculty Committee on Student Conduct.

2) Tomorrow (Oct. 5), Chancellor Strong will send out letters of appointment to members of the student-faculty-administration committee which will discuss the dispute.

3) The University has not pressed charges against Jack Weinberg (for trespassing), but re-emphasized the ad-

ministration had no authority to speak for the district attorney's office.

October 5

1. Protestors held a noon rally on Sproul Hall steps, claimed victory and voiced their approval of Friday evening's agreement. Art Goldberg said:

> "We ask only the right to say what we feel when we feel like it. We'll continue to fight for this freedom, and we won't quit until we've won."

Approximately 1000 students gathered in the mall between Sproul Hall and the Student Union to listen to the protest speakers.

Mario Savio, one of the demonstration leaders who negotiated the agreement with President Kerr and who urged the students to accept the agreement, stated that "although the whole war is far from over, we have won the biggest battle." That battle, he explained, was to gain "jurisdictional recognition" from President Kerr of a faculty-student-administration committee to negotiate the "free speech" issue.

To answer what he considered President Kerr's implication of a Communist tinge to the anti-ban movement, Savio decried the "great bogeyman raised . . . whenever a group is working for social change. No one wants to admit that large numbers of people are sick and fed up with the way things are."

A number of speakers addressed the assembled students, including several of the eight suspended students, Professor John Leggett of sociology, Professor Charles Sellers of history, and Warren Coats of the Young Republicans. Statements of support were read, including a document signed by 43 political science and economics teaching assistants, commending demonstrators' goals.

The rally was technically illegal under university regulations regarding non-student speakers. It was permitted, however, under a "special waiver" signed by Dean of Students Katherine A. Towle. Dean Towle explained:

> "We are honoring the spirit of the President's agreement and therefore have granted a special waiver for this meeting today, so that leaders of the demonstration may discuss the written agreement of last Friday."

> (*University regulations require non-student speakers to wait 72 hours after officially requesting permission from the Dean's office to speak on campus. Most of the leaders of the current demonstrations are either suspended or non-students. No one requested permission for them to speak at this rally.*)

(*The* DAILY CALIFORNIAN *speculated, on Oct. 6, that both sides had maneuvered behind the scenes to persuade the other to back down on the rally issue. The Administration wanted the students to postpone the rally—or, hold it on city property—apparently to avoid embarrassment over allowing anti-ban students to again break University regulations. The student protestors wanted to hold it on Sproul steps, in order to honor their Friday night announcement of the rally's location and time. Apparently, the students won.*)

2. In an effort to atone for damage to the police car during the Thursday and Friday demonstrations, the students began a collection of funds to help pay the $334.30 in damages to the police car.

3. Chancellor Edward W. Strong turned the cases of the suspended students over to the Faculty Committee on Student Conduct, in accord with the agreement between the demonstrators and President Kerr to submit the suspensions to adjudication within one week. Unfortunately, as the chancellor found out—and everyone soon knew—there was no "Student Conduct Committee of the Academic Senate," as specified in the agreement. The Faculty Committee on Student Conduct is a duly constituted committee, and, even if it had been asked to do so, the Academic Senate would have been unable to set up an *ad hoc* committee to hear these cases before October 13, well beyond the one-week deadline stipulated in the agreement.

4. Chancellor Strong also announced appointments to the faculty-student-administration Study Committee on Campus Political Activity. They were:

Faculty: Robley Williams, professor of virology; Theodore Vermeulen, professor of chemical engineering; Joseph Garbarino, professor of business administration; and Henry Rosovsky, professor of economics.

Students: ASUC President Charles Powell and Marsha Bratten, both winners of the 1964 Robert Gordon and Ida W. Sproul Awards. Two additional student members will represent the demonstrators.

Administration: Katherine A. Towle, dean of students; Milton Chernin, dean of the School of Social Welfare; William Fretter, dean of the College of Letters and Sciences; and Alan Searcy, recently appointed vice chancellor for academic affairs.

October 6

1. The FSM Steering Committee met with Vice Chancellor Alan Searcy to protest Chancellor Strong's "unilateral" appointment of the Committee on Campus Political Activity

without consulting the demonstrators and to express dissatisfaction with the way student-administration negotiations were
proceeding. Arthur Goldberg said the chancellor's action was
"almost a breech of good faith by the administration . . .

"It is dangerous to start out so arbitrarily. The University has put us in an impossible position before we
start."

President Kerr had agreed to accept recommendations from
the demonstrators, and failed to do so, according to protest
leaders. The protestors also claimed Chancellor Strong's action put them in a position of inequality, since, they claimed,
ten of the chancellor's appointments were opposed to the
students' position.

The protestors argued that a special committee of the Academic Senate should choose the faculty members; the students
would choose the student members.

2. The ASUC Senate passed a resolution asking President
Charles Powell to meet with President Kerr "to determine
whether the administration has violated the spirit of Friday's
agreement . . ." The Powell-Kerr meeting would center on
two points:

1) The manner of the Administration's appointment of
faculty members to the faculty-student-administration
committee agreed to on Friday, and
2) The Administration's referral of the cases of the suspended students to the Faculty Committee on Student
Conduct.

The Senate also decided that, if the students approve, it
would negotiate with the Regents for detachment of the controversial Bancroft-Telegraph area from the university and
its establishment as a "free area for political and social action."

The ASUC Senate's first move would be a poll to determine
whether "the students wish it to attempt to secure control of
the Bancroft-Telegraph area . . . and if they would assent to
the use of ASUC funds for the purchase of the land." The
senate would consider itself bound by the poll's results.

If the students approved, two possible alternatives would
be considered:

1) The ASUC would purchase the land and donate it to
the City of Berkeley, or to a trust of the Senate's choosing, or
2) The land will be donated or sold outright to the City of
Berkeley.

During the ASUC Senate meeting, Commuter-Independent
Representative Ed Wilson charged that the administration had

failed to live up to the spirit of Friday's agreement. Specifically:

1) The Administration tried to force the anti-ban students to postpone Monday's rally for seventy-two hours (in conformance with the University's rules regarding non-student speakers).

2) The Administration should let the Academic Senate choose the faculty members of the negotiating committee, rather than select them itself, which the Administration already had done.

3) The district attorney was pressing charges against Jack Weinberg, even though the Administration had agreed not to. (*President Kerr, in announcing the agreement, carefully pointed out that the University's decision not to press charges against Weinberg did not prohibit the district attorney's doing so.*)

4) The Academic Senate Committee on Student Conduct does not exist. According to Friday's agreement, the cases of the suspended students were to be referred to this group. Instead, Wilson charged, the cases have been referred to the Faculty Committee on Student Conduct, which is appointed by the Administration.

3. The Advocate Young Republicans, a group of Boalt Hall School of Law students, issued a statement "disagreeing with, and expressing condemnation of lawless behavior." The group also announced that it disagreed with the rules set up by the university with regard to the restriction on political conduct of students on campus.

October 7

The Committee on Campus Political Activity held its first meeting. Ten FSM spokesmen appeared, presented a statement condemning the committee as illegally constituted and asked it to disband, then left. The statement read, in part:

"As the duly elected representatives of the Free Speech Movement (FSM), we cannot in good conscience recognize the legitimacy of the present meeting.

"This present meeting is a result of unilateral action by the Administration, and as such we cannot participate . . .

". . . We were not even officially notified of this meeting.

". . . We respectfully request this body consider itself illegally constituted and disband."

The Study Committee's purpose, announced as the meeting convened, was to recommend action to the administration on the problem of political action on campus.

Following a three-hour session, minus FSM representatives, the Study Committee issued two statements:

1) The Committee will conduct discussions, hold hearings, and finally draft recommendations to the Administration as to proper University policy.
2) The Committee will hold its first public hearing at 7:30 p.m., Tuesday (Oct. 13) in a room to be announced.

October 8

1. An FSM spokesman claimed the demonstrators were surprised to discover the purpose of the committee was study—not negotiation. (*The first announcement of the committee's name and purpose was made in statements issued last night.*)
Jack Weinberg said:

"The Administration feels they have the sole right to say what this committee is supposed to do."

Weinberg, the former student whose arrest touched off the October 1 and 2 "police car" demonstrations, is a member of the FSM Steering Committee. He claimed FSM representatives had attempted to meet with administration officials for two days, but had been unable to do so.
2. Two conservative groups took issue with the political ideas of the two students who may ultimately represent the demonstrators on the study committee. In a joint statement, the University Young Republicans and the Cal Students for Goldwater charged:

"These two are, in fact, being chosen by a sub-caucus called the 'Steering Committee,' a group which believes in unlawful solutions to legitimate problems, and which represents solely left-of-center political groups."

FSM's press relations group answered the above charges:

1) FSM's Steering Committee had attempted to reach the conservative groups, but had been unable to do so.
2) The Steering Committee had been democratically elected from members of the Executive Committee (which is composed of representatives of all student groups involved in the demonstrations).
3) FSM intended to add four independent students to its Steering Committee at a 7:00 p.m. meeting tonight.

3. ASUC President Charles Powell was unable to meet with President Kerr, as requested in the ASUC Senate resolution, because President Kerr was in Southern California.
4. President Clark Kerr, during a speech before the San Diego Chamber of Commerce, said:

"The situation (at Berkeley) is new in that students are

more activist than before and that diverse groups . . . are attacking the historic policies of the University. Students are encouraged, as never before, by elements external to the University."

Kerr also described the incident as "one episode—a single campus, a small minority of students, a short period of time."

5. President Clark Kerr answered student charges of "bad faith" on the part of the administration in a statement released tonight:

"A question has been raised about the appointment of the joint advisory committee. The minutes of the meeting show the following:

" 'Kerr: This committee would have to be appointed by the administration.'

"It was noted that it was the only agency with authorization to appoint faculty, students and administrators.

"A question has also been raised about the 'Student Conduct Committee of the Academic Senate.' This is a misnomer. It was used in a draft prepared by an informal group of faculty members. I did not catch the misstatement at the time; nor did anyone else. The only such committee that exists is the 'Faculty Committee on Student Conduct' which is composed of faculty members. The minutes show the following:

" 'Kerr: We need to understand that the Committee does not make final determinations. You would have to be aware that you would be dependent also on whatever confidence you have in the decency and fairness of the Administration and respect for it.'

"The campus administration went ahead promptly to show its good faith in appointing the joint committee and submitting the suspension cases to the Faculty Committee on Student Conduct. The campus administration reserved two of four student places for representatives of the demonstrators as they clearly represent only a minority of students."

6. Following President Kerr's statement, the faculty advisory group which proposed most of the six-point agreement of October 2, issued the following statement:

"We who have sought to mediate some of the issues growing out of the recent demonstration, deeply regret that the present steering committee of the demonstrators took during the negotiations a rigid and unreasonable position on the question of student representatives, jeopardizing the successful organization of the student-faculty-administration committee.

"We continue to believe firmly in the importance of

maximum freedom for peaceful student political action, and in company with all individuals whose primary interest lies in this end, we shall bend every effort to realize that objective."

7. Richard W. Jennings, chairman of the Berkeley Division of the Academic Senate, said the senate will consider directing the Committee on Academic Freedom and the Committee on Educational Policy to inquire into the recent university rulings on student political activity, the students' protest of the rulings, and the problem of the students' rights to the expression of political opinion on campus.

8. Dean of Men Arleigh Williams sent letters to the eight suspended students, informing them that in accordance with the agreement, their cases had been referred to the Faculty Committee on Student Conduct. The letters also asked the students to appear in the dean of students office to set times for hearings. (*Two students appeared, but none submitted himself to the committee.*)

9. The Northern California branch of the American Civil Liberties Union announced it had agreed "to intervene on behalf of the students recently suspended by the university . . .

"The ACLU's position is that the regulations which the students were alleged to have broken violate their political rights as guaranteed by the first amendment . . . the ACLU will challenge the suspensions as a violation of due process of law."

10. Dean of Men Arleigh Williams received a petition signed by about 650 members of 37 fraternities and sororities, asserting that FSM was "composed of responsible students" and declaring support of its goals.

11. A petition was circulated among student leaders by Sharon Mock, ASUC second vice president. The petition expressed a belief . . .

". . . that rational democratic procedures should be used to voice opinion and to revise laws, since we as Americans have benefitted by this process for years.

"We condemn the methods . . . used by a minority of students and non-students which are disrupting the educational process through the deliberate violation of present University and State regulations. We also wish to preserve the Open Forum Policy which now exists on our campus as a result of orderly democratic procedure."

(*The petition was signed by the presidents of Inter-Fraternity Council, Winged Helmet, Deutsch, Davidson, Griffiths and Cheney Halls, Treble Clef, the Commuter-Independent Association, Golden Guard, and the Spirit and Honor Society. It also was signed by the entire Pan-*

hellenic Council, most of the Board and Cabinet of the Associated Women Students, and by 29 Oski Dolls.)

October 12

1. The FSM Steering Committee met with Chancellor Strong and called for suspension of activities of the Study Committee until representatives of the administration and the FSM could reach agreement on "the interpretation and implementation of the pact of October Second" and either immediate reinstatement of the suspended students, or submission of their cases to an *ad hoc* committee of the Academic Senate, with the provision that the administration would abide by their decision.

The FSM representatives stated that they could not recognize the legality of the Study Committee without jeopardizing their leadership and control of the situation. They also maintained that, not only the students, but also the faculty members selected to serve on the committee should be appointed by negotiations between the FSM and the Chancellor on selections acceptable to the FSM.

Chancellor Strong answered that, since the Study Committee had been appointed and was meeting, he would ask it for advice on the propriety of suspending its activities. He also said that, since interpretation of the intent of the agreement was best referred to the signers, they might discuss that point with the president. Chancellor Strong also explained that he had referred the cases of the suspended students to the only existing appropriate committee that could have been meant by the October 2 agreement.

2. A petition, signed by 88 members of the faculty, was presented to the chancellor, urging reinstatement of the suspended students.

October 13

1. The Academic Senate passed two motions:

1) The first noted "with pleasure the general improvement in recent years in the atmosphere of free inquiry and free exchange of opinion within the University." This motion also declared in favor of "maximum freedom of student political activity," and directed the Committee on Academic Freedom to inquire into recent events and report to the Senate as quickly as possible.

2) The second motion recognized "the welfare of the University can only be maintained if the peace and order of an intellectual community are also maintained," and called upon all parties "to resolve the dispute in peaceful and orderly fashion" and "make full use of the joint

faculty-student-administration committee for that purpose."

2. FSM leaders contacted Earl Bolton, university vice-president-administration, and subsequently sent telegrams to Governor Edmund G. Brown and Edward W. Carter, chairman of the Board of Regents, requesting that they be allowed an hour to present their case to the Regents. The FSM leaders promised "mass demonstrations" if they were not given "some clear indication . . . that the administration is not playing."

3. The Study Committee on Campus Political Activity held its first public meeting at 7:30 p.m. in Harmon Gymnasium. Approximately 300 students attended. The committee heard testimony from 50 students, all but one of whom, as instructed by an insert in the *FSM Newsletter,* stated that the committee was illegally constituted and should disband.

October 14

Professor Arthur Ross, chairman of the Committee on University Welfare, met with the FSM Steering Committee and agreed to discuss with the administration proposed modifications of the interpretation of the Agreement of October 2.

October 15

1. Agreements were reached with the FSM, the administration, the Regents and the Study Committee, and were announced to a meeting of the Academic Senate by a communication from President Kerr and Chancellor Strong, both of whom were attending the Board of Regents meeting at Davis. The points of the new agreement were:

1) The Study Committee was expanded from 12 to 18 members. The new members will include two faculty members named by the Committee on Committees of the Academic Senate; two administration members to be named by the President to represent the University-wide administration; and two additional student members plus the two members initially assigned them to be named by the FSM Steering Committee. The Study Committee would hold two or three public hearings a week and finish such hearings within three weeks. No more than five silent observers and two silent attorneys were to attend all meetings, and all findings and recommendations were to be by consensus.

2) The Academic Senate was asked to appoint an *ad hoc* committee to hear the cases of the eight students suspended two weeks ago. The *ad hoc* committee was to be advisory to the administration.

2. The Academic Senate, meeting in Berkeley, unanimously

granted the administration request to establish an *ad hoc* committee. The Committee on Committees appointed Ira M. Heyman, professor of law, as chairman. Other committee members were Robert A. Gordon, professor of economics; Mason Haire, professor of psychology and research psychologist in the Institute of Industrial Relations; Richard E. Powell, professor of chemistry and chairman of the department of chemistry; and Lloyd Ulman, professor of economics and industrial relations and director of the Institute of Industrial Relations.

The Academic Senate, during the same meeting, also passed a motion introduced by Frank C. Newman, dean of Boalt Hall School of Law:

> "Whereas, the Berkeley Division of the Academic Senate recently has gone on record as favoring maximum freedom for student political activity and the use of peaceful and orderly procedures in settling disputes;
>
> "And, whereas, the attitude of the Division has been widely misunderstood as condoning lawlessness, now, therefore, this body reaffirms its convictions that force and violence have no place on this campus."

3. Edward W. Carter, chairman of the Board of Regents, sent a telegram to Mario Savio following the Regents meeting at Davis:

> "The Regents have concluded that in view of the study being conducted by the appropriate committee, no useful purpose would be served by considering whether your group should be heard by the Regents at this time."

4. President Clark Kerr, during a news conference following the Regents meeting, reiterated his belief that some of the demonstrators "had Communist sympathies."

5. The FSM Executive Committee met briefly this evening and accepted the changes in the Study Committee and in the appointment of the *ad hoc* Academic Senate committee. Following this meeting, Art Goldberg said:

> "For the first time in the history of the University, an administration treated its students as representative members of the University community. This is a major event in the life of the University and for all the students on campus."

October 16

1. The FSM Steering Committee issued a statement at 12:30 a.m.:

> "The FSM has every hope that the negotiations which we are entering into with the administration can be productive.

"However, we hope that President Kerr's attack upon us is not an indication of an unhealthy attitude with which the administration is entering these negotiations.

"It is regrettable that the President has resorted to such attacks and that the Board of Regents has permitted President Kerr's attack."

2. The Board of Regents, meeting for the second day at Davis, commended President Clark Kerr for his handling of the "regrettable" demonstrations at Berkeley.

The Regents also "reaffirmed the university's traditional policy of encouraging maximum freedom with responsibility and disapproving resort to force or violence."

October 18

The FSM Executive Committee nominated its representatives to the Committee on Campus Political Activity: Mario Savio, Bettina Aptheker, Sydney Stapleton, and Suzanne Goldberg.

October 20

1. Chancellor Edward W. Strong appointed the four FSM candidates to the Study Committee. Upon nomination of the Committee on Committees of the Academic Senate, he also appointed Earl F. Cheit, professor of business administration, and Sanford H. Kadish, professor of law.

2. Particle Berkeley, an on-campus group devoted to encouraging student scientific research, was warned by the Dean of Students Office that it faced the possibility of losing on-campus status, if it joined the Free Speech Movement.

Jack Weinberg, as FSM spokesman, said:

"We hope this is not an indication of future punishment to be given on-campus groups involved in the FSM.

" 'On- and off-campus' means 'what we like and what we don't like' to the Administration.

"This is a bad omen, especially at the start of negotiations on the free speech issue."

(*Particle Berkeley has no official connections with* PARTI-CLE MAGAZINE, *a student scientific journal, published by an off-campus corporation. Two members of the group represent Particle Berkeley on the FSM Executive Committee.*)

3. Chancellor Edward W. Strong issued a statement warning of possible further demonstrations led by "hard core demonstrators":

"The hard core demonstrators still are going to try to open the campus," he said. Chancellor Strong identified "hard core demonstrators" as activists who had spent the summer in Mississippi as civil rights workers. Strong went on to say: "The University will not be used as a bastion for the planning and implementation of political and social action." He said the activists returned to Berkeley thinking the University should become more directly involved in social justice, and that some of those involved were "professional demonstrators, but I won't smear all the other good kids by calling it Communist-led." As far as freedom of speech was concerned, Strong said, "the University has truly an Open Forum policy, but we have to draw a line between the freedom and the planning and implementing of political action."

4. Arthur Goldberg, speaking for FSM, answered Chancellor Strong's statement:

"If 'hard core demonstrations' means that we are still going to fight for our principles and the Free Speech Movement, then Chancellor Strong is right." Goldberg said it was possible that some of the demonstrators had been in Mississippi during the summer.

There are two types of "political action," Goldberg explained. "It's sort of like the double standard—we (FSM) are the girls, with lock-out, and the administration is the boys, with no limitations. When they want to talk about their Democrat and Republican politics, it's 'university policy.'

"But, if we say anything about social action, or something that might make people think, it becomes 'too political.' If the University has a true Open Forum, why can't we advocate social action? It seems we have a closed Open Forum."

5. Commuter-Independent Representative Edward Wilson introduced a motion in the ASUC Senate which called for a test case in the courts to settle the problem of administration responsibility on the free speech issue. Wilson withdrew his motion in anticipation of a similar case to be initiated by the American Civil Liberties Union.

6. The expanded Committee on Campus Political Action agreed that all decisions would be by consensus of students, faculty and administration, each voting as a bloc with one vote.

October 25

The Ad Hoc Academic Senate Committee on Student Suspensions (known as the Heyman Committee) requested that the eight suspended students be reinstated during the course of the committee's hearings.

October 26

1. Chancellor Edward W. Strong refused the Heyman Committee's request for reinstatement of the eight suspended students.

2. The FSM Steering Committee issued a policy statement, charging "the Regents have had legislation drafted which would make certain forms of otherwise legal demonstrations on campus misdemeanors." The Steering Committee also accused President Kerr of changing the regulations governing political activity on campus (presumably, subsequent to the changes made at the beginning of the semester). The Steering Committee also stated:

> "If the administration refuses to acknowledge the right to advocate off-campus political and social action, we shall have to consider action as well as talk."

The three-page FSM statement indicated a general dissatisfaction with the course of negotiations to date:

> "We may soon have to admit that the administration does not mean to deal fairly with us."

Specifically, the FSM statement charged:

1) Instead of stating he supported the work of the Committee on Campus Political Activity, President Kerr attacked the FSM as "non-students and Communists."
2) Chancellor Strong has refused to reinstate, for the duration of their hearings, the eight students suspended for their part in the free speech demonstrations. Thus, "apparently the students are guilty until proven innocent."
3) The Committee on Campus Political Activity will not allow the FSM counsel to question witnesses on points of law.

The FSM statement further "demands that the administration acknowledge these on-campus rights:"

1) Freedom to advocate off-campus political and social action.
2) Freedom to recruit for off-campus political organizations.
3) Freedom to solicit funds for off-campus political causes.
4) Freedom from harassment of '72-hour rules' and the mandatory presence at meetings of tenured faculty moderators and police.

3. Ernest Bessig, director of the Northern California chapter of the American Civil Liberties Union, threatened to take

the university to court. If the Heyman Committee fails to resolve the question of student political rights, "we will undertake legal action," Bessig said. Any court action would challenge the constitutionality of the disputed administration regulations and the procedure by which the eight students were suspended, Bessig explained.

Peter Franck, head of the Berkeley ACLU chapter, proposed two alternative methods of testing the constitutionality of the university regulations:

1) Challenge directly the suspensions of the eight students, or
2) Have someone else violate the regulations.

Franck indicated the second proposal would probably be utilized, if court action became necessary. Franck, who also is an attorney advising FSM members, also claimed the university counsel's office asked the Regents for permission "to draft legislation which would put teeth into the present antipolitical activity rules." The counsel's office would only make such a request at President Kerr's urging, Franck contended.

4. Thomas Cunningham, university general counsel, had "no comment" on the FSM-Franck charges that his office was drafting restrictive legislation. Other university sources denied knowledge of either alleged action.

October 27

1. Chancellor Edward W. Strong announced the appointment of two university-wide administration representatives to the Committee on Campus Political Action, bringing the committee to full complement. The administration representatives were Robert B. Brode, academic assistant to the president and professor of physics, and Frank L. Kidner, university dean of educational relations and professor of economics.

2. Two university faculty members attacked the university regulations governing student off-campus political activity during an open forum meeting of the Graduate Coordinating Council.

Seymour M. Lipset, professor of sociology and director of the Institute of International Studies, described the rules as "irrelevant and destructive to the purposes of the university. Social action is relevant" to both graduate and undergraduate education. He said that while the university has liberalized a great deal in the last six years, it still has not gone far enough. He said he felt President Kerr has been responsible for "very significant changes" in the liberalization of the university.

John R. Searle, associate professor of philosophy, claimed that, while the avowed function of the regulations is to keep the campus politically neutral, the actual result is an "increase in the alienation, hostility and contempt" of the students toward the administration.

October 28

1. The Committee on Campus Political Activity considered a recommendation that the First Amendment of the U. S. Constitution be the only policy regarding political expression on campus. The recommendation was introduced by FSM representative Sid Stapleton. Although the committee did not adopt Stapleton's motion, Mario Savio, another FSM representative, expressed pleasure with the proceedings. However, Savio said, if the committee did not adopt the First Amendment as the only policy regarding speech on campus, "we will have to consider more direct action."

The committee also heard an explanation, by Dean of Students Katherine A. Towle, of university policy regarding on-campus and off-campus groups, and activities permitted these groups. It was permissible, she said, for a speaker to recommend certain actions be taken, but it was not permissible for a speaker to advocate such actions be committed:

"A speaker may say, for instance, that there is going to be a picket line at such-and-such a place, and it is a worthy cause and he hopes people will go. But, he cannot say, 'I'll meet you there and we'll picket'."

2. The Heyman Committee, appointed by the Academic Senate to recommend action on the eight suspended students, met today for six hours and heard the cases of three suspended students: Donald Hatch, Mark Bravo and Brian Turner. All three were charged with operating a table on campus without a permit, and raising money for unauthorized purposes.

November 2

1. The *FSM Newsletter* strongly criticized Chancellor Strong and President Kerr, made several references to possible "direct action," and said:

"We repeat: when the morass of mediation becomes too thick to see through, action must let in the light."

ASUC President Charles Powell deplored the tone of ultimatum which permeated the *Newsletter:*

"The leaders of FSM must realize that if they wish the recommendations of the committee to be seriously considered by Chancellor Strong, the recommendations will necessarily need strong support of the entire committee, and threatening the committee with subtle hints that future demonstrations will ensue is definitely not the wise course to take."

2. Chancellor Edward W. Strong, addressing the Town and Gown Club, said:

"Finally, there is the problem of keeping the university true to its role and purpose in society. We cannot permit the University to be used or exploited for purposes not in accord with its charter as an educational institution in a democratic society. The University is a public trust. It was founded to enlighten the minds of its students and to prepare them for useful careers as educated men and women. Freedom of thought and inquiry is essential for the sifting of ideas, the advancement of knowledge, and the discovery of truth. No less essential, as the accompaniment of intellectual freedom, is exercise of that freedom with responsibility. No civilized society can endure if obligations are not honored in living under law. The most disturbing aspect of the recent student demonstrations was the philosophy expressed—the ends justify the means. The employment of illegal means to secure ends desired in the name of freedom would, if tolerated, be destructive of freedom. Individuals enjoy freedom in so far as the guarantees are built into the laws that protect individual rights. When these laws are flouted, protection is weakened and a society is on the road to anarchy. Living as we do under a system of representative government, the right way to effect changes in the laws is by consent and majority vote.

"The functioning of any society requires that authority be vested in some individuals, be they judges, legislators, or executives. Arbitrary exercise of authority is always to be challenged, but defamation of authority duly exercised undermines respect for high offices and demoralizes a society.

"The university is a champion of intellectual freedom; it must no less be a champion of orderly and responsible conduct. It cannot and will not tolerate deliberate violations of its rules and regulations. If it did, it would be in the position of aiding and abetting disrespect for law and order. As the twig is bent, so the tree grows. Among the lessons to be learned, even if it be by a hard way, is the lesson of responsibility. The University remains steadfast in teaching this lesson."

3. The ASUC Senate passed the following resolution:

"WHEREAS: Specific infractions of University rules and regulations occurred during the demonstrations of September 30, and of October 1 and 2 which were:
    1) Disruption of university business in Sproul Hall and of ASUC business in the Student Union.

2) Deliberate prevention of University police action by detaining a police car and an arrested man for 32 hours.

"AND WHEREAS: There have been on various occasions verbal threats on the part of leaders of the Free Speech Movement to resort to open demonstrations again in order to force individuals, the Administration, or the Hearing Committee on Campus Political Activity to be sympathetic to their demands,

"BE IT RESOLVED: That the ASUC Senate condemn mass demonstration which violates University regulations on this campus of the University of California as a means of forcing compliance on the part of those in positions of authority to student demands. Willful and blatant violation of law and order in a democracy cannot be tolerated by an ordered society, nor should it be used by those who seek changes of rules and regulations governing this campus, even when those same rules may not be agreed upon by all.

"BE IT FURTHER RESOLVED: That the ASUC Senate does recognize that there may be inconsistencies in the University laws regulating campus political activity and urges all who are concerned about the existing regulations in one way or another, to support the efforts of the Hearing Committee on Campus Political Activity and to communicate their concerns to the individuals on that committee.

"BE IT FURTHER RESOLVED: That subsequent to the report of the Hearing Committee the ASUC Senate calls upon all students to express their sentiments through the processes of the ASUC Senate, their constituted student government.

"BE IT FURTHER RESOLVED: That the ASUC Senate encourages all other on-campus and off-campus organizations to go on record as supporting the stand of the Senate in an effort to prevent future unlawful demonstrations."

November 3

The Heyman Committee completed hearings on the eight student suspensions.

November 4

1. Two letters, one bearing the typewritten name of Clark Kerr and the other the typewritten name of Thomas Cunningham, university general counsel, were introduced by FSM as "documentary proof" that the administration "had been drafting legislation without waiting for the report of the Committee on Campus Political Activity." Both letters were photostatic

copies; neither had been signed. The letters dealt with university rules and were dated October 13, 1964.

President Kerr said the letter bearing his name had been prepared by a staff member; he disagreed with it and never signed it. "I made no proposals for any changes in the rules at the October (Regents') meeting, neither those in the letter nor any others," Kerr said. The Kerr letter included an addition to University Regulations on the Use of University Facilities:

"University facilities may not be used for the purpose of recruiting participants for unlawful off-campus action."

The second letter, bearing the name of Thomas Cunningham, was presented to the Regents. Cunningham said he had been authorized to study the situation and to prepare proposed legislation for the State Legislature, if he deemed it necessary:

"They (the Regents) told me to go ahead and study the problem and report back to them. I am. There has been absolutely no legislation prepared at all, and I am still studying the problem. My letter has nothing to do with University rules."

Regarding the first letter, with Kerr's name, Cunningham said:

"I prepared it. The president discussed it with the chief campus officers, and decided he would not recommend it. He said the students were studying it at that time."

2. Between 50–60 picketers took part in a demonstration on Sproul Hall steps. The picket line was established "to bring to light the misunderstanding" and "to focus attention on the Free Speech Movement," according to Skip Richheimer, a graduate student in history.

The pickets' specific purpose, Richheimer said, was to call attention to the afternoon meeting of the Ad Hoc Academic Senate Committee (Heyman Committee). FSM intends to ask the committee if the students should be able to enjoy their constitutional rights as citizens in certain geographical areas of the campus. The answer to this question, Richheimer said, will determine whether the administration intends to be sincere in its negotiations. If FSM concludes the administration is not sincere, and that nothing can be gained from the committee, the FSM "will have to resort to other measures," Richheimer said.

November 5

The Committee on Campus Political Activity continued to debate a faculty proposal introduced by Earl Cheit, professor of business administration, during yesterday's (Wednesday,

Nov. 4) meeting. The debate centered around phrases which the administration claims are necessary to protect the university, but which the students contend would give the university the right of "prior restraint."

The first part of Professor Cheit's proposal read:

"That in the Hyde Park areas, the University modify its present regulations by dropping the distinction between 'advocating' and 'mounting' political and social action. Although we could find no case in which this distinction has been in issue, the position of the students and the recent resolutions of the Academic Senate and the Regents all support a University policy which (subject only to restrictions necessary for normal conduct of University functions and business) permits free expression within the limits of the law. Subject only to these same restrictions, off-campus speakers invited by recognized student groups to speak in the Hyde Park area should be permitted to do so upon completing a simple registration procedure which records the inviting organization, the speaker's name, and the topic of the talk."

An amendment to this paragraph, passed Nov. 4, added the phrase: "and his willingness to answer questions."

An amendment proposed by Sanford Kadish, professor of law, would have rephrased Professor Cheit's original sentences dealing with action "within the limits of the law." It would have inserted two new sentences after the first:

"The advocacy of ideas and acts which is constitutionally protected off the campus should be protected on the campus. By the same token, of course, speech which is in violation of law and constitutionally unprotected should receive no greater protection on the campus than off the campus."

The students and faculty representatives seemed agreed on this amendment, but administration representatives felt the emphasis on prohibiting unlawful action was not strong enough.

The committee adjourned for an hour while Kadish, Kidner and Attorney Malcolm Burnstein attempted to find suitable phraseology acceptable to all three factions. They returned with this amendment:

"If, as a direct result of the advocacy on the campus, acts occur in violation of U.S. or California laws, the University should be entitled to take appropriate disciplinary action against the speakers and their sponsoring organizations, to the extent that the person or organization can fairly be found to be responsible for the unlawful acts."

Mario Savio, speaking for the student representatives, claimed the compromise amendment would, in effect, give the university the right of prior restraint, as it leaves interpretation of unlawful acts up to the university. The students were not in favor of the amendment.

The meeting adjourned.

November 7

The Committee on Campus Political Activity reached an impasse over the first resolution proposed by the faculty for recommendation to Chancellor Strong. The question again was over whether the university should be able to take action against students involved in illegal acts off campus when the acts were advocated or organized on campus (even though, at the time the acts were advocated or organized, they were legal).

Frank Kidner, university dean of educational relations and an administration representative, offered an amendment to the faculty motion which read:

> "If acts unlawful under California or Federal law directly result from advocacy, organization or planning on the campus, the students and organizations involved may be subject to such disciplinary action as is appropriate and conditioned upon as fair hearing as to the appropriateness of the action taken."

According to the *Daily Californian,* a heated discussion between Dean Kidner and Mario Savio followed, during which Dean Kidner expressed the view that an act would not have to be proclaimed unlawful for the administration to take action.

Sid Stapleton, student committee member and a member of the Young Socialist Alliance, said he felt the university would be unable to conduct a fair hearing because of political pressures. Vice Chancellor Alan Searcy responded, "the administration is made of men of good will."

Dean Kidner's amendment failed. The administration representatives voted affirmatively, the faculty abstained, and the students voted negatively.

The student representatives then offered this amendment:

> "In the area of first amendment rights and civil liberties, the university may impose no disciplinary action against members of the university community and organizations. In this area, members of the university community and organizations are subject only to the civil authorities."

Sanford Kadish, professor of law, offered a substitute amendment which, he said, defined the notion of collective responsibility and incorporated into general law the problem of the responsibility of one person or a number of people.

Professor Kadish's substitute amendment failed by one vote. The student amendment was defeated, with the administration and faculty voting negatively.

When it was obvious the committee could not reach agreement, Professor Cheit proposed the committee report agreement on points two through seven of the faculty recommendations, and that the students and the faculty prepare a statement of the nature of their differences and present it to Chancellor Strong and the university community.

Mario Savio agreed to make the disagreement public, but he indicated he did not agree that point one was the only point of disagreement.

It was agreed that no action would be taken until everyone agreed.

The meeting adjourned.

November 8

The Free Speech Movement issued the following statement:

"Ever since Oct. 2 the organizations composing the Free Speech Movement have voluntarily refrained from exercising their constitutional liberties on the Berkeley campus of the University of California. The FSM imposed this moratorium in the hope that agreement with the administration regarding any regulations could soon be reached. Although we continue to be a party to the Campus Committee on Political Activity, we feel that we must lift our self-imposed moratorium on political activity because the committee is already deadlocked over the issue of political advocacy and appears headed for a long series of radical disagreements . . . We must exercise our rights so that the University is not permitted to deny us those rights for any long period and so that our political organizations can function to their maximum capacity. Many students and organizations have been hampered in their efforts in the past election and in civil rights activity because of the moratorium.

"Saturday the CCPA became deadlocked over the issue of the student's right to advocate off-campus political activity.

". . . (the proposed) amendment is directly aimed at student participation in the civil rights movement and is totally unacceptable to the students. The administration would give themselves the right (1) to decide on the legality and the 'appropriateness' of the students' off-campus political activity, (2) to decide the legality of the students' on-campus advocacy of off-campus action, and (3) to discipline the students in the area of their civil liberties.

". . . The Free Speech Movement proposed (an) amendment which is the position of the American Association of University Professors and the American Civil Liberties Union.

". . . the administration vetoed our position and insisted on the ability of the University to discipline students in the area of their civil liberties. The FSM believes that the University is not a competent body to decide questions concerning civil liberties, especially since it is subject to strong political pressure. Because students' rights have great political impact as well as legal significance, the courts should be the only body to decide upon them.

"The AAUP has declared that 'students should enjoy the same freedom of religion, speech, press and assembly, and the right to petition the authorities that citizens generally possess.' The Free Speech Movement intends to exercise those freedoms on Monday (Nov. 9)."

November 9

1. The following statement by Chancellor Edward W. Strong appeared in the *Daily Californian:*

"If the FSM returns to direct action tactics, this will constitute a clear breach of the agreement of October 2. Students and organizations participating will be held responsible for their actions."

2. The following statement by the faculty representatives of the Committee on Campus Political Activity appeared in the *Daily Californian:*

"In view of the continuing newspaper reports that the FSM has threatened demonstrations in violation of the agreement under which the committee was constituted, the faculty representatives wish to reiterate their statement made at the Saturday morning meeting.

"It is our belief that substantial progress has been made and will continue to be made so long as no action is taken which jeopardizes the continuation of the good work of the committee.

"Once again, therefore, we call upon FSM to abide by the terms of its agreement."

3. Because of the lack of agreement and action by the Committee on Campus Political Activity, the FSM Steering Committee declared it was lifting "its self-imposed moratorium on political activity" and held a rally on Sproul Hall steps at noon, the first such activity since the October 2 agreement.

According to Mario Savio, the Committee on Campus Political Activity meetings have not shown promise of reaching a solution. Savio said the FSM could not accept the administration's demand that the university have jurisdiction over the legality and "appropriateness" of off-campus political activity.

Another member of the FSM Steering Committee said:

"The University has changed its position considerably throughout the period of negotiation. Originally there was no suggestion that the Administration wanted to have jurisdiction over the legality of off-campus activities."

During the demonstration, FSM and eight other off-campus organizations set up card tables along the steps of Sproul Hall. There were donation cups and sign-up sheets on each table, in violation of university regulations. About 75 persons involved had their names taken, according to FSM spokesmen. Each table also offered a petition which stated: "We were at the tables and support those who were manning them."

Speakers addressed the rally from the top of an old dresser. The crowd sat, squatted and stood around the dresser, as it had around the stranded police car early last month. Approximately 200 students participated in the rally, while an additional 400 watched from the fringes.

4. The Graduate Co-ordinating Committee announced members of its group would set up tables tomorrow afternoon with FSM and other protesting groups. The graduates would sit under signs identifying their departments for at least an hour. They said they would man their tables until they were suspended, arrested, or their demands were met. Approximately 75 or 100 graduate students at the meeting said they would man tables. The motion to man the tables was passed with only one dissent.

Steve Weissman, Graduate Co-ordinating Committee representative to FSM, said that if the police attempt to arrest the students, the graduates will refuse all cooperation. He added that such an action might be cause for a strike by the teaching assistants and the faculty.

5. The following statement was issued jointly by President Clark Kerr and Chancellor Edward W. Strong this evening:

"FSM has abrogated the agreement of October 2, and by reason of this abrogation, the Committee on Campus Political Activity is dissolved . . .

"We shall now seek advice on rules governing political action on campus from students through the ASUC and from the faculty through the Academic Senate.

"The Academic Senate and the ASUC Senate have called for the use of peaceful and orderly procedures in settling disputes. We welcome proposals from all interested groups."

Regarding political activities, the statement said:

". . . students participating in violation of rules will be subject to penalties through established procedures."

And, the Kerr-Strong statement concluded:

"The university is devoted to rational discussion, to law and order, and to freedom for students and faculty matched with responsibility in the use of this freedom."

6. An FSM statement called the dissolution of the Committee on Campus Political Activity the "destruction of one more line of communication between the students and the administration . . . it makes the possibility of ultimate settlement even more remote."

Mario Savio added his own comments to the official FSM statement:

"By its continuing acts of political oppression, the University Administration has abrogated the Pact . . . Accordingly, the students have lifted the self-imposed moratorium on the exercise of the constitutionally-guaranteed political rights . . . No institution, except the courts, has any competence to decide what constitutes the abuse of political freedom.

"The students shall not cease in the responsible exercise of their rights."

November 10

1. Graduate student protestors continued defiance of university regulations on the steps of Sproul Hall. The university took no official notice of their actions. Tables soliciting money—in one case, for a haircut for a professor—were manned by 196 teaching assistants and graduate students who worked in large groups. The large number of workers was intended to prevent administration action against a few participants, according to FSM. Demonstrators and spectators heard a speech by Mario Savio, then members of the Graduate Co-ordinating Committee of the FSM set up tables to distribute literature and to collect funds. Savio said: "The administration is on the horns of a real dilemma. They must either take all of us or none of us."

The dean's office took no official notice of the violations, nor was any effort made to obtain names of those manning tables. The demonstrators obligingly sent a list of their names to the dean's office, however.

2. Participants in Monday's (Nov. 9) demonstration were mailed notices to appear at the dean's office for disciplinary action. Students whose names were taken in Monday's demonstration held a late-afternoon conference at Westminster

House, where Malcolm Burnstein, an Oakland attorney, counseled them on their legal rights. Burnstein told them:

"The regulations attempt to deprive you of a kind of speech, not a place to do it in. It is the opinion of all of us who have read the regulations that the University cannot legally do this."

3. Ira Heyman, professor of law and chairman of the Ad Hoc Academic Senate Committee studying the case of the eight suspended students announced the committee's decisions and recommendations will be issued Thursday, Nov. 12.

4. Faculty representatives of the Committee on Campus Political Activity met at noon to report on the status of the committee's deliberations at the time the committee was dissolved. The Faculty Representatives' report said negotiations deadlocked on "the question of the authority of the university to discipline for on-campus conduct that results in off-campus law violation." Earl F. Cheit, professor of business administration, said: "We were very concerned lest the committee go out of existence when we were so close to an agreement." Faculty representatives expressed a general disappointment over the dissolution of the committee.

5. Art Goldberg, one of the student protest leaders from the beginning, announced he was no longer a member of the FSM Steering Committee. "No comment," he said. (*He was later reinstated.*)

6. ASUC President Charles Powell announced formation of a five-man ASUC Senate committee to make recommendations regarding student political activity. Powell said he was acting because of the dissolution of the Committee on Campus Political Activity. Powell noted that the ASUC Senate was the first body to formally endorse the free speech rights of students on campus, but that the efforts of the senate and of the class officers had been undermined and destroyed by the militant demonstrations of the FSM. "Up until now, the administration has chosen or been forced to negotiate around the senate. Now, the issue is back where it started, where it should be, and where real decisions are going to be made," Powell said. Powell also said:

"Members of the ASUC Senate placed their faith in the ability of the committee to solve the problem. Now that the committee is defunct, the Senate must take decisive independent action to reach a solution.

"The whole idea is that it's time the Senate took charge of this question of political activity on campus which was so confused and distorted by demonstrations, and we intend to take charge with conviction and responsibility."

According to senior representative Dan Griset, "The new committee will be the true voice of the students. It will be the only student group to offer official recommendations to the chancellor."

Mario Savio and Dean Frank Kidner addressed the ASUC Senate in the evening. Savio demanded equal rights for students, both on and off the campus. He said: "If the FSM must resort to mass demonstrations, they will not be halted unless we receive substantial concessions from the administration." Kidner listened to Savio's remarks "with some interest and some sympathy," then reported, "the administration will continue to consider revisions in its policy."

November 12

President Kerr released the report of the faculty members of the disbanded Committee on Campus Political Activity. (*Full text, see Appendix.*) The report recommended substantial liberalization of university rules regarding on-campus political activities. In essence, the six faculty members recommended on-campus mounting of legal off-campus political and social action be permitted. Recognized student organizations, they said, should be allowed to accept donations and sign up members in designated areas on campus. However, the report said:

> "The on-campus advocacy, organization or planning of political or social action . . . may be subject to discipline where this conduct directly results in judicially-found violations of California or Federal criminal law; and the group or individual can fairly be held responsible for such violations under prevailing legal principles of accountability."

The faculty group also recommended:

1) Room should be made available for meetings of off-campus groups in the student office building, scheduled for completion next semester.
2) The experimental use of Sproul Hall steps and the adjacent area as a Hyde Park area should be discontinued.

November 13

1. The Academic Senate Ad Hoc Committee on Suspensions recommended six of the eight suspended students be reinstated as of the date of their suspensions. The committee also recommended six-week suspensions for Art Goldberg and Mario Savio, the suspensions to begin Sept. 30 and end November 16:

> "We recommend that Messrs. (Mark) Bravo, (David) Goins, (Sandor) Fuchs, (Brian) Turner, and Mrs.

(Elizabeth) Stapleton be reinstated as of the date of their suspensions. The penalty of indefinite suspension should be expunged from the record of each student . . .

"Instead, the penalty for each of these six students should be recorded as that of 'censure' for a period of no more than six weeks."

The committee recommended heavier punishment for Goldberg and Savio because of their alleged roles in organizing and leading demonstrations. Goldberg was charged with leading a picket which interfered with a university meeting on Sept. 28, and Savio was charged with leading the Sproul Hall sit-in of Sept. 30.

The committee's findings, in the form of a 14-page report, (*Full text, see Appendix*) were formally submitted to the Berkeley Division of the Academic Senate. Copies were sent to the administration and to the students involved. The next regularly scheduled meeting of the Academic Senate is Dec. 8. An emergency meeting was scheduled for Nov. 24.

Regarding the Heyman Committee report, Chancellor Edward W. Strong issued the following statement at 5:15 p.m. today:

"I have received a copy of the report of an *ad hoc* advisory committee which was established by the Berkeley Division of the Academic Senate to review the duration of suspension of eight students indefinitely suspended last September for violation of University rules. This advisory committee has been under the chairmanship of Professor Ira M. Heyman, a member of the faculty of the school of law, Berkeley.

"Although Regents, the President and I had understood that the committee was to be advisory to me, Professor Heyman has addressed the report to the Academic Senate and his committee concludes 'that it should render its report to the Berkeley Division of the Academic Senate, with copies of the report to go to the University administration and students involved.' President Kerr and I completely disagree with this procedure. Out of respect for and courtesy to the Academic Senate, however, we shall await the reaction of the Berkeley Division to the report before commenting on its recommendations.

"As the report stresses, the committee, with the assent of the parties, 'has been concerned only with events occurring through September 30, 1964, and has not been asked to, nor has, considered any events after that date.' Much has happened since September 30. Some of the students mentioned in the report have since engaged in serious misconduct since that date and with regard to those actions, regular disciplinary procedures will prevail, including the immediate filing of charges by appropriate officials and hearings before the faculty committee on student conduct. In a conversation with Professor Heyman on November 9, he agreed recent violations of rules should be referred to the faculty committee on student conduct.

"President Kerr has today sent a copy of the Heyman Committee report, together with this statement, to each of the Regents for their information in accordance with the request of the Regents made at their October meeting."

Meanwhile, a university spokesman said, the university will continue to enforce its regulations. Those people who have been called before the deans for manning tables have been given a warning, if they have not previously violated university rules, the spokesman said.

Members of the Free Speech Movement were generally pleased with the Heyman Committee findings.

Mario Savio said:

"It is gratifying that the initial contentions of the students that the rules governing political activity were obscure and their reinforcement was arbitrary have been upheld by the faculty findings."

Art Goldberg, however, was unhappy with Chancellor Strong's refusal to act on the committee's findings before hearing from the Academic Senate:

"The committee's recommendations that six of the students should never have been suspended in the first place constitutes a clear moral imperative for the administration to reinstate them immediately."

2. The recently formed ASUC Senate committee on the free speech controversy considered a compromise proposal to resolve the conflict. According to Mike Adams, a committee member, the committee re-evaluated proposals made last Thursday, and made a number of substantial improvements on them. Adams did not reveal what the "improvements" involved.

3. The FSM issued a clarification of a statement made Wednesday (Nov. 11):

"We request that an action be taken against all participating groups or students equally. It must be understood that membership in the FSM is contingent upon an organization's endorsement of the principle of full political freedom, and not necessarily upon an endorsement of the tactics of the FSM."

November 16

1. Tables again appeared on the steps of Sproul Hall for solicitation of funds and recruitment of members. FSM spokesmen said the tables would remain on the steps all week.

2. The Free Speech Movement began circulation of a petition in support of its stand on advocacy of illegal off-campus acts, in preparation for the Board of Regents meeting in Berkeley on Friday (Nov. 20). The petition, which will be presented to the Board of Regents, disagrees with point three of the recommendations of the faculty members of the former Committee on Campus Political Activity.

> "We the undersigned resolve that:
> "Only courts of law should have the power to judge whether the content of speech on campus is an abuse of constitutional rights of free speech. Only courts of law should have the power to impose punishment if these rights are abused.
> "Therefore, we ask the administration to recognize that it not usurp these powers."

(Point three of the faculty report, which is advisory to President Kerr, recommends students be disciplined by the university for advocating off-campus action only if such advocacy:

"1) Directly results in judicially-found violations of California or Federal criminal law, and

"2) The group or individual can fairly be held responsible for such violations under prevailing legal principles of accountability.")

3. Letters were sent to approximately 70 students who violated university regulations last week by manning tables, according to Arleigh Williams, dean of men. The students were asked to report to the dean of students' office for interviews. Teaching assistants who sent their names to the administration and claimed they had violated regulations also were sent letters, William said. "All the interviews will be completed before we decide what action will be taken concerning those students," Williams explained. *(Interviewed students were advised by legal counsel not to answer any vital questions, according to an FSM spokesman.)*

4. FSM announced a vigil aimed at Friday's Regents meeting. Details were not announced.

5. ASUC President Charles Powell addressed the following letter to the Berkeley student body. It appeared in today's *Daily Californian:*

> "Tonight at an emergency meeting of the ASUC Senate, recommendations will be submitted by the Senate

sub-committee on campus political activity for final approval. They will then be submitted to Chancellor Strong and President Kerr for consideration before the Chief Campus Officers meeting and the Regents meeting later this week. The Senate sub-committee will suggest modifications of the Faculty Report as well as proposing a new solution which would allow and center all student political expression in the Student Center area.

"Until such time as the Regents have considered our recommendations, as well as those of other individuals and groups, the ASUC Senate stands firmly on the positions it has taken during the entire crisis—that is:

"1. The ASUC Senate supports the ideals and freedoms sought by the FSM (Senate motion of Sept. 22 authorizing a petition supporting privileges of advocacy and of solicitation of funds and membership—a petition which has 3500 signatures) and;

"2. The ASUC Senate will not endorse a student movement such as the FSM which encourages willful violation of University regulations while those regulations are being re-evaluated (Senate Law and Order motion of Nov. 2).

"Pending the Regents' action this week the ASUC Senate may find it necessary to strengthen its position which is, in essence, in substantial accordance with the objectives of the FSM but disagrees as to the means. Until the Regents have had time to consider all the proposals to be presented and to make some decisions, I am extremely serious in my request that all students not associated with the FSM stay away from any demonstrations. Large onlooking crowds only make for greater distortions of facts by news media and for greater traffic problems.

"And to the FSM I would say that I think you have made your points clear; you've had enough to command the attention of the campus community for the first seven weeks of classes. I would suggest that it is time for us all to relax somewhat and allow the Regents a chance to consider all proposals made."

6. The ASUC Senate held a special meeting tonight, and considered three possible proposals regarding student political activity. The proposals, if approved, would be forwarded to the administration:

1) A five-member committee, formed last week by ASUC President Powell, produced a majority report favoring considerable modification and liberalization of existing regulations governing on-campus political activity.

2) Representatives-at-Large Dan Griset and Frank Rossi

submitted a minority report favoring adherence to existing University regulations.

3) Representative-at-Large Art Shartsis submitted an independent report rephrasing, but supporting, the Administration's current regulatory powers.

The ASUC Senate voted to separate control of the Bancroft-Telegraph area from the other university political activity areas. This will allow groups not permitted on campus to have an adjacent activity area.

The senate also approved a suggestion that a committee be appointed to advise the chancellor on the administration of student political action.

A debate arose between senate members over the university's right to discipline students participating in illegal political activity. The senate committee's majority report recommended that students arrested for political activity be placed on temporary probation until the legality of their actions can be determined in a civil court.

November 17

1. Tables again appeared on Sproul Hall steps. No attempt was made to remove them.

The *FSM Newsletter* stated "the illegitimate tables will remain until they have become legal, through repeal of the restrictive rulings."

The *Newsletter* also denounced the university faculty:

"They allow their colleagues to be victimized one at a time. They are loath to use their power to fight for their own freedoms or anyone else's . . . They may think like men; but they act like rabbits."

2. A meeting of the Boalt Hall Student Association overwhelmingly (402–170) approved a statement condemning the administration's political action rulings. The statement said, in part:

". . . a free society can tolerate no less than an unrestricted opportunity for the exchange of views on the political and social questions of the day . . . we believe that the University's restrictions raise serious constitutional questions.

"We believe that the spirit and perhaps the letter of our Constitution command that these restrictions be withdrawn. Where the choice is between expediency and freedom of speech, a nation of free men can have no choice."

3. The ASUC Senate tonight approved a proposal for a solution of the free speech issue. ASUC President Charles

Powell and First Vice President Jerry Goldstein will personally deliver the report to President Clark Kerr tomorrow.

The ASUC Senate's proposal recommends:

"The University shall maintain that 1) all legal activity is allowed on campus, and 2) illegal activity off the campus is, as always, the private business of the student as a private citizen."

Also suggested was a method of operation, should the chancellor "suspect that a student . . . used university facilities to incite, plan or organize illegal off-campus action or used criminal speech on campus." Under the ASUC proposal, the chancellor could convene the Faculty Committee on Student Conduct which would give the student a fair hearing. Presumption of innocence, with burden of proof to be the same as in criminal courts, would be used in the hearing. The committee's report would be advisory to the chancellor. The senate recommendation also included the suggestion that the Faculty Committee, a standing committee now appointed by the chancellor, should be appointed by the Academic Senate, beginning next semester.

The ASUC Senate also adopted an alternative proposal, introduced by Faculty Representative Lyman Porter. Porter's proposal recommends the university set off the entire student center area, including the contested Bancroft-Telegraph strip, as a region for complete freedom. Under Porter's plan, the free speech area would be completely under the control of the students. The ASUC would set up a board to administer the practical organization of the area.

November 18

1. The Free Speech Movement announced plans for a mass vigil during Friday's Regents meeting in Berkeley. The FSM Steering Committee also issued an open letter to the Regents, requesting permission for FSM leaders to appear before the Board. The letter requests permission for a five-member delegation to appear before the Board and "formally present the platform of the FSM, which consists of a carefully formulated body of proposed regulations to govern student political activity on campus."

Mike Rossman, an FSM Steering Committee member, said, "Many proposals are being taken to the Regents, but the FSM desires to plead its own case."

President Kerr indicated the Regents would rather not have anyone speak, but would review written proposals.

2. The report issued yesterday by the ASUC Senate Study Committee on Campus Political Activities also brought comment from FSM leaders.

Mario Savio admonished the ASUC committee for "failing

to endorse a principle stand of the Free Speech Movement, namely, that only the courts may judge when speech is an abuse of constitutionally guaranteed political rights."

Mike Rossman said:

"The ASUC Senate has acted too hastily. The members of the Senate have too little knowledge of legal language necessary to guarantee that any liberalizations will be implemented. The language of the Senate proposal and of the Faculty report which they have amended is too obscure and open to interpretation . . . This proposal does not provide for many of the major needs of the students, which have been expressed by the FSM."

3. Sanford Elberg, dean of the graduate division, called a meeting of all university teaching assistants. According to Elberg, the meeting was "to clear up the various aspects of the free speech issue." Faculty members of the defunct study committee and FSM representatives addressed the meeting, but it was "not intended to be a debate," Elberg said. About 450 students attended the meeting in Pauley Ballroom.

Earl F. Cheit, professor of business administration, and Henry Rosovsky, professor of economics, explained the controversial faculty position in regard to student discipline. According to Cheit, the proposals drastically limit the power of the university to discipline students. Under the proposals, students cannot be punished until they have received "a fair hearing" from a faculty committee.

Many attending the meeting were critical of Cheit's statement. Students questioned the ability of the university to grant students "a fair hearing." "The only institution which guarantees citizens a fair hearing is a civil court of law," one of the students said.

4. An unidentified man telephoned Oakland police, threatening to shoot Mario Savio. Berkeley and university police were informed.

5. The Ad Hoc Committee on Student Conduct (the Heyman Committee), issued a statement in which the committee said their report on the cases of the eight suspended students should not have been addressed to the Berkeley Division of the Academic Senate. The report was properly filed with the senate, the statement said, but it should have been addressed to the chancellor.

"By filing the report with the Division, the committee did not intend that the Division review the findings of fact and recommendations since the members did not sit at the hearings and receive the evidence and arguments which are the only relevant basis for the findings and recommendations."

November 19

The State Board of Directors of the California Democratic Council asked the university administration and Regents to protect "the constitutional liberty" of the students:

". . . advocacy of ideas and acts which are constitutionally protected off campus should be protected on campus . . ."

November 20

1. A mass student rally on Sproul Hall steps, encouraged by folk singer Joan Baez, preceded a "peaceful mass pilgrimage-demonstration" by more than 3000 persons. Following a noon rally on Sproul Hall steps, the majority of the gathering quietly marched across campus, led by a banner declaring "Free Speech," to sit on the lawn across Oxford Street from University Hall while the Regents met this afternoon.

2. A delegation of five FSM representatives requested a hearing before the Regents. Although the FSM delegation was admitted to the Regents' meeting room, they were not allowed to speak.

Michael Rossman, a member of the FSM Steering Committee, explained why FSM believes it should be "the legitimate spokesman for the students":

"Although others have proposed solutions to the problem facing the students (some of them well-meant and sympathetic), the Free Speech Movement is the legitimate spokesman for the students since it is most intimately acquainted with the needs of the students. It is only within the ranks of the Free Speech Movement that nearly all of the political, religious, and social action groups on the campus are represented."

3. As demonstrating students gathered across the street, the Regents considered the following recommendations submitted by President Kerr and Chancellor Strong:

1) That the sole and total penalty for the six students be suspension from September 30 to date.

2) That the other two students be suspended for the period from September 30, 1964, to date and that they be placed on probation for the current semester for their actions up to and including September 30, 1964.

3) That adjustments in academic programs be permitted for the eight students on approval by the appropriate Academic Dean.

4) New disciplinary proceedings before the Faculty Committee on Student Conduct will be instituted immedi-

ately against certain students and organizations for violations subsequent to September 30, 1964.

5) That rules and regulations be made more clear and specific and thus, incidentally and regretably, more detailed and legalistic; and that explicit penalties, where possible, be set forth for specific violations.

6) That the Berkeley campus be given sufficient staff in the Dean of Students Office and the Police Department so that as nearly as possible all students involved in violations be identified with the fullest possible proof since the incompleteness of identification of participants and collection of full proof have been held against the University; also that the General Counsel's office be given sufficient staff so it may participate, as necessary, in the legal aspects of student discipline cases, particularly since a more legalistic approach is being taken toward student discipline.

7) That the right and ability of the University to require students and others on campus to identify themselves be assured by whatever steps are necessary."

The Regents approved these suggestions. Six of the suspended students received suspensions from Sept. 20 to date. Arthur Goldberg and Mario Savio, demonstration leaders, were placed on probation for the rest of the semester, in addition to the suspensions.

The Board of Regents also revised university policy on political action. The Regents' resolution, introduced by President Kerr, read:

"1) The Regents restate the long-standing University policy as set forth in Regulation 25 on student conduct and discipline that 'all students and student organizations . . . obey the laws of the State and community . . .'

"2) The Regents adopt the policy effective immediately that certain campus facilities, carefully selected and properly regulated, may be used by students and staff for planning, implementing or raising funds or recruiting participants for lawful off-campus action, not for unlawful off-campus action."

(*No specific procedure on discipline for advocacy of "unlawful off-campus action" was passed. Approval for the first section was unanimous; the second section received a few "nays."*)

4. FSM leaders immediately denounced both the Regents and President Kerr for having "ignored" the Heyman Committee recommendations and FSM's own recommendations in presenting the matter for Regents' consideration.

5. During a new conference following the Regents' meeting,

President Kerr expressed the belief that the new regulations were more liberal than the previous university regulations. Asked who would decide the illegality of advocated action, President Kerr said:

> "In the usual case, you'd wait for the courts to decide. It would then go to the Faculty Committee on Student Conduct."

Specific regulations were not set down, President Kerr said, because "the question of writing rules and regulations is pretty complicated. The Regents prefer to make general policy statements."

The president also indicated the university's general counsel, Thomas Cunningham, would "probably make up the specific regulations, and the Board will take a look at them."

President Kerr also expressed doubt that the FSM would accept the Regents' action.

November 23

1. The Free Speech Movement responded to the Regents' "free speech issue" ruling with a mass rally at noon, followed by a three-hour sit-in in Sproul Hall.

The tone of the rally was sad but resolute. The demonstrators sang anti-administration songs (set to the tunes of Christmas carols and well-known folk songs); denounced President Kerr and Chancellor Strong for "ignoring" the Heyman Committee's recommendations; and verbally advocated actions which, according to some interpretations, were against university regulations.

During the rally, Vice Chancellor Alan Searcy delivered a statement by Chancellor Edward W. Strong from a small, improvised rostrum on the first landing of Sproul Hall steps:

> "This statement is directed to the action of The Regents in their meeting of November 20 . . .
>
> "The new policy provides opportunities for direct political action requested by 18 off-campus student organizations on September 18, and by the ASUC Senate on September 22.
>
> "Prior to adopting this policy, the Regents received and reviewed materials submitted by individuals and groups including a motion of the ASUC Senate, and the recommendations of the faculty group of the Committee on Campus Political Activity.
>
> "Activities of students in disobedience of the laws of the State and community are punishable in their courts. The University maintains jurisdiction over violations of its rules including those which prohibit use of University facilities for planning and recruiting for actions found to

be unlawful by the courts. There will be no prior determination of double jeopardy in matters of political and social activities organized on the campus by students and staff. The demand of the FSM that the University permit the mounting of unlawful action on the campus without penalty by the University cannot and will not be granted.

"Most of the items in the report of the faculty group of the Committee on Campus Political Activity are subject to action by the Chancellor. I will take appropriate action upon consultation with the Student Affairs Committee and through that Committee with the ASUC Senate. These items include such matters as specific rules and regulations concerning collection of funds, issuance of permits for use of tables, and so-called 'Hyde Park' areas. These rules and regulations will receive immediate attention. Pending this action the new policy will be in effect at Bancroft and Telegraph beginning today. Permits for tables may be obtained from the Office of the Dean of Students."

Vice Chancellor Searcy asked protestors to wait 24 hours, until the administration had worked out the specific application of the new Regents' policy on this campus.

At the completion of his statement, Vice Chancellor Searcy turned to leave. Mario Savio grabbed the microphone of FSM's powerful dual-speaker public address system, demanding Searcy engage in debate with him. "Hey! Get back here!" Savio demanded. The vice chancellor returned to his microphone, but refused to debate with Savio.

The chancellor's statement was met with charges of "another stall" by FSM orators, who claimed the administration, armed with the power to act against students whose on-campus advocacy caused off-campus illegal action, would be able to crush off-campus social movements at moments they would be most needed.

Following Searcy's statements, much of the remaining time was taken up with debate over whether or not to sit-in. After about an hour of debate, at 2:00 p.m., several dozen protestors arose and walked into Sproul Hall. About 300 others gradually followed them, as the debate continued.

Once inside, the demonstrators lined the second floor hall outside the deans' offices. Most of their time was spent debating their next move.

Mario Savio explained the disagreement: Either the protestors could stay in the building and face possible arrest for trespassing, or they could leave at 5:00 p.m. when the Sproul Hall offices closed. The reason for debate, Savio said, was that the FSM Steering Committee was split on whether a trespassing charge could be used as a test case for the free speech cause.

The Steering Committee finally voted, 6–5, to recommend students leave the building at 5:00 p.m. The decision was met with dissent from many demonstrators. There was more debate and, at one point, Bettina Aptheker, a member of the Steering Committee, told the crowd:

> "Damn it, if we're going to win, then we've got to abide by the decision of the Steering Committee, no matter how badly split it was."

At 5:00 p.m., the demonstrators left Sproul Hall.

2. The FSM Executive Committee met at 9:30 p.m. to plan further protest action.

November 24

1. Chancellor Edward W. Strong announced the following new rules for political activity on the Berkeley campus:

> "Authorized student organizations will be permitted in designated areas (these designated areas to include the Bancroft-Telegraph area, North entrance, and area in the Student Center to be delineated by the ASUC Senate), to accept donations and membership signups, and to distribute political and social action material from tables provided by the organizations. On an experimental basis, the administration of this activity is delegated by the Dean of Students to the ASUC President.
>
> "The following conditions shall apply:
>
> "A. Permits for tables must be obtained from the ASUC.
>
> "B. Tables for the student organizations shall be manned at all times.
>
> "C. The organizations shall provide their own tables and chairs.
>
> "D. At Bancroft and Telegraph there shall be no more than one table in front of each pillar and four at the east side, and three at the west side of the entrance way. No tables shall be placed in front of the entrance posts. No posters shall be attached to posts or pillars or set up on easels.
>
> "E. In using the tables for purposes of political action, organizations must not use the name of the University and must dissociate themselves from the University as an institution by means of a printed disclaimer.
>
> "F. Donations may be solicited at the tables.
>
> "Participation in the activities described above shall be limited to members of the University—students, staff, and faculty."

2. The Academic Senate defeated, by the narrow margin of 274–261, a motion to limit university regulation of speech, political and social activity only to the extent "necessary to prevent undue interference with other university affairs." The Academic Senate also defeated a motion to establish an Academic Senate committee to deal with questions of student political conduct.

November 28

Letters from Chancellor Edward W. Strong, initiating new disciplinary action, arrived at the residences of Mario Savio and Arthur Goldberg today. Both Savio and Goldberg were in Southern California, attempting to rally support for the Free Speech Movement on other college campuses.

The letters charged the two FSM leaders with entrapping a university police car and an arrested person:

"On October 1 and 2, 1964, you led and encouraged numerous demonstrators in keeping a University police car and an arrested person therein entrapped on the Berkeley campus for a period of approximately 32 hours, which arrested person the police were then endeavoring to transport to police headquarters for processing."

Savio's letter additionally charged him with organizing and leading demonstrators in "packing in" the hallway outside the dean of students office in Sproul Hall, "thereby blocking access to and from said office, disrupting the functions of that office and forcing personnel of that office to leave through a window and across a roof." It also charged Savio:

". . . led and encouraged demonstrators forcefully and violently to resist the efforts of the University police and the Berkeley city police in their attempts pursuant to orders, to close the main doors of Sproul Hall on the Berkeley campus," and, "On October 1, 1964, you bit Berkeley city police officer Phillip E. Mower on the left thigh, breaking the skin and causing bruises, while resisting Officer Mower's attempts to close the main doors of Sproul Hall."

Goldberg's letter also accused him of having:

". . . threatened Sgt. Robert Ludden of the University police by stating to him, in substance, that if police reinforcements attempted to remove the prisoner from your control and that of the demonstrators, he, Sgt. Ludden, and other police officers stationed at the entrapped police car, would be violently attacked by you and other demonstrators."

The letters required Savio and Goldberg to attend a hearing by the Faculty Committee on Student Conduct, and added:

"You may be represented by counsel at the hearing. The recommendations of the Faculty Committee on Student Conduct will be advisory to me."

November 29

1. The FSM Steering Committee held an emergency meeting at 4:00 p.m. At 8:30 p.m., the Steering Committee issued the following statement:

"The Administration sees the free speech protest as a simple problem of disobedience and refuses to recognize the legitimacy of the students' needs . . . By again arbitrarily singling out students for punishment, the Administration avoids facing the real issues.

"Its action violates the spirit of the Heyman Committee report and can only be seen as an attempt to provoke another October 2. We demand that these new charges be dropped."

A university spokesman admitted he knew the letters had been written, but said the administration normally makes no comment on cases dealing with the Faculty Committee on Student Conduct.

Chancellor Strong would not confirm the letters:

"Out of concern for the students, no matter what the occasion, the Chancellor's office makes no announcement of students being called up for disciplinary action."

November 30

1. Chancellor Edward W. Strong rejected FSM demands that the new charges against Mario Savio and Arthur Goldberg be dropped:

"The Heyman Committee limited itself to charges of misconduct up to and including September 30, and declined to consider charges of violations after that date . . .

"These further charges have been referred to the Faculty Committee on Student Conduct for hearing . . .

". . . In threatening to engage in direct action if the charges are not dropped, those who make such threats demand a decision based not on facts but on intimidation. The charges, properly, will be subjected to the test of evidence."

FSM spokesmen refused comment on Chancellor Strong's statement. However, an FSM Executive Committee meeting was held this evening to decide on future action.

2. The Graduate Co-ordinating Council announced a meeting "to plan for a T.A. strike" to be held tomorrow (December 1).

3. "Free Speech" enthusiasts held a rally on the UCLA campus. An FSM spokesman claimed "strong FSM movements" now exist and are planning action on university campuses at Santa Barbara, UCLA, Davis, and on other Southern California college campuses. The spokesman predicted "some statewide action will be taken this week."

4. Administration spokesmen refused comment on an FSM charge that new disciplinary action had been taken against eight organizations affiliated with FSM.

5. University President Clark Kerr addressed the following letter to the *Daily Californian*. The letter appeared, with the appended *Daily Cal* reply, in the paper's December 1 issue:

"Relying on the *Daily Californian* as a medium of information is like relying on smoke signals. You can gain an impression that something is being said, but you can never be quite sure what. My current concern is the continued unwillingness of the Editors to quote what I actually said in an item which has been discussed within the University Community from time to time, with the *Daily Californian* being the chief carrier of misquotations.

"Now I realize that misquotations may be more interesting than quotations and the *Daily Californian* succeeds in being interesting. With the hope that it might also be accurate, I am turning to the Icebox as a last resort, hoping it may be open also to the cause of accuracy as it is to so many other and sometimes quite contrary causes.

"Herewith are two actual quotations that are a lot less interesting than the misquotations:

"1. At a press conference held in conjunction with a speech before Town Hall in Los Angeles on Oct. 6 and in response to a reporter's question, I said:

" 'Experienced on-the-spot observers estimated that the hard core group of demonstrators—those who continued as part of the demonstrations through the night of Oct. 1 —contained at times as much as 40 per cent off-campus elements. And, within that off-campus group, there were persons identified as being sympathetic with the Communist Party and Communist causes.'

"2. On October 2 at a press conference in San Francisco following a meeting of the American Council on Education, I said:

" 'I am sorry to say that some elements active in the demonstrations have been impressed with the tactics of Fidel Castro and Mao Tse-Tung. There are very few of these, but there are some'."

The *Daily Californian* answered President Kerr's letter with the following statement:

"Early in the Bancroft-Telegraph 'free speech' dispute President Kerr was quoted by a metropolitan newspaper as saying that 49 per cent of the student demonstrators were Mao-Marxists.

"The *Daily Californian* never ran that so-called quotation at any time because we understood it was not accurate.

"We believe that we acted for the 'cause of accuracy'."

December 1

1. The FSM issued an ultimatum, and the Graduate Coordinating Council announced that teaching assistants would strike on Friday (Dec. 4), or sooner, "if conditions warrant."

The FSM demanded the university fulfill three major requests:

1) Disciplinary action initiated against FSM leaders Mario Savio, Arthur Goldberg, Jackie Goldberg and Brian Turner, resulting from the demonstrations of Oct. 1 and Oct. 2, be dropped.

2) Present rules on political speech be revised so that only the courts regulate the content of political speech. All regulations which "unnecessarily restrict" political activity be repealed.

3) The Administration refrain from further disciplining of students or organizations for political activity.

If the administration did not meet their demands within 24 hours, FSM said, "direct action will follow."

2. The ASUC Senate passed the following "Demonstration Resolution" during an evening meeting:

"WHEREAS all of the original requests and demands of the ASUC Senate, faculty and FSM seeking the rights of free speech have substantially been met or are in the process of negotiation on this campus, and

"WHEREAS the decisions concerning the administration of the means of free speech have been put in the hands of the students, specifically the ASUC Senate, and

"WHEREAS, in specific, the FSM has advocated a sit-in at the Chancellor's office on December 2 and a portion of the teaching assistants at this University are planning to strike,

"THEREFORE BE IT RESOLVED:

"1) That in view of continuing progress toward full on-campus political rights the ASUC Senate draws the inevitable conclusion that the FSM no longer has the extension of on-campus political rights as its goal, and that its present plans for civil disobedience are directed solely towards meaningless harassment of the University.

"2) That the ASUC Senate encourages all responsible students to avoid the scheduled sit-in December 2nd so as not to indicate that more students support this type of irresponsible action than is actually the case.

"3) That the ASUC Senate emphasizes the right of a student to an education and therefore encourages department chairmen at the University of California to make preparations to accommodate students in the event that any teaching assistants neglect their classes.

"4) That the ASUC Senate encourages all students to continue to attend their classes and, in that manner, to cooperate in continuing as normal an academic schedule as possible.

"5) That the ASUC Senate shall fully investigate the manner in which the administration has pursued prosecution of students involved in demonstrations throughout this semester.

December 2

1. Approximately 1000 persons—students, some faculty members and non-university persons—packed four floors of Sproul Hall following a huge rally in the plaza between Sproul Hall and the Student Union.

Leading the mass sit-in Mario Savio said:

"There is a time when the operation of the machine becomes so odious, makes you so sick at heart, that you can't take part; you can't even tacitly take part, and you've got to put your bodies upon the gears and upon the wheels, upon the levers, upon all the apparatus and you've got to make it stop. And you've got to indicate to the people who run it, to the people who own it, that unless you're free, the machines will be prevented from working at all."

Folk singer Joan Baez told the demonstrators:

"When you go in, go with love in your hearts."

Then, as Joan Baez sang "We Shall Overcome," the demonstrators filed through the right-hand main entrance to Sproul Hall, up the main stairway and—as the first and second floors filled—on up the inside stairways to the third and fourth floors.

Protestors sat one and two deep along all hallways, leaving an aisle for traffic down the center. Plans were laid for at least an all-night siege, and possibly as long as two or three days.

As the sit-in developed, the university closed all offices in the building, except Public Information and the Business and Finance departments. Employees were sent home.

Protest leader Mario Savio demanded admittance to the Dean of Students Office. Dean Peter Van Houten and two University police officers refused his request.

Most of the demonstrators contented themselves with singing folk songs, playing cards or studying. Folk singer Joan Baez, seated in a second floor hall, slept part of the afternoon.

As evening arrived and the 7:00 p.m. closing time for Sproul Hall approached, food was brought into the building and distributed to the demonstrators.

At 6:45 p.m., University Police Lieutenant Merrill Chandler informed the students the building would be closed. He ordered those inside to leave. At 7:00 p.m., police locked the doors, allowing anyone who wished to do so to leave, but no one could enter. Ropes dangled from the second floor balcony, used to lift some food and several demonstrators into the building.

Sit-in leaders urged juveniles, non-citizens, women with young children and individuals on probation or parole to leave, because of possible legal problems concerning their arrest.

As the evening wore on, and possibility of arrest or other administration action appeared to lessen, protestors watched movies ("Laurel and Hardy," "Operation Abolition"), attended "Freedom School" classes in stairwells and open areas, sang, attended Hanukkah services, danced, played cards, studied, talked ("This may be a lark now, but we may regret it."), or slept.

Joan Baez left at approximately 11:00 p.m.

Hallway lights were turned off and by 1:00 a.m., most of the demonstrators had settled down for the long night ahead.

2. ASUC President Charles Powell denounced the sit-in. He attacked "the FSM's insatiable hunger for full capitulation . . ." The sit-in, Powell maintained, can only result in a "showdown" from which neither the university nor the students would "escape unscathed." Powell further called the demonstrations "needless" on the grounds that the Regents already had granted the FSM the privileges it had requested.

3. University Young Republicans formally withdrew from the FSM tonight. UYR President Warren Coats stated:

"What the FSM is asking, in effect, is that the Administration cease to be an administration."

December 3

1. Beginning at 3:05 a.m., Chancellor Edward W. Strong, assisted by a portable "bull horn," delivered a terse message to students assembled on each of Sproul Hall's four floors:

"May I have your attention? I am Dr. Edward Strong, Chancellor of the Berkeley campus. I have an announcement.

"This assemblage has developed to such a point that the purpose and work of the University have been materially impaired. It is clear that there have been acts of disobedience and illegality which cannot be tolerated in a responsible educational center and would not be tolerated anywhere in our society.

"The University has shown great restraint and patience in exercising its legitimate authority in order to allow every opportunity for expressing differing points of view. The University always stands ready to engage in the established and accepted procedures for resolving differences of opinion.

"I request that each of you cease your participation in this unlawful assembly.

"I urge you, both individually and collectively, to leave this area. I request that you immediately disperse. Failure to disperse will result in disciplinary action by the University.

"Please go."

Outside the building, approximately 635 uniformed police officers had been assembling for nearly an hour. They came from the Alameda County Sheriffs Department, Oakland Police Department, Berkeley Police Department, University Police Department and California Highway Patrol.

At 3:45 a.m., California Governor Edmund G. Brown issued the following statement:

"I have tonight called upon law enforcement officials in Alameda County to arrest and take into custody all students and others who may be in violation of the law at Sproul Hall. I have directed the California Highway Patrol to lend all necessary assistance. These orders are to be carried out peacefully and quietly as a demonstration that the rule of law must be honored in California."

Simultaneously, in compliance with Governor Brown's orders, police officers entered the fourth floor of Sproul Hall, and the arrests began. It took 12 hours to clear the building. After clearing the fourth floor, police moved down to the third. After clearing a portion of the third floor, the police shifted their attention to the second floor, where demonstrators from the first and third floors had joined those on the second for a massive jam-in. Police spent most of the day clearing the second floor.

Any demonstrator was free to leave the building at any time, before his arrest. Only those who insisted on remaining in the building were arrested.

Each arrested demonstrator was given the choice of walking or being dragged. Some walked; most "went limp" and were dragged. Men were fingerprinted and searched, then taken down inside stairways to the basement. Women were taken to the Dean of Students Office, searched, then taken down an elevator to the basement. From the basement, demonstrators were loaded into buses and "paddy wagons" for the trip to one of three detention locations: Santa Rita Rehabilitation Center, Oakland City Jail, or Berkeley City Jail.

Arrests were formally made by the Berkeley Police Department on one or more counts: failure to disperse, refusal to leave a government building after being ordered to do so, and resisting arrest. (Civil rights attorney Robert Truhaft, the first person arrested, commented that this was the first time sit-in demonstrators have been charged with resisting arrest for going limp while being arrested.)

Bail for arrested demonstrators was originally set at $75 per offense, with $100 for resisting arrest (going limp and having to be dragged). Individual bails, depending upon specific charges, ranged from $166 to $276. At 9:10 p.m., Berkeley Municipal Judge Rupert Crittenden reduced the bails, lowering the range to between $56 and $110. (*Bail totals include "penalty assessment" of approximately ten per cent.*)

A group of university faculty members raised contributions (from students, T.A.'s and faculty members) of approximately $8,500 for bail bond fees for the arrested students. All demonstrators, except one being held for narcotics possession, were released by December 4. Transportation back to Berkeley also was arranged.

Charges of "police brutality," "sadism," and "torture" began even before the first arrested students were on their way to jail. FSM spokesmen, including leader Steve Weissman—who "escaped" out of a window—claimed the demonstrators were being clubbed, kicked, had their arms twisted, hair pulled, etc.

Arthur Goldberg later charged:

"The police laughed with pleasure while they inflicted pain on the students."

According to Dr. James Terry, Santa Rita medical officer, the police were to be commended for their "skill in doing what they had to do without hurting the students."

2. At 1:00 p.m., a general faculty meeting was held in Wheeler Auditorium. Nathan Glazer, professor of sociology, presided. More than 800 professors and instructors attended (T.A.'s attended, but did not vote). During the two-hour meeting, the group passed two resolutions:

1. A resolution introduced by Henry F. May, chairman of the department of history, addressed to the President, the Chancellor, and the *Daily Californian:*

"In view of the desperate situation now confronting the University, every effort must be made to restore the unity of our campus community, and to end the series of provocation and reprisal which has resulted in disaster. With this purpose, the undersigned faculty members urge that the following actions be taken immediately:

"1) That the new and liberalized rules for campus political action be declared in effect and enforced, pending their improvement,

"2) That all pending campus action against students for acts occurring before the present date be dropped,

"3) That a committee selected by and responsible to the Academic Senate be established, to which students may appeal decisions of the Administration regarding penalties for violations relating to offenses arising from political action, and that decisions of this committee are final."

Herbert McClosky, professor of political science, offered two additions, both of which were overwhelmingly accepted:

1) Retraction of the Regents' decision that the University could prosecute students for advocating illegal off-campus action, and

2) A demand that no student be prosecuted by the University for participating in any off-campus activity.

2. A telegram to Governor Edmund G. Brown, signed by 361 faculty members:

"The undersigned members of the faculty of the University of California at Berkeley strongly condemn the presence of the State Highway Patrol on the Berkeley campus. We also protest the exclusion of faculty members, including at least one member of our Committee on Academic Freedom, from Sproul Hall, at a time when the police were admitting newsmen and photographers. Punitive action taken against hundreds of students cannot help to solve our current problems, and will aggravate the already serious situation. Only prompt release of the arrested students offers any prospect of restoring the unity of campus life and of a return to normal academic functions."

The faculty assembly also heard a statement, read by John H. Reynolds, professor of physics and chairman of the Berkeley chapter of the American Association of University Professors. The statement was met with cheers, but was not introduced or passed as a motion:

"The Executive Committee of the Berkeley Chapter of the AAUP unanimously believes that the present crisis cannot be properly resolved without:

"1) Complete amnesty for past offenses in the course of the Free Speech controversy,

"2) A new chief campus officer for Berkeley who will have the confidence of the University community."

3. As arrests continued in Sproul Hall, pickets attempted to block campus entrances, encouraging faculty members, teaching assistants, and students to stay away from classes in protest over the demonstrators' arrests.

4. Governor Brown's office in Sacramento was picketed by a group from the Davis campus. Brown conferred with the pickets in the afternoon. His decision to order the arrests was based on a "consensus of opinion," he said. The governor also said:

"I assume full responsibility for this in every shape, form and manner. I felt it was the right thing to do. The overriding matter became one between the people of the State of California versus the demonstrators."

5. Later in the afternoon, President Clark Kerr issued a statement condemning the demonstration and the FSM (*Full text, see Appendix*). Kerr's statement said, in part:

"The FSM and its leaders from the start declared the police would have to haul them out. They are now finding that, in their effort, to escape the gentle discipline of the University, they have thrown themselves into the arms of the less understanding discipline of the community at large . . .

"When patience and tolerance and reasonableness and decency have been tried, yet democratic processes continue to be forsaken by the FSM in favor of anarchy, then the process of law enforcement takes over."

6. The Graduate Co-ordinating Council met late this afternoon to discuss plans to implement the strike. Significant support for the movement was evident: the *Daily Californian* reported 50 per cent or more of the T.A.'s in anthropology, English, French, geography, German, history, Italian, molecular biology, philosophy, physics, political science, Slavic languages, social science, sociology and subject A would refuse to cross picket lines.

7. Chancellor Edward W. Strong issued a statement this evening. The statement began with the statement Chancellor Strong read to the students occupying the corridors of Sproul Hall, then continued:

"Only those persons were placed under arrest who refused in subsequent hours to leave the building voluntarily. When Sproul Hall was closed at 7:00 p.m. Wednesday, warning was given at that time that further occupancy of the building by demonstrators was illegal.

"The deliberate refusal of individuals to obey the law, after being warned of consequences of disobedience, made it necessary to proceed with their arrests. Concerned for the welfare of its students, the University hoped that the warning given would be heeded. When it was not, no further recourses remained except enforcement of the law.

"The University, as a public trust, cannot default on its responsibility of maintaining law and order on its campuses. There must be no interference with nor disruption of the orderly conduct of University business.

"In his statement, President Clark Kerr places the most recent defiance of legitimate authority by the FSM in the context and perspective in which it should be viewed by all members of the campus community. I join with him in his appeal to reason in the conduct of University affairs, and in the firm expectation that reasonableness will prevail."

December 4

1. Demonstration leaders and others arrested yesterday and released on bail appeared on campus wearing large white "V's" on black backgrounds and attended a huge noon rally on Sproul Hall steps. More than 5000 persons jammed the plaza and many lined the balconies and Dining Commons roof to hear protest leaders and faculty members condemn Governor Brown, the Regents, President Kerr, Chancellor Strong and the police.

2. The student strike continued through the day, with picket lines at campus entrances and construction sites. Labor unions, asked to support the FSM pickets, generally condemned the use of police and the "denial of free speech" on the campus, but would not officially endorse or recognize the student strike. "This is not a dispute between labor and management," a local Teamster official said, although several individual delivery truck drivers were reported to have refused to cross the students' picket lines.

3. FSM set up a committee of 125–150 people to call university students during the weekend. Attempts were made to reach every Berkeley student. "I'm calling to ask for your support of the walkout," callers were supposed to say; however, many students reported receiving telephone calls from someone who said:

"I'm your T.A. in —————. It wouldn't be advisable for you to attend classes during the strike."

4. Henry F. May, chairman of the department of history,

announced formation of a Council of Department Chairmen (*Full text, see Appendix*).

5. ASUC President Charles Powell issued the following statement during a news conference this afternoon:

> "Because of the fact that the issues have become muddled and because the FSM has refused to use the right channels and have the patience to use the right channels, the majority of this campus community doesn't support the actions of this body of individuals. The campus community would support proper channels—the only two remaining channels which are available—but sit-ins, strikes, and arbitrating bodies are not going to bridge the gap which divides this campus.
>
> "Education and the normal processes of learning are of utmost importance here, and the FSM regards itself as being able to decide for everyone else on this campus that their demands are more important than the basic purpose of this University. I maintain that such disregard of others' rights to an education on this campus if it continues will have serious consequences.
>
> "Our world-renowned faculty members will leave, large numbers of students will change campuses having done poorly in courses here for lack of the proper atmosphere, and legislative influence from Sacramento is threatening more and more the autonomy of the University of California. Destroying the political autonomy of the University would be a disastrous consequence, and along with the other reasons which I have stated, make the FSM continual demonstrations and tactics completely invalid and unwanted."

December 5

1. The FSM Executive Committee and Steering Committee began a week-end-long series of meetings to plan details of their strike and future action. The strike is to continue until noon, December 8. The strike would end shortly before the Academic Senate is scheduled to meet to consider its Committee on Academic Freedom's recommendations to end the current dispute.

2. The 37-member California Alumni Council, governing body for the 50,000-member California Alumni Association, met today and issued the following statement:

> "WHEREAS recent events have seriously endangered, in the eyes of the people of the State of California, the fine reputation of the University established over nearly 100 years of creative growth; and
>
> "WHEREAS the overwhelming law-abiding majority of students, faculty and alumni have privately deplored

the threatened state of anarchy sought to be imposed on a great University by relatively few agitators and malcontents and their misguided sympathizers; and

"WHEREAS all too seldom in the past week have the voices of this majority of thinking citizens been raised to speak in defense of law and order; and

"WHEREAS the time has come for this Council to speak out on this challenge to duly constituted authority, and to speak also of civil responsibilities as well as civil rights;

"NOW THEREFORE BE IT RESOLVED by the Alumni Council of the University of California as follows:

"We are appalled and do condemn the tragic conduct of a group which has announced its intention to engage in unlawful conduct characterized by itself as 'civil disobedience.'

"We commend Governor Brown, President Kerr, Chancellor Strong and District Attorney Coakley for their forthright and vigorous action.

"We adopt and concur in President Kerr's recent statement that the means adopted by these dissidents have now 'become an instrument of anarchy and personal aggrandizement.'

"We do recommend and fully support firm disciplinary action including expulsion or dismissal where warranted.

"We urge the great majority of students, faculty and citizens of California who have an ingrained respect for law and order to speak up in its defense and support the administration's maintenance of traditional democratic principles and processes."

3. Charles Powell, ASUC president, called a news conference to issue a statement which read, in part:

"The FSM, a minority group, is imposing needless suffering on the majority of the students on the campus by illegally demonstrating for an aspect of political activity which is now not allowed and can only be changed . . . through legal means."

4. The College Federation of Young Republicans said:

"We condemn the leadership and lawless tactics of the Free Speech Movement which can in no way claim to represent the great majority of students at the University of California . . ."

5. The Berkeley chapter of the American Federation of Teachers directed a resolution to President Kerr, which declared in part:

"We would like to inform you that any punitive action taken against teaching assistants or officers of instruction would be intolerable to our group and create a situation in which class instruction could not continue . . ."

6. The ASUC Senate, holding an emergency meeting tonight, passed the following resolution:

"1) We urge all members of the faculty and all teaching assistants to immediately resume classroom instruction. We further urge all students to resume attending their classes for the pursuit of knowledge and higher education.

"2) The new and liberalized regulations regarding political and social activity on the campus, must be immediately implemented and enforced. Any inconsistencies should thereafter be corrected by the proper authorities of the stable, established bodies for orderly change. In essence the regulations are essentially these:

"1. Advocacy of off-campus action falling within legal speech areas is allowed.

"2. Solicitation of funds is allowed.

"3. Solicitation of membership is allowed.

"Means for implementing these ideas including speakers and tables, are 'subject only to restrictions necessary for normal conduct of University functions and business.'

"All students should remain within the new regulations while the student committee interprets, establishes, and defines these regulations.

"3) We recognize the arrests of the students, and realize that legitimate due process of law was and will be enacted against them, regardless of the difficulties involved in the administration of due process in such a situation.

"Before the students are tried, we wish that the following points, which have great bearing on the overall picture, be given the court's deepest consideration:

"1. The students involved were cognizant of their actions, however, reasons for their conduct were obscured by cloudy issues.

"2. Prior to the arrests, there was a breakdown in communication between all groups involved and an inconsistency in actions best exemplified by changing stands on all sides.

"3. The events have been an intermixing of emotionalism and rational conviction, the value of which, none save the courts, may hope to presume.

"Realizing that there were such extenuating circumstances involved in this issue, we hope the court will give this case a most liberal consideration and grant sufficient leniency so as not to interfere with the education of these students.

"4) The ASUC Senate will press for the initiation of legal proceedings to resolve the complex issues by immediately beginning procedures to bring a test case to the courts on the issue of jurisdiction over charges regarding illegal advocacy of off-campus political and social action.

"5) The ASUC Senate urges that charges against the four students be dropped."

Commuter-Independent Representative Joel Hacker, a member of Slate, was the only senator in opposition to the proposal.

In reaction to the ASUC Senate recommendations, Arthur Goldberg, former Slate chairman and one of the FSM leaders, said:

> "How can I go to class and learn of our country's democratic processes when I'm not allowed to practice them on campus?"

December 6

1. President Clark Kerr announced he had cancelled a planned trip to Chicago, and that he would address a special university meeting at 11:00 a.m. tomorrow (Dec. 7) in the Greek Theatre. All classes between 9:00 a.m. and noon were cancelled. President Kerr announced the meeting would serve to introduce a proposal "to inaugurate a new era of freedom under law" which had been unanimously approved by 73 department chairmen yesterday.

Kerr's announcement came after he had spent four hours in discussions with Governor Brown, members of the Board of Regents and faculty members. President Kerr previously had announced he would speak to the students on his return from Chicago, Tuesday or Wednesday.

2. The following statement was released by the Council of Department Chairmen:

> "On December 3, in the midst of the great crisis at the University, a meeting of all Department Chairmen of the Berkeley campus was convened. It carried on earnest deliberations for several hours and established a Working Committee to explore approaches to all problems concerned with the crisis.
>
> "A second meeting was convened on December 4, and almost unanimous agreement was achieved on a proposal forwarded by the Working Committee.
>
> "This proposal in its essential elements was finally approved unanimously by the Chairmen on December 6 and has the concurrence of the President. All chairmen have

been advised by the Council of Department Chairmen to hold departmental meetings at 9:00 a.m. on Monday morning, December 7. The agreement will be publicly announced at 11:00 a.m. in an extraordinary convocation in the Greek Theatre called by the Department Chairmen at which Professor Robert A. Scalapino and President Clark Kerr will speak. Department Chairmen have recommended that classes be dismissed from 9:00 a.m. to 12:00 a.m. Department representatives will speak with students about the agreement throughout the afternoon.

"All parties to this agreement are extremely optimistic that it will unite the great body of the University, strengthen faculty-student relations, and inaugurate a new era of freedom under law."

3. A new organization, University Students for Law and Order, and the ASUC announced joint sponsorship of a noon rally to be held in the lower Student Union plaza tomorrow (Dec. 7).

USLO Chairman Robert Dussault took the opportunity to issue the following statement:

"There is no need, nor is there any excuse, for civil disobedience on our campus. Those students involved in the demonstrations demand protection of their rights while, at the same time, they are violating our rights. We urge all students support the legally-constituted administration on all issues until such a time as the civil judicial system dictates otherwise."

The USLO-ASUC announcement of the noon rally brought the following statement from Brian Turner, an FSM spokesman:

"FSM has never precipitated any violence. Our presence in Sproul Hall Plaza at noon is well known. Any students who attempt to bring together opposing emotion-packed student elements must bear the responsibility for any reaction between the groups."

4. It was announced that Chancellor Edward W. Strong was admitted to the University Medical Center in San Francisco last night with abdominal pains, tentatively diagnosed as gall bladder trouble. Hospital spokesmen estimated Strong would be in the hospital for a week.

5. The Academic Senate announced its meeting Tuesday (Dec. 8) will be held in Wheeler Auditorium.

6. Eight hundred arrested demonstrators met with some of their attorneys at 7:00 p.m. at Garfield Junior High School in north Berkeley. The students, scheduled for arraignment at 9:00 a.m. tomorrow (Dec. 7), were advised on their legal position and on court procedures.

Nearly 40 lawyers were involved in defending the arrested demonstrators. They held a meeting Saturday (Dec. 5) and chose a coordinating committee to spearhead their efforts. The coordinating committee was composed of attorneys Norman Leonard, John Dunn, Malcolm Burnstein, Howard Jewell, Milton Nathan, Stanley Gold, and Spencer Strellis. The lawyers stressed they are not working for FSM, but are merely representing various students.

(Figures on the total number of sit-in demonstrators arrested on Thursday depended upon whose figures one preferred to use. The police figure was 761, a decrease from the original police total of 801, due to discovery of fictitious names, duplications and mis-numbering. The university announced, however, following a check of its records, that 814 arrests were made with the following breakdown: Students, 590 or 72.5 per cent; Non-Students, 135 or 16.6 per cent; Teaching and Research Assistants, University Employees and Unidentified Persons, 89 or 10.9 per cent.)

The district attorney's office announced demonstrators' cases will be assigned to various deputies within the department for investigation, with no distinction between students and non-students.

December 7

1. Seven hundred and sixty-eight demonstrators arrested in Sproul Hall on December 3 appeared for arraignment before Municipal Judge Rupert Crittenden in the Berkeley Community Theater at 9:00 a.m. On motion of counsel, Judge Crittenden postponed arraignment to December 14, in order to allow legal counsel an opportunity to prepare their clients' cases.

2. The following statement, signed by nine full professors of political science, appeared in the *Daily Californian*. The statement was signed by Professors Charles Aiken, Eric Bellquist, Thomas C. Blaisdell Jr., Joseph P. Harris, George Lenczowski, Albert Lepawsky, Frederick C. Mosher, Julian Towster, and Dwight Waldo:

> "We commend the preponderant number of University students who have at this time conscientiously and with good humor continued to attend their classes and pursue their studies.
>
> "We condemn the illegal occupation of University facilities by striking students and we deplore the partial disruption of University activities which such conduct has caused.
>
> "We advise any students who still remain on strike to return to their classes and resume their studies forthwith.
>
> "We especially urge them to do this immediately instead of waiting for some deadline designated by others,

so that they may demonstrate they are mature men and women capable of making up their own minds.

"Particularly in our capacity as teachers of government, do we call students' attention to the absolute necessity for pursuing orderly and legal processes in attempting, in good conscience, to correct any grievances they may have.

"Especially in a University in a democratic society, students must recognize that the derogation of due process and the disruption of normal administration in the name of Freedom of Speech is demagoguery, not democracy.

"And finally, as teachers of American government, comparative political science, and international politics and administration, along with the entire University system of the State of California which has sprung from it, has now become a national and international model for higher education, scientific research and intellectual services of vast array, with crucial contractual relationships to other institutions and governments and with prime educational responsibilities on its own burgeoning campuses abroad.

"To hamper the work of such a world-renowned and world-committed institution and to engage in behavior which subjects it to obliquy, is not solely an injury to a single University campus, but a threat to the attainment of the larger ideals of freedom, science, and service which, we are convinced, continue to motivate the minds of University students here and all over the world."

3. At 11:00 a.m., approximately 16,000 students, faculty members and staff gathered in the Greek Theatre for the unusual convocation ceremonies. University President Clark Kerr was introduced by Professor Robert A. Scalapino, chairman of the political science department and of the Council of Department Chairmen, who announced "our maximum effort to attain peace and decency."

President Kerr, flanked by all the Berkeley campus department heads on the Greek Theatre stage, publicly accepted the proposal presented to him by the Council of Department Chairmen and announced the terms:

"1. The University Community shall be governed by orderly and lawful procedures in the settlement of issues; and the full and free pursuit of educational activities on this campus shall be maintained.

"2. The University Community shall abide by the new and liberalized political action rules and await the report of the Senate Committee on Academic Freedom.

"3. The Departmental Chairmen believe that the acts of civil disobedience on December 2 and 3 were unwar-

ranted and that they obstruct rational and fair consideration of the grievances brought forward by the students.

"4. The cases of all students arrested in connection
with the sit-in in Sproul Hall on December 2 and 3 are
now before the Courts. The University will accept the
Court's judgment in these cases as the full discipline for
those offenses.

"In the light of the cases now and prospectively before the courts, the University will not prosecute charges
against any students for actions prior to December 2 and
3; but the University will invoke disciplinary actions for
any violations henceforth.

"5. All classes shall be conducted as scheduled."

Professor Scalapino provided background on the Council of
Departmental Chairmen's proposals. Scalapino praised President Kerr for the "courage and vision" in accepting it. Scalapino also said:

"No one would claim that we are presenting here a
panacea—a perfect and final answer. We are offering the
possibility of an orderly and fair atmosphere in which to
reassess our problems, a possibility that demands for its
success the good will and the good faith of all the members of this community."

President Kerr accepted the Council's proposals, and told
the meeting that the proposals would go into effect immediately:

"As President of the University, I welcome it (the proposal) and endorse it and shall present it to the Regents
of the University at their next meeting. In the interim,
until the Regents meet next week, this proposal is in full
force and effect."

4. Prior to the Greek Theatre meeting, Mario Savio, FSM
leader, conducted a heated argument backstage with Professor Scalapino. Both Assistant Professor of Sociology John
Leggett and Savio charged the department chairmen had
"usurped" the Academic Senate's authority by presenting their
proposal in advance of the Academic Senate meeting scheduled for tomorrow afternoon (Dec. 8). Savio demanded an
opportunity to address the Greek Theatre meeting. Scalapino,
who served as meeting chairman, told Savio that the meeting
was "structured" and, as such, was not an "open forum." He
refused Savio's request to speak.

During the meeting, Savio sat approximately 15 feet from
the edge of the stage. As President Kerr spoke, he shook his
head and muttered "Hypocrite!" A reporter asked Savio if he
was going to speak. Savio nodded and said, "I'm going to
speak."

As President Kerr neared the end of his remarks, Savio rose and walked to the far left (south) end of the Greek Theatre stage, mounted the stage, and stood there for two or three minutes while President Kerr completed his remarks. At the conclusion of the president's address, Chairman Scalapino moved to the rostrum and announced the meeting's adjournment.

Simultaneously, Savio moved rapidly across the front of the stage to the rostrum, clutching a scroll of paper in his hand. As he reached the rostrum, two university police officers grabbed him and pulled him away from the rostrum. Savio was dragged through the center rear stage entrance and into a small room at the south end of the backstage area used by performers.

Several of Savio's supporters attempted to assist Savio; they were pushed aside or knocked down and held in place. No arrests were made.

Scores of people—faculty and staff, newsmen, students and police—gathered in front of the building where Savio was being held. At first, no one was allowed to enter. Alex Hoffman, an attorney defending some of the arrested students, shouted through the door: "Demand to see your lawyer, Mario."

Attorney Hoffman and several departmental chairmen eventually were admitted to the room where Savio was being held.

As Savio was being held at the south end of the Greek Theatre, Arthur Goldberg pleaded with President Kerr to release him at the north end. Kerr agreed, and, it was announced Savio was not under arrest, that he would be allowed to speak.

Surrounded by well-wishers, Savio told the crowd he merely wanted to announce an FSM rally at noon in front of Sproul Hall (*President Kerr had personally given permission for this rally, so that the protestors could discuss the terms of the new agreement*). Then Savio said:

> "Please leave here. Clear this disastrous scene, and get down to discussing the issues."

Following the meeting, President Kerr indicated he was quite upset over the incident:

> "There had been some indications of threats to disrupt the meeting . . . The police were prepared. Apparently, they weren't aware the meeting was over . . .
>
> "Whether we have a new start seems somewhat doubtful . . . We wanted to walk one additional mile. There are those who think we've walked too many miles already."

5. Nearly 10,000 persons jammed the plaza between Sproul Hall and the Student Union at noon. They rejected, by acclamation, the proposals announced by President Kerr less than an hour earlier.

Jack Weinberg, a non-student member of the FSM Steering Committee, told the crowd:

"I really expected that we were going to get something today. But, we didn't. We are the ones who must save this University, but we're not going to save the University by capitulating."

Steve Weissman, also a Steering Committee member, denounced President Kerr as a "liar":

"Kerr stated, 'We agree on ends and are divided on means.' This is a lie—a bold-face lie. The sit-in did not obstruct, but rather caused, the first rational discussion of the problem on this campus."

Martin Roysher, still another Steering Committee member, read a telegram of support from British philosopher Bertrand Russell:

"You have my full and earnest support. Warm greetings."

Roysher also announced that Russell had sent the following telegram to Governor Edmund G. Brown:

"Urgently appeal to you to halt University and police oppression of students at Berkeley Campus. Appalling restrictions upon their civil liberty. All who value individual liberty are supporting their cause."

FSM leaders also announced that James Farmer, national director of CORE, would appear at an FSM rally next Tuesday (Dec. 15).

6. In anticipation of the Academic Senate meeting at 3:00 p.m. tomorrow, the FSM announced its strike would end at midnight tonight. Students were urged to attend classes tomorrow as a demonstration that the students have faith in the Academic Senate.

Jack Weinberg said:

"Clark Kerr demanded that the strike end. We can't do that. But, at midnight tonight we will temporarily end our strike and we will wait and see if they (the Academic Senate) can merge as an independent force."

Steve Weissman added:

"Let's give them tomorrow one day of real peace and quiet."

7. In response to the FSM request for suspension of strike activities, the Graduate Co-ordinating Council voted to suspend the strike of teaching assistants, readers and research assistants. The council refused, however, to delete a warning

that the strike might be resumed, if the Academic Senate fails to take initiative action in supporting the free speech activities. A council member said:

"There has been plenty of pressure from the Administration, so we might as well exert a little pressure ourselves."

The GCC also turned down motions to hold a rally and vigil tomorrow.

Steve Weissman, a Council member as well as a member of the FSM Steering Committee, said:

"Frankly, many of the strike and protest signs have alienated some members of the faculty."

8. An emergency meeting of the ASUC Senate was cancelled tonight, because a majority of the Senate failed to attend.

9. Elections for seven representative positions on the ASUC Senate were being held today and tomorrow. "If you support FSM's goals, vote for the Slate candidates," Arthur Goldberg told the noon rally.

December 8

1. The Berkeley Division of the Academic Senate met in Wheeler Auditorium at 3:10 p.m. and, after nearly three hours of debate—half of the time on an amendment introduced by Lewis Feuer, professor of philosophy—passed (824–115) unchanged "a resolution unanimously approved at a meeting of approximately 200 faculty members on December 7":

"In order to end the present crisis, to establish the confidence and trust essential to the restoration of normal University life, and to create a campus environment that encourages students to exercise free and responsible citizenship in the University and in the community at large, the Committee on Academic Freedom of the Berkeley Division of the Academic Senate moves the following propositions:

"1. That there shall be no University disciplinary measures against members or organizations of the University community for activities prior to December 8 connected with the current controversy over political speech and activity.

"2. That the time, place, and manner of conducting political activity on the campus shall be subject to reasonable regulations to prevent interference with the normal functions of the University; that the regulations now in effect for this purpose shall remain in effect provisionally pending a future report of the Committee on Academic Freedom concerning the minimal regulations necessary.

"3. That the content of speech or advocacy should not be restricted by the University. Off-campus political activities shall not be subject to University regulation. On-campus advocacy or organization of such activities shall be subject only to such limitations as may be imposed under Section 2.

"4. That future disciplinary measures in the area of political activity shall be determined by a committee appointed by and responsible to the Academic Senate.

"5. That the Division pledge unremitting effort to secure the adoption of the foregoing policies and call on all members of the University community to join with the faculty in its efforts to restore the University to its normal functions."

Professor Feuer's amendment, which was defeated, 737–284, would have amended Section 3 to read: ". . . the content of speech or advocacy *on this campus provided that it is directed to no immediate act of force or violence . . .*"

The University Board of Regents considered the Academic Senate's resolution at its next meeting, December 17 and 18, in Los Angeles.

Nearly 3000 observers gathered outside Wheeler Hall listened to the proceedings over loudspeakers. They cheered as the vote defeating Feuer's amendment was announced; they wildly cheered the announcement of the main motion's final passage.

Joseph Tussman, professor of philosophy and chairman of the philosophy department, summarized the senate's resolution:

"Anything that is illegal in the community at large is still illegal on the campus. The question is: Should the University impose more restrictions on its students in the area of political activity than exists in the community-at-large? The Senate said: No."

For Mario Savio, who returned from an attempt to see Governor Brown in Sacramento just in time for the senate's decision, the senate action was a perfect birthday present. Savio turned 22 today. He said:

"Our tactics caused the present success . . . The Senate action was a direct attack on the doctrine of *in loco parentis* . . .

"The FSM will now be a defense committee for 800 patriots."

In a statement, issued soon after the senate had adjourned

and entitled "Happiness is an Academic Senate Meeting," FSM said:

"With deep gratitude the Free Speech Movement greets the action of the faculty. The passing of the proposals of the Academic Freedom Committee is an unprecedented victory for both students and faculty. For months the FSM has fought to bring the issues to public discussion and to rouse the faculty to take action. Our efforts have finally succeeded, and our protest has been vindicated.

"Now that the University community is again united, we hope that it will work together for speedy implementation of its proposals. The faculty must see that the Regents adopt its recommendations. For our own part, the FSM will be completely at the service of the Committee on Academic Freedom in its coming efforts to formulate proper regulations.

"We regret having been forced to undertake controversial actions to begin a dialogue. The actions have weighed more heavily upon us than upon any others in the academic community. We hope that the dialogue which has at last begun will continue and increase, and that the success of this dialogue will mean that such actions will never again be necessary.

"We urge the faculty and the Academic Senate to do everything in their power to see that the court charges against the 800 are dropped. These students risked arrest to protest unfair regulations and arbitrary disciplinary actions. They made a responsible protest, and should not be punished for having fought in the only ways available for just goals which are now largely achieved. We ask that the faculty honor their dedication by taking appropriate action."

University President Clark Kerr also commented on the Academic Senate resolution:

"The action of the Academic Senate at Berkeley involves such basic changes in the policies affecting all campuses of the University, including changes in the Standing Orders of the Regents, that no comment will be possible until the Regents have next met."

2. In related action, the Berkeley Division of the Academic Senate also passed the following resolution:

"Whereas, the present grave crisis in the life of the University demands that the Berkeley Division of the Academic Senate offer leadership to the campus community;

"And whereas, the existing organization of the Division

is not well adapted to the exercise of such leadership under the emergency circumstances now prevailing;

"Therefore, be it resolved:

"1. That an Emergency Executive Committee, consisting of six elected members and the Chairman of the Division *ex officio,* be constituted to represent the Division in dealing with problems arising out of the present crisis during the remainder of the present academic year, reporting its actions regularly to the Division, and convening the Division when necessary.

"2. That the election of the six elective members shall be conducted by the Secretary of the Academic Senate and the Committee on Elections; that nominations be filed at the office of the Secretary, 220 California Hall, by 8 p.m., Wednesday, December 9; that each nomination be accompanied by the signatures of five sponsors and a signed statement that the nominee will serve if elected; that voting take place by written secret ballot in the office of the Secretary of the Academic Senate between 9 a.m. and 8 p.m., Thursday, December 10; that each voter vote for not more than six candidates; that the six candidates with the highest votes be elected; and that the committee be convened immediately after the results are determined to choose its chairman.

"3. That the Emergency Executive Committee be authorized to call on any of the Standing Committees or to appoint *ad hoc* committees to assist it; and that committees thus called on for assistance report to the Division through the Emergency Executive Committee."

3. Slate candidates swept to victories in all seven ASUC Senate positions for which elections were held Monday and Tuesday, Sandor Fuchs, Slate chairman and FSM member, said:

"The victory for Slate is a victory for the Free Speech Movement, and an independent ASUC. It comes at a time of the greatest victory for the student movement, just hours after the Academic Senate voted for full free speech on campus."

Slate officials also promised:

". . . to immediately implement its (Slate's) program upon taking office, including full freedom of speech on campus, a co-op ASUC store, low cost student apartments, and the readmission of graduate students."

4. The ASUC Senate, meeting only hours after the announcement of the Academic Senate action, unanimously passed the following resolution:

"The ASUC Senate urges all professors, instructors and teaching assistants to be most tolerant of and lenient toward students missing classes, examinations, and papers during this semester, and epecially within the last week."

Commenting on the ASUC Senate resolution, Vice President Jerry Goldstein said:

"A great deal of intolerance towards these students has been shown . . . This resolution may do something to help the students out."

Faculty Representative Lyman Porter gave the resolution his "full endorsement."

5. Charles Powell, ASUC president, evaluated the ASUC Senate's role in the "free speech" controversy:

"Overall, we've missed the boat. We have in many ways been inadequate in dealing with the free speech problem."

December 9

1. Edward W. Carter, chairman of the University Board of Regents, issued the following statement:

"The Constitution of the State of California clearly charges the Regents with full and ultimate authority for conducting the affairs of the University of California. This they exercise principally through their appointed administrative officers and by delegation of certain specific but revocable powers to properly constituted academic bodies.

"It now appears that on the Berkeley campus these traditional methods have proved inadequate to deal effectively with the extraordinary problems created there by regrettable recent incidents. Hence, the Regents will consider this whole matter directly at their next meeting now scheduled to be held on December 18 in Los Angeles."

2. Governor Edmund G. Brown, president of the Board of Regents, issued the following statement:

"I have been asked to comment on the Academic Senate at Berkeley. I have also been asked to comment on reports that I will be asked to grant amnesty to members of the FSM who were arrested on December 3. The Academic Senate proposes fundamental changes in the policies now in effect at Berkeley and the other eight campuses of the University of California. These proposals deserve and will get my careful attention. But I do not intend to make a judgment on them until the Board of Regents meets in Los Angeles next week.

"As to the request for amnesty, I will not intervene in the cases now pending before the courts, nor do I intend to intervene at any other stage. For ten weeks the campus of one of the world's leading universities has been in turmoil. The orderly pursuit of knowledge has been all but impossible. This strife and dissension has deeply disturbed the people of California who have been generous in their financial support of the University and in their defense of its need for academic freedom to grow in intellectual stature.

"The trouble on campus has been caused by a group called the Free Speech Movement which had a grievance and which had several courses to follow in petitioning for redress of that grievance. The FSM chose a chaotic course of demonstrations, sit-ins and threats against the administration of the University of California. Their actions resulted in charges against several hundred students. Whether the charges will be sustained by a court, I do not know, and I do not intend to prejudge their cases. But it should be clear to the members of the Free Speech Movement that in a society governed by law, a decision to defy the law must include a decision to accept the consequences. I have considered the question of amnesty carefully and my decision is final. I will not intervene."

3. Two hundred and fifty teaching and research assistants pledged themselves to abide by the constitution of the Union of University-Employed Graduate Students, formed today at Berkeley. The union was constituted "for the purposes of affiliation with organized labor." Teaching and research assistants from almost every department are included in the new organization, with strongest support from the mathematics and economics departments. Under the chairmanship of Michael Abromovitch, mathematics, the group passed a motion to adopt a constitution to be discussed and amended at a later date. The proposed constitution was drafted by Barry Shapiro, philosophy grad student on leave of absence; David McCullah, philosophy teaching assistant, and Michael Rabbitt, economics teaching assistant.

4. The Berkeley Chapter of the American Association of University Professors met today and heard the following statement by its Executive Committee:

"Six days ago, in the darkest hour this campus has seen, the Executive Committee of the Berkeley Chapter of AAUP called for amnesty for students and for a new chief campus officer. Our concern was for fresh leadership which could enter upon the work on restoration without the taint of past discords.

"Events of the past five days have gone a distance toward this restoration. Fresh leadership was provided by the committee of department chairmen. For future leadership in this crisis we can look toward the newly created Executive Committee of the Academic Senate.

"The amnesty we sought for students has been granted by the President of the University in an agreement with the department chairmen.

"The faculty has closed ranks in this crisis and has acted with unprecedented unity. Actions of a divisive character must be avoided in the work of re-knitting our campus community.

"For these reasons the Executive Committee presents no motion to the membership. It wishes to make two further statements.

"1. Chancellor Strong has long been a respected member of this faculty. We are immensely saddened by the news of his illness and hope for his early recovery to full health.

"2. There must always be the continuous possibility of direct and human negotiation between students and a local administrator who has full authority commensurate with his responsibility for order on the campus."

A motion from the floor, duly seconded, called for adoption of the Executive Committee's statement of December 3, requesting amnesty for students and removal of Chancellor Strong. After thorough debate, the motion was tabled.

December 13

1. Chancellor Edward W. Strong, released from the hospital yesterday, cancelled, then approved with qualifications, a pre-court client-counsel meeting scheduled at 7:30 p.m. in Wheeler Auditorium. The meeting was moved to the Berkeley Community Theater.

Dean of Students Katherine A. Towle initially approved a request, on December 10, to hold the meeting in Wheeler Auditorium for the purpose of "legal representation for arrested students." The request was submitted by Thomas Barnes, associate professor of history and a member of Campus CORE.

At the time the request was presented, Dean Towle did not realize the meeting would involve private client-counsel relationships, a university spokesman said later.

Late this afternoon, Chancellor Strong cancelled the meeting, explaining:

"State property cannot be used for the private practicing of attorneys counseling their clients."

At 6:30 p.m., one hour before the meeting was scheduled to begin, Chancellor Strong released the following statement:

> "The meeting is approved for open informational presentation of general statements of legal principles and procedures applicable to such cases. It is not proper to use University facilities for the private counsel-client relationships."

Loudspeakers outside Wheeler Hall informed the 768 students that the chancellor had refused permission to use the building, and that the meeting had been moved to the Community Theater.

2. The University Students for Law and Order denied the "implied authorship" of a leaflet being circulated on the Berkeley campus:

> "University Students for Law and Order deny the implied authorship of a ditto copy dated December 11 and distributed to departmental mailboxes referencing alternative proposals to those of the Academic Senate. This ditto copy is typical of the smear tactics which have been employed by the opposition in pursuit of their goals."

3. Sculptor Benny Bufano donated a sculpture of a crouched polar bear to the Academic Senate to help raise funds to support the "free speech" movement. Bufano estimated the sculpture could raise $5000, "if handled properly."

4. A number of meetings and programs related to the "free speech" controversy were announced over the weekend:

1) James Baldwin would give a benefit lecture for the Free Speech Movement on Wednesday (Dec. 16).

2) James Farmer, national director of CORE, would speak at noon Tuesday (Dec. 15) on the subject: "Civil Liberties and Civil Rights."

3) Students interested in participating in local forums throughout the state on the "administration-student controversy" were asked to leave their names at the Student Union information desk.

4) A meeting to discuss how "students can effectively communicate support to the Regents of the Academic Senate proposal" would be held Monday (Dec. 14) at Hillel Foundation.

5) John Hendrix, Vince Guaraldi and Les McCann would appear in a benefit jazz concert for the arrested students at 8:00 p.m. tomorrow (Dec. 14) in Wheeler Auditorium.

6) The Graduate Co-ordinating Council announced a tutoring program for persons arrested recently and who may have been hurt academically by the recent controversy.

December 14

1. Berkeley Municipal Court Judge Rupert Crittenden continued the cases of most of the persons arrested in the Sproul Hall sit-in to January 5. Judge Crittenden's action came during a hearing in the Berkeley Community Theater. The continuance allows most students to leave Berkeley for Christmas-New Year vacation.

Judge Crittenden anticipated defendants would begin entering pleas on January 5. He planned to handle 100 pleas a day.

2. Dean of Students Katherine A. Towle refused to permit use of Wheeler Auditorium for a benefit concert scheduled for 8:00 p.m. this evening. The concert was planned to raise funds for the defense of students arrested in the Sproul Hall sit-in. The concert was moved to the Finnish Hall in Berkeley.

In refusing Arthur Goldberg permission to hold the concert in Wheeler Auditorium, Dean Towle said:

> "I cannot approve Slate's request for tonight's proposed jazz concert in Wheeler Auditorium, because it includes the collection of donations prohibited by university regulations."

The application for use of the hall had been received only five and one half hours before the concert was scheduled to begin, Dean Towle said. But, even if it had been received sooner, Dean Towle noted, the request would have been denied, because it violated rules restricting collection of funds to the Sather Gate and Bancroft-Telegraph areas.

Dean Towle also criticized FSM for selling tickets and advertising the concert before asking permission to hold it. Dean Towle did, however, suggest possible alternative off-campus locations where the concert could be held.

3. The proposed appearance of author James Baldwin was cancelled because of the no-collection edict. Instead, Baldwin appeared at the Masonic Auditorium in San Francisco.

4. An initiative petition was circulated on campus, asking the ASUC Senate to pass a motion supporting the Academic Senate:

> "The ASUC Senate fully supports the position on campus regulations adopted by the Berkeley Academic Senate on Dec. 8, 1964; and urges the Regents to adopt this position as University policy."

5. The Academic Information Committee, an *ad hoc* group, began distribution of pamphlets entitled "A Message on the Proposed Solution to the Free Speech Controversy." The pamphlet is sponsored by Professors Henry Nash Smith, William Kornhauser, Sheldon Wolin, Charles Muscatine, Charles

Sellers and David Freedman. It was prepared by a volunteer committee of the university professional staff.

According to Jay Levine, professor of English and Information Committee Secretary:

"Our main purpose is to publicize the position taken by the Academic Senate . . . We are in no way connected with the FSM . . . Our fund is being used entirely to inform the public of the nature and grounds of the resolution. We're not persuading anyone to do anything."

6. The Berkeley Division of the Academic Senate today elected six members of the Emergency Executive Committee, authorized by Senate motion on Dec. 8.

Elected to the committee were Raymond G. Bressler, professor of agricultural economics; Earl F. Cheit, professor of business administration; Arthur M. Ross, professor of business administration; Carl E. Schorske, professor of history, and Robley C. Williams, professor of molecular biology. Richard W. Jennings, professor of law and chairman of the Berkeley Division, holds an *ex-officio* position on the committee. Professor Ross was elected committee chairman.

December 15

1. James Farmer, national director of the Congress of Racial Equality (CORE), addressed an FSM noon rally while standing on City of Berkeley property, outside the disputed Bancroft-Telegraph area. The rally, originally planned to be held on Sproul Hall steps, was moved as "our token of good faith," according to Steve Weissman, FSM leader. The rally was moved, Weissman said, so as not to alienate either the faculty or the administration. FSM would do nothing to make the faculty's attempt at settlement less effective, and it would do nothing where someone could claim "it's our fault," Weissman said.

The university administration invited Farmer to speak in Pauley Ballroom. But, as FSM spokesman John Sutake explained:

"It was felt it should be an outdoor rally; that is the nature of FSM rallies."

If the "battle for free speech and advocacy" is lost, Farmer warned the crowd of approximately 3,000, it would provide "a tool to turn off the faucet on the mainstay of the civil rights movement." Farmer also praised the protesting students:

"Whenever the battle for equal rights is fought, the students of the University of California are in the forefront . . . I applaud you and salute you. I come as your guest and will lend whatever support I possibly can to your ultimate victory . . ."

Farmer described charges that he was pulling strings in the Free Speech Movement as "absurd" and "ridiculous," but he said he was "not afraid" of being labeled "an outside agitator . . .

"Every housewife knows the value of an agitator. It's the instrument inside the washing machine that bangs around and gets out all the dirt."

Both Steve Weissman and Martin Roysher spoke to the crowd before Farmer was introduced.

Roysher said:

"We have definite interests as students . . . which might indeed be different from the faculty. We the students believe, yes, the faculty and students should have a voice, a determining role, but we should be as equals on this campus. There should be no paternal subordinating relationship between students and the faculty or the administration."

Jacobus Ten Broek, professor of political science who introduced Farmer, avoided the "student voice" reference when he said:

"The faculty and the students have identical interests in broad areas: that students should have the rights guaranteed to them by the Constitution, and that this is an educational institution."

That education, Professor Ten Broek added, should "encourage students' commitment to the action and passion of our time."

2. The newly elected Emergency Executive Committee of the Academic Senate requested a conference with the University Board of Regents during its meeting in Los Angeles, Thursday and Friday, December 17 and 18. The request was delivered to President Kerr's office after two meetings of the committee today. A statement issued by the committee today said:

"The newly elected Emergency Executive Committee met twice today and requested a conference with the board of Regents at its Los Angeles meeting this week. Pledged to support the faculty resolution passed December 8, 1964, by the Berkeley Division of the Academic Senate, the Committee will seek to present the resolution to the Regents as a basis for restoring a campus environment in which teaching, learning and research may be effectively resumed. Under its provisions members of the University community would be assured freedom of political expression under reasonable regulation as to time, place and manner, safeguarding the University's primary academic functions.

"In view of the Committee, these proposals of the Academic Senate fall largely within the framework of the Regents' policies governing political activity enunciated at their meeting of November 20. The committee regards the proposals which will be presented to the Regents as an extension of Chancellor Strong's interpretation of their policies. Accordingly, the committee does not regard itself as in conflict with either the Administration or the Regents.

"The resolution proposes that disciplinary measures in the area of political activity be determined by a Senate committee. The Emergency Executive Committee observed that the Academic Senate had responsibility in this area until 1938, and that present circumstances justify the return of this function to the Senate."

3. The ASUC Senate tonight approved (6–5) a recommendation that the Regents approve the five-point Academic Senate proposal to end the "free speech" controversy. The resolution was introduced by Bob Nakamura, newly elected Slate commuter-independent representative.

December 16

1. State Senator Hugh Burns (D-Fresno), chairman of the State Senate Subcommittee on Un-American Activities, said that his committee will not hold public hearings on the student revolt at Berkeley. Public hearings at this time would serve no useful purpose, Burns said. A hearing "would create a climate which would make it difficult for the University of California Board of Regents to solve the problem," Burns added. He had few kind words for the Free Speech Movement, however, describing it as "a group of malcontents, silly kids and addle-headed teachers, egged on by Communist stooges." The committee would discuss the student revolt in its next report, Burns promised.

2. The ASUC Senate, called into emergency session tonight by President Charles Powell, wrangled over the expenditure of $500 to be spent on forums to discuss the "free speech" issue throughout the state.

The senate passed a resolution last Tuesday night, authorizing the forums and an expenditure of $500 for staging them.

Mike Adams, men's residence hall representative and forum coordinator, planned to spend $200 to print a report compiled by eight graduate political science students. The 40-page report was intended to refute charges of "outside agitation" and "Communist subversion" in the Free Speech Movement.

At the emergency senate meeting, Representative-at-Large Art Shartsis proposed that the $500 could only be spent on physical arrangements. Shartsis' motion specifically forbade printing of the report. "This document (the report) is not factual. It presents only one side," Shartsis said.

The senate voted, 10–2, with one abstention, in favor of Shartsis' motion.

3. A new organization of undergraduate students, called the Undergraduate Association, has grown rapidly since its founding 10 days ago, according to an announcement by Richard Romanoff, founder of the new group. The group already had 700–800 members, Romanoff claimed. Romanoff is a senior in anthropology.

Explaining his group's growth, Romanoff said:

> "A huge number, perhaps even a majority, of the undergraduates feel the ASUC has dismally failed to represent them in any meaningful way . . .
>
> "During the Free Speech Movement crisis the ASUC did nothing whatsoever to speak for the undergraduates, or to guide and aid them. The demand for the Undergraduate Association has grown from the failures of the ASUC."

Earl Salo, a junior in history, added:

> "Many people hope the newly elected members of the (ASUC) Senate from Slate will carry ASUC government out of the sandbox.
>
> "But, it may be the ASUC is structured so it is incapable of effectively taking action for the undergraduates, no matter who its members are. We need an Undergraduate Association to do the things the ASUC Senate is too restricted to do."

Although many members of the new Undergraduate Association were also members of Slate and FSM, Romanoff said the association is entirely independent of Slate and FSM:

> "You don't have to be a member of FSM or agree with its actions to be a member of the Undergraduate Association."

The new association would be organized along departmental lines, Salo said:

> "This way, each department has its own small group to engage in activities that interest only members of that department, and also membership in the central Undergraduate Association, which will be large enough to give the students a real voice in University affairs."

One of the new organization's first activities would be establishment of a tutoring program similar to that announced by the Graduate Co-ordinating Council. Many students who are not in academic difficulty have expressed interest in tutorials as a method of individual communication between teachers, graduates, and undergraduates, Romanoff said:

"The ASUC has done nothing to help undergraduate students achieve a closer contact with graduates and faculty. This will be one of our first objectives."

Other association goals would be improvement of teaching quality, and study, and encouragement of possible course changes and other academic reforms.

December 17

1. Twelve University Regents, including Governor Edmund G. Brown, met with the Emergency Executive Committee of the Berkeley Division of the Academic Senate for two hours in Los Angeles. After the meeting, Governor Brown said he could see little misunderstanding between the faculty and the Regents. Emergency Committee Chairman Arthur Ross called it "a frank discussion." The Academic Senate Committee had requested the meeting Tuesday.

According to Ross:

"This meeting permitted the Committee to make a full presentation of the Berkeley Division resolution of December 8 as a basis for a constructive solution to the crisis at Berkeley."

2. While Berkeley faculty representatives met with the Regents, the statewide Academic Council of the Academic Senate held its own meeting at UCLA. The Academic Council issued its report and recommendations directly to the Board of Regents.

3. During a news conference, President Clark Kerr said:

"We are dealing in difficult areas, such as the distinction between advocacy and action."

The President went on to say that the Regents put up no bars against on-campus advocacy in their meeting of Nov. 20. He also emphasized that the Regents "will not respond to threats."

4. Robert Dussault, founder of University Students for Law and Order, resigned as chairman of that group's executive committee:

"This resignation has become effective, not because of internal policy disagreement or harassment by the opposition, but rather because of immediate responsibilities as indicated by my marriage and January graduation."

USLO would continue as an organization in pursuit of its original goals, Dussault added, but he will act only in an advisory capacity.

December 18

1. The University Board of Regents, meeting in Los Angeles, did not accept the Berkeley Division of the Academic Senate's proposed solution to the "free speech" controversy. Instead, the Regents adopted the following motion:

"1. The Regents direct the administration to preserve law and order on the campuses of the University of California, and to take the necessary steps to insure orderly pursuit of its educational functions.

"2. The Regents reconfirm that ultimate authority for student discipline within the University is constitutionally vested in the Regents, and is a matter not subject to negotiation. Implementation of disciplinary policies will continue to be delegated, as provided in the by-laws and standing orders of the Regents, to the President and Chancellors, who will seek advice of the appropriate faculty committees in individual cases.

"3. The Regents will undertake a comprehensive review of University policies with the intent of providing maximum freedom on campus consistent with individual and group responsibility. A committee of Regents will be appointed to consult with students, faculty and other interested persons and to make recommendations to the board.

"4. Pending results of this study, existing rules will be enforced. The policies of the Regents do not contemplate that advocacy or content of speech shall be restricted beyond the purview of the First and Fourteenth Amendments to the Constitution."

The Regents also issued a four-point statement to the university faculty:

"1. The Regents express appreciation to the Academic Council of the University-wide Senate for its constructive proposals and analysis of recent developments, and welcome the continuing discussion taking place in the divisions of the Academic Senate on the several campuses.

"2. The Regents reaffirm faith in the faculty and student body of the University, and express the conviction that this great academic community is in the process of finding the means to combine the freedom with responsibility under today's new circumstances.

"3. The Regents respect the convictions held by a large

number of students concerning civil rights and individual liberties.

"4. The Regents reaffirm devotion to the First and Fourteenth Amendments to the Constitution, and note that University policies introduced in recent years have liberalized the rules governing expression of opinion on campus. The support of all the University community is essential to provide maximum individual freedom under law consistent with the educational purposes of the University."

Edward W. Carter, chairman of the Board of Regents, stressed that the Board was standing firm on its resolution of Nov. 20, which provided that students could plan lawful off-campus political or social action, with the Regents retaining the right to regulate such activities on-campus.

2. The Emergency Executive Committee of the Berkeley Division of the Academic Senate, which met with 12 Regents yesterday, issued the following statement today:

"Members of the Emergency Executive Committee of the Berkeley Division of the Academic Senate announced today that they believe substantial progress has been made toward solving the problems which have beset the Berkeley campus.

"Our extensive discussion with members of the Board of Regents and with President Kerr, plus the actions of the Regents today, assure that the University will not restrict the content of speech or advocacy on the campus. This was the main point in the resolution passed overwhelmingly by the Berkeley Faculty Senate on December 8, and represents a desirable clarification of University policy sought by student groups.

"It is now clear that the advocacy of ideas and acts, which is constitutionally protected off the campus, will be protected on the campus.

"The Committee is satisfied that President Kerr stands committed personally to follow the policy, announced on December 7, that in view of the cases pending in court, the University will not take additional disciplinary action against students involved in the recent sit-ins.

"The Regents have established a Study Committee and charged it with the urgent mission of reviewing and, where necessary, revising University policy with respect to student political activity. If possible, this assignment is to be completed before the opening of the Spring Semester. The Regents' Committee will consult with students and faculty with the intent of providing maximum freedom with responsibility.

"The Regents reaffirmed their ultimate responsibility

for discipline, and their delegation of authority to the President and the Chancellors. The Emergency Executive Committee believes further study and negotiations must be pursued in order to guarantee procedures which will preserve impartial adjudication of violations in the area of campus political activity.

"The positive attitude of the Regents, their resolution on advocacy, and the current development of new regulations by administrative and faculty committees working with students at Berkeley, make it possible for the campus to return to its primary functions of teaching, learning and research.

"We believe that the base is being established for full political freedom within academic order, and we call on all members of the University community to join in strengthening it."

3. Free Speech Movement leaders were unhappy with the Regents' action.

In Los Angeles, Michael Klein, a Berkeley graduate student and an FSM spokesman, said the Regents' four-point resolution was "an affront to the Academic Senate." He said Free Speech Movement unhappiness with the Regents' action did not, in itself, constitute a threat of "immediate demonstrations . . . But," Klein warned, "if an atrocity is committed, we'll be prepared to take whatever actions are necessary." Such an "atrocity," he said, would be "suspension of the students who participated in the December 3 sit-ins." (*President Kerr said no action is pending against arrested students and teaching assistants.*)

FSM leaders in Berkeley termed the Regents' decision to uphold the administration's authority in discipline on political matters "a repudiation of the policy we've been fighting for."

In a prepared statement, Steve Weissman said:

"We are shocked that the Regents refused (the faculty's) recommendations . . . Despite the efforts of students and faculty, the Regents have decreed that there shall be no change in the policies repudiated by both students and the Academic Senate.

"The students, as in the past, will continue to defend the rights of the academic community. The faculty, we hope, will stand with us in this fight."

Mario Savio declared the Regents' "horrendous action" marked a "tragic day in the history of the university." FSM had not planned a specific response to the Regents' action, Savio said; but, he reminded, "we're moving into a long vacation period that will give us time to speak with the faculty, consolidate our forces, and decide what appropriate action to take."

In an aside, Savio said he was somewhat surprised by the Regents' strong stand:

> "The Board was not as tactically adept as I had suspected they were. I had expected some action less clear."

December 28

The Committee on Academic Freedom of the Berkeley Division of the Academic Senate released its recommendations concerning regulation of student political activity. The report was formally presented to the Academic Senate on January 5.

December 31

Chancellor Edward W. Strong announced the Committee on Academic Freedom's recommendations would go into effect "provisionally" on Monday, January 4, the first day of classes after the holiday recess.

January 1

Chancellor Strong revised his previous statement on implementation of the Committee on Academic Freedom's proposals, adding:

> "The recommendations of the Senate Committee on Academic Freedom contain certain minor points that require further study and clarification.
>
> "The statement by me yesterday should not be taken as implying approval of the committee's recommendations."

January 2

An emergency meeting of the Board of Regents named Martin Meyerson, Dean of the College of Environmental Design, as "acting Chancellor" for the Berkeley campus, replacing Edward W. Strong. Strong was granted a leave of absence "to recuperate from his recent illness." Meyerson's appointment was effective "immediately" and was for an "indefinite" period.

Acting Chancellor Meyerson conducted a series of meetings with faculty, administration and students over the New Year's weekend.

January 3

Acting Chancellor Martin Meyerson issued two statements. The first was addressed to "Colleagues and Students." This statement was primarily Acting Chancellor Meyerson's introduction of himself to the campus community; it included a lengthy discussion of the new chancellor's philosophy, especially as it related to the current crisis. His second statement, issued later in the day, set down provisional rules for political activity on the Berkeley campus:

"The Regents and the President have asked me to issue provisions concerning the time, place and manner of political activity on the Berkeley campus. I shall do so as soon as I have had the opportunity to hear the views of the Berkeley Division of the Academic Senate on the reports of its Committee on Academic Freedom, and the views of others, as they relate to Regents' policies.

"Meanwhile, for political activity during this interim period, the following rules will cover those matters of greatest concern during the next few days:

"1. OPEN DISCUSSION AREA: Until final plans can be developed for a suitable alternate discussion area, the Sproul Hall steps are available for temporary use for this purpose at the noon hour and between 4:00 and 6:00 p.m. Suitable voice amplification will be provided by the University.

"2. TABLES: Student organizations may set up tables in the following areas between 7:00 a.m. and 6:00 p.m.

(a) At the Bancroft and Telegraph entrance.

(b) At the Golden Bear Restaurant area, east of the low concrete wall.

(c) At the North Gate and Tolman Hall areas, and between Kroeber Hall and the Law Building.

(d) Student organizations may receive donations, distribute literature, recruit members, and engage in the sale of such items as buttons, pins, and bumper stickers at the tables. Publications of a student organization may be sold at the tables.

(e) Posters or placards identifying the sponsors are to be attached to the tables and other posters may also be attached.

"3. SPEAKER NOTIFICATION: The required advance notification for off-campus speakers is reduced to 48 hours; the Dean of Students Office will reduce or waive this requirement in those instances in which 48-hour notification is not feasible for reasons beyond the control of the sponsoring organizations.

"Students should refer to the Office of the Dean of Students for necessary clarification.

"The Emergency Executive Committee of the Berkeley Division of the Academic Senate concurs in these rules."

January 4

The Free Speech Movement held its first legal rally on the steps of Sproul Hall at noon.

Between ballads sung by folk singer Joan Baez, FSM

spokesmen expressed dissatisfaction with the proposals of the Committee of Academic Freedom, denounced the new rules for campus political activity, and announced a pending "investigation of the Board of Regents" under the auspices of the American Federation of Teachers.

Discussing the appointment of Acting Chancellor Meyerson, Mario Savio said:

> "The important comment is that the person is nowhere near as important as the pressures on the person from higher up. His statement yesterday was hopeful. He seems to understand the situation, whereas the previous Chancellor (Strong) did not."

THE UC STUDENT PROTESTS: CALIFORNIA POLL
BY MERVIN D. FIELD,
DIRECTOR, *The California Poll*

The student protest movement at the Berkeley campus of the University of California has captured the attention of the public all over the state, and the predominant reaction is one of strong disapproval of the students' actions.

The California Poll has recently completed a survey of public opinion throughout the state and finds that 92 per cent of the adult public has heard or read something about the demonstrations, and 74 per cent of the public takes a disapproving attitude toward them.

A cross section of people was interviewed in mid-January. When asked what they recalled seeing or hearing about the demonstrations, many people characterized them as "riots," "mobs," "strikes," and a significant number spontaneously mentioned that they believe the whole thing was Communist-backed or influenced by other outside sources.

The student protest movement is viewed with approval by fewer than one in five persons, and a clear majority expresses "strong disapproval." The following table shows the replies given by Californians when asked:

"On the whole, how do you personally feel about the student protest movement—would you say you approve strongly, approve with reservations, disapprove somewhat, or disapprove strongly?"

Approve strongly	4%
Approve with reservations	14
Disapprove somewhat	19
Disapprove strongly	55
No opinion	8

The impression which the demonstrations have created in

the public mind has many overtones of violence and disorder as shown by the responses when people are asked to describe what it was that they recall seeing or hearing.

Recall seeing or hearing:

Students wanted freedom of speech	20%
Sit-ins, demonstrations, riots (no mention of free speech)	15
Communist-backed, influenced	13
Students wanted political freedom	11
Mob action, strikes	10
Student riots, demonstrations for free speech	8
Violated laws, insubordinate	6
Students asking for their rights	5
About Mario Savio	5
Non-students, outside agitators involved	4
Students arrested, jailed	4
Students want to have more say, run the school	4

A number of additional items were mentioned by 2 per cent or fewer people such as: "radical, beatnik influence," "about integration," "soliciting funds for political activity," and "choosing speakers on campus."

Younger people and those with more education themselves tended to show a little more approval of the student demonstrations, but majority opinion at all ages and educational levels still is disapproving.

Education	Approve		Disapprove		
	Strongly	Reservations	Somewhat	Strongly	No opinion
Less than high school	3%	10	18	57	12
High school	4%	11	18	58	9
College	5%	29	21	44	*
Age					
21 to 29	3%	17	30	36	14
30 to 39	7%	19	20	47	7
40 to 59	4%	11	14	64	7
60 and over	1%	10	16	65	8

* Less than one-half of 1 per cent.

IV
The Voice of the Actors

It would be impossible to reproduce the sense of the count-less meetings and discussions held during the crisis at Berkeley. One way to give some sense of it all is to reproduce some of the statements issued by various sides. First and most numer-ous are the leaflets of the FSM, itself. What we have here is only a sample. Second, we have included some of the state-ments issued by student opposition groups. These are scanty because such groups only came into existence late in the strug-gle and did not put out many leaflets. Third is a sample of some of the statements issued by a few of the many small but active political groups of varying complexions that concern them-selves with Berkeley events. And finally, we have reprinted some of the statements presented by the administration, the Regents, and the faculty. In the latter case, we have included a selection of statements issued during the controversy by in-dividual faculty. The resolutions passed by the Academic Senate and the Regents have been presented in the Chronology in Section III.

THE FSM SPEAKS

THE POSITION OF THE FREE SPEECH MOVEMENT ON SPEECH AND POLITICAL ACTIVITY*

1. Regulation of Advocacy Under the First Amendment

Civil liberties and political freedoms which are constitu-tionally protected off campus must be equally protected on campus for all persons. Similarly, illegal speech or conduct should receive no greater protection on campus than off cam-pus. The administration, like any other agency of government, may not regulate the content of speech and political conduct. Regulations governing the time, place and manner of exer-cising constitutional rights are necessary for the maintenance and proper operation of university functions, but they must

* *California Monthly*, February, 1965.

not interfere with the opportunity to speak or the content of speech.

In contrast, the university regulations adopted by the Regents on November 20, 1964 and interpreted by the chancellor, read as follows:

> The Regents adopt the policy . . . that certain campus facilities carefully selected and properly regulated, may be used by students and staff for planning, implementing, raising funds or recruiting participants for lawful off-campus action, not for unlawful off-campus action.

By making the distinction between advocating "lawful" and "unlawful" action, the Regents propose to regulate the *content* of speech on campus. It is this distinction that is at the heart of FSM opposition to these regulations. The U. S. Supreme Court has made clear that advocacy of unlawful conduct cannot constitutionally be punished—even in the courts— so long as the advocacy will not clearly and presently cause some substantial evil that is itself illegal.

2. Impropriety of Nonjudicial Forums for Punishing Political Activity

Under the November 20th regulations, if the chancellor accuses a student of advocating an unlawful act, the student and his sponsoring organization are liable to punishment by the university. A student so accused may appear before the Faculty Committee on Student Conduct, whose members are appointed by the chancellor, and whose opinions are only advisory to him.

The Free Speech Movement considers this to be unconstitutional and unwise for the following two reasons.

(1) Since such a procedure allows the chancellor to assume the role of prosecutor, judge and jury simultaneously, the students have no confidence that the final verdict will be fair. In fact, the history of the treatment of civil liberties cases by the campus administration reveals an insensitivity to safeguarding such liberties.

Further, the fact that the administration is peculiarly vulnerable to pressures originating outside the university should remove it from consideration as the proper authority for determining guilt or innocence in the extremely sensitive area of speech, assembly and protest within the First Amendment. It must be emphasized that the current crisis has not developed in a vacuum. These rules work a grave hardship on the civil-rights movement in Northern California. Organizations in this movement rely heavily on negotiations, demonstrations, picketing and other such legal tactics. It is true, however, that in order to focus attention on a serious injustice and to bring pressure to bear for its correction, civil-rights workers sometimes employ tactics which result in violation of law. Without passing on the propriety of such acts, the Free Speech Movement insists that the question whether their *advocacy* is legal or illegal must be left to the courts, which are institutionally independent of the shifting pressures of the community. Moreover, the standard that the chancellor is free to apply is only one of "responsibility" of the act of advocacy for the act advocated, which is far more inclusive and vague than the "clear and present danger" test. Hence, guilt is likely to be found upon much less substantial and compelling grounds than would be necessary to obtain conviction for illegal advocacy in a court of law. Students are convinced that the regulations providing for such a hearing are the direct result of pressures generated by the civil-rights movement in the surrounding community, and enable the administration to respond to such pressures by disciplining student civil-rights workers.

(2) Even if complete mutual trust existed between the administration and the student body, and even if the university attempted to observe the requirements of due process, it would be impossible for it to provide all of the safeguards of our judicial system, or otherwise to fulfill the functions of a court. The points in controversy, relating to the degree of responsibility of an act of advocacy for an act advocated, are of such a delicate and complex nature that even the courts have not built up wholly adequate precedents. Certainly, then, a non-judicial body should be considered incompetent in this area.

On the other hand, the students' position that the courts alone have jurisdiction does not in any way imply the creation of a haven for illegal activity on the campus. On the contrary, it involves just the opposite of this—the *removal* of any special protection the university may now afford, as well as any extra-legal punishment. The student becomes subject to the same process of trial and punishment for illegal acts that all other citizens must accept.

3. On-Campus Regulation of the Form of Free Expression.

The Free Speech Movement recognizes the necessity for regulations ensuring that political activity and speech do not interfere with the formal educational functions of the university. Rallies must not be held so as to disturb classes, block traffic, damage university property, conflict with other scheduled public meetings or rallies, etc. Such regulation is purely formal; no discretion to regulate the *content* of speech can constitutionally be permitted the controlling authority. Further, the regulations must be carefully tailored to protect or promote these state interests without unduly burdening the opportunity to speak, hear, or engage in political activity on the campus.

At the present time, university regulations governing the

form of expression on the campus are promulgated by the administration, while other segments of the university community are limited to a purely advisory capacity. It is the general position of the Free Speech Movement that those persons and organizations subject to regulations must have a part in their final enactment. It is especially important as a safeguard against abuse or factual error that students share the responsibility for promulgating regulations over the form of speech. The administration has demonstrated many times its propensity to plead the necessity to regulate form as an excuse for regulating content. For example, the administration has until recently designated a place removed from the area of normal student traffic as the sole "Hyde Park area," thus seriously hampering access to listeners. As the local ACLU has pointed out,

> a denial of certain avenues of such access (such as the open areas of the campus) with the claim that there are others, which though perhaps not as desirable are nonetheless available, will not avoid violation of the First Amendment unless the government entity . . . can demonstrate that there are no available alternative means of achieving its purposes, and that the purposes in question are so necessary as to be, in the language of the Court, "compelling."

Students have thus regarded the designation of such an area as an unreasonable and unconstitutional restriction and refused to accede to it.

Because of such past experience, and because of the important principle of democratic self-government involved, the Free Speech Movement has taken the position that final regulation of the form of exercise of speech should be by a tripartite committee, consisting of representatives chosen independently by the students, faculty and administration.

OCCASIONAL LITERATURE

*The Administration: Bungling Friend or Deliberate Enemy?**

The issue is free speech.

Early this semester we were confronted with administrative rulings drastically reducing political activity on campus. The rights to solicit members, to collect funds, to advocate action in off-campus projects, rights students have always had at Cal, were abolished by administrative fiat. The rulings were the response of a single individual, Chancellor Strong, to right-

* Leaflet of October 15, 1964.

wing political pressure. They had absolutely no basis in law, reason, tradition, or general Regents' policy.

Administration officials frustrated all our attempts to explain that these rulings were unacceptable restrictions on our freedom of speech. Rights unexercised are lost, so we finally disregarded the new restrictions and continued normal campus political activity. In retaliation, the administration singled out eight participating students and suspended them. When Chancellor Strong ordered Jack Weinberg's arrest, our protest spontaneously grew to a massive sit-in around the police car. Under the pressure of this demonstration, Clark Kerr finally agreed to meet with student representatives, and thirty-three and one-half hours after Jack's arrest an agreement was signed.

In order to understand the meaning of that agreement, it is essential to consider the circumstances under which it was reached. The administration had repeatedly announced to the press, even while the negotiations were in progress, that it would not accede to the students' demands and that it would not compromise on any aspect of the new restrictions. Our minimum demands were that the eight suspended students be reinstated, that Jack immediately be released, and that the administration meet with us to discuss the new rulings. The administration could not meet our demands without losing face; we could not accept the new rulings and the administration's punitive actions without betraying our commitment to free speech. However, the situation of Friday evening was explosive. Hundreds of policemen, armed with clubs, were ready to move in on the crowd of demonstrators and make mass arrests. An agreement had to be reached.

Since the administration could not lose face, the agreement had to be worded to allow intermediate agencies to make the concessions we demanded. Thus the cases of the eight students were to be turned over to the Student Conduct Committee of the Academic Senate and acted on within a week, Jack was to be booked but then released, and a joint faculty-student-administration committee was to be set up to review the new restrictions and make recommendations to the administration. President Kerr assured us that he would consider carefully our recommendations for members to sit on this committee and told us that we had to have some trust in the administration.

Now, what has happened to this agreement? The cases of the suspended students were supposed to be referred to the Student Conduct Committee of the Academic Senate, but no such committee of the Academic Senate exists. In fact, the cases were referred to a committee appointed by Chancellor Strong. The duration of the suspensions was to be decided within a week. Almost two weeks have passed and the students have not had a hearing before any committee at all. President Kerr promised to consider student recommendations for the joint faculty-student-administration committee, yet when the Free Speech Movement tried to contact him during the weekend with its recommendations, he was consistently unavailable. Monday morning the names of the committee members appeared in the newspapers.

President Kerr had demonstrated bad faith even before this. As the students, in compliance with the agreement, dispersed from around the police car, Kerr was holding a press conference. He smeared and red-baited the entire Free Speech Movement. He said the students used "Communist tactics," whatever those are. Forty per cent of the leadership, Kerr said, were non-students (they were, of course, students suspended by the administration). He even was quoted in the *Examiner* of October 3 as saying that 49 per cent of the students "followed the Mao-Castro line"!

President Kerr told us that we should trust the administration. His statements and actions, from the moment the agreement was signed, have betrayed our trust.

The agreement is broken, but our demands remain. How can we achieve them now? It is ridiculous to think that an administration-appointed committee, whose recommendations will finally be approved or rejected by the administration, will upset the administration's rules. Why then has the study committee been set up?

The answer is simple. Committees mean delay, and delay, even for so short a time as until midterms, means the death of large-scale student protest. Furthermore, because the joint committee has no power and is ostensibly a neutral, objective body, it serves as a buffer between the students and the administration. The recommendations of a committee two-thirds composed of administration and faculty will be a compromise of our demands. The administration will then compromise with this compromise. We cannot sit back and allow a third party, however neutral, to negotiate in our behalf. We cannot settle for less than our full rights as citizens.

As long as we allow the administration to maintain the initiative, any concessions to free speech will be a dispensation, not a restoration of our rights. We therefore cannot afford to participate in their committees, under their rules and their control.

The issue is free speech.

Why Are UC Students Still Not Satisfied?!!*

The Regents' meeting of November 20 resulted in surprisingly harsh rulings concerning the dispute over political activity on the Berkeley campus.

* Leaflet of November 24, 1964.

I. Although the Heyman Committee recommended that six of the eight students suspended on September 30 *should not have been suspended at all,* the Regents voted to confirm their suspensions; in addition, while voting to reinstate all eight, the Regents decided that Mario Savio and Art Goldberg should be placed on probation for the rest of this semester. Such probation could easily result in expulsion for both, because they have been in repeated violation of university regulations since September 30.

II. The Regents voted to allow the administration to take disciplinary action against students, staff, and organizations who advocate illegal off-campus actions. The wording of the resolution is ambiguous, and the responsibility for interpreting it is given to Chancellor Strong. The Regents rejected without consideration the proposals concerning political freedom made by various faculty members, the ASUC Senate, and the FSM.

These rulings (and others not discussed here) stunned the 5000 students awaiting the Regents' decision outside University Hall. It is the consensus of students involved in the controversy that the rulings are unconstitutional and unacceptable. The university must not set itself up as a secondary court, to punish students for actions which are liable to civil court action.

Chancellor Strong said in the *Daily Cal* Monday that "there will be no prior determination or double jeopardy in matters of political and social activities organized on the campus by students and staff." That's fine, for now. But the essential thing is that he can make "prior determination" not only of the *act of advocacy* but also of the *act advocated.* He can take disciplinary action against students—whether they are subjected to court action or not—*if he decides to do so at any time in the future.* This is clearly intolerable.

The Academic Senate is meeting this afternoon to discuss the Eli Katz case. This case involves the refusal by the administration, and specifically by the chancellor, to rehire Professor Katz, despite the recommendation of the German Department that he be rehired. In that instance the chancellor interpreted his powers as the case demanded. Professor Katz was not rehired as a direct result of insisting on his constitutional rights.

There is a close connection betweeen the Katz case and the free-speech controversy, and we hope that the Academic Senate will consider this fact. Specifically, we expect the senate to take a stand against the Regents' rulings. Up until today the faculty has played the role of mediator in the dispute between the administration and the students. In so doing, the faculty has seriously compromised the principles of the First and Fourteenth Amendments. The faculty, by its compromising proposals, has allowed the administration to becloud the principles involved.

LET THE FACULTY NOW STAND UP AND UNEQUIVOCALLY
SUPPORT THE STUDENTS OF THIS CAMPUS IN THEIR JUST
DEMANDS FOR FULL POLITICAL FREEDOM.

We urge all students to attend the Academic Senate meeting today—place as yet undetermined.

WE WANT A UNIVERSITY*
(DEDICATED TO THE 800)
BY THE FREE SPEECH MOVEMENT

At present in the United States, students—middle class youth—are the major exploited class. The labor of intelligent youth *is* needed, and they are accordingly subjected to tight scheduling, speedup, and other factory exploitative methods. Then it is not surprising if they organize their CIO. It is frivolous to tell them to go elsewhere if they don't like the rules, for they have no choice but to go to college, and one factory is like another.

Paul Goodman

. . . we get a four year long series of sharp staccatos: eight semesters, forty courses, one hundred twenty or more "units," ten to fifteen impersonal lectures *per week*, one to three oversized discussion meetings per week led by poorly paid graduate student "teachers." Over a period of four years the student-cog receives close to forty bibliographies; evaluation amounts to little more than pushing the exam button, which results in over one hundred regurgitations in four years and the writing of twenty to thirty-five papers in four years in this context means that they are of necessity technically and substantially poor due to lack of time for thought.

Brad Cleaveland

Throughout the semester, the FSM has been producing leaflets and pamphlets at a furious pace. We have been patient, repetitious, sometimes boring; we have tried to explain what we're doing and who we are. As we look back at our written communications of the semester, we discover that to some extent we have failed. Each day was an emergency, a crisis, so that although we said important things, issues arose which were not of the moment—important issues which we have not

* Distributed January 4, 1965.

adequately discussed. We take this opportunity to more fully discuss our movement, the university, and our education.

The Free Speech Movement

FSM: MORAL IMPETUS, THE FACTORY, AND THE SOCIETY

I. The Moral Impetus

Our stand *has* been moral. We feel, that to a great extent, our movement has accomplished something which so many of the movements of the past few generations have failed to accomplish. We have tried, in the context of a mass movement, to act politically with moral justification. We have tried to be sensitive to each of our supporters and the individual morality he has brought to the movement. This is what has been unique about our movement.

Although our issue has been free speech, our theme has been solidarity. When individual members of our community have acted, we joined together as a community to jointly bear the responsibility for their actions. We have been able to revitalize one of the most distorted, misused, and important words of our century: comrade. The concept of living cannot be separated from the concept of other people. In our practical, fragmented society, too many of us have been alone. By being willing to stand up for others, and by knowing that others are willing to stand up for us, we have gained more than political power, we have gained personal strength. Each of us who has acted, now knows that he is a being willing to act.

No one can presume to explain why so many thousands have become part of the Free Speech Movement. All we can say is what each of us felt: something was wrong; something had to be done. It wasn't just that student political rights had been abridged; much more was wrong. Something had to be done about political rights, and in actively trying to cope with political rights we found ourselves confronting the entire Berkeley experience. The Berkeley campus has become a new place since the beginning of the semester. Many are trying to tell us that what we are trying to do may destroy the university. We are fully aware that we are doing something which has implicit proportions so immense as to be frightening. We are frightened of our power as a movement; but it is a healthy fear. We must not allow our fear to lead us into believing that we are being destructive. We are beginning to *build* a great university. So long as the students stand united in firmness and dignity, and the faculty stands behind us, the university cannot be destroyed. As students, we have already demonstrated our strength and dedication; the faculty has yet to show it can do its share. Some faculty members have stated that if what they call "anarchy" continues, then they will leave the university to seek *employment* elsewhere. Such faculty members who would leave at this point would compromise themselves by an antiseptic solution to a problem of personal anguish, rather than stay and fight for a great university. There is reason to fear these professors, for *they* can destroy the university by deserting it.

And sadly there is reason to believe that even after all of the suffering which has occurred in our community, the overwhelming majority of faculty members have not been permanently changed, have not joined our community, *have not really listened to our voices*—at this late date. For a moment on December 8th, eight hundred and twenty-four professors gave us all a glimpse—a brief, glorious vision—of the university as a loving community. If only the Free Speech Movement could have ended that day! But already the professors have compromised away much for which they stood on that day. They have shamed themselves in view of the students and their colleagues all over the country. The ramparts of rationalization which our society's conditioning had erected about our professors' souls were breached by the relentless hammerblows of conscience springing from thousands of students united in something called "FSM." But the searing light of their momentary courage became nakedness to them—too painful to endure. After December 8th most faculty members moved quickly to rebuild their justifications for years of barren compromise.

We challenge the faculty to be courageous. A university is a community of students and scholars: be equal to the position of dignity you should hold!! How long will you submit to the doorkeepers who have usurped your power? Is a university no more than a physical plant and an administration? The university cannot be destroyed unless its core is destroyed, and our movement is not weakening that core but strengthening it. Each time the FSM planned to act, it was warned that to act was to destroy. Each time, however, the campus community responded with new vigor. Too many people underestimate the resilience of a community fighting for a principle. Internally, the health of the university is improving. Communication, spirit, moral and intellectual curiosity, all have increased. The faculty has been forced to take the student body more seriously; it has begun to respect students. Furthermore, it has gained the opportunity to achieve a profound respect from the students. Those professors at Cal and other universities who love to teach, should be looking to Berkeley as the nation's greatest reservoir of students who embody the vital balance of moral integrity and high intellectual calibre. If the university community can maintain its courage, stand firmly together in the face of attacks from without, it will survive. Those who fearfully warn that we are destroying the university, are unwittingly weakening the FSM and the university. In the final analysis, only fear destroys!

II. Free Speech and the Factory

In our fight for free speech we said the "machine" must stop. We said that we must put our bodies on the line, on the machinery, in the wheels and gears, and that the "knowledge factory" must be brought to a halt. Now we must begin to clarify, for ourselves, what we mean by "factory."

We need to clarify this because the issues of free speech and the factory, of politics and education on the campus, are in danger of becoming separated. For example, the press has had the tendency to assert this separation when they insist that we return to our studies; that we are not in a center for political activity, but a center for education. Likewise, the faculty betrays the same tendency in its desire to settle the free speech issue as quickly and quietly as possible in order that we may return to the "normal conduct" of our "great university."

In contrast to this tendency to separate the issues, many thousands of *us,* the Free Speech Movement, have asserted that politics and education are inseparable, that the *political* issue of the First and Fourteenth Amendments and the *educational issue* cannot be separated. In place of "great university," we have said "impersonal bureaucracy," "machine," or "knowledge factory." If we emerge as victors from our long and still hard-to-be-won battle for free speech, will we then be returning to *less* than a factory? *Is* this a great university? If we are to take *ourselves* seriously we must define precisely what we meant when we said "knowledge factory."

The best way to identify the parts of our multiversity machinery is simply observe it "stripped down" to the bare essentials. In the context of a dazzling circus of "bait," which obscures our vision of the machinery, we get a four-year-long series of sharp staccatos: eight semesters, forty courses, one hundred twenty or more "units," ten to fifteen impersonal lectures *per week,* one to three oversized discussion meetings per week led by poorly paid graduate student "teachers." Over a period of four years the student-cog receives close to forty bibliographies; evaluation amounts to little more than pushing the test button, which results in over one hundred regurgitations in four years; and the writing of twenty to thirty-five "papers" in four years, in this context means that they are of necessity technically and substantially poor due to a lack of time for thought. The course-grade-unit system structure, resting on the foundation of departmentalization, produces knowledge for the student-cog which has been exploded into thousands of bits and is force-fed, by the coercion of grades. We all know what happens when we really get "turned on" by a great idea, a great man, or a great book: we pursue that interest at the risk of flunking out. The pursuit of thought, a painful but highly exhilarating process, requires, above all, the element of time.

Human nerves and flesh are transmuted under the pressure and stress of the university routine. It is as though we have become raw material in the strictly *in*organic sense. But the Free Speech Movement has given us an extraordinary taste of what it means to be part of something organic. Jumping off the conveyors, we have become a community of furiously talking, feeling, and thinking human beings. If we take seriously our common agreement that we stopped a "machine" how can we be accused of conspiring to destroy a "great university"? Where?

The history of rather volcanic emotions which led up to the eruption of the Free Speech Movement did not result from thin air. It came from within *us*. On November 29 a letter appeared in the *New York Times Magazine*. It is a beautiful and sad letter from a young girl, and describes well the "volcanic activity" in all of us.

To the Editor:

"I'm a student in the oldest girls' school in the country. I love my school, but your recent article on homework really hit home (Hard Day's Night of Today's Students by Eda J. LeShan). I came to this school not thinking I could even keep up with the work. I was wrong. I can keep up. I can even come out on top. My daily schedule's rough: I get up at 6:30 and have classes from 8:15 to 3:00 and stay in study hall or engage in activities until 5:30. I have majors, plus religion, speech, music, and art once or twice a week. I have gym four times a week. All this I can take. The homework I can't. I work from 3:00 until 5:00 in school.

After dinner I work until midnight or 12:30. In the beginning, the first two weeks or so, I'm fine. Then I begin to wonder just what this is all about: Am I educating myself? I have that one all answered in my mind. I'm educating myself the way THEY want. So I convince myself the real reason I'm doing all this is to prepare myself for what I really want. Only one problem. After four years of this comes four years of college and two of graduate school for me. I know just where I'm going and just what I want, but I'm impatient.

Okay, I can wait. But meanwhile I'm wasting those years of preparation. I'm not learning what I want to learn. I don't care any more whether $2 + 2 = 4$ anymore. I don't care about the feudal system. I want to know about life. I want to think and read. When? Over weekends when there are projects and lectures and compositions, plus catching up on sleep.

My life is a whirlpool. I'm caught up in it but I'm not conscious of it. I'm what YOU call living, but somehow I can't find life. Days go by in an instant. I feel nothing accomplished in that instant. So maybe I got an A on that composition I worked on for three hours, but when I get it back I find that A means nothing. It's a letter YOU use to keep me going.

Every day I come in well prepared. Yet I dread every class; my stomach tightens and I sit tense. I drink coffee morning, noon, and night. At night, after my homework I lie in bed and wonder if I've really done it all. Is there something I've forgotten?

At the beginning of the year I'm fine. My friends know me by my smile. Going to start out bright this year. Not going to get bogged down this year. Weeks later I become introspective and moody again. I wonder what I'm doing here. I feel phony; I don't belong. All I want is time; time to sit down and read what I want to read, and think what I want to think.

You wonder about juvenile delinquents. If I ever become one, I'll tell you why it will be so. I feel cramped. I feel like I'm in a coffin and can't move or breathe. There's no air or light. All I can see is blackness and I've got to burst. Sometimes I feel maybe something will come along. Something has to or I'm not worth anything. My life is worth nothing. It's enclosed in a few buildings on one campus; it goes no further. I've got to bust."

NAME WITHHELD

P.S. I wrote this last night at 12:15 and in the light of day I realize this will never *reach* you.

This letter is probably one of the most profoundly shared expressions of anguish in American life today. It is shared by millions of us.

III. The Factory and the Society

The emotions expressed in that letter reflect the problems of the society as expressed in the multiversity as well as in a small prep school for girls in the East. The university has become grotesquely distorted into a "multiversity"; a public utility serving the purely technical needs of a society. In Clark Kerr's words, it is a factory for the production of knowledge and technicians to service society's many bureaucracies.

Current federal and private support programs for the university have been compared to classic examples of imperialism and neocolonialism. The government has invested in underdeveloped, capital-starved institutions, and imposed a pattern of growth and development upon them, which if disrupted, would lead to economic breakdown and political chaos.

Research and training replace scholarship and learning. In this system even during the first two years, the student is pressured to specialize or endure huge, impersonal lecture courses. He loses contact with his professors as they turn more to research and publishing, and away from teaching. His professors lose contact with one another as they serve a discipline and turn away from dialogue. Forms and structures stifle humane learning.

The student is powerless even to affect those aspects of the university supposedly closest to him. His student "government" by political castrates is a fraud permitted to operate only within limits imposed autocratically by the administration. Thus it is constitutionally mandated to serve the status quo. Likewise, the student has no power over the social regulations which affect his privacy, and little influence in shaping the character of the dormitories in which he lives. The university assumes the role of the parent.

As a human being seeking to enrich himself, the student has no place in the multiversity. Instead he becomes a mercenary, paid off in grades, status, and degrees, all of which can eventually be cashed in for hard currency on the job market. His education is not valued for its enlightenment and the freedom it should enable him to enjoy, but for the amount of money it will enable him to make. Credits for courses are subtly transformed into credit cards as the multiversity inculcates the values of the acquisitive society.

It has been written that "The main concern of the university should not be with the publishing of books, getting money from legislators, lobbying for federal aid, wooing the rich, producing bombs and deadly bacteria." Nor should it be with passing along the morality of the middle class, nor the morality of the white man, nor even the morality of the potpourri we call "western society." Nor should it be with acting as a second household or church for the young man away from home, nor as a playground for twisters, neophyte drinkers, and pledge classes. Already the parallels between the university and the habits of the society are many; the parallels between our academic and financial systems of credit, between competition for grades and for chamber of commerce awards, between cheating and price rigging, and between statements of "Attendance is a privilege, not a right," and "We reserve the right to refuse service to anyone."

In an article in the current *New York Review of Books*,

Paul Goodman poignantly comments upon the plight of the modern student: "At present in the United States, students—middle class youth—are the major exploited class, (Negroes, small farmers, the aged are rather outcast groups; their labor is not needed and they are not wanted). The labor of intelligent youth *is* needed and they are accordingly subjected to tight scheduling, speedup and other factory exploitative methods. Then it is not surprising if they organize their CIO. It is frivolous to tell them to go elsewhere if they don't like the rules; for they have no choice but to go to college, and one factory is like another."

In saying these things it is important to avoid a certain misunderstanding. By identifying the parts of the machinery in our factory, the way in which we have described them, and their blending into our society of institutionalized greed, might lead people to assume that we have a fundamental bias against institutions as such; that we wish to destroy the structure altogether, to establish politics on the campus, and lash out against the power structure for the purposes of expressing a kind of collective orgasm of seething resentment against the "power structure." When we assert that free speech and the factory, or politics and education, are bound up together, we are again pointing to the obvious. In a twentieth-century industrial state, ignorance will be the definition of slavery. If centers of education fail, they will be the producers of the twentieth-century slave. To put it in more traditionally American terms, popular government cannot survive without education for the people. The people are more and more in the schools. But the pressure of the logistics of mass popular education combined with excessive greed has resulted in the machinery of the educational process having displaced the freedom to learn. We must now begin the demand of the right to know; to know the realities of the present world-in-revolution, and to have an opportunity to learn how to think clearly in an extended manner about that world. It is ours to demand meaning; we must insist upon meaning!

The Free University of California

The question of how to break down the machinery and build "intellectual communities worthy of the hopes and responsibilities of our people," is one of the minds of many participants in the Free Speech Movement. No one supposes he has the answers, but they can come from the Berkeley community. Our task is to generate these answers and to discover how they can be implemented. The Free Speech Movement proposes that the Free University of California be formed. We are inviting prominent intellectual and political figures to address the university community. We would like to see seminars on the educational revolution and many other topics which are not considered in the university. In the near future we hope that discussions with students, faculty, and members of the community, will take place independent of the university community. Such discussions would deal with any topic in which a sufficient number of people are interested. We would like to establish the availability of a revolutionary experience in education. If we succeed, we will accomplish a feat more radical and significant than anything the Free Speech Movement has attempted. We will succeed in beginning to bring humanity back to campus.

AN END TO HISTORY*

BY MARIO SAVIO, STUDENT IN THE DEPARTMENT OF PHILOSOPHY, BERKELEY, AND MEMBER FSM STEERING COMMITTEE

For this anthology I originally intended to revise thoroughly my article, "An End to History." I have since changed my mind, deciding to have it reprinted as first taken from a tape made in Sproul Hall, the Berkeley administration building, during the December sit-in. I find the article does not even conform to the subject of the title. But I also believe that a positive purpose would be served by preserving the text.—Mario Savio

Last summer I went to Mississippi to join the struggle there for civil rights. This fall I am engaged in another phase of the same struggle, this time in Berkeley. The two battlefields may seem quite different to some observers, but this is not the case. The same rights are at stake in both places—the right to participate as citizens in democratic society and the right to due process of law. Further, it is a struggle against the same enemy. In Mississippi an autocratic and powerful minority rules, through organized violence, to suppress the vast, virtually powerless majority. In California, the privileged minority manipulates the university bureaucracy to suppress the students' political expression. That "respectable" bureaucracy masks the financial plutocrats; that impersonal bureaucracy is the efficient enemy in a "Brave New World."

In our free-speech fight at the University of California, we have come up against what may emerge as the greatest problem of our nation—depersonalized, unresponsive bureaucracy. We have encountered the organized status quo in Mississippi, but it is the same in Berkeley. Here we find it impossible usually to meet with anyone but secretaries. Beyond that, we

* From *Humanity, an arena of critique and commitment*, No. 2, December 1964.

find functionaries who cannot make policy but can only hide behind the rules. We have discovered total lack of response on the part of the policy makers. To grasp a situation which is truly Kafkaesque, it is necessary to understand the bureaucratic mentality. And we have learned quite a bit about it this fall, more outside the classroom than in.

As bureaucrat, an administrator believes that nothing new happens. He occupies an a-historical point of view. In September, to get the attention of this bureaucracy which had issued arbitrary edicts suppressing student political expression and refused to discuss its action, we held a sit-in on the campus. We sat around a police car and kept it immobilized for over thirty-two hours. At last, the administrative bureaucracy agreed to negotiate. But instead, on the following Monday, we discovered that a committee had been appointed, in accordance with usual regulations, to resolve the dispute. Our attempt to convince any of the administrators that an event had occurred, that something new had happened, failed. They saw this simply as something to be handled by normal university procedures.

The same is true of all bureaucracies. They begin as tools, means to certain legitimate goals, and they end up feeding their own existence. The conception that bureaucrats have is that history has in fact come to an end. No events can occur now that the Second World War is over which can change American society substantially. We proceed by standard procedures as we are.

The most crucial problems facing the United States today are the problem of automation and the problem of racial injustice. Most people who will be put out of jobs by machines will not accept an end to events, this historical plateau, as the point beyond which no change occurs. Negroes will not accept an end to history here. All of us must refuse to accept history's final judgment that in America there is no place in society for people whose skins are dark. On campus students are not about to accept it as fact that the university has ceased evolving and is in its final state of perfection, that students and faculty are respectively raw material and employees, or that the university is to be autocratically run by unresponsive bureaucrats.

Here is the real contradiction: the bureaucrats hold history as ended. As a result significant parts of the population both on campus and off are dispossessed, and these dispossessed are not about to accept this a-historical point of view. It is out of this that the conflict has occurred with the university bureaucracy and will continue to occur until that bureaucracy becomes responsive or until it is clear the university cannot function.

The things we are asking for in our civil-rights protests have a deceptively quaint ring. We are asking for the due process of law. We are asking for our actions to be judged by committees of our peers. We are asking that regulations ought to be considered as arrived at legitimately only from the consensus of the governed. These phrases are all pretty old, but they are not being taken seriously in America today, nor are they being taken seriously on the Berkeley campus.

I have just come from a meeting with the Dean of Students. She notified us that she was aware of certain violations of university regulations by certain organizations. University friends of Student Non-violent Coordinating Committee, which I represent, was one of these. We tried to draw from her some statement on these great principles, consent of the governed, jury of one's peers, due process. The best she could do was to evade or to present the administration party line. It is very hard to make any contact with the human being who is behind these organizations.

The university is the place where people begin seriously to question the conditions of their existence and raise the issue of whether they can be committed to the society they have been born into. After a long period of apathy during the fifties, students have begun not only to question but, having arrived at answers, to act on those answers. This is part of a growing understanding among many people in America that history has not ended, that a better society is possible, and that it is worth dying for.

This free-speech fight points up a fascinating aspect of contemporary campus life. Students are permitted to talk all they want so long as their speech has no consequences.

One conception of the university, suggested by a classical Christian formulation, is that it be in the world but not of the world. The conception of Clark Kerr by contrast is that the university is part and parcel of this particular stage in the history of American society; it stands to serve the need of American industry; it is a factory that turns out a certain product needed by industry or government. Because speech does often have consequences which might alter this perversion of higher education, the university must put itself in a position of censorship. It can permit two kinds of speech, speech which encourages continuation of the status quo, and speech which advocates changes in it so radical as to be irrelevant in the foreseeable future. Someone may advocate radical change in all aspects of American society, and this I am sure he can do with impunity. But if someone advocates sit-ins to bring about changes in discriminatory hiring practices, this cannot be permitted because it goes against the status quo of which the university is a part. And that is how the fight began here.

The administration of the Berkeley campus has admitted that external, extra-legal groups have pressured the university not to permit students on campus to organize picket lines, not to permit on campus any speech with consequences. And the bureaucracy went along. Speech with consequences, speech in the area of civil rights, speech which some might regard as illegal, must stop.

Many students here at the university, many people in society, are wandering aimlessly about. Strangers in their own lives, there is no place for them. They are people who have not learned to compromise, who for example have come to the university to learn to question, to grow, to learn—all the standard things that sound like clichés because no one takes them seriously. And they find at one point or other that for them to become part of society, to become lawyers, ministers, businessmen, people in government, that very often they must compromise those principles which were most dear to them. They must suppress the most creative impulses that they have; this is a prior condition for being part of the system. The university is well structured, well tooled, to turn out people with all the sharp edges worn off, the well-rounded person. The university is well equipped to produce that sort of person, and this means that the best among the people who enter must for four years wander aimlessly much of the time questioning why they are on campus at all, doubting whether there is any point in what they are doing, and looking toward a very bleak existence afterward in a game in which all of the rules have been made up, which one cannot really amend.

It is a bleak scene, but it is all a lot of us have to look forward to. Society provides no challenge. American society in the standard conception it has of itself is simply no longer exciting. The most exciting things going on in America today are movements to change America. America is becoming ever more the utopia of sterilized, automated contentment. The "futures" and "careers" for which American students now prepare are for the most part intellectual and moral wastelands. This chrome-plated consumers' paradise would have us grow up to be well-behaved children. But an important minority of men and women coming to the front today have shown that they will die rather than be standardized, replaceable and irrelevant.

THE FREE SPEECH MOVEMENT
AND CIVIL RIGHTS

BY JACK WEINBERG, FORMER TEACHING ASSISTANT IN
MATHEMATICS AT THE UNIVERSITY OF CALIFORNIA,
CURRENTLY CHAIRMAN OF CAMPUS CORE AND A MEMBER
OF THE FSM STEERING COMMITTEE

Over the past several months the relationship between the
Berkeley Free Speech Movement and the civil-rights movement has become almost a cliché. Those who view the FSM
merely as an extension of the civil-rights movement, merely
as a battle to enable student civil-rights groups to maintain
the campus as a base for their operations, have a very incomplete understanding of the FSM, and probably an incomplete
understanding of the student civil-rights movement. In this article we discuss the student civil-rights movement and its relation to the FSM, the FSM as an on-campus protest, and the
implications of both the FSM and the student civil-rights movement for American society.

I. FSM and the Civil-Rights Movement

Over the past few years, there has been a change, both
quantitative and qualitative in Bay Area student political activity. Until 1963, only a relatively small number of students
had been actively involved in the civil-rights movement. Furthermore, until that time, student political activity of all kinds
was quite impotent in terms of any real effect it had on the
general community. Organizations such as peace groups raised
demands which were so momentous as to be totally unat-
tainable. Civil-rights groups, on the other hand, often raised
demands which were attainable but quite inconsequential; a
job or a house for an individual Negro who had been dis-
criminated against. In no way was student political activity a
threat, or even a serious nuisance to large power interests. In
early 1963, a new precedent in the Bay Area civil-rights movement was established; civil-rights organizations began demanding that large employers integrate their work forces on more
than a mere token basis. Hundreds of jobs would be at stake
in a single employment action. In the fall of 1963, a second
important precedent was established. Starting with the demonstrations at Mel's Drive-in, large numbers of students became
involved in the civil-rights movement. And as they joined, the
movement adopted more militant tactics. Thus with more significant issues at stake and with more powerful weapons available, the civil-rights movement became a threat, or at least a

real nuisance to the power interests. Not only was the civil-rights movement, "a bunch of punk kids," forcing employers to change their policies, but it was also beginning to upset some rather delicate political balances.

Attempts were made by the civil authorities and the power interests to contain the movement: harassing trials, biased news reporting, job intimidation, etc. But the attempts were unsuccessful, the movement grew, became more sophisticated, and began exploring other fronts on which it could attack the power structure. Throughout the summer of 1964, Berkeley Campus CORE maintained a hectic level of continuous and effective activity. The Ad Hoc Committee to End Discrimination planned and began executing a project against the Oakland *Tribune*. Since those who wished to contain the civil-rights movement found no effective vehicles in the community, they began pressuring the university. Because a majority of participants were students, they maintained that the university was responsible. After initially resisting the pressure, the university finally succumbed and promulgated restrictive regulations with the intent of undercutting the base of student support for the civil-rights movement. The reactions to these regulations should have been predictable: immediate protest and a demand for their repeal. Since the civil-rights movement was responsible for the pressures applied to the university which led to the suppression of free speech and free political expression and their interests were the ones most seriously threatened, the civil-rights activists took the lead in protesting the suppression, and many concluded that the FSM is an extension of the civil-rights movement.

II. The FSM as Campus Protest

But if we view the FSM simply as an extension of the civil-rights movement, we cannot explain the overwhelming support it has received from students who have been indifferent to the civil-rights movement and even from some who have been hostile to it. Civil-rights activists, those whose interests are really at stake, make up a very small part of the ardent FSM supporters. The vast majority of the FSM supporters have never before had any desire to sit at tables, to hand out leaflets, or to publicly advocate anything. The Free Speech Movement has become an outlet for the feelings of hostility and alienation which so many students have toward the university. Early in the movement, one graduate student who was working all night for the FSM said, "I really don't give a damn about free speech. I'm just tired of being sat upon. If we don't win anything else, at least they'll have to respect us after this." Clearly, his was an overstatement. Free speech *has* been the issue, and virtually all the FSM supporters identify with the FSM demands. The roots, however, go much deeper. The free-speech issue has been so readily accepted because it has become a vehicle enabling students to express their dissatisfaction with so much of university life, and with so many of the university's institutions.

The phenomenon we describe is not at all unprecedented, even though the FSM may be an extreme example. There have been wildcat strikes which in many ways are quite similar to the free-speech protest. The following pattern is typical: there is an industry in which the workers are discontented with their situation. The pay may or may not be low. There is hostility between the workers and the management, but it is hostility over a great number of practices and institutions, most of which are well established, and none of which have been adequate to launch a protest over the abstract issue. One of the greatest grievances is likely to be the attitude of the managers toward the workers. The union has proven itself incapable of dealing with the issue. Then one day a work practice is changed or a worker is penalized over a minor infraction. Fellow workers protest and are either ignored or reprimanded. A wildcat strike is called and the protest is on.

The same kind of forces which create a wildcat strike have created the FSM. Alienation and hostility exist but are neither focused at specific grievances nor well articulated. There is a general feeling that the situation is hopeless and probably inevitable. There is no obvious handle. No one knows where to begin organizing, what to attack first, how to attack. No one feels confident that an attack is justified, or even relevant. Suddenly there is an issue; everyone recognizes it; everyone grabs at it. A feeling of solidarity develops among the students, as among the workers.

The students at Cal have united. To discover the basic issues underlying their protest one must first listen to the speeches made by their leaders. Two of the most basic themes that began to emerge in the very first speeches of the protest and that have remained central throughout have been a condemnation of the university in its role as a knowledge factory and a demand that the voices of the students must be heard. These themes have been so well received because of the general feeling among the students that the university has made them anonymous; that they have very little control over their environment, over their future; that the university society is almost completely unresponsive to their individual needs. The students decry the lack of human contact, the lack of communication, the lack of dialogue that exists at the university. Many believe that much of their course work is irrelevant, that many of their most difficult assignments are merely tedious busy work with little or no educational value. All too often in his educational career, the student, in a pique of frustration, asks himself, "What's it all about?" In a flash of insight he sees the educational process as a gauntlet: undergraduate education appears to be a rite of endurance, a series of trials, which if successfully completed allow one to enter graduate school; and upon those who succeed in completing the entire rite of passage is bestowed the ceremonious title, Ph.D. For those who cop out along the way, the further one gets the better the job one can obtain, with preference given according to the major one has selected. All too often, the educational process appears to be a weeding-out process, regulated by the laws of supply and demand. The better one plays the game, the more he is rewarded.

To be sure, there are some excellent courses at Cal; some departments are better than others. Although a general education is difficult if not impossible to obtain, in many fields the student is able to obtain an adequate though specialized preparation for an academic career. Furthermore, successful completion of a Cal education is quite a good indication that the student will be agile and adaptable enough to adjust to a position in industry and to acquire rapidly the skills and traits that industry will demand of him.

When viewed from the campus, the Free Speech Movement is a revolution, or at least an open revolt. The students' basic demand is a demand to be heard, to be considered, to be taken into account when decisions concerning their education and their life in the university community are being made. When one reviews the history of the Free Speech Movement, one discovers that each new wave of student response to the movement followed directly on some action by the administration which neglected to take the students, as human beings, into account, and which openly reflected an attitude that the student body was a thing to be dealt with, to be manipulated. Unfortunately, it seems that at those rare times when the students are not treated as things, they are treated as children.

III. The Implications for American Society

It is inadequate, as we have shown, to characterize the FSM as a purely on-campus phenomenon, as a protest stemming from a long overdue need for university reform, or as a response to a corrupt or insensitive administration. Invariably, when students become politically and socially active, one can find that at the root, they are responding to their society's most basic problems.

Let us first consider why students have become so active in the northern civil-rights movement. The problem with which the civil-rights movement is trying to cope, the problem of the effect of our society on the Negro community, is exactly the problem of our entire society, magnified and distorted. Unemployment, underemployment, poor education, poor housing, intense social alienation: these and many more are the effects of our way of life on the Negro community, and these, to one degree or another, are the effects of our way of life on all of its members. When taking a moral stand, when doing what they can in the struggle for equality for all Americans, students invariably find that as they become more and more successful they come into conflict with almost all the established interest groups in the community. Students have turned to the civil-rights movement because they have found it to be a front on which they can attack basic social problems, a front on which they can have some real impact. In the final analysis the FSM must be viewed in this same light.

The University of California is a microcosm in which all of the problems of our society are reflected. Not only did the pressure to crack down on free speech at Cal come from the outside power structure, but most of the failings of the university are either on-campus manifestations of broader American social problems or are imposed upon the university by outside pressures. Departments at the university are appropriated funds roughly in proportion to the degree that the state's industry feels these departments are important. Research and study grants to both students and faculty are given on the same preferential basis. One of the greatest social ills of this nation is the absolute refusal by almost all of its members to examine seriously the presuppositions of the establishment. This illness becomes a crisis when the university, supposedly a center for analysis and criticism, refuses to examine these presuppositions. Throughout the society, the individual has lost more and more control over his environment. When he votes, he must choose between two candidates who agree on almost all basic questions. On his job, he has become more and more a cog in a machine, a part of a master plan in whose formulation he is not consulted, and over which he can exert no influence for change. He finds it increasingly more difficult to find meaning in his job or in his life. He grows more cynical. The bureaucratization of the campus is just a reflection of the bureaucratization of American life.

As the main energies of our society are channeled into an effort to win the cold war, as all of our institutions become adjuncts of the military-industrial complex, as the managers of industry and the possessors of corporate wealth gain a greater and greater stranglehold on the lives of all Americans, one cannot expect the university to stay pure.

In our society, students are neither children nor adults. Clearly, they are not merely children; but to be an adult in our society one must both be out of school and self-supporting (for some reason, living on a grant or fellowship is not considered self-supporting). As a result, students are more or less outside of society, and in increasing numbers they do not desire to become a part of the society. From their peripheral social position they are able to maintain human values, values they know will be distorted or destroyed when they enter the compromising, practical, "adult" world.

It is their marginal social status which has allowed students to become active in the civil-rights movement and which has allowed them to create the Free Speech Movement. The students, in their idealism, are confronted with a world which is a complete mess, a world which in their eyes preceding generations have botched up. They start as liberals, talking about society, criticizing it, going to lectures, donating money. But every year more and more students find they cannot stop there. They affirm themselves; they decide that even if they do not know how to save the world, even if they have no magic formula, they must let their voice be heard. They become activists, and a new generation, a generation of radicals, emerges.

STATEMENTS OF THE UNIVERSITY
STUDENTS FOR LAW AND ORDER

TEXT OF SPEECH DELIVERED BY R. F. DUSSAULT ON DECEMBER 7, 1964 AT STUDENT MEETING ON CAL CAMPUS*

The organization which I represent, University Students for Law and Order, was organized as an alternative course of action to the so-called Free Speech Movement. We believe that the FSM has exceeded the limits of protest acceptable to the majority of students at our university.

There is no need nor is there any excuse for civil disobedience on this campus. Those students involved demand protection of their rights while at the same time they are violating our rights.

As an organization, USLO does not pretend to know solutions to the varied and complex problems which presently confront us as students. But one fact is undeniably clear—that unless we are willing to express ourselves as a responsible body, we have no right to expect the continued financial support of the community at large.

As a course of action, USLO urges the students to support the legally constituted administration of this campus on all issues until such a time as the civil judicial authorities dictate otherwise.

We therefore request that you express your moral support of our viewpoint by signing the petition which is now being circulated and by disassociating yourself from the FSM.

PRESIDENT CLARK KERR WILL ADDRESS THE UNIVERSITY AT 11:00 A.M. IN THE GREEK THEATER.†

Before Dr. Kerr became president, the following conditions existed on campus. In 1956 Adlai Stevenson, Democratic party nominee for the presidency of the United States, was not allowed to speak on this campus. He was a political speaker and for that reason was not allowed to appear.

Before President Kerr took his present position the governor

---

* Distributed as a leaflet.
† Distributed December 7, 1964.

of California could not even address a political-science class in session here on campus. Today, speakers may talk on any subject. An example of this is the appearance of a Nazi, Sergeant Forbes, last spring.

Through the direction, support, and energies of President Clark Kerr the OPEN FORUM has been initiated, and the SPEAKERS' BAN LIFTED. More liberalization of regulations at the university has taken place in the past six years, under Kerr's direction, than happened in the ninety years before he assumed the presidency.

This man, Clark Kerr, speaks today in the Greek Theater at 11:00 A.M.!

FSM, WHERE NOW???*

"Support the Academic Senate" is the new slogan heard around the troubled Cal campus. Why?

Because the Academic Senate has supported the FSM.

"Down with the administration" is another popular but slightly hackneyed slogan resounding from the Terrace to the Steps of Sproul Hall. Why?

Because the administration will not be intimidated by the tactics or demands of the FSM. Because the laws and statutes of California say it CANNOT.

If the Regents approve the Academic Senate Resolution passed on December 8 then we can look forward to a new slogan "Support the Regents." If instead they choose to stay within the present interpretation of state law and reject the proposal we shall hear, "Down with the Regents!"

The next step is to change state law. If the voters refuse to do this, what? "Down with the State"? Will this be the next cry? Don't fool yourself. FSM is not going to stop now! A "victory rally" today at noon. Another rally tomorrow. They're not going to stop so long as so many are under their control.

In a press conference after the Academic Senate meeting yesterday Mario Savio warned the Regents and the state that if the senate resolution were not rubber-stamped then the university could expect further trouble. Mario Savio WARNED the Regents and the state.

We of the University Students for Law and Order wish to make it clear that we are firmly opposed to any further disruptions on this campus. That we continue our activity under this uneasy truce demonstrates that we do not believe the FSM will stop. No matter what concessions are granted to them,

* Distributed December 9, 1964.

they will continue towards their purpose of bringing ALL wheels to a grinding halt.

WATCH AND WAIT!!!

FSM, WHAT NEXT?????*

Pardon us for patting our own backs. But a prediction by University Students for Law and Order that the FSM is not going to stop is being proven daily. Savio and other FSM officials have taken their "crusade" to the country. Mario's departure for his national tour came shortly after revealing to the press that he was "tired of rallies" and that he was going to resume his function as a student. The next day, in New York, after directing several weak rallies on campuses across the country, he threatened a massive rally in New York City's Times Square.

Evidently Savio's "protest" across the nation is falling flat. What has he left in his wake at this university? Faculty members on both sides of the issue have threatened to resign. An unresolvable dilemma has been raised. Recruitment of new faculty, with the situation at such a crucial stage, is impossible. Democratic ideals have been flaunted in the name of democracy and threats of continuing these flaunts have been made. A Latin-American style of government is being initiated—stability is fighting against instability.

At Penn State, where Savio spoke, university President Walker said that the FBI had informed him *last March* that there would be "an organized attempt, using bogus students and bogus faculty members, to divert the energies of students into channels embarrassing to our universities." He further said that they would be using slogans like "Free Speech" to achieve their goals.

Whatever decision is made by the Regents must be accepted by the university, whether we agree with it or not. It is only when the legally constituted authority is recognized that the university can continue to function. It is only when the divisive tactics predicted last March are repudiated that the framework of law and order can prevail.

If the FSM refuses to abide by the decision of the Regents, it is their prerogative. But let them challenge this decision in the courts. Are they so afraid that their position is legally indefensible that they will refuse to do this? Or are they rallying students to revolt for revolution's sake?

What is the position of FSM? Why are its leaders turning to the nation in an attempt to heap discredit upon the university? Why do they refuse so categorically to follow the judicial

* Distributed December 14, 1964.

processes on which America was founded? When will they be satisfied? Where will their *putsch* end?

WHAT VICTORY WILL BE GAINED BY THE DESTRUCTION OF OUR UNIVERSITY?

NOW TIME TO THINK . . .*

USLO does not advocate either the acceptance or the rejection of the Academic Senate proposal. We continue to publish for one principal reason: we firmly believe that the Regents will not, in fact, accept the proposal in its entirety. The reasons behind our belief are, in part:

1. There is no reason for this governing body to abdicate any of its power. It would if it accepted the proposal.

2. In light of past decisions of the Regents, we feel that they will continue to maintain the balance of its power as the final controlling body over this university.

3. In a recent court decision, Wilkenson vs. Ohio State University, the court maintained that it was not only the right, but the *responsibility* of the president to regulate student activity both on and off campus, and that the president had the right to regulate THE CONTENT OF SPEECHES ON THE CAMPUS.

Assuming then, that the Regents do reject or at least defer the proposal, or any part of the proposal, WHAT WILL BE THE FSM's COURSE OF ACTION? We believe that renewed demonstrations and strikes will occur in an attempt to *completely* "bring the wheels to a grinding halt."

It must be emphasized that each and every student who supports or honors future FSM demonstrations and/or strikes will have to realize his responsibility for the probable consequence: legislative control of the University of California. The public at large feel that they have an investment to protect here, and that they cannot permit chaos to prevail.

The immediate goals of the FSM are exemplified in the five points of the Academic Senate proposal. Many responsible and dedicated people have worked, and continue to work, to achieve these points *through peaceful negotiation.* Don't be led into believing that strikes and demonstrations are the ONLY solution.

The ends do not justify the means, especially in regard to the ends and means now in question upon this campus.

A little foresight should reveal that a future strike, or any other disruptive action on this campus, will completely destroy any hope of attainment of these goals.

We submit, for the benefit of all, that the Regents' decision

* Distributed December 17, 1964.

be accepted. Further action *must* be limited to the courts and other legal bodies.

DO NOT SUPPORT FURTHER DEMONSTRATIONS—EMPLOY LEGAL CHANNELS!

THE GROUPS ON THE PERIPHERY
SPEAK UP

PLURALISTIC SOCIETY OR CLASS RULE?*
BY SPARTACIST

All good political science majors know how this society functions. It is a dynamic balance of various interests and pressure groups ranging from organized labor, to downtown merchants, to the John Birch Society. Of course. To speak of class rule is to exhibit naïveté and bad taste. Worse yet, it is to "use the rhetoric of the thirties."

Now Governor Brown (the good, gray "vector zero" product of the pluralistic society) has turned the cops loose on Berkeley students and is vowing to put down "anarchy and revolution." Does the governor's charge have any substance? The issue which first brought the students onto the scene was civil rights. In theory, racial equality is fully compatible with the present social order. Indeed, the abstract model of the society works better with racial equality than without it. Civil rights, therefore, is a reformist demand. The actual society, however, is so beset by internal contradictions and external conflicts, and racism so deeply imbedded in it, that the demand for racial equality in practice takes on a revolutionary character. Hence the crackdown on student civil liberties. The campus had to be sealed off from the community because, with the prospect of deepening struggles in the black ghettos, the students were not only a powerful force in their own right but also threatened to provide a link between the ghetto and potential anti-status-quo forces in the white community. The fight for civil rights led to a fight for civil liberties. Civil liberties, too, are theoretically a reformist issue and are even enshrined in the political constitution of the society. But the actual exercise of civil liberties by dissidents (as opposed to their theoretical expostulation by establishment intellectuals) is also a revolutionary threat and is reacted to as such by the authorities.

What have the Berkeley students uncovered? First, in pursuance of civil rights, they have taken on such bastions of private property as the Bank of America and the Oakland *Tribune*. The response of the UC administration, which, via the Board of Regents, is responsible to these same forces, was to curtail student civil liberties. Finding themselves unable to

* Revolutionary Socialist group leaflet distributed in early December.

secure their rights within the rules made and changed at will by their enemies, the FSM resorted to militancy, civil dis-obedience, and a traditional class weapon, the strike. While the faculty sweated and equivocated, the liberal Democratic governor, who knows what power is, called out the cops.

What the Berkeley students have exposed is not merely a vast and inept bureaucracy, but a coherent ruling-class struc-ture. It runs all the way from the agro-business, banking, min-ing, railroad, utility, and newspaper capitalists and their direct representatives on the Board of Regents through the Demo-cratic governor and the university administration down to the point of application, the police club. When Brown calls the FSM revolutionary, he speaks the truth, despite the fact that FSM fights only for rights supposedly guaranteed within a democratic capitalist society. In this struggle the students, whatever their intentions may have been, have given a clear and dramatic demonstration of how bourgeois class rule works. They have shown it too moribund and fearful to grant even those rights which are supposed to be its moral justifica-tion.

These exposures are invaluable lessons for *other* actual and potential enemies of this ruling class, such as the automation victims, farm laborers, the ghetto masses, indeed, all sections of the working class. To the extent that they learn these les-sons, and come to understand their stake in this Free Speech Movement, they will aid the embattled students with their nu-merical strength, organization, and economic power. This rev-elation of class power will mark a significant step in a process of increasing political and class consciousness which must lead to a movement that will have the strength to effect the final solution of the whole gamut of problems which are now the students' concern.

Pat Brown calls it "revolution."

BROWN CALLS COPS TO TEACH STUDENTS
BY THE PROGRESSIVE LABOR MOVEMENT*

The magnificent struggle led by the Free Speech Move-ment (FSM) for the political rights of all students has reached a new and decisive stage with the mass arrest of the sit-in demonstrators and the calling of a general student strike.

Many questions arise:

Why are Governor Brown, the Board of Regents, and the UC administration so determined to crush the FSM?

* Maoist Communist leaflet distributed in early December.

Why are they so insistent upon enforcing their undemocratic regulations?

Why don't they grant the simple but fundamental demand of FSM that students should have the same constitutional rights that all Americans are supposed to have?

It's true that Governor Brown and the UC administration don't want their authority challenged. Such a challenge frightens them and that's why Governor Brown shouts "anarchy" and calls the cops. But there's much more to it than that.

The real politics behind the free-speech struggle at UC is fundamental and of national significance. The United States ruling class, which controls the government, the economy, and the university system, is confronted with a far-reaching and growing crisis at home and abroad—that is the Negro freedom movement and the liberation revolutions in Vietnam, the Congo, and Latin America.

One of the most important sectors of the people supporting the cause of Negro freedom and demanding an end to United States foreign intervention is U.S. students. The Mississippi Summer Project was carried forth by students. The picket lines against Knowland's jimcrow hiring practices at the Oakland *Tribune* are manned mainly by students. Students led the great sit-in that forced thirty-three of San Francisco's snootiest hotels to stop discrimination in hiring. Students are publicly circulating declarations that they are unwilling to fight against the Vietnamese people. The list of examples are endless.

It's no accident that it's President Johnson's top man in California, Governor Pat Brown who's been giving the orders to UC President Kerr. President Kerr keeps his right ear open to Knowland. The university officials represent the same financial interests that control the government, that determine domestic and foreign policy, that profit from the cheap labor of colonial peoples and the Negro people.

They don't want students going to Mississippi, or picketing the *Tribune,* or circulating petitions and demonstrations against U.S. aggression in Vietnam and the Congo.

Nor do they want students circulating radical literature, or hearing revolutionary speakers, or learning about Marxism-Leninism, or joining progressive and socialist organizations.

They want students to be submissive, passive, conformist, and unthinking . . . to be mere products of a factory-type university system whose only ambition in life is to be a "success" like Governor Brown, President Kerr, William Knowland, or the representatives on the Board of Regents. In other words, they want students to come out of school in the image of and as servants of the capitalist class.

When students reject that intellectually corrupt path and instead become active, thinking, and non-conformist—when students actively challenge undemocratic rules and bureaucratic authorities by fighting for their rights, then they are given a bit of the Vietnam, Harlem, and Mississippi treatment—suspensions, expulsions, arrests, jail and police intimidation.

One of the leaders of FSM said after the mass arrests that "students have learned more about how democracy works in the United States through the Free Speech Movement than they could have through 40 years of academic classes."

How true!

One lesson learned by most students is how the daily press lies. Every student who has had any relationship with the FSM knows how the press has lied about FSM . . ." 40% outsiders and communists," "takes orders from the Progressive Labor Movement and other communist organizations," "only 50 demonstrators showed up for the rally," etc., etc.

One can now realize to what extent the news media will lie in order to mislead the American people, especially when it involves internationally vital matters (where billions of dollars are at stake) such as Vietnam, the Congo, Cuba, China, and the Soviet Union.

The student movement of the 1960s is alive with radicalism and a searching inquiry into the real nature of U.S. foreign policy and the oppression of the Negro people. Being *thinking* people, students are better able to discern bogus propaganda from truth. Being *young* people, students are alive with the enthusiasm, honesty, and idealism of youth. That is why students throughout the world are also in the forefront of the struggle for freedom and against foreign aggression.

The struggle for free speech at UC is now at a decisive stage. The fight can be won if the general strike gets the support it deserves and needs. Truck drivers, members of the Teamsters Union, set an honorable example by respecting student picket lines. The entire labor movement, the civil-rights movement, every democratic-minded person and organization should support the FSM's just demands:

Drop all charges against the sit-in demonstrators!

Reinstate all students!

Restore the Bill of Rights at the University of California!

BIG UC REVOLT—THE HOUSE THAT KERR BUILT*

BY TOCSIN

The president of the nation's largest university looked out on his vaunted "free market place of ideas" last week and found it seething with insurrection.

* From *Tocsin* (anti-Communist weekly), October 10, 1964.

The Berkeley campus of the University of California underwent a three-day "free speech" sit-in that swelled to upwards of 5000 persons, sealed off the administration building and brought in more than 500 policemen attempting to prevent disaster. The demonstration pretext was a sudden clampdown against the use of campus facilities for partisan political and social causes.

Visibly shaken by the unprecedented defiance of the demonstrators, UC President Clark Kerr took a long overdue look at the forces of civil uprising at work at his university.

If they have grown to the proportions of a monster apprentice, Sorcerer Kerr himself must take the blame.

"The University is not engaged in making ideas safe for students," he told a Charter Day audience in 1961. "It is engaged in making students safe for ideas."

Last week when a gang of idea-safe students dragged a campus policeman down a flight of stairs, they could recall this and other Kerr aphorisms.

"Our American ideals are not fragile objects . . . to be sheltered from the reality of today's world," Kerr has stated. "They are strong and resilient and as serviceable today as in 1776. They need no special care except daily exercise, and no shield but truth."

In 1962 Kerr refused to "dignify with a comment" a charge by an Alameda County law-enforcement officer that the university was a center of Communist activity. But last week he conceded that a hard core of Mao Tse-tung Communists constituted the leadership of the recent sit-in.

When two California legislators asked the university to discipline students arrested in Bay Area civil disobedience protests, Kerr only last May denounced the proposal. Far from administering punishment, arrested students boasted, the university was actually aiding them in their sit-in activities by imposing no penalty for missed class work or permitting them to defer completion of courses.

The Ad Hoc Committee to End Discrimination, which organized the San Francisco Sheraton Palace Hotel sleep-in last March, was spawned from a UC nucleus. Now staging demonstrations against the Oakland *Tribune,* it is led by Mike Myerson, a former chairman of the campus Slate party. After graduation in 1961 he became chairman of the U.S. delegation to the Communist World Youth Festival in Helsinki. The Ad Hoc Committee included three chapters of the W.E.B. DuBois Clubs, which were named for a deceased American Communist and operate at UC under the leadership of the children of two identified Communists.

These and other Marxist-backed groups operate freely at the campus under Kerr's well publicized "open forum" policy. Slate and the DuBois Club acted as whips to last year's successful drive to kill the ban against acknowledged Communist Party speakers, and presented the first "admitted" CP speaker on campus. In April 1963 Kerr "predicted" that students on the Berkeley and Los Angeles campuses would vote overwhelmingly to lift the ban. They did.

For carrying through the rescinding of the speaker ban, Kerr this year was rewarded by the American Association of University Professors with the Alexander Meiklejohn Award. The citation paid tribute to Kerr and the UC Regents for "notable service in establishing a healthy climate for academic freedom." Meiklejohn, who lives in Berkeley, is honorary chairman of the National Committee to Abolish the House Committee on Un-American Activities and has sponsored other cited Communist fronts.

Frank Wilkinson, an identified Communist who was twice permitted to speak on campus even during the "ban," named Meiklejohn as his spiritual mentor in a 1962 talk at UC.

It was Wilkinson's first appearance in 1961 that raised the "free speech" issue to fever pitch.

Convicted of contempt of Congress for refusing to reveal his Communist affiliations to the House Committee on Un-American Activities, Wilkinson in March 1961 picked UC as one of his last major stops on his way to the Federal Penitentiary. He delivered a widely publicized speech, congratulating students for their "magnificent" demonstration against the HCUA's San Francisco hearings in May 1960. FBI Director J. Edgar Hoover named Wilkinson as the architect of the riots which erupted during the hearings. A number of UC students were among sixty-four persons arrested.

Shortly after his release from prison in 1962, Wilkinson returned to his Wheeler Hall rostrum to deliver new eulogies to the students for their intelligence and ability to hear all points of view.

Kerr's frequent pronouncements supporting "academic freedom" and "the free market place of ideas" made Wilkinson's smooth defense of "civil liberties" seem familiar and acceptable.

The university is "not going to be banning people just because they are alleged to be Communists," Kerr said during the California gubernatorial race in 1962. He referred to a campaign pledge by candidate Richard Nixon that Communists and Fifth Amendment-takers would be prohibited from speaking on state campuses.

Kerr answered that UC would make its own decisions in determining who is allowed to speak. He said that there is "absolutely not" any indication that the effect of then recent speakers at UC campuses had tended to undermine the nation's way of life.

Last week's insurrection looked like a bitter answer to Kerr's statements.

Startled Bay Area residents wondered vainly last week why no successful opposition to Kerr's liberal-extremist policies had ever developed at the university.

The answer, explained a former faculty member, is that Kerr rules the UC campuses with iron-fisted control. Surrounding himself with a group of administrative yes-men, Kerr has created a climate in which disagreement with his views is equated with lack of faith in free speech.

"The chickens are merely coming home to roost," said one middle-aged Berkeleyan, viewing last week's sit-in from a window overlooking the university's "free speech" area.

STATE CAMPUS SAFETY IMPERILED*
TOCSIN EDITORIAL

The three-day, two-night siege of the University of California by an angry mob of student rebels is only the most dramatic instance in a slow process of dissolution of authority and discipline under the presidency of Clark Kerr.

Under Kerr's policies the administration has given carte blanche to left-wing extremists to practice open defiance of law and order.

Demonstrations against the House Committee on Un-American Activities, a march against the ROTC program, assorted sleep-ins, sit-ins, and shop-ins have paved the way for bigger and better nose-thumbings at constituted authority.

This was the first demonstration requiring a force of several hundred policemen (working for an estimated hourly $3000 of taxpayer money) to stand ready to prevent bloodshed.

And the demonstrators have indicated it will not be the last. When the penalty is no more than a chiding tut-tut from Kerr, what have the rebels got to lose?

Serious students on restricted budgets and schedules have no assurance, under present conditions, that their studies will not be disrupted. All entry to the administration building was forbidden October 2 during the demonstration, and study-list filing, a required step in enrollment, came to a dead halt.

Nor is there any guarantee of physical safety for either students or property when a mob with arms locked can thwart peace officers from carrying out their duties. The campus police have been reduced to the role of toy soldiers, prevented from interfering with young revolutionaries.

In the face of this continued threat to the existence of law, order and public safety at the University of California, re-

* From *Tocsin* (anti-Communist weekly), October 10, 1964.

sponsible citizens must demand the resignation of President Clark Kerr.

CLARK KERR BLAMES PEKING BUT "MUSCOVITES" ACTIVE*

BY TOCSIN

A hard core of "Castro-Mao-Tse-tung-line" Communists were blamed by President Clark Kerr for swelling last week's campus demonstrations.

Kerr came up with a figure of machinelike precision in estimating the extent of the "Maoist" influence—he put their number at 49 per cent.

The UC president also claimed that "very few" university students were actually involved in the hard-core leadership. No basis was cited either for absolving students of participation or for the 49 per cent figure.

In assigning responsibility to followers of the "bad" Peking-line Communists, Kerr made no mention of the participation of the "good" Moscow-oriented Communists.

But at least two of the leading participants in the campus insurrection are directly tied to the Moscow faction. They are UC students Bettina Aptheker, daughter of top Communist Party theoretician Herbert Aptheker of New York, and Margaret Lima, daughter of Northern California Communist Party Chairman Albert J. ("Mickie") Lima of Oakland, Calif.

The two girls have been active on the UC campus in the Marxist W.E.B. DuBois Club, Slate, Women for Peace, and in various off-campus "civil rights" demonstrations.

* From *Tocsin*, October 10, 1964.

ADMINISTRATION STATEMENTS

REMARKS BY THE CHANCELLOR TO THE UNIVERSITY MEETING, SEPTEMBER 28, 1964.
BY EDWARD STRONG

This first university meeting of the academic year 1964–65 is being held in a "Hyde Park" area—a forum to which any student or staff member of the university may come to speak his mind on controversial subjects and issues. A *forum* is a place of public discussion. The university maintains an *open* forum—a forum (1) *open* in respect to the full spectrum of political and social views that may be expressed and heard on campus; and (2) *open* in respect to invitations that can be extended to individuals to speak on campus.

In my statement in the *Daily Californian* last Wednesday, I noted that the open-forum policy of the university is being fully maintained. I noted that "Printed materials on issues and candidates can be distributed by bona fide student groups in designated places on campus, including the Telegraph-Bancroft location." Consistent with the maintenance of freedom of discussion, no line is drawn between the spoken and the written word. Some of our invited speakers between now and November 3 will be candidates for public office. They will appear on campus to present views and arguments which, they hope, will be persuasive in winning support in votes to be cast on election day. In the designated places on campus now provided for distribution of printed material by student groups, campaign literature may be made available for free distribution. Campaign buttons and bumper stickers, voting lists and argumentation recommending a vote for or against a proposition or a candidate are included in printed materials which may be distributed in the designated places.

Consistent with university policy regarding use of university facilities, no one is permitted on campus to use these facilities to mount social and political action directed to the surrounding community. President Kerr, on June 12, 1961, issued the following statement of principles:

1. Freedom to speak and to hear is maintained for students and faculty members.

2. Subversion and other illegal activities are not tolerated; and we will not employ a Communist.

3. Law and order are maintained on the campus.

4. A balanced program of speakers and ideas is presented.

5. No exploitation of the name of the university is allowed.

6. No student may be compelled to join an organization which engages in social or political action.

7. No efforts at conversion and solicitation of members by political or religious groups are permitted on campus.

I have received from the ASUC Senate the text of a motion passed by that body on September 22 requesting freedom (1) to solicit political party membership, (2) to mount political and social action on the campus, (3) to solicit funds on campus for such action, and (4) to receive funds to aid projects not directly concerned with an authorized activity of the university. This petition has received the attention of the president and the Regents of the university. University facilities are not to be used for any of these four purposes. Any student or group of students seeking to recruit members for social or political action, or to solicit funds for such action, is free to do so off campus, but is prohibited from doing so on campus.

Why does the university prohibit the mounting of social and political action on campus? In responding to this question, I want first to call your attention to University Regulation No. 5, entitled "Academic Freedom," and in particular to these three concluding sentences: The university "will not aid nor will it condone actions contrary to the laws of the State. Its high function—and its high privilege, the University will steadily continue to fulfill, serving the people by providing facilities for investigation and teaching free from domination by parties, sects, or selfish interests. The University expects the State, in return, and to its own great gain, to protect this indispensable freedom, a freedom like the freedom of the press, that is the heritage and right of a free people."

The university prohibits the mounting of social and political action on campus by reason of the following considerations. If the university permitted its facilities to be used to recruit membership in political parties and to promote social or political demonstrations in a surrounding community, the university could then no longer hold fast to a fundamental position on which it has insisted. The university respects the right of each student as a *citizen* to participate as he sees fit in off-campus, non-university courses of action. When an individual, in so participating, acts in a disorderly way or is in violation of the law, he is answerable to the civil authorities for his conduct. Some citizens demand further that the individual as a student also be disciplined by the university, that is, that he be censured, suspended, or expelled. We answer such demands by pointing out that we respect the right of our students to act in their capacity as citizens in the public domain.

On the one side, an individual as a student is held responsible by the university for compliance with its rules and regulations. On the other side, when a student goes off campus to participate in some social or political action, he does so on his own responsibility as a citizen. He has no right, acting as a citizen, to involve the university, either by using its name or by using any of its facilities to further such action. For, were the university to become involved, the consequence is clear. We ask and expect from the state an indispensable freedom residing in independence—independence that rests on fulfillment of a public trust, namely, that the university will never allow itself to be dominated nor used by parties, sects, or selfish interests. By honoring this public trust steadfastly, the university is enabled also to honor and defend the rights of its members to act freely in the public domain in their capacity as citizens. The consequence of defaulting on this public trust would be the erosion of the independence of the university and the destruction of the position maintained by the university respecting the responsibilities of an individual as a student in the university and respecting his rights and responsibilities as a citizen of the state. As a student in the university, an individual is answerable to the university for conduct coming under its rules and regulations. As a citizen of the state, an individual is answerable to the state for conduct coming under the laws of the state. This is as it should be to insure freedom with responsibility within the university and in civil society. The university extends many privileges to its students. In return, the university expects observance by its students of the university's published policies relating to students and student organizations.

STATEMENT READ AT THE MEETING OF THE ACADEMIC SENATE, BERKELEY DIVISION, NOVEMBER 24, 1964.

BY EDWARD STRONG

On October 13 the Academic Senate declared itself in favor of "maximum freedom for student political activity" at Berkeley. In the spirit of that declaration, the six faculty representatives of the Committee on Campus Political Activity submitted a report to me which went forward to President Kerr and the Regents. I conferred twice yesterday with these representatives on the ten points in their report and on my announcement published in the *Daily Californian* this morning, in response to their recommendations pertaining to the Berkeley campus.

It was our mutual concern to proceed in accordance with the enabling policy adopted by the Regents last Friday, namely, that "certain campus facilities, carefully selected and properly regulated, may be used by students and staff for planning, implementing, raising funds or recruiting participants for lawful off-campus action, not for unlawful off-campus action." Thus, students now do have maximum political freedom.

I am calling upon the assistance of the Student Affairs Committee for advice on the selection and regulation of campus facilities which may be used as specified by the Regents' enabling policy. I will be glad to have any recommendations which the Committee on Academic Freedom may wish to make as a result of the investigation which it was instructed to make by the Senate. The chairman of that committee, Professor Garbarino, has been active in formulating the statement of the six faculty representatives.

I should like to say a word also about the report of the Senate *ad hoc* committee appointed to consider the cases of the eight suspended students. I appreciate the thorough and conscientious way in which the committee performed a difficult task. The committee declared itself "troubled by the refusal of these students to respond unconditionally to Dean Williams' request for an interview." Since the university cannot function unless students respond to requests of officers and faculty, the administration must view such action as a serious matter. Indeed, the refusal of a student to appear in the office of the dean of students after appropriate notification to do so is cause for immediate removal of that student from the rolls of the university. I would like to point out, however, that although the administration did not find it possible to accept fully the recommendations of the committee, it did award suspensions which were *de facto*.

Finally, I would like to say that I cannot enough express my appreciation to those members of the faculty who have in this time of troubles expressed their concern and devoted their energies to finding solutions acceptable to reasonable men. Unfortunately, these troubles tend to polarize us, and to bring out the suspicions that the faculty always has of the administration. I understand these feelings: I have shared them, and I know they betoken the vigilance that makes free men. But, as you know, we administrators are faculty members under the skin; we are amateur administrators—if we were not perhaps we would make fewer mistakes. Out of all the confusion and misunderstanding of the past two months has now emerged a condition of maximum lawful student political activity on campus. Some of the details remain to be worked out, but surely this is a policy upon which reasonable men can agree. I seek to work together with you in overcoming divisive and destructive forces, so that we may solve our mutual problems in the most constructive way.

STATEMENT BY PRESIDENT CLARK KERR

(November 12, 1964)

The faculty members of the former Committee on Political Activity at Berkeley have now completed a report rendered in draft form on Tuesday of this week. Copies are being sent to each Regent along with this statement of mine. They are also being sent to the chancellors of each of the nine campuses of the university with the expectation that those parts relevant to each campus will be discussed, at the discretion of the chancellor, with appropriate student and faculty groups. The *Daily Californian* is being requested to publish this report and these introductory remarks of mine in full. Comments and suggestions about this report will be welcome from faculty and student groups in advance of the presentation of the report to the Regents who meet the end of next week.

The faculty members have labored long and conscientiously on this report. The members of the university community should be most appreciative of their efforts. I certainly am. The report is the unanimous consensus of these faculty members on how to handle the perplexing problems that have troubled the Berkeley campus. I have met with this group and its report reflects, in part, our discussions. I believe that this report provides a basis for constructive solutions to the current and difficult problems. Certainly it is the best available basis for the continuing discussion and consideration of these problems. I am sure there will be a variety of views about the report among students, faculty, administration and Regents, but it clearly constitutes, in my judgment, the best hope for progress.

All members of the university community and all citizens should know that the University of California is committed to the ideal of providing its faculty and students with the maximum range of political freedom consistent with standards of responsibility in its use and with the educational purposes of the university. I am committed to this ideal, and I am convinced that the great majority of faculty and students are also committed to it.

But the history of our country includes a record of disagreement among honest and earnest men about how to achieve this ideal of freedom while still maintaining law and order in society. Sometimes even men of good will participate in actions that violate the law in their efforts to achieve their ideal of freedom. Ultimately, however, if they are men of good will, they return to the law as the only viable method for the resolution of disputes and the protection of freedom.

For the past month all of us—administration, faculty and students—have witnessed a temporary and most regrettable breakdown of order on the Berkeley campus. I am convinced that most of the students and their leaders who participated in the violation of campus rules did so with heavy hearts. But this university cannot and will not permit continued violations of the rules that govern the campus, no matter how impatient some people may grow with the difficult and tedious process of discussing and negotiating differences in viewpoint. And such negotiations cannot be carried on effectively when their subject becomes the object of new violations of law. This process of negotiations carried on calmly and with good sense is just as necessary in the solution of problems within the university as within the nation and as within the world. Moderation is a virtue.

In any situation such as this, it is inevitable that men will err and misunderstandings will develop. But I have been dismayed by the assumption of some students and some staff members that any such errors or misunderstandings are part of a deliberate effort by this administration to deprive the university of its freedom. Clearly the facts are otherwise. There never has been a period in the history of this university when there has been a greater increase in freedom for faculty and students and greater protection of the freedom of faculty and students.

Whatever policy results from the current discussions is almost bound to be subject to some continuing disagreement. The university will always be ready to give careful consideration to all serious proposals about its policies. It should be noted, in this connection, that the university is devoted to the First and Fourteenth Amendments to the Constitution, and whatever it does will be in keeping with this devotion. But the detailed application of these Amendments throughout our nation has been the subject of controversy for over a century and a half. Their application to university policy may continue to be subject to controversy. If so, there are legal methods for resolving such controversy, if discussions fail to do so.

We have great hopes for the current discussions and that solutions to these difficult problems will be possible within the legal order. We intend to pursue such solutions energetically and faithfully. But I would be remiss in my obligation as president if I allowed intimidation to replace reason as the standard for making judgments, and I do not intend to see this happen. The University of California is an educational institution greatly concerned with the welfare of its students, both together and individually. It has great patience with temporary violations of proper conduct. It has great patience—but this patience is not infinite. The university has a clear obligation to take appropriate disciplinary action against specific individuals and organizations involved in improper and disorderly conduct.

Finally, may I note that for over twelve years as chancellor at Berkeley and later as president I have sought to protect and increase the freedom of faculty members and students, always with the confidence that with greater freedom would go a greater sense of responsibility. This view and the progress resulting from it is now meeting its severest test within the university and before the eyes of the entire State of California. It continues to be my view and my faith despite recent occurrences at Berkeley. As I said before Town Hall in Los Angeles shortly after the events of October 2: "the salient fact is this —and some parents may recognize an analogy in their own family experience—most of the students all of the time and all of the students most of the time do match their freedom with an equivalent sense of responsibility. This is the basis for our continued confidence in the students of today and our continuing defense of their liberties."

STATEMENT BY PRESIDENT CLARK KERR

(December 3, 1964)

Governor Brown last night decided that the unlawful sit-in in Sproul Hall must be ended immediately. He has the final responsibility for the maintenance of law and order in California. The university, which has always stood for democratic principles, including observance of the law, expects faculty, staff and students to carry on the orderly processes of the university and to reject what has become an FSM attempt at anarchy.

The FSM issued an ultimatum which had nothing to do with free speech and which it knew, and publicly stated, the university could not possibly accept. This ultimatum called for the abdication by the university of its responsibilities. The ultimatum was not accepted. The FSM then again seized Sproul Hall, as it had done before, and stated it planned to bring the university to a "grinding halt."

The FSM and its leaders from the start declared the police would have to haul them out. They are now finding that, in their efforts to escape the gentle discipline of the university, they have thrown themselves into the arms of the less understanding discipline of the community at large. They have asked that they be subject only to external law and external courts. They are learning that the community is no more sympathetic with anarchy than the university they so violently condemn.

The students at the start of this affair in September had an understandable concern. Certain practices in the "Sather Gate tradition," which lay outside university policy, had been allowed by the Berkeley campus to take place at Telegraph and Bancroft. The campus administration ended these practices on September 14 and student protest boiled up. After wide consultation within the university, the Telegraph and Bancroft area has again been made available for the earlier practices. The Regents at their November meeting went beyond this. They changed a general university policy of many years standing to permit on-campus planning, recruiting and fund raising for lawful off-campus action. They did this in response to student requests and faculty proposals, and also in the light of changing court decisions. The chancellor immediately after the Regents' meeting made a number of other adjustments, which lay within his authority, in keeping with faculty and ASUC suggestions.

This protest has never been over "free speech." There has been and is freedom of speech in the University of California. The protest has been over organizing political action on campus. This is now allowed with the one qualification that unlawful action cannot be mounted on the campus. And it has been made abundantly clear that there is no "double jeopardy" involved since students would be liable for university discipline for misuse of university facilities and would not be punished for the actual off-campus violations of law.

This protest has had the slogan of "free speech"; it has had the substance of a demand for on-campus political action and this substance has been granted within the limits of the law; but it has now become an instrument of anarchy and of personal aggrandizement.

For two months the university has encouraged discussion, emphasized the facts, examined and implemented new policies. It has counted on this process to yield better policies and more understanding. It has counted on this process to separate the well-intentioned students from the hard-core recalcitrants. This process has had some constructive results. However, passion and irrationality and rumor have still held sway in some quarters.

The university is an institution whose primary obligation is to educate its students. It has shown patience. This patience has been met with impatience and with violation of the law. The university has shown tolerance. This tolerance has been met with intolerance and distortion of the truth. The university has shown reasonableness. This reasonableness has been met with irrationality and intransigence. The university has shown decency. This decency has been met with indecency and ill-will.

When patience and tolerance and reasonableness and decency have been tried, yet democratic processes continue to be forsaken by the FSM in favor of anarchy, then the process of law enforcement takes over. This nation is devoted to freedom under the law, not to anarchy under a willful minority, whether that minority be radical students in the north or white supremacists in the south. The ends of neither group justify the means they employ. Freedom can only exist within a rule of law and this is just as true when the attack is from the radical left as when it is from the Ku Klux Klan.

The rule of law must be honored in California. Faculty, staff and students honor it by their conduct of the regular affairs of the university at the level of distinction for which this university has been noted. The Associated Students and other student groups have shown a great sense of responsibility, and many faculty members have contributed much in the way of helpful suggestions and calm good judgment. These efforts of the large majority of students and faculty deserve public recognition and the support of the citizens of California.

A MESSAGE TO ALUMNI*
BY PRESIDENT CLARK KERR

My first visit to the Berkeley campus was in the fall of 1932 to see some friends at International House. We were peacefully drinking Cokes in the coffee shop when a snake-dancing line of students came yelling and shouting through the lobby trying to gain recruits for a demonstration to be held outside Sather Gate against university policies. The placards these students were carrying painted Cal as a fascist state. I asked who was the leader of the group. It was a student who later became a prominent person on the Pacific Coast. His daughter was one of the participants in the sit-in in Sproul Hall on December 2–3, 1964.

The Sather Gate tradition, with its soap-boxes, was moved to Telegraph and Bancroft after the Student Union was built and when the north end of Telegraph Avenue, beyond Bancroft, was dedicated by the City to the University. In September 1959, I suggested that a twenty-six foot strip be returned to the City of Berkeley. The Regents approved this by a vote of 15 to 2; but the transfer was never formally made, although many of us thought it had been. It was on this twenty-six foot strip that political action became more and more intense until in September, 1964, the Berkeley campus felt it necessary to ban such activity.

The main article in this issue of the CALIFORNIA MONTHLY

* From *California Monthly*, February 1965.

gives a narrative account of what happened after the ban was announced, along with a number of pertinent documents. I should like to make some comments on this episode.

1. The intensity of student reaction took the Berkeley campus and university-wide administration by surprise. In retrospect, some of the factors explaining how it all boiled up into such a head of steam, so quickly, appear to be these:

There was a hotly contested presidential campaign which aroused the emotions of many people, students included. Also Proposition 14 on the California ballot was loaded with passion.

Civil rights constitute a great moral issue for the student generation of today. Some Cal students were just back from Mississippi and Alabama; others had lived there in spirit all summer. University and college campuses have been a primary recruiting ground for civil rights workers and demonstrators.

Some students returned to Berkeley with their plans all made for election and civil rights activity only to find the "Sather Gate tradition" seriously curtailed. They reacted immediately. The Berkeley and university-wide administrations took prompt action to respond to student protests. I returned from Tokyo on the night of September 15, after participating in the opening ceremonies for our new study-abroad center at the International Christian University. On September 16, Chancellor Strong, Vice Chancellor Sherriffs, Dean Towle and I met to discuss the problem. Several adjustments were shortly made, such as: Sproul Hall steps were designated as a temporary open discussion area, and a specified number of tables were allowed back on the Bancroft strip. But these adjustments were not taken, as they were intended, as evidence that the administration was listening and responding favorably to student requests. They did not lead to willingness to talk and be reasonable, but rather to greater and greater demands and to more and more direct action.

The current generation of students is well characterized as activist—activist through the whole political spectrum from the far right to the far left and through the middle. And religious groups also are far more active than in former years. The activists are impatient for results. They have a remarkable sense of solidarity among themselves as activists, though their goals are often strikingly diverse.

They have a new technique—civil disobedience. Some of them really believe that illegal methods are the only effective ones available to gain the ends they desire. It was very difficult, on October 2, 1964, to persuade some leaders of the demonstrators to agree to "desist from

. . . their illegal protest against university regulations."
They agreed most reluctantly; several saying that such
methods were their only hope of success. Civil disobedience is very difficult to handle on a university campus.
The administration is faced with two equally intolerable
possibilities—countenancing greater and greater flouting
of the rules or attempting to enforce the rules against
massive group violations.

The activists gained support from non-activists. The
presence of large numbers of police on campus on October 2 and December 3 antagonized many students. The
Berkeley campus is big and somewhat impersonal, particularly for the new undergraduate, and there has been
growing dissatisfaction with the quality of undergraduate
life. Many students found friendships and excitement in
the mass demonstrations.

The campus activists had support and some leadership
from the substantial numbers of "non-students" who now
live around the Berkeley campus using certain of its facilities and participating in selected aspects of its activities. Some of these are ex-students. The person in the police car on October 1 was a non-student, as was the first
person to lie down in front of the car. Political activity
on the campus generally, and this episode particularly,
also attracted the attention of some "outsiders" who
would not normally be involved in campus life.

Historically, three campuses across the nation—City
College of New York, the University of Chicago, and
Berkeley—have been known as centers for student political activity. After the HUAC riots in San Francisco in
May, 1960, Berkeley became a greater focal point for
such activity—a special aspect of the so-called "westward
tilt."

The United States is now a nation of young people;
about 46 per cent of the population is under 25 years
of age. Nearly 5 million of these young people are now
in college. This leads a few of the activists to have a
sense of potential power and a desire for actual power
—power certainly against the college or university administration; potentially against the faculty, and particularly against society at large. There is a new drive in the
minds of some student activists; they see themselves as
new men of power working in a nerve center of society.

2. The students were not the only actors on the stage:

The courts have been changing their interpretations of
the law quite substantially in recent years. The university
has liberalized its rules in many ways in recent years also
—sufficiently so to be given the Alexander Meiklejohn

Award for contributions to academic freedom by the American Association of University Professors in the spring of 1964. But, by the fall of 1964, certain of the university's rules had become of doubtful legal enforceability. The university did not permit on-campus recruitment of participants for political action off campus or on-campus organization of such action. Stanford University, in May, 1964, after reviewing the changing character of the law and of student interests had quietly revised its rules.

The administration underestimated the intensity of student reaction to the impairment of the "Sather Gate tradition," and had no experience in coping with mass civil disobedience on campus.

The faculty, except for the very small group consistently identified with the FSM, became involved rather slowly and tentatively at first. The cry of freedom always strikes a responsive chord in faculty hearts. The sight of police on campus is anathema. Faculty members face their students daily in class and have a bond of sympathy with them. In the end, the great majority of the faculty did become involved and came to play a constructive role.

The Regents acted in a sensible fashion from the beginning. They remained united around a policy of reasonable changes in the rules and maintenance of law and order on campus. Their unity was a great source of strength to the university.

3. Some claims have been made repeatedly by the FSM which have doubtful substance:

That freedom of speech was the issue. There was and is great freedom of speech. There were limitations on direct political activity organized on campus.

That no channels of communication were open. In fact, the chancellor, members of his staff, and university-wide officials talked with FSM leaders in person and by telephone at numerous times during October and November. Furthermore, exchanges of written statements between student groups and the administration are a matter of record. The renewal of direct action in November was because the tri-partite committee, which had made great progress, was moving too slowly for the FSM and was not moving in the exact direction the FSM desired. Many channels were open in addition to these—including the ASUC—but few were used.

That there was police brutality. This has not been proved.

That the administration engaged in making improper

charges. I did say in October that, among the outsiders who turned up, some had been sympathetic with Communist causes. I consider this a statement of fact.

That the strike was an overwhelming success. As a matter of fact, it hardly touched any school or college except Letters and Science and here there was very little effect in the sciences. Most of the students most of the time went about their regular affairs.

4. The episode of 1932 was not the end of the Berkeley campus; nor will that of 1964 be the end, although it was much greater in scope. The Berkeley campus is one of the great university campuses of the nation. It must rise to even greater heights for its own sake and for the sake of the whole university and the State of California. It can do so and it will. The alumni can help greatly as they have so often and in so many ways throughout the history of the university.

First, we need to understand what happened, and this may be the most difficult task of all. Among other things, we need to realize that only a small percentage of students enrolled at Berkeley was involved in violations of the law or of university regulations.

Second, we need to approach our problems in a constructive fashion. We need reasonable rules, reasonably enforced. We need improvements in the quality of undergraduate life. We need respect for democratic processes and the rights of others, exercised by all members of the university community.

Third, we need to avoid, to the greatest extent possible, new acts of retribution beyond what the law will require in the cases now before the courts, for such acts will only serve to impede the process of reconciliation. This need not be a Greek tragedy with disastrous consequences for all the actors. We can write our own happier ending if we write it with tolerance and reason and confidence in the future.

The University of California is one of the great experiments in all higher education—an experiment in combining quantity and quality, an experiment in freedom within a public context, an experiment in cooperation among campuses and with other segments of higher education, an experiment in using knowledge and training on an unprecedented scale for the benefit of all mankind. The failures in this single episode, regrettable as these failures are, are far out-weighed by the successes of the great experiment.

SOME FACULTY STATEMENTS ISSUED IN DECEMBER AND JANUARY

TO THE STUDENTS OF POLITICAL SCIENCE 113*

". . . by our silence or by the stand we take, we too shall enter the fray." Some of you have heard me speak these words of Camus before; I speak them again today, only now not as the prelude to a lecture but rather to the expression of an obligation deeply felt. It has been said that with so worthy a cause, the protesting students deserved better of their leaders. I have no doubt we all do. But the luxury rarely falls to any one man, however rational or learned, himself to set the precise terms to a debate engaged in by his fellows. The fact is that I can no longer suit my actions to whatever hopes I might previously have held for seeing some of those terms changed. Even to be silent is still to enter the fray. I have been witnessing the astonishing scene at Sproul Hall since the early hours of morning. And as I have tried to absorb the significance of what was taking place before my eyes, it became clear to me that I simply was incapable of violating the palpable air of protest which today surrounds every building on this campus.

There will be no class today.

NORMAN JACOBSON
ASSOCIATE PROFESSOR OF POLITICAL SCIENCE

STATEMENT BY PROFESSOR HENRY F. MAY
CHAIRMAN, DEPARTMENT OF HISTORY

(*December 4, 1964*)

I am making this statement with the authorization of a group of department chairmen established yesterday in an effort to establish a platform for solution of the present crisis.

It is clear that many people do not understand why faculty members are sympathetic to any extent with the rebellious students, and critical to some extent of the administration. *Of course,* faculty members do not approve of demands for capitulation, or of invasion of buildings—courses of action which are contrary to all that we believe in. But the remaining question is why such large numbers of students, including many of

* Distributed as a leaflet on December 3, 1964.

our best students, many never involved in politics in the past, are so deeply distressed and upset. Here the faculty, with regret, has no choice but to be critical of the administration.

The whole affair started when privileges long customary—collection of money, collection of signatures and the like were suddenly withdrawn by the administration. These privileges had before this been used in what seems to me an inoffensive way. At the beginning of the present semester there were many tables at the entrance to the campus. For instance, there was a Goldwater table, one against Proposition 14; there was a SNCC table, a CORE table, etc. I have heard no complaint of violence or trouble resulting from collection of money or obtaining signatures. In the opinion of students and of many of the faculty, the reasons given for the withdrawal of these privileges were unconvincing and contradictory. It was said that student political action was contrary to state law, a statement with which the law professors I know do not agree. It was stated that the reason for the action was to promote an easier flow of traffic and the like. In any case, it was this action which led to the initial protest, culminating in the drastic incident of October 2. (I might say that I refer here to the incident in which students prevented an arrest.) To prevent violence, a settlement was negotiated which involved, among other things, the setting up of a tri-partite student-faculty-administration committee which discussed these problems for a long time. These negotiations broke down, and the faculty members of the group made public their recommendations for new rules governing student political behavior. The efforts of the faculty members in this respect were praised by the president. At the same time, another faculty group, pursuant to the same agreement, made recommendations concerning punishment of students arising out of this incident. At a Regents' meeting on November 20, the recommendations of both these groups were accepted in part, though not entirely, and at a subsequent meeting of the *Academic Senate* the majority of the faculty upheld the administration, and defeated an attempt to take enforcement of rules concerning political behavior from the administration and give it to the faculty. At this point, with the announcement of the new rules, the Free Speech Movement was dwindling and losing student support quite obviously. As a result, its leadership was getting more and more radical as the more reasonable students withdrew. However, during Thanksgiving weekend it seemed to most of us that peace was returning, and that it would be possible to go forward together under the new rules.

Then last Monday, the administration announced its decision to press for *disciplinary action against students* for actions taken during the crisis two months before. I am told that this decision was made against the urging of several highly respected members of the faculty. While technically the action did not violate previous agreements, it seemed to be *contrary to the spirit of the agreement of October 2,* and subsequent negotiations. These seemed to imply that there have been mistakes on all sides, and that punishments would be minimal.

Understandably, I think, the students felt tricked, and it is at this point that the biggest demonstrations took place which had ever happened. The leadership of the FSM, reassured by this new support, made some rough threats to enter Sproul Hall. No measures were taken to prevent this action. It happened, and the governor called in the police. Now the situation is a tragic one, and the university seems almost in danger of disintegration. The faculty feels, as it said in an emergency meeting yesterday, that the new rules should be enforced, that punitive action against violations of university rules in the past should be called off, and that while the administration should continue to deal with violations of rules, a process of appeal to a faculty committee should be established. I might add that such a faculty committee might well be stricter in the enforcement of these rules than the administration, particularly if any disruption of teaching were involved. No settlement is possible which does not take account of the strong emotions now influencing our students and many of our faculty.

Final Summary Statement
(December 4, 1964)

All of the faculty speakers in this conference have said that they are deeply critical of the FSM and its leadership. I want to make clear that this is not said in order to appease hostile sentiment. All of us here would have said the same thing at any time in the past two months. We are, however, equally critical of the administration from which we expect more firmness, and in its statements, to put it mildly, more consistency than has been shown.

I said earlier in answer to a question that I believe most of our students are critical of the FSM and its leadership. To avoid misunderstanding, may I add that most are also critical of the administration. As a purely private guess, I would say that about 300 are with the FSM through thick and thin. About 1200 obviously sided with the FSM after the announcement this past Monday concerning retroactive punishments. Since the arrests, many more are involved in the present unrest. There is also a minority of students, I believe a small one, articulately hostile to the FSM, and pro-administration. Most, I believe, are bewildered, distressed, and in a state of extreme emotion.

May I say a word about what I believe to be the underlying causes of these sad and disturbing events. The first is the breakdown of communications on a large campus which is undertaking the immensely difficult task of trying to be at the same time a first-rate university and a mass institution. It is also part of a new kind of state-wide university made up of a number of equal campuses. This means that in many points it is not clear what level of the administration bears responsibility for a given action.

The second underlying cause is the emergence of new categories of political action on the borderline of legality. I believe that most of us on the faculty would agree that sit-ins in a restaurant which has peculiar racial standards are legal. We would agree that sit-ins undertaken in order to obtain the acceptance of political demands are not. Between these two categories there is a borderline which is very difficult for students as well as for other people to understand.

WHY HAS THE BERKELEY FACULTY FAILED TO CONDEMN VIOLATIONS OF THE LAW BY STUDENTS?

BY HENRY NASH SMITH, PROFESSOR, DEPARTMENT OF ENGLISH, BERKELEY

In trying to answer the question posed in my heading, I speak only for myself. There is no official "faculty position" on any aspect of our present troubles except the motions passed in meetings of the Berkeley Division of the Academic Senate.

Since the beginning of the present semester, students on the Berkeley campus have engaged in a long series of public demonstrations ranging from letters informing the dean they have violated university regulations, to a thirty-six-hour blockade of a police car on the campus late in October, a sit-in occupation of the administration building on December 2–3, and a student strike, with mass picketing, that lasted from December 4 to December 7.

My colleagues on other campuses may well be puzzled by the fact that while more than once the Berkeley Division has voted its disapproval of "force and violence," and while the policy recommended by the division on December 8 would not condone actions that interfere with the normal functions of the university, the division has consistently refused to vote a blanket condemnation of "illegal acts" or "lawlessness" on the part of students.

So far as I have been able to discover, the debate here over on-campus advocacy of off-campus illegal acts is at bottom an argument over whether students are to be allowed, at meetings held on university property, to advocate or organize sit-ins conducted in the community at large. Stated in these terms, the controversy at once becomes recognizable as part of the painful, confused, but profoundly significant national agony over civil rights for the Negro. One can of course imagine various kinds of illegal activity that might hypothetically be advocated on the campus by students if they were allowed absolute freedom of speech, but sit-ins related to the civil-rights issue are the form of off-campus political action most vividly present to the minds of both students and faculty members with whom I have discussed the matter.

The relation of our disturbances to the national civil-rights movement is indicated in various ways. The sit-in itself is a mode of action characteristic of civil-rights organizations. The most conspicuous disturbances in which Berkeley students have been involved during the past year have been efforts to create wider employment opportunities for Negroes with various businesses in the Bay Area. Several prominent student leaders of the Free Speech Movement, and many of their followers, have had firsthand experience of sit-ins in the South.

Experience with the national civil-rights movement has brought about a certain confusion in the minds of many students with respect to the absolute sanctity of all laws. In many parts of the South, state or local statutes enforce segregation, yet these laws are considered by a majority of the American people to be both immoral and unconstitutional. The idea of "law," in other words, seems to many respectable citizens not to be simple and monolithic, but highly problematical. The bald question, "Do you condemn all violations of law?" oversimplifies one of the most vital among contemporary public issues, and cannot be answered by a simple "yes" or "no."

The problem for both students and faculty here is further complicated by the belief, widely current on this campus and supported by men learned in the law, that the present university restrictions on advocacy are probably unconstitutional.

Many members of the Berkeley Division have concluded that a problem having such deep resonances for the nation at large, and involving such momentous ethical and political commitments, is of too great magnitude to be resolved in such a forum as the Academic Senate. Introduction of this question, even by implication, into academic legislation can hardly fail to obscure and impede the solution of the immediate local problems confronting us. Consigning to the courts of law the task of assessing punishment for sit-in demonstrations has seemed to a large majority of the Berkeley faculty the only feasible course.

During the past two or three months the Berkeley Division has seemed to many of us to have been placed in the position

of a spectator at a gladiatorial combat between antagonists—
Free Speech Movement and university administration—too
deeply absorbed in their own struggle to pay much attention to
the gallery. Because under existing regulations the administration has final authority over student discipline, the faculty has
found it difficult to intervene in the struggle. But as the combat has grown more prolonged and more violent, the Berkeley
Division has felt a greater and greater obligation to find some
means of entering the arena in order to serve as a mediator.
This is a dangerous and difficult role, particularly for inexperienced volunteers. But if the faculty is to have any chance
of success, it must approach its ungrateful task as an unbiased
third party. Some faculty members have proposed that the
division establish its impartiality by judicious condemnation of
both students and administration. This procedure is perfectly
comprehensible, and it has a certain moral grandeur. But from
a practical standpoint, to add invective, however austerely
phrased, to an atmosphere already befogged with abuse seems
a poor way to reduce tension and prepare the way for a workable settlement. I interpret the actions of the division over the
past weeks as showing a desire to preserve its freedom of
mediation. Instead of indicting both contestants in exactly
equal measure, it has preferred to refuse to frame accusations at all. I believe this policy to have been on the whole
sound, and I deeply regret the misunderstandings to which it
has perhaps inevitably given rise.

STATEMENT ON ACADEMIC SENATE RESOLUTION OF DECEMBER 8, 1964

BY HERBERT MC CLOSKY, PROFESSOR OF POLITICAL
SCIENCE, BERKELEY*

On December 8, the Berkeley Division of the Academic
Senate adopted a five point resolution designed to end the current controversy over student political rights and to return the
campus to its normal academic pursuits. The meaning of
the resolution and the intentions of its sponsors have aroused
some questions in the public mind. In the paragraphs that follow, I shall try to answer some of these questions.

I must caution, however, that the interpretations offered
are mine alone. They in no way bind the Committee on Academic Freedom, which introduced the resolution, the Council
of Departmental Chairmen, which supported the resolution,
or the 824 senate members—a majority of nearly 88%—who
voted for it. I shall begin with some general observations about

---

* From Berkeley *Daily Gazette*, December 15, 1964.

the meaning of the resolution, and shall then discuss each of its principal sections.

General Observations

Two concerns, I believe, lay uppermost in the minds of the resolution's proponents: the survival of the university as one of the world's most distinguished educational institutions; and the conviction that academic freedom obligates us to extend to students the widest possible latitude for political expression and advocacy.

In addressing the question of survival, the faculty was in no sense "capitulating to the mob." On the contrary, it was taking a hard, objective look at certain unpleasant realities. The most important of these realities was that the university had been plunged by a series of provocations on both sides into the most dangerous crisis in its history.

What began in a small way with the imposition of new restrictions on student freedom to support political candidates, to collect funds, to recruit members, and to man tables at certain locations on the campus had "escalated" into mass demonstrations, sit-ins, and strikes by the students, and suspensions, mass arrests, threatened dismissals of teaching assistants, and new restrictions on advocacy by the administration.

The crisis, in short, had become intolerable. Had it continued in its rampant form—and the senate's resolution or one like it not been adopted—we would now be facing a series of clearly predictable and potentially disastrous events. Among these events: a continuation of mass demonstrations and possible new sit-ins and arrests; sympathy strikes by hundreds of teaching assistants; the dismissal of these assistants, as promised by the administration; and, as an inevitable consequence, the resignation of large numbers of faculty members.

Since the most gifted teachers and scholars are in greatest demand, they would be sought out first by competing institutions and would be the first to leave. Soon, others would follow, for the university would have ceased to be the happy, intellectually exciting community that had attracted them in the first place. To judge from present evidence, these resignations would occur among faculty members of different points of view, among those favoring the students as well as those favoring the administration. The faculty members who remained would be torn for years by the quarrels spawned by this unhappy affair. These are no alarmist fantasies; signs of faculty demoralization and internal discord have already begun to appear. To replace the scholars who leave with men of equal quality would be difficult at best. In a highly competitive and expanding market, where the number of able scholars is far smaller than the number needed, it has been difficult, even under optimal conditions, to attract scholars of the first rank.

With the decline of faculty quality, it would become even more difficult than it is now to attract gifted students. The competition for qualified graduate students is, if anything, as intense as is the competition for outstanding faculty members.

The fashioning of a university of the first rank is not unlike the construction of a splendid cathedral. It requires unlimited patience, innumerable small but carefully considered decisions, the dedication of men of taste and sensibility, the cooperation of a wise and generous administration, and the financial and moral support of the community. It cannot be accomplished in a few years, often not even in a few decades. Unfortunately, however, it can be toppled in a few years, or even, it seems, in a few months.

No one would gain if the crisis were to continue and the tragic consequences I have sketched were to occur. The students would suffer an immense loss by having to attend a university of diminished intellectual quality. The administration, the Regents, and the people of California would suffer immeasurably from the loss of gifted teachers, scientists, poets, engineers, and social scientists who contribution to the intellectual and material welfare of the state has been incalculable. The faculty, of course, would suffer from a loss of *élan* and of pride of membership in the university community.

None of these losses need be suffered if the controversy is soon resolved, if differences are negotiated and long-range solutions are evolved. The resolution of December 8 may be imperfect in some respects, but it offers a focal point around which all parties can reasonably converge. For the time being, at least, it has diminished the sense of emergency and has temporarily alleviated the most pressing grievances. In this respect, it has been successful.

The resolution was not intended to assign blame or responsibility. Some of its supporters felt that the administration had contributed disproportionately to the crisis by hasty and ill-conceived actions, by failure to consult students on prospective changes in the rules, and by violations of the spirit, if not the letter, of previous agreements concerning discipline. Many also felt that the administration had meddled needlessly in the regulation of student political activity and had thereby provoked the subsequent outbreak.

Other faculty members who supported the resolution placed primary responsibility upon the students, blaming them for their impatience, for their withdrawal from the administration-faculty-student committee established to negotiate differences, and for their tactics of civil disobedience in a context in which such tactics were unjustified.

The resolution does not align the faculty with one side or

the other. It was conceived in the spirit of mediation, and in the desire to do justice to the legitimate student claims to freedom of political speech and advocacy. At the same time, however, it seeks to safeguard the authority of the university to regulate the "time, place, and manner of conducting political activity on the campus." No license is granted to either students or non-students to behave on campus in any way they please. Despite the intemperate accusations of certain editorial writers, the control of the university has not been vested by this resolution in "the irresponsible hands of student troublemakers . . ." Nor have "acts of anarchic defiance" been "condoned."

The resolution is admittedly imperfect and can doubtless be improved. It was not intended as a detailed program of legislation but as a statement of policy and principle. Its details can easily be negotiated and worked out through consultation and trial-and-error.

The terms of the resolution are in no sense radical or extreme. They do not call for any major overturning of policy. Indeed, they express support for practices that have actually been in effect at various times in the past.

The alleged "radicalism" of the proposal lies not so much in its substance as in its associations. Having been inserted into a controversy in which the contestants have been sharply polarized, the resolution has been invested by both sides and by some members of the community with radical properties. Careful examination of its principal terms, however, will confirm that it seeks to continue and to certify, by explicit documentation, a tradition of freedom that has been effectively in existence on this campus for many years.

Lifting of Penalties

This point in the resolution had already been negotiated by President Kerr and the Council of Chairmen in their meeting of December 6. Its inclusion in the December 8 resolution was prompted by the conviction that the time had arrived to wipe the slate clean and to make a new beginning. Events had taken so damaging a turn that all questions of penalties and retribution had declined in importance. The need now was to free the campus from the atmosphere of anger and panic that had overtaken it and that was preventing the achievement of a rational and equitable solution.

Although some faculty members believed that all violations of university discipline must be severely punished, others felt that the students had been provoked needlessly. Most important, however, they felt that the granting of immunity from university discipline for all acts prior to December 8 was a *sine qua non* of any settlement. Without it, we would be hopelessly mired and unable ever to extricate ourselves.

The adoption of this view was a sign not of weakness or capitulation but of realism and charity. There is a time to punish and a time to forgive. There are occasions when forgiveness for disobedience of the rules does more to strengthen the rules and the legitimate authority of the rule makers than the strict enforcement of the rules and the exacting of retribution for failure to obey them.

We should also keep in mind who the offenders were. In our distress, many of us have forgotten that the so-called "rebels" and dissenters are our own students—young men and women of quality and intelligence, the future doctors, lawyers, professors, writers, scientists, and political leaders of the society. Some have disobeyed the law, but they are not "criminals." A few are passing through youthful flirtations with revolutionary political movements (from which, as the experience of their predecessors attests, they will soon emerge), while a great many have shown themselves superior in courage and moral conscience by their activities on behalf of civil rights.

They are not without blame, and they have contributed, along with the administrative officials of this university, to an intolerable crisis from which we shall finally escape only if the men and women who judge these events do so with wisdom and forbearance. But, like the administration whom they oppose, the vast majority of students who participated in the protests are decent and civilized, liberal and tolerant, sincere and responsible. To have taken a punitive, righteous, or sanctimonious attitude toward them would have been unworthy of a great university and damaging to the settlement of this unfortunate affair.

Rules and Regulations

Although it is clear from the text, there is some confusion in the public mind about the university's authority to regulate the conduct of political activity on the campus.

Nothing in the resolution jeopardizes in any way its authority to determine the "time, place and manner" by which the political activities of students and non-students shall be regulated. Point 2 of the resolution explicitly provides for this. Not only can the university impose intramural penalties for breaches of discipline in this area, but it possesses the power granted to it by the state of California to prosecute individuals or groups who violate the law when on university property. No action by the Academic Senate could deprive the university of this power.

Just as the university can regulate the use of university facilities by students, so *a fortiori* can it control the use of those facilities by non-students. Regulations governing such uses are now being considered by the Committee on Academic Freedom, a highly respected group of faculty members who can be expected to evolve a plan of regulation that will satisfy both the normal teaching and research functions of the university as well as the rights of students to assemble, associate, and discuss in a manner befitting the requirements of a free society.

The Right of Advocacy

Here we come to what many faculty members regard as the most crucial section of the resolution, although it is by no means clear that the disagreement between the students and the administration on this question is a genuine one. The question is complex and beset with technicalities. But the principle that the faculty wished to express is simple, straightforward, and entirely in keeping with the requirements and spirit of the First Amendment.

The faculty has asked that the content of speech or advocacy on the campus shall not be restricted by the university, and that the political activities of students when they are away from the campus shall not be subject to university regulations.

This provision asks the university, therefore, to relinquish the burden of imposing intramural punishments on the content of political speech.

Apart from the First Amendment, there are many reasons of realism and prudence for adopting this recommendation. For the university to regulate these matters would involve it in a complex, technical, and rapidly changing jurisprudence. It would need to constitute itself a court, with all the attendant paraphernalia of judges, lawyers, prosecutors, witnesses, verbatim transcripts, rules of evidence, and numerous other elements of accepted judicial procedure. The university has neither the competence nor the facilities for undertaking this role. It would require the policing of political speeches by every student and visitor on the campus. It would also require the surveillance of 60,000 students as they engage in political activities in other parts of the community.

Obviously, what appears to be an innocent and plausible requirement, namely, that the students may use the campus to promote lawful but not unlawful activities, turns out, upon investigation, to involve the university in a hopeless entanglement of legal, moral, and political difficulties.

The political difficulties, of course, would arise whenever the university rendered a decision that was repugnant to some interest or political action group that favored, or opposed, the content of what had been advocated.

By imposing university punishments for alleged illegal advocacy or for advocacy leading to illegal acts beyond the campus, the university would open itself to an interminable series of litigations, student and faculty protests, petitions, unfavorable press notices, and pressures from organized interest groups. Furthermore, with the civil rights movement now at its height, it would be impossible for the university to escape the appearance (and the charge) of having interfered with the effort to achieve the rights of an oppressed minority.

The resolution, it should be observed, neither grants nor withholds immunity from civil prosecution for speech or actions judged to be illegal. The judgment, however, is left to the courts, which are best suited to deal with it.

The intention of the advocacy provision in the resolution is entirely consistent with what has been the effective policy of the university for some years. That policy has been repeatedly expressed by President Kerr when he spoke, for example, of making students "safe for ideas," or when he recently announced that student speech would not be subject either to "prior censorship or double jeopardy." It also corresponds with his previous announcements that "one punishment, not two, should fit one crime."

Careful investigation of this matter, I am certain, will persuade all parties to the controversy that the differences that have developed around this question are more shadow than substance. I trust they will also be persuaded that in matters of free speech, the university must be "more royalist than the king." The freedom to think and to express one's thoughts is the indispensable ingredient of the search for truth and the instruction of the young. Unless it is applied in fullest measure, a university is impossible.

As a center of learning and enlightenment, moreover, the university bears an obligation to the community to set a standard and to uphold the great values of the American democratic tradition against every challenge and temptation.

Some of my colleagues fear that by refusing to intervene in the regulation of speech, we shall somehow reduce the university's autonomy and its freedom from civil interference. Others, however, voice precisely the opposite charge. The resolution, they assert, seeks to convert the university into a fortress from which students can mount political activity against the society with impunity. Both charges, in my opinion, are without substance. In practice, the university will be neither more autonomous nor less autonomous for having put this provision into effect.

Academic Senate Committee

The last of the major points dealt with in the resolution calls for the establishment of a faculty disciplinary committee that would be appointed by and responsible to the Berkeley Division of the Academic Senate. Although the senate has on various occasions in the past exercised this power, the regulation of discipline has in recent years fallen primarily upon the chancellor and other administrative officers, with the advice and assistance of appointed faculty members.

If I assess correctly the opinions of most faculty members on this question, there is no great enthusiasm for reassuming the burden of enforcing discipline in the area of student political conduct. Why then have they adopted this provision?

I believe they have done so for two reasons essentially: a great number of students appear to have lost confidence in the old agencies by which political activities have been regulated and disciplined. The second reason is that many faculty members hope that with the content of advocacy freed from the burdens of regulation, and with the liberalization of the rules governing political conduct already achieved or in the making, the relatively minor matters of enforcing the time, place, and manner of conducting political activity on the campus will not prove a heavy burden. In short, many expect that this committee will have little to do.

The adoption of this proposal raises one small question about the location of "final" power over these matters. Traditionally the Regents hold final power over all matters of this type, and the resolution does not propose that the Regents can or should relinquish their constituted authority. It only proposes that the regulation of student political conduct be effectively vested in a senate committee.

The issue here is in any event a small one, easily negotiable and not difficult to resolve. One possible intermediate alternative, for example, might be to permit a senate committee to function in this area for a three-year period, with the entire matter to be reviewed at the end of the trial period. Persons with more experience and knowledge of university procedures than I possess could doubtless suggest many other alternatives.

In summary, then, the resolution expresses no principle that is fundamentally at variance with previous university practice or professed policy. All of its provisions could easily be absorbed into the existing university framework with little or no difficulty.

REFLECTIONS ON THE CRISIS AT BERKELEY
BY HENRY STAPP, LAWRENCE RADIATION
LABORATORY, BERKELEY

The events at the University of California must be recognized as a critical point in the nation's history; the issues involve basic questions of political rights and social obligations, and the outcome is likely to set a pattern for expressing grievances that will profoundly affect the entire land. That the Berkeley Academic Senate should recommend a policy judged outrageous by most citizens attests to the subtlety of the problem. Yet the seriousness of the matter requires every responsible citizen to carefully weigh for himself the issues involved.

The conflict at Berkeley is only incidentally a matter of university regulations. The central issue is the challenge to the nation's traditional precept of respect for law inevitably posed by the civil disobedience demonstrations in the South. If this type of illegal action is regarded as respectable, then the whole question of the citizen's obligation to support the law must inevitably be reassessed.

The direct immediate question is under what circumstances civil disobedience is a morally acceptable method of expressing grievances in a society where democratic principles prevail. A proposed answer is that if a person is willing to face legal punishment to dramatize his grievances, then this is a moral right that should always be respected.

This proposal is in direct conflict with the traditional view that in a society in which democratic principles prevail it is the moral and social obligation of the responsible citizen to support and obey a law regardless of his personal feelings. He does this not from fear of punishment but from respect for the rights of others as defined by majority opinion. This tradition of respect for democratic law is commonly regarded as the bedrock upon which our society is built; that without this abiding commitment by responsible citizens to a respect for law, our society would surely crumble.

The issue raised, therefore, is whether this tradition of respect for laws, regardless of opposing conviction, should be modified to give respectability to nonviolent civil disobedience as a method for expressing grievance even in a society where democratic principles prevail.

An example of the new morality is the Berkeley sit-in. There the specific cause was a university move to discipline student leaders. Previously, by a liberal policy of granting most student demands but standing firm on a rule prohibiting the mounting of illegal actions from university property (advocacy was permitted), the university had satisfied most students. But aroused by the disciplinary move, the students invoked the sit-in method used in the South by their leaders.

This case dramatizes an important question: If a move to discipline four students leads to massive civil disobedience, what is to be expected in serious situations?

A much debated point in the Berkeley dispute is whether the university is abridging a constitutional right by prohibiting the mounting of illegal actions from its premises. As the proper channel for raising this question is the courts, the debates have served mainly to obscure the central moral issues.

Separate from the legal question is one of policy: assuming the university has the legal rights to forbid the mounting of illegal actions on its premises, should these rights be exercised? The faculty said an emphatic no.

The manner in which the faculty expressed themselves has placed the Regents in the position of having to oppose the Academic Senate resolution, thereby jeopardizing the university, or in effect, to repudiate the traditional basis for social and political morality in this country. The traditional moral position calls not only for submission to the laws of a democratic society but for an active commitment on their behalf; the responsible citizen not only obeys the laws but exercises the legal means within his power to prevent illegal action. He certainly does not facilitate illegal action.

Now among the many points raised by the students is the point that a university education should provide more than book-learning; there is also the education for citizenship provided by involvement in political discussion and action. This could not be more true. That is one reason why university policy in this matter is so important. Should not the university policy itself be an example of the type of moral commitment to legality that one expects from responsible citizens? If the university abdicates the position of positive commitment to the support of law on the grounds of academic freedom, will this not be an example and precedent for the abdication of this responsibility by other groups and individuals on the basis of their own special interests?

What such questions signalize, and what every citizen must face, is that this nation is entering a genuine moral crisis; some of its most basic precepts are under serious attack from important quarters. While alternative moral structures are doubtless possible, the collapse of the present one would open the door to various rival possibilities, and the ensuing struggles could sorely distress or even jeopardize the nation. The conscientious citizen must, therefore, carefully weigh whether progress in California today toward the elimination of injustice is sufficiently unsatisfactory to warrant the desertion of our traditional principles.

Although the clash at Berkeley is just one battle in this challenge to traditional morality arising from the troubles in the South, it may be of decisive importance. For it will be an influential factor in the disposition of student and intellectual groups, which generally play important roles in situations of disorder and readjustment.

The tragedy of the Berkeley situation is that we are faced on the one hand with the perilous course of inviting chaos by officially repudiating at the outset the traditional precepts upon which this country has been based, with no clear guideline for the future, or, on the other hand, with the destruction of one of the nation's greatest universities. This latter might seem of relatively small consequence, but the resulting alienation of the nation's academic community would exacerbate an already difficult situation.

The essential source of disagreement in Berkeley is that one side is concerned mainly with a large number of grievances that are individually rather insignificant, particularly on the national scale. They are essentially grievances against administration handling of various problems. In expressing these grievances the students used methods not sanctioned by traditional morality. And in the proposed solution the traditional morality is directly repudiated. The forces opposing student demands take the perspective of the nation as a whole. They do not see that student grievances at a school administration can warrant jeopardizing the stablility of the nation by a repudiation of our traditional moral structure.

The hope and good fortune in the Berkeley situation lie in the fact that the clash occurred in Berkeley. For in Berkeley is gathered one of the nation's most illustrious faculties, at a university presided over by one of the nation's most liberal presidents. The Regents are distinguished and dedicated representatives of the people of California, and the students and graduate students are among the nation's brightest. Since the challenge was inevitable we can be thankful that an important first phase of the conflict can be acted upon by the best products of American culture in the Berkeley environment of goodwill. If toleration and understanding cannot be found in Berkeley, then the nation's fate is dark.

AN ANSWER TO A LETTER BY A PRO-FSM STUDENT PUBLISHED IN THE BERKELEY *DAILY GAZETTE*

BY DANIEL I. ARNON, UC PROFESSOR OF CELL PHYSIOLOGY

A letter (printed Feb. 4) attempts to justify the student disorders of last fall as the consequence of alleged student grievances of previous years. He suggests that the FSM leaders of 1964 were motivated by events which occurred before they were even students on the Berkeley campus. But what is the truth about these past events?

(1) The graduate students were not "disenfranchised on the basis of a dubious poll" as he writes but were allowed to withdraw from the student government (ASUC) after 1300 of them signed, in April 1959, a petition for "disassociation" from ASUC and for relief from paying the attendant fees, and when this sentiment was substantiated by a poll of graduate student opinion.

(2) Campus privileges were withdrawn from Slate (a student organization now prominent in FSM) on June 10, 1961, when this organization, contrary to its promises, failed to abide by the terms of its university recognition.

(3) The demagoguery of the leaders of Slate who opposed the allegedly more severe restrictions of the "Kerr directives" was exposed when, on November 15, 1961, President Kerr in an open letter offered to withdraw his new "directives" and return to the old "directives" on student political activity. This offer was rejected by the leaders of Slate.

Finally, we come to the point which perhaps best illustrates the inaccuracies, half-truths, and downright distortions which underlie so much of the current FSM mythology. Your correspondent states that the administration did not lift the "Communist speaker ban until students of the Santa Barbara campus took the Regents into court over the issue." It was not Santa Barbara but Riverside. The students did not win the case but lost it (Lessin vs. the Regents of UC). The Regents, despite winning the case in court, voluntarily lifted the ban on Communist speakers in the following year (1963) because they recognized that objective discussion of even the most extreme political issues and philosophies on the campus separates propaganda from truth and thereby promotes the intellectual development of students and prepares them for intelligent participation in the affairs of society.

This action of the Regents has been widely acclaimed in the academic world. In April 1964, the American Association of University Professors (AAUP) recognized it as an outstanding contribution to the cause of academic freedom and honored it by awarding to President Kerr and to the Regents the Seventh Alexander Meiklejohn Award, "an award which bears the name of one of America's most honored and redoubtable champions of intellectual freedom," as the AAUP citation reads.

How then could "free speech" become an issue in October when in April of the same year the University of California was being so generously commended for expanding free speech on the campus? The truth is that, despite repeated assertions, free speech never was an issue in the student disorders at Berkeley last semester. The use of the Free Speech Movement (FSM) label contains just that element of oversimplification best calculated to obscure facts but win followers. The dispute was, from the beginning, not over free speech but over the freedom to organize political action and collect funds on the campus.

The rest is history. What has not been stressed before is the refusal of the FSM leaders to seek a peaceful and orderly change of existing regulations. It is not good enough to say that they used threats and violence because they lost confidence in the administration. Why have they not appealed, by petition, to the Academic Senate, whom they always profess to trust and respect? Petitions from students are a fixed item on the agenda of every meeting of the Academic Senate, but none was ever received from the FSM leaders during the stormy fall semester.

It is difficult to escape the conclusion that important segments of the FSM, notably Slate, were less interested in free speech than in destroying those orderly procedures and common decencies between students, faculty and administration without which a university cannot function as an intellectual community. This conclusion is strengthened by very recent evidence. Last week Slate distributed a "Supplement to the General Catalogue" which damaged the reputation of a prominent UC professor (see the *Daily Californian,* Feb. 4 and 5). This action was publicly condemned even by those on the faculty who in the past have supported some of the FSM objectives. Another Slate Supplement, distributed at the time of registration for the fall semester (see *Daily Californian,* Sept. 16, 1964), that is, BEFORE the later disorders, carried the following appeal to students:

"This institution, affectionately called 'Cal' by many of you . . . does not deserve a response of loyalty and allegiance from you . . . organize and split this campus wide open . . . begin an open, fierce, and thoroughgoing rebellion on this campus."

The university at Berkeley, like all universities, has indeed problems to solve. But these will not be solved by the tactics of Slate or of the FSM leaders, which if not checked may well destroy the university.

INTELLECTUAL RESPONSIBILITY AND POLITICAL CONDUCT

BY ALBERT LEPAWSKY, PROFESSOR OF POLITICAL SCIENCE, BERKELEY, JANUARY 2, 1965

The university is slated to "go back to school" on Monday. As we reach this climax in the dramatic days which the Berkeley community is now living through, what are some of the hopeful lessons we might learn from this profound experience? I think there are at least two, one as to the student's role, the other relating to the faculty's responsibility.

Studentship and Scholarship

First and foremost is the lesson that university students, whether undergraduate or graduate, can no longer be treated as passive pupils but must be regarded as a critical and, it is hoped, a constructive force in the shaping of this evolving institution of higher learning.

By the same token, however, activist Berkeley students have learned or, to be more accurate, they are learning that their recently recognized maturity is posited upon the proverbial double-edged sword. For, in the course of establishing or exercising their new-found responsibilities, if they violate the laws of the surrounding society or contravene established canons of conduct in the modern university, they must be prepared to pay the same price which men and women pay for comparable missteps in the world at large.

The price students must pay is measured not merely in the legal penalties of the law—every child expects the punishment to fit the crime—but rather in the cost of lost learning; lost learning not only for those who choose to sit-in or strike, but also lost learning for the preponderance of students who shun the "Free Speech Movement" and demand their liberty to learn, but who, in the shuffle, are denied their continued freedom to be educated. And there is also the imponderable price paid by the institution itself. This takes the form not only of a damaged image but an interrupted intellectual effort at a university in which all these students are members, whether they are critical or proud of it.

Civil Rights on and off Campus

In every fight for freedom, one has to weigh the freedoms sought against those sacrificed, and not only one's own freedoms but the other fellow's as well. It is easy to say that the principle at stake in the dispute immediately at hand is so basic (to oneself and also to others who are too ignorant to recognize their best interests), that it is worth the price of other people's lost liberties as a whole and of one's own remaining liberties. In actual fact, however, there is no better way to misread the lesson for the righteous student in this whole affair than to permit him to pose it, without rebuttal, as a moral and personal impasse which justified the ultimate tactic of civil disobedience he imposed upon others.

The struggle on this campus is manifestly different from the fight for civil rights which called forth civil disobedience in the South. For a hundred years this nation has procrastinated and the South has sabotaged civil rights. All legal remedies in the fight for civil rights were exhausted. Consequently, men and women, both the disfranchised and the disillusioned in the South and their courageous defenders from the rest of the country (including some of our own "Free Speech" leaders), had no alternative but to turn to the doctrine and tactic of Thoreau and Gandhi.

In Berkeley, by contrast, the complaining students, though taxed to the limit sometimes by faculty apathy and administration ineptness, still had (and they still have) unexploited channels of appeal within this multi-university structure and in the open courts outside. They chose instead to use extraordinary means, illegal or legalistic, to press their case. Thereby, they seriously interrupted, as they promised they would, the proper functioning of the university.

Even now, under the same sort of pressures, some student leaders are demanding the immediate crossing of "t's" and dotting of "i's" as to particularized rights under the First and Fourteenth amendments, rights which in principle the Regents and administration have reaffirmed. There are here involved, some of the most intricate and still-to-be adjudicated issues of on-campus and off-campus conduct, of legal and illegal political activity, of due process and double jeopardy, and of legitimate or conspiratorial behavior.

Berkeley Campus as a Possible Model

The University of California has been "fingered," by either fate or faction, to be the "fall guy" among American universities for the decision (I hope it will be the adjudication) of these technical questions. Their determination can only be made on a case-to-case basis. No forced pronunciamentos from either students or faculty, administrators or Regents, can legalize what may possibly turn out to be unlegal.

I very much doubt that the courts of this country will hold that the preservation of political freedoms for scholars, whether students or faculty, who are members of an academic community, requires the American university, either public or private, to forego its right and responsibility to enforce certain essential regulations of conduct upon the whole body of its members acting on its own premises. How else can a viably functioning intellectual institution be maintained in an interdependent society?

Should the courts go to other extremes in interpreting the First and Fourteenth amendments, our universities will have to roll with the punch and try to maintain a genuinely free character nevertheless. But to capitulate to such a drastic "constitutional" revision, under undue pressure rather than by due deliberation, would be unworthy, if not suicidal, for any recognizable sub-community within or corporate part of the Great Society.

If protesting students or sympathetic faculty continue to employ pressureful political tactics, they will be misreading the lessons to be learned in Berkeley's present circumstance. To press the initiative or strike while the iron (more precisely, the campus) is hot may be slick politics, but it is not necessarily sound political science. It is an old tactic among power groups which our professors of political science teach about but seldom advocate.

Intellectualization and Politicization

Lesson number two, which responsible faculty may particularly wish to consider for themselves and stress for their students, may be stated thus: the main task we face is that of preserving the university not merely as a free political community but primarily as an institution which is privileged to be an intellectual sanctuary within a greater society that is now in political flux.

After all, the university's prime mission resides not in political activity but in the cultivation of the intellectual freedoms. In this respect the key question, whose answer is going to be decisive not only for this university but for other, probably all, universities in this nation, and possibly also for the nation as a whole, is: shall the politicization of the American university be permitted to escalate to a point which threatens the university's overriding responsibility for the intellectualization of American life?

The proper answer to this question is, I think, as follows: political behavior is an important part of intelligent conduct, and intellectual freedoms must therefore incorporate political freedom at the university. However, insofar as the university and its members may be concerned, any conflict arising between the intellectual and the political way of life must be resolved in favor of the primacy of the intellectual over the political.

In the last analysis political behavior does not constitute all of social conduct, and politics is not the predominant part of ethics. Some may feel otherwise. But I have never been so enamored of my own specialized discipline of political behavior or public administration as to feel that it is more fundamental to the good life than is the general search for genuine truths and the imparting of balanced bodies of knowledge.

All institutions, whether educational or otherwise, which have a recognizable role in the greater society have special objectives. The university's responsibility is teaching and learning, research and experimentation; yes, even political experimentation. But it is imperative that no one facet of the university's activities, certainly not the political, should dominate its overall responsibilities for the cultivation of the intellect.

Faculty and students can go on, as they have throughout this dispute, preaching their doctrines upon university administrators, Regents, and the supporting public. But their main opportunity now is to attain a tenable position of their own within the heart of the intellectual community itself. And if they adhere to the twin tests of valid ideas and sound experience, they cannot fail to consider, though they may not yet wish to confirm, the two lessons which may be learned from Berkeley's "Moment of Truth."

OPINIONS BY LAW SCHOOL FACULTY

TO: THE COMMITTEE ON ACADEMIC FREEDOM
OF THE BERKELEY DIVISION
FROM: R. H. COLE, H. A. LINDE AND R. M. O'NEIL,
PROFESSORS OF LAW

In November you asked us to consider certain legal aspects of state university regulation of student activities—particularly of a "political" nature—on the university campus. When we met with you on November 13, we discussed numerous issues. Some of these were of a general nature; others were concerned with the particular regulations which were then applicable to student expression and activities on the Berkeley campus. Since that meeting, we have done research on these questions, and have discussed them at length among ourselves and with various of our colleagues. We were not able, however, to transmit to you a formal opinion before the meeting of the Berkeley Division of the Academic Senate on December 8. What the present memorandum seeks to do is to summarize the views we expressed on November 13 and which subsequent consideration has confirmed. We shall be happy, if you so request, to clarify any portions of this memorandum or to supply further analysis on any points at which it may be desired. For the sake of brevity, we have omitted detailed argumentation and all legal citations.

I. *Analytical Considerations and Distinctions*

At the outset we desire to draw several distinctions that will be of recurrent importance throughout our analysis. Some of these distinctions, if not all, carry constitutional significance. First it is necessary to separate questions of (a) the substantive scope of regulations that may constitutionally be imposed upon the use of state university grounds and facilities; (b) disciplinary sanctions that may be used to enforce such regulations—including expulsion, suspension and other less drastic curtailment of academic benefits; and (c) other (usually direct and immediate) means of enforcement that involve no disciplinary consequences.

Second, it is necessary to distinguish between two classes of persons subject to university regulations—for a university may enforce certain restrictions against (a) non-students, as well as against (b) students (who are, of course, within the reach of additional forms of sanction).

Third, a distinction should be drawn between two types of regulated student conduct: (a) that which violates general law (i.e., federal, state, county or city statutes or ordinances) but does not violate university regulations; and (b) that which does violate university regulations. Conduct in the latter category may or may not also violate the general law.

Fourth, it seems appropriate to distinguish between forbidden conduct which is (a) specifically relevant to a student's qualifications as a member of the university community; and (b) conduct which is substantially irrelevant to those qualifications. Such qualifications may either be academic in nature, or be based upon protection of important non-academic interests of the university community. To illustrate: A non-resident student's violation of the traffic laws of his home state during his summer vacation, or a conviction for drunk and disorderly conduct while away from the campus, would seem irrelevant to his qualifications as a member of the university community. In similar fashion one might dismiss many other off-campus offenses. On the other hand, an assault upon a member of the faculty, or the theft of a book from the university library, seem to be material to the student's qualifications—even though the latter instances involve behavior neither more nor less punishable under the general law than the former cases.

Following this analytical framework it may be well to mention several matters with which we have not been concerned and on which we are therefore not reporting. We have not been concerned with the constitutionality of existing criminal statutes in the general law that may be applicable to student activities or offenses on or off the campus. Nor have we considered the choices that may be made among available sanctions and university discipline—although we note that certain forms of discipline (e.g., expulsion or suspension) are much more likely to inhibit student conduct than other, milder sanctions (e.g., transferring a student from one dormitory to another for "rowdiness").

II. *The State University and the Student: Constitutional Premises*

A. *The State University Is Governed by the Constitution.* A state university is clearly subject to those federal constitutional limitations and prohibitions that apply to all other branches of the state government. Thus the courts have consistently held that a state university may not refuse admission to anyone on racial or religious grounds. Nor can a state university hire or fire employees, academic or administrative or clerical, on racially discriminatory grounds. Similarly the other basic constitutional guarantees of individual liberty—including provisions of both state and federal constitutions that guarantee freedoms of expression (speech, press, assembly and petition)—apply to actions of the state university just as they do to actions of any other branch of the state government.

B. *Attendance at a State University: Right or Privilege?* For at least the last quarter century, state universities have not been free to dismiss student claims of constitutional deprivation or infringement on the ground that admission to the university is only a "privilege" and not a legal "right." A state is not constitutionally required to establish a university, or to open the doors of its university to everyone if it does establish such an institution. That does not mean, however, that the state may condition attendance at the university upon the surrender or abandonment of such activities as religious worship, lawful assembly, or voting in elections, which are constitutionally protected against direct infringement by the state. This principle is a particular application of a general legal doctrine that government may not condition the grant of a "privilege" upon the recipient's willingness to forego or surrender constitutionally protected rights. Recent decisions of the California Supreme Court have been particularly vigorous in the recognition and application of this doctrine.

C. *The State University Has Special Regulatory Interests.* A state university undoubtedly has certain general regulatory powers over the campus—powers equivalent to those of other branches of the government that operate public buildings (such as hospitals and libraries) where a degree of quiet and order are essential to the work of the institution. Thus the university may regulate activities on the campus in order to control the flow of traffic, insure the safety of those who use university facilities, prevent excessive noise, and protect the university community against fire, theft and other physical dangers.

In addition the university possesses special regulatory interests of a sort which require protection only in the academic setting. These interests are of two sorts—academic and nonacademic. For example, the university has undoubted power to prohibit and punish cheating and other misconduct during examinations, plagiarism, abuse of library privileges, and myriad other matters of this sort. In pursuit of its special nonacademic interests the university just as clearly has the power to protect students against financial fraud, the use of and exposure to narcotics, alcohol, gambling and the like on the campus.

III. *Application of the Constitutional Principles to the Problem of University Regulation*

A. *General Considerations; Regulation of the Time, Place and Manner of Speaking Are Generally Valid.* Regulations designed to vindicate special interests of the university, whether academic or non-academic, are unlikely to raise constitutional objections so long as they are drafted narrowly and specifically in terms of the interest they seek to protect. In fact, most regulations of this sort do not deal at all with expression or activity protected by the First Amendment, and we are therefore not concerned with them in this memorandum. To the extent that such regulations do affect expression and assembly on the campus, they usually do so in ways that are not thought to infringe constitutional rights. For example, it is well settled that although a city may not exclude speakers entirely from its public parks, nor permit them to speak only on certain "approved" subjects, it may forbid the use of very loud sound amplification and may require minimal registration in advance of a speech or meeting to make sure that two speakers are not vying for the same podium at the same hour. Such restrictions, although concerned only with the time, place and manner, undeniably do interfere with the absolute freedom of expression. But they withstand constitutional attack for two distinct reasons: First, they are entirely indifferent to the content of the expression (and thus do not permit censorship); and second, they do not seriously or permanently inhibit the speaker's ability to reach his audience. Those legal principles which warrant municipal regulation apply just as forcefully to the regulation by a state university of the time, place and manner of speaking on the campus.

B. *Formal Restrictions Must Not Discriminate against a Particular Class of Expression.* Regulations that appear to deal only with the time, place and manner of speaking may nevertheless involve invalid substantive restriction under certain conditions. That would be the case if a regulation were to permit certain conduct for *nonpolitical* purposes while prohibiting the same conduct for *political* purposes. To illustrate: Recently some students have taken to using dormitory windows as display places for various pictures, banners, slogans and the like. The university, to protect against damage to the windows of the dormitories it owns, could very likely forbid all use of such windows for these purposes—or could impose other less drastic restrictions (dealing, for example, with the size and number of banners or posters permitted in each room).

But the university could not, consistent with the First Amendment, permit window signs reading "Beat Stanford" and forbid signs that read "Beat Goldwater." Such a regulation would be unconstitutional because it would put the university in the business of discriminating against a particular class of protected expression—even if, as posited, the university could forbid all use of dormitory windows for such purposes. Thus many regulations on the campus that affect only the time, place and manner of expression may become invalid if they single out political activity (or any other protected category) for special treatment. (We do not, of course, mean to suggest that university regulations might not constitutionally give greater latitude to political and other protected forms of expression; that is a different question with which we are not immediately concerned.)

C. *Any Regulations of Speech Content Raise Serious Constitutional Questions.* To this point we have been concerned only with regulations of such formal aspects of speech as time, place and manner of speaking and holding meetings. We have observed that such regulations are generally valid when they are narrowly drafted to serve interests of the university that may be either of general applicability to governmental institutions, or peculiar to the academic community.

We come now to the more difficult question of regulation of the substance or content of expression. The courts have made increasingly clear in recent years that any regulations based upon the content or substance of expression are very vulnerable to constitutional challenge. But before we apply this general proposition to the matter before us, some background considerations seem appropriate.

The use of speech does not always immunize a speaker from penalties and liabilities under the general law, criminal or civil. There is much human behavior that involves language, either written or spoken, but is nonetheless subject to civil and criminal liability. In some instances the language used is merely evidence of the offense, or serves to provoke the offense; in other instances the language is itself the gist of the offense. One can hardly conspire to commit a crime, or solicit or abet others to crime, or incite a mob to crime, or defame another, or be obscene, without the use of language. But the mere fact that language is involved, even centrally, does not necessarily invoke the constitutional protections of the First Amendment. Thus a civil suit for libel, or a prosecution of one who has brought about a "clear and present danger" of a crime or a riot, does not infringe the First Amendment.

Regulations framed in terms of, or directed against the content of speech raise, however, quite different constitutional questions. Although, as we have just indicated, one may be penalized for certain conduct involving speech, the courts have consistently required that any such regulation differentiate sharply and clearly between that which is permitted and that which is prohibited. Laws that affect the content of expression must give clear warning where the line between the lawful and the unlawful lies. This is largely because unclear or vague regulations are very likely to deter or inhibit the person who wants to engage in speech that is protected, but who also desires to avoid any possible liability if his judgment is unsound. What this means, to distill the learning of hundreds of court decisions, is that regulation of obscenity, defamation, "fighting words" and other expression that may be forbidden, must be carried out with the most discriminating tools. Innumerable regulations that have attempted to differentiate between the protected and the prohibited have failed to pass constitutional muster because they left the speaker uncertain of the regulatory line. And it should be clear that some of the most socially useful speech and political activity does approach the borderline—indeed, its very utility often derives in large measure from its controversiality.

Thus we conclude: (1) Under the First Amendment the state may constitutionally regulate or prevent certain behavior even though it may involve the use of language; (2) for that reason the content of speech on the university campus may theoretically be regulated to a limited extent; and (3) the drafting of regulations to separate the protected from the unprotected is a perilous process even for experts in constitutional law. Thus we caution against any attempt to draft regulations for a state university campus dealing with expression in terms of content.

D. *University Regulation of Speech Content Is Particularly Dangerous.* We caution against regulation of speech content for two distinct reasons. First, there is the extreme difficulty of precise delineation to which we have already referred. Second, there is an additional reason to which we now turn: the absence in university disciplinary proceedings of those institutional and procedural safeguards that are available to the criminal defendant in a court of law. University disciplinary sanctions, although not "criminal" in the technical sense, are likely to be far more drastic in their effect than typical criminal penalties. Almost any student would rather pay a $25 fine, or even serve a week in jail, than be expelled from college. Thus it is no answer to suggest that the institutional safeguards afforded in court are unnecessary in the disciplinary process because criminal sanctions cannot be imposed there.

The importance of those institutional safeguards—trial by jury, right to a public trial, a full transcript, right of appeal, and the surveillance of an independent judge—has been repeatedly stressed by the courts in free speech cases. The United States Supreme Court has denied to administrative tribunals and other nonjudicial bodies certain powers to regulate the content of expression that have been given to the courts. The reason for this distinction is precisely the one we have been considering—the availability in the criminal court of institutional and procedural safeguards that cannot be provided in an administrative proceeding. Thus, for this reason as well as the reason stated earlier, we would caution against any attempt to frame regulations or restrictions concerning the content or substance of speech and expression on a state university campus.

E. *University Regulation of Speech Content Is Not Essential to the University's Interests.* One question remains: Are there, notwithstanding the constitutional doubts we have expressed, special university interests that might nevertheless warrant some regulations directed at speech content? Of course various academic interests of the university justify some regulation of speech content in the classroom and on the examination paper; the student who receives a failing grade for his erroneous answers, or the student who is suspended for his dishonest answers, can hardly claim the shelter of the First Amendment. What we are now concerned with, however, is speech in the extra-curricular context.

It may still be argued that certain non-academic interests justify additional regulations of speech content on the campus. Without deprecating these interests, we feel that they are adequately protected without content-oriented regulations on the campus. This is primarily because the general laws that make certain dangerous or highly offensive behavior "illegal" apply just as much on the campus as they do off the campus; the gates of the university afford no sanctuary from the enforcement of criminal law. Thus if two or more persons on the campus beat up a third, the police can break up the fracas and arrest the participants for assault and battery. (It is immaterial to this analysis whether the arrest be made by city, county, state or campus police.) If the attackers agree among themselves to attack the victim, or if one man calls upon the others to do so but does not himself join the fray, the ordinary principles of criminal law and accountability surely apply just as though the incident had occurred on the sidewalk.

Many offenses that may be committed on university campuses are also crimes—theft, battery, liquor and sex offenses, for example. Likewise, the law enforcement authorities have power to maintain law and order on the campus under general traffic laws, ordinances relating to excessive noise and other disturbances, breach of the peace, and many others. In all of these cases it has not been necessary to consider whether the persons involved were students; and the power of the law enforcement authorities to invoke the general law on the campus depends in no way upon the availability or actual resort to special university disciplinary sanctions.

Another factor confirms our judgment that university interests are adequately protected without regulations directed at speech content: There are, as we suggested at the outset, various means of enforcement of university rules (and of the general law) that involve no punishment and thus are unlikely to inhibit. A crowd can be controlled by skillful policemen, for example, in various ways less drastic than arresting the speaker who is addressing it. Similarly the university has many sanctions in its regulatory arsenal by which to enforce its rules, and therefore its special interests, without invoking the drastic measure of suspension or expulsion. Unless it can be shown that none of these non-punitive means of enforcement is effective, and that the application of the general law on the campus inadequately protects the university, we believe that content-oriented regulations of speech are unnecessary, as well as constitutionally unwise.

December 15, 1964

A STATEMENT ON THE LEGAL ISSUES
BY DAVID W. LOUISELL,
PROFESSOR OF LAW, BERKELEY

I wish to speak briefly on the opinion of the Legal Advisory Committee. That opinion is largely devoted to a general discussion of free speech. My purpose, if my lawyer colleagues within and without the law school will indulge me a few minutes, will be to state the several pertinent legal principles as I view them in the context of the actual problems facing us.

To begin, whether or not a university regulation ultimately will be held constitutional often cannot be predicted with the certainty one would desire. I shall never forget an experience I had as a law student returning home from school. I got a ride from a businessman outraged by some piece of New Deal legislation then under court attack. "Well," he belligerently said to me, "you're a law student, and you tell me you've had constitutional law. Is or is not that act constitutional?" I opined that it was, only to be corrected a few months later by the Supreme Court, which in turn soon thereafter received its lesson at the hands of history.

The more abstract the questions we ask ourselves here today, the more unpredictable are the courts' answers of tomorrow. As our distinguished parliamentarian stated at the last meeting, the courts do not deal in advisory opinions about abstract questions. They decide concrete cases on the basis of particular facts. For me the most relevant observation is that whether or not any regulation we may suggest will be constitutional, is largely a function of the deliberateness, fairness, and care with which we write it. We would be misled if we permitted abstract constitutional speculation to keep us from doing what we, as educators, think is wise and fair. Carefully doing what our own experience and informed judgment honestly dictates is our best practical guarantee not only of wisdom but also of legality.

I think it fair to say that no institutions are treated with higher regard and respect by the courts than colleges and universities. This is true generally, and particularly so with autonomous universities such as ours. While I was at the University of Minnesota, it was my job to defend it in litigation challenging its method of accommodation of various student religious interests. My research established that the University of California, like Minnesota, is one of but a handful of American state universities that can with accuracy be said to be autonomous. In a sense it is hardly an exaggeration to refer to our university as a fourth branch of the state government.

In the famous case of *Hamilton* v. *Regents of the University of California,* 293 U.S. 245 (1934), the *unanimous* United States Supreme Court upheld this university's power of self-government, even to the extent of sustaining its then requirement of compulsory military training, against the complaining students' cogent claim that such training violated their religiously predicated consciences. That court included four among the most eminent libertarians in the history of the tribunal: Justices Brandeis, Cardozo, Hughes, and Stone.

It seems clear to me that there is no remaining problem about free speech as such, if there ever were one. The general language "That the content of speech or advocacy should not be restricted by the University" has been taken by our Emergency Executive Committee to mean what clearly it must mean, namely, speech within the protection of the First and Fourteenth amendments. The Regents are in accord. As the Legal Advisory Committee correctly puts it:

> ". . . One can hardly conspire to commit a crime, or solicit or abet others to crime, or incite a mob to crime, or defame another, or be obscene, without the use of language. But the mere fact that language is involved, even centrally, does not necessarily invoke the constitutional protections of the First Amendment. Thus a civil suit for libel, or a prosecution of one who has brought about a 'clear and present danger' of a crime or a riot, does not infringe the First Amendment."

Further, I think it apparent that by reason of the nature of a university community it can have some restrictions even in the area of speech that would be invalid if applied by the government to people generally. A foreign-language professor could prohibit the reading by students of an English translation of an assigned book. Such a prohibition might even transcend the concept of time, place, and manner.

However, there does seem to be a serious problem as to whether the university should wholly abandon its disciplinary jurisdiction just because a student's conduct is also within the jurisdiction of the criminal courts. I think two different kinds of conduct should be clearly distinguished. First, suppose that students organize on this campus a sit-in or other activities to be carried on in a state whose regulations are themselves illegal because in contravention of paramount federal law. Such student conduct may be not only morally commendable but perfectly legal; it may in fact be in vindication of the federal law as the supreme law of the land.

Next, suppose that students organize on campus a sit-in or other activities off campus in California and carry them on under circumstances and in a manner that is clearly and palpably illegal. It can be argued that this should be left solely to criminal prosecution. Perhaps normally it should, as a matter of prudent judgment, just as other crimes, for example, homicides committed on campus, would be left to criminal prosecution. Even so, I doubt that one would seriously question the university's possible interest in suspending dangerous students during the legal proceedings if the facts indicated that necessity.

It should be remembered that the court proceedings in politically motivated offenses might well take two years or more, especially if review by the United States Supreme Court were sought. In the meantime the defendants, presumably on bail, would have the capacity to repeat the offense. I doubt that many would contend that the university should be wholly indifferent to such student conduct just because criminal proceedings were pending, particularly if the conduct were especially outrageous. It must be remembered that characterizing conduct as "political" or "politically motivated" does not diminish its criminality if in fact it is criminal.

The same kind of problem could arise respecting conduct on campus. Suppose a student commits a violent assault on, or murder of, a fellow student or professor. He is acquitted of the criminal charge on the ground of insanity at the time of the offense and discharged from custody on the ground that he is now competent. Should the university be wholly foreclosed from appraisal of his readmissibility?

These may be hard questions, especially when posed out of the context of the full facts of an actual case. We should be careful not wholly to give up all potential jurisdiction on abstract grounds lest we make wise handling of future cases difficult or impossible. I fear that such blanket abdication of responsibility historically assumed by universities will tend to undermine our autonomy by inviting increased intervention of the civil authorities.

If it is wise for the university to retain some potential jurisdiction over student criminal conduct, we should not refrain from doing so on some vague idea that the university cannot be fair and just. The courts do not insist that university disciplinary proceedings duplicate in all respects judicial proceedings; they do insist, increasingly so, and I am most grateful for it, on fundamental fairness. From my own observations, I deny that a committee of this body cannot have the requisite wisdom, learning, and courage to comply with Due Process of Law.

Further, if the university's end result is fundamentally unfair and therefore illegal, no courts in the land are more open than those of California to redress grievances should university remedies be found wanting.

If it is wise for the university to retain some potential jurisdiction over student criminal conduct—and that is our real question, is it wise?—we should not abandon this jurisdiction because of specious thinking about double jeopardy. The exercise of disciplinary jurisdiction by the university would no more constitute double jeopardy than a physician's jail sentence and suspension of license for the same illegal use of narcotics, or a lawyer's jail sentence and disbarment for the same embezzlement of his client's funds. Of course, depending on the facts of a given situation, humane considerations or factors growing out of the unique student-university relationship may dictate that the university refrain from discipline that is thought to be primarily punishment, especially when the judicial arm of the state has taken over. But we should not seek refuge from precise thinking by loose talk about double jeopardy.

In conclusion, we should do what we honestly believe to be best for the university after giving the matters our most intelligent and deliberate thought. It is not without reason that the courts place special trust in institutions of higher learning; it is not without reason that the people of California have constitutionally established an autonomous university. For us to erect a standard to which honest and wise educators can repair, is our best guarantee that we will be within the law, and that the courts will sustain us.

January 12, 1965

V

Analyses and Interpretations

Any revolutionist who studies the record of the Berkeley dispute will probably conclude that one should stay away from universities if one wants to complete a revolution. This has been a conflict in which all, or almost all, the actors seemed ready to take up their typewriters in the middle of the action to analyze what is going on. Reporters appearing on the scene found that many of those they wanted to interview had copies of their own articles in their pockets. And as if the participants had not written enough, colleagues at other institutions were not loathe to comment. Here we present a sample of what has been published.

Since the articles vary in point of view, we have tried to present them in the form of debates. In some cases this has been simple, since they represent true debates. In others, we have coupled or grouped various articles that deal with comparable materials but take different points of view.

DEBATES

WHAT HAPPENED AT BERKELEY*

BY NATHAN GLAZER,
PROFESSOR, DEPARTMENT OF SOCIOLOGY, BERKELEY

As I write this, in late December, we in Berkeley are in the Christmas lull. The university's 18,000 undergraduates are for the most part at home, many of the faculty and even some of the graduate students are away. But despite the quiet, the campus is full. The American Physical Society is meeting, which probably explains why it is still difficult to find a parking space even with a faculty sticker ($72 a year). For the first time in weeks, the steps of Sproul Hall, the administration building, are bare of demonstrators and loud-speakers, the entries to the campus are empty of tables collecting money, students handing out literature, or posters announcing meetings. But

* From *Commentary*, February 1965.

faculty studies, teaching-assistant rooms, and libraries are busy and show no signs that this is a holiday.

The Regents of the University of California met the day before the Christmas recess began, declared that they "do not contemplate that advocacy or content of speech [on the Berkeley campus] shall be restricted beyond the purview of the First and Fourteenth Amendments to the Constitution," and set up a committee to review university policies in consultation with faculty and students "with the intent of providing maximum freedom consistent with individual and group responsibility." (After an earlier meeting, on November 20, during which thousands of students were sitting outside being led by Joan Baez in singing, the Regents had said that their policy was to make campus facilities available for "planning, implementing or raising funds or recruiting participants for lawful off-campus action, not for unlawful. . . .") The Emergency Executive Committee of the Berkeley Division of the Academic Senate (the faculty) issued an optimistic statement after the Regents' meeting, asserting that substantial progress had been made.

Despite all this, I—and many other faculty members—are filled with foreboding. We see neither a clear nor a near end to the crisis. And I am afraid it will not be easy for our friends in other places to understand what is going on here; it is hardly possible for those of us closest to it to agree on an interpretation.

To begin with, we must dispose of the ingeniously simple slogan of "free speech" which has made it possible for so many who are far from the events at Berkeley to send in forthright statements in support of the Free Speech Movement or the position adopted by the faculty on December 8 (that political advocacy or organization should be limited only by minimum regulations designed to permit the university to function normally). Those of us who watched the Free Speech Movement (FSM) daily set up its loud-speakers on the steps of the administration building to denounce the president, the chancellor, the newspapers, the Regents, the faculty, and the structure and organization of society in general and universities in particular, could only admire the public-relations skill exhibited in the choice of a name for the student movement. Life, however, is not so simple as to present us with a classic free speech issue on the shores of San Francisco Bay.

During 1963–64, my first year as a teacher at Berkeley, student political activity was vigorous beyond anything I had recently seen at any other American college. In front of the concrete posts that mark the main pedestrian entrance to the campus from the busy intersection of Telegraph Avenue and Bancroft Way, one could find, on an ordinary school day, students handing out leaflets, advertising many different kinds of political meetings and actions, to be held on the campus itself and off it as well. Various student groups would set up tables stacked with literature, both free and for sale, and members of the group would be available at the tables for discussion, information, and argument. The chief groups represented were socialists—evolutionary, revolutionary, and ambiguous; civil rights organizations such as CORE, or Friends of SNCC; Young Democrats; Young Republicans; and Conservatives. One could expect to come upon supporters of Khrushchev or Mao, Castro or Ho Chi-Minh, marijuana or LSD, not to mention the more garden-variety political and social positions. (We smiled then at the backwardness of Eastern campuses where straight sex was still an issue; only homosexuality or perversion, it seemed, could make an issue at Berkeley.) Outdoor meetings were also held at this same location, often as preludes to expeditions to San Francisco, Oakland, and downtown Berkeley to picket business establishments which had failed to negotiate or sign an agreement with CORE or some other civil-rights organization. On the campus itself, large posters were always in evidence announcing a great variety of events, many of them political. Berkeley was one of the few places in the country, I imagine, where in 1964 one could hear a public debate between the supporters of Khrushchev and Mao on the Sino-Soviet dispute—there were organized student groups behind both positions.

Of course regulations existed, administered by deans of students, which these groups had to observe in conducting their activities on campus. For example, the university required 72 hours' notice for visiting speakers. If a speaker was controversial, the university would demand that a tenured member of the faculty chair the meeting. On occasion, disputes broke out between the university and a student group over who should pay for putting out the chairs on Dwinelle Plaza (the open-air area in the center of campus where particularly large meetings are held), or whether a student group sponsoring a speaker who was expected to draw a large crowd (for example, Malcolm X) should be required to pay for police protection. These disputes were perhaps portents of what was to come, but the regulations did not seem to inhibit a degree of political activity that was perhaps unique on American campuses.

Nor did they inhibit a number of actions that can only be considered questionable political stunts. Thus, Slate, a student political party, decided that it would be a good idea to bring the West Coast leader of the American Nazi party to the university. He spoke in the largest enclosed space on campus, the men's gym. I do not recall any objections from the administration. The morning of his talk, young men and women wearing Nazi uniforms were posted at the chief entrances to the campus, handing out leaflets announcing the meeting. Later

I heard an intense argument between two students at one of the entrances; it transpired that the young Nazi-clad figures were not really Nazis, but adherents of the liberal-progressive Slate, who had hit upon this as a clever way to publicize the meeting.

On another occasion, Slate invited the chief western organizer for the John Birch Society—I chaired that meeting. One could only conclude that inviting Communists to the Berkeley campus had become pretty tame, and an aspiring progressive organization had to invite John Birchers and Nazis to get an audience or to assert its absolute belief in free speech. But whatever one thought of this particular tack adopted by Slate, it was clear that free speech prevailed on the Berkeley campus.

It turned out, at the beginning of the fall semester of 1964, that this grand chaos—as it appeared—of oratory, advocacy, and action, was based on a tangle of distinctions that only the administrative staff that dealt with regulations affecting student organizations, and the leaders of the organizations they regulated, understood—and perhaps not even they. The regulations go back to a time when no political activity of any kind was allowed on campus. Under this earlier situation, even candidates for the presidency were not allowed to speak at Berkeley: to have permitted such a thing would presumably have involved the university in "politics," and as a state university it was not supposed to be involved in politics. But gradually these rules were qualified and changed to the point where the Berkeley campus, like all other campuses that are proud of their devotion to the principle of free speech, was allowed to have Communist speakers. Largely as a result of such changes, last spring President Clark Kerr was given the Alexander Meiklejohn award by the American Association of University Professors for having made a major contribution to academic freedom.

But through all these modifications of earlier restrictions, a distinction was maintained. The campus was a place for "free speech." It was not, however, a place for advocacy,* for organization, or for collecting money. Thus an "off-campus" political organization (like CORE) could run a meeting "on-campus" but would have to explain to those present that certain kinds of discussion (for example, on implementing a demonstration) must be held off-campus. This was not as great a hardship as it might have been in other colleges or universities, where the campus is separated physically from the town (as is Stanford) or where the community possesses few meeting places suitable for student groups. Further, just

---

* "Advocacy" was used throughout the ensuing dispute to mean advocacy of *action*, not of ideas.

as Berkeley is required to be free of "politics," it is also required to be free of religion in all forms—proselytization, worship, or even the organizational activities of student religious groups. The city of Berkeley, however, surrounds the university. And across the street which marks off campus from city, there is a row of institutions—YMCA, Methodist, Jewish, Episcopalian, etc.—which have often been available for political meetings banned on campus.

But to return to the distinction that underlay the regulations (or that some people in the administration believed underlay them)—that is, between "speech" on the one hand, and "advocacy and organization" on the other: traditionally, the chief area for advocacy was the sidewalk in front of the concrete posts which mark the boundary of the university. This was also the area where impromptu meetings would precede the march to the picket lines and the demonstration sites. But at the beginning of the fall semester of 1964, the university administration decided to enforce the distinction between "speech" and "advocacy and organization" on the strip of sidewalk in front of the posts (which is also the property of the Regents of the University of California).

Various reasons for this decision have been given. The administration at first asserted that the number of tables and meetings had become so great as to interfere with traffic. The students argued that there were more forceful reasons. During the preceding summer, while the Republican Convention met at the Cow Palace, students were recruited here not only for the usual civil rights activities (which included in this case blocking the entrances to the Cow Palace for a while) but to pack the galleries for Scranton. During that summer, in addition, civil rights demonstrators decided to move against the Oakland *Tribune*, owned by the family of former Senator Knowland, and the students charged that it was his complaint that led the administration to ban "advocacy and organization" on the strip of sidewalk in question.

There now began a conflict between two very unevenly matched opponents: the student political organizations and the administration of the Berkeley campus of the University of California. Berkeley has a long history of student agitation for the widening of freedom of political action on campus. This history has involved petition, picketing, demonstrating, research and argument, and the like. Many alumni of these efforts are still on and around the campus. A number of lawyers, in and outside the law school, have been involved in such past disputes and know them in detail. But the present student constellation differs markedly from that of only a few years ago, and thus a radically new style was adopted for this newest conflict with the administration over political activity.

The great new factor has, of course, been the civil rights

movement, and particularly the development of the new techniques of civil disobedience, which opened up the lunch counters of the South and then spread to the North. Nowhere
have these techniques been adopted with more enthusiasm and
success than in the Bay Area. Last year hundreds of Berkeley
students—along with students from San Francisco State College
and elsewhere, and non-students as well—"sat-in" at a chain
of lunch counters, "shopped-in" at a chain of supermarkets
(they would fill a cart with groceries, let the clerk reckon the
total on his machine, and then leave the mess of groceries on
the counter, insouciantly declaring they did not have the
money to pay for them), "slept-in" at the Sheraton Palace
Hotel, lay down in the automobile showrooms of Van Ness
Avenue. This activity led in each case to an agreement to hire
a certain number of Negro workers. It also led in some cases
to mass arrests and mass trials, which seriously strained the
court system of San Francisco. The fact that the state of California has a law banning discrimination in employment and a
commission devoted to ending discrimination in employment
seemed to leave the demonstrators unmoved. Indeed, they
often insisted that they themselves rather than the state agency
should police the agreements they had won from the employers.

The civil rights movement created a situation among the
student political groups on campus quite different from the
one which had prevailed when such groups were fighting for
the loosening of the strict regulations which once governed
their political activity. Besides introducing new tactics, the
civil rights movement developed a large body of students committed to these tactics, and a substantial body of public opinion
—in the faculty and among the liberal population of the area—
sympathetic to them. Admittedly, Berkeley was ideally suited
to serve the expansion of the radical civil rights movement in
the North. It had never been affected to the extent other colleges were by the mood of the "silent generation" of the 50's.
(In 1960, remember, when the House Un-American Activities
Committee met in San Francisco City Hall, hundreds of
Berkeley students were willing to attempt to disrupt its hearings.) Indeed, in 1957, when I visited Berkeley for the first
time, a number of socialist youth leaders from the East had
just migrated here, because they found the political climate
peculiarly congenial to their work. (In addition, it was my impression that Communism too retained more life and relevance
in the Bay Area than in the East.) Some of these socialist
youth leaders became students; some worked at the university;
others worked in the community, becoming part of the penum-
bra of campus life which at Berkeley involves many people
who are neither students, faculty, nor staff, but who may have

been part of the university at one time in the past and who possibly will again be part of it in the future.

The strains produced by the application of the new tactics in the mild racial climate of San Francisco had already been intense. Was the Bay Area Mississippi, it was asked, that actions had to be taken which destroyed private businesses when there was legal redress for the wrongs that the students believed existed? Few people in public life thought so. Even many liberals were troubled, and during 1963–64, some state legislators and others demanded that the university move against the students who had been arrested in civil-rights actions. President Kerr refused, asserting that what students did off-campus was their business, so long as they did not use campus facilities for it. Here again was the distinction between speech on the one hand and advocacy and organization on the other. On this distinction the president, the Regents, and Chancellor Strong of the Berkeley campus apparently hoped to ride out the hard year ahead, while students' leaders were attempting to produce the degree of chaos in the surrounding community that they calculated was necessary to achieve fair treatment for Negroes.

When the chancellor's office passed on to the lesser members of the administrative hierarchy the decision that the strip of land on Bancroft Way outside the concrete posts was now to become subject *de facto* (as it had been *de jure*) to the university ban on advocacy, collection, and organization, the student leaders and their constituencies were already attuned to and experienced in the use of the new tactics. The first rank of the administrative hierarchy to deal with the new regulations, on the other hand, were deans who up till now, one assumes, had been concerned principally with such matters as lock-out rules in female dormitories. Initially the student groups protested the new regulations to these deans. They were immediately able to show that the distinction between "speech" and "advocacy" was difficult or impossible to maintain and ridiculous in an election year; they also showed that traffic could easily flow despite the tables. The administration withdrew somewhat; tables were permitted and advocacy was allowed, but collection and organization were still prohibited. This was unsatisfactory to the students, who resorted to a direct test of whether the administration would enforce the new regulations: they set up their tables and collected money. A number were then directed to appear before a dean on September 29 to discuss these violations. They arrived, but with another 300 or 400 students, all demanding that they too receive the same disciplinary action as the group that had manned tables. The Dean of Men refused to deal with this large mass. They sat in—in Sproul Hall, the administration headquarters, until the early morning.

Thus, what had originally been a protest by all the student political groups—from revolutionary socialist to extreme conservative—was transformed very early into a movement run by the civil rights leaders. For as soon as the tactics of the protest "escalated" into questionably legal activities (like sitting-in at Sproul Hall, which was done for the first time on September 29) the right-wingers could not go along. They were still part of the protest movement for a few more days. But they stood aside from further escalations—the surrounding of the campus police car containing an arrested prisoner on October 1, the loose and then the tight sit-in at Sproul Hall that day which prevented the deans from leaving or anyone from entering, the decision to maintain the sit-in around the police car throughout October 2. By that time, it was clear that the leadership of the movement was now coming exclusively from the civil rights and left-wing political groups. But there were too few students directly committed to the left-wing groups to provide the necessary "bodies"—to use the term popular with the civil rights leaders. Only the civil rights groups, and only with the good issues handed to them by administration action, could raise hundreds ready to sit-in.

On October 2, the movement won its first great victory—the withdrawal of the menacing array of police that had been concentrated on the campus, and a meeting with Clark Kerr in which a pact was signed calling for an administration-faculty-student committee to deal with the issue of political activity. At this meeting with President Kerr, the right-wing and religious student groups were still represented. Then the Free Speech Movement, at a marathon two-day meeting, organized itself officially, and from that meeting neither the right-wing nor the religious groups emerged with any positions of leadership. More than that, the Young Democrats and even the right-wing Socialists, who had played an important role in the demonstration around the police car, were excluded. In a pattern similar to other and grander revolutions, the student uprising had moved to the left—into the control of the civil rights leaders identified with direct action, and of the leaders of groups in a direct or indirect line of descent from the Communist and Trotskyist student political groups of the past. As for the followers, they mainly came from students involved in or touched by the civil rights movement.

If the leadership of the student movement was rapidly concentrated into a coherent and tightly knit cadre, sharing very much the same philosophy and outlook, the other elements of the university community were split and in disarray. Let us look first at the "administration." Where in the history of American higher education has the administration of a university loomed so large as at Berkeley? In the past, presidents, faculties, and boards of trustees have been important—but *ad-*

ministrations? This is another sense in which Berkeley may be unique; and yet one fears that the future of American higher education may be foreshadowed here. Everyone—arriving faculty members, arriving deans, visiting authorities—is astonished by the size of the administration at Berkeley, and in the statewide University of California. One large building near the campus is completely devoted to the statewide administration, another on the campus to the Berkeley administration. The title "Dean," which at other universities carries dignity, is used at Berkeley to cover a wide variety of jobs, only some of them academic (where the traditional dignity still attaches to the title), but many deans have not come up through the faculty and have little to do with it. They deal with student affairs. For presumably 27,000 students provide a good number of non-academic problems which neither the faculty nor the academic deans would want to be bothered with.

Academic matters are handled by the academic deans and their assistants. The size of these staffs is impressive, and unfortunately—given certain conditions—necessary. Many students move to Berkeley from other campuses of the state university, from state colleges, from junior colleges, from other institutions outside the state. Each institution has its own requirements—for entrance, for graduation, for majors—and the work done elsewhere therefore has to be evaluated and harmonized to the Berkeley requirements. The evaluations are often argued and fought over, and the student is often frustrated in his fight. In the end a bureaucracy is probably the only system by which a vast number of cases can be managed equitably. Yet while the rules may be just, the sense of justice done is rarely communicated by a clerk or an assistant dean's determination.

Could we operate with a smaller administration? Very likely. Yet one thinks of such matters as vast numbers of migrating undergraduates to be fitted into the university, and thousands of graduate students, a large proportion of whom are also employees receiving regular checks for research assistantships, teaching assistantships, fellowships. There are also hundreds of new faculty members every year, each of whom has had to be passed on by various committees. There are scores of research institutes, hundreds of research contracts, each involving separate budgets, all to be coordinated. It is difficult to communicate any sense of the scale of the administration at Berkeley. Let me give a personal report: when I arrived in Berkeley after working for the Federal Government, my feeling was that the quality of the two settings—organization piled upon organization, reaching to a mysterious empyrean height—was remarkably similar. I understood from other faculty members that this was rather new, that it was only in recent years that the administration had become so huge.

Ironically, President Kerr, in his Godkin Lectures,* has offered the best general text—perhaps the only existing one—on what is happening. The students have been among its most avid readers, and have not shared the admiration of some reviewers of the book who see in the University of California, as described by its president, the democratic university of the future, combining high standards and mass education. President Kerr describes the shift from the liberal arts college offering a humane education, to the early university which trained men in the traditional professions and for scholarship and college teaching, to the modern "federal grant" university, half of whose budget may come from federal research grants.

It would be an error to think of these grants as being devoted only to warmaking and to statecraft. Vast sums flow for social and psychological and policy research, research as useful to a benign welfare state—or, for that matter, a modern authoritarian state—as to a cold-war America. Obviously, however, the federal grant university is not entirely dependent on federal grants. All undergraduate and graduate teaching is covered by state funds, and in many departments—languages, philosophy, history, English, art, and music—little if any part of faculty salaries comes from research grants. Nevertheless, the effect of the federal millions is larger than one would suspect from a direct accounting of where the money goes. The research funds strengthen the university's capacity to compete for faculty, for they allow members to be relieved from teaching and to supplement their regular nine-month salary from a research budget during the summer. These funds also permit the recruitment of greater numbers of graduate students, who normally expect to be supported out of research and teaching assistantships—and even if the latter are covered by state funds, the students are there because federal money will eventually support their own research.

It is easy to conclude that everyone benefits from this except the undergraduate, whose instruction is largely in the hands of teaching assistants. And yet a year ago, when I was spending my first term on the Berkeley campus, I could not find much restiveness or resentment among the undergraduates. Indeed, several told me they preferred Berkeley to the junior colleges and state colleges from which they had come, despite the fact that a layer of graduate students was interposed between them and the professorial staff. And they said that the lectures at Berkeley were more stimulating despite the size of the classes. Of course, such undergraduates had moved to Berkeley from schools with smaller classes for other reasons besides the qual-

* *The Uses of the University.*

ity of the education, whatever that might be: the life of the campus and the college town around it was undoubtedly a great attraction.

But resentment ran higher, I would judge, among graduate students, many of whom discovered that their professors were just as busy when it came to bothering with them as they were where undergraduates were concerned. Once again the pleasurable environment of learning had escaped them; they were working hard as research assistants and teaching assistants, on other men's research and courses, but they were denied the satisfaction of an intellectual community which brought students and teachers together. Their relations with faculty were too often quite businesslike, the exchanges of services for money. And how could it be otherwise when the professors were burdened with so many governmental, teaching, administrative, and research duties?

Resentment also ran high among the faculty. Many remembered an easier life as junior faculty, on the Berkeley campus or elsewhere. They could not understand why they were always so busy, and found that scholarly labors could best proceed away from the campus. Thus many protected themselves from their students and their colleagues by working at home. But there was another source of resentment for them —the incorporation of Berkeley, which had previously enjoyed a good deal of independence, into the structure of the statewide university, with its eight or nine campuses and its statewide administration, trying to coordinate the varied institutions that had been brought together or were coming into existence as parts of the University of California. Berkeley's incorporation meant that in one matter after another which affected faculty—the shift from semesters to quarters, the setting of standards of admission, the distribution of students among campuses—decisions could be and were taken that were not the decisions the faculty, or individual members of it, wanted.

As a result of these changes, and as a result of the administration's insensitivity to the problems involved, a degree of distance developed between statewide and campus administration, between administration and faculty, between faculty and students, that may well have been unique in American education. The question we must ask, however, before distributing blame is this: given the need or the desire to create an enormous system of statewide university education, how could such a situation have been avoided?

Certainly the faculty, while complaining of the inaccessibility of the administration and its insensitivity to faculty needs, was not very responsive on its own part to student needs. A public meeting some of us ran on the problems of education at Berkeley last year was attended by only a handful of faculty (and not much more than a handful of undergraduates and graduate students). The faculty does not respond enthusiastically to occasional efforts by the administration to get it to consider ways of improving undergraduate education. But at the same time it must be said that faculty members generally censor their impulses to educational reform because they are aware of the many barriers that would have to be vaulted to get the change through. The new faculty member learns rapidly enough that if he devotes himself to his research, his courses, and his *pro forma* service on committees, he is doing all that is expected of him—and all that any reasonable man, in the prevailing system, would want to undertake.

The university administration, then, was both rigid—as we all knew from experience—and fragile—as we discovered in the crisis raised by its attempt to change the *de facto* rules governing student political activity. For in the situation created first by reasonable student demands and secondly by new and radical student tactics, the administration showed itself incapable of consistent, decisive, or effective action. Again and again it was forced to withdraw from positions either because they were poor ones, or poorly argued and defended, or because the higher levels (the president) moved in and changed the positions taken lower down (the chancellor).

The confusion above, a confusion veiled by silence and inaccessibility, could only increase by geometric progression down below. Asked to enforce policies about whose rationale and stability they were uncertain, the deans could only put up a very poor show, and in the course of the crisis the student leaders—having discovered very early how to break through to the top—treated them with greater and greater insolence and arrogance. Rapidly becoming more expert in the techniques of organization and publicity, these leaders soon added a powerful wing to their original movement—the graduate students. They soon discovered too that there was little to fear in breaking the rules, for the faculty was so unsympathetic to the administration and its rigid and mechanical handling of the problem that, while it would not at first directly support the students and their tactics, it was always ready to attack the administration.

The next casualties were the chancellor and the vice-chancellors. As early as October 2 the president, ignoring the advice and actions of the chancellor's office, had intervened to make a direct pact with the students—which the chancellor was expected to carry out. More important than the structure of authority which permitted the chancellor to be overridden was the fact that neither he nor his staff could come up with a leader to handle a political crisis for which a close study of the French and Russian revolutions might well have provided the only suitable training. Certainly there was no one at this level who could influence the students or deal effectively with them. Nor, as it turned out, was there anyone at this level who could deal effectively with the faculty and convince them that the matter was being handled intelligently or morally. On at least two important occasions faculty members—including myself—who did not support the tactics of the students felt that the administration had acted against the spirit or the letter of an agreement in trying to discipline student leaders. In both cases it was unclear whether it was the chancellor, the president, or the Board of Regents—the highest authority—who had ordered the action. But whatever the facts, the chancellor's authority was weakened by these incidents.

We must now speak in more detail about the role of the faculty. At the start, the faculty for the most part looked upon the conflict between the administration and the students as detached and neutral outsiders. From the beginning, however, groups of faculty members thrust themselves into the situation as mediators. They (or some of them) were distinguished from the great majority of their colleagues by the fact that they had been involved in student politics in the past and remained interested in them in the present. The first such group of mediators (of which I was one) helped to draw up the pact of October 2. But we eventually joined the administration as casualties of the developing crisis. We became casualties, I believe, owing to the critical change in the issues of the conflict that occurred around the beginning of November. This change became apparent in the discussions of the faculty-student-administration committee that had been set up by the October 2 pact. For the first month there had been two fairly straightforward issues: the attempt of the administration to change the status quo, which all the student political groups, left and right, and all interested faculty opposed; and secondly, the student tactics, which some of the student groups and most of the interested faculty opposed, but which everyone agreed should not lead to disciplinary action (on the ground that the original issue which had occasioned the tactics had been a just one). To my mind, these two problems were settled when the administration's representatives on the committee provisionally accepted a much wider range of political advocacy and organization on campus than had been permitted before, and when a second committee (faculty) set up under the October 2 pact called for the lifting of the suspensions that had been pronounced against the students who had violated the old regulations.

Until this point, the interested faculty members and the student FSM leaders had stood together. But now the student leaders and the administration raised a new issue, created by the prospective liberalization of the rules. If the campus was to be opened up for advocacy and organization, what of advocacy and organization that led to illegal actions or was designed to produce illegal actions? This was no abstract question. The administration's insistence on a line between the legal and illegal—a line it had not drawn when no advocacy or organization was permitted on campus—was immediately seen by the students as a threat to actions they were already planning (against the Oakland *Tribune,* various local merchants, etc.) and which in their minds were being held up by the involvement of their forces in the campus dispute. (They were, of course, aware of the large number of potential recruits they had attracted on the basis of the free-speech issue.) The student leaders fully expected further mass arrests as a result of these actions, and they hoped to protect their rear against university discipline.

On this issue of illegal action the faculty-student-administration committee split in November. The student representatives insisted on a specific guarantee that nothing they advocated or organized on campus would lead to any measures by the university against them or their organizations. The administration members insisted on the right to discipline individuals or organizations who advocated or organized illegal action. The faculty group proposed a formula which neither gave the students a specific guarantee of immunity nor gave the administration a specific ban against illegal action on campus. Under this formula the students would have conducted their demonstrations and sit-ins in all likelihood safe from university interference, for the university's policy of the year before had been not to discipline those arrested for civil rights activities and it seemed improbable that this policy would be changed. If, however, the university decided on a change, the students could have tested in the courts its right to punish them for illegal action advocated or organized on campus—a contingency which, they asserted, would be "against the 1st and 14th amendments" and would constitute "double jeopardy."

This course, which would have permitted the students to turn their attention to what they felt to be such critical substantive problems as discrimination on the Oakland *Tribune,* they rejected. Their movement would not give up the issue provided them by the split on the question of illegal action. Those faculty members like myself who had been sympathetic until this time, but now withdrew their support, were denounced orally and in print as "finks" and stooges of President Kerr (who had become the *bête noir* of the students, his hand seen in every move).

On this issue the students decided to abrogate the pact of October 2 (in which they had agreed to stick to legal action), pronounced (on their own authority) new rules to govern political activity on campus, and began to operate under them. The students now hoped that the Regents would give them what the committee set up under the pact of October 2 had not, but on November 20, the Regents insisted on maintaining the distinction between lawful and unlawful actions. At this point the student leaders split, some arguing for further drastic measures, others urging *de facto* acceptance of the new rules under which they had full freedom of action, but were threatened by the possibility of university punishment for illegal action. A new sit-in was staged at Sproul Hall, which involved only 300 students; the administration did not act against it, and it was called off after a few hours.

Then, on November 30, it was learned that the administration (Strong? Kerr? the Regents?) had summoned four student leaders to appear before the Faculty Committee on Student Conduct (advisory to the chancellor) to hear charges against them stemming from their tussles with the police on October 1 and 2. As a result of this blunder, an issue that was capable of arousing the students—the disciplining of their leaders—was fortuitously tied to one that could not—immunity for advocacy or organization of illegal action. The rest of the story has been covered by the national news media. Once again, on December 2, Joan Baez—no other figure in the United States could better symbolize the tangle of protests, amorphous and specific, that moved the students—sang with them as they occupied Sproul Hall. In the early morning of December 3, a small army of police began carrying out students—about 800 of them. That afternoon, yet another impromptu group of mediating faculty, the department chairmen, met to formulate a compromise which offered full amnesty to the students for the actions of the past two months; they hoped to sell this to the president and the Regents. On December 4, a long threatened strike of teaching assistants was launched, and on Sunday, December 6, the president and the Regents accepted the department chairmen's compromise.

By this time, however, the student leaders had glimpsed the possibility of complete success. For some days a substantial number of liberal faculty members had been preparing a resolution which asserted that political activity on campus should be regulated only as to "time, place, and manner" in order not to interfere with the functioning of the university, and they were rounding up support for its adoption. The great majority of this group had little sympathy for FSM tactics, but they believed its position on the rules was right. In any case, the larger part of the faculty had now become involved, because they had been forced to confront and take a stand on the strike of their teaching assistants. Many were also shocked by the December 3 police action. The FSM hoped that the faculty resolution supporting their position would pass and they joined its drafters in campaigning for it.

On December 7 the compromise negotiated by the department chairmen was presented by Professor Robert Scalapino and President Kerr to the student body and faculty at a large open-air meeting at the Greek theater. The radicalization of the students—thousands of whom had now participated in sit-ins, strikes, and picketing—had proceeded at a frightening pace over the weekend; full victory was now seen as possible, and the compromise was denounced by the student leaders as a "sell-out." It was at this meeting that Mario Savio, head of the FSM, attempted to seize the microphone, and the campus police dragged him away.

Because of their desperate desire to settle things, because of their experience of one administration failure after another, I believe most of the faculty was by now ready to accept any agreement that might lead to peace. The administration—President Kerr and Chancellor Strong—was absent and silent when a thousand members of the Academic Senate met on December 8 and by a huge vote endorsed the resolution of the liberal faculty members mentioned above. This resolution—in addition to backing the view that political activity should be unrestricted except for time, place, and manner—demanded that responsibility for disciplinary measures in the area of political activity should be placed in the hands of the faculty. Having lived through months of non-existent or ineffective leadership and increasing disruption and disorder, the faculty also voted for the election of a strong Emergency Executive Committee to represent it. A few days later, however, as if in recoil from the resolution, the faculty elected a moderate Executive Committee, the majority of whom had not been identified with the preparation and propagation of the resolution that had been adopted so overwhelmingly.

But what of the issue of illegal political activity itself? Did the seven-to-one vote of the faculty resolve that? I do not believe so. At the December 8 meeting Professor Lewis Feuer proposed an amendment to the main resolution which would have excepted speech or advocacy "directed to immediate acts of force and violence" from the general immunity. In support of this amendment, he spoke not of the civil rights movement, which was uppermost in the minds of all the protagonists, but of Mississippi, where such a resolution as had been endorsed by the faculty would deny a university administration the right to move against a chapter of the Ku Klux Klan, and of pre-Nazi Germany, where a similar position in effect prevented university administrations from moving against Nazi students engaged in the destruction of the ground-rules of democratic society. The discussion was intense. Many of those who opposed Feuer were convinced that his amendment raised serious constitutional issues. On the whole it was obvious to those of us who supported his amendment—and had other amendments in mind as well—that the temper of the faculty did not favor any extended consideration of the issues at that time. The students were barred from the meeting, but thousands were outside, and we could hear their roars of approval or disapproval as the debate went on. It was scarcely necessary to be reminded of the terrible power of the student movement, though two professors, both of whom supported the majority resolution, did remind us that chaos was at the door. I think there was a good deal of hysteria mixed in with the action of the Berkeley Division of the Academic Senate that day. Afterward men who had been friends for years but had taken opposite sides approached each other with hesitation, and felt it necessary to reaffirm their friendship, so deeply had their emotions become involved.

I hope it is now clear why the issue on the Berkeley campus is not simply one of "free speech." The immediate issue is the student demand that the university allow them facilities for full political action and give up its right to discipline them for what it considers improper use of these facilities. If the university is to be equated with the administration, the students have a point. For the administration has the least claim to the power to determine the standards which govern the university. But what of the Regents, who represent the people of the state? What of the faculty? What of the students? Are all incapable of determining what is proper on a university campus? The constitution of the university—the distribution of powers among its various elements—may well be out of joint. At one time the faculty exercised student discipline at Berkeley; on some campuses it is the faculty and students together. Constitutions can be changed. But should the constitution of a university include a grant of immunity to any and all forms of action that go by the name of politics? If it did, the university would abdicate its responsibility to set standards for its students, its faculty, and its staff in one critical area of their life on the campus. We are now in the following ridiculously inconsistent posture at Berkeley: no religious activity of any kind is allowed on the campus and no one challenges that; students can be penalized for infractions of rules involving the consumption of liquor and the like, and no one challenges that; but it is asserted that any political action whatever should be permitted without any step being taken by the university against any person or organization as a result.

It is possible that this huge and on the whole practically oriented university has no basis on which to set any standards. I am not sure we have come to this yet. The students—now backed by most of the faculty—view any assertions of power by the university as designed only to reduce the scope of their self-evidently good and just activity. They do not see that the power to regulate on the basis of standards appropriate to a university also increases the potential scope of their activity and protects them from the civil arm. It is easier to run meetings on the Berkeley campus than on the city streets—even the streets of enlightened cities. The students and their faculty supporters do not agree that this higher degree of freedom, established under the protection of the university's authority, may be organically connected to the university's power to regulate this freedom and prevent its abuse.

How then is the dispute to be finally resolved? One can envisage circumstances that would give us a temporary peace, but it would be a very fragile one. Many of the FSM leaders are also deeply concerned with the academic conduct of the university, the curriculum, the courses, the character of the faculty, the nature of student-faculty relations. It is a concern which many faculty members applaud. But if strikes and sit-ins should be held on the campus to impose student views of how the university should be run academically—and nothing in FSM ideology prevents this—there would be an end to peace once again.

Secondly, one must see these events in the context of the students' desire to protect their university status and privileges while conducting their operations in the community. Will the community in turn, however, respect these rights and privileges if the actions of the Berkeley students maintain their intensity of 1963–64, or if, as the students hope, they increase in intensity? A number of supermarkets against which they directed some of their most powerful efforts, I notice, have closed down. Will the community, which votes hundreds of millions of dollars for the university through the state legislature, remain docile in the face of what they may consider a one-sided bargain?

At a press conference called by a group of faculty members after the mass arrests on December 3, Professor Henry May, chairman of the history department, was asked by newsmen what lay at the bottom of the crisis. He answered thoughtfully that he saw two major issues. One was the inevitable strains and pressure stemming from the attempt to create at Berkeley a mass university that would at the same time be great; the second was the rise of new forms of political action which aroused deep emotions and whose legal status was in doubt. I believe these are the two chief underlying causes of what is happening at Berkeley. We have the answer to neither problem; this is why we must be concerned and disturbed, and why what is happening at Berkeley is more than a local story.

Epilogue, January 6.— On January 1, the Regents suddenly appointed a new Acting Chancellor for the Berkeley campus, Martin Meyerson. He took office at a time when the Emergency Executive Committee of the Academic Senate was performing prodigies in negotiating with and mollifying all parties. With the advice of the Emergency Executive Committee, the new chancellor issued temporary and minimal "fail-safe" rules (the language of nuclear warfare is common in the controversy) with which to greet the students returning from vacation, and FSM is abiding by them. Meyerson has brought a new atmosphere to the campus, and every day we congratulate each other on an unaccustomed peace.

REPLY TO GLAZER*

BY PHILIP SELZNICK,
PROFESSOR, DEPARTMENT OF SOCIOLOGY, BERKELEY

Professor Nathan Glazer's account of the student protest at Berkeley, published last month, is distressing to many who have been close to the events. This is hardly surprising, for Glazer has adopted a policy (and a posture) overwhelmingly rejected by the Berkeley faculty. He has, I am sorry to say, obscured the basic issues, faltered in his assessment of the moral quality of the students' actions, and misread the role of the faculty. I am grateful for the opportunity to present a different interpretation.

Glazer says that he is "filled with foreboding." There is indeed much to worry about, and the ultimate effects of the protest cannot now be fully assessed. Nevertheless, I am not inclined to wring my hands. Something basically good has happened here. If we still have something to teach our students about the relation of means to ends (and I believe we have), it is also true that they have had much to teach us. Their mode of instruction has been passionate and in part irresponsible, but it has not been such as to justify a shrinking back in horror. Much of what the students did was clearly necessary if we were to be made to *really listen*. I think they accomplished that. And considerably more.

I shall restrict my comments to three topics: (1) the controversy over political speech and action on campus; (2) the role of the faculty; and (3) the problem of "law and order."

(1) In the early days of the crisis President Kerr denied that there was a "freedom of speech issue" at Berkeley. This point of view is adopted by Glazer. Observing the heady activity around him, he concludes that "free speech prevailed on the Berkeley campus." This approach shows a peculiar insensitivity to the fact that free speech issues in a democracy often arise out of marginal cases. We do not decide whether an issue has been raised by pointing to all the free speech that abounds. The hard case and the forlorn sect may give us

* From *Commentary*, March 1965.

trouble beyond their due, but they also summon us to reaffirm our fundamental commitments.

The basic policy was phrased as follows in a handbook for student organizations published by the Dean of Students: "University facilities may not be used to support or advocate off-campus political or social action." Action included supporting or opposing particular candidates or propositions in local, state, or national elections. One may decide that such activities are improper for a university campus, but it is strange indeed to be told that they do not represent restrictions on political speech. The whole point was: should partisan advocacy— surely a form of speech—directed to influencing specific decisions in the community be allowed on campus? Whatever the merits, that is a free speech issue.

The ban on speech directed to action was sustained by a combination of wishful fantasy and timid opportunism—both sincerely responsive to the needs of the university as perceived by the administration. The fantasy consisted in an attempt to distinguish "discussion" and "advocacy." President Kerr hoped to fulfill his own ideals, and satisfy long-standing demands for a more open campus, by enunciating an "open forum" policy. This policy provided enlarged opportunities for the hearing of all viewpoints, but the line was to be drawn against direct involvement in politics. This distinction, however defensible on abstract grounds, runs so contrary to the normal continuities of political expression, and is so little supported in the political experience of the larger community, that it had little chance of surviving a determined assault. And indeed it did crumble, almost at the first challenge.

Glazer has recounted the successive retreats of the administration on the issue of advocacy during the two weeks following the first student protest. It is interesting that the "realist" defense of the original policy, as necessary to the protection of the university from conservative criticism, was given small weight by the administration when the need to abandon untenable distinctions became apparent. This suggests that the basic policy never had any good reason for being, even as a defensive tactic, and was a needless affront to the sensibilities of the students.

Although the general ban on advocacy was swiftly eroded, a sticky problem remained. On November 20 the Regents officially accepted the idea that political activity, including recruitment and fund-raising, could be conducted on campus. However, they included the proviso that such activity must be "for lawful off-campus action, not for unlawful off-campus action." Thus free speech was still at issue, for the university apparently reserved the right to regulate speech or organization that in its judgment was directed to illegal off-campus action. Under ordinary circumstances, this might not have been a fighting issue. But civil rights-conscious students saw a direct threat to the possibility of organizing on the campus "direct action" in the community. At the same time, the energy and commitment that had already won large gains against the policy of September were still available for the achievement of unabridged freedom of speech.

That is how things stood in late November. On the 22nd, a brief sit-in was staged in Sproul Hall. On the 30th, it was announced that four leaders of the Free Speech Movement faced charges for actions connected with the demonstration of early October. There followed the massive sit-in of December 2nd–3rd, the removal and arrest of some 800 demonstrators, the student strike, the fiasco in the Greek Theater on December 7, and the critical meeting of the Academic Senate on December 8.

By the overwhelming vote of 824–115 the senate adopted a resolution whose chief provisions were:

1. "The time, place, and manner of conducting political activity on the campus shall be subject to reasonable regulation to prevent interference with the normal functions of the University."

2. "The content of speech or advocacy should not be restricted by the University. Off-campus student political activities shall not be subject to University regulation. On-campus advocacy or organization of such activities shall be subject only to such limitations as may be imposed under [the regulation of time, place, and manner]."

Glazer's interpretation of this policy is very odd. On p. 301 he speaks of "the student demand that the university allow them facilities for full political action and give up its right to discipline them for what it considers improper use of these facilities." He asks, should the university constitution "include a grant of immunity to any and all forms of action that go by the name of politics?" And then he laments that we are now "in the ridiculously inconsistent posture" that "students can be penalized for infractions of rules involving the consumption of liquor and the like . . . but it is asserted that any political action whatever should be permitted without any step being taken by the university against any person or organization as a result."

Now compare these statements with the faculty position that the "time, place, and manner of conducting political activity shall be subject to reasonable regulation to prevent interference with the normal functions of the University." In fact, of course, we did not grant immunity to all forms of action nor did we abjure all discipline for improper use of university facilities. We proclaimed freedom of speech—not without rules, but with only such rules as are truly necessary to preserve the normal tenor of university life. This would exclude rules imposed arbitrarily, or to quiet outside criticism, or to serve mere administrative convenience.

No one is against regulating "time, place, and manner," although the word "manner" may produce some future controversy. The heart of the faculty resolution is the provision that *the university should not regulate the content of public expression on campus*. If a member or guest of the university community wants to advocate the seizure of private property by Negro tenants in Harlem or Oakland, or the forcible and illegal expulsion of Negroes from Mississippi, the university is to grit its teeth and restrain its punitive hand.

It is easy to list political abominations, easy to understand the desire to restrain them. But the regulation of what people say has its own problems, not least of which is the difficulty of finding a formula that will reach the contemplated evil and no other. The constitution contains no general language defining the limits of free speech. There are such limits, but they are contained in a judicial gloss and in laws limiting such activities as conspiracy, incitement to crime, defamation, and obscenity. The angled byways of constitutional interpretation in this field are notorious, and our faculty decided that there was no need for the university, in its governance of student affairs, to go down that troubled road.

For the university's purposes, at least in this phase of American history, it is enough to regulate time, place, and manner. If in *what* they say students go beyond the pale of legal speech, then resort may be had to civil authorities who must act within the evolving framework of constitutional law. In any case, if many students are affected by offensive ideas communicated on campus, it is our job to intensify their education. Restrictive rules will avail us little and cost us much.

Glazer is understandably concerned lest a free society and a free university be unable to move against a terrorist or totalitarian movement. But the impotence of democracy, where that has been displayed, has had little to do with a Hitler's freedom to publish or to harangue a crowd. Political palsy, not constitutional freedom, toleration of abominable acts, not of abominable speech, have contributed most to the political cankers of our time.

It is instructive that the formulas offered by President Kerr (no advocacy of illegal off-campus action) or by Feuer and Glazer (no advocacy "directed to immediate acts of force or violence") have little precision as defenses against grave evils. On the contrary, they cast a wide net and would catch first of all proponents of civil rights resorting to demonstrative tactics and convicted of minor infractions. This is the classic dilemma faced by every would-be legislator against speech.

The complexities and dangers of regulating speech are compelling, but they are not the whole foundation of the faculty's policy. Even more important is the contribution we seek to make to an atmosphere of freedom. The university is not the whole polity. We have our own nature and commitments, and these include a special concern that students *feel free*. There may be something to the argument that participation in political action is a valuable adjunct to the curriculum. I do not give it great weight. Somewhat more persuasive is the view that free speech on campus permits and encourages students to hear all points of view. But to me the decisive point is that students should have a sense of belonging to a community that is completely open to the free play of persuasion and argument.

At this writing, there is apparently very close agreement between the faculty resolution and the position adopted by the Regents on December 18 that "the policies of the Regents do not contemplate that advocacy or content of speech shall be restricted beyond the purview of the First and Fourteenth Amendments to the Constitution." This still leaves some ambiguity, especially as to who shall interpret what lies beyond that purview, but most people here are confident that the basic issue is settled. The students seem content with the protections of the First Amendment.

Reference to the United States Constitution can be misleading, however. Some have argued that the university should not abridge freedom of political expression because it is a state agency and therefore subject to constitutional constraints on government. The preferable view, in my opinion, is that the university may well draw upon the experience and wisdom of the larger community in matters of speech, but its policy should be its own. It follows that the university should be free to change that policy if fresh thought and new circumstances require it. A university may wish to allow considerably greater freedom of expression, so far as its own rules are concerned, than may be protected under a current constitutional doctrine.

(2) Having stated my view of the faculty position on the main issue, I should like to turn to Glazer's assessment of the role of the faculty in this controversy. Referring to the meeting of December 8, Glazer writes (p. 301): "I think there was a good deal of hysteria mixed in with the action of the Berkeley Division of the Academic Senate that day." Earlier (p. 300) he says: "Because of their desperate desire to settle things, because of their experience of one administration failure after another, I believe most of the faculty was by now ready to accept any agreement that might lead to peace." These assessments color his entire treatment of the faculty's role. I think the facts show that Glazer taxes his colleagues unduly, and wrongfully casts doubt upon the integrity of their decision.

Until the crisis broke in late September, the faculty played no large part in the determination of policy regarding speech and political activity. Over the years a number of faculty members were actively interested in liberalized rules and, in cooperation with student leaders and President Kerr, helped to bring them about. Still others protested when, for example, a restrictive distinction was made between "on campus" and "off campus" student organizations. But passivity was more common, and the faculty dangerously allowed the president to elaborate, without dissent, his own perspectives on freedom and the university. These perspectives were very strongly influenced by his experience with trade unions. In Kerr's view, the university is an organization like other large-scale organizations in our society. Individual freedom and institutional well-being are best served if there are limited commitments on both sides. He lacked a vital theory of the university community and of the conditions under which its greatest potentialities might be realized. Perhaps the worst thing that can be said about the role of the faculty in recent years is that it failed to enter into a dialogue with the president concerning basic educational philosophy.

The disorders of early October were profoundly disturbing to many faculty members. There was considerable feeling that the administration was behaving very badly, but there was also widespread uneasiness about the students' conduct. Nevertheless, there was a quick response on the main issue, coupled with a determination to avoid open condemnation of either the administration or the students. On October 13 the Academic Senate passed by a large majority a motion favoring "maximum freedom for student political activity," and calling upon its Committee on Academic Freedom to formulate an appropriate policy. It was already clear where many of the faculty stood.

While various committees studied the matter, the agitation continued during October and November. There was of course an enormous amount of discussion within the faculty, including active work on petitions and resolutions. By late November, the impasse seemed so great that sentiment for determined faculty action grew rapidly, and various groups began to look to the meeting scheduled for December 8 as a time of decision. Immediately following the police action of December 3, an unofficial meeting of hundreds of faculty, chaired by Professor Nathan Glazer, passed a series of resolutions foreshadowing the actions of December 8. On December 6, an informal meeting of about 200 faculty members discussed, amended, and then approved unanimously a series of resolutions that had been prepared by a group of faculty liberals. These resolutions were substantially the same as those adopted on December 8. In the meantime, the Committee on Academic Freedom decided to present its own version of the same policy.

On December 7 classes were cancelled in the morning and department meetings were scheduled for the purpose of discussing a compromise agreement reached among the department chairmen, President Kerr, and some of the Regents. This was to be presented to an 11:00 a.m. convocation of the entire university community in the Greek Theater. At the same time, the resolutions of "the 200" were being widely circulated and discussed. There was much resentment of the compromise agreement, which did not speak to the basic policy issue, and even more antagonism against the idea of a full-dress convocation called to announce and celebrate a non-existent consensus and settlement. The show was an historic failure, and all eyes turned to the senate meeting scheduled for the following day.

Thus the meeting of December 8 was preceded by an unusual amount of discussion and preparation. To be sure, the atmosphere was tense and there was a crisis to be met. However, the whole pattern of faculty actions since October was consistent with the outcome. Almost everyone disliked the administration's policy, and most were now determined to say so.

If the faculty policy had been adopted by a slim majority, Glazer might have a point. Surely not everyone was equally convinced, and there must have been some who responded mainly to the desire for an end to the affair. On the other hand, there were members who agreed with the majority's policy but voted against the resolution, or abstained, because they felt under pressure. But almost the entire faculty voted, and the majority was over 7 to 1! Moreover, there has been no sign of weakening. Two days later, at a comparably large meeting, a resolution was introduced which, while reaffirming the action of December 8, could have been interpreted as a concession to the administration. Some well-known members of the "200" group supported the motion. Nevertheless it was tabled—in the context a clear indication of the majority's determination to stand fast by what it had done. The Emergency Executive Committee, though billed as "moderate," has taken the December 8 policy as its charter. In sum, the senate's decision was deliberate and firm. Nor is there any real reason to doubt that most members voted their convictions.

(3) I agree with Glazer that the issues at Berkeley have gone beyond free speech. Many have been troubled by the tactics of "direct action" applied in a university setting. Certainly the students resorted to pressure and intimidation. They relied on the model of the labor or civil rights dispute rather than on that of intellectual controversy or even normal political action. The excitement produced some excesses, both of invective and of conduct. All this is sobering, worthy of attention, in need of remedy.

Yet I feel that Glazer's disapproval of the student tactics—especially after they had won what *he* thought was enough—has obscured his vision and blunted his sensibility. He has not adequately perceived the moral character of the students themselves—their claim to our respect, support, forgiveness, and sympathy. Glazer tellingly documents the administration's rigid and inept handling of the dispute. But he does not grasp the significance of the fact that arbitrary administrative action lay at the base of the controversy, and was fuel to its flames at every step. These matters bear closely on the charge that somehow "law and order" went down the drain at Berkeley.

The obligation to obey the law is among the more subtle and variable of human commitments. In assessing that obligation, we take account of the nature of the setting, the character of the rules and of their enforcement, and the legitimate interests of the offender. Unquestioning obedience to lawful orders has more apparent point in a military organization than in business, and in both it weakens as we ascend the echelons or move from line to staff. While we cannot do without it altogether, a very strong emphasis on administrative authority is out of place in higher education. Here, if anywhere, the spirit of consultation should prevail. So too, arbitrary rule-making or administration saps its own authority and provides the offender with a defense. And if the offense carries forward a legitimate purpose, such as freedom of expression, or self-defense, it has some chance of vindication.

This approach was clearly manifest in a report of the Ad Hoc Committee on Student Conduct established to hear the cases of eight suspended students. The chairman of the committee was Professor Ira M. Heyman of the Law School. The Heyman committee made many discriminations and took account of much beyond the simple fact of rule-breaking. Two points are especially pertinent. First, the committee gave due weight to the context, namely, that a controversy over rules was raging and that the chancellor had made it clear "that the president and the Regents had rejected in final form the request of the ASUC Senate for changes in the rules. . . . The door was thus seemingly closed to any negotiation on these central points." Second, the committee took account of what the students were up to, viewing it "as a symbolic act of protest and not as an act of private delinquency."

Legality is a two-way street. He who insists on obedience to rules should be ready to justify the rules themselves. At Berkeley the administration adopted a posture of intransigeance and as much as said that it would yield only to pressure. There was little concept of true consultation with students on matters affecting their interests. In this setting, a loss of confidence and respect was inevitable. To many of the students, it seemed to justify direct action.

There has been much talk of "riots" at Berkeley. In fact there was no riot at all. One very serious incident—the surrounding and immobilization of a police car for 36 hours—could have come to that and should not be minimized. But most of the action consisted of orderly mass rallies, not less orderly sit-ins, and a brief student strike. A great many rules and some state laws were broken in the process. That is certainly regrettable, but we lose our bearings if we respond to such activities as if they were political or even academic outrages. A more appropriate response, learned long ago in other contexts, is to get at the root of the trouble.

A final word about the students and their leadership. The Free Speech Movement has been led by student radicals. In that sense, it is certainly unrepresentative of the student body as a whole. But the struggle these young radicals mounted struck a deeply responsive chord. Most of the students approved the goals of the FSM. At least a substantial minority, especially in the social sciences and humanities, approved of the demonstrative tactics as well. One survey, conducted by a class in social research methods under the direction of Professor Robert H. Somers, showed that in November 34% of all students supported the direct-action tactics of the FSM. This amounts to perhaps 9,000 student sympathizers, not counting the larger group who also supported the goals of the movement and whose sympathies could presumably be activated if the administration behaved especially badly. This was borne out by the size of some of the rallies.

On the other hand, student support was clearly tied to the issues at hand. It was not mindless or mechanical, and many had reservations about the more extreme actions, such as the use of a police car as a podium or indulgence in unrestrained invective. The FSM sympathizers did not respond to *any* appeal. They responded above all to concrete deprivations, such as the withdrawal of earlier *de facto* rights and, especially, the indefensible reinstitution of charges against the FSM leaders on November 30. (Glazer speaks of this as a "blunder," but the students more rightly perceived it as a sickness of soul.) On more abstract issues, the FSM could get large crowds for rallies but not for illegal action.

For my own part, I was offended by the posturing and scorn of a few of the FSM leaders, but I was deeply impressed by the earnestness, dedication, and basic moral enlightenment of most of the student supporters I encountered. These are among our very best students. They are not thugs or scoundrels, neither are they caught up in any impenetrable ideology. They are acting out what they have learned, without the patience and restraint of maturity. The students had a just cause and they yearned for affirmation of it. If there was an excess of zeal, it did not forfeit their claim to our sense of fellowship.

In a community of scholars, that is something we should reject, not in fearful recoil from the first signs of stirring and change, but only as a last extremity. Happily, there is no prospect of that at Berkeley.

REPLY TO SELZNICK*

BY NATHAN GLAZER

There is no disagreement between Professor Selznick and myself over the facts as to what happened at Berkeley; there is little disagreement even over the interpretation of many of the facts. We both ascribe the origins of the dispute and its continuance and revival to the ineptitude of the administration (though I would not go so far as "a sickness of soul"—these men, after all, are our colleagues and it is hard to see that they suffer from such radical defects). We both agree that the FSM was led by students whose political views were not representative of the student body but who, on the basis of the issues presented by the administration, were able to mobilize large numbers of students, in particular those moved by the civil rights revolution.

But we do disagree on three major issues: the extent to which this was a free speech fight, the wisdom of the faculty action, and the judgment of the moral quality of the students' acts.

When the representatives of the university administration in the Committee on Student Political Activity agreed early in November to the opening of the campus to the planning and preparation of political action as well as speech, then to my mind the free speech issue, to the extent that it existed, disappeared. This committee was composed of student, faculty, and administration representatives. It agreed that all the actions originally banned by the administration (collection of funds, organizing, advocacy of action) would now be permitted on campus. These were the original issues, and they were settled. The new issue that now arose—the legitimacy of the advocacy and organization of illegal action—was referred to a subcommittee of this committee, consisting of a representative of the statewide university administration, a law school professor (one of the faculty group), and a lawyer representing the FSM, and this subcommittee agreed on language which satisfied the administration and which, in the judgment of the faculty representative and the student lawyer, protected all the students' civil and political rights. This compromise was rejected by the FSM students on the committee. Professor Selznick accepts the view of the FSM leaders that

* From *Commentary*, March 1965.

the university's insistence that the campus could not be used for the launching of illegal action involved a restriction of free speech. "The university apparently reserved the right to regulate speech or organization that in its judgment was directed to illegal off-campus action." I did not interpret the Regents' action this way; nor did the faculty members of the Committee on Student Political Action interpret this position this way; nor did Chancellor Strong's regulations for student political activity, issued a few days after the Regents' meeting to implement their action, give support to such an interpretation. There was never any hint or suggestion that there would be prior censorship; nor was there any suggestion that administration action would be taken on the basis of any kind of speech—the issue was specifically illegal action and the launching of action from the campus by groups using its facilities. The specific problems at issue (e.g., who interprets what is illegal?) could have been ironed out in the Committee on Student Political Action, which was designed just for the purpose of working out these details. I attended one of these meetings, and it was clear to me that discussion in any real sense was made almost impossible by the legalistic quibbling that the students reveled in. They acted as if they were in training for service on the UN Security Council or the Korean truce commission, when they could have acted as members of an academic community trying to work out reasonable rules.

But speaking most forcefully against Professor Selznick's restrictive interpretation of the university position is that it still stands and that nothing has fundamentally changed in the administration's position of the first week of November as ratified by the Regents on November 20th, two weeks before the sit-in and arrests of December 2nd and 3rd. The Berkeley campus rules will have to abide by it; and as far as I can see, both the faculty and the students are now ready to live with the position that the campus is not to be used for the launching of illegal political action. If free speech exists on the campus (and I think everyone agrees it does) then it is clear that this position does not restrict free speech.

The Regents' position strictly interpreted can be used to penalize students and student groups who launch actions which are declared illegal by the courts. But a general declaration of principle for the university does not require the university to act in an area as uncertain, as rapidly changing, as ambiguous as present-day civil rights demonstrations. Its actions will depend on the temper of the administration, on the development of public opinion, the direction of legal decisions, the developing character of the civil rights movement. But regardless of how all these factors develop it is inconceivable to me—as it is, I am sure, to Professor Selznick—that a general university position against the use of its facilities for the launching of illegal political action can be withdrawn.

Now on the role of the faculty: Professor Selznick suggests that we still have something to teach our students about the relation of means to ends. I agree. I also believe we did nothing to advance this teaching, and the resolution of December 8, presented at the time it was, and so overwhelmingly adopted, made the task of such teaching infinitely more difficult. The previous day we had seen the collapse of an effort to compromise the issues. This collapse, we must realize, was engineered in large measure by the leaders of the FSM, and by the use of tactics to disrupt and take over meetings that extremists everywhere have made familiar to us, most recently in the unsuccessful campaign of Patrick Gordon Walker. One of the most brilliant analyses of such tactics is, of course, to be found in Professor Selznick's *The Organizational Weapon*. These tactics deny any dignity to an opponent and would deny his right to conduct a meeting with the agenda and speakers he sees fit. In this case the opponent was the president of the university and the department chairmen who had worked out the compromise. On that day, and the following day, the university was on strike. One group of graduate history students taking an examination was interrupted by an FSM activist calling upon them to go out on strike. One striking teaching assistant was prepared to put up on the door of another teaching assistant who was conducting a class a sign reading, "this class is taught by scab labor."

This was a time that required teaching as to the relations of means to ends. But it was impossible at this time to get the Academic Senate to adopt any position which could be interpreted as critical of FSM actions. What the student leaders learned from the Academic Senate meeting of December 8th was that extreme tactics could be used without censure from the faculty. (Many individual faculty members, including, of course, those in the great majority that adopted the resolution of December 8th, did, in smaller meetings, in discussion with students, criticize their actions.)

The size of the faculty vote for the resolution of December 8th was, I believe, unnaturally swelled by a number of special factors, among them the fact that there was a good deal of confusion among many faculty members who had been told that the main resolution was supported by the president and the administration, and that it was in fact a peace settlement reached to end the strike. Nothing was done to dispel this confusion; among those who supported the minority amendment no one who was considered close to the administration spoke. Every faculty member confronted the terrible dilemma that to turn down the resolution meant that the strike would continue. Our teaching assistants had been protected against reprisal for two days; could they be protected if the strike continued, and would 800 graduate students dismissed from teaching and research positions be added to 800 arrested students? I do not doubt that the resolution would have been passed in any case; the vote, however, would have been much less one-sided in the absence of this confusion and pressure.

The most difficult question is how one assesses the moral quality of the students' actions. Here is a student movement that is committed to the expansion of freedom, and many of whose leaders and members have risked the terrible dangers of fighting for justice in Mississippi. I admire and respect the students who have committed themselves to the civil rights struggle, and who have transformed the temper of our universities. Unquestionably the knowledge that the students in the FSM were also involved in the larger fight for justice and equality for Negroes made many faculty members hesitant in judging their actions, in a different place and for a different cause.

But no movement in this world is immune from the threat of distortion and corruption, even a movement for the good and the just. Power may corrupt, even when it is power mobilized for a good cause, and committed to the philosophy of non-violence. These are possibilities; at times these possibilities come close to actualization on the Berkeley campus.

A new period has opened on the Berkeley campus, one of wide communication between administration, faculty and students, one of great concern with the nature of the university, and of the process of education within it. A great wave of energy has been released here, particularly among the students, by the crisis of the past few months, and it has been wonderful to see what prodigies of work—in organization, in research, in writing—have been evoked from them by the struggle. Certainly many professors have been given quite a start to discover what stores of energy are locked in our students and untouched by the normal educational routine. This is a moment that should be seized, for there are only few moments in the history of an institution when large changes are possible. It is also clear that the new chancellor welcomes proposals for change. This can be a valuable and fruitful time for us. But this time of change can be perverted and aborted if the student leaders do not recognize how such a wide-ranging discussion concerning the character and future of the university should be conducted. Certainly the tactics of force and disruption can play no part in it. I know the faculty shares this view; I hope the radical student leaders do too. But it is just this that has not been settled in the recent crisis.

THOUGHTS ON BERKELEY*
BY PAUL GOODMAN

1

The function of administration is to expedite the essential academic business of teaching and learning, e.g., as secretary and janitor; and protectively to represent the academic community in its external relations, e.g., in court or as fund-raiser. When administration becomes the dominant force in the community, however, it is a sign that extra-mural powers are in control—State, Church, or Economy—and the administration is their agent. Notoriously, Image-burnishing and fund-raising disregard or even prevent teaching and learning.

At Berkeley, the students griped that the University of California has become a "factory, disregarding faculty and students," a factory to process professional licenses and apprentices for technological corporations, and to do extra-mural contracted research. The particular bone of contention, the Free Speech ban, seems also to have been extra-murally instigated, by backlash elements, persons like Senator Knowland, etc. The administration certainly acted with panic, under outside pressure and out of touch with its own community.

At present in the United States, students—middle-class youth —are the major exploited class. (Negroes, small farmers, the aged are rather out-caste groups; their labor is not needed and they are not wanted.) The labor of intelligent youth *is* needed and they are accordingly subjected to tight scheduling, speedup, and other factory methods. Then it is not surprising if they organize their CIO. It is frivolous to tell them to go elsewhere if they don't like the rules, for they have no choice but to go to college, and one factory is like another.

2

Thus far in the Berkeley revolt, two new factors have emerged: 1) The students want to extend the concept of Academic Freedom from *Lehrfreiheit* (freedom of professors to teach according to their lights) to include *Lernfreiheit* (freedom of students to ask for what they need to be taught, and if necessary to invite teachers, including advocates of causes.) I shall return to this later. 2) The faculty energized by the students, wants to resume prerogatives that it had given up to the administration, e.g., discipline. This is probably the more important issue; but in my opinion the administration cannot agree (and the Regents have so voted) to the faculty resumption of prerogatives, because this could go very far and en-

*From *The New York Review of Books*, January 14, 1965.

tirely unmake the academic-factory; e.g., the faculty might hire or teach in disregard of image, endowments, or research grants; they might resist huge classes or abolish grading. The question, then, will be whether there are enough professors who are concerned for the academic community to fight it out, rather than pursuing their grants and independent research.

It is useful to recall the important student strike, a few years ago, at New York State University at Oyster Bay (now Stony Brook). Here the state tried to impose a new president, to turn the Liberal Arts school into an engineering institute. The students were angered by disregard of their physical and social needs; the faculty was indignant at the attempt to fragment the divisional system into departments that could be administratively subjugated. Backed by the faculty, very many students struck and the new president had to go.

Generally speaking, student efforts to get an education befitting free men rather than slaves can succeed only with strong faculty backing, for the students are transient, they do not *definitely* know what they want, they do not know the score behind the scenes and thus they can be abashed by administrative double-talk. On the other hand, given the supine history of American faculties in our sectarian and trustee-ridden colleges, and given the present extra-mural careerism of the important professors, the students must lead if there is to be any change.

3

The extension of Academic Freedom to the claim to Freedom-to-Learn implies a revolutionary change in the status of American college-going. Up to now, American collegians have been regarded, and have regarded themselves, as late-adolescents; but the claim to *Lernfreiheit* means that they are young adults who are capable of knowing what they ought to get.

This is, of course, the (non-English) European and Latin tradition. It goes with early sexual maturity, with economic independence (often in bohemian poverty), and with active involvement in politics. Classically, in Europe, it has also involved drawn-out education, many moratoria, much changing of schools and career plans, and "being a student" as itself a kind of profession of young adults, especially of the upper class.

Some of these changes are evident in this country. Whatever parents and administrators may say about extended sexual tutelage and *in loco parentis,* the young are practicing earlier sexual maturity without apologies. The past ten years have witnessed a remarkable resurgence of youthful political engagement. And since the selective service, it becomes farfetched to deny the eighteen-year-old vote. It is hard to see

how the university can welcome recruiters for Peace Corps
or Army and disallow CORE or SNCC. (Incidentally, since
the Supreme Court's "abatement" decision the illegal activity
has turned out to be legal after all!) Administration itself has
dealt a mortal blow to the notion of late-adolescence by its
persistent attempts to abolish the fraternity system, which was
a bulwark of Youth House and Social Life ideology (leading,
for instance, to trivial student governments). I do not think
the aim of Administration has been to treat the students as
young adults; rather, the abolition of fraternities seems to be
an attempt to tighten control, increase academic performance,
and to gouge rent (since dormitories are built with Federal
funds). Nevertheless, the effect of abolition must be student
maturation, demands to live off-campus or to liberalize dormitory rules, to lower rents and improve food, and to be represented by a government that is not otiose.

On the other hand, there are strong American influences to
prevent student maturation and independence. First, the frantic career-drive, spurred by the anxiety of middle-class parents, leading to conformism, and willingness to submit to
scheduled mis-education, credits, and grading, in order to get
a diploma quick. Secondly, the students are not financially
independent; tuition is exceedingly high, so that it is impossible
to opt for independent poverty; scholarships and loans put the
student under administration control. Probably most important, the universal compulsory school-going without alternative
choices, is infantile. In 1900, only 6 per cent graduated from
high school. We thus have conflict: the direct and evident
need for the students as a working class of the economy
would tend to make the students more mature; but the conditions of their collegiate exploitation tend to make them insecure and immature.

The evolution of both faculty and student organizations in
the United States has been different from the communities of
scholars in Europe. We do not have community guilds but
rather national unions. The faculty unions—e.g., The American Association of University Professors or the Teachers
Union—were first formed as defensive leagues; my guess is
that they will now begin to take the offensive. I can conceive
of them declining to take graduate students from Ole Miss; or
defending the principles of the original Mobilization for
Youth, as a committee of the American Sociological Association has done; or attacking the entrenched Boards of Education with new ideas for the public schools. On the other hand,
the student unions—e.g., the Student Peace Union, the Students
for a Democratic Society—started largely for extra-mural political reasons; but my guess is that they will now, as at Berkeley, look to improve the academic community. In this the
National Students Association could be a leader. Hopefully,

as I have said, the student activity will revive the dormant community of the faculty.

In my opinion, the chief *political* action of students would, at present, be intra-mural—humanizing and making cultural the academic community—for the colleges and universities have become so tightly interlocked with the dominant tightly interlocked system of society that any *intra-mural* improvement will be a profound shock to the system. Also, in these matters the students can really know what they are talking about.

4

What is the role of a student government? In our contemporary conditions, it is interesting to hark back to the "Nations," the powerful student government of medieval universities.

The medieval student government was a band to bargain collectively on rent with the townspeople, on food prices with the tavern-keepers. Our present governments could bargain this way with both the town and the administration, the bookstores, the Co-op.

In medieval conditions, the Nations bargained with the faculty on tuition. With us this is wholly an administrative matter. One thinks of the students of City College in New York going to Albany on the tuition fight. A related issue is class size and immature section men. The tuition mounts, but the student gets less and less for his money. A few years ago there was a strike on this issue (I think successful) at Rochester.

A purpose of the Nations was to regulate morals and keep the peace, in order to prevent outside sanctions; and if need be to get the faculty to rescue students in trouble with the secular arm. They were also a *conjuratio,* a sworn league for mutual aid in sickness and other troubles, a kind of lodge.

Besides these medieval functions, our modern situation requires some new student government powers. In the frantic expansion, there is a vast amount of building. On visits to eighty colleges around the country, however, I have seen scarcely a single new dormitory that shows any thought (or concern) for the student users. And there are fancy façades but lousy food. The students certainly ought to have an advisory role from the beginning in any plans for a new physical plant. (The faculty, let me say, should have more than an advisory role, instead of being routinely consulted and disregarded.) Further, in the present lockstep grading and scheduling, students should have a say in rules of moratoria and transfer, so that they can shape their educations to their own current powers and concerns, and not be short-changed on "credits." Ultimately, faculty must and will control what it teaches and how it teaches, but the students must come to their studies voluntarily, when they are ready; they cannot be force-fed.

I submit that all these matters could be better dealt with by concerted self-interest than by paternalistic administrators and guidance counselors. Further, I think that professors would be delighted to be teaching mature young persons who can take care of themselves. The GI-bill without shell-shock.

REPLY TO GOODMAN*
BY NATHAN GLAZER

I understand Paul Goodman's difficulty in writing about Berkeley from a distance, but there are things in his brief article that are really odd, when read on the scene:

". . . when administration becomes the dominant force, . . . it is a sign that extra-mural powers are in control—State, Church, or Economy . . ." State was in control at the state university long before administration became dominant. Church, in any form, is banned. Administration's dominance is not explained by the extra-mural power of the economy, unless Goodman means that the university requires a good deal of money to run, and the faculty prefers to cede the management of the budget to others, so long as their salaries are sufficient. The dominance of the administration is based on the facts of 18,000 undergraduates, 10,000 graduate students, 1500 faculty members, 200,000 grades per year, etc., etc. It is not the administration that imposes a system of education involving innumerable courses and examinations—it is the faculty. Nor is it the administration alone that hampers reform. It is the indifference to educational reform of both faculty and students.

"The faculty, energized by the students, wants to resume prerogatives that it had given up to the administration, e.g., discipline." Quite untrue. Read: "The faculty, disturbed and frightened by administration ineptitude and mass student protest, was stampeded into demanding this right as the student price for peace." The faculty is not interested in exercising student discipline over liquor, sex, cheating, and other things that they are happy to leave in the hands of the administration. Nor do they relish devoting endless time to hearings in which students and administration are represented by lawyers, and in which any normal lay intelligence finds itself overwhelmed by legal technicalities and political in-fighting. Mr. Goodman should come to one of these. Faculty discipline will become the pro forma activity of faculty members dragooned into it, or willing to waste their time at it. It will become another cog

* From *The New York Review of Books*, February 11, 1965.

in the committee system that uses up faculty time and helps prevent student-faculty contact.

"At present in the United States, students—middle-class youth—are the major exploited class . . . they have no choice but to go to college." Nonsense. Intelligent youth may accept the minimal income for freedom Mr. Goodman has so effectively argued for, and which the society provides. The non-student representative in the FSM Executive Committee estimated there are 3000 non-students around the campus at Berkeley, who have done just this. Their families or the un-employment insurance system, or the many odd jobs around the university, or their friends support them. They may be unhappy, but not because they are being exploited. Mr. Goodman is making hash out of a useful and respectable word.

"The administration cannot agree to the faculty resumption of prerogatives, because . . . this could unmake the academic-factory . . . the faculty might hire or teach in disregard of image, endowments, or research grants." More nonsense. The issue is politics, not education. The administration holds on to its prerogatives because it thinks the faculty is politically irresponsible and will get the university into trouble with the legislature. But not through anyone it hires or anything it teaches. It can and does teach Marx, Goodman, Genet, Mao Tse-tung, or what you will. And it hires anybody it wants. The point is, these are guilds of scholars and researchers. To make them act differently from the way they do does not require taking power away from the administration; it requires administrations strong enough and coherent enough to break up the conservative patterns of teaching and hiring that develop within the guilds. This makes a much less Arcadian picture than Mr. Goodman, I am afraid, would care to deal with.

The student uprising at Berkeley is indeed for very mature ends: the end of a powerful student political movement with impact on the community. The educational aims are less clear, but their clearest part is that the educational process should serve the political ends. This should not be so unfamiliar to us.

". . . freedom of students to ask for what they need to be taught and if necessary to invite teachers." A grand idea, and I am sure it would work wonderfully at Bennington or Black Mountain. The student movement here may turn into that. If it does it will find that the problem is the faculty, not the administration. And Mr. Goodman, in his fine book *The Community of Scholars*, agreed that one reasonable alternative approach to setting up a university was to have the faculty teach what it felt had to be taught, and the students could come, or not, as they wished. Perhaps we will have something new on the academic scene, a faculty transformed not by an administration, à la Hutchins, but by a student body. But if it is to happen at this university, with this student body and this faculty, it will be quite a fight.

REPLY TO GLAZER*
BY PAUL GOODMAN

If Nat Glazer believes his ending, that the Berkeley movement "may" turn toward fighting for an authentic community of scholars and that "perhaps" a faculty may be transformed by a student body, I am puzzled by the zeal with which he refutes me and calls my remarks Nonsense! rather than saying sadly and firmly, "Alas, not yet true; we must yet make it true." In my article I was not sanguine: "The question will be whether there are enough professors who are concerned for the academic community" and "Given the supine history of American faculties and the present careerism of the important professors, the students must lead." But there is a conflict in the students themselves between the causes that have made them more mature and their prior and present educational exploitation that tends to make them insecure and immature.

Nevertheless, the faculty voted 7 to 1 for the students, and it seems to me presumptuous of Nat to call this being "frightened and stampeded." I have been told, rather, that it was a faculty reaction of *nausea* at the Administration lies, spineless subservience to outside pressures, infantile tantrums, avoidance of confrontation and calling the cops. I believe it, for it is this kind of nausea that indeed recalls decent but self-centered people to their plain duty. Besides, what about the 200 faculty who supported the students from very early in the game? They were not stampeded. And most important, what about the almost unanimous support of the section-men and research-assistants, who took the greatest risks by striking?

I deeply trust that faculty is not interested in exercising discipline over "liquor, sex, cheating, and other things." For they are none of its damned business, nor Administration's either. Surely Nat knows this; what is he up to? E.g., would he himself bother with grading if it were not administratively demanded?

And what are we to make of his denial that State and Economy have increased administrative dominance? Clark Kerr himself has said, "The university is being called on to respond to the *expanding* claims of national service, and to merge its activity with industry *as never before* [my italics] . . . It is a mechanism held together by administrative rules and powered by money." This is true and Kerr likes it; the students don't like it; and I call it exploitation of the young. By extra-mural

* From *The New York Review of Books*, February 11, 1965.

power of the Economy I do not mean that it costs a lot of money to run a school, but simply such bashful items as 17 billions annually for Research and Development, of which 2 billions direct from Government to university and other billions through private contracted research in the universities; lots of money from the National Defense Education Act; the piratical raiding of name-professors in order to get contracts and foundation grants; the National Science Foundation's Ph.D.-processing curriculum reforms for the lower schools; State and Economy underwriting, in the few dozen most prestigious schools, of from 40 per cent to 80 per cent of the total budget; the tuition-hikes and rent-gouges of the neglected undergraduates; the frontier testing for apprentice skills, and hot campus-recruiting by the corporations . . . Need I go on?

I am unimpressed by the theory that it is sheer numbers that have made administration dominant. Have administrations hastened to decentralize in order to lessen their burdens? Have they tried to discourage the popular superstition of school-going? Have they tried to shift the contracted research to non-academic institutes? No. They have acted as crude imperialists.

By "exploited class" I mean simply that the students' powers and time of life are used for other people's purposes; I am *not* making a hash of the word. Let us remember that 100 years ago, the young were exploited from 10 to 25 years of age in other kinds of factories. (Needless to say, middle-class youth are also pampered, but this merely confuses them in their exploitation.) The demand for *Lernfreiheit* is the student claim to learn intrinsically, when they are ready and what they are ready for, like free men. Surely Nat is not serious when he speaks of the freedom of middle-class youth to "accept the minimal income" instead of getting degrees, and he mentions the 3000 non-students in Berkeley. How oddly he puts it!—the "intelligent," who have quit school, he says, are *not* exploited; he seems to be saying that those who are pressured into remaining in school *are* exploited, which is my point. But then why does *he* continue teaching there, among the stupid?

Finally, however, there is one profoundly important statement in Nat's letter; and I am thankful for the chance to comment on it, which I failed to do in my original piece. He speaks of "the indifference to educational reform of both faculty and students." This, it seems to me, is the crux for the future of the Berkeley movement as a mass-movement.

There is a dilemma. As I have repeatedly written, the majority of these youth ought not to be in a serious scholastic setting at all, for that is a very specialized way of growing up and does not suit most, including most of the bright. In the usual present-day university, my guess is that about 50 per cent are there only incidentally, with their attention mainly on (serious or frivolous) extra-curricular activities but they need the diploma; another 30 per cent are there like sheep because they have always gone to school and done lessons, and they are clinging to the routine for another four to six years; about 15 per cent are set on some diplomated career and *want* to get competitive grades and "master the subject"; and perhaps 5 per cent would like to learn something academically (and are hampered by the others). This does not provide a mass-base for academic reform! although there evidently has been a mass-base for civil liberties, (especially when energized by civil rights for Negroes) and for being treated as human beings and not manipulated.

But now that the chancellor is gone and Senator Knowland no longer needs to have fits about the election and Proposition 14, how can the Free Speech movement live on? For the majority, the struggle against bureaucracy and exploitation cannot be posed as a claim to better teaching; it must be a claim to a more decent physical and social community of young people, less harried by petty mechanical tasks, and perhaps with more contact with the professors not as teachers but as likable friends and guides. That is, they ought to demand the B.A. at birth if it is economically necessary; or demand to be paid for doing onerous lessons; or attempt to destroy the illusion that a paper degree is good for anything, and quit the university and educate themselves in various other environments; or fight for the guaranteed decent income for everybody, with or without diploma, and meantime use the multiversity to practice cultured leisure and mount political actions. On the other hand, those who want to learn something ought frankly to conspire with favorable professors to teach them in freedom, and simply disregard the Administration as otiose. This is really quite easy, for in the essential, Administration *is* otiose. E.g., the professor can say at the opening class, "Everybody gets A; those who are not interested, need not attend; I'm not a constable and I don't hand in names." If the Administration attempts sanctions, the student community as a whole can proudly come to the defense of its proper scholars; and, it seems to me, the professors would have an academic freedom case. Lead the way, Nat! do you have Tenure?

FSM: FREEDOM FIGHTERS OR MISGUIDED REBELS?

A SPEECH BY HAL DRAPER, EDITORIAL BOARD, *New Politics*

Following is a transcription (slightly condensed) from the tape-recording made by Pacifica radio station KPFA, Berkeley, of the "Conference on the Student Revolt" sponsored by the Independent Socialist Club, held on January 9, 1965, on

*the university campus. This discussion constituted the evening
session of the conference. The tape of the entire discussion,
including the question-period exchanges and final summaries
by both speakers, is available from KPFA.*

After the chairman's preliminary remarks, I'd better tell
you that this is not supposed to be a debate. It's a—non-debate.

I think it's a very good thing that a non-debate of this sort
should take place. Everybody believes in "furthering communication," and it would be a very good idea if the ASUC or
the Committee on Arts and Lectures were to sponsor a couple
more non-debates like this, on the question of what's been
happening on the campus. Or even the Department of Sociology, for that matter. In the meantime, while these institutions
are seeing their way clear to such communication, it's a good
thing that the Independent Socialist Club has acted in the
breach.

According to the title of this non-debate, the FSM students
are "misguided rebels." I want to say, that's not so bad at all.
You've been called worse.

For example, at the debate that took place at the Academic
Senate on December 8, you were called "a bunch of rowdies"
by that eminent gentleman and scholar, W. Petersen. President
Kerr has called you "Maoists," "Castroites," "anarchists,"
and—worst of all possible epithets—"non-students." Professor
Feuer, in his article, which is perhaps the most violent, vitriolic, and virulent attack on the FSM, called the FSM a
"Soviet-style coalition." (By the way, nobody has recently
seen an FSM at the University of Moscow, I believe.) You
are a "Soviet-style coalition"; you're "forlorn crackpots,"
"limpniks," "lumpen-beatniks."

So you see, if you're merely "misguided rebels," that's practically a compliment. I feel like beaming on Mr. Glazer and
saying gratefully to him, "Thanks, the same to you." Because,
after all, Mr. Glazer is a rebel too: he's a rebel against the
majority—the majority of the Academic Senate. And as for
being misguided . . .

In this presentation I'm going to limit myself to two basic
points of contention. It's a hard choice, because there are a
great many other important aspects, most of which, however,
have been covered in a great deal of detail at other sessions
of this conference; and for that matter I have discussed many
in other talks. There's the whole problem of outside pressures
on the university, and also the civil-rights aspect of the fight,
which I don't intend to touch on in these thirty minutes.

The points that I do want to address myself to are these:
what did the FSM accomplish? Should it have been done in
some less militant way, some way less distressful to some
people?

Both of these points have to be discussed in the framework of what is *the* issue—what has been the issue from the beginning and still is the issue. That is the issue that has been called, in shorthand language, "free speech" on the campus—which includes, particularly, freedom to mount political and social action, freedom to advocate, freedom to hold meetings, to raise funds, to recruit. It's for these freedoms, and for a university climate that makes possible these freedoms that the FSM has been fighting.

Now, to grapple with these points I propose to start by taking up the new version of history that was promulgated this week, Tuesday, by President Kerr, in an interview which was published in the San Francisco *Chronicle* last Wednesday and simultaneously in the Los Angeles *Times*. In this interview President Kerr presents his apologia; and I'm willing to follow along with him in pointing back, as he does, to the inception of the free-speech issue on the campus in September.

The headline given to this interview is: "A *Candid* Interview with Kerr." So be careful. And you are told right off that "he told *with characteristic precision* of the history of the free-speech rebellion." Nobody could be more warned than that.

This history of the free-speech rebellion, which was told "with characteristic precision" by President Kerr, starts by telling us that he admits he made mistakes in judgment—"in judgment and tactics during the early stages of the uprising. When Kerr returned to the campus September 15 [we read], following a seven-week trip to Europe . . . he found that the day before [on September 14] Berkeley administrators had closed the traditional Sather Gate political arena."

"I thought that was a mistake, and that we should return this area to the students," Kerr said. "But this was difficult." [Laughter.] Well, you're going to see what the problem is in the next sentence. "It had just been taken away. We could hardly turn around and hand it right back."

The simplest question is: well, why not? It's much easier then than later!

"Kerr then suggested to the administration that students be permitted use of the Sproul Hall steps instead, and that certain other concessions be made to student political groups. He characterized these as 'retreats' and justified them on the grounds that 'I thought that we could get things back into channels of discussion if we showed reasonableness, but it didn't work.'" And he went on to say that "instead of the reasonable discussion he had hoped for, he got the Free Speech Movement." And he didn't think that was a fair exchange.

Now I have given you President Kerr's version, finally given to the world, of what happened in September: the poor president, long-suffering, patient, put-upon—he couldn't get the students to engage in "reasonable discussion."

Well now, that's a fine, candid history, and the only thing wrong with it is that it leaves out what actually happened.

Let me say this as clearly as possible: if this published interview accurately reflects the case that Kerr presented, then it adequately explains, I think, why so many in this university do not trust Clark Kerr's capacity to understand either what is going on or to tell the whole truth about it.

What actually happened at the beginning of this fateful collision?

On September 14 the clubs operating tables were told by Dean Towle: "No tables." The first reason given, by the way, was that they were blocking traffic, you remember. This was the reason presumably thought up by the "saintly" Chancellor Strong. The issue was the tables; and the eight suspensions of students that took place, took place over their activities at the tables.

Kerr tells us that he came back the next day and that he thought it was a mistake. That *what* was a mistake? There is not a word in this candid history about the tables or the eight suspended students—not a word. It has dropped out, into the Memory-hole.

The mistake, he tells us, was taking the Bancroft area away from the students, that's all. And he says he sought to rectify the mistake by permitting the use of Sproul Hall steps as a Hyde Park area—which, of course, as you know, was done. But not a word about the tables or the eight suspensions. And it is in this way that he can try to get away with the bit about "hoping for reasonable discussion and getting the FSM" instead.

Now what actually happened about "reasonable discussion"?—after Kerr had come back and had things in hand, presumably. On September 17—Kerr was already back now—the clubs submitted a request to the dean's office for restoration of their rights, including tables. Just a request: they didn't sit-in, they didn't smash windows. They introduced a request legally, through channels, practically humbly.

And on September 21 the dean met with them and rectified the mistake, that mistake which Kerr didn't even mention, that is, about the tables: okay on tables *but no fund-raising, no recruitment* there. (And at first, no advocacy of partisan positions—that was changed afterward.) Now it was in this form that the issue of the tables led to the eight suspensions, to the arrest of Jack Weinberg, the police-car blockade, and so on into the rest of the history.

Now what are tables? Well, they're articles of furniture. But in this situation what the tables meant was the right of the students to carry on unrestricted legitimate political and social action. That's what the tables meant, and that's what the issue was. Now, was Kerr open to "reasonable discussion" on this issue—the issue that moved the students to fight?

Let me tell you that, not only during those last days of September, but also on October 1–2, faculty mediators and others, including personal friends of Kerr, were told by Kerr for days running that the issue of the rules and of the suspensions was *"not negotiable."* He told everybody: *"not negotiable."* Personal friends went to see him; they reported that his reply was, "These issues are *not negotiable."* Evidence: even in that vitriolic article by Professor Feuer, he records what he knows from his personal experience to be true: "They heard . . . one phrase repeated: 'non-negotiable.' "

Now, three months later, Kerr tells the press that all he was after was "reasonable discussion of the issues." And I tell you that that is a lie, and that Clark Kerr knows the facts that show it's a lie.

Feuer writes in his article that Kerr's devotion to academic freedom is "unquestionable." Just about as unquestionable, one might add, as the halo around the "saintly" Strong; but in any case, it's "unquestionable." And if you blink at that, you have to remember that last Sunday Dr. Sidney Hook explained in the *New York Times Magazine* that academic freedom does not apply to students at all, anyway. And with that proviso, he may be right!

The reason the Kerr interview leads off with this fabricated history is, as a matter of fact, that the main bludgeon with which the enemies of the students have been making headway is precisely the tale that things are all right but the students, the FSM is intransigent, has been intransigent, has refused to parley; nothing can satisfy them; they're just malcontents, can't get along with them. You got that in the San Francisco *Chronicle* and the rest of the press. You get it in Professor Feuer's bitter polemic. You get it from the Babbitts on the faculty.

But it's not true. And the proof that it was not true came on December 8, when the "intransigents" were satisfied— weren't they, that day, when the Academic Senate's resolution was adopted, which adopted the position of the FSM?

Now remember, this is what it was all about. It was this—the question of "free speech" and the rights of social and political activity—which the Academic Senate adopted. That was *it.* That was the issue about which the students had been fighting. And it was on this issue that, at this time, the FSM smashed the "non-negotiable" position of President Kerr and the administration, and won the faculty to support *its* position.

Now I tell you that this was a titanic achievement. Not everybody in the FSM agrees with me on that; I've got perhaps an extreme point of view on it. It was, in my opinion, a titanic achievement (leaving aside the question of what will be whittled away *now*). It had never before been achieved by any student movement in this country.

I say that as an expert on the subject. As I explained in more detail at another Independent Socialist Club meeting the other week, I was, in the 1930s, a member of the first national committee of the American Student Union, which had something to do with student activity. In 1934 and '35, I and another chap organized the very largest of the student anti-war strikes of those years. And I tell you solemnly that nowhere, at no time in this country, has any student protest ever scored such a smashing achievement over a hostile administration.

I don't tell you this to make you or the FSM feel good. I tell it to you for an entirely different purpose: in order to pose a question to all the people who say so glibly that the FSM could have done even better by different methods—more "reasonable" methods, less militant, less "intransigent." And I ask a very simple question about that: *Have you ever tried it?*

All of you "reasonable" people, who think that this could have been done with marshmallows: show me your credentials; tick off all the administrations you have fought to a standstill with those methods. Or that anybody else has.

Nobody else has! And only the Free Speech Movement on this campus has succeeded in winning a victory of these dimensions for such an objective—which now the university community claims for its own, in the vote that the Academic Senate gave.

I say that this fact should give pause when we fully appreciate the size of the achievement. Look, after all, at the great change that has taken place from September 30 to December 8, when the Academic Senate met.

You may be thinking to yourself: Well, but Mr. Glazer was in the minority; he didn't agree with the decision of the Academic Senate. I'm not discussing that; that was taken care of by Professor Ten Broek and others at the Academic Senate meeting. Never mind that amendment which was made by Professor Feuer and supported by Glazer—the one about "force and violence." Never mind that: suppose it were *in* there, suppose that amendment had been added to the Academic Senate resolution.

It wouldn't have been any improvement, but the resolution still would have said that *"the content of speech or advocacy should not be restricted by the University"* (with a proviso about violence which had no application in practice to what the students had actually done). And it would have said that *"on-campus advocacy or organization of such activities shall be subject only to such limitations as"* do not interfere with *the normal functioning of the University* (with the proviso about violence which had nothing to do with what the students had done).

Now remember: you throw the Feuer amendment in, and *if* Feuer and Glazer really meant that the resolution would have been good providing only that their amendment were carried, then it still meant that they, too, the minority as well as the majority, were condemning the September line of the administration as a subversion of "free speech" and of the students' rights. They too, the minority as well as the majority! And if that isn't so, by the way, I'd like to find out.

Could the subversion of "free speech" have been stopped without the FSM and its activities? Certainly it could have been stopped without the FSM.

It could have been stopped if the faculty had risen in their wrath and said, "This is an abomination"—as in effect they said later on December 8—if they had risen and said, "This is an abomination, a violation of the university community's freedom; it must be stopped"; if they had risen on their hind legs, to their full height, and taken their responsibility and their duty in hand, and at their Academic Senate meetings in October had thundered out against this subversive attack by the administration against what is now proclaimed as basic freedoms by the faculty itself. This at a time when the *Daily Cal* was railing against the FSM position, when President Kerr was, when most professors were doing so.

But do you remember the Academic Senate meetings in October? Not December 8—in October. Nothing of the sort happened, did it?

And I've got a very simple question to ask: *Why?* What educated the Academic Senate? Why did they find out certain things by December 8 that they didn't know in October?

This is a non-debate, you understand, but I am anxious to know how Mr. Glazer accounts for this, sociologically speaking. (After all, the Academic Senate is an institution which is worthy of sociological study; maybe some day it'll get some.) Now I'm a—well, sociologist myself, in a socialist sort of way: it seems perfectly clear to me that the faculty were, in effect, educated by their students. And they were educated by their students by *action*.

What happened in that intervening period was that social forces were dramatized out in *action*, in the students' action —by the sit-ins, by the strike, and by the Greek Theater drama, which was not in their textbooks.

There on the stage—there was President Kerr, effortlessly reeling off the golden phrases about Moderation, Decency, Excellence, Tolerance . . . and while the mellifluous syllables were still bouncing off the Campanile, the armed cops of the state were there with their arms around Mario's neck to show the power behind the rhetoric. You don't usually see it in quick succession like that. It was modern education—with visual aids.

I say that the faculty was educated by what happened, and it was educated only because the FSM made it happen; while the critics of the FSM, at every stage, had little advice to give the students except one bit of advice—which was: "Capitulate. Stop fighting. If you continue the fight you'll only get a backlash from the authorities."

For two days there, on October 1 and 2, around the police car, that's what the faculty mediators told us. Two of them explained this at length on the top of the car—Professors Lipset and Glazer—with the best of good will: "Give up. Go home. President Kerr won't yield."

Now this is the only thing that I want to address directly to Mr. Glazer, because I want to give him a chance to save his soul alive. It turned out, didn't it, that the issues were *not* nonnegotiable. It turned out that in the face of that massive eruption of moral courage by the students, Kerr broke his intransigence and negotiated, didn't he? And so isn't it indisputable that that was achieved because we ignored your pleas to give up, disperse, and go home? So weren't you wrong, Mr. Glazer, and weren't the students right?

I'm asking you this because it'll give you a chance to 'fess up; it'll do you good. (I'll confess a sin myself, just to make it even. I was wrong that day too: *I* thought the administration was going to keep its agreement!)

Look at yesterday's *Daily Cal* for another insight on this question, on the methods of the FSM. The headline says: "Demonstrations Do Not Speed Administrative Changes: Kerr." And Kerr's proof of the fact that the demonstrations had nothing to do with the administrative changes was: "The President cited the lifting of the Communist speaker ban in 1962 as an instance of a major shift in policy without student incident. 'We did away with the Communist speaker ban without student demonstrations. Had there been student demonstrations I'm not sure the atmosphere would have permitted it,' Kerr said."

That's the proof in the article. Two comments on that. In the first place, as everybody knows, there was *continual* student agitation against the ban. But two: there weren't any sit-ins, there weren't any strikes; that's perfectly true. There wasn't an organized FSM. So what happened when the ban was lifted? Maybe you've forgotten that when the ban on Communist speakers was lifted, in the same action Kerr imposed that harassment rule on *all* student organizations that you can't hold meetings on the campus with an outside speaker without having a tenured professor as moderator, and a couple of other harassing rules. And nobody said a peep! Because there was no FSM, and he got away with it. But: "Demonstrations do not speed administrative changes," says Kerr.

There is no time to take up many other questions connected with this, but I want to summarize in a way I started to do a couple of months ago.

In the past three months or so, there has been a unique educational institution on this campus, one in which the faculty as well as the students have learned what it means to be educated through action as well as through books. Now, one of Clark Kerr's mistakes back in September—it's not one of the mistakes that he's confessing to, perhaps, but it was one in September—was to make that remark which so betrayed his bureaucratic mentality: in answer to the argument that students should be free to mount social and political action because this too was a part of education, that they should be free to *act* in history today instead of just reading about it, President Kerr made the immortal argument that this wasn't so because, after all, we can study Greek history but can't *act* on it, can we?

And on October 2, speaking at noon from the top of that police car, I was moved to comment on a famous episode of Greek history which that suggested. Here's a variation of that as a summary:

It seems that—in this Greek history that we cannot act on—there was a man named Socrates in Athens who went out into the agora and set up a table . . . even though it has been ascertained by reliable historians that he had no registration card and was a bona fide non-student. (I'm stretching history a bit.) The Greeks came and arrested him on the charges (I quote the Encyclopaedia Britannica) of "refusing to recognize the gods established by law"—that is, refusing to recognize the Administration on Mount Olympus—and secondly, *"encouraging the young to disobey the guardians of authority."*

So Athens condemned him to death by a democratic vote (which, by the way, was more than the administration ever gave). And there was muttering, but when the cops' chariot came, no one sat down in front of it. Because, children, the FSM had not been invented yet.

And (if you'll permit an anachronism) the members of the Academy came and explained that this was all done according to Law and Order. They told them: "Act through channels only: write a letter to your Archon!"

And (so to speak) along came Feueripides and explained: "After all, encouraging the young! This is just a Generational Conflict." And Lipsetarchis came along and said: "After all, he *was* flouting the Law; that is as bad as the Kappa Kappa Kappa." And Kerrinthius came along and said: "After all, he is undoubtedly 49 per cent a Persian agitator." And so, in full accordance with the law, Socrates was done to death, which made the law very happy, no doubt, but has made future generations less so.

Now our president tells you that you can't act on Greek history. And I say: Yes, too bad for Greek history! But Greek history is not our problem. We've got our own history to take care of. And you *can* act on your own history.

You can decide whether you will act—for justice and for your social and moral imperatives as you see them—or whether you're going to be simply another misguided Organization Man, with your eyes very firmly fixed on the gleaming goal of some day having your own, very own, Research Center, with a heart-warming flow of grant money: you know, that heaven to which all good professors go when they die . . .

You not only *can* decide that; you *must* decide that. And for the decision which the students of the FSM have made, I think we should salute them.

FSM: FREEDOM FIGHTERS OR MISGUIDED REBELS?
A SPEECH BY NATHAN GLAZER, JANUARY 9, 1965

There have been at least three *kinds* of issues in the free-speech controversy:

First have been the issues as to the proper limits of political activity or the preparation of political activity on a university campus.

Second have been the issues as to the constitution of the university: the questions as to how much control, over what kinds of activities, should be vested in the Regents, the president, the chancellor, the faculty, the students.

Third have been the issues as to what measures, what kinds of activities, what kinds of pressures, should be used in the dispute over the issues that fall into the first two categories.

I have views on all three sets of issues. But I have felt from the outset, and increasingly as the controversy went on, that the heart of the controversy was really over the question of means, of tactics; and not over the question of ends. I will confess I am less certain over my views on the first two sets of issues—the limits of political activity on a campus and the constitution of a university—than I am over the third set of issues —the legitimacy of the means by which one presses one's views.

My views on this are very simple. In a functioning democracy no one has the right to resort to force to press an argument. On a university campus on which free speech prevails, no one has the right to resort to force either. I do not think a political democracy and a university are the same thing. I think there are matters in a university which cannot be determined by majority vote of its elements, for the simple reasons that inevitably and necessarily a university was involves two classes, at least, with very different rights and privileges. By its very nature, one must assume that in a university one of these classes has greater rights and privileges and authorities than the other.

This is not to say a university is a dictatorship or must be a dictatorship. But it is to say that the mechanisms whereby change comes about cannot be the mechanisms whereby change comes about in a political democracy. There are no elections in which all the elements participate under the rule: one man one vote. Nor do I think universities in general would be improved if they operated under such a system.

Now to specifics:

The leaders of the FSM argued from the beginning that there was only one way in which they could make their voice heard: to introduce such disruption in the workings of the university that it would have no choice, if it wished to continue its work, but to accept their views.

One of their greatest successes was to convince both thousands of students and vast numbers of liberals in the community that we had on the campus of the University of California one of those extreme situations which justifies abandoning the dependence on argument and due process. The only alternative, according to this line, was to resort to the creation of circumstances in which argument and discussion becomes meaningless. In such circumstances, the opposition is left with the alternatives of either giving in or itself resorting to force. (This is, of course, the chief argument against the resort to force in the first place, and the reasons why the grounds that justify such a resort have to be examined very carefully.)

I do not think this "final resort" argument was valid in this case. I am relatively new on this campus. Yet I am aware that over a period of ten or fifteen years there has been a steady broadening of the kinds of political activities that are legitimate on this campus. I have known some of the former students involved in broadening these activities. They were on the whole leftists. If they found it unnecessary to resort to the tactics of force and disruption, I saw no reason why today's student radicals should find it necessary. Was the regime of President Sproul and Chancellor Kerr I asked myself—and I would ask you to ask yourselves—so much more liberal than that of President Kerr and Chancellor Strong that new tactics of disruption were required to continue the expansion of the limits of political action on the campus? I did not think so.

A second point convinced me of the illegitimacy of the resort to these tactics. This was the fact that they were used again and again prematurely and when alternatives existed.

Let me give you a number of examples from the very beginning. Students had set up tables and collected money in defiance of the new regulations. This to my mind was a reasonable way of continuing the discussion. I did not disapprove of this, and I believe this is not inconsistent with my views as to the means that may be used in conducting a dispute in a university. The university is not a democracy, as I have said. Ingenuity is required in conducting a discussion. To collect money means to be cited. To be cited means to have an argument with the deans, with the faculty committee on student conduct, with the chancellor and the president and the Regents. To conduct a discussion means to bring forth arguments of such power that in the rational setting of a university some concession is necessary to good arguments. Such concessions had occurred before. They would occur again. But what happened when the students were cited? I read from the report from Chancellor Strong to the faculty—I assume the facts are correct:

> At 3 o'clock that afternoon some 300 to 400 students moved into the second floor of Sproul Hall and Mario Savio announced that all of them acknowledged violating University regulations in the same manner as those students who had been instructed to make appointments with the Dean of Students, and they all wanted similar appointments. The Dean of Men declared that he was then concerned only with observed violations, and if students wanted appointments they could leave their names and he would determine if and when such appointments could be made. He . . . requested that the crowd disperse, since he had scheduled a meeting of the leaders of the student organizations and their advisers to discuss the problem at 4 o'clock. Savio responded that the group would not leave unless they were guaranteed that the same disciplinary action would be meted to all there. Unable to make such guarantees, the Dean of Men again asked the group to leave, and later announced that since, in the opinion of the administration and some of the advisers of the student groups who had come to attend the 4:00 P.M. meeting, the environment was not conducive to reasonable discussion, the meeting was cancelled. He again urged (the students who had been cited) to enter the office to discuss offences noted earlier. The indicated students did not appear for interviews, and the group remained in Sproul Hall until about 2:40 Thursday morning.

Were Savio's actions at that time calculated to conduct a reasonable discussion, or to conclude it with a show of force?

I will give a second example from the action taken after the Regents' statement of November 20, which asserted that the campus could not be used for illegal action. I think this was a very difficult position to argue against, but leaving this aside, the FSM felt it was a point of critical substance and importance. I have never understood why at that time they did not take opportunity of what to me was a great victory for their movement, a great expansion of the bounds of political activity on campus, and to begin to advocate and mount and organize (all of which was permitted) anything which they wished to advocate and mount and organize. If then the university had stepped in and said, "But this is illegal action," then the students would have had a case. If it had been an illegal action that had occurred inadvertently, or an illegal action as defined by the state of Mississippi, or an illegal action which had the support or sympathy of wide sections of the community, why, then they would have had a good case. If it was an action that aroused the antagonism and repugnance of large sections of the community, they would admittedly have had a bad case. But instead of continuing the discussion, continuing it by undertaking the actions they felt necessary or desirable, they again occupied Sproul Hall, this time unsuccessfully and with little support.

Finally, there was the major occupation of Sproul Hall of December. The cause of this new action of disruption was the fact that charges were brought against four students. These students were to appear before the Faculty Committee on Student Conduct. Now I believed this action of the administration was both unwise and unjust. Unwise, obviously, as events showed. Unjust because I believed the pact of October 2, which I and a number of other faculty members had drafted and urged on the chancellor and the president, was in effect wiping the slate clean of all the actions related to the surrounding of the police car. The question now was: what does one do about it? What after all is happening? One is to be brought up on charges before a faculty committee, of, one assumes, reasonable men to whom the facts will speak as they do to most reasonable men. I also know this is not a Star Chamber proceeding, because once earlier I had had an experience with such a hearing. The parties can be represented by lawyers. It was inconceivable to me that these four students could not have done an excellent job of demolishing the justice of the proceedings. They were not interested in demolishing the justice of the proceedings through arguments or hearings. Instead, they called upon Joan Baez to help them lead the students to the occupation of Sproul Hall again.

Thus I am unconvinced by the FSM argument that this was

the only way to be heard—the students had made themselves heard before without these tactics; they could make themselves heard again. The night of October 4 and early morning of October 5, you may know, a substantial body of professors met in Barrows Hall to ward off an impending crisis. I won't go into the details of this crisis, but in the course of that meeting we met with a lawyer who had been active as a student some years before in getting a certain rule modified. He was asked by the dean of the Law School: "How did you manage to get through such changes without going in for sit-ins and the like?" It was a good question then. It is still a good question.

A third development convinced me of the illegitimacy of these "last resort" tactics: the rapid shift in the movement from one representing all political groups to one representing the far left, and the revolutionary left, alone. Think of the power and force of a movement that included Young Democrats, Young Republicans, Conservatives! The resort to tactics of disruption made it impossible for those who opposed them on principled grounds to continue. The tactics then justified themselves. How can a leadership group composed in large part of revolutionary socialists make a good argument to public opinion, legislators, and the like? The only way is by tactics attuned to their small numbers—namely, the tactics of disruption. But then the conditions that would have made the tactics of reason possible were rejected by the FSM leaders themselves, by driving away the support they would have received from moderate and conservative elements in fighting for the restoration and expansion of political rights.

I am impressed too by the way in which the regular student organization was pushed aside. This too took the same position in favor of expanded rights of political activity that the moderate and right-wing groups had. This too was a resource in the struggle. It was a resource the leaders of FSM did not wish to use. They were more enamored of their tactics than they were of the end—expanded rights to political activity on campus.

Finally, there was another ally that was not mobilized. Again and again in those early days, I was asked by students: where is the faculty? Many faculty members were concerned with the question. The faculty would have acted. The students disdained the hard work of discussing and arguing with the faculty. They presented it with *faits accomplis* that threatened the work of the university. Time is needed to organize the sentiment and actions of a thousand men. I have no doubt that if this sentiment and action would have been organized, the administration action would have changed.

Now we are told however that, after all, the faculty was mobilized, it did support the FSM position. Were not the

FSM tactics the most efficient and expeditious way of organizing and mobilizing it? Could anything have worked better than confronting it with a strike of teaching assistants and the arrest of 800 students? How can one argue with success? And were not these tactics successful?

A university campus is the last place in the world I would think where one brings up the argument of success, or the crude argument that means have been justified by their effectiveness. Lenin too was successful and so was Stalin, and even Hitler, for a while, and this as you all know does not settle the argument.

The success of these methods is to my mind one of the most depressing things that has come out of the entire dispute. Any organized society is a very fragile thing. It is amazing that it works at all. But it works on the basis of the acceptance of rules and norms of behavior, which determine the kind of society it can be. Success in a way is an easy thing. Think how successful Oswald was. Think how easy it would be to kill most of the leaders of the world's states. Or to move to a smaller sphere, the leaders of the FSM are perfectly aware how easy it would be to disrupt the university. I need not add to the armory of disruption that has been discussed publicly and privately. You all know that one proposal has been to sabotage the registration procedure for the spring semester.

And for what ends have we seen this childish and dangerous discussion of ways of messing up the registration procedure? For the ends of achieving free speech? I have not been convinced. For the end of the building of a movement and committing people to it by action? That, certainly. For the end of inducing in as great a number of people as possible the conviction that society and all its institutions, and in particular this university, are rotten? Certainly that. And if people are convinced that an institution is rotten then they become unrestrained in their actions, indifferent to the implications of what they do and even to the larger truth that a society is kept together by agreement on the rules and on the mechanisms by which it runs.

I have been told: perhaps these other means of changing the rules—working with the right and the center, with the student organization, with the faculty, developing support in the community and legislature, etc.—maybe all this would have worked, but look at how much time it would have taken. This again strikes me as a peculiar argument to raise on a university campus. The issue of time is critical in warfare, it is critical in political action. But a university, one would think, is the one place in the world in which you can take a good deal of time to settle matters. No one after all was up for hanging.

Let me now say something briefly about the relationship between this university and political action. The university does not exist to make students effective in political combat. If they learn something about it, well and good. Nor is its prime function, as so many of the student political groups and leaders seem to think, to offer them opportunities for the most effective conduct of their work. For many of them political activity has become full-time work, and their major emphasis is the recruitment of students to play a part in the community. The university, to my mind, should take the position that this purpose is relatively low in the order of priorities. It is obvious that the conduct of the classes comes before it. The conduct of research comes before it. The preservation of conditions that permit classes and research to continue comes before it. This order was reversed by the FSM. It took the position that let everything stop, but its position as to the proper role of political activities in the university must prevail.

The politicization of institutions that should not be political is to my mind a very dangerous thing—it is indeed, the mark of totalitarianism. A free society respects the rights of people to erect special institutions, religious, cultural, academic, or what one will. It respects the rights of those institutions to determine the conditions that are best suited for the realization of their aims. Neither the right of the university to determine its nature or to determine the conditions that foster it were respected by the FSM. It had decided what was important. And it had decided to impose its views as to what was important on the university, and accept no limit as to the means it would use to compel the university to accept its views. Such an approach to dispute can destroy a university. It has been used in one dispute. There is no indication in the philosophy of the FSM that it will not be used in a second. Will it be used to determine which faculty members shall be hired, and which shall be let go? Will it be used to determine what is taught in courses? Will it be used to realize the legitimate student interest in the academic conduct of the university? If it is, then the victory in this specific matter of political action on campus will mean very little. The university as we know it and as I think most of us would want it to be will then be gone.

PERSPECTIVES OF THE EDITORS

THE LESSON OF BERKELEY*
SEYMOUR MARTIN LIPSET AND PAUL SEABURY

Improbable as it may have seemed to outsiders, events at the Berkeley campus of the University of California during the last three months of 1964 constituted a small-scale but genuine revolution. Through continuous violation of university regulations, sit-ins, almost daily mass demonstrations, and finally a strike by students and teaching assistants, the authority of both the administration and the faculty had become virtually nonexistent at Berkeley by December.

The immediate cause was the withdrawal of a privilege. In mid-September, political groups and civil-rights organizations were barred from a twenty-six-foot-long strip of pavement at the entrance to the campus that traditionally had been used as a site for informal debate. More recently, it had been used for fund raising and recruiting for off-campus activities, both forbidden on university property.

Much of the intensity of student reaction to this ruling is directly attributable to a change of attitude on the part of young people all over the country—a change brought about by their participation in the civil-rights movement. Moreover, both students and faculty members at Berkeley, as at other large universities, are unhappy about changes taking place in American higher education today. In protesting the university administration's political restrictions, they were also voicing a discontent with the nonpolitical aspects of university policy. American students today are more concerned with ultimate moral ends than with responsibility or consequences. The civil-rights movement has provided them with a moral cause, and the example of civil disobedience with a tactic.

In the last two or three years, a civil-rights movement emanating from colleges in the San Francisco Bay Area has conducted sit-ins in hotels, restaurants, banks, supermarkets, and newspapers to demand the hiring of Negroes. Of the students arrested in these demonstrations, many were strongly influenced by various leftist groups that are currently stronger in the Bay Area than anywhere else in the United States.

Steering Left

The campus protests crystallized in the organization of the Free Speech Movement (FSM) early in October, with Mario

* From *The Reporter* (January 28, 1965).

Savio, a twenty-two-year-old philosophy major, as its leading figure. Savio spent last summer in Mississippi and was arrested during a sit-in demonstration in San Francisco last spring. He is an emotional, effective speaker and calls himself a "democrat with a small *d*." Membership in the FSM was open to any individual or organization that chose to affiliate. Hard-core support was estimated at around five hundred; by December as many as three or four thousand students were committed to all-out support, and according to FSM claims three thousand nonstudents from the university community were supporting the movement. The executive committee was composed of delegates from affiliated groups, elected representatives of graduate-student organizations, unaffiliated students meeting in assembly, and elected spokesmen for the nonstudents in the university community. But the real leadership of the movement was provided by a steering committee (appointed by the executive committee) of less than a dozen members who were considerably to the left of the executive committee. The political convictions of the steering committee notwithstanding, the overwhelming majority of student followers of the FSM, including those who have engaged in the sit-ins, were moderates whose politics are limited to the civil-rights cause. A minority within the FSM attempted to restrain the more extreme elements and included at various times two democratic socialist organizations, the Young Democrats, and a variety of conservative groups, including Youth for Goldwater.

The growth of FSM must be ascribed to a series of blunders caused to some degree by the fact that various crucial decisions were made at different levels of the local campus administration as well as by the president, the regents, and the governor. Repeatedly, the university took an uncompromising position on a variety of matters, and then, under FSM pressure, backed down and accepted conditions it had previously rejected out of hand. Naturally, this behavior encouraged the FSM to increase its demands.

In mid-September, the students were demanding only the return of the "right" to carry on political activity on the twenty-six-foot strip; gradually this demand grew into an insistence on the elimination of all university restriction of political activity on campus. The FSM's position was that there should be no restrictions besides those imposed by the civil authority for any public place, and that the only enforcement agency should be the police—the reverse of the one usually taken by leftist student movements abroad and people concerned with academic freedom in this country. These groups have maintained that universities should govern their own affairs, and that public authority is a greater threat to academic freedom than university administration. Indeed, in much of Latin America, students are legally protected from arrest within university precincts. Some who opposed the FSM on this position pointed to the fact that the city and county police, summoned when a campus police car was held captive for thirty-six hours on October 1 and 2, were not sent into action against the students by President Kerr, who had authority over them. By the time of the second major sit-in on December 3, Governor Edmund G. "Pat" Brown took over control of law enforcement on campus and, against the explicit advice of the university administration, ordered police to arrest students sitting in at Sproul Hall.

The most important reason for the weak position of the university administration during the past four months was that there were few on campus, among either students or faculty, who supported its original position on the political-rights issues: that a university should restrict the collection of funds for, or the advocacy of, off-campus political activities. The administration, in fact, modified its original position by early November and agreed to all the major student demands except the right to advocate and plan unlawful actions—chiefly the sit-ins. This position was ratified by the regents, and though the FSM continued to denounce university policy, it seemed at the time that it had lost the bulk of its support. The university returned the moral advantage and mass backing to the FSM by bringing charges over the Thanksgiving weekend against Savio and three other leaders for having organized the original sit-ins and capturing the campus police car almost two months earlier. To many, this seemed an implicit violation of the signed agreement between the university and the student leaders that had brought the police-car episode to an end. The December sit-in and strike were a result of this action.

But it should be noted that Steve Weissman, leader of the FSM graduate students and, after Savio, the most influential, told a *New Yorker* writer, "that if the university had not broken the thing open again . . . by its disciplinary action against four of the FSM leaders, they would have acquired a print of . . . a Genet film that had been banned as obscene from a student film series that week—set up a portable projector and loudspeaker, and shown the film on the wall of Sproul Hall."

Kerr as Prophet

The opposition to the FSM among faculty members and students was based on antagonism to the use of illegal means, such as campus sit-ins and deliberate violations of university regulations, to attain political ends that might have been gained through conventional channels of redress. But these critics, many of whom felt that the use of illegal tactics was part of a conscious effort by extremists to undermine faith in the democratic system, were constrained to silence by their belief that the university's position was morally indefensible.

The meaning of these events cannot be understood by limiting the discussion to an analysis of the right of on-campus advocacy, or of the use of illegal and extremist methods. Despite the FSM's name, free speech was never the central issue—Savio admitted as much. The revolt was not just against the injustices of society at large but also against the university as a microcosm of that society. To fully understand the student and faculty response, one must recognize that many educators believe that the American university community is becoming increasingly restive as a result of changes in our system of higher education. Ironically, a vivid description of these changes can be found in *The Uses of the University,* by the president of the University of California, Clark Kerr.

Kerr warns that major universities have become predominately research institutions; that teaching, particularly on the undergraduate level, holds little interest for many on the faculty; that administrators tend to become preoccupied with raising funds and gaining influence; that faculties have little institutional loyalty, with many professors choosing their universities on a careerist basis. These circumstances should produce considerable resentment among students, and Kerr, in fact, predicted a sharp increase in tensions and conflicts between students and instructors.

The large degree of political free speech long enjoyed at Berkeley, the size and eminence of the university, and the high caliber of its students and teachers are the very reasons why a mass student uprising took place there. Berkeley students have always made more use of their political rights to meet and speak freely on campus than American students elsewhere. Every sort of extreme-left group is represented—the DuBois Club (Communist), the Young Socialist Alliance (Trotskyist), the Independent Socialist Club (Revolutionary Marxist Socialist), and the Progressive Labor Movement (Maoist)—and so are various rightist groups. Even the American Nazi Party has been presenting speakers on campus and has announced that it will open headquarters nearby. The new student revolt began precisely where students were most free to organize.

For years, Berkeley has been evolving into a research center perched precariously on a mountain of somewhat neglected undergraduates. Many on the faculty came to support the FSM in the hope that the revolt will help to establish better contact between students and faculty and to increase autonomy of the Berkeley campus within the vast machinery of the "multiversity"—nine campuses of the statewide university system geared into a cumbersome synchronization.

Although faculty recommendations are accepted by the administration on most matters of educational policy, it is the multiversity faculty, represented on an all-state representative body, that speaks for the professors of the university. This arrangement leaves Berkeley representatives in a definite minority. Many important decisions have been made by the statewide Academic Senate or by the president's office. While these decisions may be defended as necessary for the advancement of higher education in California, they are apt to be resented by Berkeley faculty members who, rightly or wrongly, feel that their interests and academic eminence are being sacrificed to the system. Many feel that it was a mistake to increase the student body to 27,500 and that the concept of an all-state university has taken from Berkeley the right of deciding which applicants may be admitted there. But perhaps the most burdensome decision forced on Berkeley by the need for a co-ordinated statewide approach is the establishment of the year-round four-quarter system. In the eyes of many professors, this creates an academic production line that processes larger and larger numbers of students through already overburdened facilities.

The FSM leadership has denounced all efforts to analyze the sources of the Berkeley revolt in any but its manifest civil-liberties context. Yet Mario Savio explained the student protest to a meeting of the Trotskyist Young Socialist Alliance in these terms: "The most important concept for understanding the student movement is Marx's notion of alienation. Its basic meaning is that the worker is alienated from his product, but the concept is applicable to students too. . . . The students are frustrated; they can find no place in society where alienation doesn't exist, where they can do meaningful work. Despair sets in, a volatile political agent. The students revolt against the apparatus of the university. This is the motive power of the student movement."

Though the ideology of the movement was directed mainly against the university, the idea of alienation became the intellectual rallying point for a rejection of all power centers. The tragedy is that many within the university community who had diverse grievances against aspects of the university were drawn into support of a movement many of whose leaders saw every crisis as an opportunity to humiliate the university administration and to demonstrate the hollowness of authority.

Following the arrest on December 3 of about eight hundred students for occupying the university administration building, Sproul Hall, many faculty members who had previously ignored the struggle came to the support of the few professors who had defended the FSM, in principle at least, almost from the start. Graduate students and teaching assistants went on strike. Growing faculty support for the FSM resulted not only in the passage of resolutions backing much of the FSM position by the Berkeley Academic Senate (assistant professors and above), but also in the emergence of a variety of faculty grievances against the multiversity system. This accumulation of grievances naturally gravitated to the aggressive leadership of the FSM protest. In early December, dozens of new student organizations, closely linked to the FSM leadership, sprang up to advance special causes.

Perhaps the most destructive part of this affair was the extent to which civil disobedience and its consequences pushed the external community and the university in two opposite directions. The community at large reacted to events by moving to the right as far as its attitude toward the university was concerned; within the university, the sight of eight hundred young persons being dragged off to jail brought many previously apathetic students and teachers into the FSM camp. Most of these newcomers to the struggle saw it as a fight to defend students against oppressive authority. They were ignorant of the political forces at work within the steering committee of the FSM, and of its highly developed organization.

By the time the Berkeley revolt reached its crest, from December 3 to 6, the steering committee had a highly efficient organization at its disposal. FSM members, in touch with a central command post, covered the campus from one end to the other with walkie-talkies, and were able to learn of speeches and actions taken at closed faculty meetings as they occurred. The steering committee systematically rounded up the "right" faculty members to attend meetings and vote.

The strike, which closed down close to half the university, convinced many that peace was worth any price. A number of conservatives on the faculty who disagree in principle with the FSM reluctantly agreed that the university had to give up its power to regulate political activities on campus, and on December 8 voted in the Academic Senate for a motion that incorporated almost all FSM demands. While many voted on principle, others voted for it as a strike settlement by the weaker party.

The faculty voted for the right of free speech on all issues and the right to organize for off-campus political action, including civil-rights demonstrations. The regents accepted all but two points. First, they refused to yield to a committee of the Academic Senate their authority over matters of student discipline for infractions of rules governing political matters. (They did provide, however, that the faculty could take part in local campus administration judgment of such infractions.) Second, while affirming the rights of students and their organizations to advocate anything on campus that is lawful under the provisions of the First and Fourteenth Amendments, the regents continued to insist on the university's right to prohibit *organized* efforts to prepare illegal off-campus activities—a restriction aimed primarily at the organization of civil-rights sit-ins. A special emergency faculty committee, which had been elected on December 14 to represent the Academic Senate and which had discussed these issues with the regents before they met, concluded that the new regulations granted almost all that the faculty and the FSM had demanded in the area of free speech.

The new year brought an uneasy peace. During the holidays, the faculty emergency committee worked hard to obtain a broad consensus for reasonable regulations governing "time, place, and manner" of political activity acceptable to faculty, students, and regents. On January 2, just before classes resumed, the regents appointed a new acting chancellor, Martin Meyerson, the forty-two-year-old dean of the School of Environmental Design. Meyerson has shown strength and sophistication in dealing with the crisis, and he commands wide support from all major groups within what has continued to be a badly divided Academic Senate.

The Aftermath

During the spring semester, the conflict between the university and various student groups continued apace, although since the arrests of the 800 there has been no further effort at massive civil disobedience. The most eventful crisis arose around the issue of "obscenity." Seeking to test the widest limits of the commitment to no restrictions on speech, various individuals, many of whom were non-students and some of whom were Maoists, carried signs of, or chanted, the word "fuck" in Sproul Plaza. Nine were ultimately arrested by campus police over a five-day period beginning March 3. Some of the FSM leadership, including Art Goldberg, former Slate leader and self-described "Maoist," who led the picket line that interrupted a university meeting addressed by the Chancellor in September, conducted protest meetings. As a result of language used at one of these meetings, Goldberg and others were subjected to university charges. Few students, however, showed interest in defending the "filthy speech movement."

The furor occasioned by the "obscenity" issue led a number of Regents and legislators to demand that the university take immediate punitive action. President Kerr and Acting Chancellor Meyerson suddenly resigned on March 10, in protest against being ordered by some Regents to expel the students involved at once. After considerable agitation by the faculty in support of Kerr and Meyerson, the Regents requested them to withdraw their resignations. Four students, including Goldberg, were later convicted by a faculty trial committee. Goldberg was dismissed from the university, while the three others were suspended for five months. A second "obscenity" crisis involved the suspension of two publications, *Spider* and *For Unlawful Carnal Knowledge,* by the Chancellor on March 19. After a faculty committee hearing, the Chancellor lifted the suspension of the first, but kept the one on the second permanently. Meyerson also issued regulations defining the conditions under which student groups might post announcements, locate tables to distribute materials and collect monies, and sell literature, which denied non-students the right to engage in such activities. Suggestions that these actions be met by civil disobedience did not receive much support, possibly because the two-month-long trial of the students arrested in Sproul Hall was then going on less than ten blocks from the campus. Some radical groups have followed the tactic of deliberate violations of minor regulations seeking to provoke the Administration into imposing severe penalties as in September. Thus far the Administration has refused to co-operate.

The punishments for obscenity led to bitter attacks on Chancellor Meyerson by the FSM. The conflict between them was also joined over the rights of student self-government. Slate had won all the seats up for election for the student council in December, almost half the Student Senate. Slate hoped to gain a majority by bringing the graduate students into the ASUC. Although a majority of both graduates and undergraduates who balloted endorsed compulsory graduate membership, the Regents, acting on a recommendation from Kerr and Meyerson, refused to authorize their admission on the grounds that not enough graduates had voted for it. (They wanted two thirds of half or more.) The Graduate Coordinating Committee, an FSM affiliate, protested with many mass meetings and petitions. This issue declined in early May when close to two thirds of the undergraduates chose moderate opponents of Slate in the ASUC elections, and a majority of graduates, voting in a second referendum, opted against membership.

Following these continued crises, the FSM decided to dissolve its crisis-born structure, and to form a new more permanent membership organization, the FSU (Free Student Union). The FSU is designed to carry on indefinitely, representing its members on various items of politics and educational policy. It claims three thousand dues-paying members. The Teaching Assistants Union, affiliated with the American Federation of Teachers, which was formed earlier in the conflict, spent much of the semester seeking to negotiate with various departments concerning the working conditions and job rights of graduate-student assistants.

As important as the institutionalization of conflict organizations among the students has been a somewhat comparable development among the faculty. Two and a half formal political factions have appeared within the Academic Senate. These are: the Committee of Two Hundred, formed in the late fall by faculty somewhat sympathetic to the FSM; the Faculty Forum, organized in January by others who, though voicing their support for maximum political freedom on campus, indicated their concern with the increasing politicization of the campus, and their disapproval of FSM tactics as inappropriate to a university campus in a democratic society; and a third smaller and less formally organized conservative grouping, which felt that liberalization of regulations had gone too far. The Chancellor and the Faculty Executive Committee have sought to reduce friction by consulting the leaders of the three "parties" on all controversial decisions. Such efforts, however, have not prevented sharp intrafaculty controversy. Spring Senate meetings have witnessed bitter debate and close votes. And as the term ended, it appeared that the three-party system, as well as FSU-Administration conflict, would carry on into the fall.

The Regents also became targets of attack. Many students and faculty criticized them for their interference with local campus matters. The effort of the Regents to impose new rules concerning student political behavior in April and May met with rather aggressive criticism from the "Two Hundred," less violent criticism from the Faculty Forum, and approval from the conservative group. A study commission employed by a Regental Committee to look into the causes of the Berkeley uprising reported in May, and, to the surprise of the Regents, placed much of the blame for the university's inability to meet the problems of student political activity on over-centralization of university authority, and Regental interference with the actual administration of local campuses. A structural reorganization of the university and the Berkeley campus seems the order of the day. And at this point the legislature decided to take a hand in the proceedings. Speaker of the Assembly Unruh and Senate Majority Leader Burns announced at the end of May that there would be an investigation of the problems of higher education in California, with special reference to the Berkeley crisis. The legislature also enacted a law giving university authorities power to order any non-student to leave the campus or suffer arrest.

To restore the Berkeley campus to the normal life of a first-rate American university is still an immensely difficult task. It requires a high and rare level of administrative leadership and intelligence, qualities which fortunately Martin Meyerson seems to have. (Whether the Regents will appoint him the permanent Chancellor is still unsettled at this writing.) It requires a faculty which is as sophisticated politically as it is intelligent academically, and which understands how a few extremists can exploit genuine grievances to make the large majority of moderates do their bidding.

Most shaken by this sudden crisis, however, has been the human trust that is the ethical basis of any university—or, for that matter, of any community. This delicate though often impersonal confidence between teachers and students, professors and professors, students and students, was severely breached. The wounds left by suspicion and resentment over apparent betrayals of trust will remain for a long time. This is a poignant future problem for the teacher and his students. Once classrooms have been bitterly divided with covert and overt defamation of faculty members as "stooges of the administration" or "tools of the FSM Steering Committee," the community of scholarship is clearly endangered.

The FSM leadership was first responsible for spreading this atmosphere, but everyone has become somehow involved. A divided faculty can not long command respect from its students, and extremists can be counted upon to make the most of such divisions if they continue.

The Berkeley Revolt is not just another California curiosity. This new style of campus political action may affect other campuses, and eventually our national political life. The new student generation is brilliant and aggressively serious. The number of graduate students who spend years at a university increases steadily. The student leftist movements are growing and probably will continue to grow as they demand totally moral solutions to issues of racial discrimination, and foreign policy. The indifference to legality shown by serious students can threaten the foundations of democratic order if it becomes a model for student political action. Extremism in the pursuit of liberty was quite recently a favorite slogan of the radical right. Berkeley has shown that anyone can play this game. The danger now exists that students at other universities will have learned how easily a great university can be brought to its knees if but two or three per cent of the student body are willing to engage in actions which may force the police on campus. Universities are probably more vulnerable to civil disobedience tactics than any other institution in the country precisely because those in authority, whether administration or faculty, are liberal. They are reluctant to see force invoked against their students regardless of what the students do. Now that this secret is out, it may be difficult to restrain students from having their way on many university issues much as occurs on Latin-American campuses.

THE ABUSES OF THE MULTIVERSITY*

BY SHELDON S. WOLIN AND JOHN H. SCHAAR,
PROFESSORS OF POLITICAL SCIENCE, BERKELEY

It isn't often that a great university suddenly goes smash, yet that is what happened to the Berkeley campus during the first week of last December. During that week the University of California (Berkeley), numbering 27,000 students, 12,000 faculty and non-academic employees, numerous research laboratories, institutes, old-fashioned classrooms, and boasting an annual budget of $60 million, suffered an almost total collapse. Campus authority vanished, academic routines were reduced to a shambles, and the prophecy of Mario Savio was fulfilled: the "machine" came to a "grinding halt."

This brought to a climax a succession of events, each more astonishing than the one before, that had kept the university in a continuous ferment since mid-September. It is no surprise that those outside the university community have been unable to make sense of these events, for even the participants themselves often had trouble in understanding their own behavior. Many of the student demands and tactics seemed outlandish and more appropriate to Birmingham than to Berkeley. The responses of university officials wavered between treating the student movement as a Children's Crusade, a Communist conspiracy, and "a civil rights panty raid" (as one administrator saw it). The most outlandish behavior, however, came from neither the students nor the myopic deans but from those specifically charged with governing the institution. Supporting the seemingly invulnerable institution in its moment of crisis was a broad array of interested and powerful elements: the governor and Board of Regents; interest groups that had long prospered from the services and needs of the university; and a suspicious and hostile public, misled by the local press into believing that agitators were destroying the university and moved by an urge to punish the young for their seeming lack of gratitude for all the advantages a generous citizenry had given them. Yet the authority of the university crumpled under the pressure of a few thousand students who had no other power than the moral courage to say "no" before the colossus and the tactical skill to say it at the right time and in unison.

Absurd it may have been, but trivial it was not. The events destroyed some illusions about contemporary education and disclosed the depths of the antagonism between a generation that has all but contracted out of the affluent society, and

* From *The New York Review of Books*, March 11, 1965.

the perfect, dehumanized expression of that society, the large-scale organization, which transmutes knowledge, energy, and money into technological miracles—the perfect artifact for multiplying change so as to drown out purpose. In a society that values growth and material power above all else, and that cannot comprehend why rebellion and discontent should flourish amidst plenty and opportunity, it was astonishing to observe the students making a moral protest in defense of traditional rights that their elders could not take seriously and in defense of the principles of a liberal education that their elders had mislaid somewhere among the many other functions of the "multiversity." The crisis demonstrated that socially useful functions, no matter how competently performed, are no substitute for moral authority.

Had the students not succeeded in creating an instrument to convert their moral outrage into power, their protests would have died unheard. The Free Speech Movement came into existence during the first week in October, and from then on it enjoyed a near monopoly on the expression of protest. It attracted widespread support and enlisted the energies of thousands of students for the numerous tasks demanded by a political struggle. Although its wide support gave it a heterogeneous quality—stretching from the radical right to the radical left—its political style was uniquely expressive of the new generation. It was highly conscious of political and social issues; its language was radical and its tactics aggressive but pervaded by a novel blend of moralism and impudence ("liberal" and "fink" were almost synonymous, "textbook" was made to sound like "pornography"). There is no doubt that there were devious motives among its leaders; that occasionally they became intoxicated by their sudden power and made noises as if they intended to smash the whole system; that here and there extreme leftists were to be found. Yet it would be a serious mistake to suggest, as other writers have, that the entire crisis was fabricated and dominated by subversives or riff-raff. It has been well established that the bulk of the followers was composed of intelligent students who were novices in political action. The sacrifices of many who were willing to place their careers on the line, the spontaneity of their indignation, the warm fellowship of their movement, and their unfailing good humor were too real to be explained by subterranean conspiracies. Those who believe that, by definition, a problem does not exist if it can be shown that radicals are somehow involved, are not about to acknowledge the dominating idealism of the movement. At bottom the unbelievers must fear that the situation is really worse than even the conspiracy theory suggests: if it is possible for so many—faculty and students alike—to be duped by so few, then the condition of one of the world's greatest universities is more hopeless than even its critics charge.

The many issues raised during these chaotic months can be classified under two broad headings. First, there were political and constitutional issues centering around whether the university should place any but the most minimal restrictions upon the exercise of political rights by students on campus, and whether the university should restrain and discipline political acts or advocacy performed on the campus but leading to illegal acts off the campus (e.g., a political rally called on campus to organize an illegal sit-in at a hotel). Historically, the administration had based its highly restrictive policies on a provision of the state constitution requiring that "The University shall be entirely independent of all political or sectarian influence and kept free therefrom in the appointment of its Regents and in the administration of its affairs." This became the justification for prohibiting political advocacy and activity on campus, for defining what activities were political, and for denying the use of campus facilities for organizing off-campus political actions. The policy of the administration was determined primarily by the desire to prevent the involvement of the university in public controversy.

The students' general contention was that they should have the same political rights on campus that they enjoyed as citizens off the campus, and that determinations of the legality of off-campus actions should be reserved exclusively to the courts. In addition, the students argued that the constitutional provision upon which the administration relied was intended to prevent the university itself from becoming involved in politics, and to prevent the governors of the university from applying political criteria in the conduct of university affairs but was not intended to deny students the right to engage in political action not involving the name of the university. Finally, the students argued that the administration had been highly arbitrary in the day-to-day application of its rules.

An overwhelming majority of the faculty was gradually persuaded that the student argument was generally correct. As early as October 13, the faculty had affirmed its support for "maximum freedom for student political activity" and on December 8 formally resolved that there should be only minimal regulations on the *form* of political speech and action on campus, no university controls on the *content* of expression, and no university sanctions on the off-campus political activities of its students.

The second broad range of issues related to the university itself. The gross size and population of the campus, the numerous research and service functions carried on, its intimate connections with outside interests have transformed the old categories of "teacher" and "academic community" into "researcher" and "multiversity" or "knowledge factory" (the last phrases are those of its president). Unlike many private institutions, Berkeley's character was not established by a founder or given shape by a religious sect determined to bring piety and learning to a rude society. Ungraced by traditions, its graduates lack a distinctive stamp. Above all, identities are hard to come by and definitions difficult to pronounce when an institution is determined to gear its life and growth to the needs of an ever expanding society, or at least to the needs of society's most powerful and clamorous parts. In *The Uses of the University,* President Clark Kerr writes that the multiversity has "no prophet to proclaim its vision; no guardian to protect its sanctity." The clear implication is that the multiversity dare not risk self-definition. It must remain "as confused as possible for the sake of the preservation of the whole uneasy balance" among the interests and pressures that make up its environment. If it is the multiversity's nature not to have a nature, there is comfort in knowing that it is "an imperative . . . rooted in the logic of history." The beauty of an imperative is that it provides a "justification" for virtually anything, including the mishmash of activities that have found a home in the multiversity.

Kerr's realization that the condition of the multiversity's existence is also the source of its weakness imports an element of desperation into his analysis. His use of industrial metaphors disguises the inherent anarchy of the multiversity system. There is a touch of melancholy in his conclusion that "the task is to keep this lawlessness within reasonable bounds." In the end the university is reduced to being a puppet, twitching to stimuli it cannot control, powerless to set its own direction. "The process cannot be stopped. The results cannot be foreseen. It remains to adapt."

If one is startled by this confession of drift by the head of the enterprise, how much more unprepared for his cynicism. The university is characterized as "a mechanism held together by administrative rules and powered by money." The faculty is "a series of individual . . . entrepreneurs held together by a common grievance over parking." For all their spriteliness, these epigrams sag—melancholy testimony that the realist is second to none in his illusions. Their author is the same man who early in the crisis denied that a "freedom of speech issue" existed and who, after the faculty voted overwhelmingly to eliminate restrictions on the content of expression, demeaned the motives of that distinguished body by attributing its action to petty jealousy toward the other campuses in the system.

An examination of the pattern of events shows how great is the distance and how difficult the communication between those who make the multiversity's rules and those who must live by them.

The controversy opened on an appropriate note. On September 14, the administration blandly announced that a narrow strip of land at the entrance to the campus was really university property and not, as previously assumed, the property of the city (uncertain as to its own identity, the multiversity has never been sure where it ends and the world begins). This strip had been the locus of student political activity. Since it was assumed to lie outside the campus, university regulations restricting political activity did not apply. Without consulting the students, the administration closed off the main outlet for political energies, claiming at first that these activities interfered with pedestrian traffic, but later reaffirming its position that "University facilities may not, of course, be used to support or advocate off-campus political or social action."

The students, ranging from Goldwaterites to socialists, immediately formed a united front to urge the restoration of a free-speech area and the modification of the rules. The chancellor then issued a "clarification," the first of a long series that came to follow a familiar pattern of concession and contradiction, giving an over-all impression of weakness. The students were allowed to use the steps of the administration building, Sproul Hall, as a free-speech area and to man tables on "the strip," but not for political purposes. The students proceeded to ignore this last restriction, and the administration to ignore the violations. Tables were set up and political speeches given in forbidden areas. Again the chancellor gave ground and permitted students to support candidates in the November elections and to take stands on state propositions. This gave something to everybody: the students might oppose an amendment repealing the state fair-housing law, while the university could continue its efforts for an educational bond issue. Characteristically, the chancellor followed these concessions with a show of firmness which he then undercut by his own actions. He stated on September 28 that the matter was "closed," but then had his deans select eight students, including three leaders, from among hundreds who claimed to have violated the regulations. The eight were suspended "indefinitely"—a penalty unknown to university rules.

This led to the first great blow-up: On October 1 a large rally formed in front of Sproul Hall. A police car taking to jail a person charged with manning a table unlawfully was surrounded and stranded in a sea of students. Mario Savio, respectfully barefoot, mounted the car and harangued the crowd. Two hundred students then entered Sproul for a sit-in. Faculty efforts at mediation were blocked by the chancellor's stubborn insistence that regulations and disciplinary measures were not negotiable. As the tension continued into the next day, a faculty group by-passed the chancellor and persuaded President Kerr of the need for compromise. This began the gradual eclipse of the chancellor by the president, thus underscoring the fact that each campus of the multiversity lacks autonomy and is headed only by an expendable functionary, suitably called "the chief campus officer." An agreement was reached with Kerr, but not before he had summoned 500 police and threatened to have them disperse the crowd unless an agreement were reached. The students agreed to halt the demonstrations, and in return the university agreed to restore the privileges of certain suspended groups, to submit the cases of the eight to a committee of the Academic Senate, to drop its charges against the man encapsulated in the police car, and to establish a committee of faculty, students, and administrators to study the rules.

The agreement was a disaster. Neither administration nor students acquitted themselves with honor. The chancellor appointed ten of the twelve members of the tripartite committee without seeking recommendations from either students or faculty. He also assigned the cases of the eight to a committee of his own choosing, not to one appointed by the Academic Senate. In response to protests, Kerr again intervened to retrieve the situation. The cases of the eight were transferred to a committee established by the senate. This committee, after hearings, recommended that six of the students be reinstated immediately. A six-week suspension was recommended for the other two. The committee's report was also highly critical of the administration's procedures. The chancellor announced that he would not respond to these recommendations until the following month.

Meanwhile, the tripartite committee foundered. The truculence of the FSM representatives, combined with the refusal of the administration's spokesmen to surrender disciplinary powers over "illegal" advocacy, created an impasse. The FSM resumed the manning of tables. The chancellor then dissolved the tripartite committee on the grounds that the students had violated the agreement of October 2. From November 9 to November 20, the students continued to violate the regulations while the administration enforced them selectively, now citing seventy students for infractions, now ignoring massive violations.

On November 20 the Board of Regents, highest authority in the entire university system, met. The board is wondrously representative of the genius of the multiversity. It would be difficult to design a more attractive target for students nurtured on the C. Wright Mills doctrine of the conservative power elite. It is composed mainly of high politicians, wealthy financiers, industrialists, and businessmen, and the remarkable Max Rafferty. Kerr persuaded the board to overturn its prohibition against all on-campus political activity and advocacy, although the ban against "illegal advocacy" was retained. The board's *quid pro quo* was a recommendation that students who had violated the rules during the past three months should be disciplined. It also dealt with the cases of the eight students and recommended reinstatement of the whole group but refused to expunge the charges against them.

The Regents nearly restored peace. The FSM was badly split: a sit-in in Sproul on November 23 was called off after a few hours, indicating that the remaining area of controversy was too limited to be inflammatory. Just when most faculty and students were resuming normal routines, the chancellor restored chaos by a master stroke of imprudence and bad timing. He sent letters to four students, including three top leaders of FSM, informing them that the university intended to bring charges for actions committed eight weeks earlier. By reopening a matter everyone had assumed to be closed, he, with one blow, revived FSM, outraged the faculty, and focused the question in its starkest terms: how is it possible to justify an authority so grossly insensitive to the spirit of an academic institution?

Two days later, on December 2, nearly 800 students filed into Sproul Hall for the climactic sit-in. The next day Governor Brown called in 600 police to clear the students from the building and hustle them off to jail. The faculty rallied to the students: cars were provided to return them from jail, and a bail fund was set up and quickly oversubscribed. While all this was going on, the graduate students had organized a strike which successfully halted most classes for two days. The students had fulfilled their vow: the machine had stopped.

Up to this point, the faculty as a body had remained relatively detached, though a few individuals had occasionally been involved in the controversy. But now the collapse of authority and the sight of 600 armed policemen shocked the faculty into the recognition that it alone was left to pick up the pieces. For a time, the faculty forgot its lust for research, its shameful neglect of teaching, its acquiescence in the bureaucratization of the university. Setting aside the ethos of power and growth, the faculty stirred to ancestral memories of the ideal of a community of scholars bound together in the spirit of friendly persuasion and pledged to truth rather than abundance. It had been clear all along that while the students' protests were directed against the administration, their entreaties were directed to the faculty, but it took a shattering experience to restore the faculty memories of fellowship with the students. Now that its collective conscience was awakened, the faculty found the energy and vision necessary for the task of reconstruction. A few writers have attributed subsequent faculty actions to hysteria. It is puzzling why men should find it necessary to deny the faculty its finest hour, and to equate decisiveness with panic, moral impulse with fear.

One line of faculty action was in response to the impotence of the chancellor, whose withdrawal and increasing isolation left the campus leaderless. A committee of departmental chairmen was formed to impress upon the president the gravity of the situation. After exhausting negotiations, the chairmen wrung from the president and a group of Regents a promise not to add university punishment to court sentences of the sitins. It is symbolic that the chairmen's group and the Regents never talked face to face. University rules forbid faculty members to make direct approaches to the Regents; hence the two parties were closeted in separate rooms of an airport motel and the president plied between them.

The amnesty was a necessary precondition for resolving the crisis, but the Kerr-Chairmen Agreement was silent on the fundamental questions of political freedom which the students had been raising. That silence provoked outbursts of protest when the president and a distinguished faculty member presented the terms of the armistice to the campus community assembled in the Greek Theater. Moreover, their rhetoric of affluence and order revealed a fatal ignorance of the yearnings and commitments of the present generation of students ("Today we decide whether we shall move ahead productively and in peace . . . This community has been divided not so much on ends as on means . . . We must seek added funds . . . We must face external investigations . . . We must face . . . a transition from the extensive growth of the past century to the intensive growth of the indefinite future—for growth must never stop.").

The second line of faculty action proved more successful. It led directly to the resolutions of December 8, which asserted that the rights demanded by the students could not be denied by a university. Moreover, it created the first stirrings of a faculty attempt to reform the multiversity. The success of this second attack grew out of a fusion of discontent and shame. That a university had resorted to force against its students seemed an absolute confirmation of the ineptitude and moral bankruptcy of the system. It was widely believed, therefore, that the chancellor must go. Also fresh in the minds of the faculty were the recent and shameful handling of a case involving academic freedom and the arbitrary decision to revise the entire pattern of university life ("year-round operation" of "the plant," the president described it).

Throughout November several groups of faculty members had been formulating proposals to meet the problem of student political activities, but the events of December 2 generated the passion necessary to unite the faculty. On December 4 an impromptu faculty meeting was called and the discussion there disclosed a deep sentiment among the vast majority for policies that would set no limits upon the *content* of expression and only such minimal restraints upon the *forms* of expression as were necessary to the performance of ordinary university functions. The faculty was also becoming persuaded that the intricate legal questions surrounding "illegal" speech and "conspiracy" were not the proper business of any university authority.

On December 8 these sentiments, now refined in the form of resolutions, were brought before the Academic Senate and passed by a vote of 824–115. The resolutions provided that: (1) only the "time, place, and manner" of on-campus political activity should be regulated to "prevent interference with the normal functions of the university"; (2) the content of speech was not to be restricted; (3) off-campus political activities should not be subject to university regulation; (4) disciplinary questions arising out of the minimal regulations in (1) should be handled by a faculty committee, i.e., the administration was not to touch such matters.

Two additional resolutions were passed. One created an Emergency Executive Committee to act for the faculty in further matters arising out of the crisis, and the other called for a committee to study the question of how the faculty might make itself more effective in the general governance of the university. The importance of these changes was quickly demonstrated, for the next encounter took place elsewhere, at the December 18 meeting of the Board of Regents.

The Regents have final power in almost every area of university affairs. Usually their meetings deal with ordinary matters of university business, but this was to be no ordinary meeting. More like a summit conference, it was surrounded by an atmosphere of urgency and intense public concern. What occurred is not easy to reconstruct, because part of the meeting was secret; what was decided is not entirely clear because of the muddled language of the public statement issued later. It seems that the Regents have finally recognized the First and Fourteenth Amendments, and that henceforth students will be allowed maximum political freedom on the campus. It is clear that students may now use campus facilities for organizing off-campus actions. However, the Regents continued to balk at the use of campus facilities for mounting illegal off-campus actions, and hence reserved authority to discipline students in such matters. The Regents also refused to devolve final authority over student disciplinary cases in political questions upon the faculty.

Despite the face-saving vagueness of their formulations, the Regents had come far since September. Their allusion to the First and Fourteenth Amendments was a tacit confession that most university rules affecting speech and action were unconstitutional, and their decision not to punish the arrested students raised the hope that eventually they would relinquish jurisdiction over cases where off-campus actions turn out to be illegal. Moreover, in announcing their willingness to consult with students and faculty to improve campus rules, the Regents recognized what the faculty had sensed earlier: students must be viewed as participating members of the academic community.

This summary of the Regents' action does not convey the fact that bloody fighting took place behind the scenes. There is little doubt that Kerr had persuaded the Regents to accept the broad direction of the faculty proposals and to leave undisturbed the amnesty agreement of December 7. It is equally clear that the chancellor had fought for his life by taking a "hard line" on both the question of rules and amnesty. He lost and shortly thereafter was replaced by a new acting chancellor. Once again Kerr had demonstrated his extraordinary political abilities. He had averted a calamitous showdown by persuading the Regents to alter the rules, but he had also neutralized to some degree the bid for autonomy implicit in the Berkeley resolutions. This he accomplished by his time-honored tactic of employing the machinery of the state-wide system and the envies of Berkeley represented in it, to condemn local solutions and quell assertions of local autonomy. He acquiesced to the fact that Berkeley's chancellor had lost all credit, but later, when it became apparent that the new chancellor was attracting growing enthusiasm, Kerr gratuitously reminded the campus that the old chancellor was "just tired and wanted to get away," but that he would "most likely" return.

As matters now stand, the faculty and students have gained most of the objectives contained in the December 8 resolutions. Assuming that good sense prevails among the parties, that the few zealots in the legislature do not persist in their announced aim of firing masses of students and faculty, and that the impending trial of the sit-ins does not reopen old wounds, the prospects for honorable peace are good. But peace is not necessarily the same as normalcy, for the events of the first semester cut too deep to permit a restoration of the old ways. A university is in the process of being redefined. Its president has recently proclaimed that "The primary responsibility of the university is the education of its students. A second major responsibility is research . . ." (a draft of the university's ten-year program made last fall had no mention of "primary" emphasis upon education). But the basic element in all redefinitions is the new breed of students who have appeared on the Berkeley campus.

Published accounts of the student movement have radically distorted its character. Some of these accounts have been almost delusional in quality. There is, for example, Professor Lewis Feuer's denial that there were any genuine issues at stake and his claim that very few genuine students were involved in the controversy. He attributes the uprising to the powers of a handful of crackpots, political extremists, drug addicts, and sexual libertines, most of them, thank God, not students at all, but spoiled personalities, tormented members of that underground Berkeley community of *lumpen*-intellectuals who managed to dupe thousands of innocent and true students into believing that there were real issues, thereby capturing the ever present hostility of the young against their elders and mobilizing it into a "generational uprising." Less imaginative men than Feuer have characterized the movement as the subversive work of leftist plotters. In this view, the campus will not find peace until it surgically removes these diseased members from the student body politic.

Another way to avoid the challenge of understanding is to concentrate all attention upon one aspect of the reality, and then to interpret that reality in very narrow categories. Specifically, this approach characterizes the behavior and tactics of the students as riotous and irresponsible and condemns them as illegal, thereby foreclosing the issues. Illegal some of the students' actions were, but that still leaves open the questions of whether they were necessary and morally justified. Furthermore, and contrary to the impression spread by the mass media, the students were not tempestuous and violent. With few exceptions, they behaved with dignity and restraint.

All of these accounts dissolve the real problem into a vapor of fantasies congenial to the commentator. None of them recognizes that there were real students asserting real grievances within an institutional setting that had in fact become pathological. As President Kerr himself noted, the students have been "restless" for some time. An adequate account must take a serious look at the sources of that restlessness.

For some time now, the students, especially the undergraduates, have felt themselves to be an alien presence within the multiversity, an "Other Academia" analogous to the "Other America," ill-housed, and ill-clad, and ill-nourished not in the material sense, but in the intellectual and spiritual senses. As the multiversity has climbed to higher and higher peaks of research productivity, material riches, and bureaucratic complexity, the students have fallen into deeper and deeper abysses of hostility and estrangement. The students' own favorite word for their condition is "alienation," by which they mean a number of things, and especially a sense of not being valued members of a genuine intellectual and moral community. Their feeling is grounded in reality.

The architects of the multiversity simply have not solved the problem of how to build an institution that not only produces knowledge and knowledgeable people with useful skills but also enriches and enlightens the lives of its students—informing them with the values of the intellect, preparing them to serve as the guardians of society's intellectual honesty and political health, arming them with the vision by which society seeks its own better future. It is the performance of these latter tasks that distinguishes a genuine educational community from a mere research factory and training institution. Hence, as Harold Taylor has said, "the mark of a true university is whether or not it takes its students seriously."

By any reasonable standard, the multiversity has not taken its students seriously. At Berkeley, the educational environment of the undergraduate is bleak. He is confronted throughout his entire first two years with indifferent advising, endless bureaucratic routines, gigantic lecture courses, and a deadening succession of textbook assignments and bluebook examinations testing his grasp of bits and pieces of knowledge. All too often the difference between the last two years of a student's education and the first two is chronological rather than qualitative. It is possible to take a B.A. at Berkeley and never talk with a professor. To many of the students, the whole system seems a perversion of an educational community into a factory designed for the mass processing of men into machines. The image is a bit excessive, to be sure, but like any good caricature this one distorts reality in order to clarify it. A great many faculty members have acknowledged the essential justice of the students' case against the multiversity and have confessed their own not-so-small contribution to the malaise. Faculty conversation at Berkeley is now haunted by remorseful allusions to the bleak realities of student life.

The reality seems all the bleaker by contrast with the glowing expectations students are now bringing to the university. Young people today are conditioned from the earliest age to see "education" as the magic key to all the delectable things. They come to college in search, not merely of knowledge, but of salvation. College is the real thing, they are told, and when the real thing turns out to look a lot like the sham they left behind, they are understandably distressed.

It costs relatively little money to attend the University of California, but unlike most other state universities, California has high admission standards. The freshmen class is selected from the top 12 per cent of high school seniors. This means that not only are the students of high average intelligence, but that they also have worked hard and kept "clean" throughout their high school years. Furthermore, Cal students, like all others, bring with them to college the natural exuberance of youth, but relatively little of this energy is drained off through the customary and "safe" channels of sports, organized social life, and seasonal bacchanals. Most of the energy finds other outlets.

The great bulk of the students live in private accommodations, and their private lives do seem quite experimental and free—though not as orgiastic as the fevered imaginations of some professors and deans would suggest. More importantly, over the past decade the students have become increasingly serious—about themselves, their studies, and their society. But there is still a lot of energy left, and at Berkeley, unlike most other American colleges, a good bit of this is poured into political and social causes. For example, Berkeley in particular, and the San Francisco Bay Area in general, have sent more young people to the South in the struggle for racial justice than any other place except New York. The word has gone out: things are happening at Berkeley. This reputation acts as a magnet, drawing young people with activist yearnings from all over the nation to Berkeley. The events of last semester, with all the publicity they gained, will increase this magnetic attraction—a thought horrifying enough to bring a dean to consider resigning his post.

Beyond the immediate attractions of a lively campus, many students today, especially those in the humanities and social sciences, are aware of the shortcomings of their society and are passionately looking for authentic values to replace what they perceive as the phony slogans and spiritual tawdriness of so much of the public rhetoric and action of our time. Few of them come to college with an ideology, nor do they seek one while there. Rather, theirs is an ethic of sincerity and personal encounter. They take ideals seriously and are quick to detect evasion, posturing, and doublethink. If their conception of the educational process is somewhat romantic and woolly—tending to equate the exchange of impressions and sentiments with learning, impatient with discipline, and inclined to rush off after a dozen exciting novelties at once—it is still more attractive than the emphasis on utility and training favored in the multiversity establishment. The latter is a bleakness of spirit, closed and immobile; while the former is a plentitude of spirit, open and vital. Such students constitute a university's most valuable resource, and it is a delight and a privilege to teach them. There were a great many such students, graduate as well as undergraduate, involved in the happenings at Berkeley. Given all the loose talk about student "riots" and "radicals," it is necessary to emphasize this point.

There were radicals among the leadership of the FSM, but there is no evidence to indicate that the movement's leaders were the slaves of ideologies that blinded them to reality or led them into attempts to subvert the true purposes of their mass following—which, to say it again, were freedom of political expression and educational reform. Furthermore, the vast majority of the students shared the goals of the FSM, and a near majority also supported their direct-action tactics. The "radicalism" of this mass following consisted in little more than devotion to some traditional principles that their elders had taught them, plus the impatience with the conservatism of the old that the young ought to have. Radical ideology, then, mattered little in the events at Berkeley. What mattered far more was a clear-eyed and courageous response to concrete, felt injustices.

There were no riots. Save for the incident of the "captured" police car, the mass rallies, sit-ins, and the student strike were all conducted with admirable dignity and calm. There were a few scattered episodes of excessive behavior by individuals under extreme stress. There were many intemperate words. Many university rules and a few state laws were broken.

All of this is regrettable but understandable, and not unjustifiable. These students were acting in a situation where, time and again, officials refused to listen to them, behaved whimsically and punitively, and altogether gave the impression that the student cause was without justice. The students responded with the only methods that could make the administration listen, and many of them showed a clearer appreciation than their elders of the moral burdens involved in the use of pressure tactics within an academic setting. What happened at Berkeley cannot be understood as the delinquent outbursts of fanatics and ungrateful rebels. These students broke the rules and the law in an agonizing effort to compel an administration that, by its unwillingness to listen to their just claims and to treat them as participating members of a community of the intellect, inevitably brought about its own moral downfall and forfeited its claim to willing obedience. To many of the students, such conduct left no alternative but direct action.

The events of the past semester have not cast a foreboding shadow over the future of education at Berkeley. It is clear to many of us here that the students reminded us of some basic values that were disappearing in the thoughtless rush for the future. Very much of what they did had to be done before anyone would listen. The result is, at this moment, a climate of respect and concern that offers more promise than has been present in a long time that the future of this university can be a noble one.

REPLY TO WOLIN AND SCHAAR
BY CLARK KERR*

Professors Wolin and Schaar must have written "Berkeley and the Multiversity" in a great hurry, for it is not marked by the accurate scholarship for which each of them is justly renowned. They have written more of a political tract than a careful analysis. I should like to note several points.

1. "Knowledge factory" is not "my phrase." It was a phrase used by Mario Savio. I have quoted Professor Machlup of Princeton University and former President of the American Association of University Professors on his concept of the "knowledge industry"—a concept he uses in quite a different sense than "factory." My phrase is "the City of Intellect." (*The Uses of the University,* page 94).

2. Professors Wolin and Schaar then go on to use a quotation of mine within their own sentence as follows: the university "must remain 'as confused as possible for the sake of the whole uneasy balance' among interests and pressures that make up its environment." The actual sentence in full reads this way: "A university anywhere can aim no higher than to be as British as possible for the sake of the undergraduates, as German as possible for the sake of the graduates and the research personnel, as American as possible for the sake of the public at large—and as confused as possible for the sake of the preservation of the whole uneasy balance." (*Ibid.,* p. 18.) The point was not "interests and pressures that make up its environment" but rather the sometimes contradictory internal claims of undergraduate instruction and research, for example—a point recently much discussed at Berkeley. What pure model of a university do Professors Wolin and Schaar advocate where there are no conflicting internal claims, no "mishmash"—only research, only teaching, only service? Furthermore, my original comment was a rather wry and semi-humorous one and the Harvard audience to which these lectures were given accepted it in the spirit in which it was intended.

3. Regarding a certain "lawlessness" within the university, I quoted Caplow and McGee in the *Academic Marketplace* and noted the "many separate sources of initiative and power" in any "large university" with particular reference to the "British Model." (*Ibid.,* p. 35.) Do Professors Wolin and Schaar suggest there should be only one source of initiative and power—a monolithic institution—and thus no "lawlessness" in

* From *The New York Review of Books,* April 8, 1965.

the sense that I was using the term? They then state that "the university is reduced to being a puppet . . . powerless to set its own direction." This is their view, not mine. I have declared rather that the "new problems of today and tomorrow may lend themselves less to solutions by external authority; they may be inherently problems for internal resolution. The university may now again need to find out whether it has a brain as well as a body." (*Ibid.*, pp. 122–123.) If anyone were to take the briefest look at the three new campuses of the University of California, for example, he would see the university starting off in new and university-determined directions, not just "twitching to stimuli it cannot control," as Professors Wolin and Schaar imply. And are Professors Wolin and Schaar themselves "twitching" when they talk about the "remorseful" faculty at Berkeley confessing its "own not-so-small contributions to the machine" and wishing to do something about it? Some "twitching to stimuli it cannot control" may be a good thing! Do they want an institution so unresponsive that it never twitches? A university should do more than just twitch, but it would be a sorry place indeed if it were completely unable to twitch even a little bit—it either would be or ought to be extinct.

4. They quote me as saying "The process cannot be stopped. The results cannot be foreseen. It remains to adapt." But my comment is not about the university at all, as they imply it is. It is my paraphrase of a statement by a famous scientist about the works of scientists and engineers. And I go on immediately to add this comment of my own— "And here the social sciences and humanities may find their particular roles in helping to define the good as well as the true and to add wisdom to truth." (*Ibid.*, p. 124.) Science should not go its unchecked way.

5. In the two paragraphs in their article to which I have been referring, the authors (a) start with a misquotation, which sets the tone for the subsequent comments, (b) take a phrase about internal problems of accommodation and make it appear as though it were about environmental pressures, (c) take a comment about the inherently pluralistic nature of a modern university and try to turn it into proof that the university is therefore a "puppet" and (d) end up with a comment about science as though it were made about the university. In the process they string together quotations and partial quotations from several pages as though they all flowed together about the "knowledge factory." The quotations relate to several topics—none of them the "knowledge factory."

6. May I cite four more illustrations, among others that could be chosen, from this tract: (a) "It is symbolic that the Chairmen's group and the Regents never talked face to face." It might be symbolic, if it were true, which it most definitely is

not. (b) It is interesting to note that other campuses had "envies of Berkeley" but that the Berkeley campus had no "petty jealousy towards the other campuses in the system." (c) Could Berkeley have been such a "magnet" if it really were so "bleak"; and could it have drawn so many students with "activist leanings" if there had not been opportunities quite beyond the normal for activism? (d) If one reads their own account carefully, it does appear (contrary to the FSM complaint, which they endorse, that nobody was willing to "listen") that somebody was willing to "listen", for there were several and quite prompt adjustments by the administration and the Regents. Their own account would suggest that the last major group to listen was the faculty. They might have noted, but they did not, that the American Association of University Professors in 1964 gave its Alexander Meiklejohn Award for contributions to academic freedom to the president and Regents of the University of California on nomination made by the Berkeley Chapter of the AAUP, among others. These contributions were made without benefit of sit-ins or the capturing of a police car or the biting of a policeman. Was civil disobedience necessary in the fall of 1964 to overcome a mistake in judgment by the Berkeley campus administration when it issued its September 14 edict on the 26-foot strip, when so much had been done of the university's own free will over the prior six years? As a matter of fact, the Regents had voted, 15 to 2, in September 1959 to dedicate this very same strip to the City of Berkeley so that political activities could go on there without any limitation by the university; but unfortunately, the transfer had never been made. The justification for breaking "university rules and a few state laws" and for "episodes of excessive behavior" must rest on the proof that there was no other recourse. Professors Wolin and Schaar do not prove this point, and the record of the prior six years stands rather as proof that such methods were not necessary. Then why were they used?

8. I should like to conclude with a statement by Professors Wolin and Schaar: "All of these accounts dissolve the real problem in a vapor of fantasies congenial to the commentator." They were not talking about their own account, but rather the accounts of others. But, perhaps, they might concede that their comment about others might apply, to a degree, even to themselves. Admiring them both, I like to entertain this thought.

PERSPECTIVES: FACULTY MEMBERS

WHAT IS LEFT AT BERKELEY
BY WILLIAM PETERSEN,
PROFESSOR OF SOCIOLOGY, BERKELEY

Whether it was a "student strike" that all but shut down the University of California for three days last December is, in my opinion, a moot question. Consider this freshman, whom I take to be typical of a very large number of students. She was torn between antipathy toward the Free Speech Movement and sympathy with her acquaintances who had been arrested; but on balance, after due consideration, she decided not to join the strike protesting the arrests. Her English instructor, however, dismissed the class, with a brief, uninformed statement on the issues. Her professor of psychology came to an auditorium with an overfull attendance (for students in addition to those regularly enrolled in the course had come to hear his advice), gave a speech on academic freedom so platitudinous that every television station quoted it for the rest of the day, and dismissed his class. The auditorium where her class in political science was to be held had been turned over to a meeting of several hundred professors, who were discussing whether or not to support the strike. Only two of her five classes were held. Her physics instructor lectured to well over half the normal attendance. In her French class, the instructor lost her sympathy by attacking the strikers in what she thought was vindictive language and, contrary to his usual practice, keeping a record of attendance. (In the humanities generally, those on the faculty who held out against the widespread support of the strike were under strong attack from their colleagues and sometimes overreacted.)

In a number of departments, teaching assistants consulted with the faculty on how they could omit giving their classes without running afoul of the California law that, in ambiguous terms, apparently prohibits a strike by state employees. In deference to these revolutionaries on the cheap, the faculty—who are protected by tenure—dismissed the classes of their teaching assistants. In short, these professional educators conspired with their students on how to break the law with impunity.

The Berkeley faculty is large and heterogeneous, and with respect to any of the issues involved in the crisis it is something of a misnomer even to speak of "the" faculty. Yet, however expressed—by enthusiastic or partial endorsement, by hostility, by apathy or ineffective opposition—their attitude toward the FSM has been crucial. One can accept too easily the explanation of the "generational revolt," excellently expounded by Professor Lewis Feuer in *The New Leader*. So far as I was able to judge, the vast majority of the undergraduates did their best to follow the confused and changing lead of their professors. If the main tendency of the faculty was to mislead, that is at least partially because the situation itself was misleading. Despite its resemblance to student agitation at other times and places, the rebellion that arose on the Berkeley campus is, I think, something quite new to American academic life.

The first fact one must know about the Free Speech Movement is that it has little or nothing to do with free speech. During the months of rancorous dispute and rising crisis, one of the few subjects *not* at issue was the right of students to speak on campus in support or denunciation of anything whatever. Some months ago a representative of SLATE, one of the extremist student groups, asked me to preside at a meeting at which a student would advocate the smoking of marijuana as a healthful practice. It was not my pot of tea, I replied; but the meeting took place without me. When student opponents of the FSM mounted picket signs endorsing a "Free Sex Movement," the joke fell flat: it *might* have been meant in earnest. After all, there had been a meeting demanding that the Student Union put contraceptives on sale; and more recently we have had the "Filthy Speech Movement." In a university lecture hall a self-proclaimed anarchist gave detailed advice on how to avoid the draft by pretending to various illnesses; a self-proclaimed Communist used university facilities not only to attack the government's policy in Vietnam but to collect money—illegally—for the Vietcong. A student, using the amplifying system supplied by the chancellor, described in vulgar detail his participation in a mass homosexual-heterosexual orgy, and recommended this kind of liberating experience to his fellow students.

The radical students' talk of constitutional guarantees has been echoed not only by their supporters on the faculty but, paradoxically, by administrative spokesmen, including the Regents, and responsible faculty committeemen, who have hoped to dispel the revolutionary ardor of the students by repeatedly granting them, or recommending that they be granted, the right of free speech and advocacy. Some of this repetition has helped to specify the time, place, and manner of the free speech already existent on campus, but in the main the official and quasi-official statements have served only to validate the extremist students' demagogy.

But the public, not surprisingly, was taken in. When John F. McCarthy, Republican leader of the California Senate, spoke on the Berkeley crisis before the Commonwealth Club of San Francisco, a rather conservative businessmen's group, even he found it expedient to remark that "of course" he did not condone the abrogation of constitutional liberties on campus. When on television two policemen were shown dragging FSM leader Mario Savio away from a microphone in the university's Greek Theater, the news commentator did not bother to explain to the viewers that, by Savio's novel interpretation of the First and Fourteenth Amendments, no one—not even the president of the university at a meeting convened by all the department chairmen—has the right to speak on campus without a representative of the Free Speech Movement present to rebut him.

If not free speech, what then is the issue? In fact, preposterous as this may seem, the real issue is the seizure of power. The guiding principle of the radicals heading the revolt is one of Lenin's favorite aphorisms, which he borrowed from Napoleon: *"On s'engage et puis on voit."* Roughly translated, this appeared on one picket sign as "Strike now, analyze later." If the whole of American society is evil, if our "alienation" from "the system," "the power structure," is total, as speaker after speaker blares forth through FSM loud-speakers, then where one begins to attack this monstrosity is important only in a tactical sense: the issue should be one able to attract the broadest support.

At the beginning of each semester, SLATE issues a "Supplement" to the university catalogue, in which courses are evaluated on the basis of a student poll. Last semester, the "Supplement" included also a former student's open letter to undergraduates, calling on them to "begin an open, fierce, and thoroughgoing rebellion on this campus."

"Go to the top. Make your demands to the Regents. If they refuse to give you an audience, start a program of agitation, petitioning, rallies, etc., in which the final resort will be CIVIL DISOBEDIENCE. . . . ORGANIZE AND SPLIT THIS CAMPUS WIDE OPEN!"

The language has become all too routine, but this open letter was published some time *before* the change in rules that, it is now alleged, provoked the student revolt. In early September SLATE was demanding that grades in undergraduate courses and discipline in student dormitories be abolished, and that there be "a permanent student voice which is effective (that is, independent) in running university affairs." The only carry-over from the "Supplement" to the actual struggle to date has been the standard demand that President Kerr (often called "Cur" on picket signs) resign, together with all other "top administrators who might employ slick diverting tactics."

When classes were started last September, out of the more

than 27,000 students at Berkeley, perhaps 200 to 300 radicals were primed for rebellion. In earlier semesters they had tried to engage the campus in campaigns against capital punishment or against atomic weapons or against the House Un-American Activities Committee; but these efforts had failed to muster mass support. The issue that worked was not substantive but administrative—the new enforcement of campus rules, long ignored, prohibiting the organization of political activity on campus.

Once started, the revolt grew rapidly, reaching a first climax in about two weeks. The university suspended eight students who had broken the rules by collecting money and names of supporters for various political organizations; 400 others demanded that they also be suspended. When the police attempted to arrest a former student for trespass (he was also breaking the university regulations), their car was surrounded and used as a rostrum from which student agitators denounced the "police state." Police were assaulted by Leonard Glaser, out on parole on a narcotics charge, and by Mario Savio, who bit a policeman on the thigh and, by such intransigence, developed in a few days from a junior in philosophy to the main leader of the student revolt.

The evening of October 2, some 7000 sympathizers and spectators jammed into the plaza before the administration building. Joan Baez, the beJaguared songstress of the dispossessed, had announced that she would come to sing revolutionary songs from the roof of the police car. There was to be a football game the next day, and it was rumored that at the pregame rallies liquor was flowing freely. As soon as it got dark, fighting was expected between the radicals and the fraternity crowd.

I was one of a group of about twenty faculty members who tried to negotiate a compromise to disperse the crowd. Chancellor Strong told us there was nothing to negotiate. President Kerr said that it was too late for discussions, that at six o'clock, when the police ringing the plaza were to move in to restore order, "blood would flow." If these tactics were intended to exert pressure on the radical students, they did not work. At the last moment the president reversed his stand: he signed not the agreement we had drawn up but one with a change in wording that altered its whole character. By our proposed compromise, the students were to "promise" not to break any laws to protest campus regulations; the agreement they finally signed stated merely that the students "shall desist" from breaking laws. As Savio explained both to the president and later to the mob, the radicals did not consider that this bound them to anything.

In any case, the negotiations moved indoors, with a number

of committees working to find a solution for what was still seen, with persistent naïveté, as a temporary crisis.

Whether students should be given permission on campus to organize political activities to take place off the campus is a complex and difficult question. Be that as it may, that dispute became obsolete on November 20, when the Regents revised the earlier regulations and granted the students the right to use the campus for political organization with only one proviso, that the off-campus activities be within the law. Apart from the exception, this was all that the students had originally wanted. The dispute since that date has been about one or another version of a very different question: Do college students have the right to determine, at their own discretion and without sanctions from a tax-supported educational institution, whether they shall obey any particular law? Thus, the agitation leading to the next climax was partly to protest a letter sent to four radical leaders, instructing them to appear before an administrative committee to answer charges that they had broken civil laws, and partly to support the "right" claimed by the students to use the university as a sanctuary from which to make illegal raids on the general community. In support of these demands, the administration building was illegally occupied for the third time, and when almost 800 students and nonstudents refused to leave or to walk to the police cars, they were arrested and dragged out.

That a tiny number, a few hundred out of a student body of more than 27,000, was able to disrupt the campus is the consequence of more than vigor and skill in agitation. This minuscule group could not have succeeded in getting so many students into motion without three other, at times unwitting, sources of support: off-campus assistance of various kinds, the faculty, and the university administration.

Everyone who has seen the efficient, almost military, organization of the agitators' program has a reasonable basis for believing that skilled personnel and money are being dispatched into the Berkeley battle. During demonstrations, the commanders of operations on campus—"in the field," one might say—kept in touch with FSM headquarters with walkie-talkies. A public information center of the FSM distributed an endless stream of propaganda. Around the Berkeley community a dozen *"ad hoc* committees to support" this or that element of the student revolt sprang up spontaneously, as though out of nowhere.

But the most important reason that the extremists won so many supporters among the students was the attitude of the faculty. Perhaps their most notorious capitulation to the FSM was a resolution passed by the Academic Senate on December 8, by which the faculty notified the campus not only that they supported all of the radicals' demands but also that, in effect, they were willing to fight for them against the Board of Regents, should that become necessary. When the resolution passed by an overwhelming majority—by 824 to 115 votes—it effectively silenced the anti-FSM student organizations.

Apart from a hortatory introduction and final point, and the routine clause absolving students for any misdeeds prior to the date of the resolution, it held that "the time, place, and manner of conducting political activity on the campus" shall be subject only to "the minimal regulations necessary" to prevent interference with the normal functions of the university. Moreover, "the content of speech or advocacy should not be restricted by the university. Off-campus student political activities shall not be subject to university regulation. On-campus advocacy or organization of such activities shall be subject only to such limitations as may be imposed" by restrictions already stipulated.

In part, these points said nothing new, reaffirming the freedom of speech and advocacy that already existed except in the propaganda of the FSM and its friends. In part, however, they constituted a considerable extension of constitutional liberties. In itself, the statement that on-campus organization of political activities shall be subject only to minimal regulation concerning their time, place, and manner leaves open whether these activities must be within the law. But this ambiguity was removed by a proffered amendment, specifying that the activities organized on campus must not be directed to the immediate use of force and violence off campus; and this amendment was voted down. In short, the position of the faculty is that the university should remain aloof from whether its students use its facilities to plan and organize illegal acts off campus, even when this infraction of the law intentionally involves the use of force and violence.

On the question of campus disturbances, the faculty resolved that "future disciplinary measures in the area of political activity shall be determined by a committee appointed by and responsible to the . . . Academic Senate." But that an administration may be justly criticized for its manner of coping with student offenders is no logical basis, in my opinion, for revising one's concept of how administration and faculty ought to divide their joint task. It is unreasonable to hold the administration responsible for the maintenance of order on campus and yet to shift to the faculty the sanctions by which this order can be kept. Faculty members, moreover, are notoriously unwilling to perform administrative tasks, and two striking examples from the period of crisis at Berkeley indicate how inefficiently they carry out disciplinary duties.

In September, it will be recalled, one of the original *causae belli* was that eight students had been suspended for disobeying the new regulations; and some weeks later an *ad hoc* faculty committee was chosen by the Academic Senate to judge the suspended students. Like children with a new toy, the professors set up an elaborate new juridical procedure; but at its own discretion, following the request of the suspended students' lawyers, the committee decided to limit its jurisdiction to the period up to September 30, the date of the suspensions, ignoring the fact that on October 1 and 2 some of these same students had allegedly participated in commandeering the police car and in the assault on policemen. It was like a parole board, in other words, that judged the nature of the offense and the way the punishment was imposed, but passed over the fact that the offenders had led a prison riot, destroyed prison property, and attacked prison guards.

In March, when the campus was attacked by a new plague, neither of the two relevant faculty committees was willing to initiate proceedings against the "filthy speechers." The committee instituted specifically to deal with political offenders held that this offense was nonpolitical, and the regular student-conduct committee, no less anxious to avoid responsibility, maintained that the way to handle this childish peccadillo was to ignore it. Eventually, under pressure from the Regents and the public, the acting chancellor set up yet another committee, whose sole function, it would seem, is to try to do something about student obscenity.

There is no one reason why the Academic Senate voted for this resolution by more than seven to one. If I try to describe the motives of my colleagues, as I understand them, I shall of course be accused of impugning those motives. In defense, I note only that this large body of highly vocal men offered not a tittle of the high principles they now profess until they were goaded into this position by their radical students. When professors are taught by students, as when students bite policemen, one can reasonably perceive this situation as anomalous and look for unusual motives, in addition to the statements of principle that various members of the faculty have adduced for their stand. Some of the most important motives, either alleged or underlying, are the following.

Civil Libertarians: Free speech has hardly been an issue on the Berkeley campus in any direct sense, yet many faculty members have supported the Free Speech Movement in response to the largely demagogic demand that its name implies. With respect to some, this contradiction may be the consequence of ignorance—for in the welter of rumors and false statements, it was all too easy to lose one's way. Some of the faculty, however, including three law professors, interpret the constitutional right to free speech as guaranteeing "freedom of expression"; and one may express oneself, it was pointed out, not only by talking but also by acts—such as, presumably, the occupation of a public building.

Defenders of Civil Rights: That the radical students allegedly fight for civil rights is another important reason that the FSM garners support among the faculty. As Professor Herbert McCloskey, the original author of the senate resolution, noted in an article in the Berkeley *Daily Gazette,* a great many of the students "have shown themselves superior in courage and moral conscience by their activities on behalf of civil rights." A few of the FSM leaders spent a summer in the deep South; and there has been a persistent effort to equate the situation there with that in Berkeley, which in general is a nonviolent and law-abiding community. On the Berkeley campus today, it seems, only a reactionary would suggest that those who want to further civil rights in California make use, for example, of the state's excellent agency for enforcing fair employment practices.

Students tell me that for them civil disobedience is not an ultimate weapon but the only device they can use to intimidate an opponent. I struggle to explain to them why, in terms of their avowed goals, these tactics are ultimately self-defeating. Civil rights, like democracy itself, exist only in a legal context; without a rule of law there are no rights either for minorities or for anyone else. In the South, the principal effort of the civil-rights workers has been to uphold laws broken by those in authority—for example, the laws granting suffrage irrespective of race. Sometimes bad laws—that is, those that would not be upheld by a judge—are deliberately broken in order to get the issue before a court; this was the purpose of disobeying the laws that segregated the races in schools, in buses, or at lunch counters. It is an entirely different matter to attack legal authority indiscriminately, and then protest when one is arrested.

But, the radical students argue, they do not want to evade the law; they want only to avoid "double jeopardy." They are "willing" to be subject to the jurisdiction of the courts, they say, but not to incur additional punishment as students for off-campus activities. This seemingly plausible argument has won much support for the FSM among both students and faculty, yet it is false on several counts.

In fact, the students have not been subjected to "double jeopardy," for President Kerr has protected them against this, even in the face of considerable community pressure. Indeed, while orating about "double jeopardy," the radicals have managed time and again to break laws and to be punished by *neither* the civil authorities nor the university. And when the advance agents of the civil courts, the police, came to apprehend those illegally occupying the administration building, the student radicals did not rejoice that at last, in response to their persistent demand, they were being treated like other citizens and no longer being subjected to the obnoxious paternalist protection of the university. Their howl of outrage at their arrest set off a strike that immobilized the campus.

It is not clear to me that "double jeopardy" is really involved. Even if we consider a conspiracy on campus to commit a crime and its commission off campus to be a single act, does it follow that the university should remain aloof from the responsibility of seeing that laws are obeyed? Should a student who deliberately breaks the law be permitted to retain, as a right that cannot be challenged, the privilege of attending a tax-supported institution of higher learning? Should he have this right even when he disrupts the most fundamental purpose of a university, which is to seek truth through calm and rational deliberation? For in educational terms, the strongest indictment of the Free Speech Movement is that it tries to prevent, by the exertion of brutal intimidation, the free and open exchange of ideas.

It so happens that I am in a fairly good position to judge the degree to which the faculty is seriously interested in supporting those who fight for civil rights. Last year my wife and I, with some assistance from a very few others, solicited funds from members of the university faculty and staff for the NAACP Legal Defense Fund. This organization not only initiates legal cases on its own (including the crucial 1954 school-desegregation case before the Supreme Court), but also pays for about nine-tenths of the legal costs of the entire civil-rights movement, no matter which of the several organizations is involved. Contributions to the Fund, thus, are a reasonable measure of meaningful support of civil rights. Unfortunately, we did not get anything like a seven-to-one vote for our effort: out of the faculty of about 1700, only 181 contributed. In contrast, the $8000 fee for the bail of the arrested students was oversubscribed in a day or two. One professor who tried to sabotage our campaign was highly vocal more recently in support of the FSM.

Anti-Enclavists and Pseudo-Enclavists: In the long struggle to establish and maintain academic freedom on European and American campuses, one of the key principles has always been to protect the university from direct political pressures. The Board of Regents that has ultimate control over the University of California, thus, is in fact a fourth branch of the state government, not directly responsible to the executive, the legislature, or the judiciary; and from before the First World War until the recent events, the Regents intervened in the immediate operations of the university only once, when they tried to enforce a rule that all members of the faculty had to sign a loyalty oath. The reverberations from that long and bitter struggle still echo almost two decades later.

It was in order to separate the university from the political arena that university personnel (faculty and staff as well as students) were prohibited from engaging in political activities on campus. This was the intent of the administrative regulations that the FSM successfully attacked: students were permitted freely to advocate political positions but not to "mount" political activities. Now that this distinction has been abandoned, and particularly if the university indeed becomes officially indifferent to whether the students based in its facilities break the law to gain their political ends, it would be absurdly naïve to hope that these attacks will be made along a one-way street. The volume of mail to the governor's office about the Berkeley crisis, I am told, was the largest in California's history, and by more than nine to one it was hostile to the FSM and its faculty supporters. If the radical right portion of the electorate intervenes—say, by an initiative to change the constitutional structure of the University of California—the danger to one of America's great institutions of higher learning would be serious.

There is no consensus among the faculty majority on whether the university should remain an enclave, and if so in what sense. In a composite document distributed by Professor Jacobus ten Broek, for example, we are explicitly informed that "a university is no longer an isolated enclave in which the members are content to exchange ideas among themselves and to train their successors. . . . What is learned on the campus is not remote from life, but must be made central to life." On the other hand, in the words of Professor Carl E. Schorske, "The primary task of the University [is] teaching, learning, and research—*not* political activity. Our students, however, are citizens, and should enjoy the right to political expression and activity on the campus . . . Illegal acts or expression should be punished by the law; offenses against the University community should be punished by the University." The consequence of this stand, of course, is that police must come on campus to effect the control that the university refuses to exercise. Yet many of those who advocated this division of function also have held to the traditional position that police have no right on a university campus.

Romantics: Under this catch-all heading one finds the Nobel laureate who rushes momentarily from the laboratory to sign a manifesto or issue a pronunciamento, the professor of English who is apt at referring to Milton's *Areopagitica* or Thoreau's *On Civil Disobedience* but has never read Lenin or Trotsky, those who orate on constitutional guarantees in the abstract but with no attention to how the campus has been operating in this respect, the sizable number who flirted with Communism in the 1930s or supported Wallace in the 1940s and whose middle-aged blood courses faster at the recollection of those seemingly simple fights of good against evil.

Administration Haters: One of the amazing minor elements of the Berkeley crisis is what one finds under any stone that the radical students have lifted. In supposedly serious explanations of why they had voted for the December 8 resolution, my colleagues have pointed out that the quarter system is being foisted on us by the administration, that we faculty voted against a parking fee but are forced to pay it anyway, that—in a hundred instances—the administration has been wrong and inefficient. Between two of the recurrent crises over the FSM, the Academic Senate met to consider a completely unrelated case of academic freedom and passed—correctly, in my opinion—a resolution in "condemnation" of the chancellor and president for their handling of it. A number of Berkeley professors have publicly voiced their gratitude to the FSM for conducting a more general fight than the faculty had been able or willing to undertake. The usual antipathy between administrators and professors is not enough to explain such a sentiment: on the other campuses of the university, the divisions of the Academic Senate voted to support the administration rather than the Berkeley faculty.

Administration Supporters: Paradoxically, some of those who voted for the December 8 resolution may have been influenced by their loyalty to the administration. Some time before the meeting of the senate, the department chairmen were convened and told in ambiguous terms that the resolution had the backing of President Kerr; and most of them apparently returned to their departments to report this to their colleagues. As a matter of fact, President Kerr disagreed with the resolution in four important respects. Vice-President Harry R. Wellman and various members of the faculty told him that his authority was being used to gather support for the resolution, and a number of his advisors urged him to attend the senate meeting in order to correct this false impression. As President Kerr now recalls the incident, he decided not to go to the meeting partly because he had other urgent business, partly because he did not think many of the faculty actually were misinformed about his position. However, he did give Mr. Wellman a short statement to be read at the meeting if any of the resolution's proponents stated that he supported it. When Professor McCloskey declared, "We have reason to hope that we can persuade both the university administration and the overwhelming majority of the students to accept the terms of this resolution—in principle if not in every detail," this could easily have been interpreted as confirming the earlier false rumors, but the statement was not read. The manipulation of the vote—if that is what it was—was completed by a parliamentary device to cut off debate. One of the most important decisions the Academic Senate has ever made was completed partly on the basis of false information, and with no opportunity even to hear some of the counter arguments.

FSM Tolerators: In various ways, faculty members have condescendingly depreciated the importance of "the students" or, as they are typically designated in this context, "the kids." Thus, Professor McCloskey tells us in the article already quoted that "many of us have forgotten that the so-called 'rebels' and dissenters are our own students—young men and women of quality and intelligence. . . . Some have disobeyed the law, but they are not 'criminals.' A few are passing through youthful flirtations with revolutionary political movements." Or Professor Joseph Fontenrose, in a similar vein, termed the all-night illegal occupation of the administration building "harmless loitering after hours," passing over the fact that its purpose, in Savio's words, was "to bring the university to a grinding halt."

FSM Supporters: As in the student body so also in the faculty, this was originally a small minority, but an active and vocal one. One assistant professor, for example, spoke at a number of FSM rallies, where on one occasion he termed Kerr the Mao Tse-tung of the United States. When Kerr spoke at the Greek Theater, this man lustily joined in the students' booing. One might suppose, in the abstract, that such behavior is unbecoming a member of the faculty; but in fact it constitutes a kind of moral tenure, following the pattern in Mary McCarthy's novel, *The Groves of Academe.* The protection of academic freedom is so absolute at a campus like Berkeley that political irresponsibility may actually cancel a negative judgment based on academic mediocrity.

Together with its other successes, the FSM also was given increasing support from the faculty. Some 250 professors, for example, signed a petition to the judge trying the arrested students, asking that the cases be dismissed—not as a matter of expediency or mercy, but "in furtherance of justice." In this perspective, it is the students who did not break the law who were at fault—in their lack of courage, or lack of sufficient concern about civil rights, or whatever.

Conformists: Once the organizing group, centered in the departments of Political Science, Sociology, English, and Philosophy, had got their steamroller moving, the pressure to go along with the majority was all but irresistible. I know a beginning assistant professor who disagreed with the majority; he was able to maintain his integrity only by remaining at home and avoiding the squeeze between virtually all the senior members of his department above and most of its graduate students below. Those faculty members who came out in public support of one or another of the FSM demands have been bathed in warm approbation, administered by both their students and in many cases their own teen-age offspring. The punishment of faculty who openly oppose the FSM, on the other hand, is unpleasant. In my department, the students sank to the level of writing scurrilous comments on the walls of the men's room about one of the main faculty opponents of the FSM. (Fortunately, the worst that *I* can report is that, the day after the senate vote, a professor of adult education whom I have known for years cut me dead on campus.)

Munichmen: If I had to weigh the significance of the various factors that contributed to the capitulation to the FSM, I would list fear as the most important. The FSM was holding a gun—indeed, a toy gun—to the heads of the faculty, and if we yielded the threat might go away. The debate in the senate was simultaneously broadcast to a vast throng of students outside, which cheered or booed each of the speakers. After the meeting, one of the professors who had dared speak for amending the resolution was accosted outside the building, where one of the FSM leaders asked him, "How much did they pay you for that?"

A few days after the meeting, a colleague told me, with some chagrin, "I was the Halifax to Professor X's Chamberlain. What do we do now?" My reply was, "Since you cast me in the role of Churchill, I also predict blood, sweat, and tears." As I write, all the plans offered by the administration and by the new Emergency Executive Committee of the Academic Senate have one feature in common: appeasement. Berkeley has still to learn that when one feeds a totalitarian body its appetite increases. "Peace at any price" may lead to a temporary lull, as it did at the end of the fall semester; but in the longer run it leads to no peace at a higher price, as the following spring semester demonstrated.

The course followed by the university administration—the president, Chancellor Strong acting mainly under the president's direction, and all of their various aides—could hardly have better fostered a rebellious student body if it had been devised to do so. To establish dubious regulations and when they are attacked to defend them by unreasonable argument is bad enough; worse still, the university did not impose on the students any sanctions that did not finally evaporate. As Bronislaw Malinowski once remarked, the notion that the "submission of every member of the tribe to its laws" is "instinctive" may be widespread, but it is false; there is no such thing as "automatic acquiescence." Obedience to norms is developed when it is suitably rewarded, and when noncompliance is suitably punished. That professional educators should need to be reminded of this axiom indicates how deep the roots of the Berkeley crisis lie.

The simple formula that has been followed can be illustrated by an example in microscopic scale. The scene is the outdoor Greek Theater, filled to overflowing with faculty and students who came to hear President Kerr deliver an important policy statement. At the conclusion of the meeting, Savio rushes to the microphone and is dragged off by two policemen. Only then, someone thinks of turning off the microphone, and the other FSM types, who followed Savio onto the stage, shout inarticulately and gesticulate wildly, thus comically relieving the explosive potential. As we file out, Professor Robert Scalapino, who chaired the meeting, turns on the microphone again to tell us that this had not been a denial of free speech, really; that Savio can go and talk to his own meeting on the other side of campus; that this was a faculty meeting, with a fixed agenda; and so on. Silence for a few moments, and again the voice of Professor Scalapino, saying that Professor Joseph Tussman just explained to him that "Mr." Savio merely wants to offer two announcements, which he is now allowed to make after all. (Charles Powell, the elected president of the student body, also requested permission in advance to announce a meeting in opposition to the FSM rally; his request is never granted.) Savio's first "announcement" is a denunciation of Professor Scalapino, the council of department chairmen, and President Kerr for not letting him speak. The second is to tell the crowd of the FSM meeting starting immediately, which will answer the "outrageous" proposals of the president; and an invitation to any faculty members who "dare" to come and speak there.

The formula exemplified in this episode was followed also with respect to more important decisions. Its elements can be specified as follows:

1. Define an issue, or accept the definition offered by the FSM. The matter can be large or petty; it is important only that everyone understands that here is another direct confrontation between the radical students and the administration.

2. Develop your case as fully as possible, so that whoever yields will lose face. Your argumentation need not be well based; for example, the prohibition of collecting money on campus was supported by statements from the chancellor's office that it was against state law (false), and that it would impede traffic (hardly).

3. Yield to the FSM. The president, and Chancellor Strong acting under the president's direction, established a well-nigh perfect record on this point. Until the governor sent in police to arrest the demonstrators, or until the Regents sounded a contrary note at their December meeting, the FSM had only to push for a policy to get it.

4. Attack on another front, and thus create another issue; repeat *da capo*. Thus, it will be recalled, on November 20 the

Regents set a new policy permitting the on-campus organization of any legal political activities; and this revision might have been the basis for isolating the FSM again from its supporters among the more moderate students. Five days later the chancellor cited sixty students for having broken the old regulation while it was in force, thus driving them back into co-operation with the ultras.

Administrators who had created a power vacuum at the top and, in this sense, contributed to the disruption of the Berkeley campus would soon, one would think, be replaced by men with deeper understanding and greater courage. But the most persistent demands of the FSM were that Chancellor Strong and President Kerr resign; whatever little power they might want to exert was compromised by the continual rumors that Kerr was accepting a post in Washington, that Strong was resigning because of ill health, and so on. And those on the faculty, or on the Board of Regents, who have been most appalled by the inefficiency of the administration have generally considered it necessary to defend it, in order to prevent the FSM from gaining yet another symbolic victory.

Even so, Chancellor Strong went on an extended leave in December and formally resigned some weeks later. He was replaced by Acting Chancellor Martin Meyerson, a young man relatively new to the campus. The dispute between the president, who wanted a soft policy toward the rebellious students, and the chancellor, who wanted to enforce the rules on his campus, was now to disappear. In his first press interview, Meyerson stated that until he had studied the record he could not state whether the sit-ins had been justified. He offered to act as a character witness for the arrested students from his college. He had the university furnish the FSM with a loudspeaker of greater amplification, and he permitted its use on the steps of the administration building—thus cancelling a ruling the FSM had persistently defied. In general, his initial tactics seemingly were to grant demands almost before they could be voiced, thus preventing the FSM from using any issue to muster support.

Some on the faculty hoped that the new chancellor, once he had become oriented in his post, would move against student transgressions with intelligence and energy. There is nothing in the record to substantiate this hope. He banned *Spider*, a student publication that combines infantile obscenity with revolutionary propaganda, and then some two weeks later was forced to back down and lift the ban. He permitted himself to get so involved in the new quasi-legal procedures of faculty disciplinary committees that even the judge trying some of the filthy speakers publicly advised the chancellor to exercise himself the authority associated with his position. And to justify his reversal with respect to *Spider,* the acting chancellor set an even less defensible principle: any publication can be distributed "if it can be shown to serve the purposes of a student organization." To offer that invitation to the imaginative innovators on the Berkeley campus was—to put it no stronger—unnecessary.

Chancellor Meyerson, like President Kerr, is trying to apply liberal democratic principles of administration, on the implicit assumption that he is dealing with other liberal democrats. This is not the first time that a liberal institution, or organization, has been faced with the problem of how to counter a totalitarian infiltration; and in the past many organizations have been destroyed by their failure to react soon enough to this danger.

The Free Speech Movement is reminiscent of the Communist fronts of the 1930s, but there are several important differences. The key feature, that a radical core uses legitimate issues ambiguously in order to manipulate a large mass, is identical. The core in this case, however, is not the disciplined Communist Party, but a heterogeneous group of radical sects. The careful camouflage of the archetypal front still exists, particularly in the repetitive assertions that only a minority of the students are radicals. This is true, as it has been true of every front organization; the question is, which minority? The extremists directing the revolt hardly bother to hide their radical associations.

The openly radical student groups active on campus include the following: the Young Socialist Alliance, the official Trotskyist youth group; the Independent Socialist Club, organized when a Trotskyist employee of the university split off the left wing of the democratic socialists; and the DuBois Club, the half-disguised youth group of the Communist Party. There are also several other leftist groups: Campus Women for Peace, Student Committee for Travel to Cuba, and possibly one or two more. Three of the most active radical groups are more heterogeneous: SLATE, the oldest extremist organization on campus; and CORE and SNCC, nationwide civil-rights movements with little central direction, which on the Berkeley campus are more extremist than the national bodies.

During the presidential campaign a number of Republican groups (both Goldwaterite and moderate) were active, as well as at least one that seemed to be farther to the right than Goldwater; and some of these were included in the student "united front" operating in September. When the Free Speech Movement was organized in early October, however, most of these were excluded. As window dressing the FSM has also included the Young People's Socialist League, the youth affiliate of the Socialist Party; Young Democrats; and two competing groups of Republicans. Over one weekend in October, the representatives of these last groups were dropped from the FSM Steering Committee; "bourgeois finks," one student told me, are surplus in a state of "dual power." But the momentum was not quite that great, and a few days later the YPSLs and the YDs, apparently unabashed, were back holding up the same fig leaf.

How many of the FSM leaders are "card-carrying" members of the various parties and sects represented on the campus I do not know, nor is it especially relevant to an understanding of the movement. The radical leaders on the Berkeley campus, like those in Latin American or Asian universities, are not the less radical for being, in many cases, outside the discipline of a formal political party. They are defined not by whether they pay dues to a party, but by their actions, their vocabulary, their way of thinking. The best term to describe them, in my opinion, is Castroite. That some of the leaders make a point of their sympathy with the Castro government is true, but almost beside the point—which is that in critical respects all of them imitate the Castro movement.

The FSM, that is to say, is an extremist student movement of a type new to the United States. In the 1930s the radicals in colleges were half-ashamed that they were not proletarians, working in a factory and organizing workers. Today, the radical students in underdeveloped countries—and at Berkeley—see themselves as the true intellectual leaders of the revolutionary movements, and perceive the other students as their most susceptible and potentially most useful targets. That from Marx and Lenin down virtually all revolutionary leaders were of the middle class had once to be explained away; in what we may designate the Castroite perspective, this fact is accepted, and made use of.

A second new element of the FSM is its indifference—relative to earlier student movements—to revolutionary theory. The Socialists and the Trotskyists active in the 1930s, for example, dissipated much of their energy in differentiating themselves from the Communists; if the corridors of CCNY were noisy, most of the clamor came from battles between one student group and another. Today, the spectrum of world Communism is so complex and changes so rapidly, that only solid scholarship can delimit Maoists from Stalinists, Khrushchevites from Titoists, Ceylonese Trotskyists from Vietcong Communists, and so on. A few students continue in the traditional scholasticism of earlier "theoreticians," but most of the FSM leaders seem to be content with a Castroite amalgam, heavily garnished with Castroite demagogy. To analyze where one should go is, by present standards, far less important than to get going.

If today's radical students are activist to a new degree, their mode of action is also—with an appropriate reduction in scale—reminiscent of Castro's. The group of twelve men in the Sierra Maestra Mountains, the tiny nucleus of the Castro movement, never grew to be larger than a thousand or two; yet this minute force was able not only to take power (as indeed was Lenin, in the aftermath of a devastating war), but even (unlike Lenin) to generate the conditions of its victory. Castro's hit-and-run raids provoked the Batista regime into a brutal and indiscriminate counterterror, which alienated the government's supporters and eventually the army itself. At Berkeley, provocative tactics applied not against a dictatorship but against the liberal, divided, and vacillating university administration proved to be enormously effective. Each provocation and subsequent victory led to the next. For those totally opposed to "the system," the solutions of lesser problems are but steps on the way to total social transformation, not an end to rioting.

Some believe that the major crisis is over—in the words of a statement that a faculty committee has distributed to campuses across the nation, that "the primary academic functions of teaching, learning, and research have regained their proper place." By my diagnosis, on the contrary, not only has the patient not recovered but he is sicker than ever. The fever has gone down temporarily, but the infection is spreading and becoming more virulent.

The FSM is tending to break up, hydra-like, into its component parts, and a dozen new political groups have been set up. Hardly any of their activity is at an intellectual level appropriate to a university. Much is merely silly or vulgar; the plaza in front of the administration building, with its competing barkers selling their pamphlets and protest buttons, resembles nothing so much as a circus midway. Some of the new trends are less innocuous. Several of the liberal organizations have been taken over by extremists, who soon will control also the Associated Students of the University of California, to which all undergraduates must pay a fee, and its daily newspaper. A year from now, if there are no countermoves in the interim, the two large buildings that this student organization occupies may well be the center for subversive activity throughout the Bay Area.

Indeed the situation is, I think, fundamentally as it was during the Christmas holiday, when, muddled by feverish committee meetings and competing rumor circuits, I escaped to my living room to listen to *The Messiah*—and was abruptly brought back to thought of the FSM leaders: "That is written: Death is swallowed up in victory!" And therefore: "O death, where is thy sting?" If the FSM is killed on the Berkeley campus, its well-publicized death throes can be used, in the opinion of its leaders, to generate the nationwide revolutionary student movement that Savio has begun to organize, and beyond that—for these are not reasonable or modest young people—perhaps a broader revolutionary party.

THE STUDENT REBELLION AT BERKELEY— AN INTERPRETATION

BY RICHARD M. ABRAMS,

PROFESSOR, DEPARTMENT OF HISTORY, BERKELEY

> My generation has been witness to more offers to sacrifice the world for freedom, for country, for God Himself, than we are likely to take without some revulsion and disgust. And every time we have heard the call to rally behind the "free world," to prepare ourselves for ultimate sacrifice for the "free world," don't you think we have thought of Rhee, of Chiang, of Trujillo and Salazar, Batista and Franco, Somoza and others? Don't you think we have thought of Mississippi and Emmett Till? And don't you think we have paled at the hypocrisy of it all? Does it help to think of the Russian crimes?

> [David Horowitz, *Student* (Ballantine Books, 1962), p. 9]

If the present signs are indicative, the young Americans of the 1950s will bear the rubric the Silent Generation. The mature also conspicuously lacked eloquence, but then that is not so noticeable. It was an era of severe stresses and bewildering change—Korea, "McCarthyism," loyalty oaths, the Berlin uprising, racial desegregation, computer automation, the H-bomb, Dienbienphu, Suez, Hungary, Sputnik, and so on. There was during the decade much self-congratulation for our achievement of affluence, but history will probably ascribe the absence of vocal dissent to fear rather than contentment. For despite a general abundance in matters economic, there was much to be discontented with and about. The continuing blight of racial discrimination in the face of the expressed "law of the land" was one. Rising unemployment was another: from 3 per cent in 1953 to 8 per cent in 1958 and still 7 per cent at the end of 1960, according to the N.A.M.'s figures. Perhaps above all was the pall of suspicion which the inquisitional practices of governmental and quasi-governmental agencies cast upon the daily life of Americans everywhere. Fear, of both a personal and national kind, placed a damper on expressions of discontent. The early fifties were the first winter of the Cold War, and the chill air of insecurity, almost unprecedented in our national history, helped lay on the muting blanket. "McCarthyism" was the dominant domestic syndrome. Of possibly equal importance, however, was that it was in such apprehensive times that a generation of adults, who had begun reaching their vocational maturity and who had spawned their young in the also apprehensive years of the Depression, had now entered into the central places of command in our society. It was their children who were in the colleges in the fifties.

"He wants very little because he has so much," said a contemporary Gallup Poll report on college students, "and [he] is unwilling to risk what he has. He is old before his time; almost middle-aged in his teens." The college student was typically a professionally oriented young man, looking almost single-mindedly for a place that would *keep* him, and from which place, he was told, he might fall if he "took chances." He kept his mouth shut and his eye on the main chance; he aspired only to perhaps a better place in the manner to which he was born or to which his father had so recently and with much sweat ascended.

Nor was the atypical student a rebel in any political sense. If he could accept no place at all in the world he perceived, the best he could do, it seemed, was to thumb his nose; he became "beat"—a word which tells of defeat and helplessness, not aggression—and he devoted himself like a Kerouac hero to the monotonous acting out of expletives. But most people, even young people, do come to terms with their world somehow; the moral senses of most "off-beat" students usually took them only so far as to make them uneasy and resentful in their eventual accommodation. These looked not to Kerouac but to J. D. Salinger, whose fragile heroes expressed for them their own feeling about the helplessness of Good and Innocence when confronted with the treacherous realities of our world. As a contemporary *Time* survey indicated, the novels popular with the young mostly "have the air of suspecting that life is long on treachery, short on rewards."

Helplessness may be the key to understanding the generation of the fifties. "McCarthyism" in its various forms ran amuck, poisoning community life in every corner of the country, while statesmen stood by—helpless, they said. Diplomatic brinkmanship and pollution of the atmosphere with "atomic debris" were dictated, it was understood, by our enemies; in this we were all helpless. We had a Secretary of State who boasted of a "liberation" policy that would encourage, he said, rebellion behind the Iron Curtain, but (predictably) he found himself forced to stand by, helpless, while our-friends-the-rebels were crushed—in East Berlin, in Poland, in Hungary. We wrote "God" on our dollar bills, slipped Him into our Pledge of Allegiance, and exhorted Koreans and Laotians, Vietnamese and Congolese to carry the crusade against godlesscommunism, but our President said he was helpless to persuade Americans to honor the law of the land on segregation. The behavior of the younger generation seems only to have reflected the general sense of futility.

But what has this to do with what happened at Berkeley this past fall? A great deal. We are experiencing a generation of young people today who do not suffer so greatly from want of respectable leadership and from the helplessness of bewilderment and insecurity. The Kennedy administration's deliberate appeal to the younger generation was a factor in this, and in some mysterious way the assassination of the President seems to have added significantly to the younger generation's eagerness for an active social and political role. But above all, the young people today have learned, beginning with the Montgomery bus boycott on through the Birmingham riots, the freedom rides, and the sit-ins, that they are not helpless, impotent, or futile. They are impressed with their power and, understandably (because of the example their elders have set for them), not a little unscrupulous about its use. They are often contemptuous of their elders, of authority, and of the law. To those of us who must live with them, this is often tiresome, disturbing, and even frightening. But it is hardly surprising.

Of all the issues on which Americans take a position these days, the one which affords the clearest moral choice is that of civil rights. Equal protection of the law, the right to vote, fair trial, and similar guarantees are written into our Constitution and, more importantly, into the "American consensus" which conservatives like so much to talk about as the key to America's unparalleled political success. The Supreme Court's decision in 1954 and especially the mounting racial tensions in the past six years or so have focused a public light on the issue so that even the smallest schoolboy today (outside the deep South, at least) knows that those principles are blatantly violated every day in the week, and he knows too that if there is any meaning to morality at all, such violations are immoral. Young people, especially our college students, have been the primary effective force in the movement to correct this situation, while their elders by and large have stood around counseling moderation, criticizing their "extreme" disruptive methods, and offering pragmatic alibis for a policy of glacial inertia. If it is true, as President Eisenhower pleaded, that "you cannot change men's hearts" overnight, these young people have done the next best thing: they have placed fear in some of those hearts—fear of business losses in chambers of commerce and fear of political losses in most of our national party leaders. Why should we be astonished if many college students today are contemptuous and cynical—about their cautious elders, and about those who can be moved by fear but not by principle?

In many respects the University of California in recent years, perhaps especially the Berkeley campus, has seemed like a microcosm of the general social scene. Within it has appeared a wide range of the tensions between the sensibilities of the new generation of students and the shilly-shallying practices of their elders. The university has not done well over the past ten or fifteen years in defending what it should regard as indispensable principles for a true university. The imposition of the loyalty oath in the early fifties was an extremely humbling experience. But on the grounds—conceivably sound—that the voting public cannot be made to understand what an insult to intelligence and integrity it is, it remains honored in form and substance without serious opposition today. Also to avoid entanglement in public controversy, the university long banned both political and religious activities from the campuses. Over the years, however, it was extremely difficult to maintain this policy when it meant the absurdity of prohibiting even major-party presidential candidates from addressing the students on campus. So the policy evolved to one that excluded only Communist Party speakers, or other political pariahs such as the Black Muslims, and under pressure from the students, faculty, and (it is popularly rumored) some threatened lawsuits, the administration withdrew these restrictions (with some residual qualifications) within only the past couple of years. (President Clark Kerr was given a Meiklejohn Award for this contribution to academic freedom.)

Despite these advances, administrative spokesmen have remained highly defensive in their relations with the public. They have seemed unduly sensitive to hostile gestures from outside conservative groups which tend to suspect the innovative energies of a university except when they contribute to some technological achievement. They have too often exhorted the faculty and students to remember what a hazardous path the university must tread between a potentially destructive public sentiment and the sometimes audacious demands of educational policy. Above all, they have too often seemed to respond to pressure from the educational side of the line by issuing apologies to the public instead of attempting to use the integrity of the university to help shape a sounder public sentiment.

The present controversy is a monumental case in point, but it is appropriate for some perspective to cite just one case that arose several years ago. The University of California administers to all entering freshmen an examination (called "Subject A") which tests for the barest essentials of grammar and English composition. The questions are composed by a committee of faculty members. On the May 1959 examination, one of the optional essay questions was: "What are the dangers to a democracy of a national police organization, like the F.B.I. which operates secretly and is unresponsive to public criticism?" Nine months later, the American Legion discovered the question and protested to Governor Brown that the question was "a deliberate and vicious Communist propaganda scheme" which called for a prompt investigation and punishment of the guilty. The chairman of the examination committee explained publicly, and in private session to the Regents, that essay topics are usually worded so as to stimulate thought, and that "controversial" statements contain considerable "shock value" toward that objective. This was surely a sensible answer; it should have been sufficient. But later that week the Board of Regents offered the American Legion the following apology:

> The Regents of the University of California deeply regret that an improper question appeared in the University's Subject A examination in May 1959, that casts a reflection on the F.B.I. The question has, of course, been withdrawn from use . . . and steps are being taken to prevent a recurrence of a similar unfortunate incident.
> [San Francisco *Chronicle*, Feb. 20, 1960.]

What is one to think of such abject nonsense? The suggestion that the question already used nine months earlier would be "withdrawn" seems plainly ludicrous, but the hint that "steps" were being taken to prevent a recurrence represented—if it meant anything at all—the threat of an intolerable tampering with the faculty's prerogatives on educational technique. Taken as a whole, the statement suggests either that the Regents had performed an absurd and cowardly retreat before a scarecrow attack or that the Regents shared with the American Legion an utter lack of understanding of what a university is all about. If present student opinion is any guide, there must have been many students who believed the latter, though the student newspaper at the time took the possibly less charitable view: "The Regents have goofed again. . . ." ran the *Daily Californian* editorial, February 26, 1960. "In the face of public criticism, the Regents took the easiest, rather than the best way out." The student editor went on to note how the Regents had failed to stand up for the right of the university to ask without fear whatever questions it judged would best provoke thought.

The incident is worth citing because it helps us to understand that the outbreak of student truculence this past fall, driven as it was by outspoken contempt for university authority and scorn for a "do nothing" faculty, had a substantial cumulative history. In the recent controversy, the Regents have fortunately expressed far greater wisdom and responsibility. But the public defensiveness has remained a great bane, and the students have thoroughly exploited it.

The university was ineffectual in its dealings with the students this past fall primarily because it failed to reckon with the striking difference in mood between the new generation of students and that of the 1950s. The false reckoning, moreover, extends beyond the administrative officials. Some of the articles already published on the Free Speech Movement (FSM), for example, especially those by unfriendly members of "The Academy" and including some Berkeley members, have brought some pretty heavy intellectual artillery to bear upon the students' attitudes and motivations. In doing so, I think, they have overshot the mark. It has been suggested, for example—with no intended caricature—that the students were merely expressing a transferred Oedipal animus, heightened by anti-paternalist Marxian ideology, and given effective form by the Maoist handbook for rebels. It has been suggested, too, that what the university administrators really needed in their dealings with the students was a thorough understanding of the French and Russian Revolutions. It would be wrong to dismiss such complexifications entirely, though. I suspect there is more than a little mean accusation concealed—perhaps even from their authors—in the hifalutin academic lingo employed. The belligerent contemptuousness, the vulgarly simplistic rhetoric, and the means-oriented behavior which has emerged a bit too often in the FSM has had a great deal to do with turning many well-meaning and indisputably liberal faculty members against the movement. But it is not necessary, and I think it is misleading, to search Freud, Marx, Mao, or Trotsky for the causes. Of course many, perhaps most, sensitive young people have a built-in resentment toward authority deriving from common familial experiences. Nor is evidence entirely lacking to support a popular wish-thought that a variety of Marxist influences have been "at work" among FSM leaders. But our students need hardly be affiliated radicals, mentally disturbed, or goaded by the political pariahs of our society to find all too much official university behavior worthy of resounding scorn; they have no need to stir up the ideological ashes of the 1930s.

It is a revealing paradox that the FSM won its greatest student and faculty support, by far, *after* the administration had conceded nearly every major objective. President Clark Kerr in fact attempted to bolster the case against the FSM by highlighting this point in his statement to the press the day of the mass sit-in arrests:

> The students at the start of this affair in September had an understandable concern. Certain [political activities] had been allowed by the Berkeley campus to take place

at Telegraph and Bancroft [Avenues, for traditional reasons despite general University policy against them]. The campus administration ended these practices on September 14 and student protest boiled up. After wide consultation within the university the Telegraph and Bancroft area has again been made available for the earlier practices. The regents at their November meeting went beyond this. They changed a general university policy of many years' standing to permit on-campus planning, recruiting and fund raising for lawful off-campus action. They did this in response to student requests and faculty proposals and also in the light of changing court decisions . . . This protest has had the slogan of "free speech"; it has had the substance of a demand for on-campus political action and this substance has been granted within the limits of the law; but it has now become an instrument of anarchy and of personal aggrandizement.

[San Francisco *Examiner,* Dec. 4, 1964.]

It hardly needs to be said that if the issue were so clear, one would not expect to find 645 students, including some of the university's most distinguished and able, willing to go to jail or to submit themselves to manhandling by the police (645 = the 82.5 per cent of the 781 arrested who, according to the police records, were indisputably students). Nor would the administration have experienced the resounding repudiation it suffered at the hands of the faculty the day of the arrests and again five days later in regular Academic Senate session. It was symptomatic of what was wrong that President Kerr missed the whole point. Nowhere in his thousand-word statement is there even a hint of the reason for the December 2–3 demonstration, namely, his decision five days earlier to press charges against four students for leading demonstrations two months before aimed at the very restrictions which the Regents had rescinded on November 20 (although not so unambiguously as President Kerr indicated in his December 3 statement) and which he was now acknowledging had been inappropriate and perhaps unconstitutional, as the students had claimed. The free-speech issue was indeed essentially dead by December 2, as President Kerr stated (though to argue that it had never been really alive is simply erroneous: the September regulations proscribed *advocacy* of political activities, which surely has something directly to do with speech). Most of even the FSM leaders recognized this by the week after the Regents' November 20 meeting. The attempted sit-in of November 23—which struck at the possibility that the phrase in the Regents' statement banning "unlawful" off-campus activities might be used for prior restraint of all kinds of controversial activities of indeterminate legality—failed completely because neither the mass of students nor faculty, nor a clear majority of the FSM steering committee itself, supported it. But then came the announcement of disciplinary action, in the face of a general understanding by the students, the faculty, and many administrators that the dismal events of October 2 had been appropriately buried. The activists among the FSM could hardly have been handed a better instrument with which to "document" the alleged treachery and bad faith of which they had been accusing the administration for weeks.

If the administration had in fact been willing to recognize *in September* that the students had had "an understandable concern" the FSM would never have been born. For President Kerr to have acknowledged it two and a half months later was perhaps gratifying but showed rather poor grace, especially considering the purposes for which he used it. Unhappily, from the very beginning—not without provocation from some students, it must be said—the campus officers treated the protests over the new regulations as a disciplinary matter and thereby shut off at a crucial point all serious negotiation on the substantive issues. The September 14 announcement itself, made without forewarning or consultation with the interested student groups, showed a cavalier disregard for student concern. Moreover, one of the justifications offered for the new regulations, that student activities at the Telegraph-Bancroft entrance interfered with traffic, was so patently disingenuous as to make it easy for the more belligerent student leaders to argue with great persuasiveness that the university's rules were not worthy of respect. At this point, who could doubt the popular rumors that the new regulations had been dictated in substance by the *Oakland Tribune's* William F. Knowland, and that the university had, as on so many occasions in the past, knuckled to the pressure without an objection?

The administration's habit of addressing itself to the outside public rather than to the university community exacerbated the tensions. The repeated insinuations in the press, many of them ascribed to the highest university officials, that the student rebellion was merely an exaggerated expression of a "generational revolt" brought to a hysterical peak primarily by chronic agitators, young rowdies, psychotics, dupes of "the Far Left," and outright outside Communists, played a strikingly significant role in arousing support for the FSM from among the great majority of normally apolitical students on campus. Repeated assertions that "outsiders" were an original and continuing source of the agitation particularly rankled. The students knew for themselves the sources of their views; it was singularly insulting for them to be told they were someone else's dupes.

Almost as offensive were the statements—strictly accurate in themselves—that "only a minority" of the students was directly involved in the demonstrations. The key words in such statements are "directly" and "demonstrations," and they tend, through the limitation of the reference, to obscure both the merits of the issues and the extent and intensity of the student discontent. (More recently, President Kerr used a still more limited reference of the same order in a statement addressed to the alumni: "First, we need to understand what happened, and this may be the most difficult task of all. Among other things, we need to realize that only a small percentage of students enrolled at Berkeley was involved in violations of the law or of University regulations." [*California Monthly*, February, 1965, p. 96.] The students will surely not fail to understand that "understanding" was not the purpose of the statement.) If but a small number of students share in the discontent at Berkeley—which must be the intended meaning of the pejorative "only a minority" approach —why is there such acute national interest in student unrest? Above all, why has the administration so swiftly yielded the substantive objectives of the protests if "only a minority" supported them? The point is, of course, that what has been remarkable about the demonstrations on the Berkeley campus is the *great* number of students who have been lured from their studies and private diversions to spend their attention, time, and energy on them. The students cannot be blamed for wondering, undoubtedly with much cynicism, about the motives of an administration which persists in "reassuring" the public outside that all is fundamentally well, when they know it is not.

In a very substantial way, then, the free-speech controversy at Berkeley was symptomatic of a collision between the cautious, defensive, and often disingenuous mode of the older generations and the aggressive, confident, and sometimes activist mode of the young. So far, the activism of the students at Berkeley has inspired most of the commentary. It is surely tempting, and I think appropriate, to deplore the students' seeming propensity for the weapons of disorder and intimidation in this affair. Indeed, at no time—despite possibly a popular impression inspired by imprecise press reporting or by a small number of faculty members (some friendly, some unfriendly)—has the FSM enjoyed any measurable support from the faculty for its tactics. The resort to civil disobedience on the Berkeley campus has represented an abuse of a tactic that is legitimate only when a fundamental moral principle (e.g., the equality of all human beings before the law) comes into conflict with the law or with legitimate authority, and when there is no evident redress available within the democratic process. Few of the faculty have been persuaded that such a condition existed at Berkeley at any time. But when one considers how much room the administration gave the students to distrust the effectiveness of legitimate protest procedure, their behavior is at least understandable. It is possible to ask that the students behave more rationally than the administration, but it is unreasonable to expect that they will.

The controversy over political advocacy and organization on campus has done much good in the way of opening up communication between students and faculty, between faculty and administration, and among the faculty members themselves. The informal "seminars" and "colloquia" which the controversy has inspired on educational policy and on features of contemporary society, in which faculty, administrative officers, and students have participated sometimes in spontaneous gatherings, have made the Berkeley campus in some respects more of what a university should ideally be like than possibly any campus in the country has ever been able to achieve in this century. A great many faculty members, moreover, have for the first time had an opportunity to make personal acquaintanceships with their colleagues in other departments, and the intellectual exchange that has ensued and seems likely to endure far beyond the immediate circumstance is another heartening development. Berkeley has become an even more exciting place to work in, educationally and intellectually, than it has always been.

But many serious problems also exist. Many kinds of grievances have emerged from—and sometimes merged with—the grievances about the political restraints which began the turmoil. For many of the students the restrictive regulations represented not so much a violation of their constitutional rights as an affront to their image of themselves as adults seeking a meaningful education. The effort of the university to set up an opaque wall between classwork and living in the society "outside" seemed like but another illustration of the "factory-quality" education which they argue the present "management" has encouraged for so long. Among other things, they resent the paternalism implied in the regulations. The fact is, an unusually large number of students at Berkeley, including those in the liberal arts college, are mature adults in every meaningful respect besides their temporary vocation as students. A great many of them are husbands, wives, and parents who understandably resent the "merely students" status which seems to stand out all over what the university directs at them or is implicit in the university's sometimes studied disregard for them. This includes the more general complaint about the impersonal quality of much of the teaching and of the administration ("do not fold, spindle, or mutilate," jibes one of the FSM's "Christmas carols"), about the arbitrariness of policy-making within the university community, and in general about the unwieldy size of the university (though there *are* smaller campuses in California). Graduate students have indicated special grievances of their own. Teaching assistants and readers have been organizing into unions to protest low pay and long hours, arguing that even soda jerks get paid more than most of them. They complain, too, that "success" comes not necessarily to the truly able and creative but merely to those who master "the System," a sinister Something that somehow confounds primarily those whose integrity is purest. And there are complaints about "unreasonable" course requirements, "arbitrary" grading techniques, and "excessive emphasis" on grades.

Like all grievances, all these have some substantial justification. Also, like all grievances, there is something of the simple *gripe* in them. There are three general problems which they suggest: (1) how much of the present discontent derives from genuine underlying grievances of long-gnawing existence, and how much is *simply* gripe which in the confusion and controversy is raised to the stature of serious concern; (2) how many of the legitimate grievances are truly remediable, given the also legitimate demands of the "multiversity"—that is, the demands which modern society must make upon a great university for services outside the classroom; (3) how much can be yielded to the demands for such services, as well as to the new requirements for self-respect among our new, early maturing students, without damaging the university as a refuge for pure research and contemplation.

One thing is clear; that unless the university faculty and administrative officers come to grips fully with the changed character of our students, they will tend to evoke the destructive rather than the invigorating and creative qualities among them.

PERSPECTIVES: OUTSIDERS

EXTREMISM IN THE DEFENSE OF . . .*
ROBERT E. FITCH, DEAN OF THE PACIFIC SCHOOL
OF RELIGION, BERKELEY

"Extremism in the defense of liberty is no vice." Now who
was it said that? The rightist leader of the Republican party
in a recent presidential election? Or, perchance, the leftist
leader of a student revolt disturbing the calm of the Berkeley
campus of the University of California as 1964 neared its
end?

However that may be, the state of California has found itself undergoing, for the second time within a few months, a
trial by ordeal of extremism. Some might say that the people
of California are extremism-prone just as other people are
accident-prone. During the late presidential campaign the
extremism came from the far right. The people of California
were implicated in it so far as their vote in the Republican
primaries put that extremism in a position to capture the
presidential nomination. Perhaps these people redeemed themselves at the time of the national election. At the present
moment the extremism comes from left of center. Both ex-
tremisms label themselves apostles of liberty, and the champion of each movement is a would-be liberator of his people.

It All Depends

There may be, there must be, a difference in specific liberties. But there is no noticeable difference in the pose of self-
righteousness and of purity of heart on the part of the lib-
erators. Right now it is to be remarked that those who were
most fierce in their denunciation of the evil intentions of the
extremism of the right can find nothing but impeccable recti-
tude in the extremism of the left. Perhaps the neatest trick
in ethical insight to come out of the current confusion at the
University of California is the distinction, provided by a liberal faculty member, between force and violence: the virtuous
students have practiced the first but not the second. When
their sit-down around a paddy wagon put a stop to an arrest,
that was force but not violence. When their lie-down at
Sproul Hall interfered with administrative business, that was
force, not violence. When their strike threatened the ongoing activities of an entire university, that was force, not vio-

* From *The Christian Century*, January 6, 1965.

lence. But when the police came to haul off the limp bodies of striking students, was that force, or violence?

If others of us look on this scene with troubled hearts and minds, it is because we see some monstrous but ambiguous power striking at the very foundations of a great university. It may also be because, having fought the good fight over some years and even over some decades, we have learned the bitter lesson that there can be demagogues and hoodlums on the left as well as on the right, and that liberty can be dissipated by liberals as well as annihilated by tyrants.

The Ingredients of Revolt

A good cause is the first ingredient in a good revolt. In spite of all the complication of issues, there can be no denying that the students on the Berkeley campus have that good cause. Or at least they had it at the beginning. They are asking for the right to participate as responsible citizens in the political process. They want the right to promote on campus, as they pursue further activities off campus, programs in connection with S.N.C.C., or CORE, or the Democratic party, or the Republican party, or the Black Muslims or what-have-you. Their indignation is aggravated by the fact that this right is already fully enjoyed by students in the California state college system, whether at San Francisco State or Sacramento State or elsewhere.

A good leader is a second ingredient in a good revolt. The students have one in the person of Mario Savio. This leader stands 6 feet 1 inch high, weighs 195 pounds, has been a student of physics, is now a major in philosophy, is a veteran of last summer's crusade in Mississippi, has not been attending classes recently, regrets that his grade average, which stood at 3.9 last year, has been somewhat impaired by his recent political interests. Savio is intelligent, personable, courageous, eloquent, possessed of a dynamic purpose. Or has he more than one important purpose? In a recent interview he confessed, "I suppose I'll end up as a professor."

Another ingredient in revolt is the enormous size and range of what President Clark Kerr has called the multiversity. On the Berkeley campus there are over 27,000 students. One per cent of the total will be a crowd; 2 per cent will fill an ordinary auditorium; 4 per cent will make a mob. (I try to remind myself that in the theological school where I teach 4 per cent of the students would just barely constitute a committee!) Under these circumstances it is hard to tell whether one is dealing with the fringe or with the center of the student body. And if one respects the devices of representative government, it is hard to tell whether this 4 per cent is really representative or is just another willful minority determined to impose its way upon an inert and inchoate mass.

Finally, those who have played at this kind of game before here or elsewhere know that there are three kinds of people who enter into the business. First there is the very small minority of the truly dedicated: those who know the principles for which they fight and who are ready, even eager, to receive the full penalty for whatever course they pursue. But lest some innocent folk should have got mixed up in this company, Mario Savio has promised that he will try, with a defense fund he is raising, to save from martyrdom by the courts those who do not really seek such an honor.

The other kinds of people are the sensation seekers and the power lovers. The sensation seekers are in it just for "kicks." They do not know, nor would they care if they did know, the difference between a Governor Wallace of Alabama and a Governor Brown of California. It is part of the tragedy of our times that in this category are to be found so many of our finest young people. They have been cheated—by parents, teachers, preachers—of any set of great ideals to which they might give themselves, and so they give themselves to whatever chance imperative may come along, preferring adventure to inertia, excitement to emptiness.

With a large number of sensation seekers on hand, a mere handful of power lovers can enter into great affairs. The power lovers, like the truly dedicated, also know the ends for which they strive. But their ends are not those of principle; they seek first to ruin, then to rule.

The Tactics of Revolt

The tactics of revolt call first for a shibboleth and a song and a militant minority. The shibboleth is "free speech"; the movement is known as the Free Speech Movement—F.S.M. Never mind that free speech is not the issue; it still makes a good shibboleth, and as shouted from loudspeakers on touring trucks during the first days of the revolt it stirred the hearts of true liberals all over town.

As for a song, why not appropriate "We Shall Overcome"? To be sure this battle has nothing to do with civil rights, or with the rights of Negroes. But if the song was good for Mississippi and Alabama, why wouldn't it work in California? Elsewhere this song has come from the lips of brave men and women, has been consecrated by stripes and wounds and imprisonment, has even been baptized by the blood of martyrs. But here we shall see to it that there is no immoderate martyrdom.

As for the militant minority, in a huge university student body one can find a minority of that kind for almost anything. What makes it grow into something that begins to look almost like a majority is a series of well executed maneuvers. First there is the deliberate disobedience of university discipline, with students seated at tables on the campus plaza passing out prohibited literature, while a small body of sub-deans goes about taking down names. Then there is the sit-down demonstration around a paddy wagon with a former student inside so that the police are unable to move the wagon away. Later there is the sleep-in at Sproul Hall, the administration building, cluttering the aisles until the police come in and haul out the demonstrators to book them for appearance in court. This is followed by what is intended to be a general strike—the cutting of all classes, with picket lines set up in an effort to persuade members of organized labor not to make the daily deliveries that are necessary to the maintenance of the university plant.

Escalating from a Kernel

At the start of such an effort the militant minority may be only 1 per cent; soon it is 2, then 3. The students arrested at Sproul Hall numbered 780. But a fair number of teaching assistants get into the act: they are both students and teachers. Joan Baez comes by to lend the inspiration of her presence and her songs. There are some other eager participants: former students, alumni, friends, state assemblymen. When President Clark Kerr calls a meeting of all students in the Greek Theater, it begins to look as though as many as a third are now sympathetic. And when the Academic Senate meets and votes support of the main requests of the students, it looks as though the faculty has joined the movement.

But the shrewdest—or was it purely instinctive?—element in the tactics was the escalating and sublimating of the objective of the revolt. Here are some of the magic words of Mario Savio:

> There is a time when the operation of the machine becomes so odious, makes you so sick at heart that you can't take part, you can't even tacitly take part, and you've got to put your bodies upon the gears and upon the wheels, upon the levers, upon all the apparatus, and you've got to make it stop. And you've got to indicate to the people who run it, to the people who own it, that unless you're free, the machine will be prevented from working at all.

In brief, what we are fighting is the Thing. The true enemy is the System, the Organization, all those faceless Organization Men who want to make us into the same soulless robots they are themselves. Indeed, which one of us, in this remarkably affluent and self-pitying society of ours, has not known himself to be the victim of the Thing? Who would not, if he had an opportunity, strike back at the Thing?

Of Liberty and Law

All this, of course, is in behalf of liberty. Does liberty have anything to do with law? Or, in an academic context, has it anything to do with intellectual honesty? Because the Free Speech Movement was never a movement for freedom of speech. In his famous *Bloudy Tenent*, Roger Williams gave us a sharp distinction between free speech and free action, and that distinction has been confirmed by important rulings of our own Supreme Court. Indeed, a maximum amount of free speech is possible only when this distinction is rigorously observed.

What the students want is a specific freedom for overt action, the right to recruit members and to solicit funds for off-campus organizations engaged in various kinds of political action. If I take a somewhat sardonic view of their insistence upon this right, it is because I have been a dean on two campuses where it was precisely the students who sought to curtail that right; they were being annoyed by nuisances and they were outraged by the interference and competition with their own agreed-on programs of activity. However, with an enormous student body it might be reasonable to allow the exercise of such a right in a carefully defined area.

There was a point at which the administration decided to concede this particular right to the students, but reserved for itself the right to penalize those who might later be found to have been connected with unlawful activities. The cry then arose that this was double jeopardy. But double jeopardy has reference only to the courts; if, for instance, a clergyman should be convicted of rape or robbery and were later unfrocked by the church, he would not be suffering double jeopardy. The jurisdiction of the civil corporation is distinct from the jurisdiction of the state.

Administration or Courts?

At another point in the battle the students insisted that the whole issue was not something to be decided by the university administration but one that should be settled in the courts as a question of constitutional rights. Yet when the police carried the demonstrators out of Sproul Hall, took them briefly to confinement areas, had them booked and released on bail (with funds raised by some members of the faculty) under the requirement that they appear in court to face charges for violating the law, there were cries of protest and dismay. At first one heard scattered charges of police brutality, but these were contradicted by the evidence of cameras and tape recorders. The underlying conviction, however, was that no policeman at any time has the right to touch the privileged person of a student, and that any court which gives a just judgment must give it in his behalf.

For those who care at all about representative government, it must be noted that the F.S.M. was in deliberate disobedience not only of the university administration but also of the duly elected president and senate of the student body. While sympathy came from the student officers at the beginning, there was a clear break before the sleep-in at Sproul Hall, with the student senate declaring that any more overt action could be only for purposes of harassment and of mischief. It is being alleged that the student government does not really represent the students, many of whom do not choose to take part in the political process on their own campus. But surely failure to take part in the orderly processes of government does not entitle one to promote disorderly activities outside of it. And if the duly elected government of the students does not represent them, then by what criterion can it be shown that a self-appointed minority of 2 to 4 per cent represents them?

The Value Vacuum

At the heart of all this confusion lies the value vacuum. This is the great yawning void, engendered by skepticism, relativism, impressionism, existentialism—which have cast out all structures, patterns, imperatives, laws, principles and standards, leaving only Chaos and Dark Night to rule over the ruin. This is the absence of any belief in a universal and objective moral order. This is the total lack of any moral authority anywhere.

The faculty is a chief contributor to this value vacuum. For one thing, since the good scholar wants to be free to do his research and maybe his teaching, he is tempted to withdraw from commitments to action beyond his professional community, above all to abstain from anything having to do with student discipline; he seeks to appear "nonjudgmental" in all areas except those which impinge directly upon his personal concerns. The larger and more impersonal the university, the more desperate is this struggle to achieve a private freedom.

Moreover, the prevalent teaching in our culture—not just in universities but even in churches and seminaries—cuts out the ground of any moral authority. We are historical relativists, who deny any order and direction in the course of human events. We are cultural relativists, who make plain that how they do it in Samoa may be just as good as how they do it in South Dakota, who wonder why how they do it in Mississippi may not be just as good as how they do it in Maine. We are ethical relativists, either lifted up to a transcendent reality forever beyond all ethical distinctions, or immersed in diverse contextual and situational traps where ethical discriminations become as meaningless as they are endless. We are epistemological relativists, so overwhelmed with assorted perspectives and frames of reference that we can discern the True no more than we can perceive the Good and the Beautiful.

The comedy begins when a university community which has been busily cutting out the ground of all moral authority suddenly comes up with its own pet absolute of academic freedom. Actually, devotion to the ideal within departmental rituals is exceedingly restricted. I have known a history department that would hire a confessed Marxist but would not touch a confessing Christian, a philosophy department that would take nothing but logical positivists, a psychology department that cared only for experiments in the laboratory and held the clinic in contempt, an economics department loaded with classicists or neoclassicists which refused to look at an institutionalist. If academic freedom can be bent by such ideological constraints, is it altogether intolerable that it might give an inch or two to the political necessities connected with a state university?

In any case, it makes sense that in the development of the debate at the University of California the faculty should fall in with the students. The academic senate in Berkeley voted overwhelmingly to petition the regents asking that the chief demands of the students be granted. So the isolated individuals who taken together make up the faculty and the student body of a great university fell collectively into one another's arms. But an embrace in a value vacuum, an embrace without moral authority, an embrace held together by the tenuous bond of a capriciously selected freedom which was not in fact the kind of freedom it pretended to be—what kind of embrace is that?

The Villains and the Victim

Meanwhile there was the scandal to the fair name of a great university. Someone must expiate that shame. At an early emergency meeting of some of the faculty it was proposed that a new "chief campus officer" be appointed. This meant that Chancellor Edward W. Strong was to be the appointed scapegoat. At the moment there was little opposition to the idea, although a few days later it was repudiated by the faculty. Nevertheless, at that moment there was a sudden, shocking revelation of mixed feelings of guilt, cowardice and irresponsibility.

Others would say that the real villains are former Senator Knowland, his Oakland *Tribune*, assemblyman Mulford and the whole tribe of Goldwater conservatives reaching way down south as far as Orange County. Certainly they did all they could to exploit the occasion, but they could hardly be charged with instigating it.

Another set of villains could be the members of the Board of Regents. Perhaps it was they who brought to bear intolerable pressures upon the university, who devised rules for its governance in an atmosphere remote from the realities of academic life.

Or perhaps the officers of the administration—President Kerr and Chancellor Strong—could be the guilty ones: they had failed to keep in touch with the students, had not kept open the channels of communication while making important decisions. (Incidentally, just how do you manage that with a student body of 27,000 the duly elected officers of which, it is alleged, are not properly representative?) Still others would argue, in irony, that Clark Kerr's big blunder, when he first took office, was that he began at once to liberalize the restrictions on student political activity and so showed himself to be an infirm ruler.

Maybe the faculty, for all its claims to sympathy with the students, is the real villain. Max Lerner writes: "Too many members have become so absorbed with research, graduate work, travel, that they have left the unglamorous task of teaching undergraduates to immature assistants. . . . The students resent it. If the California episode wakes up the faculty to its central task . . . it may have been worth while." Yet it is this same faculty which now proposes that it assume for itself some responsibility in policing the political activities of students. Certainly when a faculty voluntarily enters the area of student discipline, that can be something worth watching.

Again it is possible that if there is a loss of confidence in someone it is not in Chancellor Strong but in the leadership of the student revolt. When that leadership boasts of its resolve to bring the machinery of the university to a grinding halt and when it acts in defiance of its own student body government as well as of the university administration, one sees the signs of pure intoxication with power. When a Mario Savio grabs the mike after a meeting in the open air theater at which President Kerr has addressed the students, one begins to wonder just who presumes to be running the place. When, later, Mario Savio proposes to take on Governor Brown and the whole state of California and when, still later, he tours other universities to arouse students to demonstrate and to constrain their presidents to act in behalf of his cause, one begins to see not just a local liberator but a universal messiah.

Shrewd observers, moreover, must unavoidably be impressed by the professional efficiency with which maneuvers were timed and executed, and with which pamphlets and posters appeared as needed. This could scarcely be the spontaneous work of amateurs.

Doubtless the ideal villain in an age of impersonal structures would be the multiversity itself. But the very anonymity, loss of identity, in the system which both students and faculty decry is precisely what many of them have come here to seek. They want it because it provides that privacy of the person and that large measure of liberty which they cherish. In any case it takes a multiversity to provide the splendors in scholarship and teaching and research which are gathered to a focus in glory on the campus at Berkeley. You can't have it both ways. And does anyone seriously propose that General Motors, the Methodist Church or Standard Oil would serve the public better if they were all shrunk down to the size of the local Chevrolet dealership, the neighborhood church and the filling station on the corner?

Whoever may be the real villain, it is quite clear what the real victim is: the university itself. As the editor of the *San Francisco Chronicle* wrote: "It is a terrifying sight to watch a great university disembowel itself in the public square. . . . It is time this random bath of bloodletting is stopped by men of wisdom and conviction." Surely this means that students enjoy the rights to which they are entitled, as they accept the legal penalties which they have earned. It must also mean an end to cowardice and to recrimination, a fresh establishment of that moral authority which alone can undergird any other authority, and the exercise of constitutionally guaranteed liberties by responsible citizens.

NO FAIR! THE STUDENTS STRIKE
AT CALIFORNIA*
BY GENE MARINE, EDITOR AND JOURNALIST

The Free Speech Movement (FSM) at the University of California burst into headlines across the country with the sit-in by 1,000 students in Sproul Hall on Wednesday afternoon, December 2, and with the arrest, on Thursday of 800 of them. The issue underlying the sit-in we can reserve until this story of The Day of the Cops is told.

At first it looked like a weak protest. FSM leader Mario Savio came out of Sproul Hall—the administration building on the Berkeley campus—to call for more support. But by midafternoon, about 1,000 students occupied all four floors. At 7 P.M. the building was officially closed, and the law, students were told, was officially violated. Campus police guarded every door, but no attempt was made to remove the

* From *The Nation,* December 21, 1964.

students. Inside with the demonstrators were several reporters (some with tape recorders) and one attorney.

Before the building closed, students left aisles for movement and were careful not to block doorways. After 7 o'clock, they set up their own "press room," a food distribution center and a communications system. Jewish students conducted a Chanukah service. Two locked rest-rooms were opened, but carefully, by removing the hinges.

Off the campus, about 150 deputies from the Alameda County Sheriff's office gathered, along with a contingent of Berkeley police and a sizable group from the California Highway Patrol. Also among the poised group of lawmen were about 200 policemen from neighboring Oakland—a police force notorious throughout northern California, particularly among Negroes.

University President Clark Kerr and Governor Edmund G. Brown were both, as it happened, in Los Angeles. As the sit-in continued in what all witnesses agree was an orderly manner, Edwin Meese, deputy district attorney of Alameda County, phoned Governor Brown that the situation was out of hand and that enforcement action was imperative. Brown consulted with Kerr and with the president of the university's Board of Regents, department-store magnate Edward V. Carter. The three agreed that intervention by the police was necessary, and Brown gave the order.

Meese and the army of policemen moved onto the campus. FSM leaders, who had set up a public-address system inside the building, advised all demonstrators under 18, all foreign students, and one who might be on probation to leave. Meese then pointed out the first arrestee: the attorney, Robert Truehaft.

With him out of the way, the police began at the top floor, arresting one demonstrator at a time, varying the order only to single out leaders. Carrying tape recorders, they addressed demonstrators individually, taking the name, then offering the option of dispersal, then making the arrest. Refusal to get up and walk (most refused) was also recorded. Students weren't advised at this point, however, of their right to counsel—an omission on which some law professors believe their cases may eventually turn. Each arrestee was photographed with a number and taken to the basement.

Months of civil rights demonstrations have taught metropolitan police officers everywhere to handle "limp" demonstrators; it requires two officers per demonstrator, and it can be efficient and painless. In Sproul Hall, however, police chose to drag the students, male and female, by twisting their arms into hammerlocks, bending their wrists cruelly backward, and hauling them so that the pressure was on their twisted wrists and their shoulder sockets. One girl was pushed into the elevator on her face from several feet away. It should be stressed that there were reporters on the scene—but the police didn't always know it. Downstairs, they were letting no reporters go up.

After about forty arrests had been made, the police saw that the process was taking too long. They withdrew temporarily (the students now call this "the coffee break"), and when they returned had apparently decided to get rough. The new plan was to bring women down in the elevator, and men by the narrow marble stairs, although a few unfortunate women also made it down the stairs. Some were brought down by arms or shoulders, but reporters present say that most were hauled by their feet. One conscientious reporter counted the marble steps as he followed a girl whose head jarred sickeningly as she was dragged down. There were ninety.

As buses were filled, the men were taken to the Alameda County Prison Farm at Santa Rita, the women to Oakland County Jail (until it was full—then they too went to Santa Rita). The first busload of male demonstrators, whose arrests had begun three hours before, arrived at Santa Rita at 6:20 A.M., Truehaft among them. They were placed in a large cage, or bull pen, and Truehaft again asked, as he had in the Sproul basement, to make the two telephone calls which California law grants all arrestees as soon as is reasonably possible after arrest. He was refused, and when he insisted he was placed in an isolation cell. A judge's phone call got him out at 10 A.M.

Booking involved a long questionnaire, which included questions about religion and nationality, and the arrestee's signature to a statement authorizing Oakland police to open his mail. Students who balked were told that unless they cooperated and answered all questions "correctly" and signed the form, their booking would not be considered complete and they would not be allowed telephone calls or bail.

Back in Sproul Hall, the students' public-address system was still functioning, with the microphone located near the head of the stairs on the second floor, and protected by a mass of demonstrators. As a reporter stood by describing the scene into a tape recorder, the police undertook what the students now call "the charge of the Highway Patrol." (The reporters on the scene seem to have assumed that they were highway patrolmen without making positive identification.)

In any case, a mass of police suddenly burst up the stairwell from the first floor, in a flying wedge aimed at the microphone. Whether by accident or design, they crowded students against the stairwell walls and formed a double line, with a space between, down to the first floor. At the top, moving toward the microphone, they simply took each demonstrator who was in the way and shoved him or her down the stairs.

Policemen on the double line operated as a gauntlet. A student whose body stopped halfway down the stairwell was picked up and thrown again. At the bottom, witnesses saw a deputy sheriff raise one limp girl as she landed, say something to her and when she shook her head, smash his fist into her face.

At the top, the policemen had their clubs out and were pounding furiously on the demonstrators around the microphone. Witnesses outside the building, in the plaza, could see through the huge second-floor windows, and insist that the clubs were used not sporadically and at random but slowly, methodically, repeatedly. As quickly as the charge began, it ended. They got the microphone, but the students had another.

On Thursday afternoon, I watched the end of The Day of the Cops. There was no civilian authority anywhere on the campus. President Kerr was still in Los Angeles. Chancellor Edward Strong, chief Berkeley administrator (Kerr runs all nine university campuses), had disappeared. The University of California was completely in the hands of police. In every window of Sproul Hall a police guard was visible. There were guards on every door. Police patrolled the campus.

The Free Speech Movement

Student groups at the University of California have for years used an area at one of the principal campus entrances, Sather Gate, to set up tables in support of candidates or, more often, ideas: to distribute materials, to collect money, to recruit members for campus organizations, etc. Technically, there has long been a rule against such "political" activity, but the administration has pretended not to notice.

In June, during the Republican National Convention, "Students for Scranton" set up a table at Sather Gate. The head of the California Goldwater delegation, William Knowland—publisher of the Oakland *Tribune,* former United States Senator, and dominant figure in East Bay politics—protested to Chancellor Strong. When the fall semester began, Dean of Students Katherine Towle announced that the old rule would be strictly enforced: no recruiting, fund raising or "mounting political and social action." The outraged cry of "No fair!" was the beginning of the Free Speech Movement—originally, and still in part, an organization of campus organizations.

The groups hardest hit were those supporting civil rights activity, especially SNCC and CORE. Knowland's newspaper is the target of a months'-old anti-discrimination picket line, and most FSM members believe that the publisher complained, not to protect Goldwater but to protect the *Tribune.*

Also, U.C. students had participated in sit-in demonstrations in San Francisco earlier in the year, and subsequently stood trial. Serious political pressure was brought to have the university discipline them—even expel them—but Kerr, backed by many of the faculty, took no action. Some observers saw the new decision as a protection against any future accusation that such activities had an on-campus origin.

At any rate, the students resisted, and on September 30 the university "indefinitely suspended" six of them for "illegal" activity at tables near Sather Gate, and two others for participation in "illegal" meetings. The next day, Jack Weinberg, a graduate student in mathematics who had dropped out of U.C. to give his full time to civil rights, manned a CORE table in the plaza (an open area near Sather Gate) and was arrested for trespassing and taken to a campus police car.

A crowd of angry students, eventually reaching 3,000 (one of every nine enrolled) surrounded the car and refused to let it move. It stayed there for thirty-two hours, while hundreds of police massed on nearby streets and student speakers used the car itself as a platform to address the gathering. Simultaneously with the "police-car protest," a Sproul Hall sit-in took place.

The protest persuaded the administration to negotiate with the students, which it had previously refused to do. The demonstration was called off and Weinberg released when an agreement was reached on October 2. Principally it provided that the fate of the eight students would be turned over to the Academic Senate Committee on Student Conduct, which would recommend action to the administration (many students missed that point); and that a student-faculty-administration committee would examine the whole question of "political behavior on the campus."

But the Academic Senate (i.e., the tenured faculty) didn't *have* a Student Conduct Committee. The chancellor therefore appointed a Faculty Committee on Student Affairs to hear the cases of the suspended students; he also appointed the Campus Committee on Political Activity, with four members each from administration, faculty and student body—two of the student seats being given to the FSM.

Students complained that the administration was not showing good faith. The FSM refused to recognize the administration-dominated CCPA as meeting the terms of the October 2 agreement. But in mid-October, Kerr restored hope by asking the Academic Senate to appoint its own Student Conduct Committee to handle the suspensions (which the senate could have done on its own, but hadn't), and enlarging the CCPA to eighteen members, with four seats for the FSM.

The worst of the storm seemed to be over, but the public, at least, was seriously confused. So far, it had read of an argument over whether student groups could put up tables and collect money. Nobody said "civil rights" out loud. When the

CCPA meetings started, however, the FSM quickly discovered that its administration and faculty members insisted on regulating the *content* of the "free speech" involved. This issue was "not negotiable"; in fact, the FSM insists that the administration refused to negotiate at all—that they merely proposed various formulas on a take-it-or-leave-it basis. The students continued to insist that they could advocate as they saw fit, without arbitrary curbs from the administration.

It must be stressed that setting up tables was never the real issue. The real issue was, and is, the civil rights movements. Therefore, it was over "advocacy" that the talks broke down.

If a student, on campus, recruits others for an off-campus activity which the student knows to be illegal, the university claims the right to punish him. Students argue, however, that the university has no right to punish the student for what amounts to criminal advocacy until the civil authorities charge him and find him guilty. If civil authorities don't find the advocacy illegal, or don't act against it, then the student should be immune from university discipline.

To make it more involved: suppose nobody knows whether or not the advocated off-campus action is illegal? Some of those at the San Francisco sit-ins were found guilty, others innocent, by different juries. Was advocating the sit-in "illegal"? And the question becomes all but hopeless if the student is recruiting for a probably legal activity—like a picket line—which later turns into a possibly illegal one—like a sit-in. How can the university, on its own, arbitrarily decide when a student is "advocating unlawful off-campus activity"? Guilt, the FSM argues, must be judicially determined. ("Judicially determined" is taken to refer to final determination after all appeal possibilities are exhausted.)

Hidden in the question of setting up tables is the idea that even the United States Supreme Court has had a great deal of difficulty over the link between advocacy and action. If the Supreme Court hesitates to make this connection, the FSM argues, the university administration is certainly not qualified to make it arbitrarily.

Finally, in early November, the FSM withdrew from the CCPA, calling it "already deadlocked over the issue of political advocacy." Tables went up again; deans took the names of students manning them; tension rose. The CCPA's six faculty members then proposed that the tables, fund raising, etc., be allowed, but that if off-campus action were *judicially determined* to be illegal, its on-campus organizers should be subject to university discipline. The FSM rejected this, because it still allowed the administration to judge "advocacy"; but both sides seemed to regard it as a possible basis for more discussions. At about the same time, the faculty's Student Conduct Committee recommended that the suspensions of the eight students be lifted, with only mild notes in the record, and criticized the administration for "gratuitously" singling them out.

With at least the principle of judicial determination apparently recognized, and with the conciliatory Student Conduct Committee report (many students thought that the administration had agreed in advance to accept it), the FSM looked forward to a regents meeting in Berkeley on November 20. Three FSM leaders, including the dynamic Mario Savio, planned to speak there. Hopes were high.

Between 4,000 and 5,000 students—15 per cent of the student body—gathered on a lawn opposite the building in which the regents meeting was held. Inside, the regents first refused to hear the FSM leaders. Then Kerr recommended more severe penalties for those suspended than had been recommended by the faculty group. And, ignoring the ten-point proposal of the faculty members and the whole concept of judicial determination, he offered a single new rule, providing that certain campus facilities ". . . may be used . . . for planning, implementing, raising funds, recruiting participants for lawful off-campus action, not for unlawful off-campus action."

"Students," said the San Francisco *Chronicle*, "stood and sat in stunned silence, and many of the coeds burst into tears." Thousands of students were (and are) convinced that the regents and Kerr had revealed themselves as "finks"— that they betrayed completely any trust the students or faculty may have placed in them. The assembled students voted for a sit-in the following Monday, and they conducted it in Sproul Hall for a few hours to show their indignation.

There seemed no place to turn. In the eyes of the public, the students appeared to have won. They had protested about the tables and the fund raising—well, they got the tables and the fund raising, didn't they? Few understood that the real issue was advocacy.

At that point, the FSM may have been beaten, but on November 27, the university sent letters (now called "The Thanksgiving Letters") to four FSM leaders, summoning them to disciplinary action for their roles in the "police-car demonstration" two months before. The initiation of disciplinary action against six campus organizations, including SNCC and CORE, was also announced. All except die-hard anti-student forces now agree that the FSM had every reason to believe it had been outrageously tricked. In bitter, frustrated anger, with hundreds of students cheering, FSM leaders presented five demands as the price of avoiding a sit-in:

(*1*) The dropping of all charges against FSM leaders and organizations;

(2) a guarantee against further disciplinary action until a final settlement;

(3) no *unnecessary* regulations against political activity on campus;

(4) an attempt by Kerr to persuade the regents that only the courts should regulate the *content* of on-campus political expression;

(5) agreement that the *form* of such expression (location on campus, use of sound equipment, etc.) should be determined by a student-faculty-administration committee.

The demands were ignored, and The Day of the Cops began.

Graduate students, assembled into an astonishingly democratic body, called a strike as soon as the police moved in— a strike certainly effective enough to be seriously disruptive. A large segment—almost certainly a majority—of the faculty was sharply critical of the administration. A much-heralded "peace plan" a few days later turned out to ignore the advocacy question, and further offended students because it was worked out in detail and handed down from on high without any consultation with them.

The fight is not yet over. As of this writing there is a lull, for the Academic Senate on December 8 offered a new compromise settlement that was enthusiastically endorsed by the students. Kerr, however, has said that the proposal involves basic changes of policy which will have to be studied by the Board of Regents. The regents meet on December 18, so Berkeley could have fireworks for Christmas.

But whatever the outcome, one already evident result is that the faculty is awake and involved—The Day of the Cops did that. When the university has to be turned over to the Oakland police, something must be seriously wrong—and many faculty members think they know what it is.

The Multiversity

The word is Clark Kerr's. He also speaks of "the military-industrial complex"—not with the faintly derogatory tone which even Dwight Eisenhower gave it, but as a simple description of what's there. And the multiversity, Kerr says, must not only come to terms with the complex; it should "invite" collaboration.

The role of the multiversity, he said in the 1963 Godkin Lectures, is that of a "factory," which produces ideas in the form of research, and idea men in the form of graduates for the use of the military, industry and the government. In return, the multiversity is paid in grants and contracts. The university president's role, he said, is that of mediator in this process—and mediator to the community, because the multiversity "is particularly sensitive to the pressure of its many particular publics."

The administration of the University of California *is* Clark Kerr. Chancellor Strong, a distinguished philosopher, is as an administrator little more than a rubber stamp; to know Kerr is to know "the administration." (Assistant Professor John Leggett, of the department of sociology at Berkeley, believes that in Kerr's writings lie the keys to the FSM and The Day of the Cops.)

All of us who witnessed that day were puzzled to understand how such a situation could have come to pass. That it involved "administrative ineptitude," in one professor's phrase, was undeniable; whatever their motives, Brown, Kerr and Strong were all convicted of ineptitude by the fact that the police were not only present on the campus but in command of it. That it involved student intransigence was equally undeniable; at the very least, there was little honest effort in the FSM to see the other side objectively. But why the ineptitude and why the intransigence?

The key to the first question, Leggett suggests, is in the relationship between Kerr's multiversity and the civil rights movement. As a number of observers have pointed out, the civil rights movement is genuinely revolutionary; it threatens a number of established standards. As one example, a completely new look at the economy is necessary if we are genuinely to open the job market to Negroes at a time when automation dominates the future.

This, in turn, is an open threat to the military-industrial complex. In the process of Kerr's "invited" collaboration, the civil rights movement on campus is disruptive, and being disruptive, it must be stopped.

Clark Kerr is far from being an evil man; few university presidents, in California or elsewhere, have shown as much concern for freedom. But he is caught, it would seem, in the dilemma of his concepts. He would doubtless be horrified at the idea of deliberately collaborating with racism; but from the point of view of the civil rights movement, that is what his concept of the multiversity requires. "There are some things," he said in the Godkin Lectures, "that should not be compromised—then the mediator needs to become a gladiator." The point is as valid as it is apt. But Kerr also says that students may not use the university as "a fortress from which they can sally forth with impunity to make their attacks on society."

Perhaps the best comment on those two quotations is in a statement adopted unanimously by the anthropology faculty on The Day of the Cops, in which they said that the issue on the campus is the civil rights movement, and that the administration must recognize its dynamism and decide clearly whether it is for or against—without hiding behind euphemisms like "off-campus political activity." Or one might add, "attacks on society."

There are, of course, matters of law and order, and democratic procedure. But to the FSM, it seems that *their* appeals to law and order and democratic procedure go unheeded. The administration, they argue, has all the power—arbitrary power, from the students' point of view—and, like Negroes, the students are not treated as equals, not allowed a sufficient governing role in their own affairs, forced into a second-class status. Thus, like Negroes and their supporters, the students turn to new weapons—the mass demonstration, the march, the sit-in. Yet, rightly or wrongly, most of us (or perhaps most of us over 30) would have bent a little, would have sought the common interest, would have worked at the behind-the-scenes political side a little harder. Why insist on a total victory which is so hopeless from the start?

Leggett refers—not without amusement, but yet seriously—to a paper co-authored by Kerr and dealing with the relative propensity of some labor unions to become involved in protracted, class-struggle-type strikes. The paper examines the characteristics of those workers—longshoremen, miners, loggers—who tend to be most militant as union members, whose labor disputes become polarized, who are disposed, in a word, to be intransigent.

First of all, their working conditions are usually terrible—they have the hardest, dirtiest jobs. Second, they tend to be isolated from the "respectable," middle-class elements in the community. Third, they are apt to be homogeneous—frequently there is an ethnic identity. Fourth, as a result of these factors, they form closed communities—they have their own folk-dancing groups or hang out in their own bars or whatever, so that there is a lot of internal communication to counter the isolation from the community.

It needs little imagination for anyone who has ever been on a university or college campus to apply these criteria to that group of students who tend to be well informed and what we used to call socially conscious. The conditions under which they can pursue their own intellectual and political interests are abominable. They're isolated, often voluntarily, from the fraternity-sorority, rah-rah life of the "respectable element." In their isolation, they form their own groups; their talk is cross talk; they dig music and poetry, political theory and political action that is foreign to the middle-class orientation of most students and most faculty members.

And out of this isolation comes distrust—distrust of a university administration that can bend to a Knowland, distrust of anybody over 30, distrust of anyone who seems to be paternal or patronizing. A promise is a promise, and fair is fair, and why all this pussyfooting around?

Balance and perspective, and a willingness to look at the other guy's side, do not come from such an environment. The tragedy of the University of California would seem to be that there was no third force—one is tempted to say, in Clark Kerr's words, no "mediator"—to bring balance and perspective to the polarized positions. The role would seem to have belonged to the faculty—not a few individuals, but the body as a whole; certainly many faculty members now think so. But beyond that, there are a few who have a more radical position (a position, incidentally, with which Mario Savio appears to agree): that the university ought in fact, not merely in principle, to be run by the students and the faculty. In Savio's phrase, the job of the administration should be merely "to see that the sidewalks get swept."

"We on the faculty," Leggett says, "have allowed the administration, over the years, to take the university away from us, to turn it into the multiversity. It isn't easy, but we're going to have to try to take it back. The students and the faculty, together, should control the university. The administration should administrate."

BERKELEY REVOLT*
BY MARSHALL WINDMILLER, ASSOCIATE PROFESSOR
OF INTERNATIONAL RELATIONS, SAN FRANCISCO
STATE COLLEGE

On the day after the free speech sit-in at the University of California's Berkeley campus, the San Francisco EXAMINER front-paged a photograph of a badly littered Sproul Hall corridor, silent testimony to the mess that the demonstrating students apparently had made of the university.

What the photo caption did not say was that almost all of the litter consisted of numbered sheets of paper which the police had held in front of each student as he was "mugged" and which they, the police, then threw on the floor.

The EXAMINER withheld this significant bit of information and thus helped to spread the impression that the Free Speech Movement was nothing but a mob of vandals.

The EXAMINER'S lack of regard for the truth was typical of what the Free Speech Movement has had to contend with from its beginning in September, not only from the mass media, but from the university administration as well. For University President Clark Kerr, from the moment he stated

* From *The Liberal Democrat*, January 1965.

falsely that the limitations he was imposing on student political action were prescribed by state law, to the time he falsely accused the students of vandalizing President Emeritus Robert G. Sproul's office ("It's always messy," Sproul later told the press in correcting the report), was so disingenuous that he gradually destroyed any feeling among the students that they were dealing with an honorable man. Indeed, the behavior of the Berkeley administration throughout the affair transformed a controversy about free speech into a test of the entire institution's integrity—a test that it began to pass only when the Academic Senate adopted by a vote of 824–115 a motion that put the faculty solidly behind the students.

The fate of anyone who depended upon the mass media for an understanding of what was happening at Berkeley was, inevitably, confusion.

From the press, one learned that the administration had always supported free speech, that it had liberalized the rules only to have the students turn them down, that the regents had further liberalized them, and that the students had turned them down again.

"The University has shown tolerance," said Clark Kerr on December 3. "This tolerance has been met with intolerance and distortion of the truth. The university has shown reasonableness. This reasonableness has been met with irrationality and intransigence. The university has shown decency. This decency has been met with indecency and ill-will."

In the face of all of this tolerance, reasonableness, and decency, why did almost 800 students insist on defying the administration by courting arrest and going to jail? And why did one of the most distinguished faculties in the world back them up and within 24 hours raise over $8,000 in bail money?

These questions require answers at two levels: the immediate and the long range.

The immediate focus of the rebellion was the insistence by the university administration and the Board of Regents on the right of the university to punish students for the content of political speeches made on campus *if* those speeches could be linked to subsequent illegal actions off the campus.

If a student on campus called for a civil-rights demonstration, and the demonstrators were then arrested, the university claimed the right to punish the student for his advocacy of illegal actions. This issue came to be known somewhat inaccurately as the "double jeopardy issue."

The double-jeopardy issue acquired more emotional weight as a consequence of the peculiar attitude of Clark Kerr toward it.

In an address delivered at the Charter Day ceremonies on the university's Davis campus last May, Kerr said, quite unequivocally:

"I say again as I have said before that the activities of students acting as private citizens off-campus on non-University matters are outside the sphere of the university. (1) The student is an individual and his individuality should be respected by the university. The university should seek to govern him and discipline him only in areas of direct university concern. (2) The student is also an independent citizen. As student, the university assumes certain responsibilities for his proper conduct. As citizen, the state assumes certain responsibilities. (3) The punishment, for students and citizens, should fit the crime. *One punishment, not two, should fit one crime.* A citizen because he is a student should not be penalized more than his fellow citizen who is not a student. There should be equal treatment under the law." (Emphasis added.)

On that day last May, Kerr further explained the impossibility of trying to administer a policy which would hold students responsible for their off-campus actions.

This position seemed to the students to be the only one that made any sense, and when Kerr, having endorsed it so forcefully in May, abandoned it for more restrictive policies in September, they felt that he was a hypocrite who had yielded to outside pressure, allegedly from William Knowland's OAKLAND TRIBUNE, which students had been picketing because of its discriminatory hiring policies. Was the Goldwaterite Knowland to decide free-speech policy on the Berkeley campus, they wanted to know.

The double-jeopardy issue became the point on which the administration refused to budge, and over which the sit-in of December 3 took place. But that was only the immediate controversy.

Underneath were two long-range issues of greater importance. The first had to do with an intellectual ferment about the role and purpose of a university in a democratic society. Ever since the university had begun expanding with the population explosion and the fantastic infusion of federal defense contracts, faculty and students alike had begun to wonder whether the traditional values of the academy were being destroyed.

The rebel leader Mario Savio summed up a widespread campus feeling when he said that "UC is a factory where the faculty are employees and the students are material to be processed."

Overly large classes, professors who were too busy meeting pressures of non-teaching functions to have meaningful contact with students—emphasis on research and publications, the downgrading of teaching, policy-making by administrative fiat without democratic channels for participation or appeal, paternalism, bigness, IBM machines, mechanization, the breaking down of a sense of community, and the growth of alienation—all of these factors had created a deep undercurrent of discontent, which finally exploded over the issue of free speech.

The second long-range issue underlying the struggle was civil rights. Berkeley, like many other northern universities, has become a major source of leadership and support for the great social revolution of this century.

Here is where the money is collected to support the freedom schools in Mississippi, where the students are recruited to lead the demonstrations in the north or to go south to "put their bodies on the line."

Given the impact of the Sheraton-Palace and Cadillac sit-ins in San Francisco, it is not inaccurate to say that Berkeley is a major nerve center of a movement which threatens to shake the power structure of the entire metropolitan Bay Area.

Small wonder that the full weight of the business elite and its press should lean on Clark Kerr and force him to repress the students.

The repression had been building up for a long time—the restrictive measures of September were merely the last straw. "This protest has never been over 'free speech'," said Kerr on December 3. "There has been and is freedom of speech in the University of California." Once again, Kerr was distorting the facts.

It would have been much more accurate to say that the university administration has always pursued a policy of making it difficult and sometimes impossible to hear controversial speakers and advertise controversial causes. The Free Speech Movement has documented this impressively in a 100-odd page report which it is now attempting to raise the money to have printed. Here are three typical examples from the report:

"In 1956 the Administration prohibited distribution of pro-voluntary ROTC literature while at the same time allowing the Military Department to distribute pro-compulsory ROTC pamphlets in all of its classes.

"In 1962 Malcolm X was forbidden to speak on campus on the grounds that he was a religious leader who 'might proselytize.' But Episcopal Bishop James Pike had spoken on campus the previous day, and in recent on-campus speeches had discussed birth control and the consequences of there being a Catholic in the White House . . .

" 'Students for Lodge' and 'Students for Scranton' . . . *could not put the names of the candidates on posters advertising meetings of the clubs; thus they could not make their nature known.*"

Freedom to do things of this nature existed at San Francisco State College and many other campuses across the nation. The Berkeley students were fed up with such discriminatory and undemocratic policies and so they finally marched into Sproul Hall on December 2 and began their sit-in.

I was present as a reporter in Sproul Hall that night and the next day during the arrests. It was an extraordinary experience. The demonstrators were a remarkably well-disciplined group. Monitors patrolled the halls to keep order and make sure no damage was done to the building. The fourth floor was set aside for a study hall and was kept quiet. Classes were held in the stairwells and elsewhere.

There were all kinds of students—those with beards and beatnik dress got the most attention from the press. I talked with teaching assistants, fellowship holders, and serious students. For those who wanted entertainment there were movies, and folksinger Joan Baez wandered about singing inspirational songs to small clusters of students. This was no rabble.

The behavior of the police was not so impressive. They clearly saw their role as one of punishing the students, not merely arresting them and removing them from the building.

I saw students dragged down three flights of stairs at high speed, bashed against the wall as corners were turned. Making these observations was difficult, for the police made every effort to prevent press coverage by declaring large sections of the building off-limits to the press, by pasting newspapers over the windows overlooking the stairwells, and by turning off the lights in crucial areas.

As a further precaution, an officer was assigned to accompany every photographer wherever he went, a procedure I had never experienced before even while covering President Kennedy and Nikita Khrushchev.

What went on in the basement I do not know, but at one point I managed to look down the stairwell in time to see an Oakland policeman violently jerk a demonstrator off the floor by his hair.

When I attempted to photograph a girl at the moment she went limp, an Oakland policeman held his hand over my lens.

From the moment the Berkeley Academic Senate adopted its free-speech resolution on December 8, a resolution that embraced the main parts of the Free Speech Movement's demands, the controversy took on an added dimension.

The senate resolution asked "that future disciplinary measures in the area of political activity shall be determined by a committee appointed by and responsible to" the Academic Senate.

This was a demand to reclaim important power from the administration, and it raised a critical question: who shall regulate the intellectual life of the university—the faculty and students, or the administration and the regents? It was not a demand which either the administration or the regents could be expected to accede to gracefully.

Prior to December 8, the Free Speech Movement had not shown great confidence in the capacity of the faculty to make a fight over a matter of principle.

The November 17 *FSM Newsletter* said: "academicians do not have a tradition of solidarity. Unlike less skilled workers, they have never stuck together and struck together. They allow their colleagues to be victimized one at a time. They are loath to use their power to fight for their own freedom or anyone else's. When a professor is hounded out of the university, the faculty forms a committee. They want us to use their tactics. They think they are on our side; but they have an innate instinct for submission. They may think like men; but they act like rabbits . . . Will the rabbits save us from the wolves? Will they even try?"

In 1950 the faculty had a loyalty-oath fight, but its instinct for submission proved stronger than its instinct for battle.

On December 8 the professors honorably got themselves into another struggle. They now have a second chance to prove to their students that they aren't rabbits by making an organized fight for the principles they have endorsed. The students wait and hope they will be men—realistic and tough.

Meanwhile, a lot of people who were previously unconcerned will be digesting a number of lessons powerfully taught through the efforts of the Free Speech Movement, namely:

—that campus policies which are not intellectually tenable are not administratively expedient.

—that police brutality is not the mere myth of junkies and beatniks.

—that on matters of political significance the press is not to be trusted.

—that university bureaucrats, administrators, and presidents, like politicians, are less impressed by reason than by force.

—that non-violent civil disobedience works.

—that there is still something in the First Amendment that can inspire men to sacrifice.

Teaching this took a lot of courage and cost some young people a great deal. We ought not to forget it.

THE BERKELEY AFFAIR: MR. KERR VS. MR. SAVIO & CO.*

BY A. H. RASKIN,

ASSISTANT EDITOR OF THE EDITORIAL PAGE, NEW YORK *Times*

BERKELEY, Calif.

What turned the University of California's world-renowned campus here into a snake pit of unrepressed animosities? As my helicopter rattled across the moon-dappled water of San Francisco Bay on its way toward this strangely riven academic center, it seemed to me two men were probably best equipped to supply the answer. In the process, they could go far toward explaining a simmering unrest on other campuses across the nation, and in every corner of our corporate society.

One man was Dr. Clark Kerr, 53, the quiet-spoken Quaker whose duties as president of the university make him Big Daddy to 72,000 students on nine California campuses. The other was Mario Savio, the charismatic 22-year-old undergraduate who had emerged as the archangel of student revolt at Berkeley.

My effort to get the answer from Savio got off to a rocky start. We had arranged to meet at the headquarters of the Graduate Coordinating Committee. This is a key unit in the Free Speech Movement (F.S.M.), the coalition of undergraduates, graduate students and teaching assistants that grew out of an ill-timed, worse-explained and now-rescinded administration order that barred all on-campus solicitation for political or civil-rights demonstrations mounted off the campus.

The committee office is a garret over the university's drama workshop, not far from the main gate to the huge, hillside campus. The visitor climbs a flight of wooden outside stairs and finds himself in a barren room that is dark despite the dazzling sunlight outside. The nearest thing to a real piece of furniture is a battered green sofa, with sags where the springs should be. A square table with a telephone fills one corner, and there are a half-dozen camp chairs. Under the table is a mound of picket signs. The mood is "Waiting for Lefty" done off-Broadway.

Savio, a slim six-footer with frizzy pale hair, peeled off the short, fleece-lined coat that has become a sort of personal trademark. His first words were a flat refusal to participate in any interview if I intended to focus on him as *the* communicator for the F.S.M. "Anything like that will just perpetuate a misrepresentation that the press has already done

* From *The New York Times Magazine*, February 14, 1965.

too much to build up," he said. "This is not a cult of one personality or of two personalities; it is a broadly based movement and I will not say anything unless it is made clear that the F.S.M. is not any single individual."

A way around that roadblock was ready at hand—a joint discussion with the six other members of the collective leadership who had accompanied Savio to the conference. It started with everybody sounding off against Sidney Hook's view in *The Times Magazine* (Jan. 3) that academic freedom was primarily for teachers and that the only imperative right for students was freedom to learn. Savio said they wanted equal space to reply; also they wanted to sue. I told them to go ahead if they thought they had a case. Finally, we got to what I wanted to talk about—namely, what they thought the issue at Berkeley had been and whether there was still any real issue left.

It was a somewhat formless encounter, a blend of a graduate seminar in political science and "Catch-22." People wandered out and others filled their chairs; getting in questions was harder than getting back answers. Yet, it was an engaging group—lucid in exposition, quick in rebuttal, manifesting no unease at differences of interpretation or emphasis within their own circle.

The Berkeley mutineers did not seem political in the sense of those student rebels in the turbulent Thirties; they are too suspicious of all adult institutions to embrace wholeheartedly even those ideologies with a stake in smashing the system. An anarchist or I.W.W. strain seems as pronounced as any Marxist doctrine. "Theirs is a sort of political existentialism," says Paul Jacobs, a research associate at the university's Center for the Study of Law and Society, who is one of the F.S.M.'s applauders. "All the old labels are out; if there were any orthodox Communists here, they would be a moderating influence."

The proudly immoderate zealots of the F.S.M. pursue an activist creed—that only commitment can strip life of its emptiness, its absence of meaning in a great "knowledge factory" like Berkeley. That is the explanation for their conviction that the methods of civil disobedience, in violation of law, are as appropriate in the civilized atmosphere of the campus as they are in the primordial jungle of Mississippi. It was an imaginative strategy that led to an unimaginable chain of events.

Trouble began on Sept. 14, a week before the opening of classes, when the dean of students suddenly shut off the only area on campus where students had been free to collect funds and enlist adherents for off-campus political or social action. This island for activists was a 26-by-60-foot patch of bricked-over ground, called the Bancroft Strip, just outside the principal pedestrian entrance.

The decision to embargo the Strip, made in the climactic days of an election campaign that would settle both the Presidency and the fate of California's controversial fair housing law, forged a united front of protest extending from campus Goldwaterites to Maoist members of the Progressive Labor Movement.

With the memory of the mutiny thick in the gloomy garret, the collective leadership of the F.S.M. spent the next three hours telling me what they thought the rebellion was *really* about.

They are convinced that the abrupt decision to close the Bancroft Strip represented a university capitulation to right-wing forces angered by student picketing and sit-ins to compel the hiring of more Negroes in Bay Area businesses. Specifically, they blame former Senator William F. Knowland, editor of The Oakland Tribune, whose paper was a special target. (Knowland says he didn't do it.)

The cutoff in political recruitment confirmed a conviction already held by some of the students that bankers, industrialists, publishers and other leaders of the Establishment in the Board of Regents were making a concentration camp out of the "multiversity"—a term coined by Kerr in a series of lectures at Harvard nearly two years ago to describe the transformation of a modern university, like Cal, into a vast techno-educational complex.

This conviction was not diminished by the extreme freedom the university has long allowed students to express their own political views, however unorthodox, at "Hyde Park" areas inside the campus. Even during the ban on the use of campus property for organizing off-campus political action, students retained their liberty to invite Communists, Nazis or Black Muslims to address meetings at the university. They also could—and often did—agitate for the right to smoke marijuana, to be able to buy contraceptives at the University Bookstore or for other far-out objectives.

All this has been going on for years in an atmosphere particularly congenial to the flowering of undergraduate rebellion. The whole Bay Area has a long Left Bank tradition of hospitality to radical movements and off-beat behavior. Czeslaw Milosz, a Polish poet, who is on the faculty, reports that among Bohemians Berkeley and Greenwich Village are regarded as "the only two places in America you can be free." The mild year-round climate also helps. "There is no place in the world where uncomfortable people can feel so comfortable," said a visiting British professor.

Taken aback by the vehement student reaction to the recruitment taboo, the Regents in November restored the right to mount political action—not only in the Bancroft Strip but in several areas where it had never been allowed before. How-

ever, the F.S.M. is still unhappy because the new ruling speci-
fies that only "lawful" off-campus activities can be planned
on campus.

The rebels argue that students should have the same right
as other citizens to participate in the political and social
affairs of the outside community. What is "unlawful" ought
to be determined solely by civil and criminal courts, not by
a university administration or faculty. The university's only
area of proper regulation over political activity should be the
establishment of minimal time-place-manner rules to guarantee that anything the students do on campus does not interfere
with classes or the orderly conduct of university business.
Such is the current focus of what is left of the "free speech"
issue.

Remembering centuries of "town vs. gown" controversies
all over the world, in which universities had always fought to
keep their campuses from coming under police rule, I asked
the F.S.M. leaders whether their insistence on leaving disciplinary authority to the municipal law-enforcement agencies might not destroy the whole concept of academic sanctuary and expose them to much harsher treatment.

Savio, a philosophy major who graduated at the top of his
class from New York City's Martin Van Buren High School,
had a blunt answer: "That is a specious argument. The campus is already crawling with cops of the most insidious kind
from the 'Red squad' and every other kind of undercover
agency." Myra Jehlen, a comely, solemn Phi Beta Kappa
from C.C.N.Y. and a Woodrow Wilson graduate scholar in
English, added a postscript: "Immunity from police prosecution only applies to panty raids and fraternity guys. We're
not interested in that."

She was the only coed in the group. Across the room was
her husband, Carl Riskin, who had gone to Cambridge in
England on a fellowship after graduating *magna cum laude*
from Harvard and was now completing his Ph.D. thesis at
Berkeley. He spoke seldom, but with force and precision.

Next to him sat Martin Roysher, a sophomore from Arca-
dia, Calif., whose casually correct clothes reflected the freshman year he spent at Princeton. He looked so young it was
hard to believe he was out of high school, yet he, too, spoke
crisply about everything from alienation to the importance of
erasing any differentiation between the freedom of students
and citizens to act upon their political beliefs.

Here, too, was Jack Weinberg, a former graduate student
in math and now a civil-rights activist in CORE, who gained
fame overnight as "the man in the police car" in the first of
the mass upheavals last Oct. 1. Stephan Weissman, the red-
bearded chairman of the Graduate Coordinating Committee,
pulled a few picket signs from under the table and squatted

on the floor. Robert Starobin, a Cornell B.A., who has been a teaching assistant in history at Berkeley for three years, is writing his Ph.D. dissertation on industrial slavery before the Civil War. Stocky and assertive, his talk bristled with complaints about the "power structure" and its determination to stifle civil-rights activity at Berkeley.

The one whose views evoked least challenge was the youth group's senior citizen, Hal Draper, a part-time librarian at the university who graduated from Brooklyn College in the Great Depression and is now fiftyish. A leader of the old American Student Union, he drifted through various wings of the Trotskyite movement and is currently an editor of New Politics, a journal intended to offer an outlet for all shades of Socialist thought. A Draper pamphlet called "The Mind of Clark Kerr" has become the F.S.M.'s bible in its fight against "the university factory." Dedicated to the students who immobilized the police car, the leaflet depicts Kerr as the preacher of docile submission to a technocratic juggernaut that will stamp out all individuality and all liberty.

The longer my conversation with the students went on, the clearer it became that the political battle was only a symptom of a larger revolt against the bigness and impersonality of the "multiversity" itself. If Clark Kerr is the high priest of the multiversity, social critic Paul Goodman is its Antichrist and thus beloved of the F.S.M. The opening theme of an F.S.M. pamphlet is a declaration by Goodman that in the United States today, "students—middle-class youth—are the major exploited class. . . . They have no choice but to go to college." Rejecting their role as factory workers on an academic assembly line, the F.S.M. demands a humanized campus, a "loving community" based on comradeship and purpose.

"We must now begin the demand of the right to know; to know the realities of the present world-in-revolution, and to have an opportunity to think clearly in an extended manner about the world," says the F.S.M. credo. "It is ours to demand meaning; we must insist upon meaning!"

What is behind this manifestese? Does it betoken a desire to dismantle the University of California, or to establish a student soviet that would make all educational policy? The F.S.M. leaders disclaim such grandiose ideas.

"This is not a matter of rolling back the multiversity," says Myra Jehlen. "But it is our view that this university does neglect its students. We have no contact with the community of scholars, except to see a professor across 500 feet of lecture hall. Teaching assistants have to serve as parents for the students."

Savio deplores the extent to which the university's professors and facilities are involved in research for the Government and giant corporations. "It is a distortion, and too bad, that the university does not stand apart from the society as it is. It would be good to return to an almost totally autonomous body of scholars and students. But what we have now is that the Pentagon, the oil and aircraft companies, the farm interests and their representatives in the Regents consider the university as a public utility, one of the resources they can look on as part of their business."

And who should run things? Says Starobin: "Our idea is that the university is composed of faculty, students, books and ideas. In a literal sense, the administration is merely there to make sure the sidewalks are kept clean. It should be the servant of the faculty and the students. We want a redemocratizing of the university. Courses are clearly up to the faculty, but students should be able to convey their ideas. Dormitory regulations should be up to the students who live in the dorms. A bipartite or tripartite committee should have the final say in promulgating minimal rules on the time, place and manner of political activity."

There was much, much more before I asked whether they felt that the turmoil had accomplished anything. Myra Jehlen answered first: "Of course, you never win finally. New problems will always arise. But there has been a great strengthening of democratic institutions on the campus. The kind of actions we've taken, the important function of students in society—these have been vindicated. Yes, we have won, though how much is not clear."

Savio was more succinct: "We committed the unpardonable sin of being moral and being successful."

The setting was very different that evening when I visited Kerr at his home in El Cerrito, five miles from the campus. It is a glass-walled ranch house on a lofty bluff overlooking the Bay. Velvety lawns roll down to an old quarry in the canyon far below. There is a swimming pool, and flowers, shrubs and vines grow in junglelike profusion in a great glass-roofed patio.

But Kerr is not a man for rich living, even though his salary of $45,000 a year puts him $900 ahead of Governor Edmund Brown as the state's highest-paid official. He is frugal even of time. If Kerr gets to an airport and discovers the plane will be 15 minutes late, he is furious at the lost time. But if it will be an hour late, he is contented; he will sit quietly in a corner of the airport, begin writing memos, speeches, articles or even a chapter for a book.

Kerr works with the same intensity at home. Each afternoon a squad of eight secretaries at his office in University Hall pack a great sheaf of papers into a cardboard box. A driver returns them before noon the next day. Each carries a notation in green ink written in an incredibly pinched, yet distinct, hand—the marching orders by which the biggest of big universities is run.

The commander's invariable uniform is a navy blue suit and white shirt. His mind has extraordinary range and a rare capacity for turning discord into consensus. Kerr ranks among the country's half-dozen most effective peacemakers in the volatile realm of labor-management warfare—a skill that has prompted every President since Harry S Truman to enlist his help. In the middle of the disturbances at Berkeley there were rumors that President Johnson asked him to accept appointment as Secretary of Health, Education and Welfare. All Kerr will say about that or any other post is that he still expects to be president of Cal on its centenary in 1968.

Among the many ironies of the Berkeley explosions is that Kerr now finds himself under savage attack from the left after more than a decade of demands for his ouster by right-wing critics. Leading the fight against a loyalty oath, he became so popular with the rest of the Berkeley faculty that in 1952, when the Regents decided to restore the goodwill they had lost in two bitter years, they named Kerr as chancellor. In 1959, a year after the Regents moved him up to president, Kerr again aroused right-wing ire by granting an honorary degree to Prof. Edward C. Tolman, who had been forced to resign for refusing to sign the oath. A year later he induced the Regents to name a new building in Tolman's honor.

When Berkeley students were arrested in 1960 for disrupting a hearing of the House Un-American Activities Committee in San Francisco, Kerr resisted demands to suspend or expel the demonstrators. He ignored similar conservative outcries last summer when undergraduates were arrested for a civil-rights sit-in at the Sheraton-Palace Hotel.

The liberalization of faculty and student rights during the Kerr administration earned for him and the Regents the American Association of University Professors' 1964 Alexander Meiklejohn award for conspicuous contributions to academic freedom. Less than six months later he was being denounced as an enemy of free expression by many on his own campus.

Kerr was not consulted on the fateful order shutting the Bancroft Strip. He was in Tokyo on his way home from a seven-week economic mission to the Iron Curtain countries on the day it was issued.

"It was perfectly apparent," Kerr says, "that the decision was a mistake, both in the action itself and in the way it was done. There was no advance consultation with the students, the over-all university administration or anyone else. When a privilege had been extended as long as that had been, there should have been consultation—and especially against the background of an impending national election and intense student involvement in civil rights."

(A Dostoevskian bit of background, still unknown to the students: Kerr foresaw in September, 1959, that the Strip would eventually be a source of trouble because there was no logical basis for exempting it from the no-politics rule that applied everywhere else on campus. He got the Regents to agree that it ought to be turned over to the city for use as a public plaza. But, for reasons still unexplained, the university's treasurer never carried out the instructions to deed over the Strip. If he had, the whole melancholy chain of events might never have begun.)

Kerr agrees with the F.S.M. thesis that students should have as much political freedom as anyone else in the community. The only difference is that he thinks they already have it. In his judgment, the rules governing political expression on campus, including the right to invite heretics of all political persuasions to speak at student meetings, give Berkeley undergraduates more freedom than bank clerks, factory workers or 99 per cent of the general citizenry.

He ridicules the notion that the university has been succumbing to the "power structure" in the dispute over civil-rights activity. "I had to fight some extremely tough battles against some very powerful legislators who felt we should kick out students who were arrested for sit-ins in the Bay Area, but we never yielded an inch," Kerr says. "It just would not have been in character for us to say that the only place the students could fight for Negro rights was in Mississippi."

As for the Bancroft Strip, Kerr says that "whatever pressure preceded the order involved the loading of the galleries at the Republican convention with Berkeley students whooping it up for Scranton against Goldwater."

The F.S.M. indictment of the "multiversity" brings a special twinge to Kerr because every charge the insurgents now raise he foresaw with greater incisiveness as long ago as April, 1963, when he gave the Godkin Lectures at Harvard.

Those talks described, with apparent fatalism but decided unenthusiasm, the evolution of a "mechanism held together by administrative rules and powered by money." Kerr predicted that undergraduates would feel so neglected and depersonalized that the revolt they once engaged in against the faculty *in loco parentis* would turn into an even more destructive uprising against the faculty *in absentia*. Everything Kerr warned of then is embodied now in the F.S.M. lament that the student is being downgraded to the status of an I.B.M. punch card in a computerized multiversity.

Kerr concedes that the multiversity is a disturbing place for many students, but he disputes that it is devoid of meaning. "One of the advantages of a big city or a big university

—as against a smaller and more monolithic closed community —is that people can find those things which may mean something to them," he says. "They are given a choice.

"It would be terribly stultifying to find yourself in a place which has a single meaning, and that meaning is the same for everyone. The only kind of society that has only a single meaning is an authoritarian one. It seems to me that is a place where you would really expect rebellion. Essentially, what the F.S.M. are saying is that they are rebelling against freedom of choice."

When I noted that the students objected not to too many meanings, but to the absence of any, Kerr replied:

"In fact, there is a lot of opportunity to participate, only it takes a little longer and requires more initiative to find it. Many tend to be overwhelmed by their opportunities; there are so many lectures to choose from, so many things to do, that they tend to become lost. They are torn too many ways and wind up condemning the whole structure."

The notion that the university, for all the magnitude of its Federal and industrial involvement (it is receiving $246 million this year for operating three giant atomic installations, plus $175 million in research grants and contracts), has become an arm of the Pentagon or big business also draws a rebuttal from Kerr. "The university," he says, "is intertwined with all society. And if it is overbalanced in any direction as compared with the surrounding society, it is in the fact that it is a source of dissent and social criticism. You could say it is a tool of the critics, and that is one of the things that makes it so dynamic."

All this brought us back to the students' overriding complaint—the enormous size of Berkeley, with 27,500 students on a single campus, and the obliteration of the individual's relationship to faculty and administration. Kerr's answer dwelt more on society's inescapable needs than confidence that alienation could be overcome.

"Every day makes it clearer that the university's invisible product, knowledge, is likely to be the most powerful single element in our culture," he says. "With so many young people pounding at our gates, we're up against a tremendous assignment. To take the position that we won't grow would be a terribly irresponsible thing."

Kerr is a philosopher-pragmatist of the technocratic society, probably the ablest and most creative in the educational field. His guiding principle is individual disengagement. He preaches the idea that each person can best protect his own happiness in a society of bigness by developing pluralistic attachments. "If you invest all of yourself in an institution," he says, "you become a slave. It becomes a prison, not an agency of liberation." This road to the independent spirit is just the opposite of that traveled by the F.S.M. and its leaders. Their goal is commitment, but there is a good deal of confusion about precisely what it is they are committed to.

And who is listening, now that the clear-cut issue created by the closing of the Bancroft Strip and the blackout of political recruiting has been resolved? The signs are that the overwhelming support for F.S.M. aims among students of all political hues and of no hues has evaporated along with the issue.

Moreover, there are strong indications of strain inside the F.S.M. steering committee, now a much more ingrown group than in the initial days of across-the-board coalition. Many would like to disband the movement. Hal Draper said frankly that it might go into "an inactive phase." Ed Rosenfeld, the F.S.M.'s press officer, says that one thought under consideration is to establish a cooperative coffeehouse, on a nonprofit basis, near the campus. "It would be a civilized gathering place in the best European manner," he says, "a suitable forum for debates and discussion."

Back at the heliport for the return flight, I tried to evaluate the Berkeley uprising against the memories of my own days of rebellion as president of the C.C.N.Y. class of '31. It was a time when one worker in four was jobless and the misery of the Great Depression was beginning to grip the land. We had been ready to picket our own commencement in cap and gown, but we chickened out at the last minute for fear of losing our degrees.

These students, for all their talk of setting up an espresso joint as a monument to their mutiny, were a tougher, smarter breed, more ready to go for broke.

But what did they accomplish, besides effecting the cancellation of an order the university admits never should have been issued?

They have done one important thing that may prove of considerable help to Berkeley and all other big universities. They have cut through the multifarious concerns of an administration that must deal with every agency of government, including those in 50 countries abroad, and forced it to recognize that it is sitting on a volcano of neglected, seething students.

Kerr, who has always recognized the need for diversity in multiversity, already is hard at work on measures to improve the quality and the immediacy of instruction. He aims to break down the idea that research, not teaching, is the mission of the good professor. Both roles are vital, Kerr believes, and so does the man he has brought in as acting chancellor, Dean Martin Meyerson of the College of Environmental Design.

Last fall's earthquake also has shaken the administration

and faculty into a heightened awareness of the need for team-work to lessen the students' belief that no one cares whether they go or stay, that undergraduate needs are passed over in favor of lucrative research contracts, book-writing projects and traveling lectureships all over the world. Professor Arthur M. Ross, the enterprising chairman of an emergency executive committee elected by the faculty in the blackest period last December, expresses confidence that a genuine educational overhaul is in prospect. Most of his colleagues agree.

What goes into the curriculum and who teaches what courses will be a matter for the faculty to determine, but both Kerr and Ross feel students can have a useful advisory role. A larger area of authority for students in disciplinary committees and in other forms of self-government also is in prospect. All these developments should help still the discord at Berkeley, but—much more important—they will help make it a better institution of learning.

One of the imponderables in trying to guess whether peace has really come to the campus is that some F.S.M. activists obviously have developed a vested interest in finding things to fight about. They seem to operate on the theory that, in a system they believe is basically corrupt, the worse things get, the easier it will be to generate mass resistance.

This is not a novel theory in radical movements, but it is not one that makes for stability. When the police dragged Savio and the 800 others out of Sproul Hall, he exulted, "This is wonderful—wonderful. We'll bring the university to our terms." When Paul Jacobs told an F.S.M. leader that he had advised Kerr to enter Sproul on the night of the sit-in and talk to the students (advice Kerr did not take), the insurgent asked sourly, "What side are you on?"

The reckless prodigality with which the F.S.M. uses the weapon of civil disobedience raises problems no university can deal with adequately. Mass discipline carries the danger of martyrdom and a spread of sympathetic disorders to other campuses.

Garrisoning the grounds with police runs so counter to the essential concept of the university as a redoubt of tolerance and reason that it is perhaps the worst solution of all. At Berkeley it brought the faculty into open alliance with the students against the administration. Yet, the alternative of giving students total immunity could engender a situation akin to that in the University of Caracas, where student revolutionaries use the campus as a fortress from which to sally forth to attack the general society.

"We fumbled, we floundered, and the worst thing is I still don't know how we should have handled it," Kerr acknowledges. "At any other university the administrators wouldn't have known how to handle it any better."

Menacing as is this new disruptive device, one even graver danger sign outranks all others raised by the mess at Berkeley. That is the degree to which it evidences a sense of lost identity, a revulsion against bigness, that is affecting all of our society. On the campus it takes the form of antagonism against the multiversity. In the mass production unions this same feeling of impending obliteration recently spurred rank-and-file strikes against General Motors and Ford, and may erupt again in the basic steel industry this spring. The longshoremen, fearing the shiny face of automation, voted down contracts that gave them lifetime job security and a generous wage guarantee—principally because they felt the machine was grinding them and their jobs into nothingness.

A similar mood of irrationality, of vaporous but paralyzing apprehension, stalks all our institutions in a time of unmatched material prosperity and individual well-being. Young people, in particular, study the unemployment statistics and decide that society is in a conspiracy to provide security for the older generation at the expense of the youngsters outside waiting to get in. Education is the magic carpet over the hurdles that make the dropout the shutout in our society. But, even at this most distinguished of universities, bigness robs many students of individual dignity or purpose. This feeling helps explain the spread of drug addiction and senseless crime among many well-to-do youngsters. All are part of an alienation that turns even affluence and security into worthless prizes.

This may prove to be the nation's critical challenge, potentially more damaging than the international crises that monopolize so much of our concern and our budget. If Berkeley cannot imbue life with a sense of fulfillment and content, where will we find it? Kerr, the mediator-innovator, must become a gladiator—pioneering new paths in intergroup relations and giving new vitality to democratic standards that rest on knowledge.

ACADEMIC FREEDOM

ACADEMIC FREEDOM AND THE RIGHTS OF STUDENTS*

BY SIDNEY HOOK, PROFESSOR OF PHILOSOPHY,
NEW YORK UNIVERSITY

Americans are accustomed to reading about universities as storm centers of political disturbance in Latin and Asiatic countries. In a country like the United States, however, most criticism of student bodies in the past has been directed against their political apathy. The fact, therefore, that a building was seized by students at the Berkeley campus of the University of California, bringing all administrative activities to a halt, that a strike was declared, paralyzing teaching, and that the governor of the most populous state in the Union, after the arrest of some 800 students, felt it necessary to appeal for problems to be solved "by evolution not revolution," should give not only educators but all reflective citizens pause. It has focused attention upon a question of considerable complexity —the rights, and the responsibilities, of students.

Since so much of current controversy and agitation swirls around the slogans of freedom, the first question to be asked is: do students enjoy the right of *academic* freedom? This depends on what is meant by "academic freedom." Perhaps the best short definition was offered by Arthur O. Lovejoy, the founder together with John Dewey, of The American Association of University Professors.

> "Academic freedom," he wrote, "is the freedom of the teacher or research worker in higher institutions of learning to investigate and discuss the problems of his science and to express his conclusions whether through publications or the instruction of students, without interference from political or ecclesiastical authority, or from the administrative officials of the institution in which he is employed, unless his methods are found by qualified bodies of his own profession to be clearly incompetent or contrary to professional ethics."

A number of interesting implications may be drawn from this definition. First, academic freedom exists primarily for "teachers" in the comprehensive sense of that term. Strictly

* A shorter version of this article was published in *The New York Times Magazine*, January 3, 1965, pp. 8–9, 16, 18.

speaking, it is nonsense to speak of "academic freedom" for students. Students have a right to *freedom to learn*. The best guarantee of freedom to learn is the academic freedom of those who teach them. Where teachers are deprived of academic freedom, students are *ipso facto* deprived of the freedom to learn.

The converse, however, is not true. It is simply false both logically and historically to assert that "freedom to teach and freedom to learn are indivisible." For many things may interfere with the student's freedom to learn, e.g., poverty, racial discrimination, inadequate transportation, which have no relevance whatsoever to academic freedom. The latter may flourish in institutions to which students are unjustly denied the opportunity to enter. The movement to abolish poverty, discrimination and other social evils in order to give students access to education and to effective freedom to learn, flows from their *moral* rights as persons and from their *civil* rights as citizens. They are not corollaries of academic freedom. To deny this would make the university responsible for the entire state of society and its reform. The educational task which the university faces is heavy enough—the development of mature, thoughtful, imaginative, and knowledgeable students capable of making their own personal and political decisions in our changing social world. To expect the university, in addition to maximizing the student's opportunity and freedom to learn when it accepts him, to take on also the tasks of other social and political agencies is to divert it from its primary responsibility.

Secondly, academic freedom is not a civil right like freedom of speech. A teacher who is dropped or refused a post on grounds of incompetence, say because in an attempt to convert his students to a sect or party he teaches that the earth is flat or that the Elders of Zion are engaged in conspiracy to destroy America or that Communists are twentieth century Jeffersonian democrats, is not being deprived of freedom of speech. For he can still proclaim his discovery from the housetops. As a citizen he can talk nonsense without let or hindrance. But in order to talk "nonsense" in the academy with impunity—and strange things can be heard within it—a teacher must win the right to do so by certification from his peers as competent, and have acquired tenure. Sometimes what sounds like nonsense to the plain citizen may be the birth of a revolutionary discovery.

What is the relation between the student's freedom to learn and his freedom of speech? Here, too, there is no direct connection. The controlling consideration on the campus must be the student's freedom to learn. Whatever restrictions exist on the student's freedom of speech—aside from those which exist on the freedom of all citizens—must be justified by the educational needs of students and of reasonable institutional provisions for their expression. It is one thing to set up a miniature Hyde Park on some corner of the campus and encourage students to use it. It is another to allow them to call a mass meeting on Prexy's lawn at dawn.

Thirdly, responsibility for the certification of competence, and for interpreting and applying the rules of tenure, must ultimately lie in the hands of the faculty whose agency the administration is or should be. This also extends to the educational standards students are required to measure up to. Students may be free to learn but sometimes unfortunately they don't learn enough. Students, too, therefore must earn the right to continue as students. Higher education therefore is not a civil right. A person does not have to earn the right to a fair trial or freedom of speech, press or assembly. But he must earn the right to become and remain a university student.

Fourth, an important aspect of the faculty's responsibility for the entire educational enterprise is its ultimate control of the educational facilities of the campus, classrooms and meeting halls, etc., and over the conditions of their exercise. This has a bearing, as we shall see, on some crucial questions.

The extent to which these implications can be implemented is affected by the fact that in some American higher institutions of learning *legal* authority is vested in a Board of Regents, and in all other institutions in a corporate governing Board of laymen. There is no practicable way of reversing this historical trend. Immense progress, however, has been made in winning over those who have legal authority to the acceptance of enlightened principles of academic freedom, which in effect entrust the determination and execution of educational policy to the faculties. The future to a large extent depends upon the persuasiveness and wisdom of the faculties themselves in shaping sound educational policy.

The observance of these principles of academic freedom in America has been a gradual and sometimes painful development. Today academic freedom is in a more flourishing state than it has ever been in its history. Only when one realizes how many and how onerous were the religious, political and social restrictions upon the teacher's freedom of teaching and inquiry in the past, can one grasp the remarkable progress made. What is true for the teacher's academic freedom is also true for the student's freedom to learn. My own life time spans a period from relative classroom tyranny to open inquiry. I recall that during my freshman year in college, I gave two reports in a class in political science. In the first I defended Beard's approach to the Constitution to the manifest disapproval of the teacher. In the second, I argued that Calhoun's logic in the famous debates was superior to that of Webster's. This was too much for the instructor who interrupted and ejected me from the class with the indignant observation: "When you aren't preaching sedition, you are preaching secession!"

Conditions today, of course, are not uniform and the situation which obtains at New York University and Harvard and other large liberal institutions will not be found in some small colleges especially in the South. But almost everywhere the climate of opinion and practice on these matters is healthier than it was. The battle is never finally won, for even one violation of academic freedom is one too many. But whenever a case arises, the odds for victory are today heavily in favor of the protagonists of academic freedom.

The issues which agitate campuses today are more likely to arise from the behavior of students than from the actions of members of the faculty. The causes for this are many, and too complex for adequate treatment in brief compass. Some observers locate the source of student restlessness in the conflict of generations but this is unconvincing since generational conflict, to the extent that it exists, is constant, while student moods of revolt are not. Others explain it by the fact that not all students can be caught up in the intellectual excitement created by the rising standards of excellence in the colleges, and the increasing intellectual demands being made on them. This leaves a considerable group of students frustrated and alienated, unable to find satisfaction in curricular studies oriented more and more to graduate and professional work. They find outlets by raising hell under the banner of any apparently good cause. Still other observers seek the causes of students' malaise in the world situation and its succession of crises. But, how then, explain the very few who are affected? For the noise of students' disturbances and rebellions is rarely a reliable index of the numbers involved. A small, well-organized determined group can throw an entire campus into uproar and keep it there by provoking ill-considered actions by faculty or administration and then progressively broadening student opposition.

Whatever the causes and whatever the extent of student restlessness, there are various kinds of issues over which difficulties are likely to arise on the campus, leading to student agitation and protest. Some flow from the rules governing the students' personal and social behavior on the campus; some from efforts to regulate the extra-curricular political activities of students both on and off the campus.

Fundamental confusion, and sometimes needless controversy, have developed over the rights and responsibilities of students because of a failure to distinguish between two sets of related questions. The first arise from the area of conduct in which students may justifiably exercise their rights as persons and citizens. The second arises from activities that have a direct educational bearing, that are related to the specific function of the college and to the business which presumably brings the student to school rather than elsewhere. These are questions on which the student should have ample opportunity to discuss, inquire, criticize and consult with the faculty but with respect to which the faculty must ultimately exercise its professional, educational authority. This cannot be challenged whether by administrators, public or students without undermining academic freedom.

To indicate the relevance and fruitfulness of this distinction let us examine some of the concrete issues which have provoked controversy in recent years. The first concerns the personal morality of students. Unfortunately personal morality for many people refers exclusively to sexual behavior. Properly understood, it embraces every form of individual conduct whose consequences have some bearing on the welfare of others. On the assumption that in institutions of higher learning, we are not dealing with children, the standards of personal deportment should initially be left to the students themselves. It is necessary, however, in the interest of the safety of students to establish rules and regulations governing the use of cars, liquor, drugs, smoking and visits to dormitories. Wherever possible these rules should be administered by the students themselves. Anything students can properly do for themselves as adults should be left to them. To student self-government, broad-based and representative, can be entrusted many of the functions incidental to organized student life in the college community. Since in time, friction and faction may generate student feuds, the faculty cannot forego exercising some oversight as a kind of appeals body to see that fair play is done. But at the age at which most students attend the university, educators cannot stand *in loco parentis* to them. A proper education requires that students achieve some independence of their parents. Otherwise they unduly prolong their childhood and stunt their intellectual and emotional growth.

What about fraternities and sororities? Do not these traditional forms of student life fall completely within the sphere of the students' personal freedom to choose their friends and associates? If these are student affairs, why should faculties meddle with them? The answer is that the faculty always retains the right of intervention in student school affairs whenever they adversely affect the integrity of the educational process. The faculty should possess enough expertise to know not only what an education is good for, but what a good education is. It is therefore justified in controlling and even abolishing fraternities altogether, whenever there is evidence that the consequences of fraternity life are prejudicial to the kind of educational experience deemed desirable for the students. It is of the first importance, when such restrictions are necessary, that the educational grounds of the action be spelled out and carefully explained. The appearance of arbitrariness should be avoided and the students treated as responsible adult persons until they give evidence to the contrary.

Should students be permitted to organize political groups on the campus or invite speakers of extremist political views to address them? It is problems of this kind which have occasioned the bitterest campus controversies and not problems of purely personal behavior. And here the failure to define the issue properly prevents asking the right kinds of question and bringing the relevant considerations to bear. A student request which may have considerable educational validity may be wrongfully denied because it is mistakenly put forward as a political demand or a demand for "free speech." This is particularly true with respect to who should be allowed to speak on a university campus. This normally has nothing to do with the question of free speech or academic freedom. Political speakers can reach students in many ways and by various media. The control of college facilities, as we have seen, must ultimately lie in the hands of the faculties. If they do not permit the use of college facilities to individuals outside of the academic community, they are not denying the civil right of freedom of speech to speakers, who can easily address students off-campus, or the civil right of freedom to listen to students who have ready access to such speakers. This is a false issue.

The genuine issue is the *educational* one. It is on educational, not on political grounds, that the valid case can be made for the rule permitting recognized student organizations to invite speakers of their choice to the campus to discuss any topic no matter how controversial. The educational process cannot and should not be confined merely to the classroom. Students should be encouraged to pursue their educational interests on their own initiative. Contemporary issues which convulse society are legitimate subjects of inquiry. They naturally will spill over any boundaries that may be erected between school and society.

Faculties and administrations often suffer from educational timidity. They are unduly fearful of the effect on their "public image" (horrid phrase!) when a speaker of extremist views, Fascist or Communist, is invited to the campus. Actually if a college is doing a proper educational job, it doesn't require Fascist or Communists to give students instruction about Fascism or Communism. But so long as students want to hear such speakers—often to see them in the flesh and to find out how they mentally tick if they tick at all—there can be no reasonable *educational* objection to their appearance, particularly if it is made clear that such speakers do not represent the views of the student body or faculty. If the students and faculty cannot cope with the rhetoric and "argument" of the Lincoln Rockwells and Gus Halls, then the college is failing badly in its educational task. In an open and honest forum, the cause of freedom and democracy can triumph over all challengers. And as for the vaunted "public image" of the college, usually the controversies and newspaper publicity attendant upon banning a speaker are far more damaging than the one-day sensation provided by his appearance. For one thing seems assured by experience. A prolonged controversy over an invitation to an extremist almost always guarantees him an overflow audience when he does finally appear.

Viewing matters primarily from the standpoint of the students' educational growth is difficult for faculties because most members think of themselves merely as teachers of specialized, individual subjects only, and not as educators concerned with the total educational pattern. It is proper educational concern, and not political consideration, which suggests where to draw the line of control on student activities, if and when there is need to draw it. In the rare cases in which the need for control does arise, the failure on the part of the faculty to draw the line means that it has abdicated from its educational responsibilities. Sometimes students, unfortunately abetted by junior faculty assistants who are themselves still emotional adolescents, will try to break up the meetings of speakers with whom they disagree. Whether these elements are subversives or patrioteers, a self-respecting faculty cannot tolerate such activities. From time to time, outside groups send professional organizers onto the campus of large metropolitan universities to recruit students and to provoke incidents with the administration and faculty. Sometimes they pose as graduate students, sometimes not. They are exceptionally skilled in the art of fanning sparks of discontent into fire storms. Only a few are necessary to make students feel that minor grievances are matters of life and death.

Occasionally, a small group of genuine students, zealots in some cause, will under false pretenses violate rules of fair discussion and honest advocacy. I could fill a volume describing the stratagems of this kind I have observed over a life-time. On a certain campus, for example, a few students will organize a "Free Speech Forum" or something else with a libertarian flavor. Their first speaker will be Lincoln Rockwell or some one of his kidney. Thereafter, featured as "a reply" to Fascism, will come a succession of Communist or extreme left-wing speakers, sometimes paid from general student or school funds. Great care is taken not to invite an anti-Communist liberal to present a genuine alternative. The "educational" point of the Forum is to build up Communism in its various disguises as the only real answer to Fascism. Complaints are met with the statement that liberals *have* been invited but they have refused to come. The evidence? A carbon letter of an invitation to a liberal figure two thousand miles or more distant, the original of which, on inquiry, it turns out he never received. Where representatives of the student body are unable to prevent dishonest educational practices of this kind, the faculty is justified in stepping in.

The same general principles should govern student publication. On educational grounds, students should be encouraged to publish their own newspapers, periodicals, and brochures, exchanging ideas, commenting on great issues, testing and challenging their teachers' views. But it would be ridiculous to say that this freedom is absolute and exempts them from those restraints against slander and libel which would be legally actionable if published off-campus. In fact where the institution is the publisher, it is legally liable for what appears in the student press. Particularly obnoxious is the circulation of anonymous literature on campus defaming members of the student body or faculty. Only those who imagine they can be liberal without being intelligent will deny that faculty intervention in situations of this character is justifiable. Just as there may be some actions by teachers (like plagiarism from something in the public domain) which may not violate a law, and yet violate basic standards of professional ethics, so there may be some student actions and false charges that may not be strictly illegal in the community at large but which cannot be countenanced on a campus if orderly educational procedures are to be maintained. The very fact that speech can be used not only for advocacy—which is permissible—but for *incitement* to illegal action—which is not—as well as to defame and slander, shows how absurd it is to hold that the "content" of speech can never be relevant, or its utterances penalized. There should be no prior censorship, of course, unless there is convincing evidence that a speaker plans to incite to violence. Some ritualistic liberals unable to distinguish between heresy and conspiracy contest this. We do not have to wait for a mob to actually move to lynch someone before we justifiably stop the agitator who is inciting them. In general if an act is criminal, then words which *incite* to its performance are criminal.

What about the organization on-campus of off-campus illegal activity? If it does not concern a direct educational interest of the university, like illegal picketing, discipline should be left to the civil authorities. But if it affects an educational interest, like objectionable conduct against faculty or fellow-students, the university may exercise discipline independently of the civil power. Each case must be judged separately. Demands for complete immunity from university discipline for such activity or rules penalizing all such activity are equally absurd.

The irony of the situation is that students in our mass institutions of learning suffer today far more from the failure of faculties to attend to the students' individual *educational* needs than from alleged suppression of their freedom of speech. The students' freedom to learn is frustrated by the crowding, the inferior staffing, by the indifference of many faculties to the best methods and techniques of effective classroom teaching. Colleges still operate on the absurd assumption that anyone who knows anything can teach it properly, and rarely train their teachers in the elements of the difficult art of teaching. It is an open scandal that the worst teaching in the American system of education take place on the college level. In some universities large introductory sections, where skillful teaching is of strategic importance in arousing student interest, are turned over to young, inexperienced graduate assistants at the outset of their studies who stumble along by trial and error, and groping imitation of models of teaching vaguely remembered. No wonder they sometimes play up to students, join them in their inchoate resentments against the educational establishment out of a kind of compensatory *camaraderie* for their own educational inadequacy. Some observers charge that unless conditions change, the real revolt on the campus will some day be directed against the shoddy educational treatment to which students have been subjected. As the numbers of students grow, the educational situation deteriorates. The excellent scholar-teacher sees less of the students than the mediocre teacher.

No paradigm case, no set of rules governing student-faculty relations can settle in advance all problems that arise on a campus. A sense of proportion, a pinch of humor, and a draught of common sense are wonderful specifics against friction but they obviously cannot be prescribed. They vanish, however, in a display of the ultimatistic spirit on either side. Both students and faculty have a shared interest in keeping the educational enterprise going. When problems and difficulties arise, they should be routed through recognized channels of petition, complaint and protest. The officially elected representatives of the student body should meet periodically with the representatives of the voting faculty which, when grave issues are at stake, should sit as a committee of the whole.

Actions on the part of any group of students, even when they feel they have a legitimate grievance, to short-circuit official school channels, to appeal over the heads or behind the backs of the representative student body for mass demonstrations, strikes, to threaten force and violence or to resort to passive resistance should be condemned by both students and faculty. For such tactics are not only disastrous to the preservation of an atmosphere in which teaching and learning can take place, they prejudice the chances for reaching mutually satisfactory settlements. The so-called Free Speech Movement at the University of California had every right to press for the modification of university rules governing campus and off-campus activities of students. What was shocking, however, was its deliberate boycott and by-passing of the Associated Students, the elected representatives of the student body. It neither used all the existing channels of protest or sought to avail itself of some remedies open to it. Offensive also was the demagogic and odious comparison drawn by some students between the situation at the university, which despite all existing restrictions is still more liberal by far than most other institutions, with the situation in the state of Mississippi. Worst of all was the resort to the tactic of mass civil disobedience, justified only in extreme situations in behalf of basic principles of freedom. Except in such extreme situations, changes in the laws of a democratic community must be made by practices *within* the law.

According to some observers, almost as shocking as the action of the students (more than 10% of whom were outsiders, and not students at all!) in seizing university property was the failure of the faculty of the university to condemn the action. Indeed, by failing to couple their appeal for an amnesty for the offenders with a sharp condemnation of their action, the faculty indirectly seemed to condone the students' behavior. Apparently those who wanted to be heroes were to be spared the consequences of their heroism. If a faculty does not teach that grievances in a democratic community as a rule must be corrected by procedures provided by the democratic process, what can be expected of their students? And for teachers to dismiss classes out of sympathy with a student strike against the university is a dereliction of professional duty.

The administration of the University of California is blameworthy in its arbitrary abrogation of existing campus practices. It failed to read properly the signs of student unrest and dissatisfaction. The faculty should have been brought into the picture much earlier, entrusted with the formulation of the rules of discipline, after consultation with the official representatives of the student body, and with the enforcement of the rules when they were breached.

The most disquieting aspect of the situation at the University of California was the extremism of the student leaders, the extent to which they were willing to go, the contemptuous and disingenuous account its organizers give of their behavior. One of them called illegal actions which might easily have resulted in mass hysteria, panic and loss of life "controversial measures to begin a dialogue." Students' concern with the proper content and method of their education is sure to grow and should be encouraged. But if they are going to lie down, seize buildings and call strikes whenever their demands are not granted by faculty and administration, it bodes ill for the educational future.

Even before recent events transpired, I read literature distributed by a strong student group at the University of California calling for "the total elimination of course, grade, and unit system of undergraduate learning", and urging other proposals not all of them as silly. But what definitely is not silly or funny, in the light of what has happened, is the injunction to the students to resort ultimately to "civil disobedience" to get their way! This would open the doors to educational chaos. There apparently are some groups on the campus that want their victims and martyrs.

I do not belong to that school of thought, if it can be called that, which always accepts "the argument of the slippery slope." In the present instance this is tantamount to believing that once a concession is made to students or a disciplinary violation overlooked, the result is necessarily anarchy. But it is a safe bet to anyone who knows the psychology of students, that once they get away with the tactic of civil disobedience in protesting a *minor* rule which, if unjust, can be modified by negotiation, their demands will grow wilder and more unreasonable, and their conduct apace.

In the long run a deplorable educational situation in a college or university, reflects more on the faculty than on the students. For the faculty must take the responsibility for the education of the students and hopefully for what they learn. The overwhelming majority of students are reasonable except when carried away in moments of excitement by well-organized pressure groups. It is a sobering thought that hundreds of thousands of American students took "the Oxford Oath" in the mid-thirties pledging themselves never to bear arms in defense of their own country just when Hitler was girding himself for war against the democracies. Many of them withdrew that pledge with their lives. The disguised leadership of the Oxford pledge movement was mainly Communist.

No service is done to students by flattering them or by giving them the impression they can acquire an education in any other way than by accepting the hard intellectual disciplines of the logic of ideas and events. They cannot be encouraged too much to broaden their intellectual interests, and they certainly should not be discouraged from giving expression to their generous enthusiasm for civil rights, for human welfare, for peace with freedom. But good works off the campus cannot be a substitute for good work on the campus. Ultimately, the good causes for which our society always stands in great need, have a better chance of triumphing if their servitors equip themselves with the best education our colleges and universities can give them.

ACADEMIC FREEDOM AND STUDENT POLITICAL ACTIVITY*

BY JACOBUS TEN BROEK, NORMAN JACOBSON, AND
SHELDON S. WOLIN, PROFESSORS OF POLITICAL SCIENCE,
BERKELEY

What distinguishes man from the other species is that in addition to wishing to live, he wishes to live well. Living well, the search for the good life, means living not only in the here and now but in the past, not only in the past, but for the future. From this perspective, the function of a university is to contribute to the possibility, for all men, of living well. This contribution has seemed most obvious in the realm of science and technology where the goods involved appear most tangible and beyond dispute. But even here it will be seen that rarely is the entire society immediately grateful for the discovery of a new process or the development of a new instrument. Fear of the unknown and distrust of the unfamiliar are a powerful motive against novelty. It is no wonder then that ideas, and especially ideas about politics and society, should also engender fear and distrust. The part of us that wishes simply to live as distinguished from the part that wishes to live well is marvelously conservative. Living within a familiar and comfortable reality is not only more pleasant, it serves as a salutary check upon constant experimentation likely to end in chaos. Form is a good not to be despised. But after all, the responsibility for the defense of the familiar is so generously diffused throughout society, and manifest in such a preponderance of our institutions and practices, that there exists a danger of atrophy through thoughtlessness. The university, alone among all our institutions, has traditionally upheld the responsibility for maintaining intact a necessary dedication to the creation and testing of new ideas.

So far so good, sound doctrine bearing the seal of ancient theory and practice. Yet, in a strange reversal of customary roles, it is not the society against which the academician now seeks protection for his ideas and experiments. He finds himself in the anomalous position of having to defend them against his erstwhile protectors, those charged with the authority to administer the academy itself.

The finest passions of our people are presently enlisted in the cause of redressing profound political and social injustice. From the highest courts of the land, from the Congress and

---

* This is a selection from a legal brief prepared on behalf of the students arrested during the sit-in of December 2 and 3, 1964.

the state legislatures, from the words and deeds of Presidents, as well as from the exhortations of great men in and out of the universities, young people are instructed in the part they may play in the quest for justice. No wonder that our students feel bewildered when their own university impedes realization of the teaching of the times. No wonder they feel betrayed in their search for justice when those who run the university, and who of all people might be expected to sympathize with the nobility of their passion, have worked instead to hinder them. Where once the members of the academy had been forced to fall back upon privilege to carry out their necessary tasks, they now find themselves seeking to defend their rights as citizens against those within the university who would deprive them of these rights.

Academic freedom has traditionally centered around three types of activities: inquiries aimed at extending the boundaries of knowledge and testing new ideas and theories; the critical re-examination of accepted ideas, theories, and beliefs; and the communication, sharing, and refinement of ideas, knowledge, and theories with other interested members of the academic community and with the community at large. Both principle and experience testify that these activities are best performed if a university is able to sustain an environment which encourages these activities to the fullest and protects them from invasion from without as well as erosion from within.

As a result of its efforts to protect freedom of inquiry, criticism, and teaching, the university has acquired a special character. It has, for example, separated itself from the larger society in many ways: by physical location, by developing a distinctive way of life, by attempting to supply its own form of governance, and by providing a place where ideas and theories, known to be repugnant or strange to the rest of society, could be critically examined. Although there have been periods in which society or its authorities have challenged the immunities of the university and have inflicted severe penalties on its members, the distinctive nature of the university, as well as the special conditions of life which it requires, have come to be accepted in most parts of this nation. Today it is not difficult to persuade informed citizens that academic freedom is a vital necessity if there is to be scientific advance, technological innovation, and greater knowledge about man and society. What is not so readily understood is the relationship between freedom of inquiry and the activity of teaching, as well as the bearing of this relationship upon the political or social beliefs and actions of members of the academic community. No one doubts that university scientists ought to be free to test, to experiment, and to impart knowledge to their students. But there are many who might grow uneasy if this conception of academic freedom were applied to more controversial areas, such as political rights and social equality. So the Board of Regents and the university administration appear to have believed. The threat to academic freedom posed by their attitudes to student advocacy was immediate and substantial.

Certainly, academic freedom is peculiarly attached to the idea of a university and the aims of a university education. But it is not the only freedom possessed by the citizen to speak, to write, and to discuss. True, academic freedom has its own distinctive and honorable tradition, at least as old and perhaps older than that which governs the general freedom of speech. But the importance of speech and discussion to the university is first and foremost instrumental: it is indispensable to learning and indispensable to teaching. The very activity of education, for student and teacher alike, is the free exercise of open minds. Whenever in the pursuit of knowledge speech is guarded and minds are sealed, the educational dialogue deteriorates into monologue, arguable hypotheses harden into dogma, and the will to stimulate active inquiry yields to the demand for passive acceptance.

What transpires in such an atmosphere does not deserve the name of learning, but of conditioning. Closed minds, on the part of students, can doubtless be indoctrinated; they may even be trained; but they cannot be taught. Closed minds, on the part of professors, can issue directives; they may even give lectures; but they cannot teach. And closed circuits of communication between students and teachers can never conduct the intellectual spark by which the minds of students and teachers alike are ignited.

Academic freedom then is not an end in itself. It is an indispensable means to the unique objective of the university: that of the cultivation of minds and the provocation of thought. "Academic freedom and tenure," as Alan Barth has written in *The Loyalty of Free Men,* "are not privileges extended to the teaching profession, but a form of insurance to society that the teaching profession will be able to discharge its function conscientiously." To this it may be added that freedom of speech and advocacy are not privileges extended to students, but equally a form of insurance to society that the next generation of citizens will be able to discharge their functions and conduct their affairs conscientiously, reasonably, and responsibly.

It was this general conception of the purpose and spirit of academic freedom which Justice Frankfurter had in mind when he reminded us (*Wieman* v. *Updegraff,* 344 U.S. 183 [1952], at 195–197) that "public opinion is the ultimate reliance of our society only if it be disciplined and responsible. It can be disciplined and responsible only if habits of open-mindedness and of critical inquiry are acquired in the formative years of our citizens. . . . It is the special task of teachers to foster those habits of open-mindedness and critical inquiry which alone make for responsible citizens, who, in turn, make possible an enlightened and effective public opinion." And he warned that "unwarranted inhibition upon the free spirit of teachers . . . has an unmistakable tendency to chill that free play of the spirit which all teachers ought especially to cultivate and practice; it makes for caution and timidity in their associations by potential teachers."

Justice Frankfurter's reference to "potential teachers" points to a further aspect of academic freedom as it bears upon students. College students are not only citizens-in-training; they are also scholars-in-training. They are apprentice or junior members of the scholarly community, whose interest in open inquiry, speech and discussion is identical with that of their seniors. Of course not all will become teachers; but some of them will and any of them might. If they have learned their trade in a restrictive or fearful environment, they cannot be expected to practice it fearlessly and wisely when their turn comes to teach.

In the community of scholars which embraces teachers and students alike, the paramount need is to create and perserve a climate conducive to the growth of critical inquiry and independent thought. On its negative side, that need requires the exclusion of all irrelevant pressures and restraints which would interrupt the dialogue or qualify its practice. Affirmatively, it demands the provision of opportunities and incentives for the members of the community to enrich and enliven that joint activity. Such opportunities are not limited to the classroom, with its somewhat formal procedures and methods of instruction. The entire campus is but an extended classroom, replete at every turn with provocations to thought and prods to conversation. Anyone who has been a student knows the corollary and complementary values to formal education of such occasions as speeches, debates, group discussions, even coffee klatches and bull-sessions. It follows that these occasions and opportunities should be not merely tolerated but assiduously cultivated.

There is growing recognition today that students can no longer be treated as mere transients who "receive" an education from their teachers, but they must be accepted as a constituent part of the academic community. The rights and privileges of membership include not only the freedom to learn, to inquire, and to discuss, but the right to be treated with dignity and to be allowed to take a responsible part in the affairs of the community. The harassment, petty vindictiveness, and arbitrariness suffered by the students throughout the fall semester of 1964 indicate the utter failure of the university administration to understand how members of an ancient and proud community ought to treat one another.

A university is no longer an isolated enclave in which the members are content to exchange ideas among themselves and to train their successors. In every field of endeavor from science to social work, from literature to civil rights, there are representatives from the university in close contact with the outside world: as consultants, as decision-makers, as training-advisers, and as participants. The insularity of the university is rapidly falling before a growing belief that what is learned on the campus is not remote from life, but must be made central to life, and that this includes not only scientific knowledge, but the humane values which have been nourished in a climate of academic freedom and which call for translation into the relationships among men in the larger society.

If, in the present age, the boundaries of a campus symbolize a free community pledged to rational inquiry and not a closed community separated from the public world, there is pressing need to reaffirm the political rights, as well as the academic freedom of the members of the university. What is often denied them, not only outside the campus boundaries, but more recently inside, is the right to take their ideas seriously. Freedom to discuss and to inquire has been granted members of the academic community presumably in order to allow them to reflect, among other things, upon questions of human conduct, the dignity of the person, and the values of liberty, equality, and voluntary consent. But when students have sought to translate these ideas into campus practices and social realities, they have been hampered and discouraged by university restrictions severely infringing their rights as participating members of an academic community and as citizens of American society. Idle thought and idle talk make idle citizens.

It is no less true of freedom in the academy than of freedom in society that it requires regular and vigorous exercise if it is to survive and serve its ends. That exercise is found in continuous contest and criticism, the free competition of the academic marketplace. Students and faculty members who seek personal safety in the avoidance of all uncertain commitments and outrageous hypotheses do no service to the cause of higher education. In this connection, not the least of the constructive consequences which have followed upon the past semester of student activity at Berkeley has been the shock of recognition it has produced in the ranks of the faculty—the recognition, at last or once again, of the necessity to take their vocation seriously: to practice in the concrete what they have always preached in the abstract.

Recognition, not discovery, is the proper word, for there is nothing novel or uniquely modern about it. Wise men in other ages, concerned for the future of human liberty, have emphasized that rights and freedoms may be lost as readily by default as by defeat. In his majestic defense of freedom of thought and expression, *Areopagitica,* John Milton wrote: "Well knows he who uses to consider, that our faith and knowledge thrive by exercise, as well as our limbs and complexion. Truth is compared in Scripture to a streaming fountain; if her waters flow not in a perpetual progression, they sicken into a muddy pool of conformity and tradition." Two centuries later, John Stuart Mill returned to that theme in his essay *On Liberty:* "There have been, and may again be, great individual thinkers in a general atmosphere of mental slavery. But there never has been, nor ever will be, in that atmosphere an intellectually active people. . . . However unwillingly a person who has a strong opinion may admit the possibility that his opinion may be false, he ought to be moved by the consideration that, however true it may be, if it is not fully, frequently, and fearlessly discussed, it will be held as a dead dogma, not a living truth."

The recent events on the Berkeley campus were an expression of the deep concern of students for their rights of membership both in the university community and in the larger political society. It is a concern intimately connected to academic freedom, for it asks those who teach and those who administer whether the values encouraged by a free academic atmosphere could be taken seriously. Contrary to widespread impression, the students never contended that academic freedom constituted a license for breaking the law. What they have denied is that the perpetuation of the functions of a university requires that the political rights of students be inferior to those of citizens, and that political and social values must not be taken so seriously that members of the academic community would attempt to advocate or promote those values by political means.

THE NATURE OF A UNIVERSITY AND ACADEMIC FREEDOM

BY MARTIN MALIA,

PROFESSOR, DEPARTMENT OF HISTORY, BERKELEY

The present time is a troubled and potentially a tragic one for the University of California at Berkeley. Nevertheless, as far as the faculty is concerned, the crisis of this fall has had at least one fortunate if unintended consequence; for it has led us to think through, often for the first time, the meaning of a university whose nature and purpose we had hitherto taken for granted.

Much has already been done to clarify some of the issues at

stake, notably in the resolution of the Berkeley Division of the Academic Senate of December 8 calling for maximum freedom of speech, advocacy, and political action for the student body. Through this resolution, through the constructive initiatives of the Emergency Executive Committee of the Berkeley Division, and through the declaration of the Regents of December 18, great progress has been made toward guaranteeing to the students the effective exercise of their political rights under the First and Fourteenth Amendments. At the same time reasonable provisional rules governing the "time, place and manner of conducting political activity on the campus" have been put into effect by the acting chancellor. All responsible members of the faculty can only support these various actions and work for the successful consolidation of what has so far been accomplished.

However, other equally crucial issues raised by the present crisis have thus far remained unclarified by any public utterance of the faculty. Until now we have addressed ourselves solely to the problem of implementing on campus the political rights of the students; but we have said nothing about the problem of safeguarding the primary vocation of the university as an intellectual community and an educational institution; nor have we mentioned the role of the faculty itself, as the most enduring element of the university and the one most vitally interested in defending the academic, as distinguished from the political, liberties of all members of this community. In the *Interim Report* of the Emergency Executive Committee it is pertinently noted that: "The Resolution (of December 8) is based on the premise that the primary and central tasks of the University are teaching, learning and research." In accordance with this principle, the time has now come when the first concern of the faculty must be to define clearly, and to declare publicly, our primary responsibilities as scholars and educators both toward ourselves and toward the university community as a whole; by the same token, we must reassert those liberties necessary to the continuance and development of this institution as a sanctuary of free intellectual inquiry.

Throughout the present crisis there has existed considerable confusion as to the meaning and scope of "academic freedom." In an endeavor to dispel uncertainty on this all-important principle, the following distinction between academic and political freedom may be advanced. Political freedom in a democracy means the equal right of all members of society as citizens to speak out their convictions and to act upon them, subject to no restraints other than those that may be defined by the Constitution. It is only normal and just, therefore, that as citizens the members of an academic community should enjoy the same political liberties as all other members of society. Obversely, these liberties in no way derive from, nor are they augmented by, the status of teacher or student. Academic freedom, on the other hand, has a more restricted aim and applies to only one group in society. Membership in this group is not determined by any birthright of citizenship; it is conferred by attainment of a certain level of intellectual competence and by virtue of an enduring commitment to the quest for knowledge and understanding, pursued as a profession or, some might say, a vocation. Thus academic freedom refers only to the guarantee of effective conditions for the unfettered pursuit of this group's professional and intellectual, rather than civic, concerns.

Concretely, in the historical tradition of Western universities, academic freedom means that right for the members of a corporate intellectual community to inquire after truth and to disseminate the results of their investigations free from all extra-intellectual pressures, whether political, sectarian, or social; concomitantly, it means the right for the members of an educational institution to teach and to learn in similar freedom from outside interference. It is to guarantee this freedom of research and teaching, for example, that professors enjoy tenure—a privilege bestowed on no other group in modern society —which is not a form of social security, but a necessity deriving from the very nature of the profession and designed to confer immunity from political and economic reprisals on those whose calling is to pursue the quest for truth wherever it may lead.

To this view it might be objected that academic freedom is simply the application to a particular profession of the general, political right of free speech, and that academic freedom therefore increases only insofar as political freedom in surrounding society increases. Historically speaking, however, academic freedom is older than political freedom, and indeed was first successfully asserted in societies that otherwise permitted no liberty of expression, still less of action. Later on, of course, in the process of definitively emancipating universities from the sectarian control of churches or from the political control of authoritarian states, the progress of academic freedom came, in practice, to be ever more closely associated with that of political liberty; and it is certain that, under conditions of a modern mass society, a return to the authoritarian state would spell the end of the academic sanctuary. Nonetheless, our long association in arms with liberalism and democracy should not lead us to forget that there exist other potential menaces to academic freedom than traditional authoritarianism. One of these is the conformist or obscurantist pressure of society, even democratic society; another is the over-zealous pursuit of political causes, including even the noblest, and the indiscriminate resort to extremist tactics. For if the social utility or political relevance of ideas were to become a criterion for determining our right to profess them, academic freedom would be destroyed just as surely as by the demands of a sectarian church or an authoritarian state.

The concept of academic freedom set forth here will no doubt appear narrow, even asocial in its implications, to many members of the university community. To this it can be answered that in a democratic society we do not abdicate our status as citizens for assuming that of academics; and in the former role each of us is free to subscribe to the idea that knowledge, in order to be complete, must serve the needs of men, and to act accordingly through the political organization of his choice. But the faculty, as a faculty, cannot be committed to more than is outlined here. No conceivable political position can furnish a basis for consensus among the members of an academic body. Such a consensus can be founded only on dedication to the corporate interests of the university as an intellectual community and an educational institution.

In the context of the present crisis the practical consequences of the idea of the university stated here are, first of all, the following: so long as the fundamental conditions of academic freedom are met by society, the prime duty of the faculty, as the most permanent part of the university community, and the one most deeply committed to the intellectual calling, is to insure at all times the continued functioning of the university; this is incumbent upon us as inquirers after truth and as teachers, whatever may be our political convictions as citizens. Concretely, this means that we must refuse to condone, either implicitly or explicitly, the use, or the threatened use, of techniques of political coercion turned inward against the university and designed to disrupt or to halt its proper functioning; likewise, we must attempt by every intellectual means to dissuade both undergraduate and graduate students from having recourse to such techniques. For the employment against the university, with the intent to obtain political ends by hampering its research or teaching activities, of such practices as sit-ins and strikes in fact constitutes a violation of academic freedom, a subordination of the intellectual to the political, and a denial of the scholarly and educational purposes for which the university exists. The university is not the same as civil society, but is instead set off from it by dedication to a specific purpose and by possession of a constitution and usages peculiar to it alone. The political techniques that may be appropriate to the causes of surrounding society, when transferred to the campus, only undermine those privileges which alone have made universities possible. By this it is not meant that the faculty, speaking as the faculty, must declare itself for the maintenance of law and order in society at large, or pass on the appropriateness of civil disobedience in the furtherance of civil rights; for to do so would be to pretend to the exercise of judicial and political functions which are not ours as an academic body. Obversely, of course, the restricted scope of our corporate role in no way limits our freedom as citizens to participate in the political struggles of society.

Secondly, in the context of the current situation, the concept of the university defended here means that we must bend every effort to remedy the grave defects of Berkeley as an educational institution which, it is no exaggeration to claim, are the root-cause of the present crisis. Much that has been said in recent months by the students about the "factory" and the "machine" is true. Much that the faculty has long felt about the defects of the university's administrative and constitutional structure is equally worthy of attention. Much that all parties have experienced by way of insensitivity to legitimate grievances gives similar cause for concern. In the course of the present crisis mention has often been made of Berkeley as one of the "world's greatest universities." It would be more exact to say that Berkeley is an impressive assemblage of scholars, but an ill-structured organization, and an uneven or an indifferent school. In particular, we are distinctly more of a success as a research center and an intellectual community for the faculty than we are as an educational institution for the students. Much thought and long effort will be required to reform this situation; and no matter more urgently demands the consideration of the senate. But such consideration can be given, and such reform come about, only if an ordered and reasonable atmosphere is first restored on the campus.

VI

Berkeley Students under
the Social Scientist's Eye

The favorite subject of study by social psychologists and sociologists for many years was their own students. An instructor could always give out a questionnaire to the captives sitting in front of him. Some would still argue that social psychology is essentially a study of sophomores who take Psychology I. We do not believe this. In any case academic progress has been made, and the opinion survey now permits students of opinion formation to gather data on general populations.

In Berkeley, however, social scientists have a good rationale for continuing to study students, since they are not just a captive audience, they also are political actors. And a sizable literature exists concerning the opinions of the students here. The current crisis has produced another crop of studies by faculty and students, and we know of more to come. In future months and years, many elaborately analyzed studies will be published. But those which are now available have much to say about the issues and the causes of the student reactions.

This section begins with a perspective on student politics by a member of the History Department. It shifts to two studies by sociologists of past student opinions on comparable issues. These studies are relevant to the present since they indicate the kinds of factors that affected reactions to civil-liberties issues before the present controversy are similar to those at work most recently. The final group of two articles are based on questionnaires distributed during the heat of the fight.

THE STUDENT MOVEMENT AT BERKELEY:
SOME IMPRESSIONS
BY HENRY MAY,
PROFESSOR, DEPARTMENT OF HISTORY, BERKELEY

This is not a historical survey of the Free Speech Crisis at Berkeley. The events of the fall of 1964 have been well and repeatedly summarized. Here in Berkeley these events—the sudden suspension of certain student political privileges, the defiance and violations, the attempted arrests and the blocking of the police car, the agreements and negotiations which always broke down, the concessions which came too late, the final student occupation of Sproul Hall, the resultant mass arrests and the ensuing strike—all these have become as familiar as the events which led up to the French or Russian revolutions. And like the events of these big revolutions, the events of our little one sound distressingly different in the versions given by equally honest men of differing political emotions.

Another thing—this is not an attempt to assess the blame for our conflict. The ineptness of the administration and the unwieldiness of our huge institution, both major causes of the trouble, have been dealt with again and again. Here, my sole concern is with the students. They were, as I saw it, the actors: faculty and administration merely reactors. They won major victories, they have great power here, and they are being watched—with anticipation or foreboding—on other campuses of the nation.

My approach toward the Free Speech Movement and its constituency is necessarily that of an outsider, though I have talked to members and sympathizers a good deal and attended a good many of the open rallies. To supplement what immediate knowledge I have, I must rely on two kinds of analogy. First, in the mid-thirties I was a student at Berkeley and cannot help comparing this generation of students to my own. Second, I am by profession a student and teacher of American intellectual history, and I cannot talk or think about any popular movement without other movements coming to my mind.

In some ways students in Berkeley have changed a lot since the thirties. They are more intelligent now. The university is harder to get into, and many enter from "enriched" high school courses. Telegraph Avenue, the "Left Bank" area near the campus, now offers an intellectual bill-of-fare of almost indigestible richness. It is easier to find Italian, French, or Japanese movies than Hollywood products near the university. Bookstores offer everywhere overwhelming displays of the latest paperbacks in philosophy, religion, and pornography. A wide range of magazines and newspapers of dissent, displayed everywhere around the campus, plead all possible and impossible causes.

Many students are nourished and stimulated by this fare. It is not surprising to find sophomores who read Sartre and Camus in the time they can spare from their assignments. Yet now, even more than in the thirties, range and excitement are commoner than intellectual discipline. Languages, including English, are seldom a bright student's strongest point. History, particularly European history, attracts great numbers, but this does not indicate that students are at all traditionalist. Institutions of the past make few claims on people who have not yet managed to feel any great identity with institutions in the present. Formal systems of thought—abandoned anyway in philosophy departments, attract no allegiance; the students are likely to be eclectic and experimental. The more rigid simplifications, including Marxist ones, fall apart under their uncommitted scrutiny.

The best quality of Berkeley students is their uncompromising effort to be honest with themselves and others. The defensive, pseudo-sophisticated pursuit of intellectual fashion which plagues some colleges is the last thing one need worry about here. Whether one talks to our students about politics, religion, or art one feels that as they listen they are trying to decide, somewhat warily, what they believe and like—not what is In or Out. Despite all that has been said, justly but too simply, about the university's concentration on research; despite the heartbreaking problems of teaching undergraduates in such numbers; I know some faculty members who refuse high salaries elsewhere and stay in Berkeley not for prestige, libraries, or climate but for Berkeley's undergraduate students.

The nature of the student body in general has much to do with the shape of the radical movement which has grown up here. In the thirties, notoriously and also in actuality, the student movement was ranged in concentric circles around a Communist core. The Communists, open or secret—and there were both kinds—repelled most students by their pomposity of manner and language. Yet the causes Communists espoused in those days of the United Front were everybody's causes: liberal unemployment relief, racial equality, and particularly international peace. In the late thirties, among "student leaders," it actually became fashionable and respectable to dabble a little in the movement. Thus there was a fairly clear series of stages or levels of radicalism, from fellow-travelers to on-and-off sympathizers and beyond them to respectable but worried liberals. Beyond all these, of course, was a very large group—larger then than now, of students who were interested in dates and athletics and not at all in politics.

Today, a free-form figure, or even a mobile, has to be used instead of a system of concentric circles to symbolize the political make-up of the Berkeley campus. At the center there is still a group of dedicated, more or less full-time radical leaders. At the edge of the picture a large semi-student fringe fades by imperceptible shadings into the immediate background. And in between is a large and rapidly shifting mass of students, sometimes indifferent, but occasionally, in particular crises that involve their strong feelings, suddenly moved to dramatic action in thousands. Each of these three parts of our picture, the radical leadership, the semi-student fringe, and the shifting, potentially active mass needs separate definition before a pattern can even begin to emerge.

In discussing the full-time leadership, one is led, regrettably but inevitably, to the Communist question. In discussions of the FSM, as of other American radical movements, Communist influence has been both irresponsibly exaggerated and uncritically denied, and probably given too much importance in both cases. Grizzled and battle-scarred Stalinist veterans of the thirties are certainly on hand in Berkeley, as are shrill young devotees of Mao and Castro. A few of the leaders of the Free Speech Movement have themselves linked the student struggle with the Cuban Revolution and the super-militant tactics of the Progressive Labor Movement. Yet insiders report that the orthodox Marxist minority in the movement has often opposed the direct-action tactics—to them unrealistic—that have proved so successful. In the leadership, Communism exists but is probably unimportant. Various kinds of socialism, unaffiliated radicalism, and above all ultra-militant devotion to the civil rights movement are inextricably mixed together.

The relation between radical leadership of any kind and large-scale student support is very tenuous. It has been demonstrated that the thousand who occupied Sproul Hall were mostly without political affiliation or experience, and this is doubtless true also of the thousands more who supported the student strike. Yet it is not irrelevant that an experienced radical leadership has existed in Berkeley since long before the administrative mistakes that immediately produced the current crisis. At least since the so-called "San Francisco riots" of 1960 (the much misinterpreted protest against the House Un-American Activities Committee) Berkeley has been something of a radical Mecca. Some administrative quarters, here and elsewhere, have claimed that Berkeley is the first target of a deliberate nationwide drive which will later hit all major campuses. I have no knowledge whatever that this is (or is not) so, but more than one graduate student has told me frankly that he chose Berkeley partly because of the movement. Some former undergraduate leaders stay around and lend a hand.

Since 1960, the student movement has carried on guerrilla war with the Kerr administration over a set of presidential directives which then attempted, plausibly but unrealistically, to define the rights and duties of several distinct and complicated categories of undergraduate organizations. Since then, important concessions have been made and student victories won. By this fall, it was nonsense to talk about a "climate of oppression" in Berkeley. Students, by observing certain forms and rules, could *say* (though in theory they could not *do*) what they wanted. The climate was rather one of bureaucracy. It is particularly hard to explain to our students why a given kind of organization can have open meetings but not membership meetings on the campus, why Communism or free love may be advocated here but not there, as long as one has an associate or full professor—but not an assistant professor —as chairman. All these rules had their historical *raisons d'être,* but this kind of history is not a favorite subject here.

Last year, the movement's center of attention shifted with new intensity to the compelling cause of civil rights. Berkeley contributed a few students to Mississippi and many to militant demonstrations in the Bay region. And finally, at the beginning of the fall term of 1964, before administration errors revived the question of campus political action, a publication of the left student organization called Slate seemed to suggest another major shift of emphasis, this time to the alleged outrages of the academic "system" itself. A Slate pamphlet called for "AN OPEN, FIERCE, AND THOROUGHGOING REBELLION ON THIS CAMPUS," demanding that grades be eliminated in the social sciences and humanities, rules be abolished in university housing units, and negotiations undertaken about the question of examinations. Ways suggested to achieve these dazzling goals included civil disobedience at university public ceremonies and maybe "a mass student strike . . . something which seems unthinkable at present."

Thus, before the outbreak of the recent controversy and the formation of the Free Speech Movement, an experienced, tough, continuing radical leadership existed. The leadership of the new movement consisted partly of oldtimers, partly of newcomers.

In one unpleasant way the Free Speech Movement seems more reminiscent of the Communist-led "United Front" movements of the thirties than it really is. These always started with lists of respectable constituent organizations and impeccable liberal objectives. The key posts however were always filled by the tried and true, who somehow ended in firm control. The FSM, formed this October to protest new political regulations, originally included representatives of radical, liberal, and even conservative student groups, and also of student religious organizations. Before long, however, the moderate groups fell away, and it became obvious that the movement was dominated by militants. The process in the two instances was different. In the thirties, radical caucuses consciously arranged to run the "United Fronts." In the FSM, extreme tactics, derived from the civil-rights movement, were I believe invoked without much planning in response to administration blunders. These tactics alienated moderates but drew sudden waves of student mass support which far outran, for short periods, the expectations of the most radical leaders.

Much has been said about the non-students, radical or Bohemian, who surround our campus in considerable numbers. Tourist buses stop near Telegraph Avenue, so that sightseers can goggle at the "beatniks," with their bare feet, beards, and long, dirty hair. With luck, they may even hear a speech, by a well-known non-student character, in favor of marijuana.

Nothing irritates the FSM more than the newspaper charge that it is made up of a bunch of beatniks. During the height of the crisis some sitters-in and other protesters wrote to the local newspapers insisting angrily on their own high grades, clean clothes, and bourgeois habits. Yet to some, beards and sandals do represent part of a general protest against confining restrictions. And people who *look* like extreme caricatures of nineteenth-century Bohemians appear at all demonstrations. The FSM is indeed not Beat, but Beats favor, and perhaps slightly affect, the FSM.

Real Beats are usually non-students. Semi-students, a group more important here, may or may not be unconventional in behavior and dress. Many bright, attractive, and serious young people, often from bourgeois families, cannot bring themselves to accept for long either the discipline of grades and requirements, or the professional goals these sometimes imply. Disaffected by the campus program but fascinated by campus life, many are in and out of the university.

Among those who are in, out, and halfway, some students here and elsewhere suffer deeply, like many young people everywhere, from various kinds of psychic malaise. Resort to psychotherapy is almost as commonplace as getting treatment for mononucleosis. Student worries and even student neuroses are not peculiar to Berkeley or America. To some extent—I suspect a slight one—their immediate cause may indeed lie in the system of grades and examinations the student movement is always condemning. Students here take, as they took in the thirties, five courses at a time. Ambitious and even devoted professors have sometimes raised the requirements of individual courses to quite unrealistic levels. Thus students are harassed by too many examinations and papers—a fault which the crisis has brought to the university's attention and one which will be corrected. But it is hardly necessary to point out that student malaise comes from a whole range of causes, individual and cultural, which lie far beyond the power of the university to deal with.

The relation of psychic disorder to political unrest is complex. But I suspect that it is important, for the understanding of the Berkeley crisis, to remember that a considerable minority of young people here has withdrawn, in whole or in part, from conventional competition. These are, admirably in their way, impossible to deter by appeals for individual prudence. Fear of the security check and the police record has declined together with career ambition. For secession, some have paid a heavy price. Others are willing to pay it, and many more contemplate joining the seceders but keep one foot in respectability.

The main body of students who have supported the FSM in action belongs neither to the radical core nor to any kind of semi-student fringe. Many are apparently well-adjusted and highly successful students even in the most conventional terms of grades. Yet even among these, even among those least identifiable with any obvious source of unrest, many are asking ultimate questions in immediate and personal terms.

The most striking fact about the present generation, to me, is that large groups are both more idealistic and more alienated than any but a handful in the radical thirties. Not only is this student generation critical of the parents and the parental social order; it is often trained to be critical by the parents, themselves perplexed and somewhat guilty in their attitude toward their own times. Exposed early to a quite unprecedented range of ideas and committed to none, they will follow no leader consistently. But for the kind of immediate cause that stirs them, they will follow any leader or none very far.

The alienation of our students is social rather than political, and it is to this alienation that Mario Savio, far the most effective of the FSM leaders, is best able to speak. Always extreme but never sectarian, at times Messianic and—to adult ears—often skirting the edges of the ridiculous—Savio is the only leader who seems to represent a new genre, as different from the Slate leaders of 1960 as from the Marxists of the thirties. Many students, he says, find "that for them to become part of society, to become lawyers, ministers, business men, people in government, very often they must compromise those principles which were most dear to them, they must suppress the most creative impulses that they have; this is a prior condition for being part of the system." In the thirties most students, and particularly the Marxists, took the "system" more for granted than this.

The sort of potential radicalism I am describing finds few easy outlets. Normally, I believe, our students are not much stirred by politics. They will turn out to work against laws that interfere with free speech or menace racial integration, and the Peace Corps offers one real outlet for their zeal for personal, concrete involvement with the problems of the world. Johnson's profound political practicality fails to attract them; still less are most of them drawn toward the disciplined ruthlessness of the Communist world. I cannot imagine that sexual freedom presents, today, much of a fighting cause; the question now is more what to do with it than how to get it. Thus the civil-rights movement is the one organized effort which can claim their complete allegiance; it is personal, immediate, and revolutionary. The local sit-ins, shop-ins, and the like roused much white resentment, but scored some undeniable successes in forcing the employment of Negroes. The high purpose of these efforts, their achievements, and also the courage they demanded gave them unrivaled prestige.

From civil rights to free speech proved to be an easy road. One participant in the Sproul Hall FSM sit-in told me that he had long felt guilty about not participating in civil-rights civil disobedience. Perhaps, he thought, because of his conventional upbringing he had never been able to persuade himself that real integration could be brought about in this manner. The Sproul Hall sit-in, on the other hand, took place in the name of free speech—a cause he had been taught to consider an absolute, and this gave him a chance to prove his courage. This honest self-analysis may well be representative. Many argue plausibly that the relation between the two causes is a more concrete one, that the restrictions on campus political action were tightened because of outside resentment at civil-rights demonstrations. Some students devoutly believe that the efforts to suspend leaders of the demonstrations were intended to cripple the civil-rights cause.

In my opinion the links between the movements should not be allowed to obscure the differences. Surely it is not the same thing to stay in a restaurant for the purpose of insisting on one's moral and even legal rights and to occupy a university building for the stated purpose of obtaining a "capitulation" on matters of university regulations. Defying a dean, or even risking academic units, does not call for the same kind of heroism—or the same degree of anger—as defying an Alabama sheriff and risking one's life.

No cause other than these two could have made so many students follow the FSM leaders into the startling actions of this fall. And nothing but the cause of free speech—not even civil rights—could have drawn together the amorphous and shifting mass, together with some of the disaffected fringe, behind the experienced leadership. No other cause could have combined so many resentments, dispelled so many misgivings, and brought to the surface so much frustrated idealism.

If one looks, as I cannot help looking, to analogies in other times, one passes fairly quickly by the various forms of American proletarian radicalism. The IWW, with its free-speech fights and its insistent toughness of language and manner is closer than any kind of Marxism. But at its most effective, the FSM speaks a language very different from the studied truculence of syndicalist revolt. Like other movements of youthful rebellion in America, the FSM is far more deeply rooted in the national tradition than it seems, or than its members always realize.

In the person of Savio, the movement speaks with a voice that has been heard in America since the beginning, the voice of an exalted, quasi-religious romantic anarchism. For all of their toughness, some of the FSM are crypto-transcendentalists and neo-antinomians. It is interesting that the movement has been patronized by some though not all, of the Christian chaplains who surround our non-religious campus like holy wolves, waiting to pick off anyone who strays away from the secularist campfire. One of the most eloquent and penetrating early appraisals of the movement came from a Methodist minister who could not but approve moral outrage in the face of depersonalization. Despite the FSM's frequent ugliness of speech and action, this observer found to his own surprise "a remarkable gentleness and sweetness of spirit which comes out here and there as the life of the movement goes on."

In terms of standard American transcendentalism, Emerson is obviously too decorous and optimistic to furnish much support. The American ancestor most nearly admitted is Thoreau. In his wake Tolstoi and Gandhi, with their methods of passive resistance and their hatred of the machine, obviously provide some precedent for the sit-ins and also for the continual FSM denunciations of IBM cards and factory methods. One of the few relieving light moments in the tense day when students lay down around the police car and hundreds of police waited around the corner for the word of attack occurred in the name of the Indian saint. The harsh and unpleasantly professional exhortations coming from the improvised speakers' stand on top of the car were interrupted by an announcement that it was Gandhi's birthday, and the crowd, lying and standing, responded by singing "Happy Birthday to You." Actually the intensely individualistic discipline of Thoreau contrasts sharply with the FSM's dependence on crowd emotion. And Gandhi's insistence that in an unjust society one must remain in jail is sharply different from the FSM's confusing insistence that court punishment of demonstrators is an outrage and a grievance.

In terms of religious and quasi-religious precedent, modern existentialism seems closer than Tolstoian non-violence. What Savio was demanding, when he urged in a peak of passion that students throw their bodies on the administrative machine and bring it to a grinding halt, was something like an existentialist *acte gratuit*, a gesture of self-identification.

Radical democracy, with its love of liberty and dangers of tyranny, its trust in the mass and its contempt for institutions, seems to me to pervade the movement as it has many American movements. At times Whitman, that protean patron of American cranks and prophets, democrats and loners, furnishes texts that might well be used by the FSM:

I hear it was charged against me that I sought to destroy
    institutions
But really I am neither for nor against institutions,

(What indeed have I in common with them? Or what
with the destruction of them?)
Only I will establish . . .
Without edifices or rules or trustees or any argument,
The institution of the dear love of comrades.

The FSM would agree with Walt about rules and trustees,
and also about love, a word it often invokes. Joan Baez, the
FSM's Maid in Armor, urged them to go into Sproul Hall
with love in their hearts. And several of their leaflets have
talked about the need for a "loving university," instead of a
brutal and bureaucratic one.

Knowing that the movement proceeds partly from alienation, one is tempted to look to the 1920s for precedents. The
literary rebels of that period interest our students, but they
were very different. Sometimes frivolous, but often as serious
as Savio, the writers of the twenties were more interested in
literature than politics, sometimes inclined to dabble in
Menckenish elitism, and concerned about Negroes mainly in
terms of art and music. Perhaps significantly, the less completely alienated rebels of 1912 seem to offer a closer parallel.
Their mixture of socialism and anarchism has its similarities
to the present mood, especially when, as in the case of Randolph Bourne, it developed tragic implications.

One contemporary analogy that has often occurred to me
I hesitate to bring up, because it is partly—only partly—misleading. This is the analogy to the Goldwater movement.
When I hesitantly suggested this to a pro-FSM graduate
student of my acquaintance, he surprised me by saying that
the same analogy had haunted his own dreams. The resemblance does not rest on the actual temporary co-operation
between the Goldwaterites and leftists in the earliest days of
the movement, when in protest against prohibition of certain
kinds of political activities, students sang "Left and Right
together, we shall Overcome." The relation I am speaking of
is less direct and more lasting. Both the so-called conservative
political movement and the radical student movement are
protests against bigness, bureaucracy, and official liberalism.
Clark Kerr is actually a rather better symbol of the Liberal
Establishment than is Lyndon Johnson, who has his archaic
side. Both protest movements express vague wishes for immediate and simple solutions to complex problems. No statement could better summarize the whole FSM defense of its
methods than "In Defense of Liberty Extremism Is No Vice."
And both movements appeal to the heart—by implication,
sometimes, against the head.

So far I much prefer the anarchism of the left to that of
the right. On the whole, the causes in which laws have been
violated by the Bay Area Movement or the FSM are to

me noble causes, though I think their tactics have distorted these causes. And even discounting its disastrous "Southern" strategy, the Goldwater movement had far more hate and less love than the FSM, though skeptics have to expect harsh treatment from both.

All these analogies seem to me to help, and none to explain fully the student movement which came of age in Berkeley. To go further one must, in the first place, keep in mind the place and time, the American mass university in a time both of quickening intellectual life and collapsing patterns. And finally, one must admit that one never understands a new generation, though one deals with it every day.

Not understanding entirely, one may either accept or oppose the student movement. Perhaps one can defend certain boundaries against it. What one cannot do—and this one faculty group after another has learned with considerable cost—is to bargain or compromise. Essentially, the movement is absolutist. It is therefore very hard to fit into the habits or structure of our campus institutions, based, like all our institutions, on consensus or compromise.

What remains in doubt is not the existence of the student movement, though it will continue to have its ups and downs, nor its militance, though this too will wax and wane. It is rather its direction. Having won nearly everything it could ask in terms of campus free speech, will the movement turn its energies once more completely outward into civil rights or some other major cause, or inward into further university revolt. Some leaders call for the "free university," the new kind of academic community without grades and rules, in which students share in all academic decisions. In Berkeley, moreover, faculty and administration have been so shaken that it is not clear that either has the moral authority or the will to draw clear lines and defend them if necessary. Like modern parents, deans and professors find it easy to sympathize with revolt, very hard to act their traditional roles.

Even if the program of the free university collapses, as it may, for lack of support, and even if no further "internal" causes emerge, a student body so deeply committed to off-campus causes presents many subtle problems. In the midst of conflict, with slogans screaming from the placards and blaring from the loudspeakers on the edge of the campus, can the faculty insist on the values, never the easiest to defend in America, of precision and complexity and patience, even of humility before one's subject? How great will be the continuing appeal of subjects which have—at least on the surface—little to do with current controversy. American education has long been plagued by utilitarianism, and there is a utilitarianism of the left as well as of the Dewey-to-Kerr center.

A few years ago many professors, I among them, were deploring the passivity and complacency of American students and of American life, and wishing for a revival of campus radicalism. Somewhat wryly, we are forced to realize that radicalism never comes in the shape or size one has asked for. It is the breath of life, and it is full of danger. Our campus now is lively and dangerous. Divided between hope and anxiety, I can look for comfort only to the very considerable reserves, in Berkeley and elsewhere, of intelligence and honesty.

OPINION FORMATION IN A CRISIS SITUATION*
BY SEYMOUR MARTIN LIPSET

Studying the opinion making processes is the principal objective of public opinion research. In the main, however, such research has been forced to analyze the factors related to existing attitudes and sentiments rather than the formation of attitudes toward new problems or issues. The controversy at the University of California over the requirement that all faculty members sign an oath affirming that they were not members of the Communist Party created an opportunity to study the opinion forming process in a comparatively closed environment.[1] Both students and faculty were faced with the necessity of making up their minds about an issue that had not previously existed.

A study was undertaken during the height of the controversy, between March 15 and April 21, 1951, to find out how the student body was reacting to this crisis situation.[2] Ideally, such research could best have been conducted as a panel study, through which it would have been possible to see how the crisis situation actually affected the opinions of many students. Since the opportunity to do research on attitudes toward the oath did not arise until the controversy was about nine months old, the panel method, unfortunately, could not be used. It was hoped, however, that a single survey of student attitudes at that time would enable the testing of hypotheses about opinion formation that had been derived from panel studies of other situations in which the immediate crisis ele-

* From *Public Opinion Quarterly*, Spring 1953.
[1] On the background and history of the controversy, see George R. Stewart, *The Year of the Oath*, New York: Doubleday, 1950.
[2] This study was originally undertaken as a class project in a course in research methods. The number of students who contributed to it are too numerous to be mentioned here. I would, however, like to express my thanks to them. Mr. Morgan Yamanaka, who served as the assistant in this course, aided greatly in both the collection of data and the analysis. Funds for analysis were obtained from the University of California, Institute of Social Sciences.

ment and the need of the participants to form new opinions
were not present. In undertaking the study, a basic assumption
was made for which there was little empirical evidence, but
which seemed to be logical. This assumption was that the
controversy itself did not result in a change in the various
factors which are treated as independent variables in the
analysis. Specifically, it was assumed that a person's stand on
the loyalty oath did not change his general political predisposition, significant group affiliations, newspaper reading
habits, or his participation in the university community. If
this assumption is made, then one can attempt retrospectively
to identify the factors which would have enabled one to predict the attitudes and behavior of individuals faced with a
new issue such as this one.

Study Design

Between March 15 and April 31, 1950, a representative
sample of the student body of the Berkeley campus of the
University of California was interviewed concerning its opinion about the loyalty oath and the non-Communist hiring
policy. Every fortieth student was selected systematically from
the files of the Registrar. The study was planned after February 24, when the Regents issued their ultimatum to every
non-signer of the oath to sign or get out. Interviewing began
on March 15 and ended on April 21, the day that the Regents
lifted the ultimatum and accepted the Alumni proposal of a
contract form and committee hearing.

The 480 students who were interviewed during the five
weeks of the student survey represented a cross section of the
student body of the Berkeley campus. Table 1 shows the
relationship between the population statistics and the sample.
The differences between the two are within the error which
could result from chance factors. There is no reason to sus-

TABLE 1

SAMPLE STATISTICS RELATED TO POPULATION DATA

Trait	Population (N:21,903)	Sample (N:480)	Not Interviewed (N:56)
Males	74%	71%	82%
Females	26	29	18
	100	100	100
	(N:21,428)	(N:479)	(N:56)
Graduates	24%	24%	25%
Undergrads	76	76	75
	100	100	100

pect that there is any consistent biasing factor resulting from sampling. About 13 per cent of the original, 56 students, were not interviewed. Of these, 31 were refusals while 25 were never reached by the interviewers. The short duration of the interviewing period, plus the fact that all the student interviewers did not show equal enthusiasm in securing their interviews, were largely responsible for the fact that the sample design was not entirely completed. The 56 students who were not interviewed did not differ from the respondents by class standing in school. There were more females interviewed than males, but sex did not differentiate on the issues.

The interview schedule was designed to obtain the students' opinions on the issue of the oath and the policy of exclusion of Communists from teaching. Information was also secured on various social background characteristics of the group, as well as on their attitudes on a variety of political subjects which were not specifically related to the issues of academic freedom and civil liberties. The attitudes of the students as a group paralleled the official position of the faculty and its supporters. That is, the students were opposed to faculty members being required to take an oath affirming that they were not members of the Communist party.[3] They were, however, more divided on the issue of employing Communists in the university. Table 2 presents the results for the entire sample.

TABLE 2

ATTITUDE OF 480 STUDENTS TO THE LOYALTY OATH AND THE POLICY OF EMPLOYING COMMUNISTS*

Loyalty Oath		*Communist Employment*	
Approve oath requirement	26%	Oppose Communist employment	45%
Disapprove oath	64	Approve Communist employment	39
Don't know	10	Qualified approval	
No response	0	Approve if known as a Communist	4
		Approve if not a propagandist	4
		Approve if non-controversial subject	2
		Don't know	4
		No response	2

* For the purpose of analysis the students were divided into nine groups on the basis of their attitudes to both the oath and the policy. Only five of these groups contained enough cases to warrant inclusion. In succeeding tables these groups will be represented by letter abbreviations: PP-PO, pro-policy of barring Communists and pro-oath requirement; PP-AO, pro-policy and anti-oath requirement; AP-PO, anti-policy and pro-oath; AP-AO, anti-policy and anti-oath; and DK for the "don't knows" on either question.

[3] In a study of student attitudes toward this same controversy on the campus of the University of California at Los Angeles [See Daniel M. Wilner and Franklin Fearing, "The Structure of Opinion: A 'Loyalty

Predispositions

Various studies have indicated that attitude formation is related to the basic predispositions of individuals. That is, attitudes on any given issue are rarely if ever independent of the general cluster of attitudes that people bring to any situation in which they participate. In the case of the loyalty oath controversy, one would expect that general political predisposition would have affected students' reactions to issues of academic freedom. In order to test this hypothesis, the respondents were asked about their past and present political preferences, and were presented with a six question attitude scale designed to rank them as conservatives or liberals.[4] The

TABLE 3

PREDISPOSITION GROUPS

Attitude on Oath and Policy	Extreme Liberal (N:161)	Moderate Liberal (N:84)	Moderate Conservative (N:130)	Extreme Conservative (N:97)
PP-PO	5%	18%	25%	32%
PP-AO	25	23	18	26
AP-PO	2	6	10	8
AP-AO	58	34	29	24
Don't know	10	19	18	10
	100	100	100	100

Oath' Poll," *The Public Opinion Quarterly*, Vol. 15. No. 4 (Winter 1950–51] pp. 729–744], the authors asked the question: "Are you in favor of requiring all faculty members on this campus to sign a loyalty oath which includes a declaration that the individual is not a member of the Communist Party"? They got a response distribution of Yes, 41.3 per cent; No, 50.2 per cent; No opinion, 8.5 per cent. The apparently more conservative distribution of attitudes among the students at Los Angeles as compared wih those at Berkeley may be partly accounted for by the following two factors: (1) Impressionistically, it appears that faculty sentiment against the oath was stronger and more articulate at Berkeley than at Los Angeles. The faculty fight was launched at Berkeley, and it is likely that a larger proportion of the Berkeley faculty was actively opposing the oath. (2) Two major San Francisco papers, one of which was widely read on the Berkeley campus, vigorously supported the faculty's opposition to the anti-Communist oath, while none of the Los Angeles papers supported the faculty's position.

However, to be more than speculative, these independent indications of faculty and newspaper influence on student opinion call for direct evidence on the relative activity of the Berkeley and Los Angeles faculties in the controversy, and the nature and weight of the influence of the Los Angeles papers on student opinion at that campus.

[4] The six questions were agree-disagree statements concerning the Taft-Hartley Law, socialized medicine, government breakup of large corporations, government ownership of public utilities, belief that most strikes are unnecessary, and belief that the British Labor Government deserved to be reelected. A conservative answer was given a score of 2,

data shown in Table 3 appear to confirm the hypothesis that attitudes on the loyalty oath and non-Communist hiring policy were not independent of general political predispositions.

A similar pattern occurred when opinions on the two issues were compared with the respondents' party identifications. As compared with Republicans, Democrats were disproportionately against the loyalty oath and the policy of barring Communists. The supporters of minority political parties were, as one would expect, even more definitely in favor of the rights of Communists than were the Democrats. The differences between adherents of the two major parties were much less, however, when the question of liberalism or conservatism was held constant than when such partisans were compared independently (Table 4). General liberalism or conservatism appears to have been more important than party affiliation as such. Nevertheless, Democrats as a group were more prone to oppose the loyalty oath than were Republicans.

Table 5 shows that seniors and graduate students, particularly the latter, were much more liberal on the academic freedom issues than the members of the three lower classes, but this difference also decreased when liberalism and conservatism were held constant. Most of the difference between the two groups of students was contributed by the variation in the proportion of liberals, the graduate students in particular being the most liberal group in their general attitudes. While there are few data which help to account for this fact, it is possible to suggest some hypotheses. During the course of the loyalty oath controversy, students were exposed to more propaganda from the liberal or faculty side than from the conservative or Regents' side. The data indicate that senior and graduate students had more information about the controversy than lower classmen. Upper classmen and graduate students, who had closer contact with their instructors than lower classmen, may have been exposed to more discussion about the issues. Public opinion research has suggested that propaganda is more effective with people whose basic predispositions are already in line with the propaganda themes, and, moreover, that its effectiveness is increased if it is conveyed at least in part through face to face contacts.[5] In this case, therefore, it may be suggested that seniors and graduate students received more of the preponderately "anti-oath, anti-policy" propaganda, received it most directly and effectively in the context of personal relations, and that this propaganda

---

a liberal answer 0, and don't know a score of 1. A perfect conservative score, therefore, would be 12, while an extreme liberal score would be 0.

[5] Lazarsfeld, Paul F. and Robert K. Merton, "Mass Communication, Popular Taste and Organized Social Action" *Communication of Ideas*, Lyman Bryson, ed., New York: 1948, pp. 95–118.

Table 4

Relation Between Attitudes and Academic Freedom Issue—Party Held Constant

Issue:	Democrats			Republicans		
	Liberals (N:96)	Moderates (N:90)	Conservatives (N:36)	Liberals (N:18)	Moderates (N:62)	Conservatives (N:66)
Communists May Teach						
Yes	65%	44%	33%	50%	40%	32%
No	28	50	61	50	57	67
Don't know	7	6	6	0	3	1
	100	100	100	100	100	100
Loyalty Oath	(N:96)	(N:93)	(N:35)	(N:18)	(N:64)	(N:67)
Approve	3	26	34	17	39	45
Disapprove	91	60	54	72	47	49
Don't know	6	14	12	11	14	6
	100	100	100	100	100	100

TABLE 5
COLLEGE CLASS AND POLITICAL ATTITUDES

Issue:	Freshmen, Sophomores and Juniors			Seniors and Graduates		
Communists May Teach	Conservative (N:65)	Moderate (N:111)	Liberal (N:49)	Conservative (N:49)	Moderate (N:103)	Liberal (N:95)
Yes	39%	44%	51%	33%	48%	73%
No	58	50	39	65	48	24
Don't know	3	6	10	2	4	3
	100	100	100	100	100	100
Loyalty Oath	(N:66)	(N:115)	(N:49)	(N:48)	(N:104)	(N:95)
Approve	39	33	16	36	31	2
Disapprove	54	53	76	56	54	93
Don't know	7	14	8	8	15	5
	100	100	100	100	100	100

influenced most those individuals with liberal predispositions. The fact that the distribution of attitudes among the moderates and conservatives differed only slightly from class to class becomes understandable in terms of this hypothesis, since one would expect that those with non-liberal predispositions would not be greatly affected by the liberal propaganda of the faculty.

The pervasive influence of basic predispositions can also be seen when the students are compared by religious background (Table 6). Considering religion alone, it would appear that, of the four religious preferences given, Jews were most liberal on the academic freedom issues, those with no religious preference next, followed by Protestants, with the Catholics most conservative. Breaking down religious preference by position on the political predisposition scale indicates, however, that, with the partial exception of the Catholics, the differences among the different religious denominations were in part contributed by the varying proportions of liberals or conservatives within them. The Catholics deviate with regard to permitting Communists to teach—even liberal Catholics were opposed to this; however, a majority of liberal Catholics are opposed to the loyalty oath.

One of the most interesting findings of this study concerns the 78 students who reported having no religious beliefs of their own, but gave their parents' religious affiliation. In each case, the students answering "none" were more liberal than those students who had a religious affiliation, but the direction of the differences among the three religious groups remained the same among those who reported no religion. That is, irreligious Catholics were more conservative than irreligious Protestants, who in turn were more conservative than irreligious Jews (Table 7). It is evident that the religious group into which one is born remains an effective determinant of attitudes even among those who have broken with the group.

In the *Authoritarian Personality*, R. Nevitt Sanford reports that subjects who were religious and reported the religion of their mothers were more prejudiced (ethnocentric) than those who reported a maternal religious affiliation but were irreligious themselves.[6] If the attitudes toward the academic freedom issues are correlated with ethnocentrism, then the findings of this study also indicate that breaking with a familial religious pattern is related to liberalism.

The Authoritarian Personality materials do not discuss differences in prejudice between Catholics and Protestants, and therefore, no comparison is possible as to whether religious attitude clusters continue to affect apostates. The data of the

[6] Adorno, T. W., *et al.*, *The Authoritarian Personality*, New York: Harper, 1950, p. 216.

TABLE 6

ATTITUDES AND RELIGION

Issue:	Conservatives			Liberals			
Communists May Teach	No Religion (N:8)	Catholic (N:17)	Protestant (N:83)	No Religion (N:55)	Catholic (N:11)	Jew (N:17)	Protestant (N:51)
Yes	37%	23%	36%	78%	27%	71%	53%
No	50	77	62	13	64	29	43
Don't know	13	0	2	9	9	0	4
	100	100	100	100	100	100	100
Loyalty Oath							
Approve	25	53	36	5	18	6	8
Disapprove	63	41	57	89	64	94	88
Don't know	12	6	7	6	18	0	4
	100	100	100	100	100	100	100

TABLE 7

RELIGIOUS AFFILIATION AND ATTITUDES TOWARD ACADEMIC FREEDOM ISSUES

Issue:	Respondent's Religious Affiliation Given			Respondent's Religious Affiliation None–Father's Religion		
	Catholic (N:57)	Protestant (N:263)	Jew (N:24)	Catholic (N:10)	Protestant (N:58)	Jew (N:10)
Communists May Teach						
Yes	33%	43%	75%	50%	64%	80%
No	63	53	25	50	29	10
Don't know	4	4	0	0	7	10
	100	100	100	100	100	100
Loyalty Oath						
Approve	37	31	4	20	19	0
Disapprove	53	60	92	60	71	90
Don't know	10	9	4	20	10	10
	100	100	100	100	100	100

loyalty oath study are too skimpy and the number of cases too small to support any extensive generalizations. They do suggest, however, the necessity for further work on the relationship between past and present group affiliations. Under what conditions do past membership groups continue to determine the frames of reference within which individuals operate? When does breaking with a group result in overreacting against the norms of the group? One might have expected, for example, that apostate Catholics would be more likely than apostate Protestants to reject their past group's norms.

The Press

The newspapers of the San Francisco Bay Area played an important role in the entire loyalty oath dispute. All of them agreed on the policy question—that is, that no Communists be employed by the university. They divided sharply, however, on the question of the loyalty oath. The *San Francisco Chronicle* and the *San Francisco News* both vigorously supported the faculty's opposition to the non-Communist oath with many editorials and favorable news stories. The three Hearst papers in the area, the *San Francisco Examiner,* the *San Francisco Call-Bulletin,* and the *Oakland Post-Enquirer,* supported the Regents in their efforts to impose a loyalty oath, and repeatedly denounced the faculty opposition as being Communist inspired. The *Oakland Tribune* took the same position as the Hearst press, but did not print as many editorials and was somewhat more objective in its news presentation. The *Berkeley Gazette* printed many objective news stories and avoided taking an editorial position. These were the papers which were being read by the student body while the controversy was on.

The students were asked which papers they had read in the last two days before being interviewed. The information obtained, shown in Table 8, gives some indication of the influence of the press on the attitudes of the student body.

There appears to have been a definite relation between the editorial opinions and news policy of the various newspapers, and the attitudes of their readers. One could not conclude from this fact alone, however, that the newspapers of the Bay Area played an important factor in the development of opinion on the oath and hiring issues. It is possible that the readers of the different papers differentiated on other factors, such as class in school or political sympathies. One would have expected that liberals would have been more prone to read a liberal newspaper.

The study permits an approximation of a controlled experiment on the influence of newspapers. The newspapers all agreed on the policy of barring Communists but differed on the oath issue. If the papers had any influence on students'

TABLE 8

NEWSPAPER READING HABITS*

Respondent's Attitude to Oath and Policy	Pro-Oath Hearst and Tribune	Both Sides Chronicle, Hearst and Tribune	Anti-Oath Chronicle and News
	(N:83)	(N:90)	(N:147)
PP-PO	34%	19%	12%
PP-AO	18	21	27
AP-PO	11	7	4
AP-AO	30	41	49
Don't know	7	12	8
	100	100	100

* The other combinations contain too few cases to be meaningful.

attitudes, it should have been primarily on the issue of the loyalty oath rather than the policy. The data indicate that readers of the more conservative papers tended to be more conservative on the policy issue of Communist employment than did the readers of the liberal papers. This was at least in part a result of selective purchasing of newspapers, as the readers of the *Chronicle* and the *News* were in general more liberal according to the attitude scale than the readers of the Hearst papers and the *Tribune*. Holding respondents' positions on the non-Communist hiring policy constant, readers of liberal papers were more opposed to the oath than were readers of the conservative papers. The pro-policy people who read the *Chronicle* and the *News* were almost two-to-one against the oath, while the pro-policy students reading Hearst and the *Tribune* were almost two-to-one for the oath. Over one-quarter of the students who were in favor of allowing Communists to teach and who read the pro-oath papers were for the oath, as compared to seven per cent of those who read the anti-oath papers (Table 9). It is interesting that the majority of the students who answered "no opinion" to the oath question also reported that they had not read any newspapers during the two days before being interviewed.

Readers of the anti-oath papers tended to be more liberal than readers of the pro-oath papers. So far it is possible that the relationship indicated in the Table 8 is spurious—that, in other words, it is basic liberalism or conservatism which is actually being compared, not the influence of the papers. By holding political attitudes, as revealed by the predisposition scale, constant, it should be possible to see whether the newspapers had an effect over and above these other related attitudes; this is done in Table 10.

TABLE 9

NEWSPAPER INFLUENCE: OPINION ON HIRING POLICY HELD CONSTANT

Papers Read	Against Communists Teaching					For Communists Teaching				
	N	Approve Oath	Disapprove Oath	Don't Know	Total	N	Approve Oath	Disapprove Oath	Don't Know	Total
Chronicle and News	(77)	34%	66%	0%	100%	(101)	7%	83%	10%	100%
Hearst and Tribune	(47)	64	36	0	100	(43)	26	70	4	100
Both sides	(48)	48	50	2	100	(57)	12	79	9	100
None	(36)	17	25	58	100	(25)	12	72	16	100

TABLE 10

NEWSPAPERS READ AND ATTITUDES ON THE ISSUES; PREDISPOSITION CONSTANT

Communists May Teach

Papers Read	Conservatives N	Yes	No	Don't Know	Total	Moderates N	Yes	No	Don't Know	Total	Liberals N	Yes	No	Don't Know	Total
Chronicle and News	(45)	33%	62%	5%	100%	(85)	51%	46%	3%	100%	(63)	68%	27%	5%	100%
Hearst and Tribune	(36)	28	69	3	100	(54)	42	41	7	100	(22)	68	27	5	100
Both sides	(23)	29	61	0	100	(53)	45	51	4	100	(38)	66	29	5	100

Loyalty Oath

Papers Read	Conservatives N	Ap-prove	Disap-prove	Don't Know	Total	Moderates N	Ap-prove	Disap-prove	Don't Know	Total	Liberals N	Ap-prove	Disap-prove	Don't Know	Total
Chronicle and News	(43)	28%	65%	7%	100%	(88)	21%	64%	15%	100%	(63)	8%	87%	5%	100%
Hearst and Tribune	(36)	47	47	6	100	(46)	52	44	4	100	(20)	15	70	15	100
Both sides	(25)	44	56	0	100	(53)	34	47	19	100	(38)	3	92	5	100

Though the number of cases is unfortunately small, the evidence shows that, regardless of the newspaper they read, persons with similar basic political attitudes did not differ greatly on the question of the right of Communists to teach. In other words, the newspaper read did not have an independent influence on this issue. This is not surprising, since the newspapers were all agreed on the question. On the oath question, however, those reading the *Chronicle* or the *News* tended to be more pro-faculty than those reading the Hearst press or the *Oakland Tribune*, even when basic political attitudes were held constant. The newspapers which maintained a barrage of slanted stories and editorials for the duration of the conflict appear to have had a real effect on student opinion. Liberals who read both sides were similar in their attitudes on the oath to the liberals who only read the anti-oath papers, while conservatives who read both sides were similar to conservatives who read the pro-oath papers. Apparently, when exposed to the cross-pressures of conflicting newspaper reporting and editorial policy, the students were more likely to accept the point of view which fitted in best with their basic political predispositions.

Since this relationship between newspaper policy and attitude appears to contradict the findings in some other public opinion studies, it should be worthwhile to see whether any other factors, other than general political attitude, may account for the differences in the attitudes towards the oath of the readers of the various papers.

The relationship between papers read and attitude toward hiring policy, holding class in college constant as in Table 11, is largely related to the fact that the more liberal students tended to read the *Chronicle*, while the more conservative ones tended to read the Hearst press or the *Oakland Tribune*. It is significant, however, that the relationship between newspaper read and attitude toward the oath was greater than the one between the paper and attitude toward the policy, suggesting again the influence of the newspapers on students' attitudes toward the oath. The same pattern holds true for political party as well, as is shown in Table 12. Democrats and Republicans reading the *Chronicle* or the *News* were far more likely to be opposed to the oath than were those who read the papers which supported the Regents.

The data of this study suggest that the newspapers had a great influence in this controversy. They do not prove this conclusively, however, as it is possible that a selective element other than the factors considered was present and differentiated among the readers of the various papers. Liberal *Chronicle* readers, for example, may have been basically more "liberal" than liberal Hearst readers. A panel study in which the sample's members were interviewed as the controversy

TABLE 11

COLLEGE CLASS AND NEWSPAPERS READ

Communists May Teach

	Freshmen, Sophomores and Juniors					Seniors and Graduates				
Papers Read	N	Yes	No	Don't Know	Total	N	Yes	No	Don't Know	Total
Chronicle and News	(64)	48%	47%	5%	100%	(113)	56%	42%	2%	100%
Hearst and Tribune	(61)	38	54	8	100	(40)	43	50	2	100
Both sides	(49)	43	49	8	100	(65)	54	43	3	100

Loyalty Oath

	Freshmen, Sophomores and Juniors					Seniors and Graduates				
	N	Approve	Disapprove	Don't Know	Total	N	Approve	Disapprove	Don't Know	Total
Chronicle and News	(81)	25%	63%	12%	100%	(113)	14%	78%	8%	100%
Hearst and Tribune	(62)	44	48	8	100	(40)	43	52	5	100
Both sides	(53)	38	58	4	100	(65)	19	66	15	100

TABLE 12

POLITICAL PARTY AND NEWSPAPERS READ

Communists May Teach

Papers Read	Democrats					Republicans				
	N	Yes	No	Don't Know	Total	N	Yes	No	Don't Know	Total
Chronicle and News	(99)	58%	37%	5%	100%	(57)	35%	63%	2%	100%
Hearst and *Tribune*	(44)	45	50	5	100	(35)	34	66	0	100
Both sides	(55)	53	40	7	100	(40)	40	58	2	100

Loyalty Oath

Papers Read	Democrats					Republicans				
	N	Approve	Disapprove	Don't Know	Total	N	Approve	Disapprove	Don't Know	Total
Chronicle and News	(99)	11%	80%	9%	100%	(60)	33%	62%	5%	100%
Hearst and *Tribune*	(46)	30	61	9	100	(35)	60	31	9	100
Both sides	(55)	18	71	11	100	(40)	38	52	10	100

proceeded, would have been necessary to evaluate definitely the influence of the newspapers. It is also necessary to remember that all of the interviewees were college students and were exposed to repeated slanted news stories and editorials about a situation which was very close to them. One would expect that they read many of the detailed stories about the university controversy.

Socio-Economic Status

Socio-economic status is one of the most important factors differentiating conservatives from liberals in the society as a whole. In general, the lower a person's socio-economic status, however defined, the more liberal that person is likely to be. It is difficult, however, to categorize a university student population in socio-economic terms. Almost all students aspire to some sort of non-manual—and usually high status—position after leaving school. The high cost of a university education means that a disproportionate number of students will come from the well-to-do sectors of the population. There are, however, certain objective and subjective indices of status in this study which should enable us to analyze roughly the effect of this factor in the loyalty oath controversy.

The relation of father's occupation to student attitudes is shown in Table 13. Father's occupation, as such, does not

TABLE 13

OCCUPATION OF FATHER

Attitude to Oath and Policy	Professional	Farmer	Proprietor	Business Executive	Employed Worker
	(N:109)	(N:34)	(N:112)	(N:56)	(N:129)
PP-PO	24%	32%	14%	13%	14%
PP-AO	22	21	28	25	19
AP-PO	11	3	2	9	6
AP-AO	34	23	46	41	42
Don't know	9	21	10	12	19
	100	100	100	100	100

appear to have influenced opinions on the issues. The children of professionals and of farmers were most conservative, although it is hard to see why they should have been more conservative than the children of business proprietors or executives. The lack of consistent differences related to father's occupation does not necessarily mean that socio-economic status was unrelated to these issues, since the occupational categories which were employed did not actually differentiate between high and low non-working class status.

The means that a student uses to finance his way to school

should be a better clue to the socio-economic position of his family. Presumably, the more well-to-do the family, the more likely that the student will be supported by his parents. If this assumption is true, then Table 14 confirms the relationship established between occupational position of parents and attitudes on academic freedom. Those students who relied completely on parental support were more conservative than those going through school by other means. Those working their way through school or completely dependent on the G.I. Bill contributed proportionately more to the anti-Regent group.

TABLE 14

How FINANCED THROUGH SCHOOL

Attitude on Issues	Work (N:64)	G.I. Bill (N:85)	G.I. Bill & Work (N:63)	Family & Work (N:97)	G.I. Bill & Family (N:48)	Family (N:93)
PP-PO	8%	18%	19%	18%	21%	26%
PP-AO	23	16	18	30	29	18
AP-PO	13	2	9	6	2	6
AP-AO	42	45	41	38	29	33
Don't know	14	19	13	8	19	17
	100	100	100	100	100	100

These data would seem to suggest that the higher the socio-economic position of the parents, the more likely the student was to be pro-Regent on the question of the oath or policy. This factor was also probably related to general conservatism-liberalism; that is, higher socio-economic status and general societal conservatism go together.

The status aspirations of the students may also have played a role in the development of their attitudes on the oath and other issues. Information was secured on the future job as-

TABLE 15

FUTURE JOB ASPIRATIONS

Attitude to Oath and Policy	Teacher (N:124)	Engineer (N:41)	Independent Professional (N:78)	Salaried Professional (N:154)
PP-PO	14%	27%	18%	14%
PP-AO	22	17	21	26
AP-PO	4	5	9	7
AP-AO	47	24	40	39
Don't know	13	27	11	14
	100	100	100	100

TABLE 16

OCCUPATIONS AND MAJOR SUBJECT

Loyalty Oath	Social Sciences		Humanities		Physical Sciences	
	Teachers (N:34)	Non-Teachers (N:79)	Teachers (N:37)	Non-Teachers (N:39)	Teachers (N:9)	Non-Teachers (N:27)
Approve	20%	20%	14%	13%	22%	26%
Disapprove	71	76	78	77	67	63
Don't know	9	4	8	10	11	11
	100	100	100	100	100	100

pirations of the students and also on how much money they expected to earn ten years after leaving school. Table 15 appears to indicate that prospective teachers were more opposed to the Regents than students might have been expected to identify with members of their own future profession. Actually, however, this relationship appears to be spurious, at least in part. Almost all of the prospective teachers were majoring in the social sciences, the humanities, or the pure physical sciences. These three disciplines were the most liberal on the issues. If major subject is held constant, as in Table 16, there was little difference, especially on the oath issue, between the opinions of prospective teachers in these fields and those intending to go into other occupations.

Campus Activities

The students at the University of California are differentially involved in the campus life. Some of them simply attend classes and live with their parents or wives in various parts of the San Francisco Bay Area. Others spend their entire time at the university living in a fraternity house, a student cooperative, or a boarding house. These different out-of-class environments should affect student attitudes and interest in campus affairs. Students living at home should be affected more by general community opinion than those living on or near campus.

The data presented in Table 17 tend to confirm this hypothesis. The students who lived within the university community were more prone to support the faculty in the oath controversy than those living with their families at home. One might expect such a finding on the assumption that students living away from school would have been more likely to be exposed to pro-oath sentiments than those living on campus, while the students spending their entire school life within the school community would have been subject to influence by the faculty, and to the pro-faculty activities organized by various student groups.

Holding constant class in school, political attitudes, and political party affiliation did not invalidate the finding, as in each case students living within the university community were more likely to oppose the oath than either students in the same class or students who had the same political attitudes and party affiliations but lived away from the campus. Certain interesting differences appeared, however, when the two residence groups were compared holding parental socio-economic class constant. The children of "upper-class" fathers (professionals, proprietors, and business executives) who lived with their families were more prone to be against Communists teaching and in favor of the loyalty oath than

TABLE 17

RESIDENCE

Attitude to Oath and Policy	Lives with Family (N:195)	Lives with Schoolmates (N:275)
PP-PO	21%	16%
PP-AO	26	21
AP-PO	7	6
AP-AO	32	43
Don't know	14	14
	100	100

persons from the same social class background who lived within the school community. There was, however, no difference between the children of wage workers living at home and those living around the school, as Table 18 shows. The original finding regarding the residence groups, therefore, must be qualified insofar as it applies to the entire sample.

Looked at in another way, three of the groups in Table 18 had similar attitudes on both the oath issue and the non-Communist policy. Only one group, the children of persons with high socio-economic status who "live with family," was deviant. This finding may be related to a number of alternative hypotheses, none of which can be evaluated on the basis of the data. It may be possible that the community as a whole differed along socio-economic lines on the communist teacher or loyalty oath issues. The differences between the two groups of students living with their families may, therefore, have reflected exposure to different community reference groups. While there is no evidence concerning attitudes among the people of California, it is extremely dubious that a large proportion of persons on any socio-economic level was in favor of Communists being allowed to teach; the hypothesis that different social class attitudes as such were reflected in the student body does not satisfactorily explain the differences.

A second possible hypothesis is that the classification of "upper class" was too broad, and that the students living at home with their families actually belonged to a different layer of the "upper class" than those living on campus. This hypothesis, also, does not appear likely in terms of other related data. It is true, however, that those living at home differed from those in school according to home community. Those living at school came disproportionately from the smaller cities and towns of California, although many of them were from Los Angeles and from outside of the state.

TABLE 18

RESIDENCE AND OCCUPATION OF PARENTS

Communists May Teach	Upper Class		Wage Earners	
	Lives with Family	Lives with Schoolmates	Lives with Family	Lives with Schoolmates
	(N:122)	(N:188)	(N:64)	(N:64)
Yes	37%	57%	55%	55%
No	59	41	36	40
Don't know	4	2	9	5
	100	100	100	100
Oath				
Approve	34%	22%	22%	23%
Disapprove	60	67	64	65
Don't know	6	11	14	12
	100	100	100	100

The variable of community of origin did not, however, differentiate students on the issue.

There is a third hypothesis, more plausible on the basis of impressionistic evidence, which assumes that an off-campus general community and a campus community constituted two alternative reference groups toward which students could orient themselves. There is evidence that off-campus community opinion was overwhelmingly against Communists teaching and generally unsympathetic to the faculty's position on the oath, while the campus opinion, shaped by the faculty's stand, was opposed to the loyalty oath. Moreover, a majority of students supported the right of Communists to teach.

Faced with this conflict between the two reference groups, "working-class" students, regardless of where they lived, and "upper-class" students living on the campus took the liberal position on both questions, thereby disproportionately orienting toward the campus community as the effective positive reference group on this question. The "upper-class" students living at home, however, disproportionately reacted toward off-campus opinion. This latter group was least exposed to the "climate of opinion" dominant on campus, and had least reason for taking their cues from the faculty, whose status in the non-academic community at large is not high compared with other more conservative authorities. For all of the workers' sons, including those who lived off campus, the university community was a locus and vehicle for their mobility aspirations and striving; as part of the total process of rising, they tended to assimilate the attitudes and orientations of the college community, and especially of its leaders.[7]

This hypothesis calls for direct evidence on the effective use of positive and negative reference groups by different groups of students, and especially points up the need for additional research on the comparative influence of multiple-reference groups operating at cross-purposes. The data here suggest that the social status of different reference groups, as compared with that of the subjects being analyzed, may be one of the principal variables determining which reference group will prevail in a cross-pressure situation.

Perception of the Situation

W. I. Thomas many years ago laid down the theorem: "If men define situations as real, they are real in their consequences." It has long been apparent that perception of an external phenomenon is largely determined by the frame of reference—the supplied context—within which it is perceived. Both perception and attitude formation are heavily affected by the nature of the meanings, the frame of reference, the predispositions that individuals bring to a situation. In the controversy over the loyalty oath and the issue of Communists teaching, one would expect that people not only differed in their opinions on the issues but also in their awareness of the presence of Communists. It is to be expected that persons who feared Communists most would "see" more Communists in their environment than would those who disparaged the Communist threat.

The data set forth in Table 19 tend to confirm this hypothe-

TABLE 19

HOW MANY STUDENTS DO YOU THINK ARE COMMUNISTS?

	Pro-Policy Pro-Oath (N:81)	Pro-Policy Anti-Oath (N:106)	Anti-Policy Anti-Oath (N:179)
Don't know	27%	18%	14%
Under 50	7	17	17
51–500	25	30	46
501 and over	41	26	23
	100	100	100

[7] This hypothesis is similar to that advanced by Theodore Newcomb in his study of the political attitudes and behaviors of "upper-class" girls at Bennington College. Newcomb found that students integrated into the campus community tended to adopt the attitudes of the faculty, while those who retained strong home ties, or were unintegrated for other reasons tended to retain the conservative attitudes of their families. See Newcomb's discussion in terms of reference group concepts in Muzafer Sherif, *An Outline of Social Psychology* (New York: Harper, 1948), pp. 139–155.

sis. The students who supported the oath and the Regents' policy believed that there were many more Communists in the student body than did the students who were opposed to both. Over two-fifths of the pro-Regents students thought that there were over five hundred Communist students on the campus, as compared with less than a quarter of the anti-policy anti-oath group making a similar estimate. Here one can see the operation of a perceptual self-confirming hypothesis. Those fearful of Communism saw the justification for such fears in their social environment, while those who were not as fearful did not see the same picture of what should have been an objective fact—the number of Communists in the student body. The question, of course, was actually a projective question; no student, unless he were a member of the Communist Party, would have had accurate information on the number of Communists on the campus. The answers, therefore, give us some insights as to the sentiments and attitudes that different groups of students brought to the situation, including perhaps varying definitions of a "Communist." Those most fearful of the Communists may have operated under broader definitions.[8]

The variation in the students' perception of the situation also carried over to the knowledge of other facts. Some students, for example, did not know that the university had a policy barring Communists from employment. The figures are given in Table 20.

TABLE 20

UNIVERSITY POLICY ON COMMUNIST PARTY MEMBERS

	Pro-Policy Pro-Oath (N:86)	Pro-Policy Anti-Oath (N:107)	Anti-Policy Anti-Oath (N:183)
Bars Communists	77%	87%	87%
Don't know or Wrong	23	13	13
	100	100	100

Note that the supporters of the oath requirement include a large minority who, in the spring of 1950, one year after the oath controversy started and ten years after the policy was established did not know that the university bars Communists from employment. This finding is probably related to the data

---

[8] The same pattern appears in response to the question, "How many unions in the United States do you think are controlled by the Communist Party?" Less than a third of the pro-oath group, as compared with half the anti-oath group, believed that less than ten of the roughly 150 national unions are controlled by the Communist Party. The pro-oath group believed many unions were controlled by Communists.

on the perception of Communists presented earlier. Not only do the pro-Regents students see more Communists than do other people, but they are less aware of restriction on them. In their minds the threat is great—and apparently also unchallenged.

Perceptual framework can also be analyzed from the point of view of the controversy itself. One would expect that the opposing groups of students would differ in their conception of the faculty's and public's attitude on the oath as well as on their general information on the subject. The students were asked what per cent of the faculty they thought favored the oath. Almost all of the students recognized that the majority of the professors were opposed to the oath, but, as Table 21 shows, there were substantial differences in the proportions that different groups believed supported it.

TABLE 21

WHAT PER CENT OF THE FACULTY FAVOR THE OATH?

	Pro-Policy Pro-Oath (N:86)	Pro-Policy Anti-Oath (N:108)	Anti-Policy Anti-Oath (N:183)
Don't know	17%	7%	9%
Under 1%	6	20	13
1–10%	18	30	36
10–25%	21	26	25
25–50%	23	14	10
Majority	18	3	7
	100	100	100

What Do You Think the Public Thinks of the Oath?

	(N:85)	(N:108)	(N:183)
Don't know	7%	5%	11%
Support	51	30	44
Opposed	19	34	15
Not interested	16	23	27
Split	7	8	3
	100	100	100

The dominant view among the students was that the public supported the oath while the faculty opposed it. The pro-oath group, however, believed that a larger group of faculty members supported the oath than did the anti-oath students. The same pattern was true of estimates of the public's position; more pro-Regent than anti-Regent students believed that the public was in favor of the oath. The most interesting set of responses to these questions were the "don't knows" and those who said that the public was uninterested in the question. In this case, "don't know" and "no interest" were meaningful answers. Almost twice as many pro-oath students (17 per cent) as anti-oath students (9 per cent) said that they did not know what proportion of the faculty favored the oath. On the other hand, there were more "don't knows" among the anti-oath students (11 per cent) than among the pro-oath students (7 per cent) when it came to the question of the public's opinion about the oath. Over one-quarter of the anti-oath, anti-policy students also said that they thought the public was uninterested in the oath question.

With regard to the attitudes dominant in the two major communities of reference, disproportionate numbers in both the pro- and anti-oath groups apparently held a point of view which supported or at least did not conflict with their own position. This disproportionate ignorance and distortion of the facts is understandable in the light of the known connections between attitudes and perception. "Because perception is functionally selective, and because beliefs and attitudes play a role in determining the nature of this selectivity, new data physically available to an individual but contradictory to his beliefs and attitudes *may not even be perceived.*"[9] Moreover, "The lack of relevant facts and the frequent conflicting facts provided for us by different authorities frequently operate so as to force the creation or invention of facts that may bear no real relation to the external situation. Those pressures which work toward the formation of beliefs work in the absence of adequate data and may force the emergence of facts that support and are congruent with the beliefs."[10]

It is not known how accessible or well disseminated were the facts regarding the attitudes held by different groups in both the campus and general communities, nor do we know the nature of the channels through which this information was communicated. These factors would have had some bearing on the actual determinants of ignorance or incorrect knowledge among the students. Moreover, within each of the two opposing groups of students, there were undoubtedly those who used the community with which it differed as a negative reference group, and others who shared their attitudes but who were not reacting against any collectively held sentiments which they could identify. Perhaps the former were more aware of the attitudes held in their negative reference group, while it was the latter, who simply did not *see* the difference in group attitudes that did exist, who appear in the tables as

[9] Krech, David and Richard S. Crutchfield, *Theory and Problems of Social Psychology*, New York: McGraw-Hill, 1948, p. 190; emphasis theirs.
[10] *Ibid.*, p. 188.

"don't knows" or as holding incorrect views regarding the attitudes of other groups.

The present data, however, do not permit us to do more than speculate in these directions. What can be said is that the majority of anti-oath students refused to recognize that the public was actually against them, while over one-third of the pro-oath students either regarded the faculty as on their side or said that they did not know what the faculty thought. Given the fact that the faculty repeatedly, by almost unanimous votes, voiced its opposition to the oath, it is significant that fifty-six per cent of the pro-oath students either believed that over a quarter of the faculty supported the oath, or did not know the faculty's point of view. It seems clear that attitudes entered into and distorted the perception of some proportion of each of the major groups of students in directions that would tend to support attitudes already held.

Conclusions

This study indicates anew that opinion formation tends in large part to be a product of the activation of previous experiences and attitudes. Students at the University of California reacted to a crisis situation largely according to their group affiliations and other background characteristics. It would have been worth while to have had a panel study of opinion formation on the loyalty oath to see how this activation took place. The role of the university community, specific meaningful group affiliations, and the press, could have best been analyzed by repeated interviews with a panel as different events occurred.

The "deviant cases," those students who behave differently from the majority of those with the same characteristic as themselves, suggest that deviation in behavior is a result of being exposed to cross-pressures. Liberal students who read pro-oath newspapers were more likely to support the oath requirement than those reading a paper consistent with their basic political attitudes. Students who were in favor of barring Communists from university employment but who read anti-oath papers were more prone to oppose the oath. Conservative students who resided within the university community were exposed to the majority opinion of the student body against the oath and were, therefore, more likely to be liberal on the academic freedom issues than their co-thinkers politically who were not as exposed to campus opinion. Catholic graduate students were probably exposed to pressure from the liberal graduate student body and were less favorable to restrictions on Communists than their undergraduate co-religionists.

Another effect of cross-pressures on students exposed to

conflicting norms or expectations appears to have been a relatively high level of ignorance regarding the issues and their background. Ignorance here may have been serving the function of reducing the clarity, and thus the intensity, of the conflict; for example, this may have accounted for the greater lack of knowledge among the pro- than among the anti-Regents students. Cross-pressures not only directly affected the distribution of attitudes and the quantity and accuracy of information among different groups and categories of students, but also apparently influenced their active behavior in the controversy. In every category, those students who were against the Regents, but who had characteristics or were exposed to pressures which made for pro-Regents attitudes, were less likely to sign an anti-oath petition than those with homogeneous anti-Regent characteristics.

It is probably impossible to generalize from an analysis of the internal evidence available within one context the weight that any given item will have in a different cross-pressure situation. The two studies of student opinion on the Berkeley and Los Angeles campuses of the University of California suggest that a much larger proportion of the students at U.C.L.A. supported the position of the Regents in requiring a non-Communist loyalty oath. It is extremely doubtful that the differences between the two campuses were a result of differing proportions of students in the categories that affected opinion on this issue. For example, there is no reason to believe that there were more conservatives or Catholics at Los Angeles. In fact, the past history of student political organization would suggest that, if anything, the U.C.L.A. campus is on the whole more liberal than Berkeley. As was indicated earlier, the differential activities of the two faculties, and the unanimous pro-Regents stand of the Los Angeles newspapers, may have meant that the variables of university community influence and press influence may have had different weights in the two situations.

These differences point up a problem that arises in many opinion studies. We know, for example, that the proportion of workers or Catholics who are Democrats varies considerably from community to community, though in most cases these variables contribute to some degree to a Democratic predisposition. The analysis of why these same factors have different weights in different contexts must involve a study of the functional interrelationships among the variables which are handled in opinion research. Most such researches, including this one, necessarily handle these various factors atomistically. One cannot determine from survey data alone the ramifications for the rest of the system of changes in any one or several factors. This suggests the necessity for comparative institutional research which would attempt to locate those aspects of the social structure that result in the same nominal variable having quite different subjective meanings and objective weights in different contexts.

The evidence presented in this paper suggests that attitudes toward academic freedom are related to the same variables which influence attitude formation in other areas of life. Though supporters of civil liberties may hope that the belief in the rights of unpopular and even dangerous minorities is shared by persons regardless of personal political belief, the evidence does not warrant maintaining that hope. In general, those individuals who are characterized by the factors which make for conservatism, or who have conservative beliefs are opposed to the civil and academic rights of Communists. Those students who stand lower in socio-economic or ethnic group status, or who are liberals politically, tend to defend the rights of Communists.

It is possible, of course, to regard these patterns from another perspective. Historically, most violations of civil and academic rights in American society have been directed against liberals, leftists, trade unions, and members of minority groups. With the exception of the restrictions on Fascists during the last war, persons who are characterized by being well-to-do, having no interest in the labor movement, conservatives, white Protestants, Republicans, have not had to fear the possibility of social discrimination, loss of economic opportunities, or imprisonment as a result of their political opinions or group characteristics. American liberals, Jews, Negroes, Orientals, trade-union supporters, even though opposed to the Communist Party and the Soviet Union, may be more prone to consider the implications of any restrictions, even those directed against a totalitarian political party, as setting dangerous precedents which may afterward react against themselves. The individual members of these groups may not consciously analyze these long-term implications, but the historic experiences of their groups may have conditioned them to react in this way.

In addition to these general factors, the legal position of the Communist Party has become a political football in American politics. Conservatives and Republicans are attempting to use the widespread American antagonism towards the Communist Party against the politics of the Democrats, liberals, and Socialists. The non-Communist left-of-center groups, therefore, have painful and recent evidence for fearing that attacks on the Communist Party may be followed by attacks on themselves.

Catholics, though members of a minority group which has frequently been persecuted in this country, belong to a church which has made anti-Communism one of its principal activities. Discrimination and persecution of Roman Catholics in

Communist-controlled countries has been severe, and Catholics, therefore, may be expected to react more strongly against Communists.

In interpreting the data of this study, it is necessary to recognize the danger of generalizing these findings beyond a student population. Students operating within the intellectual atmosphere of the university may react in more rational ways than the general population. Student members of underprivileged groups may, for example, be more inclined to make rational identifications between their own group and other groups under attack, an identification which underprivileged groups outside the campus may not make.

DETERMINANTS OF SUPPORT
FOR CIVIL LIBERTIES*

HANAN C. SELVIN AND WARREN O. HAGSTROM
PROFESSORS OF SOCIOLOGY, UNIVERSITIES OF
ROCHESTER AND WISCONSIN

Can individual freedom survive in a country where most people do not support it? More exactly, do legal guarantees of such freedom remain effective when only a minority voices approval of them? In America, at least, the answer is yes. A 1954 survey of a national cross-section found that 60 per cent would not favour allowing someone to make a speech "against churches and religion" in their community.[1] Even in 1938, when tolerance for political dissent was undoubtedly greater than now, more than half of those who asserted a belief in free speech in a national survey were unwilling to let a 'radical' speak in their town. There is much evidence that freedom of speech, freedom of the press, the right to a fair trial, and other fundamentals of political democracy are not fully supported in the United States, despite the fact that they are embodied in a written Constitution that is taught in every secondary school and despite the general acceptance of "democracy" and "freedom" as essential characteristics of American society.

How can a society persist when so many of its members do not believe in its basic values? One answer is that other factors are more important to the preservation of democracy than complete consensus on democratic values. For example, Lipset has shown that the stable democracies of the world are characterized by a high level of economic development and a

* From *British Journal of Sociology* (1960).
[1] Samuel A. Stouffer, *Communism, Conformity, and Civil Liberties*, Garden City, Doubleday and Co., New York, 1955, p. 32.

widespread sense of the legitimacy of the established government.[2] Furthermore, in the area of public opinion all people are not equal. Support for democratic values by members of the government, by journalists and political writers, and by community leaders is more important than support by the politically inarticulate. On this point Stouffer's data are clear and compelling: in every section of the United States and on every issue the community leaders and the people with the most education (from whom the leaders are drawn) are more concerned about civil liberties and more tolerant of political dissent than is the general public. Lipset did not have comparative data on support for individual freedom in his countries, but we believe that no nation can maintain a tradition of individual freedom without these values being supported by the politically active and influential.

If this is true, then it is important to understand the role of universities and colleges in the transmission of these values, for university-trained men and women have come to dominate politics, government, and the mass media at all levels. We report here on a recent study of this process at the Berkeley campus of the University of California.[3] The main purpose of this study was to identify the social and psychological factors associated with more or less libertarian views—that is, more or less strong support of those provisions in the Constitution of the United States known as the Bill of Rights. These include such fundamental rights as freedom of speech, assembly, press, and worship; the right to a public trial by jury; and protection against imprisonment or seizure of property without "due process of law".

Although this study was done on one campus at one point in time (December, 1957), its implications are broader. The sample of 894 students was designed to compare significant types of groups—to study the influence of such factors as place of residence and major subject—rather than to 'represent' the total student body at this university. In other words, the sample is representative of certain kinds of social backgrounds and campus experiences, rather than of a particular collection of people. However, in our judgment the sample is sufficiently accurate to permit rough comparisons between our sample and others.

It is easy enough to support liberty as an abstract idea or even as a set of specific privileges such as are embodied in the Bill of Rights. But this support may be meaningless if it

[2] Seymour M. Lipset, "Some Social Requisites of Democracy: Economic Development and Political Legitimacy", *American Political Science Review*, 54, March 1959, pp. 69–105.

[3] The study was sponsored by the Bill of Rights Project of Stiles Hall (The University Y.M.C.A.) under a grant from the Fund for the Republic. The Bill of Rights Project was directed by Robert H. K. Walter.

TABLE I

ATTITUDES TOWARD PRINCIPLES OF THE BILL OF RIGHTS*

	Agree %	Disagree %	Don't Know %
1. The circulation of Russian or Chinese newspapers in this country should be restricted to scholars.	6	87	6
2. The Government should have the right to prohibit any group of persons who disagree with our form of government from holding public meetings.	10	85	4
3. State governments should have the power to pass laws making it illegal to speak against racial or religious groups.	10	85	5
4. It unduly hampers the police in their efforts to apprehend criminals when they have to have a warrant to search a house.	11	84	4
5. The police are justified in holding a man with a long criminal record until they have enough evidence to indict him.	12	80	7
6. It is reasonable to suspect the loyalty of a lawyer who represents accused Communists before a Congressional Committee.	13	79	8
7. A high-school teacher who "pleads the Fifth Amendment" while being questioned by a Congressional Committee should be fired at once.	13	75	11
8. The government is acting properly in refusing a passport to a Socialist.	10	67	21
9. Large-scale police round-ups of "undesirables" are proper as long as they are restricted to people with known criminal records.	19	63	18
10. Legislative committees should not investigate the political beliefs of university faculty members.	61	29	9
11. A former member of the Communist party who refuses to reveal the names of Party members he had known should not be allowed to teach in a private university.	27	60	13

12. It is wrong for government investigators to take pictures of people listening to a street-corner speech.	56	30	13
13. "Crime" comic books should be screened by some government agency before publication.	45	*47*	7
14. If a person accused of a major crime is acquitted, and if new evidence is then found that the prosecution claims indicates that he was guilty, he should be retried.	53	*39*	7
15. The government should have the right to withhold relevant FBI files from defendants in criminal cases, when opening the files to them might reveal the names of confidential informants.	56	*24*	20

* Percentages are based on the total sample size, 894. Less than 1 per cent of respondents failed to answer any one question. The questions are listed according to the frequency of libertarian responses; this is not the order in which they appeared in the questionnaire.

disappears whenever the values of individual liberty come into conflict with other values, as they inevitably do. We therefore measured students' support for the Bill of Rights by a series of fifteen statements, each embodying an implicit conflict of values. These statements are listed in Table I, along with the proportion of the total sample who agreed or disagreed with the statement or did not know enough about it to decide. The proportion giving what we consider the "libertarian" response is italicized.

The most important finding in this table is that support for the principles of the Bill of Rights depends on the specific principle in question. The proportion with libertarian attitudes ranges from the 87 per cent who uphold the freedom to read Russian and Chinese periodicals (statement 1) to the 24 per cent in favour of the right of the accused to confront his accusers in criminal cases (15). Overall, the responses are decidedly libertarian: for all but three of the fifteen questions a majority of the respondents take a libertarian stand. Most widely supported are freedom of the press (1), assembly (2), and speech (3). But among many students even these values are not strongly held. When they conflict with other values, such as protecting children against influences that are felt to be harmful, they are easily abandoned: only 47 per cent oppose pre-publication censorship of 'crime' comic books (13).

At the other extreme, the rights of persons accused of crimes were least strongly supported. More than half of the students (56 per cent) would deny some accused persons the right to confront their accusers (15), and a similar proportion would allow someone to be tried twice for the same offence (14).

These results are similar to those obtained by Raymond W. Mack at Northwestern University and by Robert McGinnis at the University of Wisconsin.[4] Mack and McGinnis paraphrased the propositions of the Bill of Rights and asked students if they agreed or disagreed with them. Their results, like ours, indicate that the freedoms of speech, press, and assembly were among those most strongly supported, while the right to confront one's accusers and the guarantee against double jeopardy were the least strongly supported. There is, consequently, good reason to believe that the order of the statements in Table I is roughly the same as would be found in other universities.

The high level of support for certain libertarian principles suggests that students may have recognized these principles as stemming from the Bill of Rights and may be responding to the source of the statements rather than to their contents. There are several pieces of evidence that this is not so. For one thing, the same principle often receives markedly different responses, depending on the situation. Freedom of the press expressed as the right to circulate Russian and Chinese newspapers is upheld by 87 per cent of the sample, but the same right when applied to the circulation of comic books without censorship, is supported by only 47 per cent. And, surprisingly, most students do not recognize that these principles derive from the Bill of Rights. Mack asked his students for the source of the statements they had been evaluating; less than 8 per cent gave even an approximately correct answer. Our California students had to choose the correct answers to three simple questions about the Bill of Rights; 46 per cent could not answer more than one of the three correctly.

Our students apparently base their responses to these fifteen questions on general sentiments of fairness or, as we prefer to term it, "libertarianism", rather than on the authority of the Bill of Rights. Because it is difficult to keep fifteen questions in mind and because the response to any one question necessarily reflects the specific wording of the question as well as the general dimension of libertarianism, we constructed a summary index of libertarianism. This is simply the number of

---

[4] Raymond W. Mack, "Do We Really Believe in the Bill of Rights?", *Social Problems*, vol. 3, 1956, pp. 264–269; and Robert McGinnis, "Teachers, Students and Belief in the Bill of Rights", unpublished paper. For reports on more extensive studies of several universities see Philip E. Jacob, *Changing Values in College*, Harper, New York, 1957; and Norman Miller, "Academic Climate and Student Values", paper presented at the Fifty-Fourth Annual Meeting of the American Sociological Association, Chicago, Illinois, September 1959.

TABLE II

DISTRIBUTION OF SCORES ON THE LIBERTARIANISM INDEX

Number of libertarian responses to 15 questions	Number of cases	
0	0	
1	3	
2	2	
3	11	20%—"slightly libertarian"
4	30	(183)
5	26	
6	41	
7	70	
8	82	
9	97	46%—"moderately libertarian"
10	114	(409)
11	116	
12	119	
13	90	34%—"highly libertarian"
14	69	(302)
15	24	

libertarian responses to the fifteen questions in Table I; the distribution of scores on this index is shown in Table II. The sample leans to the libertarian side. The mean number of libertarian responses is 9.9, almost two-thirds of the possible fifteen. Very few students, only 5 per cent, gave libertarian responses to less than five statements in the index; at the other extreme, 11 per cent made such answers to fourteen or fifteen statements. However, to understand the implications of Table II it is necessary to consider briefly what such an index means.

The libertarianism index is admittedly crude. For one thing, it attributes equal importance to all fifteen questions, where a more refined analysis would be able to take into account the varying importance of the items. And, unlike the cumulative scales now coming into wide use, knowing how many questions a person answers in a libertarian way does not identify the particular questions involved; for example, a score of 14 could be acquired in fifteen different ways. A very low score is even more ambiguous, for we have counted 'don't know enough about it to decide' as equivalent to an anti-libertarian response. (Further analysis shows, however, that this procedure is justified; the students with many "don't know" responses behave like those with many anti-libertarian responses.) Finally, this index is not unidimensional. The fifteen items may be considered as manifestations of several more basic concepts, much as questions on an intelligence test yield scores on different mental abilities.

None of these defects is serious in this study. Most of the time this index is used only to classify the students into three broad groups—"highly libertarian", "moderately libertarian", and "slightly libertarian", as indicated in Table II. This classification is sufficiently precise to show how a student's libertarianism is related to his other attitudes, his experiences at the university, and his family background. The extent to which the parts of this analysis hang together and corroborate the findings of other studies indicates that the precision of our index is adequate. (In general, highly refined scales are necessary only where the social and individual costs of error in a single case are high—for example, in deciding whether or not a specific prisoner should be paroled. Where the only "cost" of a few such errors is to change a measure of association slightly—as in studying the relationship between the family status of parolees and their rate of recidivism—then the crude technique used here is precise enough.)

How does the libertarianism of California students compare with that of other significant groups in America? Neither the libertarianism index nor its component questions can be used directly in such comparisons, for these questions differ from those used in the other studies. However, one set of questions has appeared virtually unchanged in four different studies—Stouffer's cross-section of the American public in 1954, his concurrent sample of community leaders in middle-sized cities, a nationwide sample by Lazarsfeld and Thielens of university and college teachers in the social sciences, and our sample of University of California students.[5] These five questions, which deal with the sanctions that the respondent would like to see imposed on an admitted Communist, are highly related to the index of libertarianism; students high on libertarianism are generally unwilling to impose severe sanctions. The five sanctions are listed in Table III, along with the proportion of each sample opposing the use of each sanction (i.e., giving the more libertarian response). The University of California students are very libertarian indeed. In almost every comparison that can be made they are more willing to extend civil rights to Communists than are members of the other samples. For example, in the first row of the table almost every student opposes removing a book by an admitted Communist from the public library, a position shared by less than half of the community leaders and by slightly more than a quarter of the general public. This willingness to support civil rights for Communists is apparently a matter of principle. At least, it is not based

[5] Stouffer, *op. cit.;* and Paul F. Lazarsfeld and Wagner Thielens, Jr., *The Academic Mind,* The Free Press, Glencoe, Illinois, 1958, Appendix 2, pp. 377–402.

TABLE III

CIVIL RIGHTS FOR AN ADMITTED COMMUNIST:
A COMPARISON OF FIVE SAMPLES

Percentage OPPOSING *use of the indicated sanctions*

Possible steps to be taken in the case of an admitted Communist	National cross-section	Community leaders	Social Science teachers	University of California total sample	University of California first-year students
	%	%	%	%	%
A book he wrote should be removed from the public library	27	42	*	94	90
He should be fired from a job in a supermarket†	26	45	82	89	87
He should not be allowed to teach in a private university‡	6	11	35	52	38
He should not be allowed to teach in a public high school	5	9	*	23	17
He should be fired from a defence plant	6	5	17	7	6
Number of cases	(4933)	(1500)	(2451)	(894)	(131)

* Questions not asked in this study.
† In the Stouffer and Lazarsfeld-Thielens studies this statement read: 'Suppose he is a clerk in a store. Should he be fired, or not?'
‡ In the Stouffer and Lazarsfeld-Thielens studies this statement read: 'Suppose he is teaching in a college. Should he be fired, or not?'

on widespread student "radicalism", for 71 per cent of our sample favored Eisenhower in the 1956 Presidential election.

The consistency in the ordering of the four samples is also noteworthy; they remain in the same order as across the top of the table, except for the question of firing a Communist from a defence plant.

One explanation for the greater libertarianism of the students is that they were selected from the most libertarian segments of the general population. Stouffer has shown that libertarianism increases with education and urbanization and that it is higher in the Far West than in any other region of the country. Since our students come largely from urban, middle-class, California families, this alone accounts for a good part of their greater libertarianism. But the university experience also has a profound effect on them; in fact, they become steadily more libertarian as they go through the four undergraduate years. Both factors, which we may call "selection" and "training", are clearly at work. In the following pages we shall explain how these two factors affect the libertarianism of our students.

The Influence of Family Background on Libertarianism

A student's pre-university background affects his support for civil liberties in two ways. It determines the attitudes he brings with him to the campus, and it affects the ways in which these attitudes change while he is there. The best way to study these changes is to measure the students' attitudes before they enter the university and when they leave, as well as at intervals during their stay—in short, a longitudinal or panel study. No such studies have been done yet at major universities (Theodore M. Newcomb's *Personality and Social Change*[6] is a panel study, but the small New England women's college at which it was done in the 1930's is not representative of American institutions of higher education.) A good approximation to the changes that can be observed in a panel study is to compare students who are at different phases of their education at one particular time (thus implicitly assuming that the same kinds of students are recruited each year). In this study we compare the attitudes of students in each of the four undergraduate years, as well as a small group of post-graduate students.

In order to see how different social backgrounds affect a student's libertarianism, it is helpful to examine the "changes" in libertarianism for the sample as a whole first. Table IV presents the distribution of libertarianism for the four undergraduate years and for the graduate students who came into our sample.

Libertarianism increases steadily from year to year among the undergraduates. The proportion highly libertarian almost doubles, from 21 per cent among the first year students to 40 per cent in the last year, and the proportion only slightly libertarian drops from 32 per cent to 14 per cent in the same period. Although the table shows that the graduate students are still more libertarian than the fourth-year undergraduates, this difference represents more than the simple transition from undergraduate to graduate status. The two groups of students

[6] Theodore M. Newcomb, *Personality and Social Change*, Dryden, New York, 1943.

TABLE IV

LIBERTARIANISM AND YEAR IN UNIVERSITY

	First year	Second year	Third year	Fourth year	Graduate Students
	Undergraduates				
	%	%	%	%	%
Highly libertarian	21	29	34	40	54
Moderately libertarian	47	44	50	46	30
Slightly libertarian	32	27	16	14	16
Total	100	100	100	100	100
Number of cases	(131)	(226)	(216)	(266)	(50)

differ in many ways, and these differences cannot be examined when our sample includes only fifty graduate students. We have therefore largely confined our discussion to undergraduates.

The Effects of Socio-Economic Status

There is ample reason to expect the social position of a student's family to affect his libertarianism. Stouffer and others have shown that tolerance for political and religious nonconformists decreases as one goes down the scale of occupational prestige.[7] Our data in Table V show something very much like this, a moderate association between the occupational sta-

TABLE V

LIBERTARIANISM AND FATHER'S OCCUPATION

Father's Occupation	Percentage highly libertarian (Undergraduates only)	Number of cases
	%	
Blue collar workers	44	(135)
Free and salaried professionals	35	(170)
Upper-level managers and officials, and large-scale proprietors	31	(249)
Farm owners and operators	30	(47)
Small businessmen	27	(98)
Clerical, sales, and public-service workers	25	(116)

tus of the student's family and his libertarianism. But there is one surprise here: the children of blue-collar workers (skilled,

[7] Stouffer, *op. cit.*, pp. 138 ff.; and Martin Trow, "Small Businessmen, Political Tolerance, and Support for McCarthy", *American Journal of Sociology*, 54, November 1958, pp. 270–281.

semi-skilled, and unskilled workers and foremen), instead of having the poorest showing on libertarianism, turn out to have the best.

The most plausible explanation rests on the relations between these students and their parents. Of all occupational groups in Table V, blue-collar workers' children are most likely to report being more libertarian than their parents. This attitudinal independence in turn results from greater economic independence; this group is the only one in which those who earn more than half of all their university expenses outnumber those who are fully supported by their parents. Greater economic independence, in the sense of self-support, is strongly associated with having more libertarian attitudes than one's parents.[8]

Although initially large, the effects of socio-economic status on libertarianism diminish markedly as students move through the four years of undergraduate education. To show this, we shall examine the relationship between father's occupation and libertarianism separately for students in the first two years and in the last two years.

TABLE VI

LIBERTARIANISM BY FATHER'S OCCUPATION
AND YEAR IN UNIVERSITY

| | Proportion highly libertarian | | | |
| | First two years (Lower division) | | Last two years (Upper division) | |
Father's Occupation	Percentage	Number of cases	Percentage	Number of cases
Blue collar workers	52	(48)	40	(87)
Professionals	32	(82)	37	(88)
Managers and officials	22	(104)	37	(145)
Farm Owners and operators	*	(15)	38	(32)
Small businessmen	21	(48)	32	(50)
Clerical, sales, and public service	11	(53)	36	(63)

* Too few cases for stable percentages.

The order of the occupational categories is roughly the same among upper-division as among lower-division students. In both cases children of blue-collar workers are most likely to be highly libertarian, and children of small businessmen are among those least likely to be highly libertarian. The im-

[8] This explanation was first suggested to us by Audrey Wipper, Faith Denitch, and Maurice Zeitlin, of the University of California, who made an intensive re-analysis of the original data.

portant finding of this table, however, is not so much the order of the occupational groups as the size of the differences between them. The differences are much smaller in the last two years than in the first two years. The extreme categories in the lower division are separated by 41 percentage points, in the upper division by only 8 percentage points. This table also serves to support the finding that libertarianism increases as students go through the university. In four of the five comparisons that can be made the upper-division students are more likely to be highly libertarian than the lower-division students. This shows that the results in Table IV cannot be attributed to differences in the occupational strata from which each year's class is recruited, and it also helps to reject the rather implausible hypothesis that these year-to-year differences could have arisen "by chance". However, the curious result that the children of blue-collar workers are less libertarian in the upper division than in the lower division probably does stem from such differences in recruitment—for example, the greater proportion of blue-collar workers' children who have transferred to the University of California after one or more years at a less libertarian community college or junior college.

Table VI exemplifies one of the major processes that occur at a university—"homogenization". The university takes in students of varied social backgrounds and attitudes. The differences in attitudes are steadily reduced, so that the graduates are appreciably more homogeneous than is the general public. University education "declassifies" students (and then usually reclassifies them). As long as they live with their parents and attend high school in their home communities, the students automatically assume the social position of their parents. But entering the university is like moving to a new town, even for those who live at home and commute to the campus, and students become aware that they will ultimately acquire their own statuses. As with their parents, the main determinant of this status will be their occupations (for the women, their husbands' occupations). But this is largely in the future. Most students have only a general idea of what life will be like for them in their future occupations, even if they have already made definite occupational choices. In a very real sense their social statuses are more similar than they were before entering the university and than they will be after graduation. And what is important here, they have lost the support for the beliefs and attitudes they had before entrance. No longer surrounded primarily by people of the same social background, they take on some of the dominant values of their new environment if these were not present in their pre-university environment. Since both the faculty and the students are predominantly libertarian, the result is a marked lessening of the effects of father's occupation as students move through their four years.

Political Party Identification and Libertarianism

Some attitudes are more resistant to change than others; one example is the choice of a political party. Most Americans retain their allegiance to the same party year in and year out.[9] This is easy for those who are apathetic about political issues. For the politically concerned it is facilitated by the ideological fuzziness of the two parties. Both contain liberals and conservatives, and they often advocate substantially the same programmes. This has been true of libertarianism in recent years; the defence of civil liberties and the attacks on them have been bipartisan. Nevertheless, party identification has significant effects on libertarianism in the community and in the university.

Studies of cross-sections of the national population have shown Republicans to be slightly more tolerant of nonconformists than Democrats. For example, Stouffer found 32 per cent of the Republicans in his 1954 study in the "more tolerant" group, as against 27 per cent of the Democrats.[10] Among university and college social-science instructors the reverse association exists. Lazarsfeld and Thielens found that 91 per cent of the "highly permissive" instructors (roughly equivalent to the more tolerant or the more libertarian) had supported the Democratic candidate in 1952, while only 30 per cent of the "clearly conservative" instructors (roughly equivalent to the less tolerant) did so.[11]

Among students at the University of California the association between party preference and libertarianism is more like it is among the professors than among the national population as a whole: 24 per cent of those who consider themselves Republicans fall into our highly libertarian category, as against 43 per cent of the Democrats and 46 per cent of the self-styled Independents. This is a consistent association: even when students alike in many other respects are compared those with Democratic preferences are more often highly libertarian than those with Republican preferences.

Since libertarianism is not an expression of the differences between the two parties, the connection between party affiliation and libertarianism may lie in characteristics of the individual students. There is some evidence that interest in national and world affairs is one connecting link, for the Democrats in our sample are more interested than the Republicans,

[9] For example, see Bernard R. Berelson, Paul F. Lazarsfeld, and William N. McPhee, *Voting*, University of Chicago Press, 1954, p. 345.

[10] Stouffer, *op. cit.*, p. 211.

[11] Lazarsfeld and Thielens, *op. cit.*, p. 185. The percentages reported in the text were based only on those who expressed a preference for the candidates of the two major parties. "Highly permissive" and "clearly conservative" are the extremes of five categories.

and the interested students are more libertarian. Is the greater libertarianism of the interested students merely an expression of their more Democratic leanings, or do interest and party affiliation contribute independently to libertarianism? To answer this question it is necessary to see how interest and party affiliation are simultaneously related to libertarianism, as in Table VII.

This table makes it possible to compare the libertarianism of Democrats, Republicans, and Independents at each level of interest in politics. Looking at the bottom row first, there is almost no difference in the libertarianism of Republicans (19 per cent) and Democrats (21 per cent) and a relatively small difference between them and the Independents (29 per cent). However, among those with greater interest the Democrats and the Independents are much more likely than the Republicans to be highly libertarian. In the top row, among students with a great deal of interest, the Democrats and Independents are twice as likely as the Republicans to be highly libertarian (57 and 60 per cent, as against 24 per cent).

Although we do not know why interested Democrats are more libertarian than interested Republicans, the fact that they are helps to explain why Democrats are more libertarian in our sample of university students, even though this is not true in the country at large. The general population is undoubtedly more apathetic than university students; and, as in Table VII, party preference has little effect on libertarianism where interest is low. Among university students and professors interest is relatively high, and party preference therefore has a pronounced effect on libertarianism.

Religion and Libertarianism

Like party preference, religious affiliation is relatively stable among university students. And like party preference, it is significantly related to libertarianism, apparently through the sentiments that religion engenders towards deviants. People who would deprive others of the protection of the Bill of Rights often have two kinds of deviants in mind. On the one hand are those, like common criminals, who violate the established norms of society without necessarily doubting their legitimacy. On the other hand are the "heretics", who attack the legitimacy of the norms, even though they may not actually violate them. Public attacks on the civil rights of the accused are often based on the feeling that these alleged deviants exploit the Bill of Rights to escape their just punishment. In recent years heresy, notably in the form of international Communism, has probably been seen as the greater menace. Religious people, especially those of rigid and orthodox beliefs, are more likely to be sensitive to the dangers of heresy than others, and

TABLE VII

LIBERTARIANISM, PARTY PREFERENCE, AND INTEREST IN NATIONAL AND WORLD AFFAIRS

Interest in National and World Affairs	Proportion highly libertarian among:					
	Republicans		Democrats		Independents	
	Percentage	Number of cases	Percentage	Number of cases	Percentage	Number of cases
A great deal	24	(87)	57	(81)	60	(52)
A moderate amount	25	(251)	39	(116)	54	(118)
Only a little	19	(96)	21	(29)	29	(38)

they often react by advocating the denial of rights to heretics or suspected heretics.

"Religion", however, is not a single characteristic. In this study we asked our students two distinct questions: "In which religion were you raised?" and "How much of your non-class time have you spent per week in church or synagogue services this semester?" The first question concerns denomination, the second attendance at religious services. The effect of denomination on libertarianism is shown in Table VIII. Almost

TABLE VIII

LIBERTARIANISM BY RELIGIOUS DENOMINATION

Religious Denomination	Proportion highly libertarian	Number of cases
Jewish	49	(65)
None	45	(77)
Protestant	32	(570)
Roman Catholic	30	(155)

half of the Jews (49 per cent) are highly libertarian, as against less than a third of the Protestants and Roman Catholics. And those who reported not being raised in any religion are almost as prone to be highly libertarian as the Jews; 45 per cent of them fall in this category.

The full effect of religion on libertarianism emerges when those who go to church and those who do not are compared within each denomination. In all of the major denominational groups the non-churchgoers are more often highly libertarian than the churchgoers; overall, 40 per cent of the non-churchgoers and 28 per cent of the churchgoers are highly libertarian, a difference of 12 percentage points, but the effect of church attendance varies from one denomination to another in Table IX. Churchgoing makes the most difference in the

TABLE IX

LIBERTARIANISM BY RELIGIOUS DENOMINATION AND CHURCH ATTENDANCE

Religious Denomination	Proportion highly libertarian			
	Some church attendance		No church attendance	
	Percentage	Number of cases	Percentage	Number of cases
Jewish	45	(22)	51	(43)
None	—	(7)	46	(70)
Protestant	28	(303)	36	(264)
Roman Catholic	25	(122)	48	(33)

libertarianism of the Roman Catholics; it has much less effect on Protestants and Jews, probably because regular attendances at services is not as much an act of faith in these religions as it is among Catholics.

Since these findings are essentially similar to Stouffer's national surveys,[12] we can use some of his other results to support our hypothesis that the lesser libertarianism of the churchgoers represents a reaction to perceived heresy. When asked to state what they thought were the beliefs of Communists, the most frequent response (from 24 per cent of the national cross-section) was that Communists were "against religion". Those believing Communists to be dangerous were asked to explain why they felt that way. They were much more likely to mention the spreading of "bad ideas" and the conversion of Americans to Communism than such activities as sabotage or espionage. Extreme anti-Communism and its associated political intolerance and anti-libertarianism seem to be stimulated more by threats to vaguely defined values than by the possibility of attacks on the power and integrity of the government.

The Effects of University Experiences on Libertarianism

The experiences that change students' libertarianism are of three kinds. First, courses in fields like history, political science, and law are necessarily concerned with the individual freedoms and legal safeguards of the Bill of Rights; perhaps the greater libertarianism of some students results from this kind of experience. Second, the training that results from academic work not directly concerned with civil liberties—for example, exposure to the varied beliefs men have held in different times and places—often induces a greater tolerance for new and strange ideas, even when courses are not designed to produce such tolerance. Third, students are affected by experiences that occur outside the classroom—discussions with other students, exposure to college nonconformists, participation in the activities of student groups, and so on. College year makes a much greater difference for the relatively successful than for the relatively unsuccessful students in Table X. Among those with low grades there is only a 4 percentage-point difference (25 minus 21) between upper- and lower-division students; the difference increases to 10 points for those with moderately high grades, and to 27 points for those with the highest grades. The most successful student is the most likely to increase his libertarianism as he goes through college.

Looking at these results in another way, it may be that libertarian attitudes enhance learning; perhaps the non-

[12] Stouffer, op. cit., pp. 140–149.

TABLE X

LIBERTARIANISM BY COLLEGE YEAR AND GRADE-POINT AVERAGE

| | Proportion highly libertarian | | | |
| | First Two Years (Lower division) | | Last Two Years (Upper division) | |
Grade-point average	Percentage	Number of cases	Percentage	Number of cases
High (A to B+)	27	(120)	54	(97)
Medium (B to C+)	27	(140)	37	(247)
Low (C and below)	21	(75)	25	(110)

libertarian, intolerant student is incapable of success in most areas because he lacks the capacity to consider unusual ideas objectively. Table X suggests, however, that the effect of learning on libertarianism is more important; if non-libertarianism resulted in less learning and lower grades, there should be an association between grade-point average and libertarianism in both lower and upper divisions. But grades make a much smaller difference in the libertarianism of students in their first two years, where only 6 percentage points separate the extreme grade-point classes, as against 29 percentage points in the third or fourth years. This reinforces the conclusion that the greater libertarianism of those with high grade point averages is the result of accumulated learning.

Major Subject

Academically, the most important academic fact that differentiates students from one another is their "major subject" of study. Whatever their speciality, students in most American colleges take courses in a variety of subjects, but some fields of study—political science, history, and journalism, among others—necessarily deal with questions of public policy and civil rights, while others, such as the physical sciences and engineering, never consider such questions. Consequently, differences in libertarianism tend to develop between students specializing in various fields. This process, by which the university *differentiates* students, works in the opposite direction to the homogenization discussed above.

"Major subject" means different things to different students; this must be taken into account in considering the influence of major subject on libertarianism. Men and women obviously attach different meanings to their major subjects. For men, a major subject is usually a stepping stone to a career, and their choices are of crucial importance. Most women, on the other hand, expect to be housewives; in our sample, 31 per cent anticipate being occupied only as housewives within five years of graduation, and another 35 per cent expect to be housewives and hold down a job at the same time. Even when college-educated women practice the calling for which they are trained it is often a secondary interest in their lives.

The effect of major subject areas on libertarianism is best observed in the column for men in Table XI. In the social

TABLE XI

LIBERTARIANISM BY MAJOR SUBJECT AREA AND SEX

	Proportion highly libertarian			
	Men		Women	
Major Subject Area	Percentage	Number of cases	Percentage	Number of cases
Applied social sciences (social welfare, criminology, etc.)	—	(9)	45	(20)
Social sciences (political science, sociology, etc.)	63	(30)	34	(32)
Humanities (literature, philosophy, history, classics, etc.)	62	(45)	34	(112)
Life sciences (medical and biological sciences, pure and applied)	41	(37)	35	(60)
Physical sciences (and mathematics)	39	(31)	—	(17)
Engineering and other applied physical sciences*	30	(245)	—	(2)
Education†	29	(24)	23	(73)
Business administration	24	(33)	—	(10)

* This category is 93 per cent engineers; it also includes a few architects, foresters, and agricultural technologists.

† Since the University of California does not permit undergraduates to major in "education" by itself, this category is perhaps too small. It includes those students who identified themselves as education majors (even if the university regards them as other majors) and students in an upper division course in the education department required of those planning to become teachers.

sciences and the humanities men are about twice as likely to be highly libertarian as in engineering, education, and business administration; the physical sciences and the life sciences fall between these extremes. Approximately the same order of categories exists among the women, but the differences in libertarianism are of course smaller. The libertarianism of women is less influenced by their choice of major than that of the men; however, as we shall demonstrate later, women are more affected by certain non-academic aspects of university life, notably the place where they live.

The relatively low position of the students whose major subject is education—that is, who intend to become elementary and secondary school teachers—is important and puzzling. Their attitudes are important because many will occupy positions where they will affect the attitudes of a generation of students. Their low degree of libertarianism is puzzling because it cannot be attributed to a lack of emphasis on liberty and freedom in education courses; these values are stressed more in the education curriculum than in business administration, engineering, or science courses. Two of our findings explain part, but not all, of the low libertarianism of students planning to go into education. The libertarianism of education students is particularly low among those dissatisfied with their choice of fields and among those with low grade-point averages, of whom education recruits a disproportionate number.

Although what students learn in their courses accounts in part for these differences in libertarianism, there is also a strong selective process operating. If accumulated learning were the only important factor, the differences between the majors would be much smaller for those just beginning their college education. In fact, there is a large association between major subject and libertarianism among lower-division students. For example, 35 per cent of those in the social sciences are highly libertarian as against 25 per cent in engineering and 10 per cent in business administration. Furthermore, many students change their major fields of study in the first year or two. We do not have data on such changes, but Morris Rosenberg has shown that many students in America change to subjects whose emphases are consistent with their own values.[18]

Type of Residence

The total university experience includes more than classes and books. Especially in matters of taste and social attitudes, informal contacts between students are of great importance. For many students a good part of this interaction takes place in organized residence groups. In these groups lasting personal attachments are formed, and strong social pressures often promote a uniformity of taste and opinions that distinguishes the members of different groups. As a result, residence groups provide one of the major channels by which American college students become differentiated in their ideas and in their behaviour.

There is a wide variety of living arrangements. Some students live with parents or relatives. Others, mostly men and older women students, live by themselves or with one or two

[18] Morris Rosenberg, *Occupations and Values*, The Free Press, Glencoe, Illinois, 1957.

friends in apartments. But most undergraduate students live in more highly organized groups. First, there are university facilities or "dormitories". Second, there are "fraternities" and "sororities". These groups largely recruit among the wealthiest students; they have elaborate social programmes, and they are controlled by their alumni more than by the university. Finally, there are housing "co-operatives", which provide low-cost room and board for students on a first-come, first-served basis; such groups recruit mostly among students from poorer families. There is considerable variation from group to group. The proportion who are highly libertarian ranges from a low of 11 per cent in one sorority to a high of 43 per cent in a co-operative house. To provide a more complete analysis of the effects of residence groups it is necessary to consider types of groups rather than individual houses; the percentage of highly libertarian students in each of several types is presented in Table XII for men and women separately. Among the men

TABLE XII

LIBERTARIANISM BY TYPE OF RESIDENCE AND SEX

| | Proportion highly libertarian (Undergraduate students only) | | | |
| Type of living arrangement | Men | | Women | |
	Percentage	Number of cases	Percentage	Number of cases
Apartment with spouse	41	(51)	—	(14)
Apartment (no spouse)	36	(74)	46	(35)
With parents or relatives	38	(37)	38	(39)
Co-operative	35	(65)	35	(62)
University dormitory	37	(86)	34	(59)
Fraternity	32	(104)		
Sorority	—		17	(175)

there are only very small differences between types of residences. Differences are somewhat larger among the women; the most unusual group is the sorority women, of whom only 17 per cent are highly libertarian. Sororities apparently attract and select women who are not highly libertarian. This is suggested by the fact that sorority women who are in their first two years of college are even more extreme; among seventy-seven of them, only 9 per cent are highly libertarian—as against 33 per cent of lower division co-op women and 39 per cent of lower-division women living in dormitories. Upper-division sorority women are also less likely to be highly libertarian, although the differences between them and the other upper-division women are smaller.

Sororities exert more control over the private lives of their members than do other kinds of residence groups, especially in matters of dress, dating, and even studying. According to reports we have collected, in many sororities there are social and physical pressures *against* studying and other forms of intellectual activity—for example, members may have a *maximum* time allowed for study. Conditions are quite different among the most independent students, those who are unmarried and live in apartments. For a man, nothing except his own preferences, his money, and the availability of an apartment prevents him from living in one; the university has no rules about where men students must live. It does have such rules for women: an unmarried woman student under twenty-one must have the written permission of her parents to live anywhere else than in an approved, organized residence group. Thus the unmarried women who live in apartments are probably more mature—at least mature enough to have convinced their parents to let them depart from the protection of an organized group. And it is only these mature women who are more libertarian than the men in comparable situations; in fact, they have the highest rate of libertarianism in Table XII.

As noted earlier, the academic aspects of university life make a greater difference in the libertarianism of men, and here we have shown that an important non-academic aspect makes a greater difference among women. This follows from the greater likelihood of men to see the university as a stepping-stone to a career and from the greater likelihood of women to see it as an introduction to a distinctive style of life. Where circumstances have selected a group of emotionally mature women and put them in a situation of social independence, as in the apartment dwellers, women are likely to be highly libertarian. But where they live in an intellectually narrow and socially homogeneous environment, women are often very low in libertarianism.

Leadership

In all sections of America and for all types of organizations —even the Daughters of the American Revolution and the American Legion, which have been noted for their frequent attacks on "liberals" and "radicals"—leaders of community organizations are more libertarian than are the rank-and-file.[14] These findings seem paradoxical. Common sense and the findings of small-group research[15] suggest that leaders typically embody the values of their groups. Why, then, should leaders of groups with anti-libertarian ideologies (in the sense in

[14] Stouffer, *op. cit.*, ch. II.
[15] See Cecil A. Gibb, "Leadership", ch. 24 in Gardner Lindzey (ed.), *Handbook of Social Psychology*, vol. II, Addison-Wesley, Cambridge, Massachusetts, 1954.

which "libertarianism" is used here) be more libertarian than their followers?

One possible explanation is that the leaders are more highly educated. If this were the major explanation, then we would expect little difference between leaders and non-leaders with the same amount of education. In our sample leaders and non-leaders do have roughly the same level of education, live in the same surroundings, and do much the same kind of work. Nevertheless, even under these conditions, leaders are more libertarian than non-leaders. Something more than formal education is needed to account for the greater libertarianism of leaders.

In our definition a leader is anyone who has held an elected position in a living group, honour society, campus publication, religious group, or any other campus or off-campus organization. The more leadership positions a student holds, or has held, the more likely he is to be highly libertarian, as reported in Table XIII.

TABLE XIII

LIBERTARIANISM BY NUMBER OF ELECTED LEADERSHIP POSITIONS

Number of elected positions	Proportion highly libertarian	Number of cases
Three or more	67	(15)
Two	42	(57)
One	38	(213)
None	31	(598)

Leaders are more libertarian despite the fact that we have included a great diversity of positions, some of them trivial: we would have classified as leaders everyone from the president of the organized student body of the university to the corresponding secretary of the Chess Club, had these students been in our sample. Actually, the type of leadership position makes considerable difference. If elected presidents and chairmen are considered separately from other elected positions, as in Table XIV, the former are more libertarian.

TABLE XIV

LIBERTARIANISM BY TYPE OF ELECTED POSITION

Highest position achieved	Proportion highly libertarian	Number of cases
President or chairman	51	(81)
Other elected positions	36	(208)
No elected positions	31	(598)

The leaders and non-leaders in our sample do not have exactly the same amount of education; students who have been in college longer are more likely to be elected to offices in student groups. But when only students in the same year are considered, leaders are still more likely to be highly libertarian than non-leaders, and the differences are not much smaller than those reported in the preceding two tables.

The greater libertarianism of leaders holds up in a wide variety of social contexts. Just as Stouffer found that leaders of veterans' organizations were more libertarian than non-leaders, so the leaders of our least libertarian groups, the sororities tend to be more libertarian than the other members of these groups. And even where many members of a group are highly libertarian, as in the co-operative houses, the leaders are even more so. The same is true among categories of students that do not represent organized groups: among men and among women, in all of the major subject areas we have studied, and among supporters of both major political parties, those who have held some kind of elected position are more libertarian than the rest.

All of this demonstrates the importance of distinguishing leaders from the general population. Herbert Blumer and other critics of public-opinion research have assailed the practice of treating everyone's opinions as equally important—that is, of not distinguishing between the mass and those in positions of power.[16] Both Stouffer's study and ours demonstrate that the failure to make this distinction leads to a serious underestimate of support for libertarianism, for people who are or have been leaders are more likely to be in positions that determine the behaviour of others in times of crisis. People with anti-libertarian sentiments are less often in positions where these sentiments can lead to collective action.

There are two main types of explanations for the greater libertarianism of leaders. First, the leader's role usually requires him to seek consensus among the group members on various questions. For the group to function effectively, he must frequently reconcile divergent views, and some measure of tolerance for dissent may be developed in this task. Furthermore, as his group's spokesman and representative to other organizations, a leader is exposed to a more diverse assortment of people than in his own group. Experience with people unlike those with whom one has previously associated is often a key factor in the acquisition of libertarian attitudes.

This explanation of the greater libertarianism of leaders has focused on what happens to them after they assume their positions. A second and complementary explanation stresses

[16] Herbert Blumer, "Public Opinion and Public Opinion Polling", *American Sociological Review*, 13, October 1948, pp. 542–549.

the process by which leaders are selected. Because he is intolerant of the rights and views of others, the anti-libertarian person may well be less popular and therefore less likely to be honoured by election to a position of leadership, especially in groups where most members are libertarian.[17] Then, too, the members of groups may anticipate that an intolerant person will not be able to function effectively as a leader. In sum, libertarianism may be a factor in the selection of leaders as well as an outcome of the experience of being a leader.

The University and the Larger Society

This paper explores the ways in which university education changes students' support for individual liberties and civil rights. Essentially the same processes take place beyond the campus, but much less is known about them. It would be important, for example, to see how the processes of selection and training are carried on after students graduate from the university, for changes in values do not stop with the end of formal education. And next to nothing is known about the processes by which young adults who do not go to universities develop and change their values. A satisfactory assessment of the effects of university training on the development of values must compare the changes produced in university students with the changes in those who do not attend institutions of higher education.[18]

For sociologists, however, the study of the university and its students has a special appeal, apart from accessibility: the university is a miniature society with many smaller social systems within it. It also has the great advantage over the community that its "life cycle" takes only four years for most students. Such processes as socialization into the norms of the community, recruitment into organizations, and selection for positions of leadership can all be studied easily. And the individual life cycle in the university is so standardized that a panel study of change can be approximated, as in the present case, by comparisons between students at different stages of their university education. Nothing comparable exists in the open community. Finally, comparative analyses of the same processes in different social contexts can be carried on more easily within and between universities than within and between other large organizations, communities, or entire societies. Sociologists are only now beginning to take advantage of these possibilities.[19]

[17] For evidence from small group research see Gibb, *op. cit.*, pp. 909–912.

[18] Allan H. Barton, *Studying the Effects of College Education: A Methodological Examination of "Changing Values in College"*, Edward W. Hazen Foundation, New Haven, Connecticut, 1959.

[19] Some examples are the works of Lazarsfeld and Thielens and of Norman Miller, noted above, and Robert K. Merton, George Reader,

THE POLICE CAR DEMONSTRATION:
A SURVEY OF PARTICIPANTS

GLEN LYONNS,

UNDERGRADUATE PHYSICS STUDENT, BERKELEY

The encirclement and holding of a police car for thirty-two hours on October 1 and 2 by Berkeley students was the first clear sign that the student protest, was of a different caliber both in depth of feeling and in base of support, from the minor protests that have occurred on other college campuses over various issues.

Three weeks after these events, I prepared a questionnaire that was eventually completed by 618 persons who had participated in the demonstration. I hoped to gain information which would make clearer the base of student support, the degree of commitment held by the students, and the motivation for their protest. The analysis of the questionnaire data was to provide one article for a large project, edited by Michael Rossman, that was to deal with campus political activity over the last fifteen years. Looking back, some of the major conclusions indicated by the questionnaire results now seem obvious. However, I shall try to present the salient information it provided and also offer some interpretations that have benefited by events that have occurred since the data were collected.

The questionnaires were completed by students between October 24 and October 27. This was a period when no demonstrations or rallies were held, and in terms of mass participation this was the least active period of the Free Speech Movement.[1] It was also the period when the newspapers were quite consistent in categorizing the demonstrators as a small, discontented, radical minority group.

The background information which led to the sit-in in October is contained elsewhere in this volume; however, some details concerning the demonstration of October 1–2 will help provide a background for the following discussion. The police car was surrounded by students at approximately 11:30 A.M., October 1, to protest the arrest and prevent the removal to police headquarters of Jack Weinberg, who was held inside the police car. Soon after, the police-car roof became a podium. From then on, almost continuously until the end of

---

and Patricia L. Kendall, *The Student-Physician*, Harvard University Press, Cambridge, Massachusetts, 1957.

[1] Before the police-car demonstration a "United Front" composed of the campus political and social action groups led the fight against the administration's action. Immediately after the end of the October 1–2 demonstration the Free Speech Movement was formed.

the demonstration, arguments concerning the free-speech is-sue, the effects of the administration's actions, the morality and wisdom of the tactics, the past actions of the administration, and other such questions were discussed. Many of the issues that would become more important later on in the controversy were first aired on the police-car roof. From 1 to 7 P.M., October 1, there was also a sit-in on the second floor of Sproul Hall. The night of October 1, a crowd of hecklers surrounded the student sit-ins and threw lighted cigarettes into the crowd. The hecklers finally left after a minister's plea. The next day the sit-in continued. Over 500 police were called in, and under a threat that the police would otherwise arrest the demonstrators, the leaders of the demonstration signed an agreement with President Kerr.

For many of the students this demonstration provided a first and very intense introduction to political activity. The demonstration provided a highly emotional experience, and at various times it was an extremely tense and potentially dangerous situation. All of this should be borne in mind when we try to describe the demonstrators, their attitudes and motivation, and the effect the demonstration had on them.

The data are most conveniently summarized in two tables. The first table gives the important results from the total sample and, where available, comparative figures for the university student population as a whole. The figures for the university student population are from data collected by Robert Somers. The second table compares students who had participated previously in one or more demonstrations of any kind with those students who had never participated in a demonstration prior to the October 1–2 demonstration.

The manner in which the sample was drawn introduces a definite bias toward the more active and committed FSM supporters. The questionnaire was available at a table sponsored by FSM at the now famous Bancroft-Telegraph strip of land, and this may have had some influence in determining who did or did not pick up questionnaires. One would assume that the more interested and involved students would take the trouble to pick up, fill out, and return the rather lengthy questionnaire. If this assumption is correct, then the proportion of students who were politically active prior to the demonstration should be considerably higher in the sample than among the total population of demonstrators. There is also a probable bias toward the left of the political spectrum, since the more active students tend to be somewhat more leftist. Finally, the degree of commitment to the movement would probably be lower if all demonstrators were included. This bias in sampling toward the more politically active and committed students should thus be borne in mind when looking at the results.

TABLE 1

DEMONSTRATORS COMPARED TO UNIVERSITY POPULATION

	Demonstrators*	University Student Sample**
	%	%
1. Sex		
Male	63	63
Female	37	37
2. Age		
17–18	19	
19–20	35	
21–22	26	
23 or over	21	
3. Years at Cal	Semesters at Cal	
0–1	36 First	32
1–3	48 2nd–3rd	27
3 or more	15 4th–5th	14
	6th–7th	12
	8 or more	15
4. Living group		
Home with parents	9	6
Fraternity or sorority	2	15
Dormitory	13	17
Co-op	5	6
Apartment	71	57
5. Income of parents	Family Income	
5,000 and under	8 Closest to 5,000 or under	15
5,000–10,000	27 " to 10,000	26
10,000–15,000	24 " to 15,000	19
15,000–25,000	22 " to 20,000	11
25,000 and over	16 " to 25,000 or over	16
6. Church attendance		
Once a month or more	13	29
Never or almost never	87	71
7. Political affiliation†		
Conservative Republican	2	10
Liberal Republican	6	20
Conservative Democrat	6	8
Liberal Democrat	43	28
Democratic Socialist	26 Independent	20
Revolutionary Socialist	10 Other	11

TABLE 1 *(cont'd)*

	Demonstrators* %	University Student Sample** %
8. Belongs to a campus political or social action group.		
Yes	26	
No	71	
9. Participated in any demonstrations before.		
Yes	50	
No	48	
10. How many demonstrations have you previously participated in.		
None	48	
1–3	22	
4–7	13	
7 or more	17	
11. Number of hours spent in Berkeley demonstration		
1 to 12	30	
12 to 20	26	
20 or more	44	
12. Did you sit in Sproul Hall October 1.		
Yes	41	
No	58	
13. Were you sitting in at the end of the demonstration		
Yes	70	
No	30	

14. At the beginning of the demonstration were you unwilling to demonstrate; or willing to demonstrate but not risk arrest and expulsion

48

Possibly risk arrest and expulsion

37

Risk arrest and expulsion 15

15. If negotiations break down and similar demonstrations are called for would you:

Risk arrest and expulsion 56

Demonstrate but not risk
arrest and expulsion 40

Not demonstrate 1

16. What factors motivated your first joining the demonstration. (only percentage totals for four factors which had highest total under choice, strong factor)

Feeling about past campus
oppression, this being
last straw 27

Indefinite suspension of 8
students 33

Need to take stand on free
speech issue   60
Administration's handling
of the affair‡   63
17. Expression of some degree of dissatisfaction with courses, exams, professors, etc.:   40   17

* The sample of demonstrators is based on 618 questionnaires: each
question was answered by between 600 to 618 persons. Where the percentages do not add to 100 it is because a few did not answer the question, since percentages are all based on the total of 618.
** The sample of students was 287 and percentages are based on this
number. Where percentages do not add up to 100 it is because some did
not answer the question.
† Percentages arrived at by extrapolation as first 200 questionnaires
did not contain the liberal Democrat choice.
‡ Based only on those questionnaires which provided this as a choice;
this factor was not in the original questionnaire, but was added later because many students wrote in this response.

TABLE 2

FIRST-TIME DEMONSTRATORS COMPARED TO EXPERIENCED
DEMONSTRATORS

	First-time demonstrators	Participants in one or more previous demonstrations
	%	%
1. Age		
17–18	23	15
19–20	36	33
21–22	23	28
23 or over	17	24
2. Living groups		
Home with parents	11	7
Fraternity or sorority	2	1
Dormitory	20	7
Co-op	4	5
Apartment	63	79
3. Church attendance		
One or more a month	17	10
Never or almost never attend	83	90
4. Parents' Income		
5,000 or under	7	9
5,000–10,000	23	31
15,000–25,000	27	21
25,000 or over	26	18

TABLE 2 (*cont'd*)

	First-time demonstrators %	Participants in one or more previous demonstrations %
5. Political affiliation		
Conservative Republican	3	0
Liberal Republican	10	2
Conservative Democrat	10	2
Liberal Democrat	48	39
Democratic Socialist	17	35
Revolutionary Socialist	3	18
6. Were one or more parents actively involved in politics during the period 1930–1950		
Yes	21	42
No	77	58
7. Are your parents presently involved in politics		
Yes	23	34
No	75	65
8. Did you sit in inside Sproul Hall, October 1		
Yes	35	47
No	64	52
9. Were you sitting in at the end of the demonstration		
Yes	68	72
No	32	28
10. Students expressing some degree of dissatisfaction with courses, examinations, professors, etc.	32	48
11. At the beginning of the demonstration were you willing to:		
Not demonstrate or demonstrate but not risk arrest or expulsion	59	39
Possibly risk arrest or expulsion	32	41
Risk arrest or expulsion	9	20
12. At the end of the demonstration had your position changed to*:		
Possibly risk arrest and expulsion	23	15
Risk arrest and expulsion	41	37
13. If negotiations break down and similar demonstrations are necessary would you:		
Risk arrest and expulsion	51	62
Demonstrate but not risk arrest or expulsion	44	37

* (Only 1% of those whose position changed had decreased their support of FSM)

14. Time spent in demonstration:

Up to 12 hours	35	26
12–20 hours	28	23
20 or more hours	37	51

15. Since the demonstration have you been:

Active (worked 3 or more hours for FSM)	18	20
Very active (worked 15 or more hours for FSM)	6	11

16. In the future will you be:

Politically active in other areas	69	44
About the same	29	54
Less active	0	1

General Comments on Data

Generally the demonstrators seem to be more liberal politically and to live in less restrictive housing than the total University student population. This is not surprising; one would expect that the demonstrators would be comprised of this type of student. He generally falls into the academic intellectual and the non-conformist intellectual groups that sociologists Martin Trow and Burton Clark refer to in their typology of student subcultures. The other two groups of this typology are a collegiate "Joe College" group and the vocationally oriented student, both less likely to be intellectually or politically active.

Some of the differences between first-time demonstrators and those who had demonstrated previously may be explained in part by the ages of the two groups. The first-time demonstrators are younger and have had less time to become involved in demonstrations. As students get older at Berkeley they tend to move into apartments and out of more restrictive environments like dormitories.

When the activity records of the liberal Democrats and democratic Socialists are compared it is clear that most democratic Socialists are like liberal Democrats, while approximately 20 per cent of the democratic Socialists resemble the revolutionary Socialists in action terms. The revolutionary Socialists prior to, as well as during, the demonstration were considerably more active than those in other groups. For example, over 60 per cent of those students who had participated in seven or more previous demonstrations considered themselves revolutionary Socialists. This is the group of students that can most legitimately be called radical. There were approximately 300 students in campus political and social action groups at the beginning of the semester. The fact that 150 completed the questionnaire gives another indication of how previously politically active students are over-represented in the questionnaire.

The question concerning demonstrating in the future was of course speculative, and when viewed in October the percentage who said they would risk arrest in the future (56) seemed quite high. When one considers that 800 people were arrested later on at the Sproul Hall sit-in, December 8, the results of the questionnaire appear to be validated.

A reading of the original questionnaires revealed that the one response provided to the question concerning motivational factors, "administration's handling of the issue," was often underscored or similarly emphasized. In response to the question "If your degree of commitment has increased since the demonstrations, what factors do you feel were responsible?"—77 per cent indicated that the administration's handling of the issue was a strong factor. This bears out what most people now feel—that unilateral action compounded the problem.

The students who were demonstrating for the first time are of particular interest. At the time, one might have argued that it was simply the excitement of the situation that caused such a large demonstration and that most students would cease their participation when excitement died down. In the light of subsequent events, it is obvious this explanation is inadequate. The FSM awakened or created a lasting response in many first-time demonstrators as indicated in Table 2. At the beginning of the demonstration the students who had demonstrated before showed a much greater degree of commitment and participation, but by the end of the demonstration the gap had narrowed considerably between them and first-time demonstrators. It is clear that the demonstration considerably increased the general level of commitment to the FSM among all participants.

Relating the perceptions of students concerning the likelihood of arrest, expulsion, or violence to their willingness to risk arrest or expulsion in the future reveals that those students who felt there was a fair or good chance of such occurrences were more likely to be willing to risk arrest or expulsion (see Table 3). In other words, those students who perceived the greatest risk from involvement in the demonstrations and yet continued to demonstrate were the most committed regarding future action. This itself is not surprising, since to demonstrate in the face of danger would require a greater commitment than to demonstrate where little danger was perceived. When one looks at the sequence of events throughout the controversy it appears that the number of actions involving risks for students were considerable. The police-car demonstration, the signing of petitions requesting equal disciplinary treatment, the massive manning of the then illegal tables, and the December sit-in all had this quality. This would seem to indicate that one reason student commitment remained high throughout the controversy can be traced to the greater personal involvement that arises from participation in an event requiring continuing personal risk. Students by their participation made an implicit value judgment about the worth of the protest. To leave the FSM after such participation would either be to admit that one had made an incorrect judgment or to reveal a willingness to stay away from what one still believed to be an important and legitimate protest. An individual may very well change his mind about the value of a given decision, but such a change is usually based on new information which leads him to believe either that the situation has changed or that his original judgment was in error. In the Berkeley controversy, however, the administration's actions only served to give further evidence to the charges of bad faith and unwillingness to admit that there were issues involving free speech. Critics of the students have pointed to the blunders of the administration, and given these, it was unlikely that many students would change their initial judgments or withdraw their participation.

There is reason to believe that the questionnaire data do not provide an estimate of the general support for the FSM. Robert Somers' data, reported elsewhere in this book, show the political affiliation of those who supported both FSM goals and tactics to be: conservative Republicans 4 per cent, liberal Republicans 8 per cent, conservative Democrats 7 per cent,

TABLE 3

RELATION BETWEEN EXPECTATION OF PUNITIVE ACTION
AND WILLINGNESS TO RISK ARREST AND EXPULSION
IN FUTURE DEMONSTRATIONS

*% in each category willing to risk arrest and expulsion in future demonstration**

Perception of degree of likelihood that each of the following would occur to respondent:**	Expulsion	Arrest	Physical Violence
No chance	39% (104)	15% (50)	38% (153)
Little chance	54% (295)	37% (139)	43% (226)
Fair chance	68% (121)	63% (198)	58% (150)
Good chance	73% (42)	75% (177)	76% (26)

* Original question: "If negotiations break down and further demonstrations are necessary would you: (1) risk arrest and expulsion, (2) demonstrate but not risk arrest and expulsion, (3) not demonstrate."
** Original question: "During the demonstration how likely did you think it was that one of the following incidents would happen to you:

liberal Democrats 41 per cent, independent 25 per cent, other 11 per cent, and don't know 2 per cent. The independents seem to include both those who would be classified by others as Democrats or Republicans as well as those who would have indicated their identifications as a Socialist of some kind if such a category had been provided. The "other" category also seems to contain some Socialists.

Peripheral Remarks

Most of what follows is not derived from the survey data. The questionnaire does not really measure psychological motivation. The data do support the contention that there were strongly felt verbalized positions on issues, and any attempt to explain the controversy without reference to them would be inadequate, to say the least. The information the questionnaire gives about motivation is assumed to have validity and is an unstated justification for parts of the argument that follow. The rest of the argument must stand or fall on its own merits.

Since the arrest of the 800 sit-ins there has been a flood of articles concerning the cause and significance of the campus rebellion. The criticisms and interpretations of the controversy have been varied. The most serious criticism of the FSM has been made by those who admitted the existence of legitimate grievances, but who see the tactics used by the FSM constituting a danger to the democratic order.

However, those who make this criticism base it on important assumptions which are not made explicit and are not necessarily valid. They also fail to consider certain historical analogues and fail to note the implication of certain distinct differences between this student generation and earlier ones.

The first assumption is so sweeping it is hard to state. Critics, in particular Seymour Martin Lipset and Paul Seabury, seem to assume that all responsible people have the same ideas about the definitions of the democratic processes and the democratic order. Their assumption seems to be that one must and can use the established democratic procedures and to go beyond them constitutes a threat to the democratic order. The relation of democratic order and democratic processes to civil disobedience are not considered. What criteria, if any, justify civil disobedience? What was the situation at Berkeley in regard to these criteria? Were there other channels really open to the students? In an industrial society is it possible that civil disobedience may be increasingly necessary to aid in keeping the democratic processes functioning? These and similar questions should have been touched on by those who criticize the students so strongly.

The more explicit assumption is that the situation at Berkeley was not serious enough to warrant the tactics used by the

FSM. No doubt one might debate this endlessly. I would make two suggestions. First, it is always difficult for someone to make what amounts to historical pronouncements about a current event. It may be even more difficult if the writer has been personally close to the event. One simply does not have the advantage of a future historical perspective, and this should be borne in mind when unequivocal judgments are made. Secondly, the spontaneity and breadth of support indicate that there were some deeply felt issues bothering the students and faculty. The argument that the majority were merely manipulated by radicals or that radicals had been using the issues of capital punishment and peace marches simply to gain support misses the point. The point was that support *was* gathered by the free speech-civil rights issue. Radicals are always present and they always have issues with which to attack the status quo. The fact that they supported FSM does not make the issues invalid. Many have pointed to the administration's handling of the situation as a major cause for the growth of FSM support. I agree with that, but again this does not mean that the protest against the handling of the situation was illegitimate.

The categorical classification of the Berkeley situation as indicating a serious threat to democratic order seems to be a definite oversimplification. American history is rich in examples of the use of tactics which were condemned at the time but have seemed justified in retrospect. The tactics used have either been stopped when reform legislation or other needed responses were forthcoming or, as in the case of the strikes against management, have become institutionalized. What reason is there not to believe that the FSM's tactics will either fall into disuse upon response of concerned parties or evolve into an accepted and thus legitimate form of gaining a hearing for certain kinds of grievances that are not easily transmitted upward through the complex power structure of modern society. Clark Kerr in *The Uses of the University* has shown how complex the modern university has become. Certainly the tactic of civil disobedience as used by Martin Luther King is accepted by many, including Governor Brown, when it is used in the South.

Neither of these possibilities should be dismissed out of hand. They seem at least as likely the alternative predictions that the tactics will be used in such an indiscriminate manner as to result in a threat to the democratic order.

However, if the student is in fact a "true believer" radical, then he may go beyond the bounds of a flexible democratic system. Many, however, have criticized the students as being "true believer" radicals, suggesting such an orientation leads them to strain limits of even a flexible democratic system. Now critics of the students have pointed to the students having a moral rather than a political orientation. The implications of this have not been developed. I am writing this at the beginning of registration week of the semester following the demonstrations. There have been dire predictions of FSM sabotage of registration or new demonstrations and demands. However, I predict that in fact FSM will not exist on the Berkeley campus this semester except possibly in connection with the arrested students' trials. The reason for this is the apolitical, non-ideological nature of the student protester. He is very concerned with wrongs that he sees in society, but one is unlikely to be a revolutionary unless one has a doctrine and firm faith that one has the answers which will create a utopian society. The student of today may be less politically knowledgeable than his counterpart in the 1930s but is likely to be more sophisticated in his beliefs about the possibility of solving the world's problems. Even the use of the term "revolutionary Socialist" used by the most ideological students today rather than the term "Communist" used in the 1930s indicates their lack of faith in any system which purports to be a cure-all. The students are issue-oriented and situation-oriented. The reason the civil-rights issue was so important to the students was because it meant the students were not fighting just for the abstract principle of free speech, but rather for speech that could have possible consequences. The moral orientation is one reason they were able to laugh at themselves (something commented on by many observers). The pressure of the "true believer" conformity has, I think, been exaggerated by those who perhaps remember different times and attitudes.

Hopefully all of this suggests that the FSM critics may be somewhat pessimistic in their assessment of the meaning of the Berkeley controversy. Even worse, they may have prejudiced many against legitimate student action which may occur for a variety of social causes in the future.

THE MAINSPRINGS OF THE REBELLION: A SURVEY OF BERKELEY STUDENTS IN NOVEMBER, 1964

BY ROBERT H. SOMERS
PROFESSOR, DEPARTMENT OF SOCIOLOGY, BERKELEY

Through a fortunate coincidence of timing, my undergraduate course in social-research methods was getting under way with a class project at the same time that the recent student protest on the Berkeley campus was coming to a head. A quick change in plans allowed us to obtain rather detailed interview material from a cross section of the student body during the heat of the free-speech controversy on this campus and thus provided a unique opportunity to learn something systematic about the thinking of the students.

Interviews were conducted mostly during the early part of November with a carefully drawn sample of 285 students representing the whole student body. Although this seems like a relatively small number of interviews, the usual calculation of sampling variability indicates that our results should not depart from the population figures by more than about 6 per cent. Hence this size sample suffices to give a relatively accurate picture of the attitudes of students—at least accurate enough to make a great deal of progress beyond the speculations derived from personal observations, conversations, observations of demonstrations, and so on, which have formed the basis for rather sweeping generalizations about the situation on campus.[1]

In sampling from a population of 27,431 students registered for the fall semester, it is of course possible to obtain some information about the whole population in order to check the accuracy of this sample. Such a comparison for the categories of sex and class show that our sample departs from the actual population proportions by no more than 4 per cent, well within chance sampling error, except for one category: male graduate students have been underselected by 5 per cent. Since female graduate students were also underselected by 3 per cent, this makes the proportion of graduate students in

[1] While interviews with 285 students have been completed, the "open-ended" or qualitative answers for only 234 had been coded at the time of this analysis. This includes such items of information as major field of study, father's occupation and date of interview.

In addition, many of the precoded answers have not been rechecked ("cleaned" in the technical language), although students checked each other's coding, and the key-punching of IBM cards was verified. Consequently, because of time pressures, I have not completed all the routine attempts to eliminate the errors that may arise between time of personal contact with the respondent and presentation of the results. However, reading various selected questionnaires to add depth to the statistical analysis has produced no important errors, though occasional minor differences in judgment as to how a response should be coded.

This study grew out of an undergraduate course in social research methods, and would have been impossible without the collaboration of my two excellent teaching assistants, Kenneth Cohen and Sally Bould. Nor would we have been able to conduct this survey, requiring some 400 hours of personal interviews with a carefully selected sample of Berkeley students, had it not been for the energetic and often eager participation of the 52 students in the class. They devoted long hours to the interviewing and to recording the responses in a form suitable for processing. It is unfortunate that time pressures prevent their criticism of the following interpretations of the data, for many of them would have sensible comments to add and, undoubtedly, points of disagreement.

Finally, without access to the data processing facilities and the helpful advice of Mr. Howard Turpin at the university's Survey Research Center, these results could never have been obtained with such speed and accuracy.

our sample 8.6 per cent below the actual proportion. It is likely that many of these graduate students whom we failed to contact are not particularly involved in campus activities or particularly interested in the controversy, so there is no doubt a small systematic bias in the following results. However, this small bias is likely to have little effect on the over-all picture of the qualities of student sentiment and position. In addition, most of this report consists of a comparison of students who expressed different, but clearly formulated, positions on the controversy, and for this purpose the sample appears to be highly accurate.

This report consists first of a summary of the information we collected which describes the campus as a whole, and then turns to a comparison of the differences between students who took opposing sides in the controversy. In part these comparisons help to shed light on the origins of the revolt, and may suggest characteristics of the student body unique to this campus which have played a role. Obviously, however, I can make no systematic attempt here to compare sentiment among students at different campuses, and a primary purpose of this report is to attempt a better understanding of the nature and quality of the complaint that the rebellious students were registering, something that appears not to have been well understood throughout the controversy. As Professor Owen Chamberlain suggested in a recent meeting of the Berkeley Division of the Academic Senate, the students in their demonstrations were "trying to tell us something." With these interview materials we have an opportunity to learn more clearly what they were expressing.

The purpose of this report is to present the results of our survey of student opinion in November, and it is therefore impossible to include more than a very brief summary of the events that took place on the Berkeley campus in the fall. Various other reports on the Berkeley situation have presented the events more fully, with a selection and emphasis reflecting the viewpoint of the author. However, our survey data cannot be interpreted if divorced from the surrounding context of events, and since many of our questions focused on the demonstration of September 30 through October 2, it is well to recall that this was provoked by the university's efforts to prohibit a traditional solicitation of funds and members in designated campus locations by "off-campus" organizations. These organizations, ranging from Campus Conservatives to CORE, are referred to as "off-campus" because their activities are directed to issues external to the campus community. An attempt by the university administration to arrest a recent graduate who was manning a table for CORE led to a sit-down around the police car in which he was to be transported, an impasse which lasted some thirty hours until a negotiated agreement between President Kerr and the student leaders ended the demonstration.

The resulting agreement was the subject of continual controversy during early October, in particular the manner in which the two committees called for by the agreement, one on rules for campus political activity and the other to review the suspensions of eight student leaders, should be selected. After intense negotiation, both committees were established, and the student leaders co-operated and refrained from violating the newly interpreted rules throughout October. On November 9 the student activists, now highly organized into a "Free Speech Movement" (FSM) decided that they should resume the manning of tables, apparently viewing the administration as intransigent and believing they had a legal, or at least moral, right to pursue this activity, whereupon the administration abolished the committee on student political activity with the explanation that the October 2 agreements had been broken.

It appeared to me that more support was aroused for the FSM at this point, especially among graduate students, than had been the case before. By November 20, more than 3000 students paraded to University Hall, where the Regents were meeting. The outcome was ambiguous, however, and at their rally a few days later the FSM appeared divided as to how to proceed. Many were predicting at this time that the controversy would settle down to a simmer, but the lull was short-lived as the administration instituted new disciplinary measures against four student leaders for their part in the demonstration of October 1 and 2. This led eventually to the sit-in of over 1000 students on December 2, the arrest of some 800 of them starting in the pre-dawn hours of Thursday, December 3, and a student strike the following Monday, which was effective on a large part of the campus. In an attempt to clarify principles and provide a framework in which the university could return to its normal functioning, the faculty, in a meeting of the Academic Senate on December 8, passed by a vote of 7 to 1 a resolution which clearly defined and supported maximum freedom of political expression for students.

What issues or sentiments led to these actions by the students? How widespread was their support and what were its motivations? The following report provides a good deal of insight into the whole series of events, despite the fact that many events have taken place since our interviewing. We have obtained a "snapshot" of campus sentiment as it appeared during November, and this in itself is instructive. In addition, however, it is possible to discover many aspects of the thinking of those who supported the rebellion, and these gross characteristics are not likely to be transitory but relatively enduring. While most of us reacted to events as they occurred with various changes of opinion and evaluation, our survey helps to go somewhat beneath the surface to consider the more basic sympathies which fluctuate little from day to day, and which help to understand the motivations of the students.

A brief review of the more important findings would be useful at this point. We found sympathy for the demonstrators to be widespread and dispersed throughout the campus, even to the extent of one third of the students approving the tactics that demonstrators had used. This support was clearly concentrated among students in certain fields—the social sciences, humanities, and physical sciences—but as strong among freshmen as among graduate students, and not related to the number of semesters a student had been on this campus. Nor is support particularly related to feelings of dissatisfaction with the educational functions of the university. On the contrary, we found a remarkable amount of satisfaction with courses, professors, and so on, and appreciation of the efforts made by the administration to provide top-quality education for students here. Thus the prevailing explanation in terms of characteristics peculiar to the "multiversity" seems to have no support. Rather, it appears that students resent being deprived of their rights to political activity, being excluded from full political citizenship, and this sentiment is especially strong among those who are emotionally involved in the civil-rights movement. Thus the material we collected suggests that the mainsprings of the rebellion are an optimistic idealism about the type of society which can be shaped by the new generation, and an unwillingness to allow the paternalism endemic to college campuses to extend its coverage to the activities necessary for the furtherance of these ideals.

I

Our interview began with some general questions about the meaning of free speech, whether the free expression of certain groups should be restricted, which groups, if any, represent a threat to our society, and so on. Analysis of their answers shows that over half the students feel that the government may legitimately restrict the free speech of some persons, principally for the familiar reason that they may do potential harm to others. Although such restriction is permitted in principle, students were reluctant to name specific groups to which the restriction could legitimately be applied, and often pointed out that it was not the group as such, but the acts of individuals which should form a justification for restriction. Nevertheless, about a fourth of the students did suggest that certain groups—the Communist Party, the Ku Klux Klan, the Black Muslims, the John Birch Society—represent a threat to the United States, and many further assert that there should be restrictions on the freedom of these groups. Indeed, half (48 per cent) of the students feel that an admitted Communist Party member should not be allowed to teach in a public school, a proscription which applies also to members of several other of the radical groups about which we asked, and two thirds say an admitted member should not be permitted to work in a defense plant.

There is one aspect of this portion of the interview which helps to point out what often may not be recognized in the eyes of the general public: the distinction between teaching in a "public school" and the "free dissemination of ideas" represented by the idea of a university. Although half the students would exclude a Communist from public school teaching, only one fifth would exclude an admitted member from university teaching. This suggests a clear differentiation in many students' minds between the functions of one type of school and the other. Of course, some may be surprised that as many as 20 per cent of the students at Berkeley would impose this much restriction on a university, and this serves again to indicate the width of the spectrum of opinions represented here. We will note later how this spectrum is differentially represented in support for the Free Speech Movement.

In the second section of our interview, dealing with political attitudes, students again confirm the image of a relatively liberal, but not unusual, cross section of the nation. Had the election been held on the Berkeley campus, 73 per cent of the votes would have gone to President Johnson by our estimate (as compared to 61 per cent in the national electorate), with some 8 per cent going to minority candidates or not voting; 17 per cent preferred Goldwater. About a fourth of the students identify themselves as liberal Democrats, a fifth liberal Republicans, a fifth Independents, and a tenth are conservative Republicans.

At the time of these interviews, mostly in the few weeks before the national election, it is perhaps not surprising that a third of the students are "very interested" in national politics, and only 1 per cent not interested. Another indication of active interest is the fact that 90 per cent of them claim to read news of national or international events on at least a weekly basis. With regard to specific political issues, it may be a clue to the latent support for the initial protests that 82 per cent of the students agree that the Civil Rights Act of 1964 represents a notable step in the progress of humanity. On the other hand, not unlike the state as a whole (where a constitution amendment, "Proposition 14," outlawing fair-housing ordinances was approved by popular referendum) students are evenly split on the issue of respecting "in all circumstances" the rights of property owners to sell to whom they wish.

Turning from national politics to local issues of the "multiversity," we asked a series of questions about the attitude of students toward the administration of the university. For example, we asked whether they felt that the administration "almost always" can be counted on to give sufficient consideration to the rights and needs of students in setting university policy (slightly over half feel it can). Three quarters of them agree that the university administration indeed has "responsibilities and duties concerning student morality and behavior," and about the same proportion (probably mostly the same students) feel that they are treated as mature and responsible adults by the university administration.

If one supposes that the student protest arose from some general feeling of dissatisfaction with the university, this supposition is damaged, if not thoroughly destroyed, by the fact that 82 per cent of our sample report themselves "satisfied or very satisfied" with "courses, examinations, professors, etc." In addition, there is almost unanimity (92 per cent agreement) that "although some people don't think so, the president of this university and the chancellor (of this campus) are really trying very hard to provide top-quality educational experience for students here." In retrospect, it is amazing to find this much appreciation of the intentions of the top administrators some five weeks after the police-car incident and only a few weeks before a widespread student strike in sympathy for the free speech movement. A later section of the report will consider more directly the extent to which such sentiments entered into rebellious students' motivations.

While students thus overwhelmingly acknowledge the good intentions of the administration regarding educational policy, still about two thirds of them agree that the administration on occasion has to "sacrifice the best interests of the students" because of outside pressures. As to whether they as students have "any say about what the administration does," opinion on campus is very evenly divided. Perhaps it is remarkable that even at the multiversity during a time of crisis as many as 50 per cent of the students feel they do influence administration behavior at least a little, but of course the response to our question is totally ambiguous regarding the ways of effecting that influence.

Turning to the more specific issues involved in the dispute this fall, the image of a well-intentioned university administration suffering from outside pressures continues to appear, although a good many students raised questions about the intentions in this specific instance. Sentiment was nearly evenly split as to whether or not the original ban on solicitation of funds was justified, and those who felt it was justified gave "state property" as their principal reason. A slightly smaller proportion (45 per cent vs. 52 per cent) felt that the ban on recruitment of memberships was justified.

Essentially everyone (82 per cent) agreed that the behavior of the administration in September, in imposing the ban, was influenced by outside pressures of one sort or another. This sentiment no doubt reflects (we did not ask directly about this) the general view that the immediate but unacknowledged cause of the ban was not traffic regulations but protest by conservative Republicans against the use of students to swell the ranks of Scranton supporters at the Republican National Convention, and perhaps inquiries by ex-Senator Knowland as to the legality of recruiting pickets on campus to demonstrate against alleged discrimination in hiring at his nearby newspaper offices.

Suspicions about the intentions of the administration are reflected in the facts that a third of the students felt that once the demonstration of October 2 began, the administration "did not act in good faith," 43 per cent felt they negotiated with students too little (although 15 per cent said it was too much!) and that half the students felt the police should not have been called in.

There was considerable controversy by the time of our interviewing as to whether the issue on campus was one of "free speech" at all. Instead, there were suggestions that a few conspiratorial and charismatic student (or even non-student) leaders misled their idealistic but immature followers into acting irresponsibly over nothing. It would be surprising—and I think reflects a basic lack of faith in the democratic process on the part of such commentators—to suppose that 59 per cent (that is, some 16,000 students) could be "duped" in this fashion into claiming that there was a free-speech issue on campus. This is the figure estimated from our interviews in which we asked, in the context of questions about the October 2 demonstration, "Do you think that there is an issue of free speech on this campus?" Subsequent questioning showed that about half the students felt that collecting funds "for political and social issues" is a part of free speech, while nearly two thirds so defined the recruitment of members to politically active groups, and three fourths of our sample said "yes" when asked whether students should have these rights. This seems a clear mandate. It is not surprising that in the weeks following the demonstration the community seemed to fall apart, and that the faculty felt a growing pressure to exercise some moral leadership, to enunciate the basic principles that should govern a university, as was finally done in the December 8 faculty meeting.

It is disconcerting but instructive to note that during this time, when over half the campus apparently agreed that the demonstrations had some legitimate substantive basis, the administration never gave evidence of a desire to correct the public view of the protest movement which it had created by announcements made early in October that nearly half of the leadership of the movement were Castro and Mao sympathizers. My personal observations are that the apparent unwillingness of the administration to consider the possibility of a legitimate intellectual and ideological ferment underlying the protest pressed more and more moderates into a coalition with the early activists. Although the impetus for action in the early demonstrations came largely from undergraduates, it became apparent that at least among graduate students in sociology, widespread support for the demonstrators became manifest only rather late in November.

Since these interviews were conducted some weeks after the "police car" incident of October 2, we asked students whether they felt that the civil disobedience used during that demonstration was the only available choice of action—and two thirds of the students said "no." However, 63 per cent of our sample said they were "for the goals of the demonstrators," and 34 per cent said they were for the "tactics"—although a few of these pointed out that they took exception to the destruction of property represented by the standing on the police car. When we asked students their impressions of the demonstrators, about half of the campus responded in a favorable way, while a third were unfavorable. In other words, there was widespread sympathy on campus for the demonstrators, sufficient to tolerate, although not without criticism, the tactics that they used.

Our figures lead us to estimate that somewhere close to 9000 students favored not only the goals but also the tactics of the free-speech demonstrators at this time. Even at the largest demonstrations the estimates of numbers present were considerably below this figure—although they did reach estimates of 6000. But these figures agree with the general hypothesis that for everyone willing to get out and demonstrate over an issue, there are others who show strong sympathies in that direction.

We also asked students about the consequences of the demonstration, asking them to try and remember the way they felt during those few days when the police car was surrounded by students. About three fifths of them recalled that they felt there was a pretty good chance of "achieving nothing and doing harm," while one third of them felt that there was a pretty good chance of their "gaining full rights of freedom of speech" (including being able to recruit members and solicit funds). Asked about what they felt might happen in the long run, there was more optimism; two thirds of our sample said there was a fair to good chance of "gaining full rights of freedom of speech."

How do students view the educational process, and their reasons for being in college? In the eyes of some it may ap-

pear that they do not have much time to study, being so involved in politics. In fact, this is obviously not the case under
ordinary circumstances; one reason that graduate students, in
sociology, for example, became involved in the controversy
only rather late is because they, like most of the faculty, were
not keeping closely in touch with campus events until they
reached such proportions that they could no longer be ignored.
For what it is worth, even in our interviews we found that
fewer than half the students claimed to be "very interested" in
the course of events while a police car was captured on the
plaza in front of Sproul Hall.

We asked a few questions about the major purposes of a
college education and the relation of political involvement to
the education process. A list of six different possible purposes
of a college education was presented by the interviewer, ranging from "vocational training, development of skills and techniques directly applicable to my career," (chosen by a third)
to preparation for a happy marriage and family life (completely ignored as the most important). The majority choice,
selected by half the students as coming closest to their aim in
attending the university was the attainment of "a basic general
education and the appreciation of ideas."

How does political activity fit into these purposes? It is
clear that on this campus few students subscribe to the "Joe
College" cultural norm that:

> Students who participate in off-campus political demon-
> strations, picketing, etc. would be better advised to spend
> their time studying or in college activities.

Or rather, 6 per cent of our sample strongly agree with this
statement, but one fifth strongly disagree, and altogether some
67 per cent disagree either mildly or strongly. The campus
clearly does not fit into the traditional stereotype, therefore,
and this sentiment surely helps to characterize the new student of the 1960s, a political animal, who will not sit back
and be treated as a harmless "post-adolescent." Lest this introduce a note of panic in my report, I hasten to add that my
observations throughout this crisis have been that the extremists are very few, and that all the students want is the citizenship that honest deliberation concedes is their due. Passions at
times become inflamed, and particular activities or expressions
may be distasteful to persons reared in different times and
faced with other problems, but the typical student seems
reasonable and intelligent—yet motivated by an optimistic
idealism, and a concern with the rights he feels belong to those
in his position.

II

To learn the manner in which sentiments of this type motivated students to take a favorable attitude toward the free-speech demonstrations on this campus, I have constructed a very simple method of classifying types of students according to their support of, or opposition to the free-speech demonstrators at the time they were interviewed. This was accomplished by using responses to two questions asked during the interview. Following a discussion of the October 2 demonstration, we asked, "Were you for or against the *goals* of the demonstrators?" (and why), and then, "Were you for or against the *tactics* of the demonstrators?" I have already noted that nearly one third of the students said they were for both goals and tactics (30 per cent to be exact).[2] For purposes of discussion, I shall refer to the group of students identified this way as the "militants."

Proceeding down the scale of support, the next group are those who supported the goals but not the tactics, and this group is again 30 per cent of our sample. I shall tag these students the "moderates."

Finally we come to the students whom I shall call the "conservatives," who expressed themselves against both the goals and the tactics of the demonstrators. They constitute 22 per cent of the student body, by our estimate.

This leaves nearly one fifth of the students out of any of the three camps, for the reason that they claim to have supported the tactics but not the goals (a small proportion whose position is due either to error or to too complex a view to be incorporated into the general picture), or who preferred not to make a clear response for or against the demonstrators' goals and/or tactics. With further detailed reading of their interviews it would, no doubt, be possible to classify many of this remaining group, but such a procedure would require considerable time and does not seem necessary to our present purposes. In addition, this remaining group was much more likely to have professed interest in the demonstration, and so it may benefit our ensuing analysis if we leave out of the picture those who are relatively less interested. Most of the comparisons suggest that this residual group is closest to the moderates in their sentiments, though perhaps at times leaning to the militants, at other times to the conservatives.

The use of this index, and surely the labels given to the groups thus identified, are in part arbitrary. I have attempted to choose labels that are relatively low in evaluative content but with more connotations than a simple "Group A, B, and

[2] This excludes the 4 per cent who favored the tactics but did not give a clear response in favor of the goals, so that in all, 34 per cent stated they favored the tactics, as earlier reported.

C." Apart from the labels, the method of classification could, of course, be made more complex, for example, by incorporating some of the qualitative material suggesting the degree to which respondents qualified their categorical responses. However, the method I have used enjoys the virtue of simplicity, with consequent ease of construction and interpretation, and the remainder of this report makes it obvious that students have been classified in a meaningful way.

Before turning to those comparisons, there is one question we asked regarding the university's treatment of the demonstrators which serves to validate the index very well, since it allowed three possible responses: did the student feel that the administration treated the demonstrators "too harshly, about right, or too leniently." Only one of the 85 militants in our sample felt there was too much leniency, and on the opposite side only one of our conservatives felt they had been treated too harshly. Two thirds of the moderates felt they had been treated about right, and the remaining third of this middle group was split about evenly between too harsh and too lenient. This result shows that the index does indeed serve to differentiate students in the intended way, and also contributes further understanding of the feelings of the three groups.

It is reasonable to assume that opinions about the demonstration were fluctuating considerably on all sides as the semester progressed. We asked the question about support for the October demonstrators in the past tense, hoping students would reflect back to their feelings at that time. Obviously such retrospective questions involve a large element of selectivity, and we are able to obtain a partial check on this through our record of the date on which the interview was conducted. Analyzing by date of interview we find that only 14 per cent of the students interviewed before November 3 are "conservatives," while a third of those interviewed during the period November 3–8 are conservative. The proportion of conservatives is down again to 17 per cent for interviews conducted after that date. On the surface, this suggests that student opinion was shifting rather wildly during this period. Indeed, it may not be coincidental that on November 9 the joint administration-student-faculty committee on campus political activity was dissolved by the administration, following renewal of activity by the protesting students. However, it is also likely that students doing the interviewing found some types of respondents easier to contact and to be interviewed than others. We find conservatives on the whole were less interested in the demonstration and less knowledgeable about it, which suggests that they may also have less readily agreed to be interviewed. As a result, these fluctuations in support for the demonstrators when date of interview is taken into account may be more apparent than real.

III

Various aspects of the differences between militants and conservatives will be explored in the following sections. First, relatively permanent aspects of their position in society and in this university will be considered. Second, I shall review some of their ideas about the role of the university and its relation to their aspirations, since it will become apparent that these ideological aspects of the campus community are of major importance in understanding the rebellion. Third, some specific perceptions of the October demonstration and the behavior of both the administration and the demonstrators before and after that incident are obviously of interest, although it is perhaps more appropriate to think of them not as playing a causal role in determining the position of a student in the controversy, but rather as interpretations, justifications, and explanations that he would give for the position that he has taken.

It should be clear that for a variety of reasons, not the least of which is intellectual preference, I have not attempted to delve into psychodynamic explanations but rather approached the task on the assumption that we are dealing with rational persons who are capable of forming intelligent and mature opinions on the basis of their experiences and their ideologies, and of making interpretations of particular situations in the light of these ideas and experiences.

To begin this review, it is useful to point out some features of the different groups that run counter to expectations. I have already noted that dissatisfaction with their general university experience is low among students here and apparently has to be discounted as an explanation for the rebellion. This will be examined in a later section.

A second point to note is that there was little unanimity about certain ideological matters among any of the camps. For example, the militants are divided as to whether "the government is justified in limiting the free speech of anyone," while the conservatives, although more unanimous, still have a sizable minority (23 per cent) giving a negative answer. Again, relatively few students in the whole sample (13 per cent) believe the government is justified in limiting the free speech of groups they may interpret as a threat to the country, and the difference between militants and conservatives is not large.

There are, of course, differences in outlook. Some of these appear in a later section since they seem to have played an important role in the position the student has taken; others represent ideas that have not produced, statistically, a large proportion of militants, or of conservatives, but do serve to distinguish the outlooks of the two groups.

For example, one third of the militants believe that an admitted member of the Communist Party should not be allowed to teach in a public school, while two thirds of the conservatives take this position. In addition, to a greater extent than the rest of the student body, militants distinguish between the right of a person thus "stigmatized" to teach in a public school and his right to teach in a university. This is one indication that, on the average, the militants have a more idealistic image of a university, a view that will appear in several guises throughout the following, but which never emerges in a strikingly clear way, perhaps because of a high degree of consensus on that image in the whole student body.

Another difference that obviously stems from their political views, which will be considered later to support the hypothesis that national political issues have not been irrelevant to the local campus controversy, is that while 39 per cent of our conservatives would have supported Goldwater in the recent election, only 6 per cent of the militants reported this preference. Conversely, 83 per cent of the militants said Goldwater would make a bad President, while this view was held by only one third of the conservatives. In their political outlook, then, in contrast to their civil-liberties ideology, the conservatives are more divided than the militants. Two other differences in this area can be noted from our interviews: in accordance with their political views the militants see the John Birch Society as more of a threat to our country than the Communist Party, while the conservatives rank these in reversed order. But both groups are about equal in their impressions of the threatening character of the Black Muslims and the Ku Klux Klan—around one fourth of each give this judgment.

Later materials will show how strongly concerned the militants are with civil-rights issues. When we note that they are also strongly libertarian, then it becomes apparent that they face a dilemma when it comes to the question of restrictions on segregationist groups: are they going to back down on their libertarianism, or support this in the face of ideas which they deplore? For simplicity I have selected their response to the question of employment of a member of the White Citizens Council as a public school teacher, although other similar questions could be selected with comparable results. The evidence is that they remain libertarian. Even though an earlier question shows them to be twice as likely as the conservatives to say that the Citizens Councils are a threat to our country, only one fourth of them say a member should be prohibited from this type of occupation, as compared with 36 per cent of the moderates and 39 per cent of the conservatives. The consistency of their idealism is thus clear, naïve though some might consider it.

Another anticipated source of difference between the militants and the conservatives is the place of political activity in education. Yet the differences are negligible—three fifths of the students on campus consider it a "necessary part of the educational process," and substantially this same split recurs through the militants, the moderates, and the conservatives. One might also suspect that the militants are more interested in national news, but we find that all but a handful of students in each of the groups reads news of national or international events at least once a week. Finally, in this connection, we asked those who affirmed the importance of off-campus political activity why they felt it important to a student's education, and the principal reason given by each group was its informative value in providing an understanding of the political process, rather than the duties of citizenship or the necessity for accepting responsibility for social problems.

IV

This material on the students' support of civil liberties and the place of political awareness in their lives provides some background to the controversy but is of little help in understanding the sources of the protest. As a step in that direction, I now turn to some of those characteristics that are frequently found to be useful in explaining behavior—and especially likely to be examined by sociologists—factors in their social relations and background. While such factors, especially those delineating a student's position in the campus community, do have some explanatory value, they also provide us with a more complete picture of the supporters of the demonstrations.

For example, it is hard to overlook the fact that in our sample there is a strong relation between academic achievement and support for the demonstrators. Among those who reported to our interviewers a grade point average of B+ or better, nearly half (45 per cent) are militants, and only a tenth are conservatives. At the other end, over a third of those with an average of B— or less are conservatives, and only 15 per cent are militants.[3] Thus, even if one disposes of the whole Free Speech Movement as representing only a minority of the campus, the group thus sloughed off is a minority vital to the excellence of this university.

[3] These results accord with a survey by several political science graduate students of the 800 students arrested in the Sproul Hall sit-in of December 3, which found that half of the arrested undergraduates had an academic average of B or above while the graduate students' records were even better. Twenty of the students were Phi Beta Kappa, eight Woodrow Wilson Fellows, and so on. Incidentally, this report also suggests that less than 5 per cent of the arrested students belong to radical political groups (Socialist clubs, etc.), and that the major common bond was membership (of about one fourth of them) in civil-rights organizations, a theme which receives strong support in our survey.

Several factors that might be expected to help distinguish militants from conservatives show little or no difference. Militants are no more likely to be found among graduate students than freshmen or any other class, nor among those who have been at this campus for several semesters as compared to those who just arrived. This casts doubt on the widely held view that the motivations for rebellion came from the impersonality and bureaucratic regulation of the campus. Were this true, one would expect students who had suffered through more semesters of it to be more rebellious. That is not the case.

I have noted that there is a relation between academic ability and support for the free-speech demonstrators. This is also true of major field of concentration. Social science and humanities students predominate on this campus, together accounting for nearly half of the students, and these two groups are the most likely to be found in the more militant camp, with physical science majors coming close behind. Indeed, in our sample these three groups accounted for three fourths of the militants we identified, and only a little over one third of the conservatives. Support for the conservatives is most likely to come from business administration, engineering, architecture, and agriculture, which together account for nearly half of them. It should be noted that although most of these differences would be found to occur among the whole population of students from which we sampled, a distinction like field of concentration breaks our sample down into so many small groups that precise figures are largely meaningless.

Another aspect of campus life that can be expected to separate out clusters of like-minded students is the living-group arrangement, and this is indeed the case. It is a noteworthy characteristic of this campus that half of the students we sampled live in a private apartment or house, while only one sixth live in dormitories. The former group is not particularly distinguished for either support or non-support of the rebellion. Nearly half of the minority of "co-op" residents are militants, however, and on the other hand, no one living in a fraternity and only a tenth of the sorority girls can be counted among the militants. These last two groups, not surprisingly, are most likely to produce conservatives, with dormitories a close third, but none of these differences are very large. Since the fraternity and sorority groups account for only 15 per cent of our sample, most of the conservatives as well as most of the militants are apartment or private-house dwellers. If we add to these the students who have a room in a boarding house (8 per cent of the total) then two thirds of the militants and half of the conservatives are from these totally off-campus living groups.

Related to living arrangement, we find that the conservatives are somewhat more likely to have participated in on-campus organizations (20 per cent took part) than the militants (15 per cent took part), while the moderates occupy an intermediate position.

Thus far we have concentrated on differences of campus life. To this we might add that students who are employed, who are married, and who are somewhat older (age 23–29) are more likely to have supported the rebel cause, although these differences are not large. For example, about one fourth of the students age 17–20 are militants, 29 per cent of those age 21–22, and 40 per cent of those age 23–29. Support falls off rapidly among the few students who are 30 or over.

Again, there are slight differences regarding such informal social relations as "whether most of your friends agree with you politically." The militants were more likely to affirm the political homogeneity of their circle of friends. However, when asked if this was also true in regard to their views on the free-speech controversy, the conservatives are most likely to find their friends agreeing with them, and the moderates— beset by a problem that plagues most middle-of-the-roaders —least likely, though these differences are quite small.

So far I have not mentioned politics or religion, and both of these values are important in determining where students stood. Almost half of the students identifying themselves as liberal Democrats (a plurality on campus) were classified as militants, and fewer than 10 per cent of them opposed both the goals and the tactics of the demonstrators, i.e., were conservatives in the controversy. The figures for conservative Republicans are almost exactly the reverse. Liberal Republicans preferred the moderate camp. Those who refused to identify themselves with any of those political labels but claimed to be "independent" or had "other" political views tended to be more like the liberal Democrats than any other group, but they are also more heterogeneous in their support for the rebellion. Thus two thirds of the militants are either liberal Democrats or independents, while approximately three fifths of the conservatives came in equal numbers from each of the following groups: conservative Republicans, liberal Republicans, and independents. When students are characterized in terms of their father's political views, the correlation is much the same but less strong.

We also found that students who characterized themselves as more interested in national politics were more likely to be militants, with the exception of the conservative Republicans. Among this group, interest in national politics is negatively related to support for the demonstrators.

Students were asked a variety of other things about their parents, including level of education of mother and father, father's occupation, and approximate family income. There are slight tendencies for students from professional and semiprofessional families to be more predominant among the militants, and also those whose mother had some college education, and who were brought up mostly in the suburbs, but these differences are small. The relation between family income and support for the demonstrators is essentially nil.

In regard to another aspect of their family life, students were asked the frequency with which they discussed intellectual, political, and moral issues, and whether these conversations were amicable or tended toward conflict. Whether or not they discussed these matters with their parents does not help to differentiate conservatives from militants, but whether or not they agreed does serve to differentiate, and it is worth looking at these results somewhat more closely.

Those who strongly disagree with their parents on "intellectual issues," on "future goals," and on religion all are more likely to have "rebelled" on campus also, supporting the free-speech demonstrators' goals and tactics. The same is true of political differences with their parents, but this relationship is more complex and will be discussed separately. These findings lend support to theories of "adolescent rebellion," although this should not be used to discount the legitimacy of the issues underlying the protest. Yet it is also relevant that in the aggregate such parental conflict amounts to little, since only 8 per cent of our sample expressed strong disagreement with their parents on any of these issues. Put differently, both in terms of intellectual issues and future goals, over half of the militants are in agreement with their parents, and those who strongly disagree constitute no more than 13 per cent of this pro-demonstration group.

Conflict over political beliefs shows a pattern somewhat different from the others. Those who strongly disagree with their parents' political beliefs have a two-thirds chance of turning up among the militants, and that is a very good chance by comparison with most other predictors. But again the aggregate effect is small, since they constitute only 6 per cent of the sample. At the same time, those who strongly *agree* with their parents' political views are also more likely to be found in the militant group, although the difference is less (37 per cent militants vs. about 25 per cent for those students with either mild agreement or disagreement). Put differently, over half the militants agree with the political views of their parents, and a slightly larger proportion of the conservatives.

The pattern of religious difference is also somewhat unique, though not exceptional in the extent of agreement: militants are evenly divided between agreement and disagreement with their parents, and nearly 16 per cent of the militants are in strong disagreement (as compared to about 13 per cent on other issues). The somewhat higher level of disagreement is a reflection of the fact that within our interview questions, religion and politics are the areas where most disagreement with parents exists. However, religion differs from politics in that students who have rejected religion, or at least claim no religious preference in our interviews, are most likely to be militants. Put differently, approximately half of the militants have no religious preference, which is true for only 10 per cent of the conservatives (half of whom profess Protestantism). The results were essentially the same when we asked about church attendance.

The militants clearly have not rejected politics, however, and indeed seem to have brought national political controversies onto campus. It would be a tempting, and in some ways troubling, inference to suggest that for many of them politics has supplanted religion—troubling because passionate political convictions are anathema to community life, in spite of their important role in certain circumstances. This is surely an area that bears further investigation, and perhaps the examination of the ideology of the militants, in the next section, will provide an introduction. Before turning to that, however, I might note that among those with a religious preference, Protestants are least likely to be militants, and Jews most likely, with Catholics intermediate. The same ordering appears when we ask about parents' religion. These differences are not large, but it is initially surprising that the Protestants are so low. Further reflection suggests that perhaps the "non-believers" with a rebellious spirit come principally from the Protestant group, thus depleting that group of a large liberal segment. There is some slender evidence against this hypothesis, however, and at present I merely note this topic as one which will reward further investigation.

V

Turning to beliefs expressed by the students, it is difficult to know what role these ideas played in determining the positions taken by the student, and to what extent they are merely a *post hoc* rationale for the position taken. We have some evidence from surveys of undergraduates in previous years that there have been minor shifts of opinion suggesting the latter. However, the accumulated evidence suggests that a great deal of the steam for the protest came from the twin issues of paternalism and of civil rights, and the evidence for this conclusion will be given.

Before turning to an examination of that evidence, I shall perform the easier task of showing that our data do not support the popular explanation of the revolt: dissatisfaction on the part of students with the way they are treated in the educational process. This hypothesis has been presented by practically every commentator, including Robert Hutchins: "The students want to learn; the professors do not want to teach";

Max Lerner, "[The students] find that the great names do not teach—and leave the teaching to assistants"; the editors of *Life* magazine who quote student leader Savio, to the effect that the target of student discontent is the "machine," the operation of which at times "becomes so odious . . . you've got to make it stop"; and even the university's President Kerr, who predicted a revolt in these terms: "There is an incipient revolt of undergraduate students against the faculty; the revolt that used to be against the faculty *in loco parentis* is now against the faculty *in absentia*," in the Godkin Lectures of 1963.

While it is impossible to assert that impersonality and bureaucracy at the university have not had an *indirect* influence, and while it surely is true that sheer size permits a student to find a significant number of others who agree with him on nearly any issue, our data do not suggest that dissatisfaction with the educational process played any role at all. I have already noted that if this were the case, it would be surprising to find militants as likely to appear among relative newcomers as among those who have spent several years on campus. In addition, we asked students whether they agreed or disagreed with the following statement (which was rather tortuously worded to try and capture agreement, which I expected to be rare):

> Although some people don't think so, the president of this university and the chancellor are really trying very hard to provide top-quality educational experience for students here.

One would suppose that students who were fed up with the system, cynical and sick at heart from the facelessness, would disagree with this and join the rebellion. We found essentially unanimous agreement with this statement! Forty-four per cent of the students strongly agreed, and 48 per cent gave moderate agreement. It is true that those students who disagreed with the statement were overwhelmingly likely to be militants, but they constitute only 5 per cent of the sample and 12 per cent of the militants.

We have further and better evidence of satisfaction with the educational functions of the university. Students were also asked how well satisfied they were with "courses, examinations, professors, etc." at the university. There was, to be sure, less enthusiasm here, but still one fifth of the students are very satisfied, and another three fifths satisfied. With every opportunity to say so, only 17 per cent expressed any degree of dissatisfaction. Thus the campus is apparently not so dreary a place as many commentators have suggested.

What is even more relevant to the protest on campus this fall, is that the minority of students who *are* dissatisfied with the courses, examinations, or professors are little more likely to be found among the militants than those who are satisfied. Thus, 32 per cent of those who are very satisfied are militants, 29 per cent of those who are merely "satisfied," 33 per cent of those dissatisfied, and 40 per cent of those two in a hundred who are very dissatisfied.[4]

Finally, we asked students whether they felt that the administration treats them "as a mature and responsible adult," three fourths agreed. Assuming that this would be the opportunity for them to remark on the impersonality of the system and their feeling that they were being treated like IBM cards running through the system, we looked at the reasons given by those who did not feel so treated. Those who mentioned the impersonality of the system, the red tape, and so on were only a small minority (6 per cent of our sample), and a larger proportion, mostly militants, mentioned regulations on political behavior, including political activity. Responses to these various types of questions thus suggest that this aspect of the multiversity was of almost no significance in the protest, at least not in any direct way.

Turning to alternative explanations, there are several qualities of sentiment that may have played this role. As I noted, opinions expressed to our interviewers regarding relations between students and administration may often be justifications rather than previously held ideologies, but one attitude area that cannot plausibly be seen as a mere rationalization is the civil-rights issue. It only became apparent to us after "going into the field" that this issue played an important role. Had we realized this in time, more questions would have been asked. As it is, one question, asking for agreement with the statement that the 1964 Civil Rights Act represents a "notable step in the progress of humanity," was too popular to differentiate very well. While 89 per cent of the militants agreed with it, so did 74 per cent of the conservatives. Nevertheless, only 6 per cent of those who disagreed were found in the militant group, as compared to 32 per cent of those who agreed.

A second question on this topic shows the differentiation more clearly. As noted earlier, we asked whether or not the rights of property owners to sell to whom they wish must be

---

[4] This shows that there is little tendency for students to give support to the demonstrators out of pique with their teachers, but should not be interpreted as suggesting there are not many complaints. Rather, perhaps grievances of this sort are not unduly out of line with their expectations. In addition, our sample is too small to identify the extreme activists in the demonstrations, who may number 1000. Our sample of militants represents about 8000 students. An independent survey of about 600 demonstrators who agreed to fill out a questionnaire for Glen Lyonns, including perhaps the most rebellious students, expressed satisfaction "only" 56 per cent of the time.

protected in all circumstances. Three fifths of the militants strongly disagreed with this statement, as compared with 18 per cent of the rest of the campus. This item, a clear phrasing of the ideological wedge between the civil-rights activists and the rest of the community, was like a baited trap for those activists, and they obliged. There are few other statements in our survey which drew more unanimity from the militant group, as compared to the rest of the students. In this sense, the protest on campus was a reflection of national politics, and perhaps the insensitivity of the administration to the strength of feeling on campus regarding this issue was a major source of its inability to function effectively this fall.

Another indication of the extent to which militants and conservatives differ on the issue of off-campus politics is the "Joe College" norm referred to earlier. For the sample as a whole I noted that two thirds of the sample disagreed that "students who participate in off-campus political demonstrations . . . would be better advised to spend their time studying or in college activities." But only 37 per cent of the conservatives disagree with this, compared with 86 per cent of the militants, and 77 per cent of the moderates. Looked at the other way, nearly two thirds of the students who strongly disagree with this image can be found among the militants. However, it is doubtful that sentiment would have been this extreme during a less rebellious and contentious semester, and perhaps a student's strong disagreement with this norm should not be viewed as a reason for his being a militant so much as a justification for his militant views.

This difference in outlook between the militants and the conservatives introduces a theme which helps to integrate a series of results bearing on the issue of "paternalism." Students who reject the "Joe College" image seem to be asking for a greater degree of citizenship in the community. If the statements concerning civil-rights issues serve to characterize the militants, among other materials a dissent from the following statement seems to be a good characterization of their "anti-paternalistic" ideology:

The university administration almost always can be counted on to give sufficient consideration to the rights and needs of the students in setting university policy.

While only 11 per cent of the students disagreed strongly with this statement, three fourths of those students ended up in the militant camp. Altogether, 40 per cent of the sample disagreed with the statement, and over half (55 per cent) of them were militants. Among those who agreed, only 13 per cent were militants.

Again, one could argue that, like other matters of belief, this may have been expressed in more extreme fashion during the recent conflict-ridden semester than in more normal times. However, in this case we are fortunate in having comparative data. Both in 1960 and 1961, surveys of undergraduates asked this same question.[5] The results for those two studies are almost identical, but by 1964 we find 14 per cent more students expressing strong *agreement* than in 1961, while disagreement is 4 per cent higher. Hence there has been a tendency to move to a more extreme opinion, but it is not large, and more predominant among those who would support the administration than among those who attack it. Thus there is evidence that for most students the belief existed prior to the conflict, and formed one of the ideological motivations for the protest. At any rate, whether we assign an independent or dependent role to these beliefs, it is clear that the militant students in our sample reject the notion that the university Administration is the proper custodian of all of their "rights and needs."

Another image held by students of university structure serves to separate fairly clearly the militants from the conservatives. Of those who feel strongly that "students like myself really have no say" in what the administration does, half are classed as militants. There is divided opinion on this, since over a third of the militant students disagree with the statement, but disagreement is higher among the moderates (54 per cent) and the conservatives (58 per cent), which shows that relative to the other groups, militants not only feel the administration, on its own, will not give sufficient consideration to their rights and needs in formulating policy, but that under the present structure they have little influence on that policy.

A concept of "political efficacy" is widely used in studies of political institutions. Robert Dahl, in his study of power and influence in New Haven, Connecticut, found that citizens who were more active participants in local community affairs had a greater sense of effectiveness and understanding of the political process. We adapted a question from his study to the local scene by asking students whether or not they agreed that most of the decisions made by the administration "are too involved and complicated" for them to decide whether they are right or wrong. Most students (82 per cent) on this campus disagree with this item, but disagreement is particularly strong (92 per cent) among the militants as compared to the conservatives (75 per cent). This is not surprising, since these are the better students as measured by their reported academic ability, but one might predict the opposite when recalling that militants are somewhat less likely to have engaged in on-campus organizations. However, it suggests that the militant

[5] I am indebted to Dr. William Nichols for these earlier survey results. The results are reported for undergraduates only.

students not only feel they have less say in what the administration does, but almost to a man feel they have the capacity to help in making those decisions.

The above statement is of course ambiguous as regards what kinds of policies it refers to, and thus reflects some relatively deeper sentiment than a personal evaluation about a particular policy. Undoubtedly the militants are referring at least in part to administration policy in regard to the issues involved in the campus protest. It seems appropriate to ask whether their rejection of paternalism in this instance means they reject any kind of regulation of student behavior by the university. We queried students as to whether they felt the administration had any responsibilities and duties concerning student morality and behavior. While conservatives agreed that they did (92 per cent), and moderates were largely agreed on this (80 per cent), militants are nearly evenly split. Moreover, the 53 per cent of the militants who agreed gave responses to our further inquiry in largely the same terms as the rest of the campus, referring to general guidance and direction in matters of morality, assuming much the same role as the parents in these matters. Thus they are surely more inclined to reject "in loco parentis" but are by no means unanimous.

It is not surprising to find the militant students unanimous in asserting that the rights over which the whole controversy flared were legitimately theirs. All but two of the eighty-five students we classed as militants agreed that the collection of funds and recruitment of members for politically active groups was a right that students should have. When asked why, a larger proportion of the militants answered in terms suggesting to us an inalienable right, belonging to students as a matter of principle, rather than a right that was justified for its instrumental value, for example as being important to a student's education. On the other hand, conservatives were quite divided as to whether or not students should not be entitled to this right if it interfered with the educational process.

Hence it is clear that although the militants may have been divided on general responsibilities to oversee student behavior on campus, they were agreed that current practices of the administration were infringing on their political rights due them as citizens. It is not surprising that they tend to be somewhat older and more likely to be married and employed.

VII

Having reviewed a series of the relatively general ideas the students have in relation to politics on campus, I now turn in a concluding section, to issues that deal more specifically with the October demonstration. By virtue of the differences in background, political and religious values, and aptitudes, we may assume that the different groups of students will interpret day-to-day events in different ways, and this is clearly the case. Thus most of the following material clearly falls in the category of justifications for the position as militant, or moderate, or conservative, in which the student finds himself at the moment.

To begin, however, it might be well to note two additional aspects of the students' general views, relating to the means available to influence administration behavior. I earlier noted that militants are less likely to feel they have any say in administration policy. Consistent with this, they are less likely to feel that participation in politics on campus can influence administration policy. While three fourths of the campus as a whole feels this type of political activity to be effective at least in some degree, only somewhat over half of the militants agree. Thus the militant students are divided in their opinions here, but deviate from the rest of the campus in this skepticism.

Another series of questions dealt with appropriate means of political action on campus. We asked the respondent whether he felt that any of the following are *ever* justifiable means for the expression of student grievances: petitions, (100 per cent) organizing public protest meetings (89 per cent), picketing (80 per cent), sit-ins (56 per cent) and refraining from going to class (53 per cent). (We did not ask them in that order; the figures in parentheses show the proportion of our total sample who agreed.)

It is hard to believe that over half of the students feel sit-ins may sometimes be justifiable for expressing student grievances! In fact, one would expect that conservatives who opposed the October demonstration would have reacted against the whole movement by disagreeing with this method even more strongly than would be the case in more quiet times. We have no way of knowing if that happened, or whether the militants also expressed more extreme opinions under the press of controversy, but with so many students affirming the legitimacy of sit-ins, it is not surprising that nine out of ten militants agreed, and about half of the moderates. Three fourths of the conservatives dissented. Thus the militants and many of the moderates feel that a sit-in is a proper form of student protest, given sufficient provocation. By December 3 over 1000 students apparently agreed that the provocation sufficed, since that many actually used this method of protest, and undoubtedly many more students felt that they had justification.

These sentiments make it easier to understand why the forcible removal of the students sitting-in at Sproul Hall led to a general strike on campus. But they also suggest the magnitude of the gap between the students and those "over 30" (whom student activists, in a humorous vein, claim cannot be trusted) in interpretations of the political process. How relevant to beliefs of this sort is the curriculum at this or any university? How many of these students have discussed in their classes the relevance of civil disobedience to contemporary political action? One image I retain from the fall is that of a coed in the school cafeteria reading a new paperback edition of Thoreau's essay on this topic, while a free-speech rally dominated the plaza outside. In the context I assumed this to be extracurricular reading, and while it may not have been in this instance, one does hear the complaint that courses are not sufficiently relevant to contemporary issues and concerns.

Since our interviews were mostly conducted during the early part of November, the October demonstration was the focus of some of our questions. While we expected that students would interpret events in accordance with their support for or rejection of the demonstrators, some of the results did not confirm our expectations. For example, it seems reasonable to suppose that the militants would be more apt to see the administration responding to external pressure in their enforcement of the ban on recruitment of members and solicitation of funds, while the conservatives would be less ready to agree to this view of the situation. It is indeed true that militants saw external pressure (88 per cent), but so did moderates (85 per cent) and even three fourths of the conservatives. This suggests that a rather undesirable image of the administration existed even in the eyes of its supporters, which is given further support by a variety of questions reported below.

Those students who felt the administration was responding to external pressures were asked about the sources of those pressures and again the differences between militants and conservatives are not large, although this may be partly a function of the categorical answers which we offered. Most students picked the Board of Regents and the state legislature. Had we asked more specifically about rumors abroad at that time regarding pressures from the political right, we might have obtained more response of that nature, and more differentiated response.

Anticipated differences between the militants and the conservatives do appear in questions about the manner of response by the administration to initial protests against their rulings. It is not surprising, for example, that over half of the students who felt the administration unjustified in enforcing the ban on solicitation of funds in the Bancroft-Telegraph area are classed by us as militants. What is surprising is that nearly half the campus (46 per cent) felt this way. While the conservatives were essentially unanimous in feeling this action of the administration was justified under the circumstances, some 13 per cent of the militants also felt this way, and most of those in all camps who saw no alternative for the administration explained that the campus was state property, and that the administration of course had to conform to state law.

Of significance to the emotion behind the rebellion was the fact that 35 per cent of our sample felt that the administration had not "acted in good faith." Three fifths of those who felt this way are found in the militant camp, as opposed to 11 per cent of those who felt they had shown good faith in their statements and action. Two fifths of the students on campus felt there had been too little attempt by the administration to negotiate the issues, and half of the students with these views are found among the militants. There is considerable agreement, of course, among militants (80 per cent) that the police should not have been called in during the demonstrations and agreement among conservatives (78 per cent) that they should have been; the moderates characteristically show a fifty-fifty split.

At the end of this series of questions, we asked students whether they had any other opinions on the behavior of the administration during the demonstration, and many students took the opportunity to reaffirm what we have already seen, that there should have been better efforts on the part of the administration to communicate with students or to negotiate differences. The militants of course responded overwhelmingly in this fashion, if they added anything at all; yet even the conservatives were as likely to say this as to give approval to the administration by saying that they did all right, or did what was necessary. The conservatives were also slightly more prone to point out that the administration had been inconsistent, although they often phrased this in such a way as to mean the administration should have been consistently firm in dealing with the demonstration. Clearly this shows that the administration made too little attempt to support and explain its position in terms that could be understood by the students on this campus and could arouse at least temporary understanding and support.

There was considerable controversy on campus as to whether the whole issue which aroused the protest was or was not a matter of free speech. The militants tended toward a unanimous view on this subject (82 per cent affirming), while the conservatives largely thought not (69 per cent denied); but both camps were somewhat divided. Put differently, defining the issue as one of free speech was not sufficient to provoke a student to join the rebellion to as great an extent as other ideological issues, such as civil rights and paternalism vs. students' rights, as described above. A similar conclusion results from the responses we received to the question on whether the collection of funds and solicitation of memberships were aspects of free speech.

There was of course considerable disagreement on campus

as to whether the method of civil disobedience chosen by the demonstrators was the only available means of protest open to them at the time. In view of the reluctance on the part of many persons both on and off campus to accept that as a legitimate means of protest for students at any time, it is surprising to find that by our estimate one fourth of the students on campus believed civil disobedience was "the only available choice of action." While almost no (5 per cent) conservatives agreed with this position, and only 13 per cent of the moderates, the people I have identified as militants were by no means unanimous. One third of them said it was not. But the majority of the militants who saw no other alternative (61 per cent) comprise nearly 5000 students by our estimate. Again it appears there was a large residue of strong support behind the smaller number of students who were active participants.

Another sentiment characterizes those we have classed as militants, and that is optimism about the effectiveness of the means of protest they chose, or agreed to. We asked students to try and remember how they felt during the October 2 demonstration regarding the outcome of that demonstration, and also about the long-run chances of success of the whole protest. There was not unanimity among the militants, but nearly two thirds of them felt there was little or no chance of "achieving nothing and doing harm" while only 15 per cent of the conservatives took this view. Again, we see that for the most part students took a position they felt to be effective in achieving the social changes they believed necessary.

Regarding the prospects for success in achieving the right to solicit funds and recruit members in the long run, there is even great divergence between the militants and the conservatives. Eighty-five per cent of the former, and only 29 per cent of the latter, felt that there was a "fair to good" chance of achieving this goal in the long run. Thus in dealing with the militants, one was dealing with a group who felt their method of protest to be legitimate and effective in the long run, and, incidentally, a matter of principle rather than of personal gain. In the light of these optimistic views it is unnecessary to turn to psychodynamic or organizational explanations which may permit one to disregard the ideological principles involved. Rather, it should be clear that this protest captured the support of a great many intelligent and dedicated students, and their views deserve a fair hearing.

VII

Documentary Appendices

UNIVERSITY OF CALIFORNIA, BERKELEY
OFF-CAMPUS GROUPS
Fall 1964

Advocates, Young Republican Club

Berkeley Student Committee of Inquiry

Berkeley Student Zionist Organization

Berkeley Students for Goldwater

B'nai B'rith Hillel Foundation, Student Council

California College Republicans

Calvin Club

Campus CORE

Christian Science Organization at the University

Democratic Socialist Club

W.E.B. DuBois Club

Graduate Co-ordinating Committee

Graduates for Free Speech

Independent Socialist Club

Inter-Varsity Christian Fellowship

Law School Democratic Club

Masonic Club at the University

Newman Hall, Student Council

Norman Thomas, Young People's Socialist League

Plymouth House Executive Committee

SLATE

Stiles Hall — University YMCA

Student-Faculty Peace Center

Students for a Democratic Society

Students for Fair Housing

Students for Independent Political Action

Unitarian College Fellowship

University Church Council, Student Executive Committee

University Civil Liberties Committee

University Friends of SNCC

University Society of Individualists

University Young Democrats

University Young Republicans

Young Socialist Alliance

REPORT OF THE AD HOC COMMITTEE
ON STUDENT CONDUCT

To the Berkeley Division:

This committee was formed pursuant to the following motion adopted by the Berkeley Division of the Academic Senate on October 15, 1964:

> "The Berkeley Division instructs the Committee on Committees to appoint a five-man ad hoc committee to hear and make recommendations on the case of the eight suspended students. The committee will be appointed immediately and will promptly take up the cases. The students may be represented by counsel and may take a recording —which would include a tape recording of the proceedings."

The committee members were appointed on October 19, 1964. On October 21, the committee addressed a letter to the chancellor requesting that the students be temporarily reinstated pending action on our recommendations. This request was denied. The committee then met with counsel for the university and for the suspended students on October 22nd at a pre-hearing conference, during which general procedures were stipulated to govern the hearings. Hearings commenced on October 28th and continued on October 29th and November 3rd. They consumed approximately twenty hours. The proceedings were in large part adversary, but the committee members also extensively questioned witnesses who appeared before them. The chief witnesses for the university were Dean Arleigh Williams, Associate Dean Peter Van Houten, Assistant Dean George Murphy, and Mrs. Leone Weaver who is Dean Towle's administrative assistant. Six of the eight students appeared as witnesses; two students, Mr. Sandor Fuchs and Mr. Arthur Goldberg, failed to make themselves available when their cases were being considered.

This committee has interpreted its terms of reference to mean that it should render its report to the Berkeley Division of the Academic Senate, with copies of the report to the University Administration and the students involved. It assumes that its recommendations in these cases will form a basis for administration action concerning these students but it realizes that its recommendations are advisory. The committee, with assent of the parties, has considered only those events occurring up to the night of September 30, 1964, when the students here involved were indefinitely suspended by the chancellor. It has not been asked to, nor has it, considered any events occurring after that time.

This report is organized in six sections. The first section concerns applicable university and campus regulations. The second describes the background of relevant events occurring between September 14th and 30th. This narrative of events is based solely on evidence received at the hearings. The third section evaluates the cases of six of the eight students whose activities were substantially similar. The fourth section concerns the remaining two cases. The fifth section is concerned with administrative procedures and penalties assessed in these cases. The sixth section comprises our recommendations in all eight cases.

I

University policies regulating student activities are contained in a pamphlet entitled "University of California Policies Relating to Students and Student Activities, September 1963." Supplementary campus policies are contained in a booklet entitled "Information for Student Organizations" which is published annually. To these should be added the memoranda of clarification and modification issued by Dean Katherine Towle on September 14, 21 and 28 and Chancellor Strong's remarks of September 28th.

Six of the cases under submission involve essentially two charges. The first is that the student operated a card table for an off-campus organization without a required activity permit and for the purpose of raising money for unauthorized purposes. Two matters are central to this charge.

The first is the setting up of a table requires a permit. Nowhere in the text of the University Regulations or the Berkeley campus rules is there any explicit requirement of a permit to set up a table. To be sure, an "activity permit" from the dean of students is required if an off-campus organization is to use campus facilities for a "special event" (Types of Student Organizations I-C); but the language of the rule seems to assume that "special events" comprise a class of formal presentations, speeches, films, etc., so that the setting up of a table to distribute literature would not seem to be reasonably described as a "special event"; and in fact no officer of the administration has so described it. The requirement of a permit appears to be no more than an administrative practice. Its apparent purpose is to facilitate the enforcement of prohibitions against distributing literature in such a way as to interfere with the flow of traffic, against the raising of money for unauthorized purposes, and such other prohibitions as the dean of students believes are to be enforced. In any event, permits for setting up tables seem to have been required over a number of years and the students here involved knew of this practice.

The second is in regard to raising money for unauthorized purposes. Here the language of the relevant part of the University Regulation titled "Use of University Facilities" is specific and of long standing:

"IV. General Limitations.

A. University facilities may not be used for the purpose of raising money to aid projects not directly connected with some authorized activity of the University, except . . . that the Chief Campus Officers may authorize a limited number of fund-raising campaigns by recognized charitable or public service agencies."

The authorized exceptions have included only relatively non-controversial projects such as the Bay Area United Crusade, Cal Camp, and the J. F. Kennedy Memorial Library. In the present cases, alleged money raising was carried on for the University Friends of the Student Non-violent Coordinating Committee (SNCC), the Young Socialist Alliance (YSA), and apparent nonprofit funding of the SLATE "Supplement to the General Catalogue" which contains commentaries on courses and instructors at Berkeley. It seems clear that raising money for SNCC and YSA, no matter how laudable the objectives, is expressly prohibited by the regulation in the absence of specific authorization by the chancellor. Doubt exists whether the regulation properly interpreted forbids "sale" of SLATE Supplements. But in view of the recommendations which we make in this report we find it unnecessary to decide that question.

The second charge common to these six students is that they failed to respond to requests to come to the office of the dean of students to discuss their alleged violations of university rules. The specific written policy invoked for this charge is of a most general nature. In essence, it states that the university will take appropriate action when a student neglects his academic duty or engages in "misconduct." "Misconduct" as defined by the administration is the basis of this charge. The word "misconduct" is very broad and under certain circumstances might not fairly warn a student that conduct he is about to engage in is punishable. Failure to confer with a dean when requested, however, would not seem to raise such problems of notice and warning.

Other relevant regulations will be discussed in context below.

The committee ruled at the outset that it was not competent to rule on claims that any university regulation violated rights of freedom of expression protected by applicable Federal and State Constitutional provisions.

II

On September 14, 1964, one week before the beginning of classes, Dean Towle announced by letter to student organizations that the policies of the administration concerning use of university facilities would "be strictly enforced" in all areas of the university including "The 26-foot strip of brick walkway at the campus entrance on Bancroft Way and Telegraph Avenue between the concrete posts and the indented copper plaques on Bancroft Way which read 'Property of the Regents, University of California. Permission to enter or pass over is revocable at any time'." The letter mentioned in particular the prohibitions against soliciting party membership or supporting or opposing particular candidates or propositions in local, state or national elections (Policy on the Use of University Facilities, III); raising money to aid various projects (*Id.* IV); supporting or advocating off-campus political action (apparently an interpretation of *Id.* III and IV D, but which is nowhere stated in these terms); and placing of posters, easels or card tables in the 26-foot strip because of feared traffic interference.

The 26-foot strip alluded to in the letter is a portion of the sidewalk at the designated location. The total width of the sidewalk is approximately 36 feet. The 10-foot strip closest to Bancroft Way belongs to the City of Berkeley. Nothing differentiates the 10-foot and 26-foot strips except the small plaques, bearing the legend stated above, imbedded in the bricks.

For at least two years, according to the testimony of administration witnesses, the university policies mentioned in Dean Towle's letter were not enforced in the 26-foot strip. The area was treated by the university for these purposes as sidewalk outside the campus. Apparently the Berkeley Police Department treated the entire sidewalk area as within their jurisdiction (without university objection), since permits were issued by that department for setting up tables in the general area, although the permits did not specify exact locations.

During the two-year period prior to September 14, 1964, numerous tables were placed in the 26-foot strip by off-campus organizations to facilitate solicitation of funds and membership and to support and advocate off-campus political action. The university did not object to these activities at that location. In retrospect it is fair to say that the 26-foot strip provided an outlet for activities desired by a number of students which are barred on the campus proper.

Dean Towle's statement of September 14th apparently was issued unilaterally in the sense that no conferences with student organizations affected by the new enforcement policy were held, nor were any student organizations consulted. (Prior discussion of this sort, in fact, would have been difficult if not impossible in view of the timing of the announcement one week prior to commencement of classes.)

The new enforcement policies were met by vociferous student protests. Protesting organizations represented virtually the full spectrum of political ideologies. Representatives from such organizations constituted themselves as the "United Front" and sought and secured conferences with Dean Towle and other administration representatives. These conferences involved broad issues related to speech and political activity on campus in addition to the enforcement of university policies in the 26-foot strip. The protests led to some modifications and clarifications issued by Dean Towle on September 21st. These included three matters: (1) a small number of tables were to be permitted in the 26-foot strip on the issuance of an "activity permit," but university rules prohibiting solicitation of funds and membership and rules prohibiting advocacy of social or political action applied to the activities carried on at such tables; (2) an attempt was made to differentiate between dates, and the like and distributions urging specific action with regard to such matters; and (3) an additional "Hyde Park" area was established at the main entrance to Sproul Hall (i.e., an area which, under campus rules, may be used by students, faculty, or staff for extemporaneous speeches or rallies without prior registration with the dean of students' office).

The student organizations involved, with apparent unanimity, were dissatisfied with the concessions. It was apparently felt that solicitation of funds and members and advocacy of action should be permitted at the tables, as before September 14th, and that the distinction between presenting views and advocating specific action with regard to those views was untenable. Further meetings of the United Front, further protests (including picketing of Sproul Hall and an all night vigil), and further conferences with the administration ensued.

These events culminated in a rally in Dwinelle Plaza on Monday, September 28th, immediately before the university meeting at which Chancellor Strong spoke. At least seven, and perhaps more, students spoke at this rally. They represented organizations active in the United Front including, among others, persons identified with the ASUC Senate, SNCC, SLATE and a student Goldwater group. University policies concerning use of facilities were criticized at the rally, and the students were urged to picket the university meeting then or immediately thereafter being held in the lower plaza next to the student cafeteria. An informational bulletin concerning the rally had appeared in the *Daily Californian* on the morning of September 28th. No formal notice had been given to the dean of students' office concerning the rally. A campus regulation encourages meeting of organizations in Dwinelle Plaza but requires 24 hours advance notification.

The rally ended at approximately 11:15, and picketing of the university meeting then ensued. The pickets marched in single or double file in the upper plaza between Sproul Hall and the ASUC building and then descended the steps to the university meeting which Chancellor Strong then was addressing. Dean Williams had stated to Mr. Arthur Goldberg, who was one of the leaders of the picketing, that pickets could stand around the perimeter of the meeting but could not go down the aisles because such action would constitute interference with a university function. Nevertheless, the pickets, after standing at the perimeter, did go down the aisles. Here they remained standing thereby making it difficult for some persons in the audience to see or hear the chancellor.

By Tuesday, September 29th, various off-campus student organizations had obviously decided to "test" various of the regulations by violating them. (Violations had apparently occurred during the week previous, especially in the 26-foot strip area, although the nature and extent of these violations is not clear. A SNCC table, for instance, had been erected in the Sather Gate area on the 29th after an activity permit for its operation had been refused. And one of the charges in this proceeding [against Mr. Sandor Fuchs] is for operating a SLATE table at Sather Gate and offering SLATE Supplements for sale on September 29th.) Wednesday, September 30th, however, was the more critical day for purposes of this report. Four card tables were erected immediately in front of Sather Gate by SNCC, SLATE, YSA, and CORE, respectively. Each table was operated by a number of students in succession. Between noon and 2:00 p.m. five students were "cited" for operating these tables without required activity permits and for unauthorized money raising. The CORE table was not disturbed although open solicitation of funds occurred there also.

Sometime after 12 noon on September 30th, Deans Murphy and Van Houten, on instructions from Dean Williams, proceeded to Sather Gate and approached students manning or operating the SNCC, YSA, and SLATE tables. They were followed by a group of students who watched the proceedings. Deans Murphy and Van Houten told each of the students that they were in violation of university regulations and instructed them to cease operations. The students generally responded that they understood that they were violating an interpretation of the regulations but believed that their constitutional rights were being abridged by such interpretations and that they had a right to continue their activity. Most of the students so involved were instructed to report to Dean Williams by 3:00 p.m. that afternoon. (Deans Murphy and Van Houten returned to the area at approximately 2:10 p.m. and cited additional students.)

Neither Dean Murphy nor Dean Van Houten inspected the CORE table which was located in the same area as the SNCC, SLATE, and YSA tables. It was their understanding that CORE had been issued an activity permit good for September 30th. CORE, as a matter of fact, had been issued such a permit, but only for distributing information. The CORE table, however, was being used to raise money. This violation was later noted by Mrs. Weaver, who, however, did not approach the table to ascertain who was operating it. Other tables were then being operated by other organizations in the 26-foot strip. Whether violations were also occurring there is unknown. The administration has no record of having checked these tables on September 30th.

Following the actions of Deans Murphy and Van Houten at noon, hastily written petitions were circulated to students in the Sather Gate area. While differently worded, their general sense is incorporated in the one here quoted:

"We the undersigned have jointly manned tables at Sather Gate—realizing that we were in violation of University edicts to the contrary, and realize that we may be subject to expulsion."

Some 400 students signed such petitions.

At 3 p.m. the students who had been cited, together with approximately 300 other students (mainly, if not totally, the petition signers) appeared at Sproul Hall as a group. Dean Williams asked five of the cited students to come into his office. Mr. Mario Savio, who was not one of the five, spoke for them, undoubtedly with their consent, stating that the students would see the dean only if he consented to proceed against all of the students who had admitted committing similar violations by signing the petitions. Dean Williams refused this condition. Thereafter, in Sproul Hall a sit-in occurred which lasted until approximately 2 a.m. on October 1st. The sit-in was orderly in the sense that aisles were cleared, doorways were not blocked, and there was not an excessive amount of noise for 300 students grouped at such close quarters. It seems clear that Mr. Savio was one of a group exercising leadership among those who were sitting in.

This committee does not know in specific detail what occurred among administration officials during the afternoon and evening of September 30th. We have been told that Dean Williams conferred with the chancellor and presented to him various "working papers" (which are exhibits in the record of this proceeding) outlining the actions taken by the eight students whose cases are here under review. In any event, at 11:45 p.m. the chancellor issued a statement in which he announced the indefinite suspension of these eight students from the university. No action was taken against the signers of the petitions or against those who were sitting in Sproul Hall. (No attempt was made to obtain the names of the latter group.)

The procedures followed were unusual. Normally, penalties of any consequence are imposed only after hearings before the Faculty Student Conduct Committee. Such procedure was not followed here with the result that the students were suspended without a hearing. This must be set against the extraordinary circumstances created by the sit-in and the cited students' refusal to confer with Dean Williams except on a condition unacceptable to him. One of Dean Williams' purposes in asking for such conference was in fact to explain the hearing procedures available before the Faculty Student Conduct Committee, although this purpose had not been explained to the five students involved. Nevertheless, and in hindsight, it would have been more fitting to announce that the students were to be proceeded against before the Faculty Committee rather than levying summary punishments of such severity. We were left with the impression that some or all of these eight students were gratuitously singled out for heavy penalties summarily imposed in the hope that by making examples of these students, the university could end the sit-in and perhaps forestall further mass demonstrations.

III

Messrs. Brian J. Turner, Mark Bravo and Donald Hatch all were charged with operating the SNCC table at Sather Gate on September 30th without an activity permit and for the purpose of raising money for unauthorized purposes (i.e., for SNCC). Mrs. Elizabeth Stapleton was similarly charged with operating a YSA table, and Messrs. David L. Goines and Sandor Fuchs were similarly charged with operating a SLATE table and offering SLATE Supplements for sale. In addition, Messrs. Turner, Bravo, Goines and Fuchs and Mrs. Stapleton were charged with failing to see Dean Williams at his request.

Dean Williams stated that these violations, considered out of the context of the other events which transpired, would be innocuous. We agree with this and, therefore, we believe that these offenses warrant only a minimal punishment.

We do not agree that the context raised these violations to a plane which made them deserving of much heavier punishment. We are convinced that while each student knew that he was behaving in a manner which the administration viewed as violative of university rules, each believed that constitutional rights and principles of great importance were being violated by the administration's action in barring solicitation of funds and members. Moreover, we believe that these students viewed their actions in operating the tables as necessary to precipitate a test of the validity of the regulations in some arena outside the university. The chancellor's remarks of September 28th, while further clarifying university policy to permit free distribution of campaign literature, made it clear that the president and the Regents had rejected in final form the request of the ASUC Senate for changes in the rules to permit solicitation of funds and membership and organization of political and social action campaigns on campus. The door was thus seemingly closed to any negotiation on these central points. The contest, thus viewed, makes the behavior of these students more understandable than if no controversy had been raging.

We are more troubled by the refusal of five of these students to respond unconditionally to Dean Williams' request for an interview. But this must be viewed in context too. Over 400 students had admitted similar violations. (Undoubtedly a number of these had in fact committed, as well as sympathized in, such violations.) The cited students saw safety in numbers. Irrationally (or otherwise) they feared that they would be "picked off" one by one. Moreover, they believed (although undoubtedly erroneously) that they were being deprived of "equal protection of the laws" because they alone were being "prosecuted," and they feared that they would concede this important principle if they acceded to the dean's request.

The committee finds that these six students did in fact violate university policies (although in the cases of Messrs. Goines and Fuchs there is serious doubt whether non-profit sale of the SLATE Supplement is in fact prohibited by the Policy on Use of University Facilities). The committee does not view these as serious violations, however, and believes that only minimal punishment (for instance "official censure" with suspension from participation in extracurricular activities for a short period of time) was warranted. In recommending the punishment, the committee has taken into account the fact that numerous other students undoubtedly behaved similarly and were not cited for violations and that the punished students were engaged in what, in view of the direct support they received from many others, should be viewed as a symbolic act of protest and not as an act of private delinquency.

In this context we particularly recall Dean Williams' account of a conversation he held with Brian J. Turner who, he said, in effect told him that he was greatly distressed to find himself in defiance of a university which he loved and of persons whom he respected, but that in conscience he could follow no other course.

IV

Broader charges were stated against Mr. Mario Savio and Mr. Arthur Goldberg.

A.

Mr. Savio was charged with having caused a SNCC table to be operated in the Sather Gate area on September 29th and to have conducted the operations of a SNCC table in that area on September 30th. Mr. Savio freely admitted that he set up the table on the 29th. While there was no direct proof that he conducted the operations of the table on the 30th, it seems clear that—in his capacity as President of University Friends of SNCC, by virtue of his proximity to the table on that day, and in his conversations with Brian Turner concerning the latter's actions after being approached by Deans Murphy and Van Houten—Mr. Savio in a meaningful sense "conducted the operations of the table" at least for some period on the 30th. But these charges against Savio seem no more serious than the similar charges leveled against the six aforementioned students.

Mr. Savio was also charged with failing to respond to the request of Dean Williams to report to the latter's office. Actually the case against Savio on this score is weaker than that against the five other students. Unlike these others, he was not asked to see Dean Williams until 4:05 p.m., when the dean addressed his remarks to the whole group of students who were sitting-in. The other students had been told at the time of citation to see the dean before 3:00 p.m. and were again told to do so at 3:00 and 4:05 p.m.

Mr. Savio was charged with having called and held the rally which preceded the university meeting on September 28th. This charge does not seem proved. The administration witnesses stated that they heard Savio speaking at the rally, but they could indicate no facts leading to the conclusion that Savio called, organized or in any meaningful sense held the rally (other than being one of seven or more speakers). Mr. Savio told the committee that he was the SNCC representative to the United Front, that he participated with numerous others in planning the rally, that he was not responsible for the bulletin in the *Daily Californian* which advertised the meeting (and plans for picketing), and that he had urged that the rally be scheduled for a Hyde Park area on the campus rather than for Dwinelle Plaza. Under these circumstances, it is the committee's view that this charge has not been proved.

The most serious charge against Mr. Savio was that he "organized and led" the sit-in which occurred in Sproul Hall on September 30th. In evaluating this charge we start from the proposition that the students who sat-in were taking part in a demonstration against rules and regulations which to them are of the most questionable wisdom.

As is evident from Dean Williams' affirmation of the students' "right" to picket, the administration does not seek to bar student protest, as it should not, especially when such protest concerns issues so vital to the central educative mission of the university.

Demonstration by peaceful sit-in, however, is viewed differently. We can understand why this is so and to an extent we share the administration's concern in the use of this type of demonstration.

The sit-in differed from the other forms of protest utilized here. Most of the picketing was simply a matter of communication. This is true of the vigil also. The setting up of tables to solicit funds and members (and the holding of the rally) while violating regulations did not contain seeds of serious disruption of university functions. The sit-in was peaceful and apparently well monitored. Doorways were not blocked and corridors were left open. But the sit-in, especially by so large a group, created a circumstance potentially disrupting operations in Sproul Hall and undoubtedly producing apprehensions of disorder. In retrospect, the university's best tactic might have been to carry on operations in Sproul Hall as usual, leaving the students where they were until the demonstration ended naturally through the weariness of the demonstrators. But in fact charges were brought, at least against Savio, in connection with the sit-in and we must deal with them.

While we are not prepared to condemn on moral grounds the device of demonstration by peaceful and orderly sit-in, we recognize that those who organize and participate in a sit-in which is judged to violate valid regulations must be prepared to pay the price for such conduct. In this instance, we believe that the price must be higher than the manning of card tables (another form of civil disobedience) not because of any discernible difference in motivation or moral position, but because of the potentially more serious consequences of the action.

We believe it important to note that Mr. Savio (and Mr. Goldberg to a lesser extent as shown below) was singled out for charges relating to the sit-in. The other 400 or so students were not so charged. Elementary fairness would seem to require that there be a showing that Savio played a unique role in the sit-in to justify this special treatment.

The evidence to support the charge of organizing and leading the sit-in is as follows: Mr. Savio was the spokesman for the five (and later eight) students asked to see Dean Williams; Savio told Dean Williams in the course of these conversations that he would urge everyone to remain where they were; Savio told Dean Williams when the latter refused to agree to proceed against all the petition signers that "we sit in"; Savio "monitored" the group to keep them orderly when approaching Sproul Hall at 3:00 p.m.; Savio "instructed" the sit-ins to leave aisles open and not block the doorways; Savio reported to the students that food was to be procured and that money for the food would be collected; sometime after the sit-in started, Savio leaned out of a window in Sproul Hall and invited other students to "come and join"; Dean Williams sensed that Savio was in a leadership role.

During the course of the testimony, it became apparent that other individuals performed some of these same activities.

The committee believes that Mr. Savio played an important

leadership role in the sit-in, but that it is probable that others also shared this leadership. The committee believes that this conduct warrants punishment of a somewhat greater magnitude than that deserved by the six students whose cases are considered above. But in view of the deans' apparent failure to attempt to identify and charge others who also played a leadership role (with the exception of Mr. Goldberg) and the unusual procedures followed in this case by the administration, the committee believes that the suspension visited to date on Mr. Savio is the maximum warranted for the conduct here charged and shown.

B.

Mr. Arthur Goldberg was charged with having played an active part in setting up SLATE tables at Sather Gate on September 29th and 30th. Counsel for Mr. Goldberg argued that any of his actions in this regard were as president of SLATE —as representative of that organization—and not as an individual. We do not believe that the distinction is warranted. Nevertheless, this charge does not seem very serious, especially in view of the doubtful applicability of the Policy on Use of University Facilities to the activities being carried on at the SLATE table.

Goldberg was also charged with having called and held the rally in Dwinelle Plaza on September 28th. The proofs of this charge were no more complete here than in the case of Mr. Savio.

Mr. Goldberg was charged with failing to respond to Dean Williams' request to come into the latter's office. Goldberg's refusal must be evaluated in the same context as the other students.

Mr. Goldberg was also charged with "assisting in organizing and participating in" the sit-in. The committee, with the assent of counsel, struck the "participating in" charge on the grounds that it would be unfair to single out Goldberg from the other 400 or so because of participation alone.

Very little evidence was adduced to show that Goldberg assisted in organizing the sit-in. Dean Williams stated that Goldberg instructed students to stay against the wall and keep the aisles clear and that students responded to his directions. Dean Williams recollected, however, that others were doing the same thing. A troublesome fact with regard to this charge is that it was not included in Dean Williams' working papers which were the basis for the chancellor's actions, and it was also not included in Dean Williams' more formal memorandum of October 1 to the chancellor or in the memorandum prepared by Dean Williams for the Faculty Student Conduct Committee on October 12th. Thus it constitutes a new charge first brought in connection with this proceeding and evidently was not one of the bases upon which the indefinite suspension was imposed. Under all these circumstances the committee believes that the charge should not be considered.

The charge of greatest consequence brought against Mr. Goldberg is that he assisted in organizing and leading student pickets who interfered with the conduct of the university meeting on September 28th. The testimony of university witnesses satisfies us that Mr. Goldberg was an important leader of the pickets on September 28th, although evidence was introduced to suggest that there was at least one other person of similar or near similar importance who was not charged at all. Goldberg urged students to picket (which was permissible), was told by Dean Williams at the time that picketing at the perimeter of the audience was permissible but that the pickets could not go down the aisles, was instrumental in leading the pickets down the stairs to the university meeting and directing their initial march around the perimeter, was seen at the rear of the audience just before or just after the pickets went down the aisles and thus interfered with the meeting by making it difficult for the chancellor to present his views on the controversies in issue, and was seen at the front of the audience during the chancellor's address talking to a number of persons who apparently were pickets.

The committee views the actions of the pickets in obstructing access to the chancellor's remarks as serious, especially in view of the issues involved in the controversy between these students and the administration. The basic issue was one of free speech. The students understandably protested what they conceived to be unjustifiable fetters. But deliberately to protest in a manner which interfered with the chancellor's explaining his side of the case was inconsistent with the basis of the students' position and could only compromise their cause.

The facts related above strongly suggest that Mr. Goldberg played an instrumental part in directing the pickets down the aisles at the meeting. And while there is no direct proof that Goldberg did in fact issue such directions, the circumstantial evidence is persuasive.

Mr. Goldberg's conduct warrants heavier punishment than is justified in the cases of the six students considered in Part III above. If we had direct evidence of a deliberate effort on Mr. Goldberg's part to break up this meeting we would be moved to recommend a more substantial penalty than we feel is justified in any of the other cases. But in view of all the circumstances, the committee believes that the suspension to date is the maximum warranted.

V.

Throughout these cases two large issues seemed always to be present: On the one hand, it seems clear that the students violated regulations and interpretations of regulations. That their behavior was motivated by high principle may influence the severity of punishment recommended, but does not cause the violations to disappear. On the other hand, the procedure by which the university acted to punish these wrongdoings is subject to serious criticism. The relevant factors are: first, the vagueness of many of the relevant regulations; second, the precipitate action taken in suspending the students sometime between dinner time and the issuance of the press release at 11:45 p.m.; third, the disregard of the usual channel of hearings for student offenses—notably hearings by the Faculty Committee on Student Conduct; fourth, the deliberate singling out of these students (almost as hostages) for punishment despite evidence that in almost every case others were or could have been easily identified as performing similar acts; and fifth, the choice of an extraordinary and novel penalty—"indefinite suspension"—which is nowhere made explicit in the regulations, and the failure to reinstate the students temporarily pending actions taken on the recommendations of this committee.

We do not believe or suggest that the administration was motivated by malice or vengeance in its reliance upon these practices. Indeed, we are sympathetic to the consideration that the unprecedented and potentially menacing context of events was instrumental in shaping its conduct. Nevertheless, it is an especially heavy responsibility of a distinguished institution to make sure that its acts are in the finest tradition in the administration of justice. We have enumerated the felt shortcomings in the confident faith that the university administration will be as desirous as we are of correcting them.

VI.

The committee emphasizes again that it has been concerned only with events occurring through September 30, 1964, and has not been asked to, nor has, considered any events after that date. Further it has considered only the specific charge made against these students by the university administration. On the basis of the foregoing, we recommend that Messrs. Bravo, Goines, Fuchs, Hatch and Turner and Mrs. Stapleton be reinstated as of the date of their suspensions. The penalty of indefinite suspension should be expunged from the record of each student. Instead, the penalty for each of these six students should be recorded as that of "censure" for a period of no more than six weeks.

We recommend that the suspensions of Messrs. Goldberg and Savio should be for the specific period of six weeks beginning September 30, 1964.

The imposition of academic penalties on these eight students would amount to additional punishment, and of a severity disproportionate to the offenses. We recommend that, so far as is feasible for each student, he be permitted to complete his course work for the present semester, without academic penalty. We further recommend that each, at his option, be permitted to drop one or more courses, or to withdraw for the balance of the semester, without loss of academic credit or the imposition of other academic penalties.

Respectfully submitted,
R. A. Gordon
M. Haire
R. E. Powell
L. Ulman
I. M. Heyman, Chairman

November 12, 1964

November 10, 1964

A REPORT ON THE STATUS OF DELIBERATIONS OF THE COMMITTEE ON CAMPUS POLITICAL ACTIVITY AS OF NOVEMBER 7, 1964

BY THE FACULTY REPRESENTATIVES ON THE COMMITTEE

The following is an account of the status of the deliberations of the Committee on Campus Political Activity as of the close of its final meeting on Saturday, November 7, 1964.

The basis for the substantive discussion was the original faculty proposal, which, in its present form, appears below, together with brief commentary. This proposal was designed to recommend specific amendments to existing university regulations in order to deal with the basic issues in dispute. Discussion of these proposals centered on paragraph I.

After discussion and several proposed amendments, all three sides, administration, students, and faculty, voted to amend paragraph I to read as follows:

I. That in the Hyde Park areas, the University modify its present regulations by dropping the distinction between "advocating" and "mounting political and social action." The advocacy of ideas and acts which is constitutionally protected off the campus should be protected on the campus. By the same token, of course, speech or conduct which is in violation of law and constitutionally unprotected should receive no greater protection on the campus than off the campus. Although we could find no case in which the distinction between advocacy and mounting action has been in issue, the position of the students and the recent resolutions of the Academic Senate and the Regents all support a University policy which (subject only to restrictions necessary for normal conduct of University functions and business), permits free expression within the limits of the law. Subject only to these same restrictions, off-campus speakers invited by recognized student groups to speak in the Hyde Park area should be permitted to do so upon completing a simple registration procedure which records the inviting organization, the speaker's name, the topic of his talk, and his willingness to answer questions.

The paragraph as amended was not voted upon. The unresolved issue was how the foregoing should be further amended in order explicitly to deal with the question of the authority of the university to discipline for on-campus conduct that results in off-campus law violation.

To deal with this question, the administration proposed at the last meeting of the committee on November 7 that the following sentence be inserted after the third sentence of the paragraph reported above:

If acts unlawful under California or Federal law directly result from advocacy, organization, or planning on the campus, the students and organizations involved may be subject to such disciplinary action as is appropriate and conditioned upon a fair hearing as to the appropriateness of the action taken.

The students proposed instead the following:

In the area of First Amendment rights and civil liberties the University may impose no disciplinary action against members of the University community and organizations. In this area members of the University community and organizations are subject only to the civil authorities.

The faculty's proposal on the same issue was:

If unlawful acts directly result from campus advocacy for which unlawful acts the speaker or his sponsoring organization can fairly be held accountable under prevailing legal principles, the University should be entitled, after a fair hearing, to impose appropriate discipline.

At the last meeting of the committee, none of these proposals was accepted by all three groups. The committee was scheduled to meet again on Wednesday, November 11, 4 P.M., to take up this and other matters. There was general agreement that if consensus could not be reached upon a single set of recommendations to be made to the administration, the committee would make a report specifying the proposals upon which all agree and defining the issues upon which no consensus could be reached, with each group explaining the reasons for its position.

Original Faculty Proposal

Moved that the Berkeley Campus Committee on Political Activity report the following seven recommendations to the chancellor:

I. That in the Hyde Park areas, the university modify its present regulations by dropping the distinction between "advocating" and "mounting" political and social action. Although we could find no case in which this distinction has been in issue, the position of the students and the recent resolutions of the Academic Senate and the Regents all support a university policy which (subject only to restrictions necessary for normal conduct of university functions and business), permits free expression within the limits of the law. Subject only to these same restrictions, off-campus speakers invited by recognized students' groups to speak in the Hyde Park area should be permitted to do so upon completing a simple registration procedure which records the inviting organization, the speaker's name, the topic of his talk, and his willingness to answer questions.

II. That the present rules relating to students and student organizations be amended to permit recognized student organizations to accept donations and membership signups, and to distribute political and social action material from tables provided by the organizations under the conditions proposed by 18 student organizations in their petition delivered to Dean Towle on September 17, 1964.

These conditions are:

1. Tables for the student organizations at Bancroft and Telegraph will be manned at all times.
2. The organizations shall provide their own tables and chairs; no university property shall be borrowed.
3. There shall be no more than one table in front of each pillar and one at each side of the entrance way. No tables shall be placed in front of the entrance posts.
4. No posters shall be attached to posts or pillars. Posters shall be attached to tables only.*
5. We (students) shall make every effort to see that provisions 1–4 are carried out and shall publish such rules and distribute them to the various student organizations.
6. The tables at Bancroft and Telegraph may be used to distribute literature advocating action on current issues

---

* While this condition appears in the original student petition, the Committee sees no reason why posters could not be substituted for a card table in front of the pillars.

with the understanding that the student organizations do not represent the University of California—thus these organizations will not use the name of the University and will dissociate themselves from the University as an institution.

7. Donations may be accepted at the tables.

These conditions are illustrative of the rules which would be appropriate at each of the other campus areas designated for this activity. Participation in the activities described in this section should be limited to members of the campus community—students, staff and faculty.

III. That the liberal administration of the requirement of 72 hours notice for off-campus speakers be continued and exceptions made where conditions warrant them. In the Hyde Park areas the notice requirement would be reduced to the minimum necessary for compliance with the registration requirements of section I.

[*Commentary:* The registration requirement should be completed before the appearance in the Hyde Park areas of an off-campus speaker is publicized.]

IV. That in the new student office building scheduled for completion next semester, a meeting room (or rooms) be available for membership and regular business meetings of recognized student off-campus groups, and that the regulation of scheduling and use of these facilities be handled through student government channels.

[*Commentary:* The modifications of regulations recommended for the Hyde Park areas are not intended to apply to these rooms.]

V. That the office of the dean of students, in cooperation with the campus police department, prepare a brief statement of the criteria used to determine when police will be required at meetings, so that organizations can better determine in advance whether or not their meeting plans are likely to incur the cost of police protection.

VI. That from the student body, the chancellor appoint approximately 10 students who are representative of a wide spectrum of viewpoints, and who will serve as his committee of student advisors on the interpretation of rules relating to student political and social action. Terms should be limited to one year and appointments to this committee rotated to assure widest possible representation.

VII. That the appropriate channel for review of broad policy issues concerning student political and social action is the procedure now provided by Academic Senate rules for receiving petitions from students.

[*Commentary:* Any student wishing to petition the Berkeley Division of the Academic Senate may do so by submitting a statement in writing to the Secretary of the Division.]

VIII. Hyde Park areas to be designated.

[*Commentary:* The faculty group strongly felt that the experimental use of Sproul steps and adjacent plaza area should be discontinued, and that the Wheeler Oak area should be designated as a Hyde Park area.]

> *Earl F. Cheit*
> *Joseph W. Garbarino*
> *Sanford Kadish*
> *Henry Rosovsky*
> *Theodore Vermeulen*
> *Robley C. Williams*

AGREEMENT OF FRIDAY EVENING, OCTOBER 2, 1964

1. The student demonstrators shall desist from all forms of their illegal protest against university regulations.
2. A committee representing students (including leaders of the demonstration), faculty, and administration will immediately be set up to conduct discussions and hearing into all aspects of political behavior on campus and its control, and to make recommendations to the administration.
3. The arrested man will be booked, released on his own recognizance, and the university (complainant) will not press charges.
4. The duration of the suspension of the suspended students will be submitted within one week to the Student Conduct Committee of the Academic Senate.
5. Activity may be continued by student organizations in accordance with existing university regulations.
6. The President of the University has already declared his willingness to support deeding certain university property at the end of Telegraph Avenue to the City of Berkeley or to the ASUC.

Signed

Jo Freeman	*Clark Kerr*
Paul C. Cahill	*Jackie Goldberg*
Sandor Fuchs	*Eric Levine*
Robert Wolfson	*Mario Savio*
David Jessup	*Thomas Miller*

January 3, 1965

The following is the text of a statement issued at 5 P.M. today (January 3, 1965) by Acting Chancellor Martin Meyerson of the Berkeley Campus of the University of California:

Colleagues and students:

The development of democratic rights in our country has taken over two centuries. We are in the midst of continuing that development on the campus of the University of California at Berkeley. Many dedicated and intelligent people—faculty, students, Regents, and administrators—have devoted their energies and talents to help resolve the issues which face us and they have made extraordinary progress.

I feel confident that if we work together on our immediate problems we can achieve a solution by the beginning of the new term in February. We can even move on to deal with some of the present and future potentialities of the campus. If we deny ourselves the benefit of time for deliberation and if we do not respect each other—including respecting our differences—then we may fail. Our stakes are enormous. Each of us should want to use the present period as an opportunity for improving education at one of the world's greatest centers of learning. If we fail we shall hurt all intellectual communities everywhere; if we succeed, we shall help all.

It was only last night after Chancellor Strong's request for a leave that I was asked by him, by the Regents and President Kerr to be the acting chancellor. Because most of you do not know me well, I wish to state some of my views which I hope will be helpful in building upon the progress and understanding which has already been accomplished.

One of the absolutes in my world is that the rights of democracy have to be extended not only to all those with whom we agree but to all those with whom we disagree. This implies the rights of those who dissent and those who do not. I am against prior censorship. As the father of young children I want them exposed to all the ideas the adult world has to offer. I am against double punishment for a single violation. I believe the courts and law-enforcement agencies are better equipped than a university to handle legal questions arising out of free speech and advocacy. I also understand the reluctance of law-enforcement agencies to let universities relinquish their traditional disciplinary role. Universities have been expected to control their own discipline. As an intellectual community we must assume a mature and responsible civic posture.

The Regents have requested me to issue provisional rules consistent with their stated policies. I shall do so shortly. By definition provisional rules are expected to change. It is a rare rule that satisfies everyone. But I have always believed that the wording of rules is far less important than the policies behind these rules and the way they are administered. I pledge the utmost fairness in the administration of rules. In this connection I shall also ask the Academic Senate's Committee on Committees to nominate a panel of faculty members from whom I can appoint a committee of five to hear and consider cases involving student political activity.

You should also know that I believe civil disobedience is warranted as a last resort in our democracy—it was warranted in Boston at the famous Tea Party—it has been warranted at other times and places. But civil disobedience is warranted only when there is no recourse to reasonable deliberation. Avenues of recourse are now available on this campus.

Responsible citizenship and political understanding are requisites to education in a free society. I say this to make clear that I believe these make a contribution to the normal process of learning. Some people have suggested that our campus has grown too big to pursue truth and knowledge. I doubt that the size of our urban campus is a handicap. Just as the large metropolis provides a wonderful richness and diversity of cultural and other opportunities, so a large metropolitan university can provide a similar range of choice. The challenge to us is to provide that stimulus and diversity without the administrative apparatus getting in the way. The administrative apparatus is necessary but it must be only a means to facilitate the process of learning and research. I have no more affection for being an IBM card than anyone else.

Even within the constraints of our campus budget I hope we can develop further the opportunity for every student whether a freshman or a candidate for an advanced degree to work intimately with one or more of his professors. Registration and other mechanics of running the campus must be simplified. A greater discourse across departmental lines is needed. It may be that student efforts are fragmented by too many courses.

Our problems at Berkeley are many. They may not differ in gravity from those which have beset great universities in the past. They do, however, differ in kind. For ours is the task to reconcile the eternal traditions of a community of scholars with the needs of a modern democracy in swift evolution. It is a task we must solve, not only for the university but for the people of California. With generosity toward each other we may succeed in bringing into harmony greater quality with quantity, responsibility with freedom, teaching with research which feeds teaching, intellectual experimentation with service to the state and nation, serious accomplishment with humor and—even—age with youth.

Martin Meyerson,
Acting Chancellor

TO THE EDUCATIONAL PRESS
BY ACTING CHANCELLOR MARTIN MEYERSON

I have spent most of my adult life as a professor. Therefore, I have developed convictions as to the future of education which have influenced my actions as a teacher, as a dean and now will influence me as acting chancellor. The comments which follow should have been addressed first to my colleagues, but then you asked for them first.

In my first statement as acting chancellor, a week ago Sunday, I said we must look beyond the immediate issues surrounding student political activity on the Berkeley campus to the fundamental educational problems of a great university today. I believe that all of us here are eager to engage in this discussion, and I expect that bold innovations will be underway at Berkeley as a result of it. The world sees in the University of California perhaps the most impressive effort ever made to provide the best possible higher education to the largest possible numbers of students. Our successes in this area appear to the rest of the world as so impressive that a steady stream of observers and visitors come to learn from us. For example, in Britain today, many concerned with the plans to increase sharply the numbers attending university there point to the University of California as the proof that a democratic state may maintain excellent universities without limiting admission to a small potential elite as Britain has done up to now. It is, of course, not only those who seek to enlarge the size of their educational establishment who look to California for a model. But though others praise us, we are aware that we are only at the beginning of the effort to combine excellence and numbers. We know our defects better than do any of our observers.

However, we are not so sure of the directions we must take to improve education at Berkeley. I shall review some of the questions that we must ask ourselves. Berkeley is so preeminent as a center of research that again and again the question is asked—is not teaching, and in particular undergraduate education, slighted by the emphasis on research and the recruitment of great research scholars? I am convinced, as I believe all who have thought deeply about contemporary higher education are convinced, that the best teachers are very often the best researchers. Most disciplines are undergoing such rapid change and development that it is generally those who are contributing to the transformation of each field of study who are best able to teach it. This is true even for elementary courses; the teaching of the elements effectively requires knowing the frontiers and it is difficult in most subjects to remain in contact with new advances exclusively by reading the research literature. Our problem is how to develop a better relationship between research and teaching, and in particular between research and undergraduate teaching.

The most exciting experience students can have is to begin to understand how it is done—how one develops ideas, how scientists work in the laboratory, professionals work at a problem, social scientists undertake research, humanists explore the meaning of great texts. In all these fields, this is "research." It should be possible for undergraduates—including those freshmen who want it—to share this excitement, and to sense the delight a scholar has in new discoveries. Students should learn as soon as possible what the world of learning and scholarship and scientific exploration is like, that faculty do not publish to avoid perishing but engage in research for much the same reason that an artist paints, a musician composes, or a poet or novelist writes. I am convinced we can share this sense of excitement of creation, even with a high ratio of students to faculty. One way of doing this may be to include early in the student's career in the university a number of small classes, laboratories, tutorials, or research seminars. When he is inducted in the style and content of higher learning, he can perhaps more easily take advantage of large lecture classes.

Our objective must be to ensure that every student has meaningful educational experiences which bring him into close personal contact with one or more members of the faculty and at the beginning of his career as a student. Our point of view must always be concerned with the education of the student—and not an abstract idea of the number or distribution of courses a student must take to graduate. We can never cover all knowledge. Our aim must be to graduate students who can continue learning.

We can expand the number of these educational experiences by relating our university in more ways to its setting. There is the Bay Area in this exciting and rapidly growing state. Our interest must not be to control or limit the experiences that come out of the community onto the campus, but to expand them. And at the same time we would hope to contribute to the cultural and civic life of the Bay Area and California. Then there is the wider Pacific area. Our university is in an unrivaled position to develop interesting new courses that could be a model to the rest of the country, bringing together the work of different disciplines to illuminate the problems of Asia, the Pacific Basin, and Latin America. These interdisciplinary approaches and courses should be brought to the undergraduate, not left solely to graduate school.

In this connection I think it important to note that although we are part of a state university, no university has ever become great by exclusively serving the needs of a given area or even an entire nation. To be universalistic is the essence of university life. That we have students from other states and from foreign countries is one of the aspects of campus life which contributes most to the education of native Californians. To attend class with, to live among, to talk and argue with, to learn from, students from every corner of the earth is one of the best ways of educating California students. Californians should be proud that their university is one of our nation's chief sources of international repute, that both scholars and students the world over turn to it to further their own education and research. Any effort to improve the quality of education in Berkeley should recognize the need to maintain the campus' cosmopolitan character.

Many of our undergraduates are in parts of the university that are preparing them specifically for professions—engineering, teaching, business, architecture, forestry, criminology, and so on. We have to consider more deeply the relationship between these undergraduate professional programs and the other tasks of university education. I am not suggesting that we must be suspicious of professional education in the university. Quite the contrary. My college is a professional one. When we realize how much advancement of knowledge has come from the professions and the vocations, we understand the issue is how to integrate these approaches better into undergraduate education. The professions—such as teaching, engineering, architecture, and others—are changing very rapidly. This suggests the value of a more broadly based, less specifically vocational education, even in preparation for such fields. At the same time, when we are aware of the intellectual excitement characterizing so much in the professions today, we see elements that we can draw upon for a general liberal arts education. Once again, as in research and teaching, it is not a question of either-or—it is a question of a better relationship.

It is essential to develop centers on the campus with which students can identify. I have already indicated my conviction that size as such is not a problem. Size offers advantages. It means, for example, that students who have particular points of view and special interests, even if minority points of view and interests, can find other students and perhaps faculty who share them and thus paradoxically can overcome isolation and forced conformity in a large university where they could not do so in a smaller school. But just as these students can find a center of identification in an organization or activity, so we must make it possible for all of our students to escape from a feeling of anonymity, to find a point of location, of loyalty, of identification. We have to think seriously how this can be done. We have to consider what we can learn from other universities, and, indeed, other campuses of the University of California. Perhaps we can make better use of our various kinds of living quarters to develop stronger centers of identification for some of our students. We may be able to develop improved physical facilities for students, such as special rooms or centers for work and study, perhaps in conjunction with libraries, while students are on campus. We have to consider whether these should be organized around disciplines, or on some other basis. Certainly relations between departments and their students should be strengthened.

Our graduate education is perhaps stronger than our undergraduate program at present. Here the faculty can more readily elicit the excitement which results from drawing the student directly into the work in progress at the frontiers of knowledge. Yet even here problems remain to be solved in the establishment of a greater sense of community, a community at once social and intellectual. Should we not develop more physical centers for graduate student work and faculty-student contact? Can we make better use of our wonderful research institutes in this connection? Might we not by changes in physical placement and organizational relations adapt them to the point where they better serve graduate student education—which is obviously and necessarily based on a close relationship to research?

These are the sorts of questions concerning our educational policies that I think the university community must explore.

The role of administration in education is a subtle and complex one. Scholars must have the greatest possible autonomy. The individual departments, schools, and colleges must also have the greatest possible autonomy to develop educational policy. The administrator, to my mind, however, ought to be more than the symbolic and ceremonial head, the chief public relations officer, or caretaker. He can help initiate educational changes; he can help the autonomous units in developing their own innovations. He can sponsor new experimental programs outside of existing units which sometimes find it difficult to innovate because of traditional commitments. A subtle equilibrium is necessary between the independence and autonomy of the separate parts and the role of the administrative center. But this is true in every community, no matter what kind, and our aim must be to develop such relations between all the parts that the educational achievement is continually greater.

I hope and believe we are beginning an era of educational

innovation at Berkeley. This may cost more money. I think we will have to expect some larger measure of support for undergraduate education, which in the course of the rapid development of the university has not received the attention that it should have. But in terms of the total budget this necessary increase in support to undergraduate education will be small. I also hope that foundations, corporate and individual (private) donors will begin to provide more to the University of California. Almost all our major private universities are now heavily indebted to public sources for a large part, often most, of their budgets. Our public universities must also move toward a mixed-support economy, particularly in California, where public education constitutes so large a part of all higher education. One of our greatest weaknesses as compared with other major schools is our inability to provide enough and large enough fellowships and scholarships both for undergraduates and graduates. I knew students from California at universities elsewhere who could not afford to attend Berkeley because their families could not support them away from home. They were able to go to these other universities because of the existence of scholarships which paid all their expenses. There are many excellent graduate students at other universities who would prefer to do their work at Berkeley, since we have a number of the leading departments in the country in various fields. Such students do not do so because they have received a high-paying fellowship from another school. Few people realize that the cost to able students of graduate education in some of the leading private universities is less than in Berkeley because good students receive lucrative fellowships which cover all their expenses. This university has few such awards, a fact which sharply reduces its efficiency as an educational institution. Similarly, the university is in a weak position in the competition for the best faculty because it lacks enough positions at the top of the national academic salary scale. I hope that private donors can be convinced to increase significantly their support for research and teaching at the university.

There are many reasons to be proud of the achievements of this university. We are bringing a very good education to large numbers. But I believe yet greater achievements lie ahead. The problems of the world and of knowledge are in rapid transformation. New educational forms must be found to realize the opportunities these changes offer us.

Martin Meyerson
Acting Chancellor
University of California, Berkeley
January 13, 1965

ANCHOR BOOKS

SOCIOLOGY

ALLPORT, GORDON W.   The Nature of Prejudice, A149

BARTH, KARL   Community, State and Church, A221

BEDAU, HUGO ADAM, ed.   The Death Penalty in America, A387

BELL, DANIEL   The Radical Right, A376

BENDIX, REINHARD   Max Weber: An Intellectual Portrait, A281

BERGER, MORROE   The Arab World Today, A406

BERGER, PETER L.   Invitation to Sociology: A Humanistic Perspective, A346

BROWN, ROBERT MC AFEE, & WEIGEL, GUSTAVE, S.J.   An American Dialogue, A257

CABLE, GEORGE W.   The Negro Question, A144

CAPLOW, THEODORE, & MC GEE, REECE J.   The Academic Marketplace, A440

DARLING, F. FRASER   A Herd of Red Deer, N35

DE GRAZIA, SEBASTIAN   Of Time, Work and Leisure, A380

DOLLARD, JOHN   Caste and Class in a Southern Town, A95

ERIKSON, ERIK H., ed.   The Challenge of Youth, A438

FICHTER, JOSEPH H.   Parochial School: A Sociological Study, A420

FORTUNE, EDITORS OF   The Exploding Metropolis, A146

FREEDMAN, RONALD, ed.   Population: The Vital Revolution, A423

GATHERU, MUGO   Child of Two Worlds, A468

GOFFMAN, ERVING   Asylums: Essays on the Social Situation of Mental Patients and Other Inmates, A277

────   The Presentation of Self in Everyday Life, A174

GRANICK, DAVID   The European Executive, A397

────   The Red Executive: A Study of the Organization Man in Russian Industry, A246

HACKER, ANDREW   Corporation Take-Over, A465

HANDLIN, OSCAR   The Newcomers, A283

────   Race and Nationality in American Life, A110

HENDIN, HERBERT   Suicide and Scandinavia, A457

HERBERG, WILL   Protestant-Catholic-Jew, A195

HOOVER, EDGAR M., & VERNON, RAYMOND   Anatomy of a Metropolis, A298

HUNTER, FLOYD   Community Power Structure, A379

JONES, ERNEST   The Life and Work of Sigmund Freud, ed. & abr. in 1 vol. Trilling & Marcus, A340